T0142272

The Human–Computer Interaction Series, launched in 2004, publishes books that advance the science and technology of developing systems which are effective and satisfying for people in a wide variety of contexts. Titles focus on theoretical perspectives (such as formal approaches drawn from a variety of behavioural sciences), practical approaches (such as techniques for effectively integrating user needs in system development), and social issues (such as the determinants of utility, usability and acceptability).

HCI is a multidisciplinary field and focuses on the human aspects in the development of computer technology. As technology becomes increasingly more pervasive the need to take a human-centred approach in the design and development of computer-based systems becomes ever more important.

Titles published within the Human–Computer Interaction Series are included in Thomson Reuters' Book Citation Index, The DBLP Computer Science Bibliography and The HCI Bibliography.

More information about this series at https://link.springer.com/bookseries/6033

Human–Computer Interaction Series

Editor-in-Chief

Jean Vanderdonckt
Louvain School of Management, Université catholique de Louvain,
Louvain-La-Neuve, Belgium

Yang Li · Otmar Hilliges
Editors

Artificial Intelligence for Human Computer Interaction: A Modern Approach

 Springer

Editors
Yang Li
Google Research (United States)
Mountain View, CA, USA

Otmar Hilliges
Advanced Interactive Technologies Lab
ETH Zurich
Zurich, Switzerland

ISSN 1571-5035   ISSN 2524-4477   (electronic)
Human–Computer Interaction Series
ISBN 978-3-030-82683-3   ISBN 978-3-030-82681-9   (eBook)
https://doi.org/10.1007/978-3-030-82681-9

This Springer imprint is published by the registered company Springer Nature Switzerland AG
The registered company address is: Gewerbestrasse 11, 6330 Cham, Switzerland

Forward for Artificial Intelligence for Human Computer Interaction: A Modern Approach

From its earliest days, Artificial Intelligence has pursued two goals: to emulate human behavior, and to achieve optimal performance regardless of method. On one side, researchers argue that humans are the best example we have of intelligent systems, so AI should focus on understanding and replicating the human mind and brain. On the other side, researchers contend that selecting a good course of action is an optimization problem, so AI should focus on mathematical equations and algorithms that achieve or approximate optimality.

This book focuses on a middle ground that brings together these two approaches:

- AI should be seen as a *tool* that allows humans and computers to work better together.
- Sometimes this means a high level of automation, but a human should still have a high level of overall control and confidence in the system.
- Other times a human is immersed in the inner loop and effective human/computer dialog is crucial to success.
- Understanding human intent and mental state is a precondition of effective dialog, as is the ability for a computer to explain itself in terms a human can understand.
- Prior to any optimization, human and computer need to come to an agreement on exactly what it is that should be optimized.

In recent years we have seen the rise of powerful new AI-enabled applications in computer vision, speech recognition, natural language understanding, recommendation systems, robotics, and other subfields. Getting the full benefit from these systems requires joint HCI/AI research.

For example, hundreds of millions of people use voice assistants regularly. Breakthroughs in deep learning AI made the recognition rate acceptable, and it is HCI that makes the whole interface work. But many challenges remain:

- HCI research gave us the WIMP interface for devices with screens, but some voice assistants have no screen. They will need a new design language. This will require a partnership with AI providing ever-increasing capabilities–better speech recognition, better models of user intent, more actions that the assistant can perform–and HCI answering "how do we give users mental models that will allow them to discover and understand the ever-increasing capabilities."

- Voice assistants could grow as a platform to become as significant as the PC or mobile platforms, but only if it is easy for developers to create applications that take advantage of the power of AI with a convenient user interface. Today, many voice assistant applications are little better than the annoying phone services that say "press 1 for ..." because that is the easiest methodology for developers who are unskilled in machine learning to express the options. The full promise of AI will only be achieved if the ability to easily develop powerful innovative systems is democratized, not restricted to only PhD-level researchers.
- In traditional software, UX designers come up with guidelines that are implemented by human programmers. But what happens when the "programmer" is a machine learning system? How can UX guidelines be codified as inputs to a system that is continually learning and evolving, and doing personalization for each user?
- As AI moves from the research labs to real-world applications, we are finding that some applications can unfairly disadvantage one subgroup of users over another, due to disparities in data or to carelessness in setting the goals of the system. To achieve fairness while maintaining privacy and efficacy will require HCI tools that allow us to explore the data more thoroughly.

Of course there are many other AI applications besides voice assistants that will also benefit from a partnership with HCI: autonomous vehicles, computer vision, robots, recommendation systems, healthcare, drug discovery, elder care, and so on. Each specialized application will require in-depth understanding of the use cases for each distinct user population.

As is often the case when two fields collide, the effects are felt in both directions. HCI gains new interaction modalities and new tools to make interactions more effective. But AI gains too. Designing machine learning software is fundamentally different from designing traditional software, in that it is more a process of training than programming. Thus, the interaction between human AI developers and the machine-learning tools they rely on is a type of HCI that we are just beginning to study and learn how to improve.

This book is not the only champion of the combination of HCI and AI. There are other recent books such as Ben Shneiderman's *Human-Centered AI* and Stuart Russell's *Human Compatible*. There are new institutes for Human-Centered AI at universities including Stanford, Maryland, Berkeley, Utrecht, and the Technical University of Denmark. The field is taking root.

What is unique about this book is its *breadth*, covering topics such as behavior modeling, input modalities, data sets, crowdsourcing, and machine learning toolkits. Specific application areas include drawing, natural language, GUIs, medical imaging, and sound generation. The breadth extends to the authors as well as the topics– we have authors who typically publish in AI natural language conferences such as EMNLP, in computer vision conferences such as CVPR and SIGGRAPH, and in HCI conferences such as CHI. You may discover someone working on similar problems who comes from a very different background.

I believe that in a few years we will look back on today as a critical time in the development of a new richer interaction between humans and AI systems, and we will see this book as an important step in a better understanding of the breadth and potential impact of this emerging joint field.

Peter Norvig

Introduction

We are in the mid of an ongoing revolution in Computer Science and by extension our everyday lives that are now intrinsically interwoven with digital technology. Brought on by rapid progress in machine learning and deep learning technologies in particular, we are now about to enter the age of "real-world AI." More and more systems that we interact with on a daily basis are now driven by some form of Artificial Intelligence (AI) algorithm, even if only in the background. Likewise at the interface layer we have started to witness dramatic changes. The machine no longer passively waits for user input to perform computation, but instead, we see how smart systems, including voice assistants on our phones, TVs, and many more, actively process data and interact with us in increasingly different ways, compared to the GUI of old.

This ongoing seismic change in Computer Science, where almost no aspect of the discipline is untouched by machine learning and AI concepts, then also brings fundamental changes to the area of Human–Computer Interaction (HCI). As outlined above, the computer itself—the "C" in the name of the discipline—is changing and the nature of what humans interact with is therefore changing too. This transition clearly brings on new questions and challenges in how to design the human-facing aspects of such systems. This change also brings on questions about the nature of interaction (the "I") itself. Last but not least, how we perceive such systems and how humans can, want, and do deal with an increasingly smart and automated world is shifting rapidly (the "H"). Therefore, a very rich conversation across the boundaries of the HCI and AI community on related topics has emerged.

To build smart assistants and other AI systems that directly interact with humans, such systems must be able to perceive and understand human activities at a level that rivals our own. For example, many of our most urgent challenges including urban congestion and mobility, rising healthcare costs, an aging society, and climate change are believed to be mitigated through AI-based solutions such as self-driving cars, personalized healthcare robots, and AR/VR-based telepresence systems. Yet such advanced AI platforms will only be widely adopted and impactful if they are able to perceive and interpret humans at levels rivaling our own. Thus the question of how to sense what humans "do" (i.e., speech, action, and other forms of input) and reason about what humans "want" (i.e., their intent) are increasingly pressing research problems that a significant amount of work across industry and academia are dedicated to.

Finally, the question on what tools, interfaces and processes that humans who design machine learning powered systems use, is becoming a topic of research on its own. Due to the complexity of AI systems and the difficulty that humans have in understanding and analyzing their inner workings, this line of work is a crucial building block toward a world in which (i) engineers can efficiently build AI-based systems, (ii) designers can create interfaces that work for humans and (iii) developers have tools at hand that allow them to understand and explain how their algorithms and systems work.

These and many other interesting questions at the intersection between AI and HCI is what this book explores. In it we present a collection of work spanning HCI and AI. We selected work that study this exciting and challenging area of research from many different angles and perspectives. These include work that leverages modern approaches in AI, particularly data-driven and deep learning methods to tackle HCI problems of importance. Problems that were so far challenging or impossible to address due to the limitations of traditional technologies. Other perspectives include those of researchers that aim to understand the effect that data-driven techniques have on the interaction between AI and human and those that propose new tools for the design of such systems. Through these perspectives, we hope to bridge across the often disjoint areas of AI and HCI and hope to provide new insights, research questions, and hopefully some useful answers to important questions to researchers and practitioners from both areas. Thus we hope to accelerate the identification of new opportunities to advance both HCI and AI. We also hope to foster cross-field collaboration between HCI and AI, and disseminate best practices, resources and knowledge from both fields.

Background

The rise of deep learning [9] and the recent advance of data-driven methods [3] have fundamentally transformed the field of AI. This impact can be felt much beyond the field of AI itself, with deep learning methods aiding scientific discoveries such as solving protein structures [12] and identifying exoplanets [13]. More closely related, making user facing systems such as speech-based interfaces, self-driving cars, and personal robots has become not only feasible but actually usable. Thus new opportunities for research in HCI and at the intersection with AI emerge if the machine no longer is an explicitly programmed data processing automaton but a complex system that is capable of carrying out tasks that where previously squarely in the domain of humans and beyond.

Overview

A rich spectrum of work has emerged, which leverage the strengths of both HCI and AI. In this section, we give an overview of the trends in the research area, opportunities and challenges that have been and are being raised. Based on these we have selected a rich set of contributed articles from world-class authors that are active in the area. We now provide a brief overview over the structure of the book and hope to thus provide some guidance to the interested reader.

Interaction Behavior Modeling

The first part of the book is devoted to human behavior modeling in the context of interaction tasks. This is a classic problem in the field of HCI. Not only is it important to predict how humans will interact with a human (and how long it will take, or how error prone a task is) but also increasingly becomes a fundamental issue in AI itself, as part of the quest of AI for computational modeling of human intelligence. In addition to advancing the scientific understanding of human behaviors, these models can aid interaction designers in determining how usable an interface is without having to test it exhaustively with real users, which can be expensive and laborious. Furthermore, such technologies may allow for online adaptation of an interface or user input recognition system, ensuring optimal interaction flow and control based on various factors such as user capability and goals.

In the chapter Human Performance Modeling with Deep Learning, Yuan, Pfeuffer, and Li discussed a series of three case studies on how to use a data-driven deep learning approach for human performance modeling. These projects were set to extend classic approaches [4, 8] by allowing more complex behaviors to be modeled in an end-to-end fashion. They reduce the effort for feature engineering and need for making potentially limiting assumptions. These approaches are extensible and can address new or emerging behaviors. Meanwhile, instead of using a deep model as a black box, the works show how deep models can be analyzed to gain analytical insights, and used for optimizing an interface.

The chapter Optimal Control to Support High-Level User Goals in Human-Computer Interaction by Gebhardt and Hilliges offers a distinct perspective of interaction modeling based on control theory. They formulate the flow of HCI as a dynamic system where both human and computer adapt to achieve a high-level goal. More specifically, they offered two approaches for optimizing such a dynamic system: one based on classic control theory using model predictive control and the other based on a reinforcement learning view of control. The authors first focus on the specific domain of human-robot interaction and apply their methods subsequently to mixed reality UIs. Compared to the Chap. 1, the chapter is more focused on adaptive user interfaces where both the system and human evolve.

In the chapter Modeling Mobile Interface Tappability Using Crowdsourcing and Deep Learning, Swearngin and Li present their work on modeling UI tappability, i.e., how a user perceives whether a UI element is tappable, which is a crucial aspect for usability. The chapter resonates with the chapter Human Performance Modeling with Deep Learning by showing how deep learning can be used to address complex human behavior such as tappabilty perception [15]. The work showcases a different set of deep modeling techniques from the chapter Human Performance Modeling with Deep Learning. In addition, it demonstrates how data, which deep learning relies on, can be curated using a crowdsourcing approach. The chapter also offers analytical insights on how the model mimics uncertainty in human perception.

Expanding Input Bandwidth

The second part of the book is focused on another classic topic in HCI—input. There has been a rich body of literature on how to expand the input bandwidth between human and machine. This is often achieved by enabling new input modalities and is aimed toward reducing user effort. In light of pro-active AI systems, sensing of user action and by subsequent analysis, intent is becoming an increasingly important topic.

Systems that interact with users always rely on mechanisms for humans to specify their intentions. Traditional techniques, including mice, keyboards, and touch screens, require the user to explicitly provide inputs and commands. However, modern deep learning-based approaches are now robust enough to inherent ambiguity and noise in real-world data in order to make it feasible to analyze and reason about natural human behavior, including speech and motion but also more subtle activities such as gaze patterns or biophysical responses. Such approaches now allow us to go beyond simple gesture recognition [14] and pattern matching approaches [16], which still require the user to memorize a set of specific commands, and to be able to analyze complex human activity in a more continuous and holistic fashion. For example understanding fine-grained hand articulation for use in VR and AR [6], understanding and modeling natural handwritten text [2], or to estimate [10] and even synthesize human gaze data [7]. Such methods then form the building blocks for novel types of interactive systems in which the human and the machine interact in a more immediate fashion, leveraging new question for HCI in terms of how to design such UIs. However, AI-based techniques cannot only be used to sense user input but also to learn high level concepts such as user preference or, more generally speaking, to analyze the usage context to adapt the UI and to present information proactively, given the estimated user intention (e.g., [5]).

The four chapters in this section are representative in the endeavors for using AI to achieve these goals, including gaze estimation, text entry and gesture input.

Zhang, Park, and Feit open the section by presenting their work on gaze estimation and how to enable gaze as an additional input modality. They give a thorough survey of gaze estimation methods, and discuss how learning-based approaches can significantly advance the topic. The authors employ AI techniques such as Convolutional Neural Nets (CNN) and few-shot learning for gaze estimation. Staying true to the cross-disciplinary spirit of the book the authors also discuss how gaze can be integrated into interactive systems and provide guidelines and application examples.

Zhang et al. next address the important research topic of text entry. Text entry has been extensively investigated over several decades, and mobile text entry is a rich yet challenging research arena. Specifically, the authors focus on intelligent error correction during mobile text entry, and formulate error correction as an encoding–decoding process, which can be naturally realized using a common deep learning architecture of an encoder–decoder with attention. In addition, the authors show how interaction techniques can be designed to seamlessly work with an AI model.

Quinn, Feng, and Zhai then present their work on using deep models for detecting touch gestures on capacitive touchscreens of mobile devices. They show how deep models, using CNN backbones and LSTM cells, can detect richer expression of finger touch, based on touch sensor image sequences, than simple pointing, which can be translated to micro gestures or variations such as pressures. The work presents original insights into how touch surface biomechanics provide unique opportunities for rich gesture expressions and how a deep model can leverage these signals. The authors then discuss interaction techniques can be designed on top of such capabilities and first-hand knowledge on system integration of such a model into a mobile system.

Continuing on the topic of gesture input, Matulic and Vogel present their work on enhancing digital pen interaction by detecting grip postures. They investigated three sensing mechanisms and developed deep neural networks to recognize hand postures and gestures. The work specifically compares deep models with traditional machine learning method, and investigates a variety of task setups and difficulty levels as well as how such a model can be used in a realistic interaction scenario. This work again shows how CNNs can be useful for processing sensor input for gesture recognition.

Data and Tools

Data is at the heart of modern AI approaches, and many advances in modern AI only exist due to the availability of large datasets in computer vision [11] and natural language processing [1]. However, datasets of interaction tasks are typically much fewer and often smaller due to the cost of collecting and annotating datasets of real users. The other central infrastructure aspect pertains to tools for developing machine learning models. The section highlights four representative topics in the area.

The section starts with a chapter from Deka et al. on Rico, a highly impactful dataset containing multidimensional UI data from 9.7k Android apps, which has been widely used across the fields of HCI and machine learning. The chapter offers a retrospective about how Rico dataset was created, using crowdsourcing and automatic crawling, and how it has enabled numerous research efforts in applying modern AI methods in user interfaces.

Continuing on the topic of data collection, Krishna, Bernstein, and Li present their work for addressing more complex data collection tasks, for Computer Vision models such as visual questioning and answering. They developed advanced inter-action strategies, in the context of crowdsourcing, for significantly accelerating data collection speed. The authors offer a broad view on methods for improving worker participation and data quality, such as using automated social interventions. On the other hand, the chapter provides a set of valuable insights into how HCI can help Computer Vision research.

The following chapter is then dedicated to machine learning tools. In particular, Li, Mayes, and Yu introduce TensorFlow.js, a tool that allows rapid prototyping of machine learning apps on the web. Compared to most chapters in the book are research projects, TensorFlow.js is a reliable product that enables non-ML researcher and practitioners, such as web developers, designers, and HCI researchers, to quickly create and iterate new ideas that leverages modern AI methods such as deep learning. The authors also offer a survey of web-based ML tooling, and provide an outlook for opportunities to employ this tool for doing HCI research and development.

To follow on the topic of tools for working with modern AI, Cruz and Igarashi give us an overview of interactive Reinforcement Learning (RL). RL has been one of the most important approaches for solving complex tasks where an agent can learn based on positive and negative rewards from environments. Particularly related to HCI, interactive RL includes human in the loop to guide the learning process of an RL agent. Cruz and Igarashi outline the HCI challenges in interactive RL, specifically for autonomous behavior design, and provide a conceptual framework for HCI researchers to work in the area, showcasing how HCI can help advance AI.

Specific Domains

We conclude the book with a section that covers a collection of work showcasing new frontiers of how modern-AI approaches enable new avenues for HCI research. The topics range from interaction design, to language-based interaction, to sound individualization and to medical imaging. These topics have started to quickly gain traction in the research community and industry alike.

Huang et al. presents a collection of work they conducted to enable sketching as a communication medium for creative tasks such as UI design and drawing. They used deep models to capture rich expressions of natural sketches, which would be difficult to achieve previously with traditional machine learning methods. The chapter presents a set of approaches involved in this research, including data collection, model development, and interactive system design, as well as evaluation, which provide a useful example of how to conduct research in this area.

Aksan and Hilliges continue this discussion on ink-based forms of communication (hand writing, sketching, diagrams)—the most flexible and freeform means of human communication. It is exactly the flexibility and versatility of a quick doodle that makes it hard to model via machine learning techniques. Such algorithms need to extract underlying structure and separate it from other formative variables such as the handwriting style of a particular individual. The chapter brings together an HCI and an ML perspective and discusses both the technical challenges of modeling ink in a generative fashion and the applications in interactive tools.

Li, Zhou, and Li present their work on bridging two dominant communication mediums: natural language and graphical user interfaces. The former is the major form of communication in our everyday life, and the latter is the de facto standard for conversing with a computer system such as a smartphone. The authors elaborate on their work in two ways to bridge (1) natural language grounding that maps natural language instructions to executable actions on GUIs and (2) natural language generation that describes a graphical UI element in prose such that they can be conveyed to the user.

Continuing on the topic of combining natural language and GUIs, Li, Mitchell, and Myers then present their efforts on developing Sugilite, which is a multi-modal, conversational task learning agent on mobile devices, using both the user's natural language instructions and demonstrations on GUIs. Sugilite focuses on multiple important issues in the area such as robustness, usability, and generalizability. The chapter also highlights the authors more recent work on screen representation learning that embeds the semantics of GUI screens, which is an important building block for mobile task learning.

Using modern-AI methods to enhance medical practice has drawn increasing interest of the field. In their chapter, Liang, He, and Chen share their work on bringing modern-AI to medical imaging, a highly specialized profession that requires a physician to manually examine complex medical images. To aid physicians in such a task that is time-consuming and error-prone, the authors discuss their approach for bringing AI into the process by engaging patients with self-assessment and enabling physicians to collaborate with AI to perform a diagnosis. Based on this work, the authors offer a broad view about human-centered AI.

Lastly, Yamamoto and Igarashi introduce a method to adapt the output of the generative model to a specific user for 3D spatial sound individualization, which has been a time-consuming and expensive process requiring specialized devices. The authors first train a deep model for sound generation and then tease apart the individualization part from the general behavior using tensor decomposition. The chapter makes a great case study of how to personalize an interactive system using modern machine learning techniques. The authors generalize their findings for many other HCI problems that would benefit from personalization.

Outlook

There have been many successes in applying modern AI methods to HCI as we have seen in these chapters. We also see examples of HCI work that helps to advance AI in return. With more and more work in the field starting to embrace AI-based methods for solving HCI problems, we see a fundamental shift of HCI methodologies toward more data driven and model centric viewpoints. With these methods, we also see many hard HCI problems that can now be solved to a certain degree. We now discuss challenges for research at the intersection of AI and HCI, and and at the same time opportunities for impact.

Data challenges. Machine learning and AI techniques hold great promise in shifting how we interact with machines from an explicit input model to a more implicit interaction paradigm in which the machine observes and interprets our actions. To achieve such a paradigm shift many challenges need to be overcome. First and foremost, deep learning methods are often data hungry, yet acquiring data of human activity is much more difficult than in other domains such as computer vision or NLP. Hence new ways to collect data and to make use of smaller datasets are of central importance to HCI–AI research. We have seen examples of methods such as human in the loop of AI systems and few shot learning along this direction. Progress in this area can be made by close collaboration between AI and HCI researchers and practitioners.

Inferring un-observable user state. Novel algorithms to capture and model high-level user state and behavior, including cognitive activity and user intent could drastically change what the UI *is*. Much progress has been made in HCI, computer vision and machine learning to understand the obeservable aspects of human activty such as speech, gestures, body position, and its spatial configuration. Some examples are discussed in this book in detail. However, it remains a very hard challenge to infer the underlying source of human activity. That is our needs, plans, and wants or our intent. The difficulty stems from the fact that these states are purely cognitive and hence are not directly observable. However, we are convinced that research into this direction utlimately will be very fruitful since it would allow for the design of interactive systems and UIs that truly adapt to the users' needs and would learn how to behave to reduce or fully eradicate user frustration and dissatisfaction.

Interpretability. Having analytical understanding about machine intelligence is an important topic both in the AI and the HCI field. Deep models with millions or even billions of parameters are particularly difficult to analyze. While better modeling accuracy is of great benefit, interpretability of a model is crucial for HCI researchers to gain new knowledge and to advance the field. We feel the progress on this topic will benefit both the fields tremendously. Last but not least, model interpretability research can help answer many questions that arise on how such intelligent systems can be made usable, and discoverable in the real world. It informs AI-based system designers and developers on how to mitigate issues around privacy, user-autonomy, and user-control.

Yang Li
Otmar Hilliges

References

1. Common crawl. https://commoncrawl.org/. Accessed: 2021-04-27.
2. Aksan E, Pece F, and Hilliges O (2018) DeepWriting: making digital ink editable via deep generative modeling. In SIGCHI Conference on Human Factors in Computing Systems, CHI '18, ACM (New York, NY, USA)
3. Deng J, Dong W, Socher R, Li L-J, Li K, and Fei-Fei L (2009) ImageNet: a large-scale hierarchical image database. In *CVPR09*
4. Fitts P M (1954) The information capacity of the human motor system in controlling the amplitude of movement. J Exp Psychol 47(6):381–91
5. Gebhardt C, Hecox B, van Opheusden B, Wigdor D, Hillis J, Hilliges O, and Benko H (2019) Learning cooperative personalized policies from gaze data. In Proceedings of the 32nd Annual ACM Symposium on User Interface Software and Technology, UIST '19, ACM (New York, NY, USA)
6. Glauser O, Wu S, Panozzo D, Hilliges O, and Sorkine-Hornung O (2019) Interactive hand pose estimation using a stretch-sensing soft glove. ACM Trans Graph 38(4): 41:1–41:15.
7. He Z, Spurr A, Zhang X, and Hilliges O (2019) Photo-realistic monocular gaze redirection using generative adversarial networks. In International Conference on Computer Vision, ICCV '19, IEEE
8. Hick WE (1952) On the rate of gain of information
9. LeCun Y, Bengio Y, and Hinton G (2015) Deep learning. Nat 521(7553):436–444.
10. Park S, Zhang X, Bulling A, and Hilliges O (2018) Learning to find eye region landmarks for remote gaze estimation in unconstrained settings. In ACM Symposium on Eye Tracking Research and Applications (ETRA), ETRA '18, ACM (New York, NY, USA)
11. Russakovsky O, Deng J, Su H, Krause J, Satheesh S, Ma S, Huang Z, Karpathy A, Khosla A, Bernstein M, Berg AC, and Fei-Fei L (2015) Imagenet large scale visual recognition challenge. Int J Comput Vision 115(3):211–252.
12. Senior A, Evans R, Jumper J, Kirkpatrick J, Sifre L, Green T, Qin C, Žídek A, Nelson A, Bridgland A, Penedones H, Petersen S, Simonyan K, Crossan S, Kohli P, Jones D, Silver D, Kavukcuoglu K, and Hassabis D (2020) Improved protein structure prediction using potentials from deep learning. Nat 577:1–5.
13. Shallue CJ, and Vanderburg A (2018) Identifying exoplanets with deep learning: A five-planet resonant chain around kepler-80 and an eighth planet around kepler-90. Astrono J 155:94.
14. Song J, Sörös G, Pece F, Fanello SR, Izadi S, Keskin C, and Hilliges O (2014) In-air gestures around unmodified mobile devices. In Proceedings of the 27th Annual ACM Symposium on User Interface Software and Technology, UIST '14, ACM. New York, NY, USA, pp 319–329
15. Swearngin A, and Li Y (2019) Modeling mobile interface tappability using crowdsourcing and deep learning. In Proceedings of the 2019 CHI Conference on Human Factors in Computing Systems, CHI '19, ACM. New York, NY, USA, 75:1–75:11
16. Wobbrock JO, Wilson AD, and Li Y (2007) Gestures without libraries, toolkits or training: a \$1 recognizer for user interface prototypes. In Proceedings of the 20th annual ACM symposium on User interface software and technology, ACM, 159–168

Contents

Data and Tools

Specific Domains

Part I
Modeling

Human Performance Modeling with Deep Learning

Arianna Yuan, Ken Pfeuffer, and Yang Li

Abstract Predicting human performance in interaction tasks allows designers or developers to understand the expected performance of a target interface without actually testing it with real users. In this chapter, we are going to discuss how deep learning methods can be used to aid human performance prediction in the context of HCI. Particularly, we are going to look at three case studies. In the first case study, we discuss deep models for goal-driven human visual search on arbitrary web pages. In the second study, we show that deep learning models could successfully capture human learning effects from repetitive interaction with vertical menus. In the third case study, we describe how deep models can be combined with analytical understanding to capture high-level interaction strategies and low-level behaviors in touchscreen grid interfaces on mobile devices. In all these studies, we show that deep learning provides great capacity for modeling complex interaction behaviors, which would be extremely difficult for traditional heuristic-based models. Furthermore, we showcase different ways to analyze a learned deep model to obtain better model interpretability, and understanding of human behaviors to advance the science.

Arianna Yuan and Ken Pfeuffer conducted the work during an internship at Google Research.

A. Yuan
Stanford University, 450 Serra Mall, Stanford, CA, USA
e-mail: xfyuan@stanford.edu

K. Pfeuffer
Aarhus University, Nordre Ringgade 1, Aarhus, Denmark
e-mail: ken@cs.au.dk

Y. Li (✉)
Google Research, Mountain View, CA, USA
e-mail: liyang@google.com

1 Introduction

Seeking models for predicting human performance in performing an interaction task has long been pursued in the field of human-computer interaction [2, 4, 6, 8, 10, 11, 15, 18, 28]. In addition to advancing the science for understanding human behaviors, creating these models has practical values in user interface design and development. A predictive model allows a developer or designer to understand the expected performance of an interface without having to test it with real users, which can be expensive and effort-consuming.

Several classic predictive models of human performance have become the cornerstones for HCI research for decades, e.g., Fitts' law [15] and Hick's law [18], which are rooted in information theory and experimental psychology. However, these models only capture specific aspects of human performance in isolation, e.g., Fitts' law for motor control or Hick's law for decision-making. They are limited in modeling human performance in realistic interaction tasks where a myriad of factors interplay, in which many of these factors we know, e.g., human perception, motor control and decision-making, and probably a lot more, are yet to be discovered.

Recent work (e.g., [16, 21, 38, 39, 47]) has attempted to develop compound methods that aim at modeling more sophisticated interaction tasks. For instance, Jokinen et al. [21] proposed a computational model of visual search on graphical layouts, with the assumption that the visual system is maximizing expected utility when deciding where to look at next. The work employed both the bottom-up processing and the top-down processing in the model when estimating the utility of different visual regions. Todi et al. [39] use a predictive model of visual search to optimize graphical layouts for an individual user so that items on an unseen interface can be found quicker. While these methods have pushed the applicability of predictive models toward more realistic tasks, they are still limited to address realistic interaction tasks and surfaces, e.g., touchscreen smartphones in an uncontrolled environment. To model each specific task, it often requires a great deal of domain expertise and extensive design and experimentation to derive an effective model. It is daunting to take into account all the factors that might affect human behavior. These rising complexities of realistic tasks constantly challenge classic modeling methods, which mostly rely on analytical insights and theoretical understanding. These methods are hardly scalable to arbitrarily complex human behaviors in realistic tasks.

The advance in deep learning has shown success in transforming many fields, such as speech recognition, machine translation and object detection [14, 20, 24]. Deep learning has also started to gain traction with HCI researchers and practitioners for solving a variety of problems, including human performance modeling [26, 33, 45, 47]. These methods can directly learn complex, nonlinear features as well as their relationships from raw interaction data. The learned features would be difficult to identify manually and articulate as rules or heuristics. There often exist features that are not so evident yet important for prediction. For example, as we will discuss in this chapter, when users search for a target (a button or an image) on a busy web page, the interplay between the target and the background cannot be simply characterized by a single or a few handcrafted parameters. By learning from the human search behavior data, a deep model is capable of capturing the priors and nuances of human behaviors, such as prioritizing the top-left quadrant of the web page over the rest regions during visual search, thus saving the researcher's effort in articulating them. A deep model, using a data-driven approach, is easily extensible for incorporating new factors as long as they are manifested in the data.

On the other hand, we want to emphasize the methodological difference of our proposed usage of data-driven, deep learning approaches in HCI. In contrast to the end-to-end models that are often desired in the mainstream deep learning field, we propose that we should combine deep models with well-documented heuristics and theoretical findings. For instance, in menu selection, the length of the text name of a menu item is a useful feature. Similarly, for visual search in web pages, high-level concepts such as target types could be where users brought their prior experience to the task, and thus should be included as a heuristic-based feature. Furthermore, analytical components, for example, knowledge about the users' navigation strategy in a mobile grid, can also be incorporated into the model. These high-level concepts are difficult to learn with limited data, which is often a challenge in performance modeling. Therefore, we advocate for a hybrid approach, which combines deep learning methods for extracting features from unstructured data with well-established heuristics and analytical insights. In the case studies we are going to discuss later, we show that this hybrid approach has unique advantages over traditional methods in both achieving higher accuracy and discovering novel human behavior patterns.

The structure of this chapter is as follows. We are going to describe a series of three projects from our research group, illustrating the methods and benefits of using the hybrid deep learning approach to model human performance. In the first case study, we present a deep learning model that learns to predict human visual search time from data [45]. In the second study, we showed that deep learning models could successfully capture human learning effects from repetitive use of a vertical menu [26]. In the third case study, we describe how high-level cognitive behaviors such as navigation strategies can be embedded in a deep model in a two-dimensional scrollable grid on a touchscreen mobile device [33]. Each case study is presented with the same structure: the introduction to the problem background, the problem formulation and dataset, the model design and training, the experiments and finally an analysis. We then finish the chapter by offering a discussion of the limitations and future work.

2 Modeling Visual Search Performance on Web Pages

Modeling human visual attention in interaction tasks has been a long-standing challenge in the HCI field [5, 37, 41–43]. Building models that can accurately estimate the difficulty of various visual search tasks has significant importance to user interface (UI) design and development. Traditional approaches for examining visual search involve usability tests with real human users, and a predictive model can save time and cost for UI practitioners by offering them insights into visual search difficulty before testing with real users.

Many classic results on visual search have been established across the fields of HCI and cognitive science. For instance, researchers have differentiated two types of visual search: feature search and conjunction search. Feature search is a visual search process in which participants look for a given target surrounded by distractors that differ from the target by a unique visual feature, such as orientation, color and shape, e.g., searching a triangle among squares. On the other hand, in conjunction search, participants look for a previously given target among distractors that share one or more visual features with the target [35], such as searching a red triangle among red squares and yellow triangles. Previous studies have shown that the efficiency (reaction time and accuracy) of feature search does not depend on the number of distractors [30], whereas the efficiency of conjunction search is dependent on the number of distractors present—as the number of distractors increases, the reaction time increases and the accuracy decreases [40]. In addition, using well-controlled visual stimuli, previous studies showed that prior knowledge of the target greatly influences visual research time [46], indicating the interaction between top-down and bottom-up processing in the visual search process.

Despite the robustness and simplicity of these early findings, they are not very practical and they only focus on modeling search time in abstracted settings. For example, the effect of a number of distractors on visual search time in conjunction search is observed with oversimplified stimuli, e.g., geometric shapes or Gabor patches. This is very unrealistic in everyday visual search tasks, e.g., finding a booking button on a busy hotel home page. Later modeling studies have attempted to simulate visual search in a more realistic context, such as searching for a target in web pages, menus and other graphical interfaces [16, 21, 38]. However, those studies usually require the extraction of a set of predefined visual features of the target and the candidate visual stimuli. Although those predefined, handcrafted features are indicative of search time, there is often useful information in the visual scene that cannot be captured by those handcrafted features and is missing in previous computational models.

As mentioned in Introduction, deep learning allows us to take a data-driven approach and save us some effort on intensive feature engineering. It has become increasingly popular in the HCI field recently. For instance, Zheng et al. [47] proposed a convolutional neural network to predict where people look on a web page under different task conditions. Particularly, they predefined five tasks, i.e., signing-up (email), information browsing (product promotion), form filling (file sharing, job searching), shopping (shopping) and community joining (social networking), and they pre-trained their model on a synthetic task-driven saliency dataset. In the work we are going to present in the following sessions, Yuan and Li [45] introduced a more generalizable deep learning method for visual search prediction, in the sense that it does not assume the nature of the search task or the prior of the search pattern. It takes advantage of both traditional modeling approaches and the popular deep learning method. Particularly, they combine existing heuristic-based, structured features that have long been used to model visual search tasks, together with the unstructured image features—raw pixels of a web page—to predict human visual search time.

2.1 Problem Formulation and Datasets

Yuan and Li focused on goal-driven visual search behaviors of human users on web pages. For each task, a human user is first given a target to search for, and then locates the item on a web page by clicking on it. The task resembles common interaction behaviors on web pages. They base their research on a dataset that was collected via crowdsourcing. The web pages used in the data collection were randomly selected from the top 1 billion English web pages across 24 vertical classification categories. For each task, an element on a web page was randomly selected as the target, and the human worker was asked to find it on the web page. A target element is of one of the following five types: image, text, link, button and input_field.

Each trial starts by showing the human worker a screen that contains only the target prompt and a "Begin" button at the top-left corner of the screen. Once the worker clicks on the "Begin" button, a web page is revealed and the target prompt remains on the screen in case the worker forgets the target to look for. The trial is finished once the worker finds and clicks on the target, or clicks on the "I can't find it" button on the top-right corner of the screen to skip the trial. If the target does not contain any text, its thumbnail image is shown to the user as the prompt for the search target. Otherwise, the text content is displayed to the human worker for finding an element that contains such text. In either case, the target is ensured to be a unique element on the page. There are 28,581 task trials in the dataset, which were performed by 1,887 human workers. In the dataset, each user has at least 8 data points. The dataset was randomly split for training (1520 users, 22591 trials), validation (184 users, 3151 trials) and testing (183 users, 2839 trials). There is no overlap in users among any of these datasets—the data of each user can only appear in one of these splits.

2.2 The Model Design and Learning

To build the model, Yuan and Li draw inspiration from cognitive psychology and neuroscience, and attempt to simulate the human visual search process with deep neural networks. In neuroscience, researchers have shown that when subjects try to selectively attend to a target in a visual scene, the neural representations of the objects, either the real target or the distractors that share similarity with the target, will be enhanced [13, 27, 29]. Based on this finding, Yuan and Li capture the human attention pattern with the neural attentional algorithm in deep learning. The attentional mechanism has recently been widely adopted in image captaining and visual question answering [1], which significantly boost the accuracy of these models by

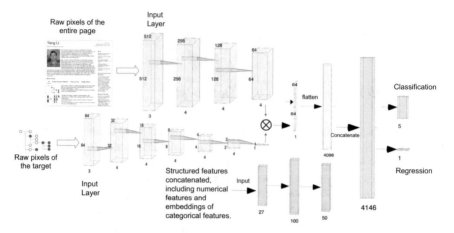

Fig. 1 The architecture of the visual search performance model. The attention map is computed as the alignment between the latent representations of the entire UI (the web page) and the target, which is then concatenated with the structured features as the input for predicting human performance in visual search

allowing the model to selectively attend specific areas in a scene given the target. The model with neural attentional mechanism also enhances the interpretability and the trustworthiness of the model because it allows us to draw analytical understanding of model behaviors by examining the attention map learned from the data.

The full architecture of Yuan and Li's model is illustrated in Fig. 1. To process a vast amount of information such as raw pixels of a web page, they use convolutional neural networks (CNN) as their image feature extractors. CNN has been widely used in object recognition, object detection and visual question answering [9, 22, 34]. This powerful architecture allows the model to capture the visual details on the web page and the interaction between the web page and the target without deliberately specifying any features. Because a target can be of variable sizes in different tasks, they first resize a target into the same dimension of 64×64, and then use a 6-layer convolutional neural network (CNN) to encode the target, which results in a target embedding of dimensions $1 \times 1 \times 4$. Similarly, for each task web page, Yuan and Li first resize them to 512×512 and then use a 3-layer convolutional neural network to encode the web page image from which results in an image embedding of $64 \times 64 \times 4$. Therefore, there are in total 64×64 super-pixel representations, each of which has dimension 4.

Computing Alignment Scores. With the embeddings of both the target (the goal) and those of the web page images computed, the model next performs a multiplicative attention mechanism [36, 44] over these embeddings. In particular, Yuan and Li compute the cosine similarity between the target embedding vector and each super-pixel representation to get a 2-D attention map. They evaluated three design choices of the attention map: (1) using the original attention map; (2) applying the attention map to the image embedding to get the attention-modulated image representation;

(3) normalizing the attention map with a softmax($\cdot$) function. In all these cases, they treat the attention map as the representation of unstructured webpage-target features (referred to as the webpage-target embedding). It is combined with heuristic-based, structured features (see next section), to predict search time. Yuan and Li find that the first method yields the best performance. Thus, the results in the following experiments are based on the first formulation of the attention map in the paper. The mathematical formula for computing the attention map $A \in \mathbb{R}^{64 \times 64}$ is the following:

$$A_{i,j} = \sum_{k=1}^{4} I_{i,j,k} T_k \tag{1}$$

where $I \in \mathbb{R}^{64 \times 64 \times 4}$ is the output from the last convolutional layer of the web page-CNN and $T \in \mathbb{R}^4$ is the output from the last convolutional layer of the target-CNN.

Combining with Heuristic-Based Features. Yuan and Li performed an analytical examination of the dataset by looking at the correlations between several well-established features in the literature of visual search time. They found that the y-coordinate of the top-left corner of the target is positively correlated with the search time: the bigger the y-coordinate, the longer it takes the participants to find the target, which implies a dominant top-down vertical search strategy employed by the human workers, since the starting position for each trial in the dataset is at the top of the screen. Regarding the size features, not surprisingly, both the width and the height of the target negatively correlate with the search time, i.e., the bigger the target is, the shorter the search time is. Based on a linear model that uses target vertical positions (y-coordinate) as one of the predictors, there is a positive correlation with the search time. Yuan and Li also analyze the influence of the number of candidate items (page complexity) over the search time. In addition to looking at how the total number of items affects search time, they conduct a finer granularity analysis by investigating how the number of candidate items in each object category would affect search time. They find that the number of certain object types are strong predictors of the search time. Images are the easiest to find whereas text is the hardest to find. Finally, target types are also an indicator for search time.

To incorporate these findings, Yuan and Li add several heuristic-based, structured features to the model. These features can be easily computed and do not require domain expertise in performance modeling to use them. The features include (1) the positional features, i.e., the (x, y) coordinates of the top-left corner of the target bounding box; the Euclidean distance between the top-left corner of the target and the top-left corner of the screen; (2) the size features, i.e., the width, the height as well as the area of the target; (3) the number of candidates or distractors, i.e., the number of leaf nodes in the DOM representation of the web page; and finally (4) the target type. There are five possible target types: `image`, `text`, `link`, `button` and `input_field`.

Except for the target types, all the other features are treated as numerical variables. For target type, a categorical variable, we use real-valued embedding vectors to encode different target types and the embeddings are learned from the data. The reason that we use embeddings instead of one-hot representation of target types is that the five target types are not entirely mutually exclusive. For instance, "link" is a special type of text and most buttons also contain text. Using real-valued embedding vectors allows the model to fully capture the similarity and the differences between various target types, which we will discuss further later. The combination of all the structured features, including the original value of the numerical variables and the embedding of the categorical variable, is then fed to a 2-layer fully connected network with the hyperbolic tangent function (tanh) as its activation function to get the feature embedding for the structured input. This embedding is then concatenated with the webpage-target embedding to jointly predict the search time using a final fully connected layer.

2.3 Experiments

Yuan and Li use the validation dataset to determine the model architecture and hyper-parameters such as the optimal stopping time and learning rate. Previous modeling work in HCI or cognitive psychology often reports performance on how well a model can fit the data. As a deep model has a vast number of parameters, it is trivial to fit the training data perfectly. Therefore, it is important to report the modeling accuracy on the test dataset, which the model has no access to during the training time. The test accuracy truly reflects the model's capability of capturing the human behavior.

Although the primary goal is predicting the search time, a regression problem, they also evaluate their model on two additional objectives: classification and ranking tasks. For the classification task, they categorize a visual search task into five difficult levels, Very Easy, Easy, Neutral, Hard and Very Hard, by bucketizing a continuous search time into one of these five categories according to the percentiles within participants. Specifically, for each participant, a data point is categorized as *Very Easy* if it is smaller than the 20th percentile of that human participant's time performance, *Easy* if it is between the 20th and the 40th percentile, *Neutral* if it is between the 40th and the 60th percentile, *Hard* if it is between the 60th and the 80th percentile and finally *Very Hard* if it is above the 80th percentile. For the classification task, the output layer is replaced with a 5-unit softmax layer, representing the probability of a search task belonging to one of the five difficulty levels. For the ranking tasks, the model is presented with a pair of randomly selected search tasks and it needs to decide which of them requires a shorter search time. The output of the regression model is used to rank the difficulty of a search task. The details of the model configuration, hyperparameters and training procedures can be found in the original paper [45].

For the regression task, the work reports the R^2 metric for both within- and cross-user cases. For the within-user case, R^2 is computed over the trials of each user. We then report the score averaged across all the users. For the cross-user case, R^2 is directly computed over all the trials from all the users. Both of them measure the correlation between the predicted and the ground-truth visual search times. Table 1 also shows the classification and the ranking accuracy. There was no repeat in performing

Table 1 The performances of different models. The first eight rows (all but the last two rows) report the results of linear models using a single feature (indicated by the Model column). The second last row (structured-all) refers to the baseline linear model that uses all the structured features. The last row reports the performance of Yuan and Li's full model, which uses both structured and unstructured inputs. The performance of the deep model is significantly better than the structured-all baseline model. $**p < 0.01$, $***p < 0.001$

Model	Within-user R^2	Cross-user R^2	Classification	Ranking
x-coordinate	0.113	0.011	0.254	0.542
y-coordinate	0.338	0.229	0.346	0.669
Target width	0.097	0.015	0.235	0.524
Target height	0.124	0.025	0.279	0.601
Distance	0.177	0.089	0.294	0.622
Target area	0.106	0.037	0.266	0.567
Target type	0.103	0.012	0.250	0.551
Total candidates	0.137	0.051	0.276	0.578
Structured-all	0.373	0.267	0.355	0.691
Deep net+structured	**0.384****	**0.288*****	**0.366*****	**0.699*****

each search task both within and across users, and all these metrics are computed based on the performance of each unique task. This metric computation is in contrast to the traditional approach of averaging performance metrics across multiple trials in HCI. Thus, in their setup, it is extremely challenging to obtain high accuracy due to noises and individual differences.

We train different models multiple times with various random seeds that control the train-test split and parameter initialization. We then reported the averaged performance metrics in Table 1. We can see that among all the single-feature baseline models, y-coordinate has the highest performance. The baseline model that uses all the structured features (structured-all) performs the best among all the baseline models. The deep model (the last row in the table) that combines both structured and unstructured input outperforms all the baseline models that use only structured features, across all the three metrics. Particularly, the within-user R^2 of the deep model is significantly greater than the structured-all baseline model, $t(4) = 4$, $p < 0.01$. The cross-user R^2 of the deep model is also significantly greater, $t(4) = 8$, $p < 0.001$. The 5-way classification accuracy is significantly greater than the structured-all model, $t(4) = 9$, $p < 0.001$. The same holds true for the ranking accuracy, $t(4) = 8$, $p < 0.001$.

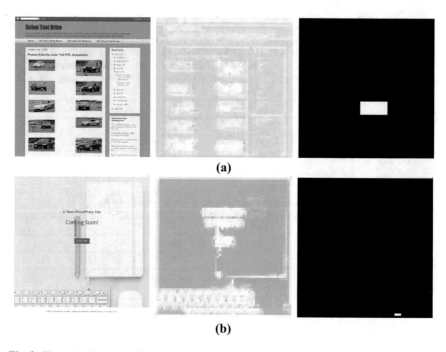

(a)

(b)

Fig. 2 The goal-driven attention map visualization of two example tasks

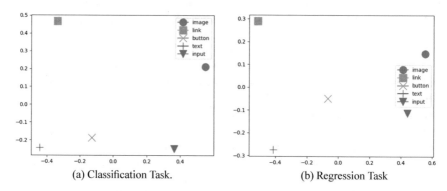

Fig. 3 The PCA projection of embeddings of each target type

2.4 Analysis

To better understand the model prediction, Yuan and Li examine the attention map learned by the model, a latent representation computed via Eq. 1. They found that the model is able to detect the content on the web page, regardless of the background color of the web page. As we can see in Fig. 2, target bounding box usually falls into one of the highlighted regions in the attention map. Interestingly, the attention map tends to capture the distractors that are visually similar to the target. For instance, in Fig. 2a, the target is an image and the model learns to highlight the images and ignore the text on the page, whereas in Fig. 2b, when the target is text, the model learns to highlight text but suppress images in the attention map.

To gain a deeper understanding of the model behavior, Yuan and Li analyzed the embeddings for each of the 5 target types learned by the model, by projecting these dimensions onto a 2-dimensional space using Principle Component Analysis (PCA) for visualization (see Fig. 3). For the first principle component, i.e., the x-axis in Fig. 3, link type is closest to text type because both types are text-based. It is followed by button, which often contain text but not always so. They are then followed by input_field and finally image. In other words, there is a sensible transition from text-like stimuli to image-like stimuli. This kind of property emerged from training for the regression task and for the classification task.

To summarize, this work shows that combining both structured and unstructured features gives the model a unique advantage to both fit the training data and generalize to the unseen data. It outperforms baseline models that use only structured features. Note that during training, the model was not explicitly supervised to form the embedding relationships in Fig. 3. Yet, these patterns naturally occur as the model learns from the data, because targets of specific types tend to manifest similar difficulties for search tasks, and thus are closer in the embedding space. Yuan and Li's methodology can be readily extended to incorporate other cognitive findings as well as emerging deep learning methods to combine the strength of both.

3   Predicting Human Performance in Vertical Menu Selection

In this case study, we look at target selection from a vertical list or menu, which has been a predominant task on modern graphical user interfaces such as a smartphone. For a task like the web page target acquisition discussed in the previous section (Sect. 2), it requires a model to address multiple performance components, such as visual search and motor control. Yet, a unique aspect of this task is the learning effect, which is not involved in the tasks in the previous section. Specifically, a user is expected to acquire a target repeatedly, and intuitively those that are often accessed by the user will become easier or faster to acquire over time.

A typical approach used by previous work is to explicitly combine multiple performance components, often via addition, and each component is designed based on a theoretical model. Specifically, Cockburn et al. [12] model menu selection time by summing pointing time (using Fitts' law), decision time (using Hick's law) and visual search time that are weighted by expertise. The visual search time is simply modeled as a linear function of the number of items present in the menu. The expertise with an item, i.e., the learning effect, is designed as a rational function in such a way that the expertise increases with the number of accesses to the item and decreases with the number of items in the menu. In the same vein, Bailly et al. [3] proposed a more complex model that is formulated based on gaze distribution for menu selection tasks, in which the total performance time is the sum of serial and direct visual search time, and the Fitts' law time. Serial search carries less weights and direct search gains more weight as the expertise increases.

While previous methods, which are mostly empirically tuned models based on theoretical assumptions, have gained substantial progress in modeling menu tasks, they are not easily extensible for accommodating various aspects of user interfaces and human factors. Learning effect is a profound factor that affects every aspect of human performance and has a complex interaction with other factors such as the visual saliency of an item, which many of these interactions cannot be easily articulated. In addition, new generations of computing devices such as touchscreen smartphones have introduced many factors that are not covered by traditional models. While it is possible to further expand existing models, there are many challenges and require a tremendous amount of effort to do so.

In this work [26], Li et al. took a departure from traditional methods by using a data-driven approach based on the recent advance of deep learning for sequence modeling. The work uses a novel hierarchical deep architecture for human menu performance modeling. A recurrent neural net, LSTM [19], is used to encode UI attributes and tasks at each target item selection. One LSTM is used to represent a menu with variable length, and incorporate UI attributes such as visual appearance and semantics. Another LSTM is to capture learning effects, a major component in human performance for repetitive tasks. The entire model is learned end-to-end using stochastic gradient descent. The model outperforms existing analytical methods in various settings for predicting selection time. Importantly, it is easily extensible for accommodating new UI features and human factors involved in an interaction task.

3.1   Problem Formulation and Datasets

A common task on desktop computers or smartphones is a user selecting a target item from a menu or list of items, e.g., choosing a song to play, a person to contact, and an application to launch. Because users often need to revisit the same item over time, it is necessary to model the task in the context of a sequence of selection tasks. Li et al. experimented with deep learning approaches on two datasets for menu selection tasks.

For menu selection on a desktop computer, Bailly et al. [3] collected a dataset from 21 participants in a controlled laboratory environment. The data collection follows a within-subjects design where each participant was asked to perform menu selection tasks for menus, with different types of sorting methods (Unordered, Alphabetical and Semantic), and lengths (8, 12 and 16 items). Participants were asked to complete 12 blocks of trials per menu. For each menu, the order of items in the menu is fixed so that participants can learn item positions over time. The experiment was conducted on a Windows PC with a 20 LCD display and a traditional optical mouse. In total, there are 189 sequences: 21 participants × 3 Menu configurations × 3 Menu Length. The length of each sequence may vary depending on the menu length: 12 blocks × (8-12-16 items) and there are 39,564 selections.

To investigate menu selection on touchscreen smartphones, Li et al. collected a dataset of menu selection tasks in the wild, from users with smartphones such as Apple iPhone 6 and Android Nexus 5. These users (workers) were recruited via Amazon Mechanic Turk. The data collection experiment was designed in a similar way to that of Bailly et al.'s dataset [3], with three menu lengths: 8, 12 and 16. Each worker is randomly assigned to a menu length with the item labels also randomly selected from a set of country names. The order of items in each menu is randomly determined for each worker and remains fixed throughout the trials. The number of trials completed by each worker ranged from 96 to 192 depending on menu lengths. In total, there were 863 sequences generated, each from a unique smartphone user (804 iPhone and 59 Android users). The mean duration of a worker session spanned 7 min (STD = 2.6 min). There are in total 159,072 selections in these sequences.

3.2 The Model Design and Learning

Li et al. designed their models [26] based on two important capabilities of recurrent neural net (RNN) [17]. First, it is capable of "reading" in a variable-length sequence of information and encoding it as a fixed-length representation. It is important as an interaction task often involves variable-length information. For example, the number of items in a menu can vary from one application to another. Second, the model is capable of mimicking users' behavior by learning to both acquire and "remember" new experience, and discard (or "forget") what it learns if the experience is too dated. While learning effects are a major component in human performance, prior works primarily use a frequency count as the measure of the user's expertise. In contrast, Li et al's model relies on LSTM [19], which offers a mechanism that is more natural in mimicking human behaviors.

Encoding a Single Selection Task. At each step, a user selects a target item in a vertical menu. As revealed by previous work, there are multiple factors in the task affecting human performance, including the number of items in the menu, the location of the target item in the menu, the visual salience of each item and whether there are semantic cues in assisting visual search. For each element in the UI, an item in the menu in our context, Li et al. represent it as a concatenation of a list of attributes (see Eq. 2). They use 1 or 0 to represent whether it is the target item for the current step. To capture the visual salience of an item, they use the length of the item name. An item that is especially short or long in comparison to the rest of the items on the menu tends to be easier to spot. To capture the semantics of an item, they represent the meaning of the item name with a continuous vector that was acquired from Word2vec [32], which project a word onto a continuous vector space where similar words are close in this vector space. m^s_j denotes the vector representation of

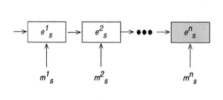 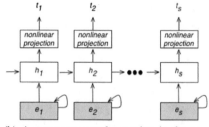

(a) The model uses a recurrent neural net to encode the selection task at a step, m_s^j is the vector representation of the jth item in the menu and e_s^j is the hidden state of the net after reading in the jth item.

(b) A recurrent neural net takes in the selection task at each step, i, and the acquired expertise (represented as the hidden state h_i), and predicts the time needed, t_i, for completing the selection task at this step.

Fig. 4 The architecture of the vertical menu selection model in [26]

the jth item in the menu at step s in the interaction sequence.

$$m_s^j = [\text{is\_target}, \text{len}(name), \text{word2vec}(name)] \tag{2}$$

To encode the selection task that involves a list of items in the menu, Li et al. feed the vector representation of each item in a sequel to a recurrent neural net [17] (see Fig. 4a). e_s^j represents the hidden state of the recurrent net after reading the jth item and seeing the previous items through e_s^{j-1}. n denotes the number of items in the menu. This recurrent net performs as a task encoder (thereafter referred to as the encoder net), and it does not have an output layer. The final hidden state of the recurrent net, e_s^n, a fixed-length vector, represents the selection task at step s. The model then concatenates a one-hot vector to indicate whether the menu items are semantically grouped, alphabetically sorted or unsorted, resulting in e_s. The task encoder can accommodate a menu with any length, n, and UI attributes.

Modeling A Sequence of Selection Tasks With the interaction task at each step of a sequence represented as e_s, it can now feed the sequence into another recurrent neural net (see Fig. 4b), which is referred to as the prediction net. Note that e_s in Fig. 4b represents the encoder net, which is a recurrent neural net itself whose outcome is fed to the prediction net. The task at each step can vary simply because the user might need to select a different target item. The UI at each step can also be different, e.g., an adaptive interface might decide to change the appearance of an item such as its size [11] to make it easier to acquire.

The recurrent neural net predicts human performance time at each step, t_i. The predictions are based on not only the task at the current step but also the hidden state of the previous step that captures the human experience performing previous tasks. Previous work in deep learning has shown that adding more layers in a deep net can improve the capacity for modeling complex behaviors [24]. To give the model more capacity, Li et al. add a hidden layer, with ReLU [31] as the activation function, after the recurrent layer, denoted as nonlinear projection in Fig. 4b. Finally, the time prediction t_i is computed as a linear combination of the outcome of the nonlinear transformation layer.

Model Learning and Loss Function. It is straightforward to compute the time prediction with the feedforward process of a neural net. The two recurrent neural nets involved in the model are trained jointly, end to end from the data by feeding in sequences of selection tasks as input and observed performance times as the target output (the ground truth), using stochastic gradient descent.

For time performance modeling, one common measure of prediction quality in the literature has been R^2 (e.g., [2, 4, 11, 15]). It measures how well predicted times match observed ones in capturing relative task difficulty or human performance across task conditions and progression. For general time series modeling regarding continuous values, there are other metrics often used, such as Root Mean Square Error (RMSE) or Mean Absolute Error (MAE). Mathematically, R^2 is the correlation between the sequence of observed times, y_i, and the sequence of predicted times, t_i, (see Eq. 3). $|S|$ represents the length of the sequence, and $\bar{y}$ is the mean of y_i.

$$R^2 = 1 - \frac{\sum_{i=1}^{|S|}(y_i - t_i)^2}{\sum_{i=1}^{|S|}(y_i - \bar{y})^2} \tag{3}$$

$\sum_{i=1}^{|S|}(y_i - \bar{y})^2$ reflects the variance of the observations in each sequence, which is independent of models. Thus, it is a known constant for each sequence in the training dataset, which we refer to as c_s. To maximize R^2, we want to minimize the squared error term $\sum_{i=1}^{|S|}(y_i - t_i)^2$, scaled by a sequence-specific constant c_s, which defines the loss function (see Eq. 4). The scaling acts effectively as adapting the learning rate based on the variance of each sequence for training the deep neural net. Intuitively, for each training sequence, the more variance the sequence has, the smaller the learning rate we should apply for updating the model parameters, and vice versa.

$$L_t = \frac{\sum_{i=1}^{|S|}(y_i - t_i)^2}{c_s} \tag{4}$$

With the loss function defined, the model can be trained using Backpropagation Through Time (BPTT) [17], a typical method for training recurrent neural nets (see more details in the following sections).

3.3 Experiments

To evaluate the model, for each dataset, Li et al. randomly split the data among users with half of the users for training and the other half of the users for testing the model. The experiment results were obtained based on the test dataset for which the model was not trained on, which truly shows how well the learned model can generalize to

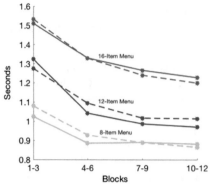 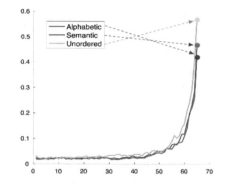

(a) The model accuracy over blocks on the smartphone dataset for menus with different lengths, with predicted times in solid lines and observed times in dashed lines.

(b) The Jacobian of Li et al.'s deep net indicates how the time performance for selecting a target item is affected by the past experience for selecting the item, in response to different menu organizations. The X axis is the trials in the sequence and the Y axis shows the magnitude of the derivative, i.e., the impact.

Fig. 5 The accuracy and analysis of the menu selection models [26]

new data that is unseen during training. They report the accuracy of the model on both target-level and menu-level R^2 that were used in the previous work [2]. Both measure the correlation between predicted and observed performance times. Target-level R^2 examines performance at each target position in a menu with a different amount of practice (blocks). Menu-level R^2 examines the average performance over all target positions in a menu with a varying amount of practice. For target-level R^2, the model achieved 0.75 on the public dataset for the overall correlation across menu organizations. In particular, R^2 for alphabetically ordered (A), semantically grouped (S) and unsorted menus (U) are 0.78, 0.62 and 0.80, respectively. Note that the single deep model here predicts for all menu organizations. In contrast, previously, Bailly et al. tuned and tested their model for each menu organization separately. Their R^2 results were reported as 0.64 (A), 0.52 (S) and 0.56 (U) [2]. For menu-level R^2, our model achieved 0.87 for overall correlation, 0.85 (A), 0.88 (S) and 0.94 (U), whereas previous work reported 0.91 (A), 0.86 (S) and 0.87 (U) [2]. Similarly, Li et al.'s model achieved competitive performance for the smartphone dataset that involves only unordered menus: target-level $R^2 = 0.76$ and menu-level $R^2 = 0.95$. It accurately predicts the time performance for each menu length (see Fig. 5a).

3.4 Analysis

While it is generally challenging to analyze what a deep model learns, Li et al. offer several analyses of the model behaviors and discuss how they match our intuition about user behavior. To understand the behavior of their deep net model, Li et al. compute its Jacobian that is the partial derivatives of the network output with respect to a specific set of inputs (see Fig. 5b)—it indicates how sensitive the time prediction is to the change in the input at each step. In particular, they want to find out how users' past experience with selecting a target affects the users' performance for selecting the target item again. Figure 5b is generated by taking the Jacobian of the deep net output, i.e., the time performance, with regards to the target feature in Eq. 2. We see that the more recent the experience is with selecting a target item, the more influence it has on the current trial for selecting the target item again. Intuitively, it might be because the user remembers where the item is on the list, as found in previous work [2, 11]. However, such an effect eventually wears off as the experience becomes dated, which is quite consistent with how human memory works. Previous work uses frequency count to represent the user expertise with an item and is insufficient to capture the profound aspects of human short-term memory such as the forgetting effect, and the interaction of learning effects with other factors. For example, Li et al. found the degree of how much the current performance relies on the past experience differs for the different menu organizations. As shown in Fig. 5b, such sequence dependency has the largest effect on unordered menus and less effect on semantically or alphabetically organized menus. A sensible explanation for this phenomenon is that semantic and alphabetic menus provide additional cues for users to locate an item, which results in less dependency on memory for completing the task.

To recap what we learn from this case study, a deep model significantly outperformed previous methods on the repetitive menu selection tasks where human experience matters. Importantly, such a deep model can easily capture essential components such as the learning effect and incorporate additional UI attributes such as visual appearance and content semantics without changing model architectures. By understanding how a deep learning model learns from human behavior, it can be seen as a vehicle to discover new patterns about human behaviors to advance analytical modeling.

4 Modeling Grid Performance on Touchscreen Mobile Devices

In the previous case studies, we have shown how deep learning can be used to model human behaviors by taking a dramatic departure from traditional methods relying on extensive feature engineering and theoretical assumptions. In this section, we are going to present a case study in which deep learning is used to enhance traditional analytical or theory-driven modeling. This is important as high-level behaviors might be difficult to learn directly from data especially when the dataset is relatively small.

The task itself, which is to find and select an item by a tap, is rather simple to the user. However, modeling this behavior is highly complex, which involves performance components such as navigation, visual search, pointing and learning, as well as the interplay among them. While many existing theories and findings are relevant, there lacks a holistic understanding of user behaviors and performance for interaction with a grid interface and a computational model for capturing many nuances when using a touchscreen smartphone.

To better understand performance factors, Pfeuffer and Li [33] first conduct an analysis of a 20-user study of mobile grid interfaces. The study reveals how components such as learning, navigation, visual search and pointing affect the user's performance in response to varying grid sizes and trial repetitions. The analysis resulted in novel findings of mobile grids. For example, users switch between two navigation strategies; users become faster over time by optimizing gesture operation and visual search; user performance depends on row regions of a grid.

Based on the findings from the study, they propose a predictive model for human performance in a grid task. A unique aspect that the model captures, via a neural net, is the probabilistic determination of user navigation strategy for deciding between starting the search from the top or the bottom of the grid. Conditioned on the strategy, the cost of navigation is linear with the row position of the target item. Once the viewport is set, users visually search across columns, and point and touch the target. After the user scrolls the screen, the target's on-screen position becomes unknown, which makes it implausible to compute the pointing cost. Therefore, they combine Fitts' law cost with a probability distribution of position across the screen, which is learned from the data.

The evaluation that measures how well Pfeuffer and Li's model predicts human performance on a test dataset shows promising results on predictive quality. As we will discuss in the following section, Pfeuffer and Li's work uses deep learning methods to enhance traditional modeling by filling the gap where certain aspects of behaviors cannot be easily designed, and by allowing end-to-end optimization of the entire model.

4.1 Problem Formulation and Datasets

Most prior performance models of menus focused on desktop computers [2, 6, 7, 11, 23], leaving mobile devices underexplored despite their large adoption in everyday life. Mobile devices provide a distinct interaction surface, with a small display and direct touch user input. Pfeuffer and Li [33] focus on a scrollable two-dimensional grid UI, a common interface on touchscreen mobile devices for presenting a large number of items on a small-form factor device, e.g., apps in a launcher, photos in a gallery and items in a shopping collection.

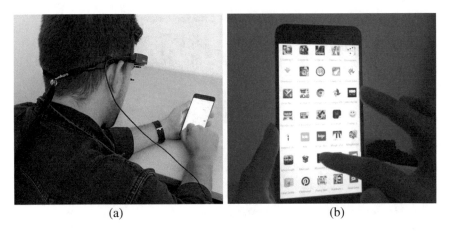

(a)   (b)

Fig. 6 The experimental study setup (**a**) and a close-up view of the grid UI used in the study (**b**)

Specifically, they conducted an eye-tracking experiment to investigate visual and manual performance components when users find and select targets from a grid UI, which informs the design of the predictive model for human performance. In the experiment, a grid interface shows a collection of mobile app icons in a two-dimensional row-by-column organization. A selection task involves 1-DOF vertical scrolling and tapping to select the target. If the target is within the initial (top) viewport, a user can directly tap on it without scrolling the grid. The UI design in this experiment was borrowed from the Android App Launcher. Typically, 6–7 rows of the grid are visible on the screen (Fig. 6). After selecting an app icon, it flashes in green or red to indicate a correct or wrong selection.

The experiment employed a within-subject repeated measures study design. The main condition is *Gridlength*, i.e., the number of rows in the grid, varying among 12, 18, 24 and 30 rows with a counterbalanced order. With the fixed number of 5 columns, there are 60, 90, 120 and 150 items in these grids, which resemble realistic number of apps. The items for each grid are randomly chosen from the top 420 apps of the Android Play Store in July 2017. Each app is used as the target at most once for each user to eliminate potential carry-over effects. The experiment used *8 blocks* per grid length to investigate learning effects. Each block consists of *15 trials* in a randomized order. For each user, the procedure resulted in 4 grid lengths × 8 blocks × 15 trials = 480 trials. 20 paid participants were recruited for the study. They were 31 years old on average (SD = 5), 8 female and 12 male, all right-handed and active smartphone users. The experiment used a Nexus 6P mobile phone and a Tobii Glasses 2 eye tracker, which sampled gaze at ≈100 hz. To map gaze data to screen coordinates, Pfeuffer and Li used computer vision to detect the phone screen within the eye tracker's scene camera.

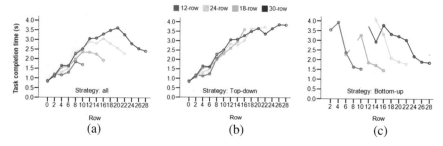

Fig. 7 Task completion time across Row×Grid, for each strategy

4.2 Model Design and Learning

At the top level, Pfeuffer and Li's model is very similar to previous models based on the linear combination of individual performance components [3, 11]. The overall selection time T_i for each item is the sum of navigation T_{nav}, visual search T_{vs} and pointing time T_{point}:

$$T_i = T_{nav} + T_{vs} + T_{point} \tag{5}$$

To model each of these components for a realistic grid task, the work uses deep learning techniques to address aspects that lack a solid theoretical basis. By analyzing the dataset, Pfeuffer and Li found an unexpected effect of the vertical grid position on task completion time, which initially increases with the row position, and then steadily decreases toward the bottom of the grid. They found that navigation strategy is the main reason for the decrease in the time required. In 80% of trials, the user navigates from the top of the grid continuously downwards (Top-Down), until the target is found. In the rest 20% of trials, the user performs a flick gesture to scroll to the bottom of the grid, and then navigates upward (Bottom-Up). As shown in Fig. 7, the time for selecting a target increases approximately linear with the row position of the target (decreasing for bottom-up). In essence, the bottom-up strategy resembles the inverse of the top-down strategy plus the initial scroll-down gesture.

Several factors seem to have strong influences on strategy usage, including the first letter of the target name. For most letters, users went for the top-down strategy, but when the initial letter is positioned toward the end of the alphabet, the user tends to use the bottom-up strategy more often. As a user becomes more experienced, the use of the bottom-up strategy increases. A shorter grid length also seems to encourage bottom-up strategy use.

Based on these observations, Pfeuffer and Li designed a novel probabilistic estimation of navigation strategy to capture the switching between the top-down and bottom-up navigation. The navigation time is a probabilistic combination of the top-down (N_{tdn}) and the bottom-up (N_{bup}) navigation costs:

$$T_{nav} = (1 - S_{btm})N_{tdn} + S_{btm}N_{bup} \tag{6}$$

where S_{btm} is a probability that the user navigates from the bottom of the grid.

The time for both navigation costs can be simply modeled with a linear function of the target's row position pos_{row}. The difference is that they use a different intercept term, because the bottom-up navigation involves the effort to reach the end of the grid, i.e., the initial swipe-down step. The bottom-up navigation counts the row position from the bottom upwards instead from the top downwards: $N_{tdn} = pos_{row}T_{row} + b_{tdn}$ and $N_{bup} = (len_{row} - pos_{row})T_{row} + b_{bup}$, where T_{row} denotes the time required for a each row, and b_{tdn} and b_{bup} are bias terms to be learned from the data. The time needed for inspecting each row, T_{row}, decreases logarithmically with expertise increase, modeled by $T_{row} = a_r\exp(-b_r t) + c_r$, similar to Bailly et al.'s model [2], where a_r, b_r and c_r are parameters to be learned from the data.

The strategy switching model has three cases determined by the grid length and viewport size, i.e., the top rows, the bottom rows in the grid and rows in-between:

$$S_{btm} = \begin{cases} 0 & \text{if } pos_{row} < view_{row} \\ 1 & \text{if } pos_{row} > len_{row} - view_{row} \\ S_{prob} & \text{otherwise} \end{cases} \qquad (7)$$

where S_{prob} is a logistic function that outputs a probability between 0 and 1, based on a linear combination of three values: the grid length, the user experience and the first letter of the target name:

$$S_{prob} = \text{sigmoid}(s_0 + s_1 len_{row} + s_2 S_{exp} + s_3 l) \qquad (8)$$

len_{row} and l are normalized to ± 0.5 by considering the range of these values in the training dataset. Sigmoid function offers a suitable numerical range of 0–1 for regulating the navigation cost. S_{exp}, the expertise of using a strategy, is computed as follows:

$$S_{exp} = \text{sigmoid}(e_0 + e_1 t) \qquad (9)$$

which is a sigmoid function taking the linear transformation of the previous encounters t as input. The sigmoid function maps an unbounded value to a range from 0 to 1. Sigmoid is appropriate in that expertise will eventually saturate with practice which will approach 1 infinitely. s_i and e_i are the parameters to be learned from the data. The entire strategy model is equivalent to a standard feedforward neural network using sigmoid as the activation function, and these parameters can be learned using general stochastic gradient descent.

In addition to the navigation strategies, Pfeuffer and Li brought deep learning to other components of the model. For example, to model the pointing time, one challenge is that the absolute position of a target on the screen is undetermined due to the human scrolling behavior. To address this issue, they use a probabilistic combination of Fitts' law time across all the vertical positions. The target's Y position on the screen is estimated using a Gaussian distribution as inspired by the study finding, while X is given by pos_{col}. They discretize the Y position as a fixed number

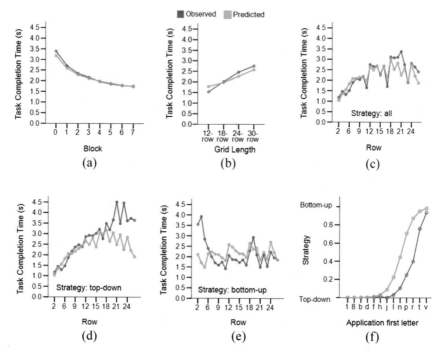

Fig. 8 Observed and predicted selection time for various grid performance factors

of rows in the viewpoint, $view_{row}$, and then compute the weighted average of the cost for each row, j, to estimate the pointing time:

$$T_{point} = \sum_{j=1}^{view_{row}} P_j T_{point_j} \tag{10}$$

The time of each row in the viewpoint is calculated by a regular Fitts' law model: $T_{point_j} = a_f + b_f \log_2 \left(1 + \frac{d([pos_{col}, j], view_{ctr})}{W}\right)$, where d is the Euclidean distance between a given target position and the viewport center, $view_{ctr}$. a_f ad b_f are learned. The probability for the target to be on each row j is determined by a probability density of normal distribution that reflects how Y positions are distributed across the screen.

$$P_j = \frac{1}{\sigma\sqrt{2\pi}} \exp(-(j/view_{row} - \mu)^2/2\sigma^2) \tag{11}$$

4.3 Experiments

To evaluate the model, Pfeuffer and Li conducted a two-fold cross-validation. For each fold, the model is trained with half of the users (10 users), and tested on the other half. See the original paper [33] for details of model implementation, parameter estimation and evaluation. Overall, the model achieves high prediction accuracy on the validation data in predicting time performance measured as average R^2, which measures the correlation between the observed time performance and predicted one (see Fig. 8).

The model predicted the user's performance across blocks with an accuracy of $R^2 = 0.99$ (8 blocks). Figure 8a shows how the power law of practice aligns well with grid interaction performance. Another main factor, grid length, has also been well modeled with $R^2 = 0.97$ (8 block×4 grid), as indicated in Fig. 8b. The row of an item defines its vertical target position, and thus is integral in capturing navigation performance. The model is able to predict performance variance across rows (12, 18, 24 and 30 rows) with $R^2 = 0.83$, and Fig. 8c shows the results of the predicted time across rows. The predicted strategy was slightly offset for the transition from the top-down to the bottom-up strategy; the model predicted users would use the bottom-up approach at earlier letters in the alphabet (Fig. 8f). One potential reason for this issue is that the targets in the experiments involve letters with very different occurrence frequencies. Nonetheless, we can see that the model still approximated the times well (Fig. 8d–e).

4.4 Analysis

In this analysis, instead of looking at model behaviors as previous case studies do, we analyze how the predictive model can help reduce user effort in a mobile grid interface. For example, in the App Launcher on Google Pixel devices, five suggestions of the next apps to use are presented at the top of the screen based on the user's current context. If a target app is among these predictions, the user can immediately launch it without searching the entire grid. A common way for deciding what items to suggest at a given step, t, is based on the probability distribution over all possible items, P_t, which are determined by an event prediction engine that is out of the scope of this chapter. The event prediction engine may score each item (representing an action) based on a range of external signals such as time of the day or user location. Note that event prediction is different from the time performance prediction that our model is designed for. For an example of an event prediction model, please see [25]. A probability-based method typically selects a given number of items (e.g., 5) that have the highest probabilities, and placed them at a convenient location such as a prediction bar at the top of the screen for easy access by the user. Let us formulate the time cost for accessing item i at trial t as the following:

$$cost_t^i = \begin{cases} C & \text{if } i \in Top5(P_t) \\ G(i, t, g) & \text{otherwise} \end{cases} \tag{12}$$

where $Top5$ picks 5 items that have the highest probabilities, and $G(i, t, g)$ is the time cost model that Pfeuffer and Li proposed that predicts time performance for accessing item i given the trial t and a grid configuration g. C is a constant time for accessing an item in the prediction bar.

Instead of only considering the probability of the item being the next app to usef, it can potentially further reduce user effort by considering the time cost for accessing each item in a grid interface. The expected utility for suggesting an item is the product of its probability and its cost.

$$U_t = P_t \odot G(t, g) \tag{13}$$

$G(t, g)$ computes the cost for each item in the grid based on the time performance model derived in this paper, which results in a vector. $\odot$ represents the pairwise product between the probability distribution and the cost vector. Thus, the utility-based optimization can be formulated as follows:

$$cost_t^i = \begin{cases} C & \text{if } i \in Top5(U_t) \\ G(i, t, g) & \text{otherwise} \end{cases} \tag{14}$$

The equation is similar to Eq. 14, except that $Top5$ selects items based on utilities instead of probabilities.

Pfeuffer and Li validated their hypothesis by evaluating the two methods, with or without expected utility computed from the grid performance model, with task sequences generated from the uniform and the Zipf [48] task distributions, which have been used in previous work for studying adaptive user interfaces [11]. In a Zipf distribution, a small number of items are frequently used while the rest in the grid are rarely used. At each trial, a probability distribution is drawn over all possible items from a Dirichlet that is seeded with one of these target distributions. The target for the trial is then drawn by sampling the probability distribution. This approach has several benefits. First, the probability distribution is valid because the target is drawn from it. Second, the resulting task sequence is mostly consistent with the desired target distribution. Last, Dirichlet can be parametrized to simulate an item predictor with different accuracy, i.e., how often the item that has the largest probability is indeed the target.

Based on 1600 interaction sequences generated from the two task distributions, with 4 grid lengths, a range of event prediction accuracy (from 10% to 70%), and the two optimization methods, they compute the total time needed for completing a sequence using a given optimization method, grid length, target distribution as well as item prediction accuracy. Figure 9a–c shows the results of the simulation for both conditions. They found the utility-based optimization outperformed the probability-based method in reducing task completion time ($F_7^1 = 35$, p < 0.0006). Across all

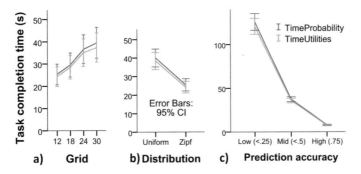

Fig. 9 Simulation of utility versus probability-based optimization for factor Grid, Distribution and Prediction Accuracy. Across these factors, the inclusion of utility reduces task completion times

conditions, the utility method is faster than the probability-based method (Fig. 9). Particularly, when the grid has more items, the advantage of the utility-based method is more pronounced (a), considering that targets that are further down the grid will acquire higher utility to be placed at the prediction bar. By discretizing item prediction accuracy to three equal bins: Low, Mid and High accuracy (Fig. 9c), we can see that when the accuracy of item prediction is low, the advantage of the utility-based method over the probability one is also more pronounced.

5 Discussion

Despite the great capacity of deep learning models, several challenges remain in using such a data-driven approach in HCI. One of the common criticisms for deep learning models is the "black-box" property of the models, i.e., these models are often hardly interpretable. In the case studies we reviewed in this chapter, we see that specific techniques are used such as examining the learned attention map (Sect. 2), or the Jacobian of the network (the partial derivatives of the network output with respect to a specific set of inputs) (Sect. 3) to get better interpretability. However, those explorations are preliminary and future research is required to investigate deeper on this issue.

Another challenge is related to the bias in data collection. Because deep learning approaches are primarily data-driven, they are very sensitive to the statistics in the training data. In other words, the models learn what they are trained on. That implies that we need to be cautious about the potential bias in our data collection. For instance, in Yuan and Li's work [45], the data they used to train the model was collected from tasks in which the "Begin" button is always positioned at the top-left corner of the screen. Consequently, the starting position of the search is the same across trials, which is different from real-life scenarios. Although the model is still useful as it can be used to examine the relative performance of alternative designs via A/B testing when the starting position is controlled, such bias needs to be corrected by collecting more training trials with different starting positions in future research.

A third challenge is to model human cognitive processes as accurately as possible using deep learning models. Take the visual search modeling on web pages [45] as an example. Despite being biologically inspired, Yuan and Li's model is not intended to replicate the real human visual search process. For one thing, it does not involve any sequential attention shifts, which is different from human behaviors. In the future, we could utilize deep learning models such as recurrent neural networks to capture the sequential aspects of visual search, which would allow us to compare model predictions and human data on a more detailed level. Similarly, in the menu modeling work, there are opportunities to extend the model for multilevel analysis of interaction by considering behaviors of finer granularity such as gazes and manual input paths.

Despite being a challenging issue, modeling human cognitive processes in HCI tasks using machine learning models is still a great opportunity. For instance, in the menu selection modeling work [26], Li et al. analyzed how human learning effects are captured and mimicked by a deep model, and how the learning effect differs across different menu organizations. The Jacobian responds differently for different menu organizations, which reflects the memory effect as manifested in the data. These findings can advance our understanding of how human behaves and thus may inspire others to design new analytical models to capture these effects. Rather than using deep models only for predictions, the deep learning approach can be seen as a vehicle to discover new patterns about human behaviors to advance analytical research.

Cognitive process modeling related to menu selection can be further expanded by manual navigation in addition to visual search. Our third use case showed that users navigate with two strategies—starting from the top or the bottom of a scrollable grid. The analytical understanding is incorporated through the probabilistic estimation of the navigation strategies. This finding first explains the last item effect [2] and proposes a modeling approach for the phenomenon. However, in general, we find fixed UI locations such as the top or the bottom of a list can act as spatial cues to the user and decrease the need for visual search over time. In contrast, dynamic UI locations such as objects in a scrollable list lead to recurring visual search processes. Thus, considering the user strategies with regards to static and dynamic UI elements can become an integral part of modeling the user performance.

Although deep learning models are not as interpretable as traditional heuristic-based models, we could still bring a lot of prior knowledge into the model by defining the appropriate model architecture. We have seen modeling work that uses hierarchically organized recurrent neural nets to capture the performance of a sequence of UI tasks [26], and convolutional neural networks for processing images for modeling search time [45]. The choice of those model types reflects researchers' prior knowledge of the nature of those UI tasks. Future work should investigate how the choice of different network architectures influences model performance.

There are several other directions for future work. In all the case studies we reviewed, although the deep models outperform the baseline models, there is still a lot of room for improvement in terms of model accuracy. In addition, in future work, we should go beyond predicting human performance, and give designers suggestions on how to optimize user experience, such as how to improve target saliency under design constraints or how to reduce menu selection time by optimizing the menu layout. Pfeuffer and Li's analyses [33] show user benefits, for reducing time cost, on using their predictive model in an adaptive user interface. Future work should further investigate the direction of optimizing user interfaces with deep learning models.

6 Conclusion

In this chapter, we discuss how data-driven, deep learning approaches can revolutionize human performance modeling in interaction tasks. In particular, we review three projects from our group, including visual search modeling on arbitrary web pages [45], repetitive menu selection on desktop and mobile devices [26], and target selection on a scrollable mobile grid [33]. Each of these projects addresses a unique interaction task and showcases different modeling strategies and techniques. These methods, based on deep learning models, significantly outperform traditional modeling techniques. Importantly, these methods are highly extensible for incorporating new factors, alleviating the efforts for extensive feature engineering and allowing end-to-end modeling. These methods also offer new avenues for modeling complex human behavior in interaction tasks and are promising for making new analytical findings that advance the science.

References

1. Anderson P, He X, Buehler C, Teney D, Johnson M, Gould S, Zhang L (2018) Bottom-up and top-down attention for image captioning and visual question answering. In: Proceedings of the IEEE conference on computer vision and pattern recognition, pp 6077–6086
2. Bailly G, Oulasvirta A, Brumby DP, Howes A (2014) Model of visual search and selection time in linear menus. In: Proceedings of the SIGCHI conference on human factors in computing systems (CHI '14). ACM, New York, NY, USA, pp 3865–3874. http://dx.doi.org/10.1145/2556288.2557093
3. Bailly G, Oulasvirta A, Brumby DP, Howes A (2014) Model of visual search and selection time in linear menus. In: Proceedings of the SIGCHI conference on human factors in computing systems. ACM, pp 3865–3874
4. Bi X, Li Y, Zhai S (2013) FFitts law: modeling finger touch with fitts' law. In: Proceedings of the SIGCHI conference on human factors in computing systems (CHI '13). ACM, New York, NY, USA, pp 1363–1372. http://dx.doi.org/10.1145/2470654.2466180
5. Borji A (2019) Saliency prediction in the deep learning era: successes and limitations. IEEE Transa Pattern Anal Mach Intell (2019)
6. Byrne MD (2001) ACT-R/PM and menu selection. Int J Hum-Comput Stud 55(1):41–84. https://doi.org/10.1006/ijhc.2001.0469
7. Card SK (1982) User perceptual mechanisms in the search of computer command menus. In: Proceedings of the 1982 conference on human factors in computing systems (CHI '82). ACM, New York, NY, USA, pp 190–196. http://dx.doi.org/10.1145/800049.801779

8. Card SK, Moran TP, Newell A (1980) The keystroke-level model for user performance time with interactive systems. Commun ACM 23(7):396–410

9. Chen K, Wang J, Chen L-C, Gao H, Xu W, Nevatia R (2015) ABC-CNN: an attention based convolutional neural network for visual question answering. arXiv:1511.05960

10. Chen X, Bailly G , Brumby DP, Oulasvirta A, Howes A (2015). The emergence of interactive behaviour: a model of rational menu search. In: CHI'15 Proceedings of the 33rd annual ACM conference on human factors in computing systems, vol 33. Association for Computing Machinery (ACM), pp 4217–4226

11. Cockburn A, Gutwin C, Greenberg S (2007) A predictive model of menu performance. In: Proceedings of the SIGCHI conference on human factors in computing systems (CHI '07). ACM, New York, NY, USA, pp 627–636. http://dx.doi.org/10.1145/1240624.1240723

12. Cockburn A, Gutwin C, Greenberg S (2007) A predictive model of menu performance. In: Proceedings of the SIGCHI conference on human factors in computing systems. ACM, pp 627–636

13. Corbetta M, Shulman GL (2002) Control of goal-directed and stimulus-driven attention in the brain. Nat Rev Neurosci 3(3):201

14. Devlin J, Chang M-W, Lee K, Toutanova K (2018) BERT: pre-training of deep bidirectional transformers for language understanding. arXiv:1810.04805

15. Fitts PM (1954) The information capacity of the human motor system in controlling the amplitude of movement. J Exper Psychol 47(6):381

16. Fu W-T, Pirolli P (2007) SNIF-ACT: A cognitive model of user navigation on the World Wide Web. Human-Comput. Int. 22(4):355–412

17. Graves A (2012) Supervised sequence labelling with recurrent neural networks. Springer, Studies in computational intelligence

18. Hick WE (1952) On the rate of gain of information. Q J Exp Psychol 4(1):11–26

19. Hochreiter S, Schmidhuber JU (1997) Long short-term memory. Neural Comput 9(8):1735–1780

20. Johnson M, Schuster M, Le QV, Krikun M, Yonghui W, Chen Z, Thorat N, Viégas F, Wattenberg M, Corrado G et al (2017) Google's multilingual neural machine translation system: enabling zero-shot translation. Trans Ass Comput Ling 5(2017):339–351

21. Jokinen Jussi PP, Zhenxin W, Sayan S, Antti O, Xiangshi R (2020) Adaptive feature guidance: modelling visual search with graphical layouts. Int J Human-Comput Stud 136:102376

22. Krizhevsky A, Sutskever I, Hinton GE (2012) ImageNet classification with deep convolutional neural networks. In: Advances in neural information processing systems, pp 1097–1105

23. Lane DM, Napier HA, Batsell RR, Naman JL (1993) Predicting the skilled use of hierarchical menus with the keystroke-level model. Hum-Comput Interact 8(2):185–192. http://dx.doi.org/10.1207/s15327051hci0802_4

24. LeCun Y, Bengio Y, Hinton G (2015) Deep learning. Nature 521(7553):436

25. Li Y (2014) Reflection: enabling event prediction as an on-device service for mobile interaction. In: Proceedings of the 27th annual ACM symposium on user interface software and technology (UIST '14). Association for Computing Machinery, New York, NY, USA, pp 689–698. http://dx.doi.org/10.1145/2642918.2647355

26. Li Y, Bengio S, Bailly G (2018) Predicting human performance in vertical menu selection using deep learning. In: Proceedings of the 2018 CHI conference on human factors in computing systems, pp 1–7

27. Liu T, Larsson J, Carrasco M (2007) Feature-based attention modulates orientation-selective responses in human visual cortex. Neuron 55(2):313–323

28. MacKenzie IS, Buxton W (1992) Extending Fitts' law to two-dimensional tasks. In: Proceedings of the SIGCHI conference on human factors in computing systems, pp 219–226

29. Martinez-Trujillo JC, Treue S (2004) Feature-based attention increases the selectivity of population responses in primate visual cortex. Curr Biol 14(9):744–751

30. McElree B, Carrasco M (1999) The temporal dynamics of visual search: evidence for parallel processing in feature and conjunction searches. J Exp Psychol: Human Percept Perf 25(6):1517

31. Nair V, Hinton GE (2010) Rectified linear units improve restricted Boltzmann machines. In: ICML: Proceedings of the 27th international conference on machine learning
32. Pennington J, Socher R, Manning CD (2014) Glove: global vectors for word representation. In: Proceedings of the 2014 conference on empirical methods in natural language processing (EMNLP), pp 1532–1543
33. Pfeuffer K, Li Y (2018) Analysis and modeling of grid performance on touchscreen mobile devices. In: Proceedings of the 2018 CHI conference on human factors in computing systems, pp 1–12
34. Ren S, He K, Girshick R, Sun J (2015) Faster R-CNN: towards real-time object detection with region proposal networks. In: Advances in neural information processing systems, pp 91–99
35. Shen J, Reingold EM, Pomplun M (2003) Guidance of eye movements during conjunctive visual search: the distractor-ratio effect. Can J Exp Psychol 57(2):76
36. Shih KJ, Singh S, Hoiem D (2016) Where to look: focus regions for visual question answering. In: Proceedings of the IEEE conference on computer vision and pattern recognition, pp 4613–4621
37. Tehranchi F, Ritter FE (2018) Modeling visual search in interactive graphic interfaces: adding visual pattern matching algorithms to ACT-R. In: Proceedings of 16th international conference on cognitive modeling. University of Wisconsin Madison, WI, pp 162–167
38. Teo L-H, John B, Blackmon M (2012) CogTool-Explorer: a model of goal-directed user exploration that considers information layout. In: Proceedings of the SIGCHI conference on human factors in computing systems. ACM, pp 2479–2488
39. Todi K, Jokinen J, Luyten K, Oulasvirta A (2019) Individualising graphical layouts with predictive visual search models. ACM Trans Int Intell Syst (TiiS) 10(1):1–24
40. Treisman AM, Gelade G (1980) A feature-integration theory of attention. Cogn Psychol 12(1):97–136
41. van der Meulen H, Varsanyi P, Westendorf L, Kun AL, Shaer O (2016) Towards understanding collaboration around interactive surfaces: exploring joint visual attention. In: Proceedings of the 29th annual symposium on user interface software and technology. ACM, pp 219–220
42. Walter R, Bulling A, Lindlbauer D, Schuessler M, Müller J (2015) Analyzing visual attention during whole body interaction with public displays. In: Proceedings of the 2015 ACM international joint conference on pervasive and ubiquitous computing. ACM, New York, NY, USA, pp 1263–1267
43. Wu X, Gedeon T, Wang L (2018) The analysis method of visual information searching in the human-computer interactive process of intelligent control system. In: Congress of the international ergonomics association. Springer, pp 73–84
44. Xu H, Saenko K (2016) Ask, attend and answer: exploring question-guided spatial attention for visual question answering. In: European conference on computer vision. Springer, pp 451–466
45. Yuan A, Li Y (2020) Modeling human visual search performance on realistic webpages using analytical and deep learning methods. In: Proceedings of the 2020 CHI conference on human factors in computing systems, pp 1–12
46. Zhaoping L, Frith U (2011) A clash of bottom-up and top-down processes in visual search: the reversed letter effect revisited. J Exp Psychol: Human Perc Perf 37(4):997
47. Zheng Q, Jiao J, Cao Y, Lau RWH (2018) Task-driven webpage saliency. In: Proceedings of the European conference on computer vision (ECCV), pp 287–302
48. Zipf GK (1949) Human behavior and the principle of least effort: an introduction to human ecology. Addison-Wesley Press, Boston. http://psycnet.apa.org/record/2005-10806-009

Optimal Control to Support High-Level User Goals in Human-Computer Interaction

Christoph Gebhardt and Otmar Hilliges

Abstract With emerging technologies like robots, mixed-reality systems or mobile devices, machine-provided capabilities are increasing, so is the complexity of their control and display mechanisms. To address this dichotomy, we propose optimal control as a framework to support users in achieving their high-level goals in human-computer tasks. We reason that it will improve user support over usual approaches for adaptive interfaces as its formalism implicitly captures the iterative nature of human-computer interaction. We conduct two case studies to test this hypothesis. First, we propose a model-predictive-control-based optimization scheme that supports end-users to plan and execute robotic aerial videos. Second, we introduce a reinforcement-learning-based method to adapt mixed-reality augmentations based on users' preferences or tasks learned from their gaze interactions with a UI. Our results show that optimal control can better support users' high-level goals in human-computer tasks than common approaches. Optimal control models human-computer interaction as a sequential decision problem which represents its nature and, hence, results in better predictability of user behavior than for other methods. In addition, our work highlights that optimization- and learning-based optimal control have complementary strengths with respect to interface adaptation.

1 Introduction

With emerging technologies like robots, mixed-reality (MR) systems or mobile devices, machine-provided capabilities are increasing, so is the complexity of their control and display mechanisms. This results in a dichotomy between the potential of these technologies and the extent to which users can leverage them to achieve

C. Gebhardt (✉) · O. Hilliges
ETH Zürich, Department of Computer Science, Stampfenbachstrasse 48, 8092 Zürich, Switzerland
e-mail: Christoph.Gebhardt@inf.ethz.ch

O. Hilliges
e-mail: Otmar.Hilliges@inf.ethz.ch

© The Author(s), under exclusive license to Springer Nature Switzerland AG 2021
Y. Li and O. Hilliges (eds.), *Artificial Intelligence for Human Computer Interaction:
A Modern Approach*, Human–Computer Interaction Series,
https://doi.org/10.1007/978-3-030-82681-9_2

their goals. For instance, robots enable users to accomplish tasks that were previously out of reach or difficult to conduct. However, they are hard to control and can be dangerous if used wrongly. MR systems promise to augment the real world with useful information, but it is conceivable that this can cause users to suffer information overload if done naively [50]. Mobile devices provide access to information always and everywhere. However, they are also constant sources of interruption, which can have severe consequences for users such as inattention [54].

To address this dichotomy, user interfaces (UIs) of emerging technologies need to reduce the complexity of interaction while preserving machine-provided capabilities. Human-computer interaction (HCI) research has demonstrated that adaptive user interfaces (AUIs) are capable of achieving this goal. Various works have shown that AUIs are able to improve the usability of PC applications. Prominent examples even achieved adoption in consumer software, e.g., the Microsoft Office Assistant [42] and Autodesk's Community Commands [64].

For an adaptive interface to be successful, the benefits of correct adaptations must outweigh the costs, or usability side effects, of incorrect adaptations [24]. For existing AUIs, the risk of incorrect adaptations is low since the non-adaptive interaction is supplemented with recommendations, which users have to deliberately activate [46]. In contrast, we argue that UIs of *emerging technologies need to continuously adapt system input and output for users to be able to fully leverage them.* The problem is that these devices confront users with a large number of controllable elements that change their state frequently. This is hard to cognitively process and, hence, users struggle when using such devices without interaction support (see Sect. 2).

The necessity of continuous adaptations causes two unresolved challenges to arise. First, *inferring users' intent is inherently hard.* The task is to derive the intent of users by observing their actions. However, observable actions only provide a fragmentary and incomplete image of intent. In addition, users do not necessarily perform actions that serve their goal. Thus, the same sequence of recorded actions can correlate with a multitude of intentions, rendering the inference of user intent an ill-posed inductive problem even when ground truth data is available. Secondly, *user intent is constantly changing.* Conceptually, HCI can be seen as a loop [11] where users specify commands using an input device and observe the effect of their actions on a display. Based on the intermediate result, they refine their intent and iteratively repeat this process until they are satisfied with the created outcome. This highlights that user intent is not stationary but shaped by the closed-loop dynamics of HCI.

To address these challenges, we propose *optimal control as a computational framework* to adapt system input and output in settings where permanent adaptation is necessary. In its classical sense, optimal control steers a dynamical system toward a goal state by relying on an underlying physical model [19]. It optimizes the input to the system for the next time step while taking future time steps into account. We employ optimal control to assist users in achieving their goal by relying on an implicit model of their intent to adapt controls and displays. It considers the closed-loop iterative nature of HCI by optimizing the UI's underlying mechanisms for a user's next interaction step while taking their long-term goals into account. Furthermore, it is robust against modeling errors of users' high-level goals since only the first step of the prediction horizon is implemented and the horizon is re-optimized with each user input. Both *inherent properties render optimal control an ideal framework to overcome the challenges* raised above and, hence, promising to improve the usability of AUIs over usual user modeling techniques.

To illustrate the usage of optimal control in interactive systems, we examine two examples of its application. First, we propose an optimization-based optimal control approach to enable quadrotor-based aerial videography for end-users. Second, we learn cooperative personalized policies that support users in visual search tasks by identifying objects of interest from their gaze-object interactions and adapt a mixed-reality UI accordingly. Before diving into the case studies, we define the problem setting in more detail, present related work and introduce the mathematical background of optimal control.

2 Problem Setting

The idea of seeing human-computer interaction as a regulatory system originated from Wiener's Cybernetics [96] and since then various control theoretic approaches have been proposed to model it (e.g., [66, 71, 87]). Commonly, the human and the computer are seen to create a coupled dynamic system [72]. Figure 1 illustrates the human-computer control loop. The coupling of human and computer constrains the system to only change its state at a rate at which humans can process the feedback and act on it. Thereby, a feasible frequency of change depends on the dimensionality of the human-controlled states (i.e., less states are allowed to change faster as humans require less time to process them). If the system violates human perceptual or cognitive constraints, it cannot be controlled by the user.

The model explains why users struggle when using emerging technologies. Such devices confront the user with large state spaces that change frequently and, hence, are hard to perceive, comprehend and control (e.g., MR systems and robots). In addition, these devices are subject to a dynamically changing user context (e.g., MR systems and mobile devices) which influences users' goals, i.e., the desired state

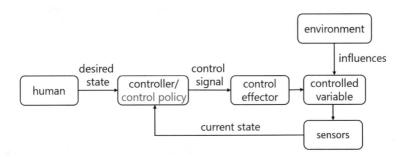

Fig. 1 Human-Computer control loop (adapted from [72])

in the human-computer control loop. As contextual changes happen frequently and implicitly (e.g., changing tasks or environments), it is infeasible for users to update the desired state manually with each context change.

To make interaction with emerging technology feasible, we propose optimal control to adapt control and display mechanisms of a system such that users are supported in achieving their high-level goal. Optimal control, in its classical sense, steers a dynamical system by extremizing a functional that defines its desired behavior [90]. In our setting, we optimize the adaptation of user input and system output according to a function that defines users' high-level goals. Classical optimal control predicts the system's behavior over a horizon and applies the first time step of the prediction to the system. Using optimal control to adapt UIs, we consider a set of future interaction steps (finite case) or all of the steps a user needs to achieve their goal (infinite case) when predicting system behavior. The first step of the prediction horizon is implemented to adapt inputs and outputs and the policy then recomputes its prediction based on a newly attained state of the system and a potentially changing desired state of the user.

Integrating this idea into the conceptual framework of the human-computer loop means replacing the controller with a predictive control policy (see Fig. 1). The policy loosens the coupling of humans and computers by mapping between system- and human-exposed states. The mapping allows users to control the high-dimensional and frequently changing state spaces of complex devices by manipulating a lower dimensional state space that is perceptually and cognitively processable.

There are two algorithms to solve the optimal control problem (OCP): model predictive control (MPC) and reinforcement learning (RL). MPC uses an explicitly formulated model to depict the dynamics of the controlled system. RL learns the system dynamics by sampling environment interactions. In this chapter, we explore how to leverage both algorithms to adapt system input and output according to user goals. First, we are going to explore how concepts from MPC can be incorporated into an end-user design tool for robotic behavior. To this end, we use MPC to optimize robotic flight plans according to high-level aesthetic criteria subject to an explicit model of a quadrotor camera. Second, we explore how such concepts can be translated to more general HCI settings. The main difference between these two is that in more traditional control settings, a model of the system is available, whereas generally it is assumed to be too involved to derive an accurate enough mathematical model of human behavior that would be useful for HCI tasks. Hence, in the latter case, we use RL to adapt mixed-reality UIs according to users' gaze behavior by learning the dynamics of gaze-object interactions.

3 Related Work

Our work touches the research areas of human-computer and human-robot interactions, control theory, as well as artificial intelligence. Due to the broadness of the topic, we focus the presentation of related work on approaches that use MPC and RL as user models or to adapt UIs.

3.1 Model Predictive Control for Adaptive Systems

Model predictive control was first introduced in the late 1970s to control chemical reactions in industrial plants [21, 82]. Through the increase of available computational power, nowadays MPC methods have been demonstrated to be able to solve complex non-linear problems which go beyond simple reference tracking. For instance, MPC methods solved over-constrained control problems for autonomous driving [61] or robotic flight [73, 74]. This capability renders MPC an interesting approach for adapting UIs according to users' high-level goals. Such problems resemble complex robotic tasks in that they are typically multi-objective, spanning complex non-linear solution spaces for which no straightforward results exist. In this section, we review related work in which MPC approaches are used to adapt interfaces to users' individual abilities or tasks to simplify the usage of the systems these UIs control.

A series of works employs MPC to simplify the control of robotic systems. Such works usually abstract the complex dynamics of a robot and allow users to control it by using more intuitive higher level commands. In this spirit, Chipalkatty et al. propose an MPC formulation that optimized inputs to a robotic system such that user intent is preserved while enforcing state constraints of the low-level robotic task [16, 17]. In another work, model predictive control was used to optimize the rendered forces of a robotic system in physical human-robot interactions by predicting the performance of the user [86]. Similarly, [48] used model predictive control with mixed-integer constraints to generate human-aware control policies. These policies optimized the assisstive behavior of a robot by maximizing its productivity while minimizing human workload. In another human-robot collaboration task, MPC was used to minimize the variations between human and robot speeds and, hence, maximize trust between man and machine [83].

Another application area in which MPC was used to adapt to human behavior is therapeutic systems. [92] estimated the joint torque of a patient from measured EMG signals and then derived the deficient joint torque to generate the target movements by considering the patient's estimated joint torque with an MPC method. The optimized joint torque of the MPC is implemented in a therapeutic robotic arm. Similarly, [86] proposed an approach that leveraged MPC to optimize the rendered forces of a therapeutic system according to the predicted performance of the user. User performance is learned continuously to account for performance changes over time.

MPC was also employed for the adaptation of UIs outside of the context of human-robot interaction. It demonstrated its capabilities as a user modeling technique for applications in which the optimal current adaptation of a UI depends on the future behavior of the user, which, in turn, can be modeled as a dynamical system. An example of such a work is presented by [75] where a model predictive controller adopts a virtual environment by adding imperceivable rotations to it to redirect the walking of a user. Other researchers proposed an MPC method to correct the parallax error of touch kiosk systems (e.g., ticket vending machines) caused by the distance of the touchable screen and the screen that displays the content [68]. Their method optimizes correction parameters based on the predicted viewpoint of the user. Furthermore, [56] introduced an MPC method for an electromagnetic haptic guidance system that assists users in pen-based tasks such as drawing, sketching or designing. Thus, their model predictive controller iteratively predicts the motion of an input device such as a pen, and adjusts the position and strength of an underlying dynamic electromagnetic actuator accordingly.

3.2   Reinforcement Learning from Human Behavior

The idea of using reinforcement learning to solve optimal control problems was first introduced in the late 1980s and early 1990s [9, 95]. With the increase in computational power, RL's problem-solving capabilities rose and it has been demonstrated to be able to learn complex system-environment dynamics from experience, and use these models to solve hard stochastic sequential decision problems. For instance, it was used to solve complex robotic control tasks (e.g., [45]) or to achieve super human performance in difficult games (e.g., [88]). In this section, we present works that use RL to adapt systems according to user behavior or learn from human data.

While RL learns a policy given a reward function and an environment, inverse reinforcement learning (IRL) attempts to learn the reward function from a behavioral policy of a human expert [76] or to directly learn a policy from the behavior of a human expert [2]. This idea was successfully applied in the robotics domain [1, 20], not only to model human routine behavior [7] but also for character control and gaming [57]. Reference [53] extend the idea of IRL by learning sub-task structures from human demonstrations and additionally identify reward functions per sub-task. Another work accounted for the fact that humans do not always act optimally and proposed cooperative inverse reinforcement learning to allow for active teaching and learning for a more effective value alignment between the human and agent [38]. IRL was also extended to deep reinforcement learning (DRL) settings where human feedback on agent behavior was used to learn deep reward functions [18].

A stream of research applied RL in combination with human motion capture data to improve policies for character animation and control [58, 63, 65, 94]. These works usually use an RL-agent to learn how to stitch captured motion fragments such that natural character motion as a sequence of clips is attained. A more recent work in character animation rewards the learned controller for producing motions that resemble human reference data [79] or directly learns full-body RL-controllers from monocular video [80]. In a similar fashion, Aytar et al. [5] use YouTube videos of humans playing video games to specify guidance for learning in cases where the normal reward function only provides sparse rewards. These works employ human behavioral sequences either as the agent's actions or as reference motion to provide additional rewards for training.

Most related to our work are approaches that treat users as the environment of an RL-agent to learn policies from explicit user feedback. For example, in the domain of dialog manager systems, RL-agents were learned based on users' responses to automated speech segments selected by a policy [27, 89]. Hu et al. [44] use Reinforcement Learning to learn an incentive mechanism which maximizes the quality and throughput of crowdsourcing workers. In this case, the agent's actions are different payment scaling factors, and its reward is based on the estimated accuracy of labels (for supervised learning tasks) provided by crowdsourcing workers. Reinforcement Learning is also used in recommender systems for domains with sequential recommendations (e.g., online video platforms and music streaming services) [12, 59, 62]. Here, the agent's actions are videos or songs available for recommendation, and the environment is users reacting to the recommended item.

Reinforcement learning was also used to predict opportune moments to post notifications in intelligent notification systems. Thus, [91] introduced a DRL agent that was trained on synthetic and real data to predict users' action toward notifications. Other authors used RL to schedule microtasks while minimizing user annoyance [40]. Thus, they modeled the problem as an MDP and used the Advantage Actor Critic algorithm to identify opportune moments for interruption based on context and history of user interactions.

In recent years, RL became a popular framework to learn control policies for human-robot interaction. For instance, [69] propose a policy gradient RL-method that reads body signals from a human and used this information to adjust interaction distances, gaze meeting and motion speed of a humanoid robot. Another example is the work by [70] who used RL to learn a control policy for a non-linear manipulator to behave like a specified robot impedance model for a human-robot interaction task. Other examples of human-robot collaboration use RL control policies to jointly balance a ball on a plank [34]. In addition, researchers proposed adjusted RL algorithms for human-robot collaboration to learn policies from real-world examples [93] or policies that can switch from autonomous to human-guided behavior [51]. Another work learned an adaptive control policy that adjusts its behavior in response to observed performance variation in their human colleagues [77].

In AUIs that support information acquisition, RL has demonstrated to help users in information acquisition tasks by learning from user interactions with keywords and guiding the search via exploration exploitation behavior [3, 35].

Recently, researchers proposed to use Partially Observable Markov Decision Processes (POMDPs) to model human-computer interaction as a constrained sequential stochastic decision process [43] where behavior emerges from the constraints imposed by human biological mechanisms for encoding information from the environment. Evidence from case studies where a visual search [13] and a decision-making task [14] were modeled within the proposed framework supports the authors' claim.

4 Background

In this section, we review problem formulations and methods of optimal control for discrete-time dynamic systems. We begin by introducing the optimal control problem (OCP) for cases where the model of the dynamic system is known. We then review model predictive control to solve these problems. After that, we establish Markov decision processes (MDPs) that are used to formulate OCPs for unknown system models. Finally, we describe how reinforcement learning is used to solve MDPs.

4.1 Optimal Control Problem

We introduce the optimal control problem (OCP) formulation for the case of a discrete system model whose progression is optimized according to a cost function. Thus, consider the following discrete-time linear time-invariant system

$$\mathbf{x}(t+1) = \mathbf{A}\mathbf{x}(t) + \mathbf{B}\mathbf{u}(t) \tag{1}$$

where $\mathbf{x} \in \mathbb{R}^n$ is the state vector, $\mathbf{u} \in \mathbb{R}^m$ is the input vector, $\mathbf{A} \in \mathbb{R}^{n \times n}$ is the system matrix, $\mathbf{B} \in \mathbb{R}^{n \times m}$ is the input matrix and $t \in \mathbb{N}_0$ is the discrete time. In the case of a non-linear system, the right part of Eq. 1 is substituted by a function that describes the evolution of the dynamic system: $\mathbf{x}(t+1) = F(\mathbf{x}(t), \mathbf{u}(t))$.

Let $\mathbf{x}(t)$ be the state vector measured at discrete time t and $\mathbf{x}_{t+k}$ be the state vector predicted at discrete time $t + k$ using Eq. 1 with initial condition $\mathbf{x}_t = \mathbf{x}(t)$. Further, consider the constraints $\mathbf{x}(t) \in \mathbb{X} \subseteq \mathbb{R}^n$, $\mathbf{u}(t) \in \mathbb{U} \subseteq \mathbb{R}^M$ where $\mathbb{X}$ and $\mathbb{U}$ are polyhedral sets containing the origin in their interiors. The general form of the cost function is defined as

$$V_N(\mathbf{x}(t)) = r_T(\mathbf{x}_{t+N}, \mathbf{u}_{t+N}) + \sum_{k=0}^{N-1} \gamma^k r(\mathbf{x}_{t+k}, \mathbf{u}_{t+k}) \tag{2}$$

with the stage cost $r(\mathbf{x}_{t+k}, \mathbf{u}_{t+k}) = \mathbf{x}_{t+k}^T \mathbf{Q} \mathbf{x}_{t+k} + \mathbf{u}_{t+k}^T \mathbf{R} \mathbf{u}_{t+k}$ and the terminal cost $r_T(\mathbf{x}_{t+N}, \mathbf{u}_{t+N}) = \mathbf{x}_{t+N}^T \mathbf{P} \mathbf{x}_{t+N}$ where N is the prediction horizon, $\gamma \in (0, 1]$ is a discount factor, $\mathbf{Q} \in \mathbb{R}^{n \times n}$ is the state weighting matrix, $\mathbf{R} \in \mathbb{R}^{m \times m}$ is the input weighting matrix and $\mathbf{P} \in \mathbb{R}^{n \times n}$ the terminal weighting matrix.

The optimal control problem (finite horizon) is then defined as

$$V_N^*(\mathbf{x}(t)) = \min_{\mathbf{U}(t)} r_T(\mathbf{x}_{t+N}, \mathbf{u}_{t+N}) + \sum_{k=0}^{N-1} \gamma^k r(\mathbf{x}_{t+k}, \mathbf{u}_{t+k}) \qquad (3)$$

$$subject\ to\ \mathbf{x}_{t+k+1} = \mathbf{A}\mathbf{x}_{t+k} + \mathbf{B}\mathbf{u}_{t+k},\ k = 0, ..., N-1$$
$$\mathbf{x}_{t+k} \in \mathbb{X},\ k = 1, ..., N$$
$$\mathbf{u}_{t+k} \in \mathbb{U},\ k = 0, ..., N-1$$
$$\mathbf{x}_t = \mathbf{x}(t)$$

with input sequence $\mathbf{U}(t) = (\mathbf{u}_t^T ... \mathbf{u}_{t+N-1}^T)^T \in \mathbb{R}^{Nm}$.

4.2 Model Predictive Control

Model predictive control solves the OCP (see Eq. 3) for the measured state vector $\mathbf{x}(t)$ to attain the predicted optimal input sequence $\mathbf{U}^*(t)$. It then applies its first element ($\mathbf{u}^*(t)$) to the system. This is repeated at each discrete time t with a receding prediction horizon. Thus, MPC is also denoted as receding horizon control (RHC). Note that MPC uses a discount factor of $\gamma = 1$.

The OCP can be reformulated as a quadratic programming (QP) problem (see [36] for the derivation):

$$\underset{X}{\text{minimize}}\ \frac{1}{2}\mathbf{X}^T\mathbf{H}\mathbf{X} + \mathbf{f}^T\mathbf{X} \qquad (4)$$
$$\text{subject to } \mathbf{A}_{ineq}\mathbf{X} \le \mathbf{b}_{ineq}$$
$$\text{and } \mathbf{A}_{eq}\mathbf{X} = \mathbf{b}_{eq},$$

where $\mathbf{X}$ denotes the stacked state vectors $\mathbf{x}_t$ and inputs $\mathbf{u}_t$ for each time-point, $\mathbf{H}$ and $\mathbf{f}$ contain the quadratic and linear cost coefficients, respectively, which are defined by (2), $\mathbf{A}_{ineq}$, $\mathbf{b}_{ineq}$ comprise the linear inequality constraints of states and inputs, and $\mathbf{A}_{eq}$, $\mathbf{b}_{eq}$ are the linear equality constraints from our model (1) for each time-point $k \in 0, \ldots, N$. This problem has a sparse structure and can be readily solved using standard quadratic programming methods. For solving non-linear dynamic systems and cost functions, non-linear programs (NLPs) can be used. In this work, we rely on numerical solvers to solve MPC problems. For completeness, we mention that OCPs can also be solved explicitly using multi-parametric quadratic programming methods. This holds for linear [8, 37] and non-linear systems [47].

4.3 Markov Decision Processes

The family of Markov decision processes (MDP) is a mathematical framework for decision-making in stochastic domains [?]. The MDP is a four-tuple (S, A, P, R), where S is a set of states, A is a set of actions, P is the state transition probability for going from a state s to state s' after performing action a (i.e., $P(s'|s, a)$), and R the reward for action a in state s (i.e., $R : S \times A \rightarrow \mathbb{R}$). The expected discounted reward for action a in s when following policy π is known as the Q value: $Q^\pi(s, a) = E_{s_t}[\sum_{t=0}^{\infty} \gamma^t R(s_t, a_t)]$, where γ is a discount factor. Q values are related via the Bellman equation: $Q^\pi(s, a) = \sum_{s'} P(s'|s, a)[R(s', s, a) + \gamma Q^\pi(s', \pi(s'))]$. The optimal policy can then be computed as $\pi^* = arg\,max_a Q^\pi(s, a)$. Classic MDPs assume a uniform discrete step size. To model temporally extended actions, semi-Markov decision processes (SMDPs) are used. SMDPs represent snapshots of a system at decision points where the time between transitions can be of variable temporal length. An SMDP is a five-tuple (S, A, P, R, F), where S, A, P, R describe an MDP and F gives the probability of transition times for each state-action pair. Its Bellman equation is

$$Q^\pi(s, a) = \sum_{s',t} F(t|s, a) P(s'|s, a)[R(s, a) + \gamma^t Q^\pi(s', \pi(s'))] , \qquad (5)$$

where t is the number of time units after the agent chooses action a in state s and $F(t|s, a)$ is the probability that the next decision epoch occurs within t time units.

4.4 Reinforcement Learning

Reinforcement learning solves Markov decision processes by learning a state-action value function $Q(s, a)$ that approximates the Q value of the Bellman equation $Q^\pi(s, a)$. There are two classes of algorithms for RL: model-based and model-free algorithms. In model-based algorithms, the state transition probabilities $F(t|s, a)$ and $P(s'|s, a)$ are known and policies are found by enumerating the possible sequences of states that are expected to follow a starting state and action while summing the expected rewards along these sequences. In this paper, we use model-free RL algorithms to solve an MDP. These algorithms learn the approximate state-action value function $Q(s, a)$ in an environment where the state transition probability functions $F(t|s, a)$ and $P(s'|s, a)$ are unknown but can be sampled from it. One model-free algorithm that learns the approximate state-action value function via temporal-difference learning is Q-learning: $Q(s_t, a_t) = Q(s_t, a_t) + \alpha \, [R_{t+1} + \gamma^t \underset{a}{max} \, Q(s_{t+1}, a) - Q(s_t, a_t)]$, where s_t, s_{t+1}, a_t and R_{t+1} are sampled from the environment.

Fig. 2 Setting of our MPC-based design tool to support users in creating robotic aerial videos

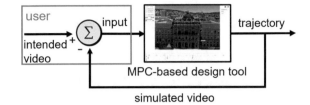

5 Model Predictive Control for Robotic Task Support

We investigate the idea of using optimal control to facilitate system use in an application which supports users in the creation of aerial videos using quadrotors. This is a cognitively demanding use case as users need to control a quadrotor and a camera simultaneously while considering the aesthetic aspects of filmmaking. During flight, they need to control the five dimensions of the quadrotor camera (x, y, z, pitch and yaw) while reacting to constantly changing state values of the moving robot.

We focus on supporting users in the creation of scenic aerial shots of the cityscapes and landscapes where the environment is static, i.e., camera targets are not moving during the shot. This allows us to move the robotic control task into an offline setting where designed quadrotor flights can be simulated and the resulting trajectories used to be tracked with a real robot. Figure 2 illustrates our setting where the controlled variable is the simulated video (resp. trajectory) as produced by our MPC-based design tool. We simplify the hard control task by allowing users to specify sparse keyframes that sketch their intended video in a realistic virtual environment (e.g., Google Earth). Based on these keyframes, our MPC method generates feedforward reference trajectories for a quadrotor camera by using an explicit model of its dynamics. It interpolates between user-specified keyframes with a function that defines the quadrotor's desired behavior according to aesthetic criteria of aerial film. In our setting, the control horizon equals the prediction horizon as all of its stages are used to adjust the controlled variable, i.e., the trajectory that produces the aerial video. The control horizon describes the stages that are implemented as input to the controlled entity. Due to the user closing the loop, the horizon is not implemented at a fixed rate, like in systems control, but every time they decide to preview their designed quadrotor flight plan in simulation. Based on the perceived match between the simulated and the intended video, users can decide to refine or specify additional inputs to better communicate their intent.

Following the problem setting in Sect. 2, we leverage MPC to abstract the high dimensionality of quadrotor camera reference trajectories (five dimensions × discretization step × temporal length of the video) by using the optimization to generate them from sparse user-specified keyframes.

In this section, we present an optimal control approach to adapt a user-robot interface that supports users in completing a robotic task. First, we identify the high-level user goals of the problem domain. Then, we introduce an MPC formulation that supports users in achieving these goals. Finally, we investigate the effectiveness of our approach in terms of improving users' efficacy and efficiency.

5.1 Aesthetic Criteria of Aerial Film

With a contextual analysis, we intend to find the main aesthetic criteria of aerial videos. The goal is to model these criteria in our MPC formulation such that end-users are capable to create videos that adhere to them. Therefore, we conduct expert interviews, to elicit aesthetic criteria of aerial footage, and a user study, to examine if existing tools [30, 49] enable the creation of videos that follow them. In the following, we present the two elicited main criteria and discuss if participants were able to design videos that adhere to them using the investigated ones.[1]

Smooth Camera Motion: The key to aesthetically pleasing aerial video is described by one videographer as *"[...] the camera is always in motion and movements are smooth"*. Another expert stated that smoothness is considered *the* criterion for shots with a moving camera (c.f. [4, 39]), whereas the dynamics of camera motion should stay adjustable (c.f. [49]).

The user study showed that participants did struggle to create videos with smooth camera motion using existing tools. The problem is that keyframe timings are kept fixed in current optimization schemes and smooth motion can only be generated subject to these hard constraints. To this end, users are required to specify a similar ratio of distance in time to distance in space in between all keyframes. This is a task most participants failed to accomplish as keyframes are specified in 5D (3D position and camera pitch and yaw) and imagining the resulting translational and rotational velocities are cognitively demanding.

Continuous and Precise Camera Target Framing: The ability to control and fine-tune the framing of a filmed subject *continuously* and with high precision is an essential aesthetic tool. The interviewees highlighted the importance of being able to precisely position an object in the image plane subject to a compositional intention (e.g., a simultaneously moving foreground and background). For this reason, aerial video shots are usually taken by two operators, one piloting the quadrotor and one controlling the camera, allowing the camera operator to focus on and constantly fine-tune the subject framing.

The results of the user study indicated that current tools do not support precise and continuous target framing, as the videos of nearly all participants featured camera targets that moved freely in the image plane. The problem is that current algorithms do not model camera targets or use overly simplified models. Our basic optimization simply interpolates camera angles between the user-specified keyframes. In [49, 85], camera targets are modeled as the intersection of a keyframe's center ray with the

---

[1] We refer the reader to [30] for details on the results and experimental design of both studies.

virtual environment and interpolated as look-at trajectories. Both approaches caused counterintuitive interpolations in between keyframes.

5.2 Method

Based on the results of the contextual analysis, we specify requirements for our MPC formulation. It should (1) automatically generate globally smooth camera motion over all specified spatial positions, while (2) giving users precise timing control (established in [49]). In addition, they should (3) precisely and continuously control the image space position of a camera target in between keyframes and (4) help users to frame camera targets at desirable image space positions. In this section, we present how we model these requirements in our optimization scheme.

5.2.1 Dynamical Model

We use the approximated quadrotor camera model in [29]. This discrete first-order dynamical system is used as an equality constraint in our optimization problem:

$$\mathbf{x}_{i+1} = A\mathbf{x}_i + B\mathbf{u}_i + g, \ \mathbf{u}_{min} \leq \mathbf{u}_i \leq \mathbf{u}_{max},$$
$$\mathbf{x}_i = [\mathbf{r}, \psi_q, \psi_g, \phi_g, \dot{\mathbf{r}}, \dot{\psi}_q, \dot{\psi}_g, \dot{\phi}_g, \ddot{\mathbf{r}}, \ddot{\psi}_q, \ddot{\psi}_g, \ddot{\phi}_g, \dddot{\mathbf{r}}, \dddot{\psi}_q, \dddot{\psi}_g, \dddot{\phi}_g]^T, \quad (6)$$
$$\mathbf{u}_i = [\mathbf{F}, M_{\psi_q}, M_{\psi_g}, M_{\phi_g}]^T,$$

where $\mathbf{x}_i \in \mathbb{R}^{24}$ are the quadrotor camera states and $\mathbf{u}_i \in \mathbb{R}^6$ are the inputs to the system at horizon stage i. Furthermore, $\mathbf{r} \in \mathbb{R}^3$ is the position of the quadrotor, ψ_q is the quadrotor's yaw angle and ψ_g and ϕ_g are the yaw and pitch angles of the camera gimbal. The matrix $A \in \mathbb{R}^{24 \times 24}$ propagates the state $\mathbf{x}$ forward, the matrix $B \in \mathbb{R}^{24 \times 6}$ defines the effect of the input $\mathbf{u}$ on the state and the vector $g \in \mathbb{R}^{24}$ that of gravity for one time-step. $\mathbf{F}$ is the the force acting on the quadrotor, M_{ψ_q} is the torque along its z-axis and M_{ψ_g}, M_{ϕ_g} are torques acting on pitch and yaw of the gimbal.

5.2.2 Variable Horizon

To attain globally smooth camera motion, it is necessary to treat trajectories as time-free. In particular, our method does not take timed keyframes as input. To this end, by taking inspiration from MPC literature [67], we make the length of the horizon an optimization variable by adding the trajectory end time T into the state space of our model ($\mathbf{x} = [\mathbf{x}, T]^T \in \mathbb{R}^{25}$ with $\frac{\delta T}{\delta t} = 0$). This has implications for the dynamical model. At each iteration of the solver, we adjust the discretization $\Delta t = \frac{T}{N}$. Here N is the number of stages in the horizon spanning the entire trajectory. The forward propagation matrices A and B are recalculated based on the current Δt.

5.2.3   Reference Tracking Metric

We require a time-free parameterization of the reference to optimize the timing of keyframes. We use a chord length parameterized, piecewise cubic polynomial spline in hermite form (PCHIP) to interpolate the user-defined keyframes [26]. The resulting chord length parameter θ describes progress on the spatial reference path defined as $\mathbf{f}_d(\theta) = [\mathbf{r}_d(\theta), \psi_d(\theta), \phi_d(\theta)] \in \mathbb{R}^5$. To prevent sudden changes of the progress parameter, we add θ into our model and formulate its dynamics with the following linear discrete system equation:

$$\Theta_{i+1} = C\Theta_i + Dv_i, \ 0 \le v_i \le v_{max}, \tag{7}$$

where $\Theta_i = [\theta_i, \dot{\theta}_i]$ is the state and v_i is the input of θ at step i and $C \in \mathbb{R}^{2 \times 2}$, $D \in \mathbb{R}^{2 \times 1}$ are the discrete system matrices. v_i approximates the quadrotor's acceleration as θ is an approximation of the trajectory length.

With this extension of the dynamic model in place, we now formulate an objective to minimize the error between the desired quadrotor position $\mathbf{r}_d(\theta)$ and the current quadrotor position $\mathbf{r}$. Thus, we minimize 3D-space approximation of lag $\hat{\epsilon}_l$ and contour error $\hat{\epsilon}_c$ of [74]. Splitting positional reference tracking into a lag error (lag in time) and a contour error (deviation from path) is important for time-free reference tracking [55], as this avoids behavior where a robot either lags behind the temporal reference or cannot trade off positional fit for smoother motion. The positional error term is then defined as

$$c^p(\theta, \mathbf{r}_i) = \begin{bmatrix} \hat{\epsilon}^l(\theta) \\ \hat{\epsilon}^c(\theta) \end{bmatrix}^T Q \begin{bmatrix} \hat{\epsilon}^l(\theta) \\ \hat{\epsilon}^c(\theta) \end{bmatrix}, \tag{8}$$

where Q is a diagonal positive definite weight matrix. Minimizing c^p will move the quadrotor along the user-defined spatial reference.

5.2.4   Smooth Progress

For the camera to smoothly follow the path, we need to ensure that θ progresses. By specifying an initial θ_0 and demanding θ to reach the end of the trajectory in the terminal state θ_N, the progress of θ can be forced with an implicit cost term. We simply penalize the trajectory end time by minimizing the state-space variable T,

$$c^{end}(T) = T. \tag{9}$$

Minimizing the end time can be interpreted as optimizing trajectories to be short temporally (while respecting smoothness and limits of the robot model). This forces θ to make progress such that the terminal state θ_N is reached within time T.[2]

To ensure that the generated motion for the quadrotor is smooth, we introduce a cost term on the model's jerk states,

$$c^{jerk}(\dddot{\mathbf{r}}, \dddot{\psi}_q, \dddot{\psi}_g, \dddot{\phi}_g) = ||\mathbf{j}_i||^2, \tag{10}$$

where $\mathbf{j}_i = [\dddot{\mathbf{r}}, \dddot{\psi}_q, \dddot{\psi}_g, \dddot{\phi}_g]^T$ is jerk and angular jerk. We minimize jerk since it provides a commonly used metric to quantify smoothness [41] and is known to be a decisive factor for the aesthetic perception of motion [10]. This cost term again implicitly affects θ by only allowing it to progress such that the quadrotor motion following the reference path $\mathbf{f}_d(\theta)$ is smooth according to (10).

5.2.5 Keyframe Timings

To give users precise timing control, we augment our objective function with an additional term for soft-constraint keyframe timings. Due to the variable horizon, we lack a fixed mapping between time and stage. To be able to map timings with the spatial reference, we use the θ-parameterization of the reference spline. Reference timings hence need to be specified strictly increasing in θ. Based on the reference timings and the corresponding θ-values, we interpolate a spline through these points, which results in timing reference function $t_d(\theta)$ which can be followed analogously to spatial references by minimizing the cost,

$$c^t(\theta, i, \Delta t) = ||t_d(\theta) - (i * \Delta t)||^2, \tag{11}$$

where i is the current stage of the horizon and Δt is the discretization of the model.

5.2.6 Reference Velocities

The above extension enables mimicry of timing control in prior methods. However, the actual purpose of specifying camera timings in a video is to control or change camera velocity to achieve the desired effect. Since determining the timing of the shot explicitly is difficult, we propose a way for users to directly specify camera velocities. We extend the formulation of our method to accept reference velocities as input. Again, we use the θ-parameterization to assign velocities to the reference spline $\mathbf{f}_d$. To minimize the difference between the velocity of the quadrotor and the user-specified velocity profile $v_d(\theta)$, we specify the cost,

---

[2] This also prevents solutions of infinitely long trajectories in time where adding steps with $\mathbf{u}_i \approx 0$ is free w.r.t. to Eq. (10)).

$$c^{vel}(\theta, i, \Delta t) = ||v_d(\theta) - \dot{\mathbf{r}}_i^T \mathbf{n}||^2, \tag{12}$$

where we project the current velocity of the quadrotor $\dot{\mathbf{r}}_i$ on the normalized tangent vector of the positional reference function $\mathbf{n}$.

5.2.7 Target Model

For our target model, we assume that in scenic aerial video shots the quadrotor camera focuses on one target per frame and targets change between frames. We believe this is a valid assumption as human perceptual constraints prevent us from focusing on more than one point at a time, which is also reflected in popular aerial video techniques [15]. For each user-specified keyframe k_j, our tool also provides the assigned camera target t_j (see [31] for details on the tool). To incorporate these targets into our optimization, we fit a bounding cylinder with radius r_t, height h_t, and a center at position $\mathbf{p}_t \in \mathbb{R}^3$. We use this primitive as its geometric properties allow us to consider the 3D expansion of a target in our optimization scheme without needing to sample vertices during optimization. Using the reference parameterization of Eq. 7, we then compute a target reference spline that interpolates position, radius and height of the consecutive targets t_j of the video. The spline is defined as

$$\mathbf{f}_t(\theta) = [\mathbf{p}_t(\theta), r_t(\theta), h_t(\theta)] \in \mathbb{R}^5. \tag{13}$$

It relates the sequence of camera targets to the θ-parameterized spline that specifies the positional reference of the quadrotor camera.

5.2.8 Framing Optimization

With our method, we optimize the degrees of freedom of the quadrotor camera to position 3D targets at desirable locations in the image frame. Therefore, we need a reference function that specifies desirable image space locations for our target reference spline $\mathbf{f}_t(\theta)$ when observed from the according quadrotor position $\mathbf{r}_d(\theta)$.

We start by specifying a set of vectors L in the camera clip space C that define desirable image space positions according to videographic compositional rules. In our implementation, L contains the center of the image plane ($\mathbf{l}^c = [0, 0, 0, 1]^T$) and the intersection points of the Rules of Thirds (e.g., $\mathbf{l}^c = [0, \frac{1}{3}, \frac{1}{3}, 1]^T$).[3] Second, we compute the directional vector $\mathbf{m}_j^v$ between the position $\mathbf{r}_{d,j}$ of each keyframe and the position of its target $\mathbf{p}_{t,j}$ in camera view space V. This vector is computed as

---

[3] These points can be seen Fig. 3 and are the intersections of the blue dotted lines.

Fig. 3 Illustration of the framing optimization cost term that optimizes the pose of the quadrotor camera such that the relative vector between the camera and target $\mathbf{p}_v$ aligns with the reference vector $\mathbf{v}_d$ that positions the target at a desirable image space position

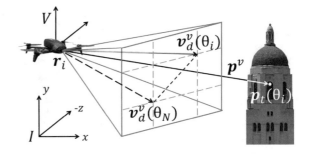

$$\mathbf{p}_j^v = \mathbf{R}_{\psi,\phi}(\psi_{d,j}, \phi_{d,j})(\mathbf{r}_{d,j} - \mathbf{p}_{t,j}) \qquad (14)$$

$$\mathbf{m}_j^v = \frac{\mathbf{p}_j^v}{||\mathbf{p}_j^v||}$$

where $\mathbf{p}_j^v$ is the view space position of t_j, $\psi_{d,j}$ and $\phi_{d,j}$ are the pitch and yaw orientation of k_j and $\mathbf{R}_{\psi,\phi} \in SO(3)$ is the rotation matrix from world frame I to camera view space C. For each keyframe, we identify the vector in L that is closest to the actual directional vector between t_j in k_j as

$$\mathbf{v}_j^v = \arg\min_{\mathbf{l} \in L} ||\mathbf{m}_j^v - w(\mathbf{R}_c^{-1}\mathbf{l}^c)|| , \qquad (15)$$

where $\mathbf{v}_j^v$ is the closest vector, $\mathbf{R}_c \in SO(4)$ is the camera matrix that performs rotations from the camera's view space V to its clip space C and w is the function that normalizes homogeneously to Cartesian coordinates. Using the θ parameterization, the reference directional vectors $\mathbf{v}_j^v$ are linearly interpolated to attain the function $\mathbf{v}_d^v(\theta)$. If users want to keep the framing they specified, one can compute $\mathbf{v}_d^v(\theta)$ by interpolating the $\mathbf{m}_j^v$ vectors. With the reference function for desired target framing in place, we can now define the cost term to optimize camera target framing as

$$\mathbf{p}^v = \mathbf{R}_{\psi,\phi}(\psi_{q,i} + \psi_{g,i}, \phi_{g,i})(\mathbf{p}_t(\theta)) - \mathbf{r}_i) \qquad (16)$$

$$c^f(\theta, \mathbf{p}^v) = ||\frac{\mathbf{p}^v}{||\mathbf{p}^v||} - \mathbf{v}_d^v(\theta))||^2 ,$$

where $\mathbf{p}^v$ is the position of the target in V and $\mathbf{r}_i$ the position of the quadrotor at a specific stage i of the optimization horizon. Figure 3 illustrates the cost term. It optimizes the pose of the quadrotor camera such that the relative vector between quadrotor and target $\mathbf{p}^v$ aligns with the directional reference vector $\mathbf{v}_d^v(\theta)$ to position the target at the desired image space position.

Fig. 4 Illustration of the visibility maximization cost term showing a camera target and its bounding cylinder from **a** side and **b** top

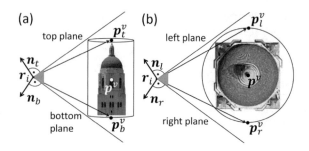

5.2.9 Visibility Maximization

With the framing optimization cost term in place, one can ensure that the camera target is at the desired position in the image plane across the entire trajectory. However, if the distance between the camera and camera target is small, it is possible that although the center of the camera target is at the desired position on the image plane, large parts of the target are not captured. While this is most likely not the case at keyframes (they are specified by users), it can occur between them where reference positions are attained via interpolation. To address this problem, we propose a second cost term that ensures that camera targets are entirely visible in each frame of the video. Figure 4 illustrates the intuition behind the objective term that introduces a penalty when any part of the bounding cylinder of a camera target intersects with a plane of the extended camera frustum and, hence, would not be visible.

For this cost term, we first calculate four points on the edges of the cylinder. As the roll of the quadrotor camera is always zero, one can attain the points at the top and bottom of the cylinder as

$$\mathbf{p}_t^v = \mathbf{p}^v + \left[0, \ \frac{h_t(\theta)}{2}, \ 0\right]^T \tag{17}$$

$$\mathbf{p}_b^v = \mathbf{p}^v - \left[0, \ \frac{h_t(\theta)}{2}, \ 0\right]^T. \tag{18}$$

To find the left and the right edges of the cylinder from the perspective of the camera, we search the points that have the z value of $\mathbf{p}^v$, the distance r_t from $\mathbf{p}^v$ and are on the plane that has $\mathbf{p}^v$ as its normal. By substituting these values into the point-normal form of this plane, we get the x-values of these points:

$$x = x_{p^v} + \frac{y_{p^v}^2 - y_{p^v} y}{x_v}, \tag{19}$$

where x_{p^v}, y_{p^v} are the respective x- and y-values of $\mathbf{p}_v$. Substituting x into the 2-norm equation that computes the distance between $\mathbf{p}^v$ and one of the points on the edge, we attain the y-values as

$$y_{1,2} = y_{p^v} \pm \sqrt{\frac{r_t^2}{\left(\frac{y_{p^v}^2}{x_{p^v}^2} + 1\right)}}. \tag{20}$$

Substituting the respective y-values back into Eq. 19, we can then specify $\mathbf{p}_l^v = [x_2, y_2, z_v]^T$, $\mathbf{p}_r^v = [x_1, y_1, z_v]^T$.

To attain the planes that describe the camera frustum, we first project the corners of the image plane into the camera view space:

$$\mathbf{q}_{tl}^v = \mathbf{R}_c^{-1}\mathbf{c}_1, \, \mathbf{q}_{tr}^v = \mathbf{R}_c^{-1}\mathbf{c}_2, \, \mathbf{q}_{bl}^v = \mathbf{R}_c^{-1}\mathbf{c}_3, \, \mathbf{q}_{br}^v = \mathbf{R}_c^{-1}\mathbf{c}_4, \tag{21}$$

where $\mathbf{c}_{1-4}$ are the four corners of the image plane defined in the camera clip space and $\mathbf{v}_{tl}$, $\mathbf{v}_{tr}$, $\mathbf{v}_{bl}$ and $\mathbf{v}_{br}$ are the top-left, top-right, bottom-left and bottom-right vectors that form the edges of the camera frustum. We then compute the normals of the planes of the frustum:

$$\mathbf{n}_t^v = \mathbf{q}_{tl}^v \times \mathbf{q}_{tr}^v, \, \mathbf{n}_b^v = \mathbf{q}_{bl}^v \times \mathbf{q}_{br}^v, \tag{22}$$
$$\mathbf{n}_l^v = \mathbf{q}_{tl}^v \times \mathbf{q}_{bl}^v, \, \mathbf{n}_r^v = \mathbf{q}_{tr}^v \times \mathbf{q}_{br}^v.$$

In addition, we define a visibility cost function that returns the squared minimum of two distances and zero if they have different signs:

$$f_{vis}(d_1, d_2) = \begin{cases} 0 & \text{if } |d_1 + d_2| < |d_1| + |d_2| \\ min(d_1, d_2)^2 & \text{otherwise.} \end{cases} \tag{23}$$

The visibility cost term is computed by summing the result of Eq. 23 for the distances between cylinder edge points and planes:

$$f_{all}(\mathbf{n}_{t-r}, \mathbf{p}_{t-r}^v) = \sum_{\mathbf{p}_m}^M f_{vis}(\mathbf{n}_t^T \mathbf{p}_m, \mathbf{n}_b^T \mathbf{p}_m) + f_{vis}(\mathbf{n}_l^T \mathbf{p}_m, \mathbf{n}_r^T \mathbf{p}_m)$$

$$c^{vis}(\mathbf{n}_{t-r}, \mathbf{p}_{t-r}^v, x_{p^v}) = \begin{cases} 0 & \text{if } x_{p^v} < 0 \\ f_{all}(\mathbf{n}_{t-r}, \mathbf{p}_{t-r}^v) & \text{otherwise,} \end{cases} \tag{24}$$

where $M = [\mathbf{p}_t^v, \mathbf{p}_b^v, \mathbf{p}_l^v, \mathbf{p}_r^v]$ is the set of cylinder edge points and $\mathbf{n}^T\mathbf{p}$ is the distance between a point $\mathbf{p}$ and a plane specified by the normal $\mathbf{n}$. Revoking the costs if $x_{p^v} < 0$ ensures that the term is only active if the target is in front of the camera.

5.2.10   Optimization Problem

We construct the objective function by linearly combining the cost terms from Eqs. (8), (9), (10), (11), (12), (16), (24) and a 2-norm minimization of v:

$$J_i = w_p c^p(\theta_i, \mathbf{r}_i) + w_{jerk} c^{jerk}(\dddot{\mathbf{r}}, \dddot{\psi}_q, \dddot{\psi}_g, \dddot{\phi}_g) + w_{end} c^{end}(T) \qquad (25)$$
$$+ w_t c^t(\theta, i, \Delta t) + w_{vel} c^{vel}(\theta, i, \Delta t) + w_f c^f(\theta, \mathbf{p}^v)$$
$$+ w_{vis} c^{vis}(\mathbf{n}_{t-r}, \mathbf{p}^v_{t-r}, x_{\mathbf{p}^v}) + w_v ||v||^2,$$

where the scalar weight parameters $w_p, w_{jerk}, w_{end}, w_t, w_{vel}, w_f, w_{vis}, w_v > 0$ are adjusted for a good trade-off between positional and temporal fit as well as smoothness. The final optimization problem is then

$$\underset{\mathbf{x}, \mathbf{u}, \Theta, v}{\text{minimize}} \sum_{i=0}^{N} J_i \qquad (26)$$

subject to $\mathbf{x}_0 = \mathbf{k}_0$ (initial state)

$\Theta_0 = \mathbf{0}$ (initial progress)

$\Theta_N = \mathbf{L}$ (terminal progress)

$\mathbf{x}_{i+1} = A\mathbf{x}_i + B\mathbf{u}_i + g$ (dynamical model)

$\Theta_{i+1} = C\Theta_i + Dv_i$ (progress model)

$\mathbf{x}_{min} \leq \mathbf{x}_i \leq \mathbf{x}_{max},$ (state bounds)

$\mathbf{u}_{min} \leq \mathbf{u}_i \leq \mathbf{u}_{max},$ (input limits)

$\mathbf{0} \leq \Theta_i \leq \Theta_{max}$ (progress bounds)

$\mathbf{0} \leq v_i \leq v_{max}$ (progress input limits),

where J_i is quadratic in $\mathbf{u}$, v, linear in Θ and non-linear in $\mathbf{x}$. When flying a generated trajectory, we follow the optimized positional trajectory $\mathbf{r}$ with a standard LQR-controller and use velocity and acceleration states of $\mathbf{x}$ as feedforward terms.

5.3 Evaluation

The goal of our method is to enable end-users to plan and record aerial videos that adhere to the aesthetic criteria of aerial film. As such, we identified smooth camera motion and precise and continuous camera target framing. In the following subsections, we first compare our method with existing approaches [30, 49] on metrics that are representative of the said criteria. After that, we investigate if our approach causes a perceptual difference of produced videos compared to the same baselines.

5.3.1 Technical Comparison with Existing Methods

Smooth Camera Motion: To assess quantitatively that our method generates smoother camera motion, we compare the averaged squared jerk per horizon stage generated

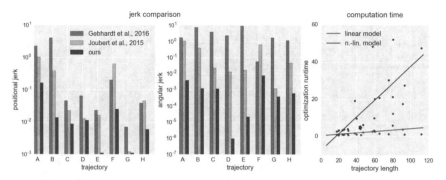

Fig. 5 Comparing average squared jerk (in $\frac{m^2}{s^3}$) and angular jerk (in $\frac{\circ^2}{s^3}$) per horizon stage of different trajectories for our method and [29, 49] (note that the latter uses a different model)

with our method and with hard-constrained approaches [30, 49]. Thus, we use user-designed trajectories from the user study in [30]. Figure 5 shows lower jerk and angular jerk values for our optimization scheme compared to both baseline methods, across all trajectories.

Continuous and Precise Camera Target Framing: To evaluate if our method fulfills our requirements with respect to target framing, we design a challenging shot and generate trajectories with four different approaches. The first is generated with the target framing method of [30] that interpolates angles between keyframes. For the second trajectory, we use the target framing method of [49] that interpolates the intersection of the center rays of keyframes with the environment. The third trajectory is generated with our method using only the framing cost term (c^f). The last trajectory is generated by using both cost terms (c^f and c^{vis}). To ensure that variations in trajectories stem from differences in target framing, we implemented the framing objectives of [30, 49] in our time-free MPC method (Eqs. 16 and 24 were replaced with the respective terms of [30, 49]).

Figure 6 shows a frame-by-frame comparison of the resulting videos of the four trajectories. For the [30] (a) and [49] (b), the camera target (the water tower) moves freely around the image plane, partly disappearing in some frames. In contrast, the video generated by using the cost term c_f (c) corrects the camera orientation of the keyframes (first and last frame) to align the target with the closest vertical line of the Rules of Thirds (see dashed white lines). In between keyframes, the tower nicely transitions between these two lines. However, when the camera approaches the target closely, the tower is not entirely visible in some of the video frames. This is corrected in the video of (d) where all cost terms of our method (c_f and c_v) are active.

5.3.2 Perceptual Study—Smooth Camera Motion

The technical comparison shows that our method generates smoother trajectories. However, it has not been validated that the generated trajectories result in the

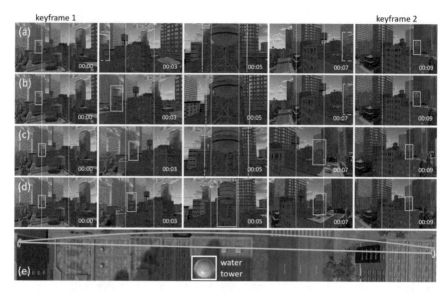

Fig. 6 The figure Illustrates the effect of the framing term on videos generated from two keyframes. For **a** [30] and **b** [49], the camera target (the water tower) moves freely on the image plane of the videos. In **c**, generated with c_f, the target is aligned with the (dashed white) vertical lines of the Rules of Thirds at the keyframes and transitions between them in between keyframes. **d**, generated with $c_f + c_v$, shows the same behavior and additionally corrects the framing such that the water tower is visible through the entire shot. **e** displays a top-down view on the trajectories of (a–c) and (d)

aesthetically more pleasing video. To this end, we conduct an online survey comparing videos which follow user-specified timings, generated with our method and the methods of [30, 49]. Thus, we compare user-designed trajectories from prior work [30, 49]. For each question, we take the user-specified keyframes of the original trajectory and generated a time-optimized trajectory of the same temporal duration using our method. We then render videos for the original and time-optimized trajectory using Google Earth. The two resulting videos are placed side-by-side, randomly assigned to the left or right, and participants state which video they prefer on a forced alternative choice 5-point Likert scale. Negative values mean that the original, timed video is aesthetically more pleasing, 0 indicates no difference and a positive value indicates a more aesthetically pleasing time-optimized video.[4]

Each of the 424 participants compared 14 videos. Results provide strong evidence that our method has a positive effect on the aesthetic perception of aerial videos (see Fig. 7). Furthermore, it has been shown that this effect is stronger for videos of *non-experts*. Looking at *expert*-created videos, the picture is different. These videos were rated as more pleasant when generated with methods which respect user-specified timings. This can be explained by the fact that *experts* explicitly leverage shot timings to create compositional effects. Optimizing for global smoothness removes this

---

[4] For more details on experimental design and results, see [33].

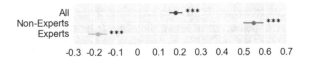

Fig. 7 Mean and 95% confidence interval of the effect of optimization scheme on *all, non-expert* designed and *expert* designed videos. Significance notation is with respect to the null effect (zero)

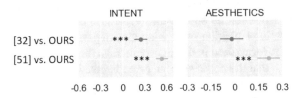

Fig. 8 Mean and 95% confidence interval of the effect of optimization scheme on the perceived match with videographer intent and aesthetics. Significance notation is with respect to the null effect (zero)

intention from the result. However, the significant positive effect of our method on *all* responses and a larger effect size for the positive effect of *non-expert-* compared to the negative effect of *expert* designed videos indicate that smooth motion is a more important factor for the aesthetic perception of aerial videos than timing. In addition, we showed in a follow-up study that experts benefit from our soft-constrained instead of baselines' hard-constrained timings [33]. Soft-constraints allow the optimizer to trade off the temporal fit for a smoother or physically feasible trajectory.

5.3.3 Perceptual Study—Camera Target Framing

In this study, we analyzed the effect of our method and the approaches of [30, 49] on the match between generated and user-intended target framing as well as on the aesthetic perception of aerial videos. More specifically, we conducted another pairwise perceptual comparison of videos generated with the mentioned approaches. Thus, we designed two questionnaires. With the first (INTENT), we investigated if video viewers perceive differences in how well the videos of conditions match with the intended result of the videographer. The second questionnaire (AESTHETICS) examined the effect of methods on the aesthetic perception of videos. To create the questionnaires, we used user-designed trajectories from a study in [31]. For INTENT, we additionally displayed the image space position at which the videographer intended to position the target. These positions were specified according to the description of the participant who designed the trajectory and were shown as a thin cross. For AESTHETICS the videos were displayed unmodified. In both surveys, the video of our method was placed side-by-side with a video from one of the baseline conditions. Videos were randomly assigned to the left or right, and participants stated which video they preferred on a forced alternative choice 5-point Likert scale.

518 participants answered both questionnaires. Negative values mean that the video of [30, 49] is perceived as more pleasing, 0 indicates no difference and a positive value means that the video of our method is perceived as more pleasing. The results of the study indicate that participants perceived the videos of our method to a better match with videographers' intent compared to [30, 49] (see Fig. 8). In terms of the aesthetic perception of videos, results are not as clear-cut. Participants found our method to produce aesthetically more pleasing videos than the framing method of [49]. However, no significant differences are found in the comparison with [30]. Aesthetic perception of framing also depends on other factors than the framing objectives formalized in the algorithm, e.g., the surroundings of the camera target. We assume that the null result can be explained by participants that attribute differences in the videos to a variety of such unmodeled factors. Nevertheless, the positive result of our approach in comparison with [49] and the fact that the INTENT questionnaire revealed a distinct significant effect in favor of our method over [30] for the same videos encourages us to suggest that our approach positively effects the aesthetic perception of videos.

6 Reinforcement Learning for Adaptive Mixed-Reality UIs

We have shown that optimal control can help users to create robotic aerial videos. Our proposed MPC approach supports users in a specific task they intend to accomplish by using a system with (quasi-)deterministic dynamics that can be modeled explicitly. Other emerging technologies, like mixed-reality systems or mobile devices, aim at supporting users in their everyday life. Hence, such systems are confronted with users that will change their task, their goals or their context without explicitly communicating these changes to the system. Thus, such systems need to consider users' state in their state space. To this end, the user state is approximated with sensors that measure their context (e.g., location) or bodily signals (e.g., eye tracking). The problem is that the same measured approximated user state can correlate with a multitude of true user states. This causes state transitions within the coupled user-system state space to not be deterministic but stochastic. All of this results in complex dynamics that cannot be modeled explicitly and, hence, model predictive control would fail to compute a control policy to support users in such tasks.

An optimal control method that is capable to cope with such challenging settings is reinforcement learning. RL can learn state transition models for complex nonlinear dynamics from experience and use these models in control policies to solve stochastic sequential decision problems. This describes the very nature of mentioned tasks. Thus, we pose such problems in the RL-framework where the user functions as the RL-environment. Figure 9 illustrates our setting and contrasts it with standard RL. Our agent makes observations about the user behavior (i.e., collected behavioral data) to learn to *support* the user in a certain task. More specifically, the agent learns to adapt system controls or displays based on a function that rewards its actions given only the observed user behavior and no form of further explicit supervision.

Fig. 9 Comparing standard
RL with our setting

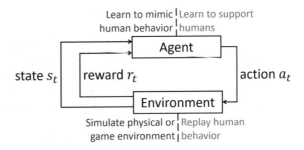

This function determines the reward based on the discrepancy of the agent's exhibited and desired behavior.

In a first case study, we investigate the applicability of this general setting in the context of a mixed-reality adaptive UI. Thus, we use RL to adapt augmentations based on users' preferences or tasks learned from their gaze interactions with a UI. We propose a method that learns to label objects by observing users' gaze interactions with objects and labels. The introduced reward function models user intent and guides the resulting policies to minimize the displayed labels in an MR-environment, without hiding relevant information. This filters information based on semantic and spatial relevance and, hence, supports users in their task by avoiding visual overload.[5]

In this section, we first introduce the behavioral data we used to build the RL-environment. We then detail our method including the RL-environment and reward function that are necessary to train MR-labeling policies. Finally, we demonstrate the capability of the method in several experiments.

6.1 Data Collection

To train our RL-agent, we require gaze trajectories. We collected this data via eye tracking in a well-defined visual search task. Participants were asked to identify targets among a set of objects that display the highest value on their label. Objects are 3D primitives positioned on a shelf-like virtual environment (see Fig. 10) and all the labels are present. The visual search environment is implemented in the Unity game engine and rendered in Virtual Reality. Participants could see the scene through an HTC Vive headset with integrated Tobii Pro eye tracking. We logged participants' gaze data relative to object and label positions, and their pupil dilation. All data were logged 120 Hz (operating frequency of eye tracker). In post-processing, we ran the eye-tracking event detection algorithm of [23] to estimate fixations and saccades. We collected 1300 visual search trials from 14 participants.

---

[5] For a more detailed version of this section, we refer the interested reader to [28].

Fig. 10 Virtual environment of the visual search task

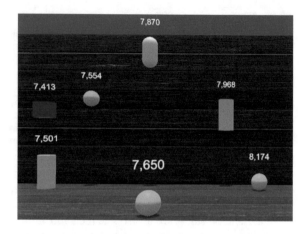

6.2 Method

We propose an agent that observes gaze trajectories and learns to label or not to label objects based on a function that rewards its actions given only the user gaze behavior and no form of further explicit supervision. In the following subsections, we will explain the individual components of our RL-method: the underlying decision process, the state action space of the agent, the RL-environment, the reward function and the learning procedure.

6.2.1 Decision Process

Saccades are considered as ballistic movements since humans cannot respond to changes in the position of a target, while undergoing rapid eye movements [81]. Therefore, the decision where to fixate next has to be made *before* the start of a saccade. To better support users, it is important that the agent decides to show or hide a label at the time the planning decision is made. Therefore, we design our RL-environment to update the state of the user gaze only at fixations (subject to the sampling frequency of the eye tracker) and to ignore state changes during saccades. The resulting setting can be seen as a dynamical system which does not update its state at a fixed sampling rate, but which provides snapshots of its state at decision points where the time between samples can vary.

This control problem can be formalized as a Semi-Markov Decision Process (SMDP; see Sect. 4.3 for its Bellman equation). In our use case, the state-action-value function $Q(s, a)$ tells us how much reward can be collected by showing the label of an object given the current gaze position (as attained from the reward function Eq. 29). The state-action value $Q(s, a)$ is formed by summing the reward of the current gaze position with the reward of all possible gaze positions that can follow normalized by their probability. Thereby, the reward of future gaze positions gets

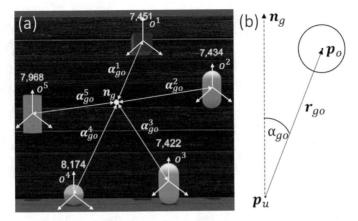

Fig. 11 **a** Angles α_{go}^{1-5} between objects o^{1-5} and gaze ray $\mathbf{n}_g$ in the local coordinate frames of the objects from the perspective of the user. **b** Geometric relations between the gaze unit vector $\mathbf{n}_g$, position of object $\mathbf{p}_o$ and user $\mathbf{p}_u$, gaze object vector $\mathbf{r}_{go}$, and the gaze object angle α_{co}

discounted. This depends on the difference between the current time and the time they are normally encountered (after visiting the current state). Note that we use model-free RL to approximate the distributions $P(s'|s, a)$ and $F(t|s, a)$ of the SMDP's Bellman equation.

6.2.2 State and Action Spaces

The agent will need to decide whether to show a label for each object in the scene. A naïve way to represent the agent's state would be to take the geometric relations of all objects with respect to the user's gaze in the world coordinate frame of the virtual scene. However, this would result in the large state and action spaces, rendering generalization to unseen scenes difficult. A more compact state-space representation is given by the geometric relation of the gaze point with respect to the center of an individual object. The agent then decides label visibility for all objects in the scene. The state space is defined in the local coordinate frame of an object with its center as the origin (see Fig. 11, a). More concretely, state and action spaces are given by

$$s = [b_o, \alpha_{go}, \alpha'_{go}] \tag{27}$$

$$a = \begin{cases} show \\ hide \end{cases} \tag{28}$$

where α_{go} is the angle between gaze unit vector n_g and gaze to object center vector r_{go} (see Fig. 11b) and α'_{go} is the angular velocity calculated by taking finite differences between two consecutive values of α_{go}. b_o is a one-hot vector encoding for object

Fig. 12 A gaze trajectory with respect to a particular object (the green sphere) specifying the progression of states and the decision sequence of actions the agent is learning

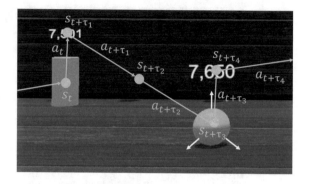

properties which in the particular case of our visual search task is a binary feature to distinguish between Os and Qs or spheres and other primitives. The actions are to show or to hide the label of an object. Euclidean distance is not included in the state space as it caused results to deteriorate.

6.2.3 Environment

Due to the high stochasticity of eye movements, it is impossible to analytically model the state transition dynamics between two consecutive samples of the eye tracker. However, if it is possible to draw a large number of samples from an RL-environment, in which state transitions follow the true transition dynamics probability distribution, model-free RL approaches have been shown to be able to learn useful policies [?]. By training on a large corpus of human gaze traces (ca. 90 visual search trials per participant) and given the small state space ($s \in \mathbb{R}^3$), we assume this assumption to hold in our case. Hence, we propose an RL-environment that enables model-free learning of policies on human gaze data.

For each object in the scene, we generate a trajectory from gaze recordings. This is constructed by transforming the gaze point from the global into an object-centered coordinate frame. For each such trajectory, we calculate the state as defined in (27) for each detected fixation. Figure 12 shows the resulting trajectory consisting of a sequence of states that depict the movement of user gaze with respect to a particular object (green sphere) in one trial. Note that state-to-state transitions of our RL-environment are independent of the chosen action, i.e., for one trajectory the transition from s_t to s_{t+1} is independent of a_t. This allows the exploration of different action sequences for the same state trajectory by simulating it multiple times. Nevertheless, we stay within the RL-framework as model-free RL learns value estimates for particular state-action pairs.

The design of this environment assumes that participants behave compliantly. That is, we assume that they only take actions that are necessary for the visual search task during data collection, looking only at the labels of target objects and ignoring distractors. In the case of complete random gaze patterns, it would not be possible to extract meaningful cooperative policies. We assume and show experimentally that the correct search behavior can be recovered by the agent when exposing it to a sufficient number of trials.

subsubsectionReward Function

In Reinforcement Learning it is necessary to provide a reward function that the agent can query in order to evaluate the goodness of a chosen action. In our case, we model the reward function to depict our goals of supporting users in the visual search tasks while reducing the amount of displayed information. This is broken down into two factors. First, we want to always show a label when it is needed, represented by the reward r_l. Second, we want to minimize the number of shown labels in total, specified with the reward r_c. The full reward function is then defined as

$$r(s, a, s') = \begin{cases} r_l & \text{if } a \text{ is } show \text{ and label is fixated in } s' \\ -r_c & \text{if } a \text{ is } show \text{ and label is not fixated in } s' \\ -r_l & \text{if } a \text{ is } hide \text{ and label is fixated in } s' \\ r_c & \text{if } a \text{ is } hide \text{ and label is not fixated in } s'. \end{cases} \qquad (29)$$

We consider a label to be fixated if α_{go} is zero and if the algorithm of [23] detects a fixation. All four if statements are necessary to avoid convergence to cases where either all or no labels are shown. Empirically, we derived that reasonable policies are attained with the reward values $r_l = 10$ and $r_c = 1$.

subsubsectionLearning Procedure With the RL-environment and the reward function in place we can now run standard algorithms like Q-learning and SARSA [?] to learn an approximation of the state action value function. Due to the small state space it is sufficient to represent the continuous state action value function $\hat{q}(s_t, a_t, \mathbf{w}_t)$ with a RBF-parameterized function approximator (cf. [84]). In our experiments more powerful function approximators, such as deep neural networks, did not yield performance improvements. For SARSA, the function's update rule is as follows:

$$\mathbf{w}_{t+1} = \mathbf{w}_t + \alpha[r_{t+1} + \gamma^{\tau_t}\hat{q}(s_{t+1}, a_{t+1}, \mathbf{w}_t) - \qquad (30)$$
$$\hat{q}(s_t, a_t, \mathbf{w}_t)] \nabla \hat{q}(s_t, a_t, \mathbf{w}_t)$$

where $\mathbf{w}_t$ is the parameter vector of the state action value function and ∇ denotes the gradient of function $\hat{q}$. In accordance with the underlying SMDP and to account for the varying duration of saccades, an action a_t can be of different temporal length, modeled by τ_t. Equation 30 corresponds to performing standard stochastic gradient descent on the state action value function. Using epsilon-greedy exploration, the agent then learns for a particular state s_t to show or to hide the label a_t in the next state s_{t+1} in correspondence to the reward provided by Equation 29 (see Figure 12).

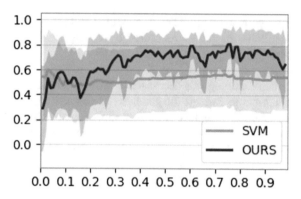

Fig. 13 Performance comparison between *ours* (in purple) versus an *SVM*-based baseline (in green). Line denotes average normalized reward on an unseen trial (y-axis) over percentage of experienced training samples (x-axis). The shaded area represents the standard deviation. Ours attains higher rewards and continues to learn from experiencing more samples, whereas the baseline converges to a low reward, displays high variance and does not improve with more samples

6.3 Evaluation

In this section, we evaluate the capability of our approach to support users in a visual search task. Thus, we first report on the results of a comparison between our method and a supervised baseline. We then present the results of a user study and, finally, demonstrate the applicability of our method to more realistic use cases.

6.3.1 Comparison with Supervised Baseline

We investigate if RL can better adapt the mixed-reality UI according to users' visual search task than a supervised baseline. Thus, we learn labeling policies in a supervised setting, using a Support Vector Machine (SVM). The SVM has comparable model complexity and discriminative power to our RBF-based function approximator. Employing the SVM as a binary classifier, we use the same state representation as in the RL-setting and assign the optimal action according to our reward function as labels to individual states.

For the comparison, we train the RL- and the supervised agent on all gaze trajectories of one trial. After every hundred samples, we test the current policy of each setting by applying it to the trajectories of an unseen trial. For each of these tests, we save the attained accumulated reward of a policy on the particular test trial. We ran the experiment on five random trials of all participants. The results can be seen in Fig. 13. Results show that policies which have been learned with explicit supervision attain a lower reward than policies learned with our method. That is they more often make decisions that are in conflict with the true user behavior. Furthermore, the shaded area in Fig. 13 indicates that the supervised policies produce a higher

Fig. 14 The labeling of policies learned in our experiment (pink dot is user's focus) for highest number task **a** pre-attentive and **b** attentive object features as well as matching-string task **d** pre-attentive and **e** attentive object features. The output of supervised policies learned for **c** pre-attentive and **f** attentive object features is also shown

variance in rewards than RL-policies and thus are less stable. Finally, we highlight that supervised policies show zero improvement with an increasing number of training samples, indicating that the SVM does not fully capture the underlying decision process of the user (see next paragraph).

To assess if learned policies are useful, we investigated their output with new users on unseen trials in the VR environment. We perform this test with policies of the SVM and our RL-method. Interestingly, policies of the supervised setting mostly converged to showing labels within a certain angle around the current fixation point (see Fig. 14b). In contrast, the RL-agent learns to distinguish between target and distractor objects and only displays the labels of targets (see Fig. 14a).

6.3.2 User Study

The goal of our method is to learn policies that support users while minimizing information overload. To evaluate the success of our approach, we conducted a user study in which a new set of participants solved the visual search task of the data collection with the help of our RL-method labeling policies. We compare participants' task performance using our RL-method with three other baselines: (1) and (2) showing labels of all objects at all time (SA = "Show All"), (3) showing the label of the object with the single closest angular distance to the user's gaze ray (CO = "Closest Object") and (4) showing labels of objects according to predictions of an SVM (SL = "Supervised Learning"). In this experiment, the tasks, object features and apparatus are identical to those used during data collection.

Figure 15 summarizes the results of our study. The data of 12 participants provides evidence that our method (RL) can learn policies that support users in their tasks while reducing the amount of unnecessarily shown labels. Statistical testing did not find significant differences in task execution time, and support between our method and the baseline of showing all labels at all times (SA). Nonetheless, RL reduces the amount of shown labels compared to SA by 87%. Likewise, the conditions CO and SL only show a fraction of the labels of SA. However, participants perceived

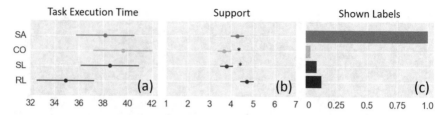

Fig. 15 Mean and 95% confidence interval of **a** task execution time (in seconds), **b** perceived support (Likert-item, higher number standing for more support) and **c** fraction of shown labels. Significance notation is with respect to the condition RL

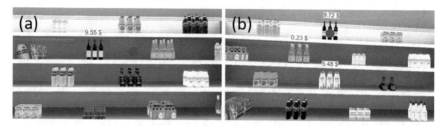

Fig. 16 *Setting:* **a** policy trained on data where the user was instructed to look for wine. **b** policy trained on trials where users are looking for wine, water and juice. *Results:* **a** The policy correctly displays only the label of a single item of interest (pink dot is user's gaze). **b** The policy displays the labels of the multiple items of interest, while hiding those of other drinks

they were significantly better supported by our policies compared to CO and SL. We attribute this to the fact, that our method decides to show the label of an object not only based on spatial information (e.g., the closest distance to gaze ray) but also learns and considers the semantic relevance of the object for the task.

6.3.3 Additional Use Cases

We also investigate the applicability of our approach to more realistic environments and tasks. Therefore, we apply our method in two additional virtual scenarios: a supermarket and an apartment.

Supermarket Scenario: More Realistic Task In this realistic task scenario, a participant was asked to search for the cheapest drink of a particular class of drinks (water, juice, soda, etc.) on a virtual supermarket shelf. There are seven different classes of drinks (water, juice, soda, milk, beer, wine and liquor), requiring to represent them as a one-hot vector of length seven in the state space of the agent (b in Eq. 27). We conducted experiments where a participant had to find the cheapest item of one and three drink categories in each trial. The policies learned on this data show that the agent can identify the drinks of interest (see Fig. 16). However, the setting is prone to flicker. This can be explained by the fact that items of different classes of drinks

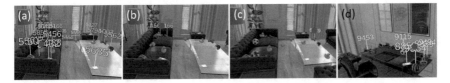

Fig. 17 Apartment scenario: **a** a realistic apartment environment with label and object occlusions makes for a difficult visual search task; **b, c** policy that identifies target objects and only shows their labels; **d** policy that shows labels of objects which are close to user's gaze

have a high visual similarity (see juice and milk cartons in Fig. 16) which causes participants to confuse items.

Apartment Scenario: Higher Visual Fidelity We ask participants to find the object with the highest number on its label in the rooms of a virtual apartment (bathroom, kitchen, living room, etc.) in which objects and labels can be occluded (see Fig. 17a). We conduct this experiment to see if the additional randomness in the participant's gaze behavior, introduced by salient features as well as object and label occlusions, prevents the agent from learning meaningful policies. Policies tend to show the labels of all objects close to participants' point of gaze since occlusions make it difficult for the agent to identify behavioral differences for target and distractor objects (see Fig. 17d). However, even in these environments, learning can converge to policies that identify target objects and only show the desired labels (see Fig. 17b, c).

Both scenarios have revealed that the quality of labeling policies depends on the compliance of participant behavior with the specified task. If users, during data collection, regularly confused target and distractor objects and checked the labels of distractors, the cooperative policy will learn to label objects wrongly. This can be seen as a drawback of our approach which we discuss further in Sect. 7.

7 Discussion

Our mixed-reality case study has shown that it is possible to *learn to assist users in their task or reproduce their behavior solely from observing their interactions with a UI*. Policies were learned from logged interactions and no costly data labeling was necessary. This is an interesting property for HCI as ample interaction log files exist from which RL could leverage to develop predictive user models.

In addition, *RL indicated to better predict user behavior compared to supervised user modeling techniques*. This can be attributed to the underlying formalism of reinforcement learning. In RL, behavioral objectives for a policy are modeled with a reward function with which they can be weighted according to their importance for a problem domain. Furthermore, it does not assume state transitions to be deterministic and models them with a probabilistic function. This allows determining the optimal action in a state even in stochastic environments. RL also considers the expected rewards in future states when deciding for an action in the current state of the agent.

The described formalism models sequential decision-making in stochastic domains and implicitly deals with challenges that arise in HCI use cases. For instance, in our work on mixed-reality labeling, RL-policies were capable of identifying target objects of a visual search task while supervised policies failed to do so. The benefit of RL was that modeling the objectives of MR labeling with a reward function better guided the behavior of the labeling policy than modeling MR labeling as a binary classification problem. Furthermore, the state transition probability function modeled the stochasticity of gaze movement. In contrast, supervised learning disregarded it with the assumption of deterministic transitions. Another work of ours, in which RL is used to model human task interleaving, has shown that considering long-term rewards for action selection helped in predicting user behavior [32]. Reinforcement learning policies better predicted task switches of participants than myopic baselines, even if these were omniscient.[6] These examples indicate the benefit of using RL as a user modeling technique for AUIs.

However, the more realistic use cases of the label agent have also revealed a fundamental problem of learning-based UI adaptation in general. Namely, the extent to which a model can support a task depends on the compliance of users' behavior with this task in training data. One possible solution to overcome this problem is to learn models on expert data (similar to [2, 76]) and use them to adapt UIs for end-users. However, such approaches would not be able to adapt to individual users.

Optimization-based methods for UI adaptation do not suffer the same problem. They are invariant against non-task-compliant user behavior as high-level goals of a problem domain are modeled directly and UIs are optimized based on these objective terms. Adaptation to individual users can be achieved by adjusting the weights of the different terms according to personal goals and preferences. Our optimization-based tool for aerial videography has confirmed these strengths. The disadvantage of MPC is that it requires the designer to model all possible user goals the optimization should adapt for in advance. This, on the other hand, is a strong suit of RL which has shown to be able to identify higher level concepts from demonstrations and execute policies that fulfill them [53]. This shows that both methods have complementary advantages and suggests their combination in future work.

Our aerial videography case study also demonstrated MPC's capabilities in the context of human-robot interaction. Optimizing robotic inputs according to a physical model abstracts the high-dimensional robot control commands and allows users to steer the robot by specifying references in a sparse and intuitive manner. By automating the hard and cumbersome parts of robotic control, the optimization acts as a support tool that allows users to focus on the high-level aspects of their tasks.

---

[6]Myopic policies only consider the attainable reward in the next state and neglect other future states when selecting an action.

8 Future Research Challenges

In this chapter, we presented first evidence on how optimal control can improve user support in challenging human-computer interaction use cases. To realize optimal control's full potential in the context of HCI, further research is necessary for which we propose interesting directions in the following paragraphs.

Extend the application of MPC in HCI: Research proposed assignment problem formulations for a large variety of HCI tasks, e.g., [6, 78]. By using mixed-integer MPC approaches [52], these could be ported into the optimal control framework. This would allow modeling iterative dependencies in such tasks that emerge from the closed-loop dynamics of HCI.

Learn to adapt for changing user goals: The ideal interface recognizes the goal or the task a user is pursuing and acts to support them accordingly. Future research endeavors should work on developing agents that are capable of such behavior. To tackle this challenge, machine learning research proposed different approaches to identify higher level tasks from demonstrations [25, 53]. These could be used to develop agents that infer possible user goals or tasks from human-interface interactions and support users in accomplishing them. Similarly, one may investigate if multi-goal adaptive UI agents can be learned via temporal integration of users' reactions to low-level adaptations in settings with shaped reward functions.

Extend adaptive capabilities of UI agents: Machine learning proposed RL algorithms for large discrete [22] and even continuous action spaces [60]. Building on this work, future research should aim at extending the display adaptation capabilities of UI agents. RL-based agents should not only decide on the assignment of content but also manipulate the content's location and properties to better suit users' tasks. This might ultimately result in agents whose actions represent pixels and that learn to create optimal UIs for observed user behavior.

Combine MPC and RL to support users in HCI: We have shown that the capabilities of MPC and RL in the context of supporting interaction are complementary. Thus, research should investigate their combination to advance the utility of AUIs. For instance, models for complex non-linear environment dynamics could be learned and used in a model-predictive optimization to compute policies without requiring retraining for changing objectives. Another example would be an MPC that provides basic guidance in situations that have not been encountered previously according to modeled user goals and a learning-based method that iteratively improves and personalizes adaptations with the increasing amount of encountered states.

Embedding UI agents into the real world: One promise of artificial intelligence are agents that act in the real world to amplify and extend human abilities. UIs are an ideal sandbox for this vision as their malfunctioning has minor consequences compared to malfunctions of robots. Thus, RL-based UI agents can contribute to turning this promise into reality. However, in realistic settings new challenges arise. Real-world user behavior is subject to sidetracking, multitasking and changing preferences, and

RL-based user modeling techniques need to be able to recover from them to provide useful UI adaptations. Future research also needs to develop policies that work in settings where learning and inference are done online. This could be achieved through off-policy learning and an agent that continuously updates a policy based on users' reaction toward the UI adaptation of a behavioral policy. The behavioral policy would regularly be updated.

9 Conclusion

In this chapter, we proposed optimal control as a framework to support users in achieving their high-level goals in HCI tasks. We reasoned that it will improve user support over usual adaptive UIs for devices of emerging technologies that require the continuous adaptation of their input and output mechanisms for users to fully leverage them. This is due to optimal control's formalism implicitly capturing the closed-loop iterative nature of HCI. More specifically, optimal control methods can optimize a system's input and output mechanisms for a user's next interaction step while taking their long-term goals into account. In addition, it should be robust against modeling errors of users' high-level goals since only the first step of the prediction horizon is implemented and it is re-optimized with each user input.

To test if optimal control methods have a positive effect on the usability of emerging technologies, we conducted two case studies. First, we introduced an MPC optimization scheme that allows end-users to plan and execute robotic aerial videos. Thus, we modeled the dynamical system of a quadrotor and its gimbal-mounted camera and enabled the generation of trajectories from sparse user-specified keyframes. The objective function models aesthetic criteria of aerial videos and generates trajectories that adhere to them. Second, we proposed an RL-based method to adapt mixed-reality augmentations based on users' preferences or tasks learned from their gaze interactions with a UI. Thus, the agent is trained model-free on human gaze recordings and guided by a reward function to fulfill two objectives: minimizing visual clutter while displaying information when needed.

Our results have shown that optimal control can better support users' high-level goals in human-computer tasks than common approaches. Optimal control models HCI tasks as sequential decision problems which represents the nature of most HCI tasks and, hence, results in better predictability of user behavior than usual approaches. In addition, our work highlighted the complementary strengths of MPC and RL with respect to automatic UI adaptation. MPC can optimize a UI for users' high-level goals without requiring task-compliant user data while RL can identify user goals autonomously without needing a user goal model.

For optimal control agents to be embedded in the real world, future research should work on approaches that learn to adapt for changing user goals that extend the adaptive capabilities of UI agents and that combine optimization-based and learning-based optimal control approaches to further increase user support.

References

1. Abbeel P, Dolgov D, Ng AY, Thrun S (2008) Apprenticeship learning for motion planning with application to parking lot navigation. In: IEEE international conference on intelligent robots and systems 2008. IROS '08. IEEE, pp 1083–1090
2. Pieter A, Ng Andrew Y (2004) Apprenticeship learning via inverse reinforcement learning. p 1
3. Kumaripaba A, Alan M, Antti O, Giulio J, Dorota G (2016) Beyond relevance: adapting exploration/exploitation in information retrieval. Association for Computing Machinery, New York, NY, USA
4. Audronis T (2014) How to get cinematic drone shots
5. Aytar Y, Pfaff T, Budden D, Le Paine T, Wang Z, de Freitas N (2018) Playing hard exploration games by watching youtube. In: Advances in neural information processing systems
6. Gilles B, Antti O, Timo K, Sabrina H (2013) Menuoptimizer: interactive optimization of menu systems. pp 331–342
7. Banovic N, Buzali T, Chevalier F, Mankoff J, Dey AK (2016) Modeling and understanding human routine behavior. In: Proceedings of the 2016 CHI conference on human factors in computing systems, CHI '16. ACM, pp 248–260
8. Bemporad A, Morari M, Dua V, Pistikopoulos EN (2002) The explicit linear quadratic regulator for constrained systems. Automatica 38(1):3–20
9. Bertsekas Dimitri P, Tsitsiklis John N (1995). Neuro-dynamic programming: an overview, vol 1. IEEE, pp 560–564
10. Bronner S, Shippen J (2015) Biomechanical metrics of aesthetic perception in dance. Exp Brain Res 233(12), 3565–3581:12
11. Chapanis A (1976) Engineering psychology. Rand McNally, Chicago
12. Chen M, Beutel A, Covington P, Jain S, Belletti F, Chi H (eds) (2019) Top-k off-policy correction for a reinforce recommender system. In: Proceedings of the twelfth ACM international conference on web search and data mining, WSDM '19. ACM, pp 456–464
13. Chen X, Bailly G, Brumby DP, Oulasvirta A, Howes A (2015) The emergence of interactive behavior: A model of rational menu search. In: Proceedings of the 33rd annual ACM conference on human factors in computing systems, CHI '15, pp 4217-4226, New York, NY, USA. Association for Computing Machinery
14. Xiuli C, Sandra Dorothee S, Chris B, Andrew H (2017). A cognitive model of how people make decisions through interaction with visual displays. Association for Computing Machinery, New York, NY, USA
15. Cheng E (2016) Aerial photography and videography using drones, vol 1. Peachpit Press
16. Chipalkatty R, Droge G, Egerstedt MB (2013) Less is more: mixed-initiative model-predictive control with human inputs. IEEE Trans Rob 29(3):695–703
17. Chipalkatty R, Egerstedt M (2010) Human-in-the-loop: Terminal constraint receding horizon control with human inputs. pp 2712–2717
18. Christiano PF, Leike J, Brown T, Martic M Legg S, Amodei D (2017) Deep reinforcement learning from human preferences. In: Advances in neural information processing systems, pp 4299–4307
19. Clarke DW, Mohtadi C, Tuffs PS (1987) Generalized predictive control-part i. the basic algorithm. Automatica 23(2):137–148
20. Coates A, Abbeel P, Ng AY (2009) Apprenticeship learning for helicopter control. Commun ACM 52(7):97–105
21. Cutler CR, Ramaker BL (1980) Dynamic matrix control - a computer control algorithm. In: Joint automatic control conference, vol 17, p 72
22. Dulac-Arnold G, Evans R, van Hasselt H, Sunehag P, Lillicrap T, Hunt J, Mann T, Weber T, Degris T, Coppin B (2015). Deep reinforcement learning in large discrete action spaces. arXiv:1512.07679
23. Engbert R, Kliegl R (2003) Microsaccades uncover the orientation of covert attention. Vis Res 43(9):1035–1045

24. Findlater L, Gajos KZ (2009) Design space and evaluation challenges of adaptive graphical user interfaces. AI Mag 30(4):68–68
25. Frans K, Ho J, Chen X, Abbeel X, Schulman J (2017) Meta learning shared hierarchies. arXiv:1710.09767
26. Fritsch FN, Carlson RE (1980) Monotone piecewise cubic interpolation. SIAM J Numer Anal 17(2):238–246
27. Gašić M, Young S (2014) Gaussian processes for POMDP-based dialogue manager optimization. IEEE Trans Audio Speech Lang Process 22(1):28–40
28. Gebhardt C, Hecox B, van Opheusden B, Wigdor D, Hillis J, Hilliges O, Benko H (2019) Learning cooperative personalized policies from gaze data. In: Proceedings of the 32nd annual ACM symposium on user interface software and technology, UIST '19, New York, NY, US. ACM
29. gebhardt c, hepp b, naegeli t, stevsic s, hilliges o (2061) airways: optimization-based Planning of Quadrotor Trajectories according to High-Level User Goals. In: ACM SIGCHI conference on human factors in computing systems, CHI '16, New York, NY, USA. ACM
30. Gebhardt C, Hilliges O (2018) WYFIWYG: investigating effective user support in aerial videography. arXiv:1801.05972
31. Christoph G, Otmar H (2020) Optimizing for cinematographic quadrotor camera target framing. In: Submission to ACM SIGCHI
32. Gebhardt C, Oulasvirta A, Hilliges O (2020) Hierarchical Reinforcement Learning as a Model of Human Task Interleaving. arXiv:2001.02122
33. Gebhardt C, Stevsic S, Hilliges O (2018) Optimizing for aesthetically pleasing quadrotor camera motion. ACM Trans Graph (Proc ACM SIGGRAPH) 37(4):90:1–90:11:8
34. Ali G, Judith B, Atsuto M, Danica K, Mårten B (2016) A sensorimotor reinforcement learning framework for physical human-robot interaction. pp 2682–2688
35. Dorota G, Tuukka R, Ksenia K, Kumaripaba A, Samuel K, Giulio J (2013) Directing exploratory search: Reinforcement learning from user interactions with keywords. pp 117–128
36. Görges D (2017) Relations between model predictive control and reinforcement learning. IFAC-PapersOnLine 50(1):4920–4928
37. Grieder P, Borrelli F, Torrisi F, Morari M (2004) Computation of the constrained infinite time linear quadratic regulator. Automatica 40(4):701–708
38. Hadfield-Menell D, Russell SJ, Abbeel P, Dragan A (2016) Cooperative inverse reinforcement learning. In: Advances in neural information processing systems, pp 3909–3917
39. Hennessy J (2015) 13 powerful tips to improve your aerial cinematography
40. Ho B-J, Balaji B, Koseoglu M, Sandha S, Pei S, Srivastava M (2020) Quick question: Interrupting users for microtasks with reinforcement learning. arXiv:2007.09515
41. Hogan N (1984) Adaptive control of mechanical impedance by coactivation of antagonist muscles. IEEE Trans Autom Control 29(8):681–690
42. Horvitz EJ, Breese JS, Heckerman D, Hovel D, Rommelse K (2013) The lumiere project: Bayesian user modeling for inferring the goals and needs of software users. arXiv:1301.7385
43. Howes A, Chen X, Acharya A, Lewis RL (2018) Interaction as an emergent property of a partially observable markov decision process. Computational interaction design. pp 287–310
44. Zehong H, Liang Y, Zhang J, Li Z, Liu Y (2018) Inference aided reinforcement learning for incentive mechanism design in crowdsourcing. In: Advances in Neural Information Processing Systems. NIPS '18:5508–5518
45. Hwangbo J, Lee J, Dosovitskiy A, Bellicoso D, Tsounis V, Koltun V, Hutter M (2019) Learning agile and dynamic motor skills for legged robots. Sci Robot 4(26)
46. Anthony J, Krzysztof GZ (2012) Systems that adapt to their users. The Human-Computer interaction handbook: fundamentals, evolving technologies and emerging applications. CRC Press, Boca Raton, FL
47. Johansen TA (2004) Approximate explicit receding horizon control of constrained nonlinear systems. Automatica 40(2):293–300
48. Jorgensen SJ, Campbell O, Llado T, Kim D, Ahn J, Sentis L (2017) Exploring model predictive control to generate optimal control policies for hri dynamical systems. arXiv:1701.03839

49. Joubert N, Roberts M, Truong A, Berthouzoz F, Hanrahan P (2015) An interactive tool for designing quadrotor camera shots. vol 34. ACM, New York, NY, USA, pp 238:1–238:11

50. Julier S, Lanzagorta M, Baillot Y, Rosenblum L, Feiner S, Hollerer T, Sestito S (2000) Information filtering for mobile augmented reality. In: Proceedings IEEE and ACM international symposium on augmented reality (ISAR 2000). IEEE, pp 3–11

51. Kartoun U, Stern H, Edan Y (2010) A human-robot collaborative reinforcement learning algorithm. J Intell Robot Syst 60(2):217–239

52. Kirches C (2011) Fast numerical methods for mixed-integer nonlinear model-predictive control. Springer

53. Krishnan S, Garg A, Liaw R, Miller L, Pokorny FT, Goldberg K (2016) Hirl: hierarchical inverse reinforcement learning for long-horizon tasks with delayed rewards. arXiv:1604.06508

54. Kostadin K, Jason P, Elizabeth WD (2016) "Silence your phones" smartphone notifications increase inattention and hyperactivity symptoms. pp 1011–1020

55. Lam D, Manzie C, Good MC (2013) Multi-axis model predictive contouring control. Int J Control 86(8):1410–1424

56. (2020) Optimal control for electromagnetic haptic guidance systems. In: Langerak Thomas, Zarate Juan, Vechev Velko, Lindlbauer David, Panozzo Daniele, Hilliges Otmar (eds)

57. Lee SJ, Popović Z (2010) Learning behavior styles with inverse reinforcement learning. In: ACM transactions on graphics (TOG), vol 29. ACM, p 122

58. Lee Y, Wampler K, Bernstein G, Popović J, Popović Z (2010) Motion fields for interactive character locomotion. In: ACM transactions on graphics (TOG), vol 29. ACM, p 138

59. Liebman E, Saar-Tschansky M, Stone P (2015) Dj-mc: a reinforcement-learning agent for music playlist recommendation. In: Proceedings of the 2015 international conference on autonomous agents and multiagent systems, AAMAS '15, pp 591–599

60. Lillicrap TP, Hunt JJ, Pritzel A, Heess N, Erez T, Tassa Y, Silver D, Wierstra D (eds) (2015) Continuous control with deep reinforcement learning. arXiv preprint arXiv:1509.02971

61. Liniger A, Domahidi A, Morari M (2015) Optimization-based autonomous racing of 1: 43 scale rc cars. Opt Control Appl Methods 36(5):628–647

62. Liu F, Tang R, Li X, Zhang W, Ye Y, Chen H, Guo H, Zhang Y (2018) Deep reinforcement learning based recommendation with explicit user-item interactions modeling. arXiv:1810.12027

63. Lo W-Y, Zwicker M (2008) Real-time planning for parameterized human motion. In: Proceedings of the 2008 ACM SIGGRAPH/eurographics symposium on computer animation, SCA '08, pp 29–38

64. Justin M, Wei L, Tovi G, George F (2009) Communitycommands: command recommendations for software applications. pp 193–202

65. McCann J, Pollard N (2007) Responsive characters from motion fragments. In: ACM transactions on graphics (TOG), vol 26. ACM, p 6

66. McRuer Duane T, Jex Henry R (1967) A review of quasi-linear pilot models

67. Michalska H, Mayne DQ (1993) Robust receding horizon control of constrained nonlinear systems. IEEE Trans Autom Control 38(11):1623–1633, 11

68. Bastian M, Andreas K (2010) User model for predictive calibration control on interactive screens. pp 32–37

69. Mitsunaga N, Smith C, Kanda T, Ishiguro H, Hagita N (2006) Robot behavior adaptation for human-robot interaction based on policy gradient reinforcement learning. J Robot Soc Jpn 24(7):820–829

70. Modares H, Ranatunga I, Lewis FL, Popa DO (2015) Optimized assistive human-robot interaction using reinforcement learning. IEEE Trans Cybernet 46(3):655–667

71. Müller J, Oulasvirta A, Murray-Smith R (2017) Control theoretic models of pointing. ACM Trans Comput-Hum Interact (TOCHI) 24(4):1–36

72. Murray-Smith R (2018) Control theory, dynamics and continuous interaction

73. Nägeli T, Alonso-Mora J, Domahidi A, Rus D, Hilliges O (2017) Real-time motion planning for aerial videography with dynamic obstacle avoidance and viewpoint optimization. IEEE Robot Autom Lett PP(99):1–1

74. Nägeli T, Meier L, Domahidi A, Alonso-Mora J, Hilliges O (2017) Real-time planning for automated multi-view drone cinematography. ACM Trans Graph 36(4):132:1–132:10
75. Thomas N, Ying-Yin H, Andreas K (2014) Planning redirection techniques for optimal free walking experience using model predictive control. pp 111–118
76. Ng AY, Russell SJ (2000) Algorithms for inverse reinforcement learning. In: Proceedings of the seventeenth international conference on machine learning, ICML '00, pp 663–670
77. Oliff H, Liu Y, Kumar M, Williams M, Ryan M (2020) Reinforcement learning for facilitating human-robot-interaction in manufacturing. J Manuf Syst 56:326–340
78. Park S, Gebhardt C, Rädle R, Feit A, Vrzakova H, Dayama N, Yeo H-S, Klokmose C, Quigley A, Oulasvirta A, Hilliges O (2018) AdaM: adapting multi-user interfaces for collaborative environments in real-time. In: ACM SIGCHI conference on human factors in computing systems, cHI '18, New York, NY, USA. ACM
79. Bin Peng X, Abbeel P, Levine S, van de Panne M (2018) Deepmimic: example-guided deep reinforcement learning of physics-based character skills. ACM Trans Graph 37(4):8
80. Bin Peng X, Kanazawa A, Malik J, Abbeel P, Levine S (2018) Sfv: Reinforcement learning of physical skills from videos. ACM Trans Graph, 37
81. Purves D, Fitzpatrick D, Katz LC, Lamantia AS, McNamara JO, Williams SM, Augustine GJ (2000) Neuroscience. Sinauer Associates
82. Rachael JA, Rault A, Testud JL, Papon J (1978) Model predictive heuristic control: application to an industrial process. Automatica 14(5):413–428
83. Mizanoor Rahman SM, Behzad S, Yue W (2015)Trust-based optimal subtask allocation and model predictive control for human-robot collaborative assembly in manufacturing, vol 57250. American Society of Mechanical Engineers, p page V002T32A004
84. Rajeswaran A, Lowrey K, Todorov EV, Kakade SM (2017) Towards generalization and simplicity in continuous control. In Advances in Neural Information Processing Systems. NIPS '17:6550–6561
85. Roberts M, Hanrahan P (2016) Generating dynamically feasible trajectories for quadrotor cameras. ACM Trans Graph 354:61:1-61:11
86. Safavi A, Zadeh MH (2017) Teaching the user by learning from the user: personalizing movement control in physical human-robot interaction. IEEE/CAA J Autom Sinica 4(4):704–713
87. Sheridan TB, Ferrell WR (1974) Man-machine systems; Information, control, and decision models of human performance. The MIT press
88. Silver D, Schrittwieser J, Simonyan K, Antonoglou I, Huang A, Guez A, Hubert T, Baker L, Lai M, Bolton A et al (2017) Mastering the game of go without human knowledge. Nature 550(7676):354–359
89. Su P-H, Budzianowski P, Ultes S, Gasic M, Young S (2017) Sample-efficient actor-critic reinforcement learning with supervised data for dialogue management. arXiv:1707.00130
90. Sutton RS, Barto AG, Williams RJ (1992) Reinforcement learning is direct adaptive optimal control. IEEE Control Syst Mag 12(2):19–22
91. Rowan S, Kieran F, Owen C (2019) A reinforcement learning and synthetic data approach to mobile notification management. pp 155–164
92. Teramae T, Noda T, Morimoto J (2018) Emg-based model predictive control for physical human-robot interaction: application for assist-as-needed control. IEEE Robot Autom Lett 3(1):210–217
93. Tjomsland J, Shafti A, Aldo Faisal A (2019) Human-robot collaboration via deep reinforcement learning of real-world interactions. arXiv:1912.01715
94. Treuille A, Lee Y, Popović Z (2007) Near-optimal character animation with continuous control. ACM Trans Graph 26(3):7
95. (1989) Christopher John Cornish Hellaby Watkins. Learning from delayed rewards
96. Wiener N (2019) Cybernetics or Control and Communication in the Animal and the Machine. MIT press

Modeling Mobile Interface Tappability Using Crowdsourcing and Deep Learning

Amanda Swearngin and Yang Li

Abstract Tapping is an immensely important gesture in mobile touchscreen interfaces, yet people still frequently are required to learn which elements are tappable through trial and error. Predicting human behavior for this everyday gesture can help mobile app designers understand an important aspect of the usability of their apps without having to run a user study. In this chapter, we present an approach for modeling tappability of mobile interfaces at scale. We conducted large-scale data collection of interface tappability over a rich set of mobile apps using crowdsourcing and computationally investigated a variety of signifiers that people use to distinguish tappable versus not tappable elements. Based on the dataset, we developed and trained a deep neural network that predicts how likely a user will perceive an interface element as tappable versus not tappable. To demonstrate the capability of the trained tappability model, we developed TapShoe, a tool that automatically diagnoses mismatches between the tappability of each element as perceived by a human user—predicted by our model, and the intended or actual tappable state of the element specified by the developer or designer. Our model achieved reasonable accuracy: mean precision 90.2% and recall 87.0%, in matching human perception on identifying tappable UI elements. The tappability model and TapShoe were well received by designers via an informal evaluation with 7 professional interaction designers.

1 Introduction

Tapping is arguably the most important gesture on mobile interfaces. Yet, it is still difficult for people to distinguish tappable and not tappable elements in a mobile interface. In traditional desktop GUIs, the style of clickable elements (e.g., buttons)

A. Swearngin (✉)
University of Washington, Seattle, WA, USA
e-mail: amaswea@cs.washington.edu

Work conducted during an internship at Google Research, Mountain View, USA

Y. Li
Google Research, Mountain View, CA, USA
e-mail: liyang@google.com

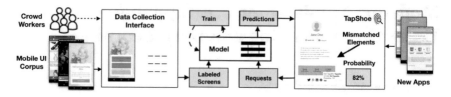

Fig. 1 Our deep model learns from a large-scale dataset of mobile tappability collected via crowd-sourcing. It predicts tappability of interface elements and identifies mismatches between designer intention and user perception, and is served in the TapShoe tool that can help designers and developers to uncover potential usability issues about their mobile interfaces

are often conventionally defined. However, with the diverse styles of mobile interfaces, tappability has become a crucial usability issue. Poor tappability can lead to a lack of discoverability [27] and false affordances [12] that can lead to user frustration, uncertainty, and errors [3, 10].

Signifiers [27] can indicate to a user how to interact with an interface element. Designers can use visual properties (e.g., color or depth) to signify an element's "clickability" [3] or "tappability" in mobile interfaces. Perhaps the most ubiquitous signifiers in today's interfaces are the blue color and underline of a link, and the design of a button that both strongly signify to the user that they should be clicked. These common signifiers have been learned over time and are well understood to indicate clickability [26]. To design for tappability, designers can apply existing design guidelines for clickability [3]. These are important and can cover typical cases, however, it is not always clear when to apply them in each specific design setting. Frequently, mobile app developers are not equipped with such knowledge. Despite the existence of simple guidelines, we found a significant amount of tappability misperception in real mobile interfaces, as shown in the dataset that we discussed later.

Additionally, modern platforms for mobile apps frequently introduce new design patterns and interface elements. Designing these to include appropriate signifiers for tappability is challenging. Additionally, mobile interfaces cannot apply useful clickability cues available in web and desktop interfaces (e.g., hover states). With the flat design trend, traditional signifiers have been altered, which potentially causes uncertainty and mistakes [10]. More data may be needed to confirm these results, however, we argue that we need more data and automated methods to fully understand the users' perceptions of tappability as design trends evolve over time.

One way that interface designers can understand tappability in their interfaces is through conducting a tappability study or a visual affordance test [34]. However, it is time-consuming to conduct such studies. In addition, the findings from these studies are often limited to a specific app or interface design. We aim to understand signifiers at a large scale across a diverse array of interface designs and to diagnose tappability problems in new apps automatically without conducting user studies.

In this chapter, we present an approach for modeling interface tappability at scale through crowdsourcing and deep learning. We first collected and analyzed a large dataset of 20,000 tappability labels from more than 3,000 mobile app screens. Our analysis of this dataset demonstrate that there are many false and missing signifiers potentially causing people to frequently misidentify tappable and not tappable interface elements. Through computational signfier analysis, we identified a set of findings on factors impacting mobile interface tappability. Using this dataset, we trained a deep learning model that achieved reasonable acccuracy with mean precision 90.2% and recall 87.0% on identifying tappable elements as perceived by humans. To showcase a potential use of the model, we build TapShoe (Fig. 1), a web interface that diagnoses mismatches between the human perception of the tappability of an interface element and its actual state in the interface code. We conducted informal interviews with 7 professional interface designers who were positive about the TapShoe interface, and could envision intriguing uses of the tappability model in realistic design situations. Based on our work on tappability modeling [31], we discuss the following contributions in this chapter, and generalize them towards other scenarios:

1. An approach for understanding interface tappability at scale using crowdsourcing and computational signifier analysis, and a set of findings about mobile tappability;
2. A deep neural network model that learns human perceived tappability of interface elements from a range of interface features, including the spatial, semantic, and visual aspects of an interface element and its screen, and an in-depth analysis about the model behavior;
3. An interactive system that uses the model to examine a mobile interface by automatically scanning the tappability of each element on the interface, and identifies mismatches with their intended tappable behavior.

While this chapter describes a method to model and predict tappability which can enable automatic usability analysis, tappability is only one aspect of usability. There are potentially other such aspects of usability that can be modeled. We discuss some of these aspects and potential areas to apply deep learning in Sect. 9.

2 Background

The concepts of signifiers and affordances are integral to our work. We aim to capture them in a systematic way to construct a predictive model and to understand their use in a large set of real mobile interfaces. Affordances were originally described by [13] as the actionable properties between the world and actor (i.e., person). References [25, 26] popularized the idea of affordances of everyday objects, such as a door which has an affordance of opening. A "signifier" indicates the affordance of an object [26]. For example, a door handle can signify the direction a door will open. Norman, later, related the concept of signifiers to user interfaces [26]. Gaver [12], described the use of graphical techniques to aid human perception (e.g., shadows or rounded corners), and showed how designers can use signifiers to convey an interface element's perceived affordances. These early works form the core of our current understanding of what makes a person know what is interactive. By collecting a large dataset of tappability examples, we hope to expand our understanding of which signifiers are having an impact at scale.

3   Related Work

While there are many methods to assess the design quality and usability of interfaces (e.g., cognitive walkthrough, heuristic evaluation), there are few methods to automatically assess an interface for its usability. Creating such automated methods can help designers avoid the time and cost required for manual usability testing, and can help them discover patterns that they may not have been able to discover without computational support. In this chapter, we present a method to automatically model a specific aspect of usability—tappability; however, we review work that applies large scale data-collection and modeling to assess some aspect of interface design or usability. This work falls into two main categories: (1) large-scale data collection to assess interface design and usability (2) machine learning methods to assess interface design and usability.

3.1   *Large-Scale Data Collection to Assess Interface Design & Usability*

There have only been a few small-scale studies on the factors influencing clickability in web interfaces [3, 10]. Usability testing methods have also adopted the idea of visual affordance testing [34] to diagnose clickability issues. However, these studies have been conducted at a small scale and are typically limited to the single app being tested. We are not aware of any large-scale data collection and analysis across app interfaces to enable diagnosis of tappability issues, nor any machine learning approaches that learn from this data to automatically predict the elements that users will perceive as tappable or not tappable.

To identify tappability issues automatically, we need to collect data on a large scale to allow us to use a machine learning approach for this problem. Recently, data-driven approaches have been used to identify usability issues [7], and collect mobile app design data at scale [6, 8]. Perhaps most closely related to our work is Zipt [7], which enables comparative user performance testing at scale. Zipt uses crowd workers to construct user flow visualizations through apps that can help designers visualize the paths users will take through their app for specific tasks. However, with this approach, designers must still manually diagnose the usability issues by examining the visualizations. In this chapter, we focus on identifying an important usability issue in mobile interfaces automatically—identifying cases where false affordances or missing signifiers will cause a user to misidentify a tappable or not tappable interface element.

Similar to Zipt [7], our work uses crowdsourcing to collect user data to aid the diagnosis of usability issues. We used Amazon's Mechanical Turk that has previously provided a platform for large-scale usability [24] and human subjects experiments [16, 17, 30], and in gathering data about the visual design of user interfaces [14, 21, 37]. Our work goes beyond data collection and analysis by developing machine learning models to automatically examine tappability.

3.2 Machine Learning Methods to Assess Interface Design & Usability

Deep learning [19] is an effective approach to learn from large-scale datasets, and recent work has begun to explore applying deep learning to assess various aspects of usability. In our work, we trained a deep feedforward network, which uses convolutional layers for image processing and embedding for categorical data such as words and types, to automatically predict human tappability perception.

Recent work has used deep learning approaches to predict human performance on mobile apps for tasks such as grid selection [29], menu selection [20], and visual search time [38]. Deep learning models have also been built to identify salient elements in graphic designs and interfaces to help designers know where their users will first focus their eyes [4, 5, 39], and to predict user engagement with animation in mobile apps to help designers examine user engagement issues [36]. Beyond a single app design and layout, others have built deep learning models to automatically explore design solutions [40] and generate optimized layouts [9] for mobile app designs. No previous work has yet applied deep learning to predict the tappability of interface elements. Deep learning allowed us to leverage a rich set of features involving the semantic, spatial, and visual properties of an element without extensive feature engineering, and to address the problem in an end-to-end fashion, which is easily scalable to complex problems.

4 Understanding Tappability at Scale

A common type of usability testing is a *tappability study* or a visual affordance test [34]. In these studies, designers have crowd workers or lab participants label interfaces for which elements they think are tappable and not tappable digitally or on paper. Based on this data, designers can construct heatmaps to visualize where users would tap in the app being tested. These studies can help designers discover which elements have missing or false tappability signifiers. However, in general, there is a lack of a dataset and deep understanding about interface tappability across diverse mobile apps. Having such a dataset and knowledge is required for us to create automated techniques to help designers diagnose tappability issues in their interfaces.

4.1 Crowdsourcing Data Collection

We designed a crowdsourcing task to simulate a tappability study across a large corpus of Android mobile apps [6], using the interface shown in Fig. 2. The left side of the interface displayed a mobile app screenshot. The right side of the task interface displayed instructions for the task, and an explanation about what we meant by tappable and not tappable. For tappable elements, it was "*When you tap this element in a mobile interface, an action will happen*", and for not tappable, the explanation was "*When you tap on this element, no action will happen*".

To collect our tappability dataset, we selected a set of 3,470 unique, randomly chosen screens from the Rico dataset [6] and had crowd workers label elements randomly sampled from these screens as either `tappable` or `not tappable`. We selected the elements for the workers to label in the following manner. Each UI screen in the Rico dataset has an Android view hierarchy—JSON tree structure of all of the interface elements on the screen, similar to a DOM tree for a web interface. Each element in the hierarchy has a `clickable` property that marks whether

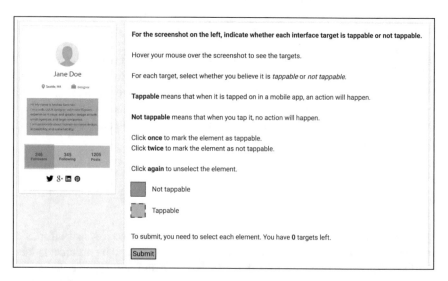

Fig. 2 The interface that workers used to label the tappability of UI elements via crowdsourcing. It displays a mobile interface screen with interactive hotspots that can be clicked to label an element as either tappable or not tappable

an element will respond to a tapping event. For each screen, we selected up to five unique `clickable` and non-`clickable` elements. When selecting `clickable` elements, starting from a leaf element, we select the top-most `clickable` element in the hierarchy for labeling. When a clickable element contains a sub-tree of elements, these elements are typically presented as a single interface element to the user, which is more appropriate for the worker to label as a whole. When a clickable container (e.g., ViewGroup) is selected, we do not select any of its child elements, thus preventing any duplicate counting or labeling. We did not select elements in the status bar or navigation bar as they are standard across most screens in the dataset.

To perform a labeling task, a crowd worker hovers their mouse over the interface screenshot, and our web interface displays gray hotspots over the interface elements pre-selected based on the above process. Workers click on each hotspot to toggle the label as either tappable or not tappable, which are colored in green and red, respectively. We asked each worker to label around six elements for each screen. Depending on the screen complexity, the amount of elements could vary. We randomized the elements as well as the order to be labeled across each worker.

4.2   Results

We collected 20,174 unique interface elements from 3,470 app screens. These elements were labeled by 743 unique workers in two rounds where each round involved different sets of workers (see Table 1). Each worker could complete up to 8 tasks. On average, each worker completed 4.67 tasks. Of these elements, 12,661 of them are indeed tappable, i.e., the view hierarchy attribute `clickable=True`, and 7,513 of them are not.

How well can human users perceive the actual clickable state of an element as specified by developers or designers? To answer this question, we treat the `clickable` value of an element in the view hierarchy as the actual value and human labels as the predicted value for a precision and recall analysis. In this dataset

Table 1 The number of elements labeled by the crowd workers in two rounds, along the precision and recall of human workers in perceiving the actual clickable state of an element as specified in the view hierarchy metadata

	Positive class	#Elements	Precision (%)	Recall (%)
R1	clickable=True	6,101	79.81	89.07
	clickable=False	3,631	78.56	61.75
R2	clickable=True	6,560	79.55	90.02
	clickable=False	3,882	78.30	60.90
All	clickable=True	12,661	79.67	89.99
	clickable=False	7,513	78.43	61.31

of real mobile app screens, there were still many false signifiers for tappability, potentially causing workers to misidentify tappable and not tappable elements (see Table 1). The workers labeled non-clickable elements as tappable 39% of time. While the workers were significantly more precise in labeling clickable elements, workers still marked clickable elements as not tappable 10% of the time. The results were quite consistent across two rounds of data collection involving different workers and interface screens. These results further confirmed that tappability is an important usability issue worth investigation.

4.3 Signifier Analysis

To understand how users perceive tappability, we analyzed the potential signifiers affecting tappability in real mobile apps. These findings can help us understand human perception of tappability and help us build machine learning models to predict tappability. We investigated several visual and non-visual features based on previous understandings of common visual signifiers [2, 3, 22] and through exploration of the characteristics of the dataset.

4.3.1 Element Type

Several element types have conventions for visual appearance, thus users would consistently perceive them as tappable [25] (e.g., buttons). We examined how accurately workers label each interface element type from a subset of Android class types in the Rico dataset [6]. Figure 3 shows the distribution of tappable and not tappable elements by type labeled by human workers. Common tappable interface elements like Button and Checkbox did appear more frequently in the set of tappable elements. For each element type, we computed the accuracy by comparing the worker labels to the view hierarchy `clickable` values. For tappable elements, the workers achieved high accuracy for most types. For not tappable elements, the two most common types, TextView and ImageView, had low accuracy percentages of only 67 and 45%, respectively. These interface types allow more flexibility in design than standard element types (e.g., RadioButton). Unconventional styles may make an element more prone to ambiguity in tappability.

4.3.2 Location

We hypothesized that an element's location on the screen may have influenced the accuracy of workers in labeling its tappability. Figure 4 displays a heatmap of the accuracy of the workers' labels by location. We created the heatmap by computing the accuracy per pixel, using the `clickable` attribute, across the 20,174 elements we collected using the bounding box of each element. Warm colors represent higher

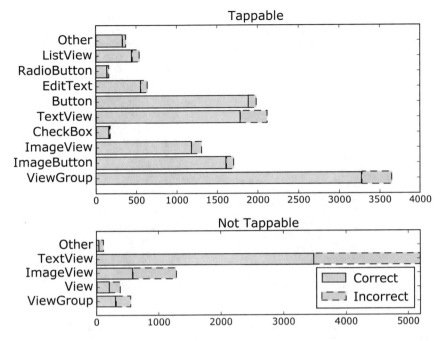

Fig. 3 The number of tappable and not tappable elements in several type categories with the bars colored by the relative amounts of correct and incorrect labels

accuracy values. For tappable elements, workers were more accurate towards the bottom of the screen than the center top area. Placing a not tappable element in these areas might confuse people. For tappable elements, there are two spots at the top region of high accuracy. We speculate that this is because these spots are where apps tend to place their Back and Forward buttons. For not tappable elements, the workers were less accurate towards the screen bottom and highly accurate in the app header bar area with a corresponding area of low accuracy for tappable elements. This area is not tappable in many apps, so people may not realize any element placed there is tappable.

4.3.3 Size

There was only a small difference in average size between labeled tappable and not tappable elements. However, tappable elements labeled as not tappable were 1.9 times larger than tappable elements labeled as tappable indicating that elements with large sizes were more often seen as not tappable. Examining specific element types can reveal possible insights into why the workers may have labeled larger elements as not tappable. TextView elements tend to display labels but can also be tappable elements. From design recommendations, tappable elements should be labeled with

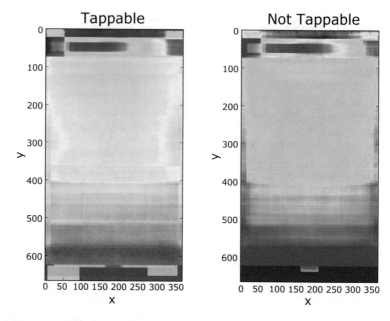

Fig. 4 Heatmaps displaying the accuracy of tappable and not tappable elements by location where warmer colors represent areas of higher accuracy. Workers labeled not tappable elements more accurately towards the upper center of the interface, and tappable elements towards the bottom center of the interface

short, actionable phrases [32]. The text labels of not tappable TextView elements have an average and median size of 1.48 and 1.55 times larger respectively than those of tappable TextView elements. This gives us a hint that TextView elements may be following these recommendations. For ImageView elements, the average and median size for not tappable elements were 2.39 and 3.58 times larger than for tappable elements. People may believe larger ImageView elements, typically displaying images, to be less likely tappable than smaller ImageView elements.

4.3.4 Color

Based on design recommendations [3], color can also be used to signify tappability. Figure 5 displays the top 10 dominant colors in each class of labeled tappable and not tappable elements, which are computed using K-Means clustering. The dominant colors for each class do not necessarily denote the same set. The brighter colors such as blue and red have more presence, i.e., wider bars, in the pixel clusters for tappable elements than those for not tappable ones. In contrast, not tappable elements have more gray and white colors. We computed these clusters across the image pixels for 12 thousand tappable and 7 thousand not tappable elements and scaled them by the

Tappable

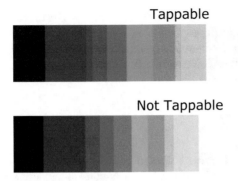

Not Tappable

Fig. 5 The aggregated RGB pixel colors of tappable and not tappable elements clustered into the 10 most prominent colors using K-Means clustering

proportion of elements in each set. These differences indicate that color is likely a useful distinguishing factor.

4.3.5 Words

As not tappable textual elements are often used to convey information, the number of words in these elements tend to be large. The mean number of words per element, based on the log-transformed word count in each element, was 1.84 times greater for not tappable elements (Mean: 2.62, Median: 2) than tappable ones (Mean: 1.42, Median: 1). Additionally, the semantic content of an element's label may be a distinguishing factor based on design recommendations [32]. We hypothesized that tappable elements would contain keywords indicating tappability, e.g., "Login". To test this, we examined the top five keywords of tappable and not tappable elements using TF-IDF analysis, with the set of words in all the tappable and not tappable elements as two individual documents. The top 2 keywords extracted for tappable elements were "submit" and "close", which are common signifiers of actions. However, the remaining keywords for tappable elements, i.e., "brown", "grace" and "beauty", and the top five keywords for not tappable elements, i.e., "wall", "accordance", "recently", "computer", and "trying", do not appear to be actionable signifiers.

5 Tappability Prediction Model

Because it is expensive and time-consuming to conduct user studies, it is desirable to develop automated techniques to examine the tappability of mobile interfaces. Although we can use the signifiers previously discussed as heuristics for this purpose, it would be difficult to manually combine them appropriately. It is also challenging to capture factors that are not obvious or hard to articulate. As such, we employed a deep learning approach to address the problem. Overall, our model is a feedforward neural network with a deep architecture (multiple hidden layers). It takes a concatenation of a range of features about the element and its screen and outputs a probability of how likely a human user would perceive an interface element as tappable.

5.1 Feature Encoding

Our model takes as input several features collected from the view hierarchy metadata and the screenshot pixel data of an interface. For each element under examination, our features include (1) semantics and functionality of the element, (2) the visual appearance of the element and the screen, and (3) the spatial context of the element on the screen.

5.1.1 Semantic Features

The length and the semantics of an element's text content are both potential tappability signifiers. For each element, we scan the text using OCR. To represent the semantics of the text, we use word embedding that is a standard way of mapping word tokens into a continuous dense vector that can be fed into a deep learning model. We encode each word token in an element as a 50-dimensional vector representation that is pre-learned from a Wikipedia corpus [28]. When an element contains multiple words, we treat them as a bag of words and apply max pooling to their embedding vectors to acquire a single 50-dimensional vector as the semantic representation of the element. We also encode the number of word tokens each element contains as a scalar value normalized by an exponential function.

5.1.2 Type Features

There are many standard element types that users have learned over time (e.g., buttons and checkboxes) [25]. However, new element types are frequently introduced (e.g., floating action button). In our model, we include an element type feature as an indicator of the element's semantics. This feature allows the model to potentially account for these learned conventions as a users' background plays an important role in their decision. To encode the Type feature, we include a set of the 22 most common interface element types, e.g., TextView or Button. We represent the Type in the model as a 22-dimensional categorical feature, and collapse it into 6-dimensional embedding vector for training, which provides better performance over sparse input. Each type comes with a built-in or specified clickable attribute that is encoded as either 0 or 1.

5.1.3 Visual Features

As previously discussed, visual design signifiers such as color distribution can help distinguish an element's tappability. It is difficult to articulate the visual perception that might come into play and realize it as executable rules. As a result, we feed an element's raw pixel values and the screen to which the element belongs to the network, through convolutional layers—a popular method for image processing. We resize the pixels of each element and format them as a 3D matrix in the shape of $32 \times 32 \times 3$, where the height and width are 32, and 3 is the number of RGB channels. Contextual factors on the screen may affect the human's perception of tappability. To capture the context, we resize and format the entire screen as another visual feature. This manifests as a 3D matrix in the shape of $300 \times 168 \times 3$ and preserves the original aspect ratio. As we discuss later, a screen contains useful information for predicting an element's tappability even though such information is not easy to articulate.

5.1.4 Spatial Features

As location and size can be signifiers of tappability, we include them as features. We capture the element's bounding box as four scalar values: x, y, *width*, and *height*, and scale each value to the range of 0 and 1 by normalizing them using the screen width and height.

Fig. 6 A deep model for tappability leverages semantic, spatial, and visual features

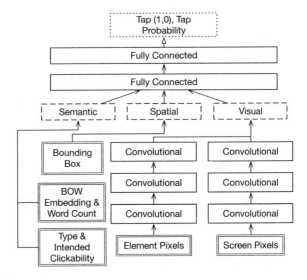

5.2 Model Architecture & Learning

Figure 6 illustrates our model architecture. To process the element and screenshot pixels, our network has three convolutional layers with ReLU [23] activation. Each convolutional layer applies a series of 8 3 × 3 filters to the image to help the model progressively create a feature map. Each convolutional layer is followed by a 2 × 2 max pooling layer to reduce the dimensionality of the image data for processing. Finally, the output of the image layers is concatenated with the rest of the features into a series of two fully connected 100-dimensional dense layers using ReLU [23] as the activation function. The output layer produces a binary classification of an element's tappability using a sigmoid activation function to transform the output into probabilities from zero to one. The probability indicates how likely the user would perceive the element as tappable. We trained the model by minimizing the sigmoid cross-entropy loss between the predicted values and the binary human labels on tappability of each element in the training data. For loss minimization, we used the Ada adaptive gradient descent optimizer with a learning rate of 0.01 and a batch size of 64. To avoid model overfitting, we applied a dropout ratio of 40% to each fully connected layer to regularize the learning. We built our model using Tensorflow [1] in Python and trained it on a Tesla V100 GPU.

5.3 Model Performance Results

We evaluated our model using tenfold cross validation with the crowdsourced dataset. In each fold, we used 90% of the data for training and 10% for validation, and trained our model for 100,000 iterations. Similar to an information retrieval task, we examine how well our model can correctly retrieve elements that users would perceive as tappable. We select an optimal threshold based on Precision-Recall AUC. Our model achieved a mean precision and recall, across the 10 folds of the experiment, of 90.2% (SD: 0.3%) and 87.0% (SD: 1.6%). To understand what these numbers imply, we analyzed how well the clickable attribute in the view hierarchy predicts user tappability perception: precision 89.9% (SD: 0.6%) and recall 79.6% (SD: 0.8%). While our model has a minor improvement on precision, it outperforms the clickable attribute on recall considerably by over 7%.

Although identifying not tappable elements is less important in real scenarios, to better understand the model, we report the performance concerning not tappable elements as the target class. Our model achieved a mean precision of 70% (SD: 2%) and recall of 78% (SD: 3%), which improves precision by 9%, with a similar recall, over the clickable attribute (precision 61%, SD: 1% and recall 78%, SD: 2%). One potential reason that not tappable elements have a relatively low accuracy is that they tend to be more diverse, leading to more variance in the data.

In addition, our original dataset had an uneven number of tappable and not tappable elements (14,301 versus 5,871), likely causing our model to achieve higher

Table 2 Confusion matrix for the balanced dataset, averaged across the 10 cross-validation experiments

	Predicted tappable	Predicted not tappable
Actual tappable	1195	260
Actual not tappable	235	1170

precision and recall for tappable elements than not tappable ones. Therefore, we created a balanced dataset by upsampling the minority class (i.e., not tappable). On the balanced dataset, our model achieved a mean precision and recall of 82 and 84% for identifying tappable elements, and a mean precision and recall of 81 and 86% for not tappable elements. Table 2 shows the confusion matrix for the balanced dataset. Compared to using view hierarchy `clickable` attribute alone, which achieved mean precision of 79% and recall of 80% for predicting tappable elements, and 79 and 78% for not tappable ones, our model is consistently more accurate across all the metrics. These performance improvements show that our model can effectively help developers or designers identify tappability misperceptions in their mobile interfaces.

5.4 Human Consistency & Model Behaviors

We speculate that our model did not achieve even higher accuracy because human perception of tappability can be inherently inconsistent as people have their own experience in using and learning different sets of mobile apps. This can make it challenging for the model to achieve perfect accuracy. To examine our hypothesis, we collected another dataset via crowdsourcing using the same interface as shown in Fig. 2. We selected 334 screens from the Rico dataset, which were not used in our previous rounds of data collection. We recruited 290 workers to perform the same task of marking each selected element as either tappable or not tappable. However, each element was labeled by 5 different workers to enable us to see how much these workers agree on the tappability of an element. In total, there were 2,000 unique interface elements and each was labeled 5 times. In total, 1,163 elements (58%) were entirely consistent among all 5 workers which include both tappable and not tappable elements. We report two metrics to analyze the consistency of the data statistically. The first is in terms of an agreement score [35] that is computed using the following formula:

$$
A = \frac{\sum\limits_{e \in E} \sum\limits_{r \in R} \left(\frac{|R_i|}{|R_e|} \right)^2}{|E|} \times 100\%
\tag{1}
$$

In Eq. 1, e is an element in the set of all interface elements E that were rated by the workers, R_e is the set of ratings for an interface element e, and R_i is the set of ratings

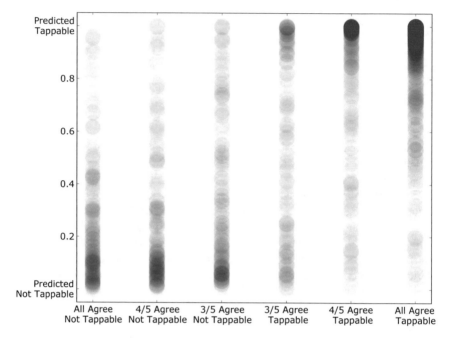

Fig. 7 The scatterplot of the tappability probability output by the model (the Y axis) versus the consistency in the human worker labels (the X axis) for each element in the consistency dataset

in a single category (0: not tappable, 1: tappable). We also report the consistency of the data using Fleiss' Kappa [11], a standard inter-rater reliability measure for the agreement between a fixed number of raters assigning categorical ratings to items. This measure is useful because it computes the degree of agreement over what would be expected by chance. As there are only two categories, the agreement by chance is high. The overall agreement score across all the elements using Eq. 1 is *0.8343*. The number of raters is 5 for each element on a screen, and across 334 screens, resulting in an overall Fleiss' Kappa value of 0.520 *(SD = 0.597, 95% CI [0.575,0.618], P = 0)*. This corresponds to a "Moderate" level agreement according to [18]. What these results demonstrate is that, while there is a significant amount of consistency in the data, there still exists a certain level of disagreement on what elements are tappable versus not tappable. Particularly, consistency varies across element *Type* categories. For example, *View* and *ImageView* elements were labeled far less consistently (*0.52, 0.63*) than commonplace tappable element types such as *Button* (94%), *Toolbar* (100%), and *CheckBox* (95%). View and ImageView elements have more flexibility in design, which may lead to more disagreement.

To understand how our model predicts elements with ambiguous tappability, we test our previously trained model on this new dataset. Our model matches the uncertainty in human perception of tappability surprisingly well (see Fig. 7). When workers are consistent on an element's tappability (two ends on the X axis), our model tends to give a more definite answer—a probability close to 1 for tappable and close to 0 for not tappable. When workers are less consistent on an element (towards the middle of the X axis), our model predicts a probability closer to 0.5.

5.5 Usefulness of Individual Features

One motivation to use deep learning is to alleviate the need for extensive feature engineering. Recall that we feed the entire screenshot of an interface to the model to capture contextual factors affecting the user's decision that cannot be easily articulated. Without the entire screenshot as input, there is a noticeable drop in precision and recall for tappable of 3 and 1%, and for not tappable, an 8% drop in precision but no change in recall. This indicates that there is useful contextual information in the screenshot affecting the users' decisions on tappability. We also examined removing the *Type* feature from the model, and found a slight drop in precision about 1% but no change in recall for identifying tappable elements. The performance change is similar for the not tappable case with 1.8% drop in precision and no drop in recall. We speculate that removing the Type feature only caused a minor impact because our model has already captured some of element type information through its pixels.

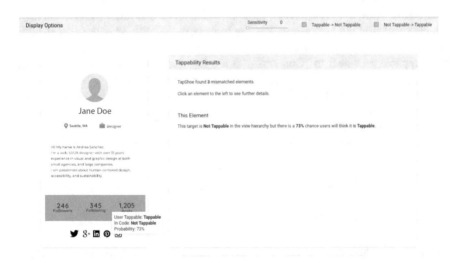

Fig. 8 The TapShoe interface. An app designer drag and drops a UI screen on the left. TapShoe highlights interface elements whose predicted tappability is different from its actual tappable state as specified in its view hierarchy

6   TapShoe Interface

We created a web interface for our tappability model called TapShoe (see Fig. 8). The interface is a proof of concept tool to help app designers and developers examine their UI's tappability. We describe the TapShoe interface from the perspective of an app designer, Zoey, who is designing an app for deal shopping, shown in the right hand side of Fig. 8. Zoey has redesigned some icons to be more colorful on the home page links for "Coupons", "Store Locator", and "Shopping". Zoey wants to understand how the changes she has made would affect the users' perception of which elements in her app are tappable. First, Zoey uploads a screenshot image along its view hierarchy for her app by dragging and dropping them into the left hand side of the TapShoe interface. Once Zoey drops her screenshot and view hierarchy, TapShoe analyzes her interface elements, and returns a tappable or not tappable prediction for each element. The TapShoe interface highlights the interface elements with a tappable state, as specified by Zoey in the view hierarchy, that does not match up with user perception as predicted by the model.

   Zoey sees that the TapShoe interface highlighted the three colorful icons she redesigned. These icons were not tappable in her app but TapShoe predicted that the users would perceive them as tappable. She examines the probability scores for each element by clicking on the green hotspots on the screenshot to see informational tooltips. She adjusts the sensitivity slider to change the threshold for the model's prediction. Now, she sees that the "Coupons" and "Store Locator" icon are not high-lighted and that the arrow icon has the highest probability of being perceived as tappable. She decides to make all three colorful icon elements interactive and extend the tappable area next to "Coupons", "Store Locator", and "Website". These fixes prevent her users from the frustration of tapping on these elements with no response.

   We implemented the TapShoe interface as a web application (JavaScript) with a Python web server. The web client accepts an image and a JSON view hierarchy to locate interface elements. The web server queries a trained model, hosted via a Docker container with the Tensorflow model serving API, to retrieve the predictions for each element.

7   Informal Feedback from Designers

To understand how the TapShoe interface and tappability model would be useful in a real design context, we conducted informal design walkthroughs with 7 professional interface designers at a large technology company. The designers worked on design teams for three different products. We demonstrated TapShoe to them and collected informal feedback on the idea of getting predictions from the tappability model, and on the TapShoe interface for helping app designers identify tappability mismatches. We also asked them to envision new ways they could use the tappability prediction model beyond the functionality of the TapShoe interface. The designers responded positively to the use of the tappability model and TapShoe interface, and gave several directions to improve the tool. Particularly, the following themes have emerged.

7.1 Visualizing Probabilities

The designers saw high potential in being able to get a tappability probability score for their interface elements. Currently, the TapShoe interface displays only probabilities for elements with a mismatch based on the threshold set by the sensitivity slider. However, several of the designers mentioned that they would want to see the scores for all the elements. This could give them a quick glance at the tappability of their designs as a whole. Presenting this information in a heatmap that adjusts the colors based on the tappability scores could help them compare the relative level of tappability of each element. This would allow them to deeply examine and compare interface elements for which tappability signifiers are having an impact. The designers also mentioned that sometimes, they do not necessarily aim for tappability to be completely binary. Tappability could be aimed to be higher or lower along a continuous scale depending on an element's importance. In an interface with a primary action and a secondary action, they would be more concerned that people perceive the primary action as tappable than the secondary action.

7.2 Exploring Variations

The designers also pointed out the potential of the tappability model for helping them systematically explore variations. TapShoe's interface only allows a designer to upload a single screen. However, the designers envisioned an interface to allow them to upload and compare multiple versions of their designs to systematically change signifiers and observe how they impact the model's prediction. This could help them discover new design principles to make interface elements look more or less tappable. It could also help them compare more granular changes at an element level, such as different versions of a button design. As context within a design can also affect an element's tappability, they would want to move elements around and change contextual design attributes to have a more thorough understanding of how context affects tappability. Currently, the only way for them to have this information is to conduct a large tappability study, which limits them to trying out only a few design changes at a time. Having the tappability model output could greatly expand their current capabilities for exploring design changes that may affect tappability.

7.3   Model Extension and Accuracy

Several designers wondered whether the model could extend to other platforms. For example, their design for desktop or web interfaces could benefit from this type of model as well. Additionally, they have collected data that our model could already use for training. We believe our model could help them in this case as it would be simple to extend to other platforms or to use existing tappability data for training.

We also asked the designers how they felt about the accuracy of our model. The designers believed the model could be useful in its current state even for helping them understand the relative tappability of different elements. Providing a confidence interval for the prediction could aid in giving them more trust in the prediction.

8   Discussion

Our model achieves good accuracy at predicting tappable and not tappable interface elements and the TapShoe tool and model are well received by designers. Here we discuss the limitations and directions for future work.

One limitation is that our TapShoe interface, as a proof of concept, demonstrates one of many potential uses for the tappability model. We intend to build a more complete design analytics tool based on designers' suggestions, and conduct further studies of the tool by following its use in a real design project. Particularly, we will update the TapShoe interface to take early stage mockups other than UI screens that are equipped with a view hierarchy. This is possible because designer can mark up elements to be examined in a mockup without having to implement it.

Our tappability model is also only trained on Android interfaces, and therefore, the results may not generalize well to other platforms. However, our model relies on general features available in many UI platforms (e.g., element bounding boxes and types). It would be entirely feasible to collect a similar dataset for different platforms to train our model and the cost for crowdsourcing labeling is relatively small. In fact, we can apply a similar approach to new UI styles that involve drastically different design concepts, e.g., emerging UI styles in AR/VR. This is one of the benefits to use a data-driven, deep learning approach, as shown in this work, which can be easily scalable across new interaction styles or UI platforms without extensive feature engineering and model redesign.

9   Future Work

From our consistency evaluation, we learned that people's perception of tappability is not always consistent (see Fig. 7). Future work can explore improving the model's performance with inconsistent data. These methods could extend our tappability annotation task beyond a simple binary rating of tappable versus not tappable to a rating incorporating uncertainty, e.g., adding a "Not sure" option or a confidence scale in labels.

The tappability model that we developed is a first step towards modeling tappability. There also may be other features that could add predictive power to the model. As we begin to understand more of the features that people use to determine which elements are tappable and not tappable, we can incorporate these new features into a deep learning model as long as they are manifested in the data. For example, we used the Type feature as a way to account for learned conventions, i.e., the behavior that users have learned over time. As users are not making a tappable decision solely based on the visual properties of the current screen, we intend to investigate more high-level features that can capture user background, which has a profound effect on user perception.

Additionally, identifying the reasons behind tappable or not tappable perception could potentially enable us to offer designers recommendations for improving the users' tappability perception. This also requires us to communicate these reasons with the designer in a human-understandable fashion. There are two approaches to pursue this. One is to analyze how the model relies on each feature, although understanding the behavior of a deep learning model is challenging and it is an active area in the deep learning field. The other approach is to train the model to recognize the human reasoning behind their selection. Progress in this direction will allow a tool to provide designers a more complete and useful tappability report.

Finally, we believe there are potentially many other aspects of usability that can be assessed in the way that our work assess tappability. Some work has already explored predicting some new usability aspects like visual search time [38] and user engagement with animations [36]. However, such works have been limited to predicting usability issues for a single screen. Some aspects of usability (e.g., difficulty or predictability of a task, user task completion) that span across multiple screens have not yet been modeled. Automating such analyses will require creating methods to collect and label relevant data at a large scale and operationalize them in models for prediction. Deep learning is again well equipped to do so as techniques for sequence modeling has been substantially advanced [15, 33]. We already see models such as LSTM [15] been successfully applied in interaction sequence modeling for interaction tasks such as menu selection [20].

10   Conclusion

In this chapter, we described an approach to model interface tappability at scale. We discussed how we collected a large dataset of tappability examples via crowdsourcing and conducted data science for a variety of tappability signifiers based on the dataset. We then discussed the design and training of a deep model that achieved high accuracy in predicting human perception on tappability. We offer further insights by analyzing the model behavior in relation to uncertainty in human tappability perception. As a proof of concept, we introduced TapShoe, a tool that uses the deep model to examine interface tappability, which received positive feedback from 7 professional interaction designers who saw its potential as a useful tool for their real design projects. This work serves as an example of how we can apply state-of-the-art deep learning methods such as Convolutional Neural Nets to assess a crucial aspect of interface usability—tappability, and showcase bolts and nuts for conducting research at the intersection of interaction design and deep learning. We hope that this work can serve as an inspiration to researchers to further investigate methods for data collection and automated assessment of usability using deep learning methods, so that designers can leverage AI to more quickly and thoroughly evaluate their interfaces.

References

1. Abadi M, Barham P, Chen J, Chen Z, Davis A, Dean J, Devin M, Ghemawat S, Irving G, Isard M et al (2016) Tensorflow: a system for large-scale machine learning. In: OSDI, vol 16, pp 265–283
2. Affordances and Design (2015). https://www.interaction-design.org/literature/article/affordances-and-design
3. Beyond Blue Links: Making Clickable Elements Recognizable (2015). https://www.nngroup.com/articles/clickable-elements/
4. Borji A (2019) Saliency prediction in the deep learning era: successes and limitations. IEEE transactions on pattern analysis and machine intelligence
5. Bylinskii Z, Kim NW, O'Donovan P, Alsheikh S, Madan S, Pfister H, Durand F, Russell B, Hertzmann A (2017) Learning visual importance for graphic designs and data visualizations. In: Proceedings of the 30th annual ACM symposium on user interface software and technology, UIST'17. ACM, New York, NY, USA, pp 57–69. https://doi.org/10.1145/3126594.3126653
6. Deka B, Huang Z, Franzen C, Hibschman J, Afergan D, Li Y, Nichols J, Kumar R (2017) Rico: a mobile app dataset for building data-driven design applications. In: Proceedings of the 30th annual ACM symposium on user interface software and technology, UIST'17. ACM, New York, NY, USA, pp 845–854. https://doi.org/10.1145/3126594.3126651
7. Deka B, Huang Z, Franzen C, Nichols J, Li Y, Kumar R (2017) Zipt: zero-integration performance testing of mobile app designs. In: Proceedings of the 30th annual ACM symposium on user interface software and technology. ACM, pp 727–736. https://doi.org/10.1145/3126594.3126647
8. Deka B, Huang Z, Kumar R (2016) Erica: interaction mining mobile apps. In: Proceedings of the 29th annual symposium on user interface software and technology, UIST'16. ACM, New York, NY, USA, pp. 767–776. https://doi.org/10.1145/2984511.2984581
9. Duan P, Wierzynski C, Nachman L (2020) Optimizing user interface layouts via gradient descent. In: Proceedings of the 2020 CHI conference on human factors in computing systems, CHI'20. Association for Computing Machinery, New York, NY, USA, pp 1–12. https://doi.org/10.1145/3313831.3376589
10. Flat UI Elements Attract Less Attention and Cause Uncertainty (2017). https://www.nngroup.com/articles/flat-ui-less-attention-cause-uncertainty/
11. Fleiss JL (1971) Measuring nominal scale agreement among many raters. Psychol Bull **76**(5):378
12. Gaver WW (1991) Technology affordances. In: Proceedings of the SIGCHI conference on human factors in computing systems, CHI'91. ACM, New York, NY, USA, pp 79–84. https://doi.org/10.1145/108844.108856

13. Gibson JJ (1978) The ecological approach to the visual perception of pictures. Leonardo 11(3):227–235
14. Greenberg MD, Easterday MW, Gerber EM (2015) Critiki: a scaffolded approach to gathering design feedback from paid crowd workers. In: Proceedings of the 2015 ACM SIGCHI conference on creativity and cognition', C&C '15. ACM, New York, NY, USA, pp 235–244. https://doi.org/10.1145/2757226.2757249
15. Hochreiter S, Schmidhuber J (1997) Long short-term memory. Neural Comput 9(8):1735–1780
16. Kittur A, Chi EH, Suh B (2008) Crowdsourcing user studies with mechanical turk. In: Proceedings of the SIGCHI conference on human factors in computing systems, CHI'08. ACM, New York, NY, USA, pp 453–456. https://doi.org/10.1145/1357054.1357127
17. Komarov S, Reinecke K, Gajos KZ (2013) Crowdsourcing performance evaluations of user interfaces. In: Proceedings of the SIGCHI conference on human factors in computing systems, CHI'13. ACM, New York, NY, USA, pp 207–216. https://doi.org/10.1145/2470654.2470684
18. Landis JR, Koch GG (1977) An application of hierarchical kappa-type statistics in the assessment of majority agreement among multiple observers. Biometrics 363–374
19. LeCun Y, Bengio Y, Hinton G (2015) Deep learning. Nature 521(7553):436
20. Li Y, Bengio S, Bailly G (2018) Predicting human performance in vertical menu selection using deep learning. In: Proceedings of the 2018 CHI conference on human factors in computing systems, pp 1–7
21. Luther K, Tolentino J-L, Wu W, Pavel A, Bailey BP, Agrawala M, Hartmann B, Dow SP (2015) Structuring, aggregating, and evaluating crowdsourced design critique. In: Proceedings of the 18th ACM conference on computer supported cooperative work & social computing, CSCW'15. ACM, New York, NY, USA, pp 473–485. https://doi.org/10.1145/2675133.2675283
22. Material Design Guidelines (2018). https://material.io/design/
23. Nair V, Hinton GE (2010) Rectified linear units improve restricted boltzmann machines. In: Proceedings of the 27th international conference on machine learning (ICML), pp 807–814
24. Nebeling M, Speicher M, Norrie MC (2013) Crowdstudy: general toolkit for crowdsourced evaluation of web interfaces. In: Proceedings of the SIGCHI symposium on engineering interactive computing systems. ACM, pp 255–264. https://doi.org/10.1145/2494603.2480303
25. Norman D (2013) The design of everyday things: revised and expanded edition, Constellation
26. Norman DA (1999) Affordance, conventions, and design, Interactions 6(3):38–43. https://doi.org/10.1145/301153.301168
27. Norman DA (2008) The way i see it: signifiers, not affordances. Interactions 15(6):18–19. https://doi.org/10.1145/1409040.1409044
28. Pennington J, Socher R, Manning C (2014) Glove: global vectors for word representation. In: Proceedings of the 2014 conference on empirical methods in natural language processing, EMLNP'14, pp 1532–1543
29. Pfeuffer K, Li Y (2018) Analysis and modeling of grid performance on touchscreen mobile devices. In: Proceedings of the SIGCHI conference on human factors in computing systems, CHI'18. ACM, New York, NY, USA, pp 288:1–288:12. https://doi.org/10.1145/3173574.3173862
30. Schneider H, Frison K, Wagner J, Butz A (2016) Crowdux: a case for using widespread and lightweight tools in the quest for ux. In: Proceedings of the 2016 ACM conference on designing interactive systems, DIS'16. ACM, New York, NY, USA, pp 415–426. https://doi.org/10.1145/2901790.2901814
31. Swearngin A, Li Y (2019) Modeling mobile interface tappability using crowdsourcing and deep learning. In: Proceedings of the 2019 CHI conference on human factors in computing systems, CHI '19. Association for Computing Machinery, New York, NY, USA, pp 1–11. https://doi.org/10.1145/3290605.3300305
32. Tidwell J (2010) Designing interfaces: patterns for effective interaction design. O'Reilly Media, Inc
33. Vaswani A, Shazeer N, Parmar N, Uszkoreit J, Jones L, Gomez AN, Kaiser L, Polosukhin I (2017) Attention is all you need. In: Guyon I, Luxburg UV, Bengio S, Wallach

H, Fergus R, Vishwanathan S, Garnett R (eds) Advances in neural information processing systems, vol 30. Curran Associates, Inc. https://proceedings.neurips.cc/paper/2017/file/3f5ee243547dee91fbd053c1c4a845aa-Paper.pdf

34. Visual Affordance Testing (2018). http://practicaluxmethods.com/product/visual-affordance-testing/
35. Wobbrock JO, Aung HH, Rothrock B, Myers BA (2005) Maximizing the guessability of symbolic input. In: Proceedings of the SIGCHI conference on human factors in computing systems extended abstracts. ACM, pp 1869–1872. https://doi.org/10.1145/1056808.1057043
36. Wu Z, Jiang Y, Liu Y, Ma X (2020) Predicting and diagnosing user engagement with mobile ui animation via a data-driven approach. In: Proceedings of the 2020 CHI conference on human factors in computing systems', CHI'20. Association for computing machinery, New York, NY, USA, pp 1–13. https://doi.org/10.1145/3313831.3376324
37. Xu A, Huang S-W, Bailey B (2014) Voyant: generating structured feedback on visual designs using a crowd of non-experts. In: Proceedings of the 17th ACM conference on computer supported cooperative work & social computing. ACM, pp 1433–1444. https://doi.org/10.1145/2531602.2531604
38. Yuan A, Li Y (2020) Modeling human visual search performance on realistic webpages using analytical and deep learning methods. In: Proceedings of the 2020 CHI conference on human factors in computing systems, CHI'20. Association for Computing Machinery, New York, NY, USA, pp 1–12. https://doi.org/10.1145/3313831.3376870
39. Zheng Q, Jiao J, Cao Y, Lau RW (2018) Task-driven webpage saliency. In: Proceedings of the European conference on computer vision (ECCV)
40. Zhou J, Tang Z, Zhao M, Ge X, Zhuang F, Zhou M, Zou L, Yang C, Xiong H (2020) Intelligent exploration for user interface modules of mobile app with collective learning. In: Proceedings of the 26th ACM SIGKDD international conference on knowledge discovery & data mining, KDD'20. Association for Computing Machinery, New York, NY, USA, pp 3346–3355. https://doi.org/10.1145/3394486.3403387

Part II
Input

Eye Gaze Estimation and Its Applications

Xucong Zhang, Seonwook Park, and Anna Maria Feit

Abstract The human eye gaze is an important non-verbal cue that can unobtrusively provide information about the intention and attention of a user to enable intelligent interactive systems. Eye gaze can also be taken as input to systems as a replacement of the conventional mouse and keyboard, and can also be indicative of the cognitive state of the user. However, estimating and applying gaze in real-world applications poses significant challenges. In this chapter, we first review the development of gaze estimation methods in recent years. We especially focus on learning-based gaze estimation methods which benefit from large-scale data and deep learning methods that recently became available. Second, we discuss the challenges of using gaze estimation for real-world applications and our efforts toward making these methods easily usable for the Human-Computer Interaction community. At last, we provide two application examples, demonstrating the use of eye gaze to enable attentive and adaptive interfaces.

1 Introduction

The human eye has the potential to serve as a fast, pervasive, and unobtrusive way to interact with the computer. Reliably detecting where a user is gazing at allows the eyes to be used as an explicit input method. Such a new way of interaction has been shown to outperform traditional input devices such as the mouse due to the ballistic movement of eye gaze [42, 52]. Moreover, it allows interaction under

X. Zhang (✉) · S. Park
ETH Zürich, Department of Computer Science, Stampfenbachstrasse 48, 8092 Zürich, Switzerland
e-mail: Xucong.Zhang@inf.ethz.ch

S. Park
e-mail: Seonwook.Park@inf.ethz.ch

A. Maria Feit
Saarland University, Saarland Informatics Campus, Saarbrücken, Germany
e-mail: feit@cs.uni-saarland.de

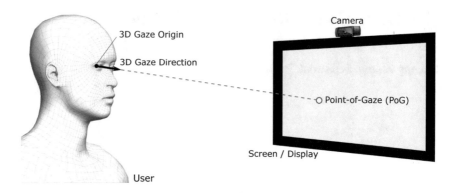

Fig. 1 The standard setting for remote camera-based gaze estimation. A camera captures images of the user's face region. The problem of gaze tracking is to infer the 3D gaze direction in the camera coordinate system or the 2D point-of-gaze (PoG) on the screen from the image recorded by the camera

circumstances where no external input device is available or operable by the user [27]. Beyond explicit input, the movement patterns of a user's eyes reveal information about the cognitive processes, level of attention, and interests or abilities [6]. This offers exciting opportunities to develop novel intelligent and interactive systems that truly understand the user.

In this chapter, we focus on remote camera-based gaze estimation and its applications. This is typically done in a setting such as that depicted in Fig. 1 where a camera is positioned at a certain distance from and facing the user's eyes. The problem these methods aim to solve is to infer the 3D gaze direction or the 2D on-screen point-of-gaze (PoG) from images recorded by the camera. The 3D gaze origin is often defined to be at the center of the eye or face. Note that these gaze estimation approaches can also be adapted to head-mounted devices such as those used in AR and VR settings, though we do not discuss them in this chapter [23].

Estimating the gaze position of a user is a challenging task. Subtle movements of the eyeball can change the gaze direction dramatically and the difficulty of the task varies greatly across people. Reliably determining where a user is looking on a screen or inside a room has been an active research topic for several decades. Classic gaze estimation methods often use high-resolution machine vision cameras and corneal reflections from infra-red illuminators to determine the gaze direction [16]. These methods can provide reasonable gaze estimation accuracy of around one degree after personal calibration in well-controlled environments. However, dedicated hardware is essential for their performance, which limits their use in real-world applications.

The rise of AI methods, such as deep learning approaches, has advanced the use of *learning-based gaze estimation methods*. In contrast to classic methods, learning-based methods are based on purposefully designed machine learning models, for example, neural networks, for the gaze estimation task. These learning-based methods either estimate the gaze position directly from an image of the user's eye or face [24, 56, 61], or derive intermediate eye features for gaze direction regression [33, 47]. This group of methods often assume an unmodified environment. That is, no additional infra-red illumination is available to provide reflections on the surface of the cornea. Hence, learning-based gaze estimation methods can work with a single off-the-shelf webcam [33, 34, 36, 55, 56]. This makes these approaches more widely and more easily applicable for human-computer interaction (HCI) in everyday settings [54, 57].

Still, many challenges persist in making gaze tracking practicable for computer interaction. For example, personal calibration plays a major role in gaze estimation and also has an impact on user experience. The calibration procedure often requires users to focus on designated points for a period of time. This can be cumbersome or in some cases even impossible and disturbs the user experience. Nevertheless, personal calibration is crucial for many gaze estimation methods to perform accurately. Thus, recently researchers have built on AI-based techniques for gaze redirection to generate additional eye images for personalization and thus reduce the number of calibration samples [51]. Other researchers have worked on providing easy-to-use software toolkits for making learning-based gaze estimation methods accessible to HCI researchers and developers [59].

Designing useful and usable gaze-aware interfaces is another major challenge. In practice, tracking accuracy and precision vary largely depending on factors such as the tracking environment, user characteristics, and others [7]. In comparison to mouse or touch input, eye tracking might yield a highly noisy signal with poor accuracy. Still, information about eye gaze, even from noisy data, can enable novel and useful interactions. However, design guidelines developed for traditional interfaces cannot be applied here. Instead, we need new design approaches making efficient use of the noisy gaze signal.

In this chapter, we first provide some background on the problem of gaze tracking. We then offer an overview of recent approaches toward improving performance on the gaze estimation task with the power of AI. We then discuss the practical challenges when applying gaze estimation methods for computer interaction and designing gaze-aware interfaces, offering concrete design guidelines and actionable insights for the HCI community. Finally, we describe two application examples: (1) gaze-aware interaction with real-life objects and (2) automatic interface adaptation by assessing information relevance from users' eye movements. These examples showcase the exciting opportunities gaze tracking offers for Human-Computer Interaction.

2   Background

In the following, we start with a brief introduction to the human eye, its movements, and the relation to human attention. We then discuss different categories of gaze estimation methods and introduce learning-based methods. Lastly, we briefly discuss the need for the personal calibration of gaze estimators and how this has been done in existing works.

2.1 The Human Eye Gaze

The human visual field is about 114° [20] large of which we can only see sharply in an area of 1° [2] during so-called *fixations*, when the gaze is focused on a fixed position in the environment. To perceive information from a larger area, the eyes perform *saccades*, fast ballistic movements that allow us to move between fixation points to integrate information from other areas. See, for example, [40] for further introduction into the working principles of the human eye gaze. The duration and frequency of such fixations and saccades can provide information about a user's attention. It can be used by interactive systems in combination with their awareness of the visual stimulus or interface to enable explicit gaze input or make further inferences about a user's cognitive state.

However, a person does not always consciously control their eye gaze. Often, it is stimulus-driven and attracted by visual features, or "idles" in uninteresting regions. Thus, there is a difference between the eyes focusing on a point and a person's covert attention (i.e. their *mental* focus). Even when focusing on a certain point, people can shift their conscious attention within the larger field of view similar to a spotlight and to some extent independent of the gaze position. This allows them to not just passively perceive information but visually process and encode it for further cognitive processing [39]. A major challenge for using gaze for HCI is to isolate and analyze the underlying cognitive processes from such noisy gaze behavior where overt and covert attention are mixed. In the later part of this chapter, we describe some applications that aim to make sense of noisy gaze behavior [7, 54].

2.2 Gaze Estimation Methods

The gaze estimation methods considered here try to infer information about where a person is looking from an image of the users' eyes or face image. They can be categorized into three groups: model-based, feature-based, and appearance-based methods [16]. In both model- and feature-based methods, key landmarks are often required to be detected, such as the pupil center, eye corner, and iris contour. Generally speaking, model-based methods fit a pre-defined 3D eyeball model to the detected eye landmarks and take the direction from eyeball center to the pupil center as the gaze direction [48, 49]. The eyeball model can optionally incorporate an offset parameter which can be determined with personal calibration data [46]. Feature-based methods take eye-region landmarks as features for the direct regression of gaze direction [41]. Since the input feature dimension is limited by the number of determined key points, these methods often cannot handle complex changes such as large head movements. Both model-based and feature-based methods conventionally demand accurate eye landmark detection, often necessitating complex or expensive hardware setups. For example, multiple high-resolution infrared-light cameras along with optimal infrared-light sources are the standard hardware configuration for most of these methods. Appearance-based methods directly learn the mapping from the eye or face image to the gaze direction [44]. Since there is no need for explicit eye landmark detection (and corresponding training data annotation in the real world), appearance-based methods can work with a single webcam without any additional light source. However, these methods can be sensitive to illumination condition changes or unfamiliar facial appearances due to the scarcity of training data.

2.3   Learning-Based Gaze Estimation Methods

Recent developments in deep learning have given rise to a large array of promising learning-based gaze estimation methods. We refer to these methods as being *learning-based*, in order to encompass hybrid methods [34, 50] as well as appearance-based methods that benefit from large amounts of training data and highly complex neural network architectures [24, 53]. In particular, appearance-based gaze estimation methods work with just a single webcam under challenging lighting conditions even over long operating distances of up to 2 m [10, 59]. This is because deep convolutional neural networks—when given large and varied amounts of training data—are effective at defining useful image-based features, and thus often outperform hand-defined features. Importantly, this allows for the new task of person-independent gaze estimation. That is, a generic learning-based gaze estimation model can be directly applied to a previously unseen user and achieve 4°–6° of mean angular error even in very challenging conditions.

Integrating known priors such as the 3D structure of the eyeball or eyelids into neural networks is a promising direction of research. A hierarchical generative model has been proposed for improving gaze estimation by understanding how to control and generate eye shape [47]. A so-called *gazemaps* representation has been used to implicitly encode a 3D eyeball model and then taken as an intermediate output for gaze direction regression [33]. Applying deep learning-based landmark localization architectures for eye-region landmark detection has also been shown to be more effective than traditional edge- or contour-based methods [11, 34].

2.4   Person-Specific Gaze Estimator Calibration

While learning-based methods perform well in the person-independent setting, the error of 4°–6° may be unsuitable for applications that require higher accuracy. When sufficient data is provided from the target user, such methods were shown to perform at an average gaze estimation error of 2.5° in-the-wild [56]. Reducing this performance gap increases the efficacy and applicability of learning-based methods greatly. In this section, we describe why this performance gap exists and discuss how recent learning-based methods reduce it.

A primary reason for this performance gap is the so-called "angle kappa" as the angular difference between the line-of-sight of a user (actual axis along which an eye "sees") and the optical axis of their eyeball (defined by the geometry of the head and eye). For a more principled definition of angle kappa, please refer to [29]. This difference varies greatly across people with typical differences being two–three degrees [29]. Importantly, the line-of-sight cannot be measured by a camera alone as it is defined by the position of the fovea, which cannot be observed. The optical axis, on the other hand, can be reasonably estimated from the appearance of the eye region.

The classic literature tackles this issue by explicitly defining the kappa angle as a parameter to an optimization problem. In all gaze estimator calibration methods, a user is asked to gaze at specified points on a screen or in space. An optimization-based scheme is then often applied to determine the user-specific parameters of the model. An important consideration in these schemes is in requiring minimal "calibration samples" from the end-user such as to make the experience less cumbersome and also to enable spontaneously interactive applications in everyday scenarios. Conventional approaches are quite effective in clean and controlled laboratory settings where the position and shape of the iris and eyeball can be reasonably measured. In-the-wild settings and unconstrained head movements of the user, however, pose significant challenges that learning-based methods can easily address. However, learned models can be tricky to adapt as user-specific parameters are usually not explicitly defined.

Several feasible calibration strategies have been suggested recently for learning-based gaze estimation, either via optimization of user-specific parameters defined at specific parts of the network or via eye-region image synthesis for personalized training data generation. The more direct and effective approaches define parameters which can be adapted based on a few labeled samples from the target user. Approaches have been proposed to apply these parameters at the input [17, 25] and output [4] of the neural network. As the primary factor in the difference between users is the angle kappa, such low-dimensional definitions of user parameters are surprisingly effective. Yet other approaches have been proposed for learning a light-weight regression model from penultimate layer activations [24, 34], or gradient-based meta-learning as a method for effective few-shot neural network adaptation [35]. A unique approach suggests correcting an initially estimated gaze direction based on changes in the appearance of the presented visual stimuli [36]. Importantly, this approach does not require any explicit calibration but instead relies on the model having been trained on paired eye gaze and visual stimulus data.

An alternative area of research is in "gaze redirection", where the objective is in accurate and high-quality eye image generation with control of gaze direction. While earlier learning-based methods in this area focused only on the image synthesis aspect [13], later works have shown that generating person-specific eye images with varying gaze directions can allow for an alternative method of personal calibration. That is, given a few samples from the target user, gaze redirection methods can be used to create a training dataset tailored to the target user [51]. Though not directly related to personal calibration, later works [18, 62] have further improved the accuracy and quality of generated images and have shown that limited gaze datasets can be augmented via such synthesis schemes.

3   Learning-Based Gaze Estimation Methods

We refer to "learning-based gaze estimation methods" as the set of methods that take advantage of modern machine learning techniques for the gaze estimation task. Nowadays, these are mostly enabled by deep learning techniques together with a large amount of training data. The input to these methods are monocular images of the eye or face region, and the models either directly estimate eye gaze, extract intermediate features for the gaze task, or otherwise work toward the improvement of gaze estimation performance via approaches such as data synthesis. Such strategies have been advancing rapidly with the recent development of convolutional neural networks. Alongside, several datasets have been introduced covering an increasingly wider variety of human appearances and temporal information to improve generalization and provide novel challenges to existing data-driven models.

3.1   Gaze Estimation Method Pipeline

The gaze estimation method we proposed in [53] was the first work to use a convolutional neural network architecture for gaze estimation. Our later works extended the architecture to much deeper networks such as VGG-16 and ResNet-50 [56, 60]. These works introduce a basic pipeline for image-based gaze estimation. That is, given an input image taken from a single webcam, we learn a direct mapping to the gaze direction (see Fig. 2). The first step in this pipeline is face detection and facial landmark localization. Then, we fit a pre-defined 3D face model to the detected facial landmarks to estimate the rotation and translation of the head. With this head pose information, we perform a procedure known as "data normalization" to cancel the rotation around the roll-axis and crop the eye or face image to a consistently defined size [43]. This data normalization procedure was later optimized further to increase its effectiveness toward improving gaze estimation performance [58]. Finally, the cropped image, together with the head pose, is fed into the convolution neural networks to regress to the final gaze direction in the camera coordinate system. The gaze direction can be presented as a three-dimension vector in the Cartesian coordinate system. We choose to convert it to a two-dimensional vector in the spherical coordinate system representing the polar angle and azimuthal angle. In this way, we reduce one degree of freedom from the gaze direction vector and center the output values around zero, for better ease of regression.

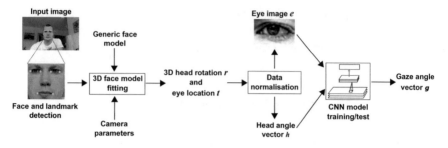

Fig. 2 The gaze estimation pipeline proposed in [56] describes a pre-processing procedure for extracting eye patches which are then input to a convolutional neural network that directly predicts the gaze direction of the imaged eye

3.2   3D and 2D Gaze Estimation

The final output of the pipeline shown in Fig. 2 is a 3D gaze direction value. Alternatively, a different group of methods directly output the 2D gaze location on a screen that the user is assumed to be gazing at. See [55] for an example of experiments directly comparing between 2D and 3D gaze estimation. Apart from a change in the dimensionality of the output value, 3D and 2D gaze estimation differ in practice in terms of how the head position is integrated into the estimation pipeline. 3D gaze estimation methods typically insert the 3D head orientation value (often referred to as head pose) directly into the network as input to one of the last fully connected layers. The task of 2D screen-space point-of-regard regression (2D gaze estimation), however, theoretically requires more complex information such as the definition of the pose, scale, and bounds of the screen plane as well as a reliable estimation of the translation of the head in relation to the screen. This can be approximated by providing a binary "face grid" where the number of black pixels (as opposed to white pixels) indicates the size and position of the user's face [24]. While this alternative 2D problem formulation tackles the gaze estimation task more directly, its main drawback is that the trained model is specific to the device used in the training data. Hence, 2D models are not robust to changes such as the camera hardware, screen size and pose, and other factors pertaining to the camera-screen relationship. 3D gaze direction estimation is thus a more generic approach that can consolidate data samples from different devices both at training time and test time.

3.3   Input for Gaze Estimation Methods

Early works in gaze estimation only take a single eye image as input since it is often deemed to be sufficient in inferring gaze direction [43, 53]. However, learning-based methods can be surprisingly effective in extracting information from seemingly redundant image regions and thus regions beyond the single eye could be helpful for training neural networks. Taking a face image along with both eye images [24] or simply the two eye patches [5, 10] as input for gaze estimation can achieve better performance than a model taking single eye input. We were the first to use a single full-face image as input for the gaze estimation task [55] showing that this achieved the best results compared to other kinds of input regions. Furthermore, to fully use the information of the full-face, we proposed a soft attention mechanism [55] and a hard attention mechanism [61] to efficiently learn information from the full-face patch. In [55], we allow the neural network to self-predict varying weights for different regions of the input face in order to make model training efficient. However, in contrast to object classification tasks where the scale of activation values of each feature map is correlated to the importance of a template or object class, gaze estimation as a regression task can benefit from an attention mechanism that goes beyond activation value modulation. Our later work proposes a hard attention mechanism to force the model to focus on the sub-regions of the face [61]. Taking a full-face patch as input, our method first crops sub-regions with multiple region selection networks. These sub-regions are then passed as input to the gaze regression network which predicts gaze direction. Since each sub-region is resized to be the same as the original input face image, the receptive field is enlarged, thus, the gaze regression model can extract large and informative feature maps from the sub-regions. This method successfully picks the most appropriate eye region for gaze estimation depending on different input image conditions such as occlusion and lighting conditions. However, the model itself can be difficult to train and take much time to converge. How to efficiently learn the information from the full-face patch is still an ongoing research topic.

3.4 Representation Learning for Gaze Estimation

In addition to studying various methods of input region selection for gaze estimation, we also suggest various approaches to learning unique gaze-specific representations in neural networks. Such representations can be explicitly defined or implicitly learned. The first representation as proposed in [34] is explicitly defined as being eye-region landmark coordinates. The fully convolutional network proposed in this work is able to detect eye-region landmarks from images captured with a single webcam, even under challenging lighting conditions. Compared to the classic edge-based eye landmark detection method [16, 48], the convolutional network provides more robust landmark prediction. These detected landmarks are then used for model-based or feature-based gaze estimation. However, since it still requires eye landmark detection, this method can only work in settings with a close distance between the user and camera such as the laptop and desktop setting [59] and relies on high-quality synthetic training data. We further improve our method by first predicting a novel pictorial representation that we call a "gazemap", then use it as input for a light-weight gaze regression network [33]. In this work, the proposed method leverages the power of hourglass networks to extract this image-based "gazemap" feature

which is composed of silhouettes of the eyeball and the iris. It is an abstract, pictorial representation of eyeball structure which is the minimally essential information
necessary for the gaze estimation task. The gazemap representation is not explicitly
correlated with key landmarks in the input eye image and can be generated from the
3D gaze direction labels. Hence, the latter approach can be applied to models that
need to be trained directly on real-world data. The alternative is to train on synthetic
data, which can result in a model that does not perform sufficiently well due to the
domain gap between synthetic and real data domains.

3.5   Gaze Estimation Datasets

To train a generic gaze estimator that can be applied to a large variety of conditions
and devices, it is critical that learning-based gaze estimation methods are trained with
datasets that have good coverage of real-world conditions. Unless the model has had
a chance to encounter data with large variations, it could suffer due to over-fitting to
the more limited training data and perform in unexpected ways outside of the original
data regime. Essentially, we should not expect learned models to handle samples that
are out-of-distribution. Specifically, for assessing a dataset for the gaze estimation
task, there are several factors that should be considered, such as the range of gaze
direction, range of head poses, diversity of lighting conditions, variety of personal
appearances, and input image resolution.

Early datasets mainly focus on the head pose and gaze direction coverage under
controlled lighting conditions such as UT-Multiview [43] and EYEDIAP [12]. Our
MPIIGaze dataset, as the first of its own kind, brought the task of gaze estimation out
from the conventional and controlled laboratory setting out into the real-world setting
which covers different lighting conditions [53, 56]. This was done by installing a
data recording software on 15 participants' laptop computers and prompting the
participant every 10 min to ask for 20 gaze data samples. In this task, participants
were asked to look at dots on the screen as they appear, then press the space button to
confirm that he/she was looking at the dot. In this way, we could record the dot that
the participant was looking at, and at the same time, the position of the on-screen
dot was stored, along with an image of the participant's face taken with the built-in
camera of the laptop. Since the data samples were collected without restriction on
location and time, we were able to collect samples under many different lighting
conditions with natural head movement. However, since the MPIIGaze dataset was
collected with laptop devices, the head pose and gaze direction ranges are limited
to the size of typical laptop screens. Therefore, models trained only on MPIIGaze
data may not apply well to settings with larger displays and viewing distances, for
example, participants gazing at a TV in a public space.

Such limitation by the capture device appears in many existing datasets. Similar
to our MPIIGaze, the GazeCapture dataset limited itself with small ranges of head
poses and gaze directions due to using mobile phone and tablet devices for data
collection [24]. The EYEDIAP dataset is designed specifically for head poses and

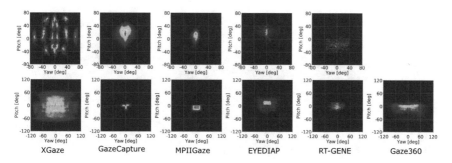

Fig. 3 Head pose (top row) and gaze direction (bottom row) distributions of different datasets. The head pose of Gaze360 is not shown here since it is not provided by the dataset. The figure is adapted from [60]

gaze directions of the desktop setting [12]. The RT-GENE dataset tried to use a head-mounted eye tracker to provide accurate gaze direction ground-truth and large spatial coverage of head poses and gaze directions [10]. The recent Gaze360 dataset used a moving camera to simulate different head poses [21]. However, the image and ground-truth quality were not guaranteed with these datasets, and the coverage of head poses and gaze directions was not properly designed.

We provide the ETH-XGaze dataset consisting of over one million high-resolution images of varying gaze directions under extreme head poses [60]. This dataset was collected with a custom setup of devices including a screen to show visual content from a projector, four lighting boxes to simulate different lighting conditions, and 18 digital SLR cameras which can capture high-resolution (6000 × 4000 pixels) images. The cameras were arranged such as to cover different perspectives of the face of the participant, effectively making each camera position correspond to one "head orientation" in the final processed dataset. Since the participant was placed close to the screen, a large range of gaze directions was captured during each recording session. A comparison of head pose and gaze direction ranges is made between our ETH-XGaze dataset and other datasets in Fig. 3. From the figure, we can see that our ETH-XGaze dataset provides the largest range of head poses and gaze directions compared to previous datasets. ETH-XGaze is a milestone toward providing full robustness to extreme head orientations and gaze directions and should enable the development of interesting novel methods that better incorporate understandings of the geometry of the human head and the eyeball within.

In addition to exploring the spatial dimension with the 18-camera ETH-XGaze dataset, we chose to explore the temporal dimension of gaze tracking in an end-to-end fashion. That is, we aimed to go beyond the static face images provided by most gaze estimation datasets by providing video data. In addition, we observed that when humans gaze at objects or other visual stimuli, their eye movements are often correlated with particular changes or movements in the stimuli. Yet, no large-scale video-based dataset exists to relate the change in the appearance of the human directly to a video of the visual stimulus. To fill this gap, we proposed another novel

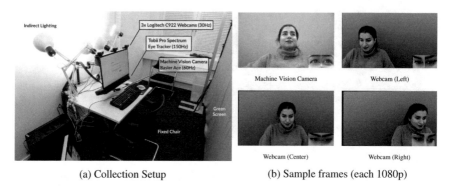

(a) Collection Setup   (b) Sample frames (each 1080p)

Fig. 4 EVE data collection setup and example of (undistorted) frames collected from the 4 camera views with example eye patches shown as insets [36]

dataset called EVE to provide temporal information of both the human face and corresponding visual stimulus for improving the temporal gaze estimation task [36]. The EVE dataset was recorded with four video cameras facing the participants, with various visual contents shown on the screen. The custom multi-view data capture setup and example frames are shown in Fig. 4. The custom setup synchronized information from three webcams running 30 Hz, one machine-vision camera running 60 Hz, and one Tobii Pro Spectrum eye tracker running 150 Hz. A large variety of visual stimuli were presented to our participants including images, videos, and Wikipedia web pages. We ensured that each participant observes 60 image stimuli (for 3 s each), at least 12 min of video stimuli, and 6 min of Wikipedia stimulus (three 2-min sessions). To our understanding, EVE is the first dataset to provide continuous video recordings of both the user and the visual stimuli while the user is free-viewing the presented visual stimuli. Alongside the dataset, we propose a method which shows that when a video of the user and screen content are taken as input, it is possible to correct for biases in a pre-trained gaze estimator by relating changes in the screen content with eye movement. Effectively, this allows for calibration-free performance improvements, finally yielding 2.5° of mean angular error.

3.6   Comparison of Learning-Based and Commercial Gaze Estimation Methods

Learning-based gaze estimation methods have developed rapidly and now begin to challenge classical methods. However, an accurate comparison of different gaze estimation methods is not a trivial task since they have different requirements in terms of capture hardware and lighting conditions. In [59], we compared three typical gaze estimation methods including two of our webcam-based methods [34, 55] and the commercial Tobii EyeX eye tracker on data collected from 20 participants. Our method proposed in [34] uses a neural network to predict eye-region landmarks which are then used for model-based gaze estimation. Our method proposed in [55] directly learns the mapping from the input face image to the gaze direction with a neural network as an appearance-based method. We do not know what exact method the commercial Tobii EyeX eye tracker uses for gaze estimation and calibration.

We mounted both a webcam and the Tobii EyeX below a screen, and then asked participants to look at displayed point stimuli from different distances to the screen. In this way, we collected the gaze direction ground-truth of the participants. We resized the region on the screen to show the visual stimuli according to the different distances such that gaze direction ranges for each distance were the same. We recorded 80 samples of which the first 60 were for personal calibration and the rest (20 samples) were for testing. The data collection setup was designed to be highly controlled to allow for a reliable comparison of performance across different gaze estimation methods for varying amounts of user-camera distances and the number of gaze tracker calibration samples. This was done by fixing the lighting conditions in the environment, asking the participants to keep their heads relatively still, and collecting the calibration and test samples in a single session.

The main results of our comparison are shown in Fig. 5. From the figure on the left, we can see that our model-based method [34] can work well for close distances while it becomes much worse when the distance between the user and camera increases. This is because this method relies on accurate estimations of eye-region landmarks. The Tobii EyeX eye tracker achieves the best performance (with the lowest gaze estimation error) since it has dedicated hardware including high-resolution cameras and active lighting sources. However, our appearance-based method [55] provides the robust gaze estimation performance across different distances between the user and camera. This means that the appearance-based gaze estimation method can be applied to many more applications, for example, room-level human attention estimation from cameras placed far away from the users. On the right of Fig. 5, we can see that the

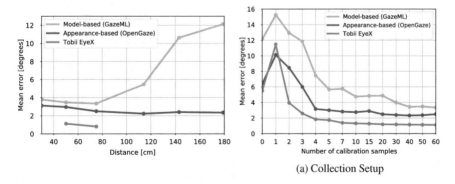

(a) Collection Setup

Fig. 5 Gaze estimation errors of different methods in degrees across distances between the user and camera (left), and a number of samples for the personal calibration. Dots are results averaged across all 20 participants and we linked them by lines [59]

three approaches only need a few personal calibration samples to reach reasonable accuracy. However, the number of necessary calibration samples may increase for real-world applications compared to this simple setting.

4 Making Gaze Tracking Practicable for Computer Interaction

Applying webcam-based gaze estimation methods to real-world interactive applications poses practical challenges. One of the key issues is that collecting personal calibration data is tedious for the user. However, without it the gaze estimation accuracy is poor. Even after personal calibration, the predicted gaze positions often show a large amount of noise, also for commercial eye trackers. Therefore, using gaze for interaction requires carefully designed user interfaces (UI) that take into account this potential noise and thus the uncertainty of the input signal. Otherwise, it results in a bad user experience or interaction is not even possible. Another problem is that, unlike existing commercial eye-tracking devices that can be directly used out-of-the-box, learning-based methods are still under development and may not lend themselves as simple solutions for novice users. In this section, we discuss our efforts toward making gaze tracking practicable for human-computer interaction.

4.1 Personalizing Gaze Tracking Methods

In principle, there are two main challenges for learning-based gaze estimation methods caused by personal differences. The first one is the kappa angle which varies by around two–three degrees on average across people [29]. The second challenge is personal eye appearance differences such as the shape of the eye and color of the iris. The eye appearance is also affected by changes in gaze directions and head poses, which is further connected to the image capturing or personal computing device. For example, a gaze estimator trained on images captured on a smartphone device that is held closer to the user may not perform well when directly applied to a large public display such as an advertisement board in a shopping mall. This could be caused by loss of image resolution and quality and unfamiliar head poses during operation. Due to these challenges, learning-based methods may benefit from further adaptation in challenging conditions that are not covered by the training data.

A basic experimental observation is that increasing the number of dataset participants results in improved general gaze estimation performance [24]. That is, learning from more peoples' data allows for a method that generalizes better to previously unknown users. However, as introduced in Sect. 2.4, there still exists a large performance gap that can be recovered when using just a few samples from the final target user to adapt learned models.

Nevertheless, collecting personal calibration data is still an effective way for good gaze estimation performance. In our work [57], we proposed to use multiple types of devices to collect samples for specific users, then aggregate all of these samples to train a joint model for that specific user across devices. The intuition behind this work is that the personal appearance should be the same for different devices which we can learn with the shared layers in the middle of our model. Our approach can benefit applications that are expected to be used by a user over a long period of time and across multiple devices, with personal calibration data being collected occasionally.

An alternative and promising method of increasing the amount of training data for specific persons is generative modeling. Given a few labeled samples, a high-quality generative model would be able to create tailored training data from which a robust yet personalized gaze estimation model could be learned. Our first work in this direction used an architecture based on CycleGAN [63] for realistic eye image generation, where gaze direction is provided as an input condition to the network, and training is supervised via perceptual and gaze direction losses [18]. Although this method is successful at generating photo-realistic images of the eye, it is not aware of head orientation and cannot easily be trained with noisy real-world images. We later proposed a transforming encoder-decoder architecture to tackle these issues, where features pertaining to gaze direction, head orientation, and other appearance-related factors are explicitly defined at the bottleneck of the autoencoder [62]. To truly enable training on in-the-wild datasets, we allow for the definition of implicitly defined "extraneous" factors at the bottleneck. The reconstruction objectives allow for these extraneous factors to encode information that is task-irrelevant yet allows for the satisfaction of the image-to-image translation objective. This approach, in particular, was shown to improve performance in the person-independent cross-dataset setting, but with further development, it should be possible to demonstrate improvements in the personalizing of gaze trackers. While personalized data collection is a promising and active direction of research, much work is yet needed for it to be effective.

Alternatively, our other research works show that learning-based gaze estimator calibration is definitely possible with tens of samples using simple regression schemes and with as few as one to three samples when using a more advanced meta-learning scheme. By defining input features using eye-region landmarks detected by a fully convolutional neural network, we show that a support vector regression model is capable of improving performance significantly with as few as 10 calibration samples. An appearance-based gaze estimator taking full-face input images was shown to be effective in tandem with a simple polynomial regression scheme taking point-of-regard as input, resulting in less than 4° of error with just 4 calibration samples [59], albeit in controlled experimental settings. When training on real-world data, a transforming encoder-decoder architecture coupled with a gradient-based meta-learning scheme was shown to be highly effective, with as few as one to three calibration samples yielding close to 3° of error on challenging in-the-wild datasets [35]. The code for the latter two systems is open-source and thus contributes toward effecting real improvements with regards to the applicability of learning-based gaze estimation methods to HCI applications.

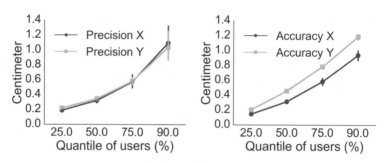

Fig. 6 Accuracy and precision of gaze tracking vary largely across users. Values increase steeply for different percentiles of users both in x- and y-directions

4.2 Design of Robust Interfaces

The estimated gaze data can be highly noisy and inaccurate. Nevertheless, it can be used for computer input, to improve user experience or otherwise enable new interaction if potential noise is taken into account during the design of gaze-aware interfaces. To this end, we have studied tracking performance in practical setups to derive design guidelines and actionable insights for the design of robust gaze-aware interfaces.

In [7], we collected eye-tracking data of 80 people in a calibration-style task, where participants were asked to fixate randomly positioned targets on the screen for 2 s. We used two different eye trackers (Tobii EyeX and SMI REDn scientific, both 60 Hz) under two lighting conditions (closed room with artificial lighting, room with large windows facing the tracker) in a controlled but practical setup. In contrast to many lab studies, we did not exclude any participant due to insufficient tracking quality. Instead, we were interested in learning about the possible variations in tracking accuracy (the offset from the true gaze point) and precision (the spread of tracked gaze points). These could be due to the independent variables of our study (lighting, tracker, screen regions), as well as due to external factors that we did not control but that are typical for real-life setups (participants wearing glasses or mascara, varying eye physiology, etc.).

The collected data reveals large variations of tracking quality in such a practical setup. Figure 6 shows the average accuracy and precision across all focused targets for different percentiles of participants. Very accurate fixations (25th percentile) are only 0.15 cm in the x-direction and 0.2 cm in the y-direction offset from the target. On the other hand, inaccurate fixations (90th percentile) can be as far offset as 0.93 cm in the x-direction and 1.19 cm in the y-direction—a more than six-fold difference— similar to the spread of the gaze points. Additionally, we found the precision of the estimated gaze points to be worse toward the right and bottom edges of the screen, as shown in Fig. 7. The ellipses represent the covariance matrix computed over all gaze points from all participants. In contrast, we found no significant variation across the screen for accuracy.

Fig. 7 The precision of the estimated gaze points varies for different screen regions. For each target, the ellipse shows the 2D Gaussian distribution fitted to the estimated gaze points of all participants fixating that target [7]

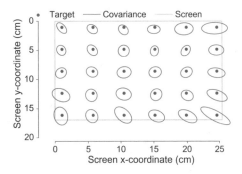

With data from such a calibration-style task, we can derive appropriate sizes for gaze targets, i.e. the regions in a UI that recognize if the user's gaze falls inside its borders. Given the gaze points belonging to a fixation, we can assume they are normally distributed in x- and y-directions independently, with an offset $O_{x/y}$ (accuracy) from the center of the fixated target and a standard deviation $\sigma_{x/y}$ (precision). From these, we can compute the necessary width and height for a gaze-aware element to be usable under such tracking conditions with the following equation:

$$S_{w/h} = 2(O_{x/y} + 2\sigma_{x/y}) \tag{1}$$

Multiplying $\sigma_{x/y}$ by 2 results in about 95% of gaze points falling inside the target, according to the properties of a normal distribution. While this seems conservative, an error rate of more than 5% (every 20th gaze point falling outside the target area) might slow down performance and lead to errors that can be hard to recover from. Figure 8 visualizes the size computation and shows two example cases with good and bad tracking quality. In [7], we give explicit target sizes for different percentiles of users. They vary from 0.94 × 1.24 cm for users that track well (25th percentile) up to 5.96 × 6.24 cm if we want to allow robust interaction for nearly all users in the dataset (90th percentile).

Target sizes can be significantly reduced if the gaze data is first filtered to remove noise artifacts and reduce signal dispersion. However, in contrast to laboratory studies, interactive applications cannot post-process the gaze data but must filter it in real time. This makes the recognition of outliers and artifacts difficult since it can introduce delays of several frames. Gaze filters must also account for the quick and sudden changes between saccades and fixations. In contrast, eye tremors, microsaccades, and noise should be filtered in order to stabilize the signal and improve precision. This makes commonly used methods, such as moving average, Kalman filter, or Savitzky-Golay filter, less useful [45].

The choice of the filter and its parameters can be seen as a trade-off between the target size required for robust interaction and the signal delay in following a saccade. In [7], we proposed a method to optimize the parameters for any filter given gaze data from a calibration-style data as described earlier. In a grid search, it instantiates

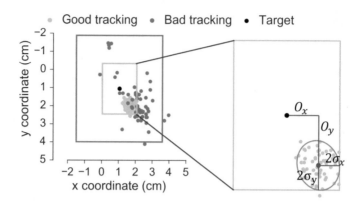

Fig. 8 Using the accuracy ($O_{x/y}$) and precision ($\sigma_{x/y}$) of the estimated gaze points belonging to a fixation, we can compute target sizes that would allow for robust interaction with an interface. The plot shows examples from fixations of two different users one with good and one with poor tracking quality [7]

a filter with each possible parameter, computes the resulting target size after filtering the data, and simulates saccades between such targets to determine any signal delay. The result is a Pareto front of parameter combinations that yield the minimum target size for a specific delay.

Using this method, we compare five commonly used gaze filters with three different kernel filters: the Stampe filter, the 1€ filter, a set of weighted average filters with linear, triangular, and Gaussian kernel functions, an extension with saccade detection, and one with additional outlier correction. See [7] for a description of each filter. The filters differ in the trade-offs they achieve for target size and signal delay. Generally, we found that a weighted average filter with a saccade detection performs best in terms of target size when signal delay should be short (up to one frame or 32 ms with 30 Hz tracker). The best performance is achieved with additional outlier correction at the cost of 2–2.5 frames delay.

The use of a filter with optimized parameters can reduce the target sizes by up to 42% (see Table 1). However, the filter can only improve the precision of the data, not its accuracy. Simulation based on real data yields important insights into the effect of filters on the signal. Filters that by design should not introduce any or only a short signal delay, in practice, introduce much larger delays to the gaze signal. For example, depending on the noise and set parameters, it may wrongly detect saccades as outliers or as part of fixation and either remove them or heavily smooth the signal. In such cases, an additional delay occurs before the filtered signal follows a saccade to a new fixation point. See [7] for an in-depth discussion of the tested filters.

We can summarize our analysis in a set of concrete design guidelines for gaze-enabled applications:

- **Target sizes** of at least 1.9×2.35 cm allow for reliable interaction for at least 75% of users if optimal filtering is used.

Table 1 Recommended target sizes for robust interaction by eye gaze. The values for raw and filtered show the improvement that can be achieved by filtering the gaze data. The percentiles show how much target sizes can vary for different levels of tracking quality [7]

	Width (cm)			Height (cm)		
	Raw	Filtered	Improv	Raw	Filtered	Improv
Overall	3.0	2.02	33%	3.14	2.19	30%
Percentile						
25%	0.94	0.58	38%	1.24	0.8	35%
50%	1.8	1.12	38%	2.26	1.48	35%
75%	3.28	1.9	42%	3.78	2.35	38%
90%	5.96	3.9	35%	6.24	4.24	32%

- **Target dimensions** should take into account the larger spread of gaze points in the y-direction we observed. Thus, the height should be somewhat larger than the width.
- **Visual representation** of elements can be smaller in which case the element should have a transparent margin that is also reactive to the user's gaze.
- **Placement** of targets should avoid the bottom or right edge of the screen, for which accuracy and precision were found to be significantly worse.
- **Filter** gaze points using a weighted average filter (over 36/40 frames in x/y direction) with a Gaussian or Triangular kernel and saccade detection (threshold of 1.45/1.65 cm in x/y direction). Additional outlier correction can further improve precision but at the cost of a two-sample delay.

4.3 Make Single-Webcam-Based Methods Accessible for HCI Researchers

To allow learning-based gaze estimation methods to be used out-of-the-box in a similar manner to commercial eye trackers, we published OpenGaze.[1] OpenGaze includes the entire gaze estimation pipeline, beginning from the acquisition of a single RGB image to the prediction of the gaze direction in the camera coordinate system. Therefore, it can be used with just a single webcam as the input device. OpenGaze is based on the appearance-based method in [55] that directly learns the mapping from input face image to the gaze direction without explicit eye landmark detection. Therefore, it is particularly effective when the distance between the user and camera is high. The full description of OpenGaze and evaluation can be found in our paper [59].

---

[1] http://www.opengaze.org.

We also publish GazeML[2] which is a demonstration of the approach in [34]. It uses stacked-hourglass networks to predict eye-region landmark heatmaps and an estimate of gaze direction. As it was only built for demonstrative purposes, its outputs are not suitable for actual gaze estimation nor can the software be easily adapted for HCI applications. Yet, it is an interesting demonstration of the possibility of real-time gaze estimation using deep convolutional neural networks.

5 Applications

Eye tracking provides information on where a user is looking, the dynamics of the gaze behavior, or the simple presence of the eyes on an object or screen. Such information offers a range of opportunities for computer interaction (see, for example, [28]). On the one hand, *explicit eye input* allows controlling an interface by fixating the corresponding UI elements or executing a prescribed series of fixations, saccades, or smooth pursuits. This requires users to consciously control their eyes which can be difficult but useful when other input modalities are not available or impractical. Explicit gaze input is used, for example, in virtual or augmented reality applications [19, 22] or to enable interaction for people with motor impairments [27]. On the other hand, *attentive interfaces* use information about the natural gaze behavior of users often without them noticing. They can obtain insights on the user's experience with an interface, their cognitive processes, their skills or struggles, and their intentions or preferences [14, 26]. In this section, we focus on such attentive interfaces that make implicit use of the gaze information. We present two applications that use this data in different ways: (1) as a way to establish a user's intention to interact with a device by tracking the location of their natural gaze, and (2) for adapting the interface to make the displayed information more relevant to a user by observing their gaze behavior over time.

5.1 Gaze-Aware Real-Life Objects

Gaze-awareness, that is, recognizing when a user is looking at a specific element, is an important functionality of an intelligent interactive system and the core of attentive interaction [3]. Also in real-life settings, interactive systems can benefit from sensing where or which object a user is looking at in their environment. However, the position of interactive devices can be arbitrary inside a room, making it difficult to identify the layout of multiple potential objects. In our work [54], we proposed a novel method for user-object eye contact detection that combines state-of-the-art learning-based gaze estimation [55] with a novel approach for unsupervised gaze target discovery, i.e. without the need for tedious and time-consuming manual data annotation.

---

[2] https://github.com/swook/GazeML.

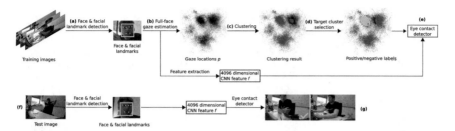

Fig. 9 Overview of our method in [54]. Taking images from the camera as input, our method first detects the face and facial landmarks (**a**). It then estimates the gaze directions p and extracts CNN features f using a full-face appearance-based gaze estimation method (**b**). During training, the gaze estimates are clustered (**c**) and samples in the cluster closest to the camera get a positive label while all others get a negative label (**d**). These labeled samples are used to train a two-class SVM for eye contact detection (**e**). During testing (**f**), the learned features f are fed into the two-class SVM to predict eye contact on the desired target object or face (**g**)

Our method works with the assumption that the target object is the one closest to the camera, thus, our method only requires a single off-the-shelf RGB camera placed close to the target object. Once the camera is placed, the approach does not require any personal or camera-object calibration . As illustrated in Fig. 9, the input to our method is the video sequence from the camera over a period of time. During the training, our method runs the gaze estimation pipeline introduced in our work [55] to obtain the estimated gaze direction. Assuming dummy camera parameters, the estimated gaze direction vector g is projected to the camera image plane and converted to on-plane gaze locations p. While the gaze estimation results are used for sample clustering, we extract a 4096-dimensional face feature vector f from the first fully connected layer of the neural networks.

As we stated in [55], the estimated gaze direction g is not accurate enough without personal calibration, and it cannot be mapped directly to the physical space without the camera-object relationship parameter. However, it indicates the relative gaze direction of the user from the camera position. Hence, these estimated gaze directions can be grouped into multiple clusters corresponding to several objects in front of the user. Given that our method assumes that the target object is the one closest to the camera, the sample cluster of the target object is identified as the cluster closest to the origin point of the camera coordinate system. Other clusters are assumed to correspond to other objects, and samples from these clusters are used as negative samples.

Labeled samples obtained from the previous step are used to train the eye contact classifier. This is a two-class classifier that determines if the user is looking at the target object or not in the current input frame. We use a high-dimensional feature vector f extracted from the gaze estimation network to leverage richer information instead of only gaze locations. Furthermore, we apply principal component analysis (PCA) to the training data and reduce the dimension of feature vector f that the subspace retains the 95% variance.

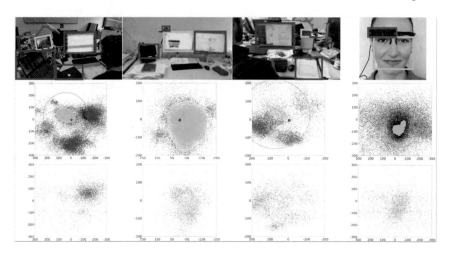

Fig. 10 Examples of gaze location distribution for the object-mounted (tablet, display, and clock) and head-mounted settings from [54]. The first row shows the recording setting with marked target objects (green), camera (red), and other distraction objects (blue). The second row shows the gaze location clustering results with the target cluster in green and the negative cluster in blue. The third row shows the ground-truth gaze locations from a subset of 5,000 manually annotated images with positive (green) and negative (blue) samples

During testing, input images are fed into the same pre-processing pipeline with the face and facial landmark detection, and feature f is extracted from the same gaze estimation neural networks. It is then projected to the PCA subspace, and the SVM classifier is applied to output eye contact labels. Note that during both the training and test phases, we neither need to label the input frame sample nor calibrate the camera-object relationship.

To evaluate our method for eye contact detection, we collected two datasets for two challenging real-world scenarios: office scenario and interaction scenario. The example of the two scenarios is shown in Fig. 10. For the office scenario, the camera is object-mounted as the camera was mounted or placed very near to the target object, and we aimed to detect eye contact of a single user with these target objects during everyday work at their workplace. We recorded 14 participants in total (five females) and each of them recorded four videos for different target objects: one for the clock, one for the tablet, and two for the display with two different camera positions. The recording duration for each participant ranged from three to seven hours.

In the interaction scenario (see far right of Fig. 10), a user was wearing a head-mounted camera while being engaged in everyday social interactions. This scenario was complementary to the office scenario in that the face of the user became the target and we aimed to detect eye contact of the second person who talked with the user. We recruited three users (all male) and recorded them while they interviewed multiple people on the street.

The example of gaze location distribution for the two scenarios is shown in Fig. 10. In the first row, we show the recording settings for the different target objects. We mark the target object (green rectangle), camera (red rectangle) positions, and other distraction objects (blue rectangle) in the figure. The second row of Fig. 10 shows sample clustering results where we mark the target cluster with green dots while all other negative sample clusters are marked with blue dots. Noise samples are marked as black and the big red dot is the camera position as the origin of the camera coordinate system. The third row shows the corresponding ground-truth annotated by two annotators.

From the second row of Fig. 10, we can see that the grouped sample clusters can be associated with objects in front of the camera, especially for the office scenarios as object layout is fixed. For the interaction scenario, we can observe one centered cluster and other random distributed samples. This is due to the fact that there is no fixed attractive object next to the user's face. Our sample clustering method can achieve good clustering results and successfully pick the cluster that belongs to the target object. It can also be easily extended to include objects that are newly added to the scene by updating the clusters. However, our method requires sufficient data for good clustering—usually about a few hours of recording. Besides, the target object should attract enough attention to the user, and it has to be isolated from other objects. Nonetheless, our method provides a way of eye contact detection with a single RGB camera without neither tedious personal calibration nor complex camera-object relationship calibration.

5.2 Adapting a UI to Improve Information Relevance

The user's gaze behavior can reveal whether the content displayed to a user is useful and relevant to their current task. In particular when making a decision, showing the right information to the user is crucial for the decision quality [31]. For example, a user might look at the details of a product for deciding whether to buy it or check the weather forecast to decide whether to go for a hike. If important information is missing from an interface, a user might be affected and make a wrong decision. On the other hand, displaying all available information might not be effective due to device constraints (e.g. on a small screen of a mobile phone) or because it might lead to information overload and a bad user experience. What makes the design of such interfaces challenging is also that users perceive the relevance of information differently [30], an aspect that cannot be foreseen at design time but must be detected and accounted for at run-time. However, the challenge is how to infer the relevance of the displayed information online, without having to interrupt users in their task.

Eye gaze has proven to be an unobtrusive and objective measure for a person's attention [37]. In this section, we show how we can analyze this data during the decision process of a user to obtain insights on the relevance of the displayed infor- mation [8]. This requires no explicit user input but analyzes the natural gaze behavior of the user while they focus on their decision-making task. In contrast to simpler, visual search tasks, the challenge is that the gaze behavior varies drastically during

Table 2 For recognizing information relevance from gaze behavior, we combine six well-established gaze metrics which we can associate with the three cognitive stages of decision-making [8]

Orientation		
TFF	Time to first fixation	The time elapsed between the presentation of a stimulus and the first time that gaze enters a given AOI. A low TFF value indicates high relevance
FPG	First Pass Gaze	The sum of duration of fixations on an AOI during the first pass, i.e. when the gaze first enters and leaves the AOI. A high FPG value indicates high relevance
Evaluation		
SPG	Second pass gaze	The sum of duration of fixations on an AOI during the second pass. A high SPG value indicates high relevance
RFX	Refixations count	The number of times an AOI is revisited after it is first looked at. A high RFX value indicates high relevance
Verification		
SFX	Sum of fixations	The total number of fixations within an AOI. A high SFX value indicates high relevance
ODT	Overall Dwell Time	The total time spent looking at an AOI including fixations and saccades. A high ODT value indicates high relevance

the decision process as users transition from obtaining an overview of the UI to comparing relevant information to finally validating their decision [15, 38].

To account for this variation, we select six different gaze metrics which were all shown to effectively infer a person's covert attention in simpler search tasks. However, gaze behavior during decision-making is more complex and is affected by the three cognitive stages the user goes through. Each metric captures a different aspect of these stages. Following Russo and Leclerc [38], we refer to them as (1) Orientation, (2) Evaluation, and (3) Verification. In the first stage, the user obtains an overview of the available information, characterized by a scanning pattern of shorter fixations without many return-fixations. The user then compares the information determined as relevant going back and forth between the same UI elements. Finally, short fixations on the most relevant information are used to validate the decision. While a clear separation of these stages is difficult, they inform our selection of gaze metrics that capture the different gaze characteristics during decision-making. These are shown in Table 2.

Each metric can be seen as a weak classifier which outputs a binary decision whether a UI element is considered relevant by the user or not. By allowing multiple metrics to vote on an element's relevance, we imitate a multiple-classifier system while avoiding the need for training data. We say that a metric casts a vote for a UI element as being relevant if its standard score (z-score) for the element is positive.

Fig. 11 Two alternative ways to adapt a room search interface. Left: relevant content is highlighted through color boxes. Right: irrelevant information is suppressed by graying it out [8]

Intuitively, this means that for that element, the gaze metric deviates from the average across all elements indicating a different gaze behavior of the user. To establish the relevance of an element, we count the number of votes cast by the 6 metrics and compare it to a threshold. Requiring a higher number of votes yields a lower number of elements being detected as relevant. This is further discussed below. In any case, this approach does not assume a fixed number of relevant elements a priori. Also, it is training-free and requires no ground-truth data.

Once we know whether the displayed information is relevant for the user's decision, we can adapt the interface to facilitate the decision process. Broadly speaking, many of the adaptation techniques proposed in the literature (see e.g. [9]) can be divided into two types: (1) emphasizing relevant content (e.g. coloring, rearranging or replicating elements) and (2) suppressing irrelevant information (e.g. graying out, removing, and moving elements to less prominent positions). See Fig. 11 for an example application. To obtain a benefit from adaptation, it is critical to minimize the risk of usability issues due to wrong adaptations. For example, wrongly highlighting seldom used elements in a menu can induce a performance cost that exceeds the benefit of adaptation [9]. On the other hand, failing to highlight an important menu item might not bring any benefit to the user but induces no cognitive cost either. Thus, when emphasizing content, a successful relevance detector should identify the subset of relevant UI elements (i.e. true positives) while minimizing the risk to detect irrelevant ones as important (i.e. false positives). When suppressing content, on the other hand, we are interested in recognizing the non-relevant elements (i.e. true negatives) while avoiding suppressing any relevant ones (i.e. false negatives) which might induce a high cognitive cost.

We can easily tune the different recognition rates of the relevance detector (true/false positive/negative) by varying the number of votes required to recognize an element as being relevant. Different voting schemes are possible. We can require a minimum of 1–6 gaze metrics to cast a vote, or we can be more selective and consider votes from metrics of the same stage (see Table 2) as redundant. In this case, we might require votes from a minimum of 2 different or all 3 stages. Figure 12 shows the resulting trade-off between the true positive (relevant elements correctly detected) and the false positive rates (irrelevant elements detected as relevant) depending on

Fig. 12 The number of
votes required to detect an
element as relevant changes
the trade-off between the
true positive and false
positive rates. This voting
approach allows to choose
the right trade-off must
depend on the adaptation
scheme. VoteXMetrics
denotes a minimum of 1–6
votes. VoteXStages refers
to a minimum of 2 or 3 votes
which must come from
different stages [8]

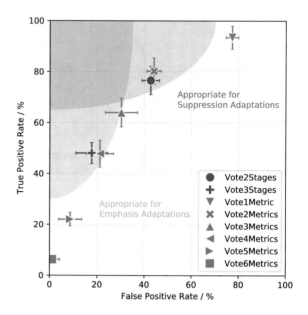

the voting scheme. The shaded areas indicate rates that seem acceptable for emphasizing or suppressing information. Data comes from an empirical study capturing the gaze behavior of 12 participants during interaction with a financial trading interface with information about a specific stock. Participants should decide whether to invest in the stock or not. Details are given in [8].

The figure shows that the true/false positive rate of the recognizer can easily be adjusted in a predictable manner to account for the requirements of different adaptation schemes. We recommend the following vote thresholds:

- For **emphasizing** relevant information, we recommend a minimum of 3 votes each from a different stage (Vote3Stages in Fig. 12). This yields a low false positive rate, reducing the risk of inducing any cognitive dissonance by emphasizing irrelevant information. At the same time, it ensures that only the most relevant information is emphasized.
- For **suppressing** irrelevant information, we recommend a minimum of any 2 votes (Vote2Metrics in Fig. 12). This yields a high true positive rate, ensuring that relevant information is not suppressed in any way, which could lead to higher interaction costs. A high false positive rate is acceptable in this case, which means that some less relevant content is not suppressed.

6 Discussion and Outlook

The improvements in AI have given rise to a new class of learning-based gaze estimation methods which make eye tracking more practicable and more widely applicable in everyday computer interaction. In contrast to traditional gaze estimation methods, the recently developed learning-based approaches do not require specialized hardware and can operate with just a single webcam and at a much larger operation distance. As these methods further improve, they will allow for HCI applications to consequently use gaze outside the lab and in the everyday interaction with computers.

Two major challenges remain open in enabling out-of-the-box learning-based gaze estimation solutions. One is in improving the generalization of models to previously unseen users, environments, eyeglasses, makeup, camera specifications, and other confounding factors. This can be tackled by the non-trivial task of collecting datasets with high-quality ground-truth annotations from a large number of people [36, 60] and designing novel neural network architectures for better generalization [33, 55]— both directions which we have extensively studied. The other challenge is due to person-specific biases, which must be accounted for when higher performance is required by the interactive application. This challenge exists not only because of the kappa angle but also the variations in the appearance of the eye and face regions in the real world. While we have explored several methods to this end in terms of few-shot adaptation [35, 59], further research must be conducted to efficiently collect data from the end-user without compromising user experience, such as via so-called implicit calibration [57].

A problem in developing gaze-based interfaces is that the accuracy and precision of the tracked gaze vary largely depending on many factors, such as the tracking method, the environment, human features, and others. The application receiving the gaze information must process a series of noisy data points. We have shown how, to some extent, a signal can be stabilized by filtering data. However, this does not account for its inaccuracy. For that, we have made recommendations for designing gaze-aware applications in a robust way such that they are usable under most conditions [7]. However, such a conservative approach might unnecessarily slow down or complicate interaction in cases where the gaze is tracked well. An alternative approach is to develop *error-aware applications* that recognize the uncertainty in the signal and adapt to it [1, 7]. As tracking quality decreases, a gaze-aware UI element could be enlarged, replaced by a more robust alternative, or deactivated entirely to avoid errors that might be hard to recover from. For such an approach to be useful, it is crucial to optimize for the time-point of UI adaptation. To this end, future work is needed that investigates how to trade-off potential gains through adaptation with the cost for the user to get used to a new interface. For taking into account personal preferences, such adaptations could even be done after explicitly querying the user.

We have seen that data about where a user is looking can not only be used for explicit interaction but also to make predictions about the user's cognitive processes, abilities, or intentions. Such attentive applications do not require the user to consciously control their gaze which can be cumbersome. Instead, they process the natural gaze behavior of the user with the goal to facilitate interaction. However, approaches to interpreting the eye gaze are often tailored to specific application cases and general solutions are rare. The voting scheme presented in this chapter (Sect. 5.2) is a first attempt to develop a more general approach for estimating the relevance of displayed information to a specific user and was shown to work across different decision-making tasks [8]. More work is needed though to develop general methods for inferring a user's intent, difficulties, or preferences from their gaze data and thus facilitate the design of intelligent user interfaces.

Once we can reliably derive information about the user's attention and intention from the estimated gaze, it is important to consider how to make effective use of this data in practice. In a user study conducted in [8], the large majority of participants confirmed that the tested application could correctly detect content relevant for their decision-making. Many also preferred the adapted version of the interface. However, the specific highlighting and suppression adaptations (see Fig. 11) did not lead to measurable improvements in terms of task execution time, users' perceived information load, or their confidence in their decision. Future work needs to develop better approaches to utilize such relevant information and develop UI adaptation schemes that facilitate the decision-making process for the user [14, 26]. Such work should also consider how adaptive interfaces can build trust to resolve users' concern of being manipulated by the interface [8, 32].

7   Conclusion

The advancement of AI techniques is boosting gaze estimation to become one of the major interactive signals for modern human-computer interaction. New learning-based methods have been developed for appearance-based, model-based, and hybrid gaze estimation methods. In particular, these learning-based methods can work with just a single webcam under challenging lighting conditions even over long operating distances of up to 2 m. The gaze estimation error is maintained to about 4° without personal calibration and 2° with personal calibration under variant challenging conditions. However, learning-based methods rely on large and varied datasets of different conditions and devices. Therefore, multiple datasets have been proposed that capture variations in head poses, gaze directions, lighting conditions, personal appearances, or input image resolutions. Although there is still a gap between methods using a single webcam and those with dedicated hardware, the presented research indicates promising efforts yield a performance that is close to that of traditional methods.

One of the key issues of the gaze estimation task is that collecting personal calibration data is tedious for the user. There are two ways to tackle this issue. The first one is efficiently using the personal calibration data with few-shot learning or synthetically generating more training samples with a few calibration images. The second effective way is carefully designing user interfaces (UI) that take into account this potential noise and thus the uncertainty of the input signal. We proposed actionable design guidelines for gaze-enabled applications including appropriate target sizes, target dimensions, visual representations, placement, and optimal parameter settings for different gaze filters. In addition, we introduced the OpenGaze and GazeML open-source toolkits which make the entire gaze estimation pipeline easily accessible to HCI researchers.

We presented two examples that show how the use of implicit gaze information can enable entirely new interactive concepts. Gaze-aware real-life objects can recognize when a user is looking at them without any specific camera-object or user calibration. In the second case, we showed that the user's gaze behavior can reveal whether displayed content is useful and relevant to the current task of a user. Such information can be used, for example, to adapt the user interface accordingly. Both examples work without requiring the user to explicitly control their eye gaze but analyze their natural gaze behavior during interaction.

In summary, AI-inspired methods have revolutionized approaches for estimating where a person is looking on a screen or in the 3D world. Already now, learning-based approaches enable sufficiently good gaze estimation in many real-world environments with just a single camera, bringing eye tracking out of the lab and into our everyday interaction with computers. This not only makes gaze a viable input method in situations where keyboard or touch input is not available or not feasible but also opens the doors for entirely new interactions and applications that can take into account gaze as an additional information source about the user's state.

References

1. Barz M, Daiber F, Sonntag D, Bulling A (2018) Error-aware gaze-based interfaces for robust mobile gaze interaction. In: Proceedings of the 2018 ACM symposium on eye tracking research & applications, association for computing machinery, New York, NY, USA, ETRA'18. https://doi.org/10.1145/3204493.3204536
2. Blignaut P (2009) Fixation identification: the optimum threshold for a dispersion algorithm. Atten Percept Psychophys 71(4):881–895
3. Bulling A (2016) Pervasive attentive user interfaces. IEEE Comput 49(1):94–98
4. Chen Z, Shi B (2020) Offset calibration for appearance-based gaze estimation via gaze decomposition. In: Proceedings of the IEEE/CVF winter conference on applications of computer vision (WACV)
5. Cheng Y, Zhang X, Lu F, Sato Y (2020) Gaze estimation by exploring two-eye asymmetry. IEEE Trans Image Process 29:5259–5272
6. Eckstein MK, Guerra-Carrillo B, Singley ATM, Bunge SA (2017) Beyond eye gaze: what else can eye tracking reveal about cognition and cognitive development? Dev Cogn Neurosci 25:69–91
7. Feit AM, Williams S, Toledo A, Paradiso A, Kulkarni H, Kane S, Morris MR (2017) Toward everyday gaze input: accuracy and precision of eye tracking and implications for design. In: Proceedings of the 2017 CHI conference on human factors in computing systems, association for computing machinery, New York, NY, USA, CHI'17, pp 1118–1130. https://doi.org/10.1145/3025453.3025599
8. Feit AM, Vordemann L, Park S, Berube C, Hilliges O (2020) Detecting relevance during decision-making from eye movements for ui adaptation. In: ACM symposium on eye tracking research and applications, association for computing machinery, New York, NY, USA, ETRA'20 Full Papers. https://doi.org/10.1145/3379155.3391321

9. Findlater L, Gajos KZ (2009) Design space and evaluation challenges of adaptive graphical user interfaces. AI Mag 30(4):68–73. https://doi.org/10.1609/aimag.v30i4.2268
10. Fischer T, Jin Chang H, Demiris Y (2018) Rt-gene: real-time eye gaze estimation in natural environments. In: Proceedings of the European conference on computer vision (ECCV), pp 334–352
11. Fuhl W, Santini T, Kasneci G, Rosenstiel W, Kasneci E (2017) Pupilnet v2. 0: Convolutional neural networks for CPU based real time robust pupil detection. arXiv:171100112
12. Funes Mora KA, Monay F, Odobez JM (2014) Eyediap: a database for the development and evaluation of gaze estimation algorithms from RGB and RGB-D cameras. In: Proceedings of the symposium on eye tracking research and applications, pp 255–258
13. Ganin Y, Kononenko D, Sungatullina D, Lempitsky V (2016) Deepwarp: Photorealistic image resynthesis for gaze manipulation. In: European conference on computer vision. Springer, pp 311–326
14. Gebhardt C, Hecox B, van Opheusden B, Wigdor D, Hillis J, Hilliges O, Benko H (2019) Learning cooperative personalized policies from gaze data. In: Proceedings of the 32nd annual ACM symposium on user interface software and technology, association for computing machinery, New York, NY, USA, UIST'19, pp 197–208. https://doi.org/10.1145/3332165.3347933
15. Gidlöf K, Wallin A, Dewhurst R, Holmqvist K (2013) Using eye tracking to trace a cognitive process: gaze behaviour during decision making in a natural environment. J Eye Mov Res 6(1). https://doi.org/10.16910/jemr.6.1.3, https://bop.unibe.ch/index.php/JEMR/article/view/2351
16. Hansen DW, Ji Q (2009) In the eye of the beholder: a survey of models for eyes and gaze. IEEE Trans Pattern Anal Mach Intell 32(3):478–500
17. He J, Pham K, Valliappan N, Xu P, Roberts C, Lagun D, Navalpakkam V (2019a) On-device few-shot personalization for real-time gaze estimation. In: Proceedings of the IEEE international conference on computer vision workshops, pp 0–0
18. He Z, Spurr A, Zhang X, Hilliges O (2019b) Photo-realistic monocular gaze redirection using generative adversarial networks. In: Proceedings of the IEEE international conference on computer vision, pp 6932–6941
19. Hirzle T, Gugenheimer J, Geiselhart F, Bulling A, Rukzio E (2019) A design space for gaze interaction on head-mounted displays. In: Proceedings of the 2019 CHI conference on human factors in computing systems, association for computing machinery, New York, NY, USA, CHI'19, pp 1–12. https://doi.org/10.1145/3290605.3300855
20. Howard IP, Rogers BJ et al (1995) Binocular vision and stereopsis. Oxford University Press, USA
21. Kellnhofer P, Recasens A, Stent S, Matusik W, Torralba A (2019) Gaze360: physically unconstrained gaze estimation in the wild. In: Proceedings of the IEEE international conference on computer vision, pp 6912–6921
22. Khamis M, Oechsner C, Alt F, Bulling A (2018) Vrpursuits: interaction in virtual reality using smooth pursuit eye movements. In: Proceedings of the 2018 international conference on advanced visual interfaces, association for computing machinery, New York, NY, USA, AVI'18. https://doi.org/10.1145/3206505.3206522
23. Kim J, Stengel M, Majercik A, De Mello S, Dunn D, Laine S, McGuire M, Luebke D (2019) Nvgaze: an anatomically-informed dataset for low-latency, near-eye gaze estimation. In: Proceedings of the 2019 CHI conference on human factors in computing systems, pp 1–12
24. Krafka K, Khosla A, Kellnhofer P, Kannan H, Bhandarkar S, Matusik W, Torralba A (2016) Eye tracking for everyone. In: Proceedings of the IEEE conference on computer vision and pattern recognition, pp 2176–2184
25. Lindén E, Sjostrand J, Proutiere A (2019) Learning to personalize in appearance-based gaze tracking. In: Proceedings of the IEEE international conference on computer vision workshops, pp 0–0
26. Lindlbauer D, Feit AM, Hilliges O (2019) Context-aware online adaptation of mixed reality interfaces. In: Proceedings of the 32nd annual ACM symposium on user interface software and technology, pp 147–160

27. Majaranta P (2011) Gaze interaction and applications of eye tracking: advances in assistive technologies. IGI Global
28. Majaranta P, Bulling A (2014) Eye tracking and eye-based human–computer interaction. Springer, London, pp 39–65. https://doi.org/10.1007/978-1-4471-6392-3_3
29. Moshirfar M, Hoggan RN, Muthappan V (2013) Angle kappa and its importance in refractive surgery. Oman J Ophthalmol 6(3):151
30. Orquin JL, Loose SM (2013) Attention and choice: a review on eye movements in decision making. ACTPSY 144:190–206. https://doi.org/10.1016/j.actpsy.2013.06.003
31. Papismedov D, Fink L (2019) Do consumers make less accurate decisions when they use mobiles? In: International conference on information systems, Munich
32. Park S, Gebhardt C, Rädle R, Feit A, Vrzakova H, Dayama N, Yeo HS, Klokmose C, Quigley A, Oulasvirta A, Hilliges O (2018a) AdaM: adapting multi-user interfaces for collaborative environments in real-time. In: SIGCHI conference on human factors in computing systems. ACM, New York, NY, USA, CHI'18
33. Park S, Spurr A, Hilliges O (2018b) Deep pictorial gaze estimation. In: Proceedings of the European conference on computer vision (ECCV), pp 721–738
34. Park S, Zhang X, Bulling A, Hilliges O (2018c) Learning to find eye region landmarks for remote gaze estimation in unconstrained settings. In: Proceedings of the 2018 ACM symposium on eye tracking research & applications, pp 1–10
35. Park S, Mello SD, Molchanov P, Iqbal U, Hilliges O, Kautz J (2019) Few-shot adaptive gaze estimation. In: Proceedings of the IEEE international conference on computer vision, pp 9368–9377
36. Park S, Aksan E, Zhang X, Hilliges O (2020) Towards end-to-end video-based eye-tracking. In: European conference on computer vision. Springer, pp 747–763
37. Qvarfordt P, Zhai S (2005) Conversing with the user based on eye-gaze patterns. In: Proceedings of the SIGCHI conference on human factors in computing systems, association for computing machinery, New York, NY, USA, CHI'05, pp 221–230. https://doi.org/10.1145/1054972.1055004
38. Russo JE, Leclerc F (1994) An eye-fixation analysis of choice processes for consumer non-durables. J Cons Res 21(2):274–290. https://doi.org/10.1086/209397, https://academic.oup.com/jcr/article-pdf/21/2/274/5093700/21-2-274.pdf
39. Salvucci DD (2001) An integrated model of eye movements and visual encoding. J Cogn Syst Res 1:201–220. www.elsevier.com/locate/cogsys
40. Salvucci DD, Goldberg JH (2000) Identifying fixations and saccades in eye-tracking protocols. In: Proceedings of the 2000 symposium on Eye tracking research & applications, pp 71–78
41. Sesma L, Villanueva A, Cabeza R (2012) Evaluation of pupil center-eye corner vector for gaze estimation using a web cam. In: Proceedings of the symposium on eye tracking research and applications, pp 217–220
42. Sibert LE, Jacob RJ (2000) Evaluation of eye gaze interaction. In: Proceedings of the SIGCHI conference on Human Factors in Computing Systems, pp 281–288
43. Sugano Y, Matsushita Y, Sato Y (2014) Learning-by-synthesis for appearance-based 3D gaze estimation. In: Proceedings of the IEEE conference on computer vision and pattern recognition, pp 1821–1828
44. Tan KH, Kriegman DJ, Ahuja N (2002) Appearance-based eye gaze estimation. In: Proceedings of the sixth IEEE workshop on applications of computer vision, 2002. (WACV 2002). IEEE, pp 191–195
45. Špakov O (2012) Comparison of eye movement filters used in HCI. In: Proceedings of the symposium on eye tracking research and applications, association for computing machinery, New York, NY, USA, ETRA '12, pp 281–284. https://doi.org/10.1145/2168556.2168616
46. Wang K, Ji Q (2017) Real time eye gaze tracking with 3d deformable eye-face model. In: Proceedings of the IEEE international conference on computer vision (ICCV)
47. Wang K, Zhao R, Ji Q (2018) A hierarchical generative model for eye image synthesis and eye gaze estimation. In: Proceedings of the IEEE conference on computer vision and pattern recognition, pp 440–448

48. Wood E, Bulling A (2014) Eyetab: Model-based gaze estimation on unmodified tablet computers. In: Proceedings of the symposium on eye tracking research and applications, pp 207–210
49. Wood E, Baltrusaitis T, Zhang X, Sugano Y, Robinson P, Bulling A (2015) Rendering of eyes for eye-shape registration and gaze estimation. In: Proceedings of the IEEE international conference on computer vision (ICCV)
50. Yu Y, Liu G, Odobez JM (2018) Deep multitask gaze estimation with a constrained landmark-gaze model. In: Proceedings of the European conference on computer vision (ECCV), pp 0–0
51. Yu Y, Liu G, Odobez JM (2019) Improving few-shot user-specific gaze adaptation via gaze redirection synthesis. In: Proceedings of the IEEE conference on computer vision and pattern recognition, pp 11937–11946
52. Zhai S, Morimoto C, Ihde S (1999) Manual and gaze input cascaded (magic) pointing. In: Proceedings of the SIGCHI conference on human factors in computing systems, association for computing machinery, New York, NY, USA, CHI'99, pp 246–253. https://doi.org/10.1145/302979.303053
53. Zhang X, Sugano Y, Fritz M, Bulling A (2015) Appearance-based gaze estimation in the wild. In: Proceedings of the IEEE conference on computer vision and pattern recognition, pp 4511–4520
54. Zhang X, Sugano Y, Bulling A (2017a) Everyday eye contact detection using unsupervised gaze target discovery. In: Proceedings of the 30th annual ACM symposium on user interface software and technology, pp 193–203
55. Zhang X, Sugano Y, Fritz M, Bulling A (2017b) It's written all over your face: full-face appearance-based gaze estimation. In: Proceedings of the IEEE conference on computer vision and pattern recognition workshops, pp 51–60
56. Zhang X, Sugano Y, Fritz M, Bulling A (2017c) Mpiigaze: real-world dataset and deep appearance-based gaze estimation. IEEE Trans Pattern Anal Mach Intell 41(1):162–175
57. Zhang X, Huang MX, Sugano Y, Bulling A (2018a) Training person-specific gaze estimators from user interactions with multiple devices. In: Proceedings of the 2018 CHI conference on human factors in computing systems, pp 1–12
58. Zhang X, Sugano Y, Bulling A (2018b) Revisiting data normalization for appearance-based gaze estimation. In: Proceedings of the 2018 ACM symposium on eye tracking research & applications, pp 1–9
59. Zhang X, Sugano Y, Bulling A (2019) Evaluation of appearance-based methods and implications for gaze-based applications. In: Proceedings of the 2019 CHI conference on human factors in computing systems, pp 1–13
60. Zhang X, Park S, Beeler T, Bradley D, Tang S, Hilliges O (2020a) Eth-xgaze: a large scale dataset for gaze estimation under extreme head pose and gaze variation. In: European conference on computer vision. Springer, pp 365–381
61. Zhang X, Sugano Y, Bulling A, Hilliges O (2020b) Learning-based region selection for end-to-end gaze estimation. In: British machine vision virtual conference (BMVC)
62. Zheng Y, Park S, Zhang X, De Mello S, Hilliges O (2020) Self-learning transformations for improving gaze and head redirection. Adv Neural Inf Process Syst 33
63. Zhu JY, Park T, Isola P, Efros AA (2017) Unpaired image-to-image translation using cycle-consistent adversarial networks. In: 2017 IEEE international conference on computer vision (ICCV)

AI-Driven Intelligent Text Correction Techniques for Mobile Text Entry

Mingrui Ray Zhang, He Wen, Wenzhe Cui, Suwen Zhu, H. Andrew Schwartz, Xiaojun Bi, and Jacob O. Wobbrock

1 Introduction

Text entry techniques on touch-based mobile devices today are generally well developed. Ranging from tap-based keyboard typing to swipe-based gesture typing [64], today's mobile text entry methods employ a range of sophisticated algorithms designed to maximize speed and accuracy. Although the results reported from various papers [46, 55] show that mobile text entry can reach reasonably high speeds, some even as fast as desktop keyboards [55], the daily experience of mobile text composition is still often lacking. One bottleneck lies in the text correction process. On mobile touch-based devices, text correction often involves repetitive backspacing and moving the text cursor with repeated taps and drags over very small targets

Portions of this chapter are reproduced with permission of the ACM from the following previously published papers [10, 66].

M. R. Zhang (✉) · J. O. Wobbrock
The Information School, University of Washington, Seattle, WA 98195, USA
e-mail: mingrui@uw.edu

J. O. Wobbrock
e-mail: wobbrock@uw.edu

H. Wen
The Robotics Institute, Carnegie Mellon University, Pittsburgh, PA 15213, USA
e-mail: tigermored@gmail.com

W. Cui · H. Andrew Schwartz · X. Bi
Department of Computer Science, Stony Brook University, Stony Brook, NY 11794, USA
e-mail: wecui@cs.stonybrook.edu

H. Andrew Schwartz
e-mail: has@cs.stonybrook.edu

X. Bi
e-mail: xiaojun@cs.stonybrook.edu

S. Zhu
Grammarly, Inc., San Francisco, CA 94104, USA
e-mail: suwzhu@gmail.com

© The Author(s), under exclusive license to Springer Nature Switzerland AG 2021   131
Y. Li and O. Hilliges (eds.), *Artificial Intelligence for Human Computer Interaction:
A Modern Approach*, Human–Computer Interaction Series,
https://doi.org/10.1007/978-3-030-82681-9_5

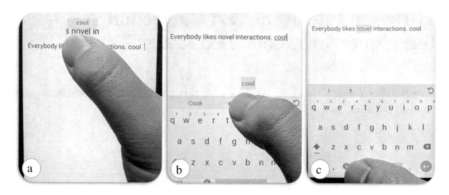

Fig. 1 The three correction interactions of Type, Then Correct: **a** *Drag-n-Drop* lets the user drag the last word typed and drop it on an erroneous word or gap between words; **b** *Drag-n-Throw* lets the user drag a word from the suggestion list and flick it into the general area of the erroneous word; **c** *Magic Key* highlights each possible error word after the user types a correction. Directional dragging from atop the magic key navigates among error words, and tapping the magic key applies the correction

(i.e., the characters and spaces between them). Owing to the fat finger problem [56], this process can be slow and tedious indeed. In this chapter, we will introduce two projects that apply techniques in Natural Language Processing (NLP) to improve the text correction interaction for touch screen text entry.

Correcting text is a consistent and vital activity during text entry. A study by MacKenzie and Soukoreff showed that backspace was the second most common keystroke during text entry (pp. 164–165) [36]. Dhakal et al. [12] found that during typing, people made 2.29 error corrections per sentence, and that slow typists actually made and corrected more mistakes than the fast typists.

For immediate error corrections, i.e., when an error is noticed right after it is made, the user can press backspace to delete the error [53]. However, for overlooked error corrections, the current cursor movement-based text correction process on smartphones is laborious: one must navigate the cursor to the error position, delete the error text, re-enter the correct text, and finally navigate the cursor back. There are three ways to position the cursor: (1) by repeatedly pressing the backspace key [53]; (2) by pressing arrow keys on some keyboards or making gestures such as swipe-left; and (3) by using direct touch to move the cursor. The first two solutions are more precise than the last one, which suffers from the fat finger problem [56], but they require repetitive actions. The third option is error-prone when positioning the cursor amid small characters, which increases the possibility of cascading errors [3]; it also increases the cognitive load of the task and takes on average 4.5 s to perform the tedious position-edit-reposition sequence [18].

The two projects in this chapter are based on the same premise: What if we can skip positioning the cursor and deleting errors? Given that the *de facto* method of correcting errors relies heavily on these actions, such a question is subtly quite radical. *What if we just type the correction text, and apply it to the error?* The first project,

"Type, Then Correct" (TTC) contains three interactions (Fig. 1): (1) *Drag-n-Drop* is a simple baseline technique that allows users to drag the last-typed word as a correction and drop it on the erroneous text to correct substitution and omission errors [59]. (2) *Drag-n-Throw* is the "intelligent" version of Drag-n-Drop: it allows the user to flick a word from the keyboard's suggestion list toward the approximate area of the erroneous text. The deep learning algorithm finds the most likely error within the general target area and automatically corrects it. (3) *Magic Key* does not require direct interaction with the text input area at all. After typing a correction, the user simply presses a dedicated key on the keyboard, and the deep learning algorithm highlights possible errors according to the typed correction. The user could then dragging atop the key to navigate through the error candidates and tap the key again to apply the correction. All three of our interaction techniques require no movement of the text cursor and no use of backspace.

The second project, JustCorrect, is the evolution of the TTC project. It simplifies the concept even further by reducing the need to specify the error position. To substitute an incorrect word or insert a missing word in the sentence, the user simply types the correction at the end, and JustCorrect will automatically commit the correction without the user's intervention. Additional options are also provided for better correction coverage. In this way, JustCorrect makes post hoc text correction on the recently entered sentence as straightforward as text entry.

We evaluated the two text correction projects with multiple text entry experiments and compared their performances. The results revealed that both TTC and JustCorrect resulted in faster correction times, and were preferred over the *de facto* technique.

2 Related Work

In the following subsections, we first review research related to text entry correction behaviors on touch screens. We then present current text correction techniques for mobile text entry and multi-modal text input techniques. Finally, we provide a short introduction to natural language processing (NLP) algorithms for text correction.

2.1 Text Correction Behaviors on Touch Screens

Many researchers have found that typing errors are common using touch-based keyboards and that current correction techniques are left wanting in many ways. For example, sending error-ridden messages, such as typos and errors arising from autocorrection [27], is of greatest concern when it comes to older adults. Moreover, Komninos et al. [28] observed and recorded in-the-wild text entry behaviors on Android phones, and found that users made around two word-level errors per typing session, which slowed text entry considerably. Also, participants "predominantly employed backspacing as an error correction strategy." Based on their observations,

Komninos et al. recommended that future research needed to "develop better ways for managing correction," which is the very focus of this chapter.

In most character-level text entry schemes, there are three types of text entry errors [35, 59]: substitutions, where the user enters different characters than intended; omissions, where the user fails to enter characters; and insertions, where the user injects erroneous characters. Substitutions were found to be the most frequent error among these types. In a smart watch-based text entry study [30], out of 888 phrases, participants made 179 substitution errors, 31 omission errors, and 15 insertion errors. In a big data study of keyboarding [12], substitution errors (1.65%) were observed more frequently than omission (0.80%) and insertion (0.67%) errors. Our correction techniques address substitution and omission errors; we do not address insertion errors because users can just delete insertions without typing any corrections. Moreover, insertion errors are relatively rare.

2.2   Mobile Text Correction Techniques

While much previous work focused on user behaviors during mobile text entry, there have been a few projects that improved upon the text correction process. Previous work often adopted a cursor-based editing approach. For example, previous research proposed controlling the cursor by using magnifying lens [2], pressing hard on the keyboard to turn it into a touchpad [2], or adding arrow keys [58]. Gestural operations have also been proposed to facilitate positioning the cursor. Examples included using left and right gestures [18], sliding left or right from the space key [22] to move the cursor, or using a "scroll ring" gesture along with swipes in four directions [65].

The smart-restorable backspace [4] project had the most similar goal to that of this chapter: to improve text correction without extensive backspacing and cursor positioning. The technique allowed users to perform a swipe gesture on the backspace key to delete the text back to the position of an error, and restore that text by swiping again on the backspace key after correcting the error. To determine error positions, the technique compares the edit distance of the text and the word in a dictionary. The error detection algorithm is the main limitation of that work: it only detects misspellings. It cannot detect grammar errors or word misuse. By contrast, the two projects in this chapter could detect a wide range of errors based on deep learning techniques.

Commercial products exhibit a variety of text correction techniques. Gboard [34] allows a user to touch on a word and replace it by tapping on another word in a suggestion list. However, this technique is only limited to misspellings. Some keyboards, such as the Apple iOS 9 keyboard, support indirect cursor control by treating the keyboard as a trackpad. Unfortunately, prior research [48] showed that this design brought no time or accuracy benefits compared to direct pointing. The Grammarly keyboard [23] will keep track of the input text, and provide corrections in the suggestion list. Grammarly uses NLP algorithms to provide correction suggestions, and it is able to detect both spelling and grammar errors. The user simply taps the suggestion to commit a correction. However, because Grammarly provides correction suggestions without guidance (e.g., it provides all possible error correction options without knowing which one the user wants to correct), the suggestion bar can become cluttered in the presence of many suggestions.

Different from the above techniques, the correction techniques presented in this chapter have the user enter a correction first, typed at the end of the current text input stream. Informed by the correction, the techniques can better understand what text the user wants to correct. Thus, they can not only correct "real errors" such as misspellings or grammar errors but also address other issues, such as offering to substitute synonyms.

2.3   Multi-Modal Text Input

Many soft keyboards (e.g., Gboard [34]) support entering text via different modalities, such as tap typing, gesture typing, and voice input. Previous research has explored fusing information from multiple modalities to reduce text entry ambiguity, such as combining speech and gesture typing [41, 51], using finger touch to specify the word boundaries in speech recognition [50], or using unistrokes together with key landings [25] to improve input efficiency.

JustCorrect also investigated how different input modalities affected the performance. It was particularly inspired by ReType [52], which used eye-gaze input to estimate the text editing location. We advanced it by inferring the editing intention based on the entered word only, making the technique suitable for mobile devices, which typically are not equipped with eye-tracking capabilities.

2.4   NLP Algorithms for Error Correction

The projects in this chapter use deep learning algorithms from natural language processing (NLP) to find possible errors based on typed corrections. We therefore provide a brief introduction to related techniques.

Traditional error correction algorithms utilize N-grams and edit distances to provide correction suggestions. For example, Islam and Inkpen [24] presented an algorithm that uses the Google 1T 3-gram dataset and a string-matching algorithm to detect and correct spelling errors. For each word in the original string, they first search for candidates in the dictionary, and assign each possible candidate a score derived from their frequency in the N-gram dataset and the string-matching algorithm. The candidate with the highest score above a threshold is suggested as a correction.

Recently, deep learning has gained popularity in NLP research because of its generalizability and significantly better performance than traditional algorithms. For NLP tasks, convolutional neural networks (CNN) and recurrent neural networks

Fig. 2 Our customized keyboard interface. The undo key is located in the top-right corner. The *Magic Key* is the circular key immediately to the left of the space bar

(RNN) are extensively used. They often follow a structure called encoder–decoder, where part of the model encodes the input text into a feature vector, then decodes the vector into the result. In TTC, we utilize an RNN in this encoder–decoder pattern. A thorough explanation of these methods is beyond the current scope. Interested readers are directed to prior work [6, 54, 61].

Most researchers treat the error correction task as a language translation task in deep learning because their input and output are both sentences—for error correction, the input is a sentence with errors and the output is an error-free sentence; for language translation, the input is a sentence in one language and the output is a sentence in another language. For example, Xie et al. [60] presented an encoder–decoder RNN correction model that operates input and output at the character level. Their model was built upon a sequence-to-sequence model for translation [6], which was also used in the algorithm of the TTC project for error detection.

3   Type, Then Correct: The Three Interactions

We present the design and implementation of the three interaction techniques of Type, Then Correct (TTC). The common features of these interactions are: (1) the first step is always to type the correction text at the current cursor position, usually the end of the current input stream; (2) all correction interactions can be undone by tapping the undo key on the keyboard (Fig. 2, top right); (3) after a correction is applied, the text cursor remains at the last character of the text input stream, allowing the user to continue typing without having to move the cursor. A current, but not theoretical, limitation is that we only allow the correction text to be contiguous alphanumeric text without special characters or spaces.

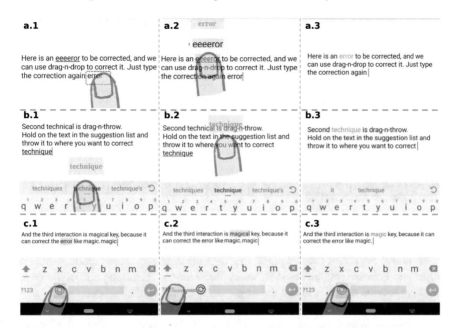

Fig. 3 The three interaction techniques. *Drag-n-Drop*: **a.1** Type a word and then touch it to initiate correction; **a.2** Drag the correction to the error position. Touched words are highlighted and magnified, and the correction shows above the magnifier; **a.3** Drop the correction on the error to finish. *Drag-n-Throw*: **b.1** Dwell on a word from the suggestion list to initiate correction. The word will display above the finger; **b.2** Flick the finger toward the area of the error: here, the flick ended on "the," not the error text "technical"; **b.3** The algorithm determines the error successfully, and confirming animation appears. *Magic Key*: **c.1** Tap the magic key (the circular button) to trigger correction. Here, "error" is shown as the nearest potential error. **c.2** Drag left from atop the magic key to highlight the next possible error in that direction. Now, "magical" is highlighted. **c.3** Tap the magic key again to commit the correction "magic"

3.1 Drag-n-Drop

Drag-n-Drop is the simplest interaction technique. With *Drag-n-Drop*, after typing the correction, the user then drags the correction text and drops it on the error location. As shown in Fig. 3a.1, if the finger's touchdown point is within the area of the last word, the correction procedure will be initiated. The user can then move the correction and drop it either on another word to substitute it, or on a space to insert the correction.

While moving the correction, a magnifier appears above the finger to provide an enlarged image of the touched text; text to be corrected will be highlighted in a yellow background (Fig. 3a.2). When the finger drags over an alphanumeric character, we highlight its surrounding text bounded by any special character or space. When the finger drags over a space character, we highlight the single space character. The correction text also displays above the magnifier during the drag to remind the user what the correction is.

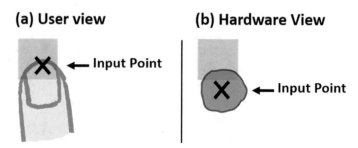

Fig. 4 Perceived input point: **a** the user views the top of the fingernail as the input point [21]; **b** but today's hardware regards the center of the contact area as the touch input point, which is not the same. Figure adapted from [56]

Similar to Shift by Vogel and Baudisch [56], we adjusted the input point to 30 pixels above the actual contact point, to reflect the user's perceived input point [21]. Vogel and Baudisch suggested that "users perceived the selection point of the finger as being located near the top of the finger tip" [7, 56], while the actual touch point was roughly at the center of the finger contact area [49], as shown in Fig. 4. After the correction is dropped on a space (for insertion) or on a word (for substitution), there is an animated color change from orange to black, confirming the successful application of the correction text.

3.2 Drag-n-Throw

Similar to *Drag-n-Drop*, *Drag-n-Throw* also requires the user to drag the correction. But unlike *Drag-n-Drop*, with *Drag-n-Throw*, the user flicks the correction from the word suggestion list atop the keyboard, not from the text area, allowing the user's fingers to stay near the keyboard area. As before, the correction text shows above the touch point as a reminder (Fig. 3b.1). Instead of dropping the correction on the error position, the user throws (i.e., flicks) the correction to the general area of the text to be corrected. Once the correction is thrown, our deep learning algorithm determines the error position, and corrects the error either by substituting the correction for a word, or by inserting the correction. Color animation is displayed to confirm the correction. The procedure is shown in Fig. 3b.1–3.

We enable the user to drag the correction from the suggestion list because it is quicker and more accurate than directly interacting with the text, which has smaller targets. Moreover, our approach provides more options and saves time because of the word-completion function. For example, if the user wants to type "dictionary," she can just type "dic" and "dictionary" appears in the list. Or, if the user misspells "dictonary," omitting an "i," the correct word still appears in the list because of the keyboard's decoding algorithm.

Throwing the text speeds up the interaction beyond precise drag-and-dropping. The user does not have to carefully move the finger to drop the correction. Our deep learning algorithm will output candidate positions for substitution or insertion within the general finger-up area. (More implementation details are explained below.) In our implementation, if the candidate is within 250 pixels of the finger-lift point in any direction, the error will be corrected and confirmed by color animation. Otherwise, there will be no effect. The 250-pixel threshold was derived empirically from iterative trial-and-error. Larger thresholds allow corrections too far away from the finger-lift point, which can cause unexpected results and user frustration. Smaller thresholds reduce the benefits of "throwing" and eventually start to feel like "dropping."

3.3 Magic Key

Drag-n-Drop required interaction within the text input area; Drag-n-Throw kept the fingers closer to the keyboard but still required some interaction in the text input area. With Magic Key, the progression "inward" toward the keyboard is fulfilled, as the fingers do not interact with the text input area at all, never leaving the keyboard. Thus, round trips [15] between the keyboard and text input area are eliminated.

With Magic Key, after typing the correction, the user taps the magic key on the keyboard (Fig. 3c.1), and the possible error text is highlighted. If a space is highlighted, an insertion is suggested; if a word is highlighted, a substitution is suggested. The nearest possible error to the just-typed correction will be highlighted first; if it is not the desired correction, the user can drag from atop the magic key to left to show the next possible error. The user can drag left or right from atop the magic key to rapidly navigate among different error candidates. Finally, the user can tap the magic key to commit the correction. The procedure is shown in Fig. 3c.1–3. To cancel the operation, the user can simply tap any key (other than undo or the magic key itself).

4 Type, Then Correct: The Correction Algorithm

In this section, we present the deep learning algorithm for text correction and its natural language processing (NLP) model, the data collection and processing procedures, and the training process and validation results.

4.1 Expected Correction Categories

We first list error types that our model should correct:

Typos A typographical error ("typo") happens when a few characters of a word are mistyped. For example, *fliwer (flower)* or *feetball (football)*. Among typos, misspellings can usually be auto-corrected by current keyboards; however, auto-correction might yield another wrong word. For example, *best (bear)* or *right (tight)*. Our model should be able to handle different types of typo errors.

Grammar Errors Grammar errors caused by one mistaken word should be corrected, such as misuse of verb tense, lack of articles or pronouns, subject–verb disagreement, etc.

Semantic Substitution Our model should also be able to substitute words that are semantically related to the correction, such as synonyms and antonyms. For example, "what a nice day" can be corrected to "what a beautiful day." Semantic substitution is not necessarily correcting an error, but is useful when the user wants to change the expression.

4.2   The Deep Neural Network Structure

Inspired by Xie et al. [60], we applied a recurrent neural network (RNN) encoder–decoder model similar to the translation task for text corrections. The encoder contains a character-level convolutional neural network (CNN) [26] and two bidirectional gated recurrent unit (GRU) layers [9]. The decoder contains a word-embedding layer and two GRU layers. The overall flow of the model is shown in Fig. 5, and the encoder–decoder structure is shown in Fig. 6.[1]

Traditional recurrent neural networks (RNN) cannot output positional information. Our key insight is that instead of outputting the whole error-free sentence, we make the decoder only output five words around the proposed correction position, e.g., the correction word and its four neighboring words (two before, two after). If there are not enough words, the decoder will output the flags *<bos>* or *<eos>* instead for beginning-of-sentence and end-of-sentence, respectively. To locate the correction position, we compare the output with the input sentence word-by-word, and choose the position that aligns with most words. For the example in Fig. 5, we first tokenize the input and add two *<bos>* and two *<eos>* to the start and end of the tokens. Then we compare the output with the input:

```
Input: <bos> <bos> thanks the reply <eos> <eos>
CS:          <bos> thanks for the    reply
CI:          <bos> thanks the reply
```

Above, "CS" means compare for substitution, which finds the best alignment for substitution (it uses all five words of the output trying to align with the input); "CI" means compare for insertion, which finds the best alignment for insertion (it only uses the first and last two words of the output for alignment, as the center word is the insertion correction). In the example, CI has best alignment of four tokens (*<bos>*,

---

[1] The model and data processing codes are available at https://github.com/DrustZ/CorrectionRNN.

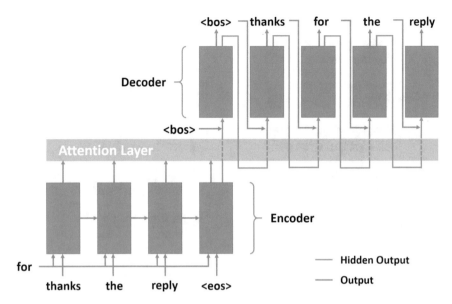

Fig. 5 The encoder–decoder model for text correction. The model outputs five words in which the middle word is the correction. In this way, we get the correction's location

thanks, the, reply), thus "for" will be inserted between "thanks" and "the." If the number of aligned tokens is the same in both comparisons, we would use insertion in our implementation.

We now explain the details of the encoder and the decoder (Fig. 6). For the encoder, because there might be typos and rare words in the input, operating on the character level is more robust and generalizable than operating on the word level. We first apply the character-level CNN [26] composed of *Character Embedding, Multiple Conv. Layers* and *Max-over-time Pool layers* (Fig. 6, left). Our character-level CNN generates an embedding for each word at the character level. The character embedding layer converts the characters of a word into a vector of $L \times E_c$ dimensions. We set E_c to 15, and fixed L to 18 in our implementation, which means the longest word can contain 18 characters (longer words are discarded). Words with fewer than 18 characters are appended with zeroes in the input vector. We then apply multiple convolution layers on the vector. After convolution, we apply max-pooling to obtain a fixed-dimensional (E_w) representation of the word. In our implementation, we used convolution filters with width [1, 2, 3, 4, 5] of size [15, 30, 50, 50, 55], yielding a fixed vector with the size of 200. E_c was set to 200 in the decoder.

We also needed to provide the correction information for the encoder. We achieved this by feeding the correction into the same character-level CNN, and concatenated the correction embedding with the embedding of the current word. This yielded a vector of size $2E_w$, which was then fed into two bi-directional GRU layers. The hidden size H of GRU was set to 300 in encoder and decoder.

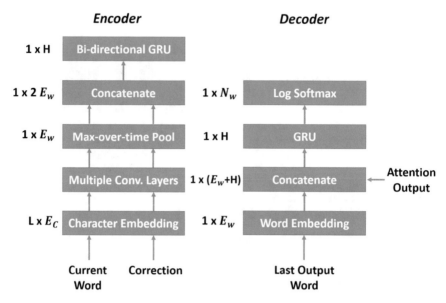

Fig. 6 Illustration of the encoder and decoder, which is every vertical blue box in Fig. 5. L is the length of characters in a word; E_c is the character embedding size; H is the hidden size; E_w is the word embedding size; N_w is the word dictionary size

The decoder first embedded the word in a vector of size E_w, which was set to 200. Then it was concatenated with the attention output. We used the same attention mechanism as Bahdanau et al. [6]. Two GRU layers and a log-softmax layer then followed to output the predicted word.

4.3 Data Collection and Processing

We used the *CoNLL 2014 Shared Task* [40] and its extension dataset [6] as a part of the training data. The data contained sentences from essays written by English learners with correction and error annotations. We extracted the errors that were either insertion or substitution errors. In all, we gathered over 33,000 sentences for training.

To gather even more training data, we perturbed several large datasets containing normal text. We used the Yelp reviews (containing two million samples) and part of the Amazon reviews dataset (containing 130,000 samples) generated by Zhang et al. [67]. We treated these review data as if they were error-free texts, and applied artificial perturbation to them. Specifically, we applied four perturbation methods:

1. **Typo simulation**. In order to simulate a real typo, we applied the simulation method similar to Fowler et al. [16]. The simulation treated the touch point dis-

tribution on a QWERTY layout as a 2-D Gaussian spatial model, and selected a character based on the sampling coordinates. We used the empirical parameters of the spatial model from Zhu et al. [68]. For each sentence in the review dataset, we randomly chose a word from the sentence, and simulated the typing procedure for each character of the word until the simulated word was different from the original word. We then applied a spellchecker to "recover" the typo. This maneuver was to simulate the error of auto-correction functions, where the "corrected" word actually becomes a different word. We then used the "recovered" word as a typo if it was different from the original word, or used the typing simulation result if the spellchecker successfully recovered the typo.

2. **Dropping words** To enable the model to learn about insertion corrections, we randomly dropped a word from a sentence, and labeled the dropped word as the correction. We prioritized dropping common stop words first if any of them appeared in the sentence, because people were most likely to omit words like a, the, my, in, and very.

3. **Word deformation** We randomly changed or removed a few characters from a word. If the word was a verb, we would replace it with a word sharing the same lexeme. For example, we would pick one of broken, breaking, breaks, or broke to replace break. If the word was a noun, we would use a different singular or plural word. For example, we would replace star with stars. Otherwise, we would just remove a few characters from the word.

4. **Semantic word substitution** This perturbation enabled the model to learn semantic information. For a given word in the sentence, we looked for words that were semantically similar to it and made a substitution. We used the GloVe [44] Twitter-100 model from Gensim [45] to represent similarity. Synonyms and antonyms were generated using this method.

For each sentence in the review dataset, we randomly applied a perturbation method. We then combined the perturbed data with the CoNLL data, and filtered out sentences containing less than 3 words or more than 20 words. In all, the final training set contained 5.6 million phrases.

For testing, we used two datasets: *CoNLL 2013 Shared Task* [39], which was also a grammatical error correction dataset, and the Wikipedia revision dataset [62], which contains real-word spelling errors mined from Wikipedia's revision history. We generated 1665 phrases from the CoNLL 2013 dataset and 1595 phrases from the Wikipedia dataset.

4.4 Training Process

We implemented our model in PyTorch [43]. We only included lowercase alphabetical letters (a–z) and ten numerals (0–9) in the character vocabulary of the encoder. We used the Adam optimizer with a learning rate of 0.0001 (1e-4) for the encoder and 0.0005 (5e-4) for the decoder, and a batch size of 128. We applied weight clipping of $[-10, +10]$, and a teacher forcing ratio of 0.5. We also used dropout with probability 0.2 in all GRU layers. For the word embedding layer in the decoder, we labeled words with frequencies less than 2 in the training set as *<unk>* (unknown).

4.5 Results

Table 1 shows the evaluation results on the two testing datasets. The recall is 1 because all our testing data contained errors. We regarded a prediction as correct if the error position predicted was correct using the comparison algorithm described above.

4.6 Other Implementation Details

We developed a custom Android keyboard and a notebook application to implement our three text correction interaction techniques. Our keyboard was based on the Android Open-Source Project (AOSP)[2] from Google. In building on top of this keyboard, we added the long-press interaction on suggested words for *Drag-n-Throw*.

The notebook application was built on an open-source project Notepad,[3] and most of the interactions were implemented as part of the notebook application. For *Drag-n-Drop*, when a user touched within the last word area (within 100 pixels of the *(x, y)*-coordinate of the last character), the interaction was initiated. We used the default magnifier on the Android system and added a transparent view showing the correction above the finger as it moves.

For *Drag-n-Drop* and *Magic Key*, the keyboard needed to communicate with the notebook application. The keyboard used the Android Broadcast mechanism to send the correction and endpoint of the throw gesture of *Drag-n-Throw*. When the information was received, the notebook would search within the three lines near the release point. For each line, the notebook extracted up to 60 surrounding characters near the release point, and sent them to a server running the correction model. The server then replied with possible correction options and the corresponding probabilities. The notebook then selected the most likely option to update the correction. To avoid

Table 1 The performance of our correction model on the two testing datasets

Dataset	Accuracy (%)
CoNLL 2013	75.68
Wikipedia revisions	81.88

---

[2] https://android.googlesource.com/platform/packages/inputmethods/LatinIME/.

[3] https://github.com/farmerbb/Notepad.

the correction happening too far away from the throwing endpoint, we constrained the x-coordinate of the correction to be within 250 pixels of the finger-lift endpoint.

For the *Magic Key* technique, the keyboard notified the notebook when the magic key was pressed or dragged. The notebook would treat the last word typed as the correction, and sent the last 1000 characters to the server. The server then split the text into groups of 60 characters with overlaps of 30 characters, and predicted a correction for each group. When the notebook received the prediction results, it first highlighted the nearest option, and then switched to further error options when the key was dragged left. For substitution corrections, it would highlight the whole word to be substituted; for insertion corrections, it would highlight the space where the correction was to be inserted.

The server running the correction model handled responses via HTTP requests. To increase the accuracy of the model for typos, we first calculated the matching score between each token of the input text and the correction using the Levenshtein algorithm [31]. The score equaled the number of matches divided by the total character number of the two words. If the score of a word in the sentence was above 0.75, we treated the word as the error to be corrected. Otherwise, we fed the text and correction into the aforementioned neural network model.

5 Type, Then Correct: Experiment

We evaluated three aspects of our correction techniques: (1) timing and efficiency; (2) success rate of *Drag-n-Throw* and *Magic Key*; and (3) users' subjective preferences. We conducted an experiment containing two tasks: a correction task and a composition task. The correction task purely evaluated the efficiency of the interactions, and the composition task evaluated the usability and success rate of the intelligent techniques in more realistic scenarios.

5.1 Participants

We recruited 20 participants (8 male, 12 female, aged 23–52) for the study. We used emails, social media, and word-of-mouth for recruitment. All participants were familiar with entering and correcting text on mobile devices. The experiment lasted 1 hour, and participants were compensated $20 USD for their time.

5.2 Apparatus

A Google Pixel 2 XL was used for the study. The phone had a 6.0" screen with a 1440–2880 resolution. We added logging functions from the notebook application to record correction time. The server running the correction model had a single GTX 1080.

5.3 Phrases Used in the Correction Task

Both tasks utilized a within-subjects study design. For the correction task, we chose 30 phrases from the test dataset on which the correction model had been 100% correct because we wanted purely to evaluate the performance of the interaction technique, not of the predictive model. We split the phrases evenly into three categories: *typos, word changes,* and *insertions. Typos* required replacement of a few characters in a word; *word changes* required replacing a whole word in a phrase; and *insertions* required inserting a correction. For each category, we had five *near-error* phrases where the error positions were within the last three words; and five *far-error* phrases where the error positions were farther away. The reason was to see whether error positions would affect correction efficiency. Examples of phrases in each category are provided in the appendix.

5.4 Procedure

Participants were first introduced to our different interaction techniques, including the categories of errors that *Drag-n-Throw* and *Magic Key* were able to correct. Then participants practiced the three techniques with three practice phrases each. After practicing, the 30 phrases as well as their corresponding corrections were presented to the participants. Then they began to correct the phrases using four techniques: (1) today's *de facto* cursor-positioning and backspace-based method, (2) *Drag-n-Drop*, (3) *Drag-n-Throw*, and (4) *Magic Key*. The order of the four techniques was counterbalanced using a balanced Latin Square.

When the correction task started, the participant would be shown the next phrase to be corrected on a desktop computer screen, as well as how to correct it. The notebook application would display the phrase with an error. After the participant corrected the error, a dialog box appeared asking the participants to enter the next phrase. The experimenter then showed the next phrase on the computer. When the participant was ready, she entered the next phrase by tapping the OK button. The interface is shown in Fig. 7. The rationale for showing how to correct the phrase on a computer screen was to filter out the learning effect and visual search time caused by the unfamiliarity of the phrases, and to isolate the interaction time.

After the correction task, the participants started composing messages freely. They were told to type for 3 minutes as they would in normal messaging situations. However, they were told not to correct any errors during typing. After finishing their compositions, they then corrected all errors with the four interaction techniques. This composition task endeavored to evaluate usability in a more realistic scenario.

Fig. 7 a The notebook application showing the test phrase. **b** The intended correction displayed on the computer screen. **c** After each correction, a dialog box appeared

When participants were correcting errors with *Drag-n-Throw* and *Magic Key*, the experimenter recorded whether any failure happened in order to calculate the error rate.

When the two tasks ended, participants filled out a NASA-TLX survey [47] and a usability survey adapted from the SUS questionnaire [8] for each interaction.

6 Type, Then Correct: Results

For the correction task, 2400 phrases were collected in total. For the correction task, we focus on task completion times; for the composition task, we focus on the success rate of the two intelligent interaction techniques and users' preferences.

6.1 Correction Time

Figure 8 shows correction times for the four techniques. In addition to overall times, the correction times for *near-error* and *far-error* phrases are also shown. We log-transformed correction times to comply with the assumption of conditional normality, as is often done with time measures [32]. We used linear mixed model analyses of variance [17, 33], finding that there was no order effect on correction time ($F(3, 57) = 1.48, n.s.$), confirming that our counter-balancing worked. Furthermore, technique had a significant effect on correction time for all phrases ($F(3, 57) = 26.49, p < 0.01$), *near-error* phrases ($F(3, 57) = 29.02, p < 0.01$), and *far-error* phrases ($F(3, 57) = 17.04, p < 0.01$), permitting us to investigate *post hoc* pairwise comparisons.

We performed six *post hoc* paired-sample t-tests with Holm's sequential Bonferroni procedure [20] to correct for Type I error rates, finding that for all phrases,

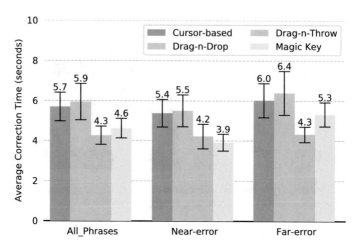

Fig. 8 Average correction times in seconds for different interaction techniques (lower is better). *Drag-n-Throw* was the fastest for all phrases and far-error phrases, while *Magic Key* was the fastest for near-error phrases. Error bars are +1 SD

the *de facto* cursor-based method was significantly slower than *Drag-n-Throw* ($t(19) = 6.66$, $p < 0.01$) and *Magic Key* ($t(19) = 4.79$, $p < 0.01$); *Drag-n-Drop* was also significantly slower than *Drag-n-Throw* ($t(19) = 7.49$, $p < 0.01$) and *Magic Key* ($t(19) = 5.62$, $p < 0.01$). For near-error phrases, the *de facto* method was significantly slower than *Drag-n-Throw* ($t(19) = 5.58$, $p < 0.01$) and *Magic Key* ($t(19) = 7.02$, $p < 0.01$); *Drag-n-Drop* was also significantly slower than *Drag-n-Throw* ($t(19) = 5.00$, $p < 0.01$) and *Magic Key* ($t(19) = 7.44$, $p < 0.01$). For far-error phrases, *Drag-n-Throw* was significantly faster than all other interactions: the *de facto* method ($t(19) = -5.64$, $p < 0.01$), *Drag-n-Drop* ($t(19) = -6.60$, $p < 0.01$), and *Magic Key* ($t(19) = -3.68$, $p < 0.01$).

We then looked at different correction types. Figure 9 shows the average correction times for *typos*, *word changes*, and *insertions*. Again, we used linear mixed model analyses of variance [17, 33] on log correction time [32]. Technique had a statistically significant effect for all correction types: *typo* ($F(3, 57) = 5.11$, $p < 0.01$), *word change* ($F(3, 57) = 10.87$, $p < 0.01$), and *insertion* ($F(3, 57) = 55.55$, $p < 0.01$).

We then performed *post hoc* paired-sample *t*-tests with Holm's sequential Bonferroni procedure, finding that for *typos*, the *de facto* cursor-based method was significantly slower than *Drag-n-Throw* ($t(19) = 3.80$, $p < 0.01$); *Drag-n-Drop* was also significantly slower than *Drag-n-Throw* ($t(19) = 2.70$, $p < 0.05$). For *word change*, the *de facto* cursor-based method was significantly slower than all other techniques: *Drag-n-Drop* ($t(19) = 3.54$, $p < 0.01$), *Drag-n-Throw* ($t(19) = 5.58$, $p < 0.01$), and *Magic Key* ($t(19) = 3.74$, $p < 0.01$). For *insertion*, *Drag-n-Drop* was significantly slower than all other interactions: the *de facto* method ($t(19) = 5.72$, $p < 0.01$), *Drag-n-Throw* ($t(19) = 11.17$, $p < 0.01$), and *Magic Key* ($t(19) = 10.92$, $p <$

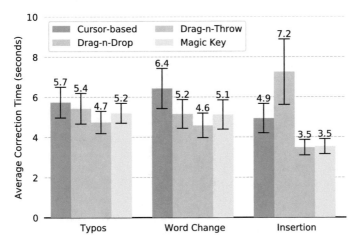

Fig. 9 Average correction times in seconds for different correction types (lower is better). *Drag-n-Throw* was the fastest for all three types. Error bars are +1 SD

0.01); also, the *de facto* cursor-based method was significantly slower than *Drag-n-Throw* ($t(19) = 5.45$, $p < 0.01$) and *Magic Key* ($t(19) = 5.20$, $p < 0.01$).

6.2 Success Rate

In the text composition task, we recorded errors when participants were using *Drag-n-Throw* and *Magic Key*. With *Drag-n-Throw*, participants made 108 errors in all, and 95 of them were successfully corrected, a success rate of 87.9%. Among the successfully corrected errors, nine were attempted more than once because the corrections were not applied to expected error positions. With *Magic Key*, participants made 101 errors in all, and 98 of them were successfully corrected, a success rate of 97.0%.

6.3 Subjective Preference

The composite scores of the SUS usability [8] and TLX [47] surveys for different interaction techniques are shown in Fig. 10. Participants generally enjoyed using *Magic Key* and *Drag-n-Throw* more than the *de facto* cursor-based method and *Drag-n-Drop*. Also, the two deep learning techniques were perceived to have lower workload than the other two.

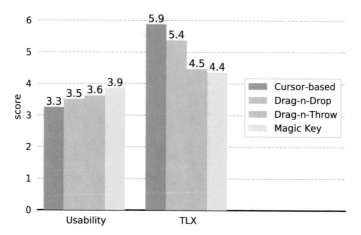

Fig. 10 Composite usability (higher is better) and NASA-TLX (lower is better) scores for different techniques. *Magic Key* was rated as the most usable and having the lowest workload

7 JustCorrect: Simplifying the Text Correction Based on TTC

In this section, we present the second project, JustCorrect, which is an extension of the Type, Then Correct (TTC) project, and simplifies the correction interaction one step further. The interaction flow is demonstrated in Fig. 11. Before explaining the technical details, we first show a usage scenario.

Sarah was texting a message to her friend Tom when she typed: *We worked on the project lsst week*. She discovered a mis-spelling: *lsst*. Instead of moving the cursor five characters back, deleting the wrong characters, and typing the correct characters, Sarah simply typed the word *last* and pressed the edit button. JustCorrect automatically replaced *lsst* with *last*. Sarah also noticed that it might be better to replace *worked* with *focused*, so she typed *focused* at the end and pressed the edit button again to correct the word. Lastly, she wanted to insert the modifier *mainly* before *focused*. She gesture typed *mainly* and JustCorrect automatically completed the task for her. In this case, JustCorrect was triggered by switching from tap typing to gesture typing. The final sentence then became *We mainly focused on the project last week*. In this example, Sarah successfully corrected a typo, substituted a word, and inserted a new word without ever adjusting the cursor position.

7.1 The Post hoc Correction Algorithm

The key to JustCorrect lies in successfully inferring a user's editing intention based on the entered word and the prior context. The post hoc correction algorithm takes

1. Sentence with errors

a quick fox jimo over a lazy dog

2. Input 'jumps' to correct 'jimo' with JustCorect-Tap (2a) or JustCorrect-Gesture (2b)

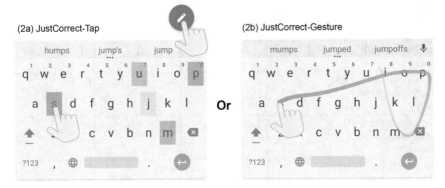

(2a) JustCorrect-Tap

Or

(2b) JustCorrect-Gesture

3. Outcome

a quick fox jumps over a lazy dog

a quick fox ∧jumps jimo over a lazy dog

a quick fox jimo ∧jumps over a lazy dog

Fig. 11 This figure shows how JustCorrect works. 1. The user enters a sentence with an error *jimo* using tap typing; 2. To correct *jimo* to *jumps*, they can either tap-type *jumps* and press the editing button (**2a**), or switch to gesture type *jumps* (**2b**). 3. JustCorrect then substitutes *jimo* with *jumps*. Two alternative correction options are also presented. The editing procedure involves no manual operations except entering the correct text

Table 2 An example of eight substitution candidates. They are generated by replacing a word in the sentence "a quick fox jimo over a lazy dog" with "jumps." S_i means that ith word in the sentence w_i is replaced by w^*. $SubScore_i$ is substitution score for ranking substitution candidates. SS_i, ES_i, and WS_i are scores from Sentence channels, Edit Distance, and Word Embedding, respectively

Substitution candidates	$SubScore_i$	SS_i	ES_i	WS_i
S_1: **jumps** quick fox jimo over a lazy dog	0.56	0	0	0.56
S_2: a **jumps** fox jimo over a lazy dog	0.89	0.2	0.2	0.48
S_3: a quick **jumps** jimo over a lazy dog	0.42	0.42	0	0
S_4: a quick fox **jumps** over a lazy dog	1.71	1	0.6	0.11
S_5: a quick fox jimo **jumps** a lazy dog	0.75	0.18	0	0.57
S_6: a quick fox jimo over **jumps** lazy dog	0.56	0	0	0.56
S_7: a quick fox jimo over a **jumps** dog	1.11	0.11	0	1
S_8: a quick fox jimo over a lazy **jumps**	0.48	0.18	0	0.31

the current entered sentence S and an editing word w^* as input, and revises S by either substituting a word w_i in S with w^*, or inserting w^* at an appropriate position. The post hoc correction algorithm offers three post hoc correction suggestions, with the top suggestion automatically adopted by default and the others easily selected with only one additional tap.

Take the sentence $S = $ *a quick fox jimo over a lazy dog*. The user inputs *jumps* as the editing word w^*. Because the sentence has eight words, there are eight substitution and nine insertion possibilities: *_a_quick_fox_jimo_over_a_lazy_dog_*. The nine possible insertion positions are indicated by the underscores. The post hoc correction algorithm then generates eight substitution candidates ($S_1 - S_8$), as shown in Table 2, and nine insertion candidates ($I_1 - I_9$) as shown in Table 3.

The algorithm then ranks the substitution candidates according to the substitution scores, and ranks the insertion candidates according to the insertion scores. These scores are later compared to generate ultimate correction suggestions.

Table 3 An example of nine insertion candidates. They are generated by inserting "jumps" before or after every word in the sentence "a quick fox jimo over a lazy dog." I_i means w^* is inserted at the ith insertion location. $InserScore_i$ is insertion score for ranking insertion candidates

Insertion candidates	$InserScore_i$
I_1: **jumps** a quick fox jimo over a lazy dog	0.06
I_2: a **jumps** quick fox jimo over a lazy dog	0.04
I_3: a quick **jumps** fox jimo over a lazy dog	0.52
I_4: a quick fox **jumps** jimo over a lazy dog	1
I_5: a quick fox jimo **jumps** over a lazy dog	0.91
I_6: a quick fox jimo over **jumps** a lazy dog	0.24
I_7: a quick fox jimo over a **jumps** lazy dog	0
I_8: a quick fox jimo over a lazy **jumps** dog	0
I_9: a quick fox jimo over a lazy dog **jumps**	0.5

7.2   Substitution Score

The substitution score reflects how likely a substitution candidate represents the user's actual editing intention. We look for robust evidence of the substituted word along three dimensions: orthographic (i.e., character) distance, syntactosemantic (i.e., meaning) distance, and sequential coherence (i.e., making sense in context). More specifically, for the ith substitution candidate S_i, its substitution score $SubScore_i$ is defined as

$$SubScore_i = ES_i + WS_i + SS_i, \tag{1}$$

where ES_i is editing similarity, WS_i is word embedding similarity, and SS_i is the sentence score for substitution candidates (explained below). The edit distance channel ES_i is intended to handle spelling corrections. The edit distance between a typo and a correct word is usually small [57].

On the other hand, when replacing a word with a more preferred choice, e.g., replacing "great" with "fantastic," or replacing "road" with "path," the two words are both valid spellings and usually close in meaning. The word embedding channel WS_i captures similar meanings. Finally, the sentence channel SS_i ensures the overall coherence of the word choice or replacement within its context.

7.2.1   Edit Distance Channel

The edit distance channel calculates the editing similarity for each substitution candidate. The Levenshtein edit distance [31] between two strings is the minimum number of single-character edits including deletions, insertions, or substitutions needed to transform one string into another string. The editing similarity ES_i is defined as

$$ES_i = \frac{L(w^*, w_i)}{max(|w^*|, |w_i|)},\tag{2}$$

where w^* is the correction and w_i is the ith word in the previous text. $max(|w^*|, |w_i|)$ denotes the max length of w^* and w_i.

7.2.2   Word Embedding Channel

The word embedding channel estimates the semantic and syntactic similarity WS_i between the editing word w^* and the substituted word w_i in S_i. In this channel, words from the vocabulary are mapped to vectors derived from statistics on the co-occurrence of words within documents [13]. The distance between two vectors can then be used as a measure of syntactic and semantic difference [1].

   We trained our word embedding model over the "Text8" dataset [37] using the Word2Vec skip-gram approach [38]. The cosine similarity $WS_C(w^*, w_i)$ is then calculated as the WS_i [1]. WS_i was normalized in the range [0, 1].

7.2.3   Sentence Channel

The sentence channel estimates the normalized sentence score of S_i using a language model—a model that estimates the probability of a certain sequence of words.

   To compute the language model probability for a given sentence, we trained a 3-gram language model using the KenLM Language Model Toolkit [19]. The language model takes each substitution candidate sentence S_i as the input, and outputs its estimated log probability $P(S_i)$. By normalizing $P(S_i)$ in the range of 0 to 1, we get the normalized sentence score SS_i:

$$SS_i = \frac{P(S_i) - min(P(S_j))}{max(P(S_j)) - min(P(S_j))}, (j = 1, 2, \ldots, N),\tag{3}$$

where $min(P(S_j))$ and $max(P(S_j))$ are the minimum and maximum sentence channel scores among all the N substitution possibilities, assuming the sentence S has N words. The language model itself was trained over the Corpus of Contemporary American English (COCA) [11] (2012 to 2017), which contains over 500 million words.

7.3   Insertion Score

For insertion candidates, we only use the *sentence channel* for insertion scores, as there are no word-to-word comparisons for insertion candidates. Assuming S has N words and therefore $N + 1$ candidates for insertion, the insertion score $InserScore_i$

for the candidate I_i is calculated as

$$Inser Score_i = \frac{P(I_i) - min(P(I_j))}{max(P(I_j)) - min(P(I_j))}, (j = 1, 2, \ldots, N + 1), \quad (4)$$

where $min(P(I_j))$ and $max(P(I_j))$ are the minimum and maximum sentence channel scores among all the $N + 1$ insertion possibilities $(I_1, I_2, \ldots, I_{N+1})$. $Inser Score_i$ is also normalized in $[0,1]$.

7.4 Combining Substitution and Insertion Candidates

The post hoc correction algorithm combines the substitution and insertion candidates to generate correction suggestions by calculating each candidate's scores. We compare substitution and insertion candidates by their sentence channel scores because it is the common component in both score calculations. The candidates with the highest top-3 scores would be shown on the interface. If all three candidates are of the same error kind (substitution/insertion), we change the last candidate with the top one of the other kind to ensure the diversity of the suggestions. The top suggestion will be automatically committed to the text (see Sect. 7, Part 3).

8 JustCorrect: Experiment

We evaluated the usability of three forms of JustCorrect: JustCorrect-Gesture, JustCorrect-Tap, and JustCorrect-Voice. These variations are different JustCorrect techniques with different input modalities, as explained below.

8.1 Participants

We recruited 16 participants (4 females) from 19 to 40 years old ($Mean = 26.4$, $Std. = 4.4$). All were right-handed. The self-reported median familiarity with tap typing, gesture typing, and voice input (1: not familiar, 5: very familiar) were 5.0, 3.5, and 2.5 respectively. Seven participants had gesture typing experience. The participants were instructed to use their preferred hand posture throughout the study.

8.2 Apparatus

A Google Nexus 5X device (Qualcomm Snapdragon 808 Processor, 1.8 GHz hexa-core 64-bit Adreno 418 GPU, RAM: 2 GB LPDDR3, Internal storage: 16GB) with a 5.2-inch screen (1920×1080 LCD at 423 ppi) was used for the experiment.

8.3 Design

The study was a within-subjects design. The sole independent variable was the text correction method with four levels:

- *Cursor-based Correction*. This was identical to the existing *de facto* cursor-based text correction method on the stock Android keyboard.
- *JustCorrect-Tap*. After entering a word with tap typing, the user presses the editing button to invoke the post-hoc correction algorithm (see Fig. 11).
  Taking the sentence "a quick fox jimo over a lazy dog," for example, if the user wants to replace "jimo" with "jumps," she tap types the editing word "jumps" and then presses the editing button (see Fig. 11). The post-hoc correction algorithm takes "jumps" as the editing word and outputs "a quick fox jumps over a lazy dog."
- *JustCorrect-Gesture*. A user performed JustCorrect with gesture typing [29, 63, 64]. After entering the correction word w^* with a gesture and the finger lifts off, the system applied the post-hoc correction algorithm to correct the existing phrase with the word. The other interactions were the same as those in JustCorrect-Tap. The only difference is that in JustCorrect-Tap, a button was used to trigger JustCorrect because tap typing required a signal to indicate the end of inputting a word, while this step is omitted in JustCorrect-Gesture because gesture typing naturally indicates the end of entering a word when the finger lifts.
- *JustCorrect-Voice*. A user performed JustCorrect with voice input. The user first pressed the voice input button on the keyboard and spoke the editing word. The post-hoc correction algorithm took the recognized word from a speech-to-text recognition engine as the editing word w^* to edit the phrase. We used the Microsoft Azure speech-to-text engine [5] for speech recognition. The remaining interactions were identical to the previous two conditions.

8.4 Procedure

Each participant was instructed to correct errors in the same set of 60 phrases in each condition, and the orders of the sentences were randomized. We randomly chose 60 phrases with omission and substitution errors from mobile typing dataset of Palin et al. [42]. This dataset included actual input errors from 37, 370 users when

Table 4 Examples of phrases in the experiment. The first three sentences contained substitution errors. The last sentence contained an omission error

Sentences with errors	Target sentences
1. Tjank for sending this	Thanks for sending this
2. Should systematic manage the migration	Should systems manage the migration
3. Try ir again and let me know	Try it again and let me know
4. Kind like silent fireworks	Kind of like silent fireworks

typing with smartphones and their target sentences. We focused on omission and substitution errors since the post-hoc correction algorithm was designed to handle these two types of errors. We also filtered out sentences with punctuation or number errors because our focus was on word correction. Among 60 phrases, 8 contained omission errors and the rest contained substitution errors. The average (SD) edit distance between the sentence with errors and target sentences was 1.9(1.2). Each phrase contained an average (SD) of 1.1(0.3) errors. The average length of a target phrase in this experiment was 37 ± 14 characters. The largest phrase length was 68 characters, and the shortest was 16 characters. Table 4 shows four examples of phrases in experiment.

In each trial, participants were instructed to correct errors in the "input phrase" so that it matched the "target phrase" using the designated editing method. Both the input phrase and the target phrase were displayed on the screen. The errors in the input phrase were underlined to minimize the cognitive effort required to identify errors across conditions, as shown in Fig. 12. The participants were required to correct errors in their current trial before advancing to their next trial.

Should a participant fail to correct the errors in the current trial, they could use the *undo* button to revert the correction and redo it, or use the *de facto* cursor-based editing method. We kept the cursor-based method as a fallback in each editing condition because our JustCorrect techniques were proposed to *augment* rather than *replace* it. We recorded the number of trials corrected by this fallback mechanism in order to measure the effectiveness of each JustCorrect technique.

Prior to each condition, each participant completed a warm-up session to familiarize themselves with each method. The sentences in the warm-up session were different from those in the formal test. After the completion of each condition, participants took a 3-minute break. The order of the four conditions was counterbalanced using a balanced Latin Square.

In total, the experiment included: 16 participants $\times$ 4 conditions $\times$ 60 trials = 3,840 trials.

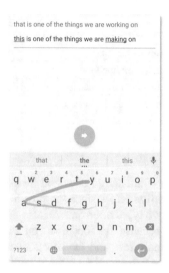

Fig. 12 A user editing a sentence using *JustCorrect-Gesture*. The target sentence is displayed at the top of the screen, and the sentence with errors is displayed below. The underlines show two errors in the phrase: this –> that, making –> working. The user is shown gesture typing the word *that* to correct the first error

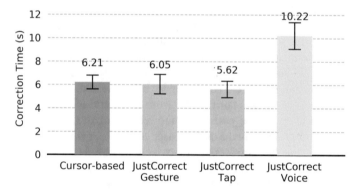

Fig. 13 Mean (95% CI) text correction times for each method for successful trials

8.5   *Results*

8.5.1   Text Correction Time

We defined the "text correction time" as the duration from when a sentence was displayed on the screen to when it was submitted and completely revised. Thus, this metric conveys the efficiency of each JustCorrect text correction technique.

Figure 13 shows text correction time for trials that were successfully corrected using the designated editing method in each condition (unsuccessful trials are

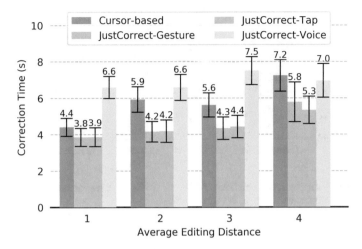

Fig. 14 Mean (95% CI) text correction times for the tasks successfully completed on the first attempt

described below in the next subsection). The mean $\pm$ 95% CI of text correction time was 6.21 ± 0.59 s for the *de facto* cursor-based technique, 6.05 ± 0.83 s for JustCorrect-Gesture, 5.62 ± 0.70 s for JustCorrect-Tap, and 10.22 ± 1.14 s for JustCorrect-Voice. A repeated measures ANOVA showed that the text correction technique had a significant main effect on overall trial time ($F_{3,45} = 71.96$, $p < 0.001$). Pairwise comparisons with Bonferroni correction showed that differences were statistically significant between all pairs ($p < 0.001$) except for JustCorrect-Tap versus JustCorrect-Gesture ($p = 0.17$) and JustCorrect-Gesture versus the cursor-based technique ($p = 0.67$).

To understand the effectiveness of the algorithm under different conditions, we analyzed cases that were successfully edited in the first editing attempt. In total, there were 3328 such trials, among 3840 total trials. We grouped these trials by edit distance between the target sentence and the incorrect sentence. The average text correction times on different methods are shown in Fig. 14. When the edit distance was 1, the correction times in *de facto* cursor-based technique were close to those in the gesture-based and tap-based techniques. When the edit distance was 2, 3, or 4, the gesture- and tap-based techniques were faster than the *de facto* baseline.

8.5.2 Success Rate

We define the success rate as the percentage of correct trials out of all trials for a given correction technique. Figure 15 shows success rates across conditions. The mean $\pm$ 95% CI for success rate for each input technique was: $100.0 \pm 0\%$ for the *de facto* cursor-based technique, $96.2 \pm 2.2\%$ for JustCorrect-Gesture, $97.1 \pm 0.03\%$ for JustCorrect-Tap, and $95.1 \pm 0.03\%$ for JustCorrect-Voice. A repeated measures

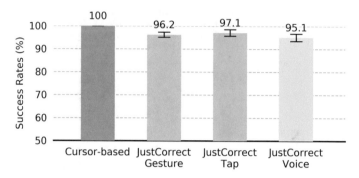

Fig. 15 Success rate by input technique. While not 100%, the three interactions of JustCorrect achieved pretty close success rate to the cursor-based interaction

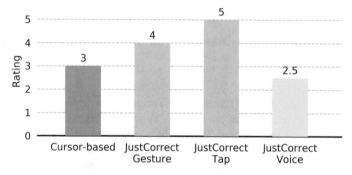

Fig. 16 The median preference rating for cursor-based correction, JustCorrect-Gesture, JustCorrect-Tap, and JustCorrect-Voice. JustCorrect Tap received the highest rating

ANOVA showed that text editing technique had a significant effect on the overall success rate ($F_{3,45} = 14.31$, $p < 0.001$). Pairwise comparisons with Bonferroni correction showed the difference was significant between JustCorrect-Tap versus cursor-based, JustCorrect-Gesture versus cursor-based, JustCorrect-Voice versus cursor-based ($p < 0.01$). All other pairwise comparisons were not statistically significant.

8.5.3 Subjective Feedback

At the end of the study, we asked the participants to rate each method on a scale of 1 to 5 (1: dislike, 5: like). As shown in Fig. 16, the median rating for cursor-based editing, JustCorrect-Gesture, JustCorrect-Tap, and JustCorrect-Voice were 3.0, 4.0, 5.0, and 2.5, respectively. A non-parametric Friedman test of differences among repeated measure was carried out to compare the ratings for the four conditions. There was a significant difference between the methods ($X_r^2(3) = 17.29$, $p < 0.001$).

Participants were also asked which method(s) they would like to use during text entry on their phones. Twelve participants mentioned they would use JustCorrect-Tap and eight would also like to use JustCorrect-Gesture. Six participants also considered the *de facto* cursor-based method useful, especially for revising short words or character-level errors. Only two participants liked to use JustCorrect-Voice for text editing, while most participants had privacy concerns about using it in a public environment.

8.6   Discussion

We introduced two projects in this chapter: Type, Then Correct (TTC), and JustCorrect. We first discuss the user study results of TTC, followed by the discussion of JustCorrect.

In TTC, *Drag-n-Throw* performed fastest among different correction types. Moreover, its performance was not affected by whether the error was far away or not (Fig. 8). *Magic Key* also achieved reasonable speeds across different correction types. For *near-errors* within the last three words, it even surpassed *Drag-n-Throw*, because the errors would be highlighted and corrected with just two taps. For *far-errors*, participants had to drag atop the *Magic Key* a few times to highlight the desired error, leading to longer correction times. *Drag-n-Drop* performed the slowest over all phrases, which was mainly caused by the insertion corrections. As shown in Fig. 9, it was faster than the de facto cursor-based method for typos and word changes, but significantly slower than other interactions for insertions. To insert a correction between two words, a user had to highlight the narrow space between those words. Many participants spent a lot of time adjusting their fingers in order to highlight the desired space. They also had to redo the correction if they accidentally made a substitution instead of an insertion. Our undo key proved to be vital in such cases. To evaluate the performance of our algorithm in more realistic scenarios, we analyzed the results from text composition tasks. *Drag-n-Throw* achieved a success rate of 87.9%. A failure was when two possible error candidates were too close to each other. For example, if the user wanted to insert "the" in the phrase "I left keys in room," there were two possible positions (before keys and before room), but only one of them would be corrected. *Magic Key* achieved a higher success rate of 97.0%, as it searched every possible error in the text.

As for participants' subjective preferences, 12 of 20 participants liked *Magic Key* the most. The major reason was convenience: all the actions were done on the keyboard. P1 commented, "Just one button handles everything. I don't need to touch the text anymore. It was also super intelligent. I am lazy, and that's why I enjoyed it so much." Another reason was that *Magic Key* provided feedback (highlights) before committing the correction, making the user confident about the target of their actions. As P4 pointed out, "It provides multiple choices, and the uncertain feeling is gone." The main critique of *Magic Key* was about the dragging interaction required to move among error candidates. P5 commented: "If the text is too long and the error is far away, I have to drag a lot to highlight the error. Also, the button is kinda small, and hard to drag."

Interestingly, we found that all three participants above age 40 had positive feedback about the two intelligent correction techniques, and negative feedback about the *de facto* cursor-based method. P14, aged 52, commented, "I dislike the cursor-based method most. I have a big finger, and it is hard to tap the text precisely. Throw is easy and works great. I also like *Magic Key*, because I don't need to interact with the text." Older adults are known to perform touch screen interactions more slowly and with less precision than younger adults [14], and the intelligent correction techniques might benefit them by removing the requirement of precise touch. Moreover, people walking on the street or holding the phone with one hand might also benefit from the interactions, because touching precisely is difficult in such situations.

In JustCorrect, our investigation led to the following findings. First, both JustCorrect-Gesture and JustCorrect-Tap showed good potential as correction methods. Both JustCorrect-Gesture and JustCorrect-Tap successfully corrected more than 95% of the input phrases. They both saved average correction time over the *de facto* cursor-based correction method. These two methods were especially beneficial for correcting sentences with large editing distances relative to the target sentences. As shown in Fig. 14, for sentences with an editing distance of 4, JustCorrect-Gesture and JustCorrect-Tap reduced correction time by nearly 30% over the cursor-based method.

Second, JustCorrect-Gesture and JustCorrect-Tap exhibited their own pros and cons. Participants had differing preferences: users who were familiar with gesture typing liked JustCorrect-Gesture because it did not require pressing the editing button, while other participants preferred JustCorrect-Tap because they mostly used tap typing for text entry. JustCorrect-Gesture saved the editing button-tap compared to JustCorrect-Tap because gesture typing naturally signals the end of entering a word by the lifting of the finger. On the other hand, in JustCorrect-Gesture, gesture typing is used to correct text only, limiting its scope of usage.

Third, contrary to the promising performance of JustCorrect-Gesture and JustCorrect-Tap, JustCorrect-Voice under-performed. The reason was that JustCorrect required a user to first enter the editing word. However, the existing speech-to-text recognition engine often performed poorly when recognizing a single word in isolation, especially for short words. We discovered that entering common words such as *for*, *to*, and *are* are challenging when using voice, which caused difficulty in correcting phrases with errors on these words.

There is an exciting point in both projects: employing the power of machine learning to automate the text correction and realize interactions that were not possible before. The advantage of deep learning is that longer context can be incorporated in the language models than the traditional n-gram-based methods, which enables the models to "understand" the intention of the user on a deeper level.

8.7   Future Work

On the basis of our work here, we propose four possible future directions: (1) Punctuation handling: currently both TTC and JustCorrect do not handle punctuation, so errors like "lets" (let's) currently cannot be corrected. (2) Adding better feedback mechanics to reduce the uncertainty of the outcome: although the interactions were intelligent and did the work right most of the time, they were not transparent to the user, and the outcome of the interactions was not obvious. For example, participants felt unconfident when using the *Drag-n-Throw*, as there was a lack of feedback as to where the corrections would be applied. Adding proper feedback, such as highlighting the surrounding text of the throwing position to provide cues about where the correction will occur. (3) Multilingual correction support: the two interaction techniques could be applied to other languages as well, such as the Chinese language. (5) Interactions beyond keyboard correction: the concept can also be applied to other correction scenarios, such as voice input and handwriting.

9   Conclusion

In this chapter, we demonstrated how artificial intelligence could be applied to the text correction interaction on touch screens. The first project, Type, Then Correct (TTC), includes three novel interaction techniques with one common concept: to type the correction and apply it to the error, without needing to reposition the text cursor or use backspace, which break the typing flow and slow touch-based text entry. The second project, JustCorrect, brought the concept further by removing the need to manually specify the error position. Both projects utilized machine learning algorithms in NLP fields to help identify the possible error text. The user studies showed that both TTC and JustCorrect were significantly faster than *de facto* cursor-based correction methods and garnered more positive user feedback. They provide examples of how, by breaking from the desktop paradigm of arrow keys, backspacing, and mouse-based cursor positioning, we can rethink text entry on mobile touch devices and develop novel methods better suited to this paradigm.

References

1. Agirre E, Cer D, Diab M, Gonzalez-Agirre A, Guo W (2013) *SEM 2013 shared task: semantic textual similarity. In: Second joint conference on lexical and computational semantics (*SEM), Volume 1: Proceedings of the main conference and the shared task: semantic textual similarity, Association for Computational Linguistics, Atlanta, Georgia, USA, pp 32–43. https://www.aclweb.org/anthology/S13-1004
2. Apple (2018) About the keyboards settings on your iphone, ipad, and ipod touch. https://support.apple.com/en-us/HT202178. Accessed 22 Aug 2019

3. Arif AS, Stuerzlinger W (2013) Pseudo-pressure detection and its use in predictive text entry on touchscreens. In: Proceedings of the 25th australian computer-human interaction conference: augmentation, application, innovation, collaboration, Association for Computing Machinery, New York, NY, USA, OzCHI '13, p 383–392. https://doi.org/10.1145/2541016.2541024

4. Arif AS, Kim S, Stuerzlinger W, Lee G, Mazalek A (2016) Evaluation of a smart-restorable backspace technique to facilitate text entry error correction. In: Proceedings of the 2016 CHI conference on human factors in computing systems, Association for Computing Machinery, New York, NY, USA, CHI '16, pp 5151–5162. https://doi.org/10.1145/2858036.2858407

5. Azure M (2019) Text to speech api. https://azure.microsoft.com/en-us/services/cognitive-services/text-to-speech/. Accessed 25 Aug 2019

6. Bahdanau D, Cho K, Bengio Y (2016) Neural machine translation by jointly learning to align and translate. 1409.0473

7. Benko H, Wilson AD, Baudisch P (2006) Precise selection techniques for multi-touch screens. In: Proceedings of the SIGCHI conference on human factors in computing systems, Association for Computing Machinery, New York, NY, USA, CHI '06, pp 1263–1272. https://doi.org/10.1145/1124772.1124963

8. Brooke J (2013) Sus: a retrospective. J Usability Studies 8(2):29–40

9. Cho K, van Merriënboer B, Gulcehre C, Bahdanau D, Bougares F, Schwenk H, Bengio Y (2014) Learning phrase representations using RNN encoder–decoder for statistical machine translation. In: Proceedings of the 2014 conference on empirical methods in natural language processing (EMNLP), Association for Computational Linguistics, Doha, Qatar, pp 1724–1734. https://doi.org/10.3115/v1/D14-1179. https://www.aclweb.org/anthology/D14-1179

10. Cui W, Zhu S, Zhang MR, Schwartz A, Wobbrock JO, Bi X (2020) Justcorrect: Intelligent post hoc text correction techniques on smartphones. In: Proceedings of the 33rd annual ACM symposium on user interface software and technology, Association for Computing Machinery, New York, NY, USA, UIST '20, pp 487–499. https://doi.org/10.1145/3379337.3415857

11. Davies M (2018) The corpus of contemporary American english: 1990-present

12. Dhakal V, Feit AM, Kristensson PO, Oulasvirta A (2018) Observations on Typing from 136 Million Keystrokes, Association for Computing Machinery, New York, NY, USA, pp 1–12. https://doi.org/10.1145/3173574.3174220

13. Erk K (2012) Vector space models of word meaning and phrase meaning: a survey. Lang Ling Compass 6(10):635–653

14. Findlater L, Froehlich JE, Fattal K, Wobbrock JO, Dastyar T (2013) Age-related differences in performance with touchscreens compared to traditional mouse input. In: Proceedings of the SIGCHI conference on human factors in computing systems, Association for Computing Machinery, New York, NY, USA, CHI '13, pp 343–346. https://doi.org/10.1145/2470654.2470703

15. Fitzmaurice G, Khan A, Pieké R, Buxton B, Kurtenbach G (2003) Tracking menus. In: Proceedings of the 16th Annual ACM symposium on user interface software and technology, Association for Computing Machinery, New York, NY, USA, UIST '03, pp. 71–79. https://doi.org/10.1145/964696.964704

16. Fowler A, Partridge K, Chelba C, Bi X, Ouyang T, Zhai S (2015) Effects of language modeling and its personalization on touchscreen typing performance. In: Proceedings of the 33rd Annual ACM conference on human factors in computing systems, Association for Computing Machinery, New York, NY, USA, CHI '15, pp. 649–658. https://doi.org/10.1145/2702123.2702503

17. Frederick BN (1999) Fixed-, random-, and mixed-effects anova models: a user-friendly guide for increasing the generalizability of anova results. Advances in social science methodology, Stamford. JAI Press, CT, pp 111–122

18. Fuccella V, Isokoski P, Martin B (2013) Gestures and widgets: performance in text editing on multi-touch capable mobile devices. In: Proceedings of the SIGCHI conference on human factors in computing systems, ACM, New York, NY, USA, CHI '13, pp 2785–2794. https://doi.org/10.1145/2470654.2481385, http://doi.acm.org/10.1145/2470654.2481385

19. Heafield K (2011) KenLM: faster and smaller language model queries. In: Proceedings of the EMNLP 2011 sixth workshop on statistical machine translation, Edinburgh, Scotland, United Kingdom, pp 187–197. https://kheafield.com/papers/avenue/kenlm.pdf
20. Holm S (1979) A simple sequentially rejective multiple test procedure. Scand J Stat 6(2):65–70. http://www.jstor.org/stable/4615733
21. Holz C, Baudisch P (2011) Understanding touch. In: Proceedings of the SIGCHI conference on human factors in computing systems, Association for Computing Machinery, New York, NY, USA, CHI '11, pp 2501–2510. https://doi.org/10.1145/1978942.1979308
22. Inc E (2018) Messagease - the smartest touch screen keyboard. https://www.exideas.com/ME/index.php. Accessed 22 Aug 2019
23. Inc G (2020) Grammarly keyboard. https://en.wikipedia.org/wiki/Grammarly. Accessed May 2020
24. Islam A, Inkpen D (2009) Real-word spelling correction using google web it 3-grams. In: Proceedings of the 2009 conference on empirical methods in natural language processing: Volume 3 - Volume 3, Association for Computational Linguistics, USA, EMNLP '09, pp 1241–1249
25. Isokoski P, Martin B, Gandouly P, Stephanov T (2010) Motor efficiency of text entry in a combination of a soft keyboard and unistrokes. In: Proceedings of the 6th Nordic conference on human-computer interaction: extending boundaries, ACM, New York, NY, USA, NordiCHI '10, pp 683–686. https://doi.org/10.1145/1868914.1869004. http://doi.acm.org/10.1145/1868914.1869004
26. Kim Y, Jernite Y, Sontag D, Rush AM (2016) Character-aware neural language models. In: Proceedings of the Thirtieth AAAI conference on artificial intelligence, AAAI Press, AAAI'16, pp 2741–2749
27. Komninos A, Nicol E, Dunlop MD (2015) Designed with older adults to support better error correction in smartphone text entry: the maxiekeyboard. In: Proceedings of the 17th international conference on human-computer interaction with mobile devices and services adjunct, Association for Computing Machinery, New York, NY, USA, MobileHCI '15, pp 797–802. https://doi.org/10.1145/2786567.2793703
28. Komninos A, Dunlop M, Katsaris K, Garofalakis J (2018) A glimpse of mobile text entry errors and corrective behaviour in the wild. In: Proceedings of the 20th international conference on human-computer interaction with mobile devices and services adjunct, Association for Computing Machinery, New York, NY, USA, MobileHCI '18, pp 221–228. https://doi.org/10.1145/3236112.3236143
29. Kristensson PO, Zhai S (2004) Shark2: a large vocabulary shorthand writing system for pen-based computers. In: Proceedings of the 17th annual ACM symposium on user interface software and technology, ACM, New York, NY, USA, UIST '04, pp 43–52. https://doi.org/10.1145/1029632.1029640. http://doi.acm.org/10.1145/1029632.1029640
30. Leiva LA, Sahami A, Catala A, Henze N, Schmidt A (2015) Text entry on tiny qwerty soft keyboards. In: Proceedings of the 33rd annual ACM conference on human factors in computing systems, Association for Computing Machinery, New York, NY, USA, CHI '15, pp 669–678. https://doi.org/10.1145/2702123.2702388
31. Levenshtein VI (1965) Binary codes capable of correcting deletions, insertions, and reversals. Soviet Phys Doklady 10:707–710
32. Limpert E, Stahel WA, Abbt M (2001) Log-normal distributions across the sciences: keys and clues: on the charms of statistics, and how mechanical models resembling gambling machines offer a link to a handy way to characterize log-normal distributions, which can provide deeper insight into variability and probability–normal or log-normal: that is the question. BioScience 51(5):341–352. https://doi.org/10.1641/0006-3568(2001)051[0341:LNDATS]2.0.CO;2. https://academic.oup.com/bioscience/article-pdf/51/5/341/26891292/51-5-341.pdf
33. Littell R, Henry P, Ammerman C (1998) Statistical analysis of repeated measures data using sas procedures. J Animal Sci 76(4):1216–1231. https://doi.org/10.2527/1998.7641216x
34. LLC G (2020) Gboard. URLhttps://en.wikipedia.org/wiki/Gboard. Accessed May 2020

35. MacKenzie IS, Soukoreff RW (2002) A character-level error analysis technique for evaluating text entry methods. In: Proceedings of the second nordic conference on human-computer interaction, Association for Computing Machinery, New York, NY, USA, NordiCHI '02, pp 243–246. https://doi.org/10.1145/572020.572056

36. MacKenzie IS, Soukoreff RW (2002) Text entry for mobile computing: Models and methods,theory and practice. Hum-Comput Int 17(2-3):147–198. https://doi.org/10.1080/07370024.2002.9667313. https://www.tandfonline.com/doi/abs/10.1080/07370024.2002.9667313

37. Mahoney M (2011) About text8 file. http://mattmahoney.net/dc/textdata.html. Accessed May 2020

38. Mikolov T, Chen K, Corrado GS, Dean J (2013) Efficient estimation of word representations in vector space. arXiv:1301.3781

39. Ng HT, Wu SM, Wu Y, Hadiwinoto C, Tetreault J (2013) The CoNLL-2013 shared task on grammatical error correction. In: Proceedings of the seventeenth conference on computational natural language learning: shared task, Association for Computational Linguistics, Sofia, Bulgaria, pp 1–12. https://www.aclweb.org/anthology/W13-3601

40. Ng HT, Wu SM, Briscoe T, Hadiwinoto C, Susanto RH, Bryant C (2014) The CoNLL-2014 shared task on grammatical error correction. In: Proceedings of the eighteenth conference on computational natural language learning: shared task, Association for Computational Linguistics, Baltimore, Maryland, pp 1–14. https://doi.org/10.3115/v1/W14-1701. https://www.aclweb.org/anthology/W14-1701

41. Ola Kristensson P, Vertanen K (2011) Asynchronous multimodal text entry using speech and gesture keyboards. In: Proceedings of the international conference on spoken language processing, pp 581–584

42. Palin K, Feit A, Kim S, Kristensson PO, Oulasvirta A (2019) How do people type on mobile devices? Observations from a study with 37,000 volunteers. In: Proceedings of 21st international conference on human-computer interaction with mobile devices and services (Mobile-HCI'19), ACM

43. Paszke A, Gross S, Massa F, Lerer A, Bradbury J, Chanan G, Killeen T, Lin Z, Gimelshein N, Antiga L, Desmaison A, Kopf A, Yang E, DeVito Z, Raison M, Tejani A, Chilamkurthy S, Steiner B, Fang L, Bai J, Chintala S (2019) Pytorch: an imperative style, high-performance deep learning library. In: Wallach H, Larochelle H, Beygelzimer A, d' Alché-Buc F, Fox E, Garnett R (eds) Advances in neural information processing systems 32, Curran Associates, Inc., pp 8024–8035. http://papers.neurips.cc/paper/9015-pytorch-an-imperative-style-high-performance-deep-learning-library.pdf

44. Pennington J, Socher R, Manning C (2014) GloVe: global vectors for word representation. In: Proceedings of the 2014 conference on empirical methods in natural language processing (EMNLP), Association for Computational Linguistics, Doha, Qatar, pp 1532–1543. https://doi.org/10.3115/v1/D14-1162. https://www.aclweb.org/anthology/D14-1162

45. Řehůřek R, Sojka P (2010) Software framework for topic modelling with large corpora. In: Proceedings of the LREC 2010 workshop on new challenges for NLP frameworks, ELRA, Valletta, Malta, pp 45–50. http://is.muni.cz/publication/884893/en

46. Ruan S, Wobbrock JO, Liou K, Ng A, Landay JA (2018) Comparing speech and keyboard text entry for short messages in two languages on touchscreen phones. Proc ACM Interact Mob Wearable Ubiquitous Technol 1(4). https://doi.org/10.1145/3161187

47. Rubio S, Díaz EM, Martín J, Puente J (2004) Evaluation of subjective mental workload: a comparison of swat, nasa-tlx, and workload profile methods. Appl Psychol 53:61–86

48. Schmidt D, Block F, Gellersen H (2009) A comparison of direct and indirect multi-touch input for large surfaces. In: Gross T, Gulliksen J, Kotzé P, Oestreicher L, Palanque P, Prates RO, Winckler M (eds) Human-computer interaction - INTERACT 2009. Springer, Berlin, pp 582–594

49. Sears A, Shneiderman B (1991) High precision touchscreens: design strategies and comparisons with a mouse. Int J Man Mach Stud 34:593–613

50. Sim KC (2010) Haptic voice recognition: Augmenting speech modality with touch events for efficient speech recognition. In: 2010 IEEE spoken language technology workshop, pp 73–78. https://doi.org/10.1109/SLT.2010.5700825
51. Sim KC (2012) Speak-as-you-swipe (says): A multimodal interface combining speech and gesture keyboard synchronously for continuous mobile text entry. In: Proceedings of the 14th ACM international conference on multimodal interaction, ACM, New York, NY, USA, ICMI '12, pp 555–560. https://doi.org/10.1145/2388676.2388793. http://doi.acm.org/10.1145/2388676.2388793
52. Sindhwani S, Lutteroth C, Weber G (2019) Retype: Quick text editing with keyboard and gaze. In: Proceedings of the 2019 CHI conference on human factors in computing systems, ACM, New York, NY, USA, CHI '19, pp 203:1–203:13. https://doi.org/10.1145/3290605.3300433. http://doi.acm.org/10.1145/3290605.3300433
53. Soukoreff RW, MacKenzie IS (2004) Recent developments in text-entry error rate measurement. In: CHI '04 extended abstracts on human factors in computing systems, Association for Computing Machinery, New York, NY, USA, CHI EA '04, pp 1425–1428. https://doi.org/10.1145/985921.986081
54. Sutskever I, Vinyals O, Le QV (2014) Sequence to sequence learning with neural networks. In: Proceedings of the 27th international conference on neural information processing systems - Volume 2, MIT Press, Cambridge, MA, USA, NIPS'14, pp 3104–3112
55. Vertanen K, Memmi H, Emge J, Reyal S, Kristensson PO (2015) Velocitap: Investigating fast mobile text entry using sentence-based decoding of touchscreen keyboard input. In: Proceedings of the 33rd annual ACM conference on human factors in computing systems, Association for Computing Machinery, New York, NY, USA, CHI '15, pp 659–668. https://doi.org/10.1145/2702123.2702135
56. Vogel D, Baudisch P (2007) Shift: a technique for operating pen-based interfaces using touch. In: Proceedings of the SIGCHI conference on human factors in computing systems, Association for Computing Machinery, New York, NY, USA, CHI '07, pp 657–666. https://doi.org/10.1145/1240624.1240727
57. Wagner RA, Fischer MJ (1974) The string-to-string correction problem. J ACM (JACM) 21(1):168–173
58. Weidner K (2018) Hackers keyboard. http://code.google.com/p/hackerskeyboard/. Accessed 22 Aug 2019
59. Wobbrock JO, Myers BA (2006) Analyzing the input stream for character- level errors in unconstrained text entry evaluations. ACM Trans Comput-Hum Interact 13(4):458–489. https://doi.org/10.1145/1188816.1188819
60. Xie Z, Avati A, Arivazhagan N, Jurafsky D, Ng A (2016) Neural language correction with character-based attention. ArXiv:1603.09727
61. Young T, Hazarika D, Poria S, Cambria E (2018) Recent trends in deep learning based natural language processing [review article]. IEEE Comput Intell Mag 13:55–75
62. Zesch T (2012) Measuring contextual fitness using error contexts extracted from the Wikipedia revision history. In: Proceedings of the 13th conference of the European chapter of the association for computational linguistics, Association for Computational Linguistics, Avignon, France, pp 529–538. https://www.aclweb.org/anthology/E12-1054
63. Zhai S, Kristensson PO (2003) Shorthand writing on stylus keyboard. In: Proceedings of the SIGCHI conference on human factors in computing systems, Association for Computing Machinery, New York, NY, USA, CHI '03, pp 97–104. https://doi.org/10.1145/642611.642630
64. Zhai S, Kristensson PO (2012) The word-gesture keyboard: reimagining keyboard interaction. Commun ACM 55(9):91–101. https://doi.org/10.1145/2330667.2330689
65. Zhang MR, Wobbrock OJ (2020) Gedit: keyboard gestures for mobile text editing. In: Proceedings of graphics interface (GI '20), Canadian information processing society, Toronto, Ontario, GI '20, pp 97–104
66. Zhang MR, Wen H, Wobbrock JO (2019) Type, then correct: intelligent text correction techniques for mobile text entry using neural networks. In: Proceedings of the 32nd annual ACM symposium on user interface software and technology, Association for Computing Machinery, New York, NY, USA, UIST '19, pp 843–855. https://doi.org/10.1145/3332165.3347924

67. Zhang X, Zhao J, LeCun Y (2015) Character-level convolutional networks for text classification. In: Proceedings of the 28th international conference on neural information processing systems - Volume 1, MIT Press, Cambridge, MA, USA, NIPS'15, pp 649–657
68. Zhu S, Luo T, Bi X, Zhai S (2018) Typing on an invisible keyboard. In: Proceedings of the 2018 CHI Conference on human factors in computing systems, Association for Computing Machinery, New York, NY, USA, CHI '18, pp 1–13. https://doi.org/10.1145/3173574.3174013

Deep Touch: Sensing Press Gestures from Touch Image Sequences

Philip Quinn, Wenxin Feng, and Shumin Zhai

Abstract Capacitive touch sensors capture a sequence of images of a finger's interaction with a surface that contain information about its contact shape, posture, and biomechanical structure. These images are typically reduced to two-dimensional points, with the remaining data discarded—restricting the expressivity that can be captured to discriminate a user's touch intent. We develop a *deep touch* hypothesis that (1) the human finger performs richer expressions on a touch surface than simple pointing; (2) such expressions are manifested in touch sensor image sequences due to finger-surface biomechanics; and (3) modern neural networks are capable of discriminating touch gestures using these sequences. In particular, a *press* gesture based on an increase in a finger's force can be sensed without additional hardware, and reliably discriminated from other common expressions. This work demonstrates that combining capacitive touch sensing with modern neural network algorithms is a practical direction to improve the usability and expressivity of touch-based user interfaces.

1 Introduction

Touch interaction is predominantly driven by two-dimensional pointing—where a user's contact on a surface is reduced to a single point (its *centroid*), with criteria placed on its spatiotemporal properties to define various gestures [14, 15]. The most common of these gestures in contemporary touch interaction are *tapping, long press-*

P. Quinn · W. Feng · S. Zhai (✉)
Google, Mountain View, CA, USA
e-mail: zhai@acm.org

P. Quinn
e-mail: philip@quinn.gen.nz

W. Feng
e-mail: wenxinfeng@google.com

© The Author(s), under exclusive license to Springer Nature Switzerland AG 2021   169
Y. Li and O. Hilliges (eds.), *Artificial Intelligence for Human Computer Interaction:*
A Modern Approach, Human–Computer Interaction Series,
https://doi.org/10.1007/978-3-030-82681-9_6

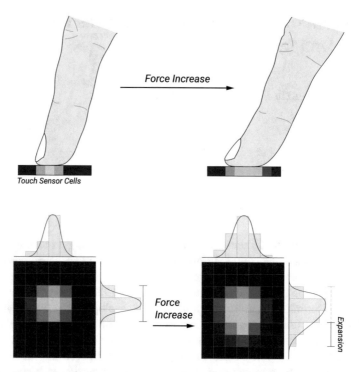

Fig. 1 An illustration of a *press* gesture: a user's finger contacts a touch sensor and deforms as the force behind it increases (top); this deformation is observed as a unilateral expansion on the sensor image (bottom)

ing (*touch and hold*), and *scrolling* (panning, dragging, flicking, and surface-stroke gestures, etc.), which are modelled using a set of three heuristics: (1) if the distance from the initial contact location exceeds a hysteresis threshold, the gesture is a *scroll*; (2) if the duration since the initial contact exceeds a time threshold, the gesture is a *long press*; (3) otherwise, the gesture is a *tap* when the contact is lifted. Although this model has nurtured a broad and successful design space for interaction, it belies the rich signal that touch sensors produce. In particular, capacitive touch sensors capture an 'image' of the finger's contact shape that can reveal the evolution of a finger's posture during its contact (Fig. 1).

As *long press* relies on a latency threshold, it is the least direct, discoverable, usable, or expressive of the three gestures described. Force sensing has been explored—both academically and commercially—as a method for rectifying these problems by creating a *force press* gesture that is directly connected to an active parameter of the user's input: their finger's force. However, force sensing requires additional hardware that suffers from practical challenges in its cost and integration.

Observations and analyses of the human finger's biomechanics and the underlying touch sensor technology (capacitive sensing) suggest a complementary approach to the latency-based *long press*. In many cases, a press gesture is manifest in the subtle signals that are captured by the image sequence from a capacitive touch sensor: as a user increases their finger's force on a screen, its contact mass increases unilaterally as the strain on the most distal finger joint increases and the finger rolls downward (Figs. 1 and 6).

These raw images are difficult to analyse heuristically due to the high dimensionality of the data, temporal dependencies in the gesture, sensor noise under different environmental conditions, and the range of finger sizes and postures that may be used. However, modern neural learning techniques present an opportunity to analyse touch sensor images with a data-driven approach to classification that is robust to these variances.

We call this approach *deep touch*: a neural model for sensing touch gestures based on the biomechanical interaction of a user's finger with a touch sensor. To differentiate between gestures we use a neural network to combine complex spatial (convolutional) features from individual images with temporal (recurrent) features across a sequence of touch sensor images. We identify a set of biomechanical patterns to shape the learned features and minimise the number of parameters so that the resultant model can be used in real time without impairing system latency or responsiveness. Although this does not allow force sensing per se, it can recognise a user's intention to *press* as a discrete gesture.

In this chapter, we first present an overview of touch sensing hardware, finger-surface interaction, and the touch input design space. The overview highlights a weakness of the current touch interaction system: the lack of a direct *pressing* gesture. We then describe the deep touch model: the biomechanical patterns, neural model design, data collection methodology, and training procedure. Finally, we describe how this model was integrated into the Android gesture classification algorithm as part of Google Pixel 4 and 5 devices without incurring additional input latency.

2 Touch Sensing and Finger Interaction

2.1 Touch-Sensing Hardware

Of the techniques for detecting the presence of a human finger near an object [22, 55, 63], the most common for small-medium size mobile devices is Projected Capacitive Touch (PCT or 'p-cap'). PCT is based on the principle of *capacitive coupling* [7, 55]: when two conductive objects (*electrodes*) are brought close together, they can hold a charge between them—their *capacitance*—which becomes disrupted when another conductive object encroaches. The capacitance C of two such electrodes, separated by a dielectric material (usually glass or plastic), is given by

$$C = \epsilon_k \epsilon_0 \frac{A}{d}, \tag{1}$$

Fig. 2 A projected
capacitive touch (PCT)
sensor: two electrodes
separated by a dielectric. A
capacitive coupling is created
with a field projected from a
drive electrode and measured
on a sense electrode. This
field is disrupted when
another conductive object
(e.g. a finger) comes close

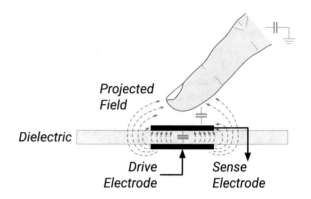

where ϵ_k is the dielectric constant of the separating material, ϵ_0 is the constant permittivity of a vacuum, A is the area of overlap between the electrodes, and d is the distance between them. When one electrode is driven (the transmitting electrode), it projects an electric field that allows C to be measured on the other (the sensing electrode). When another conductive object approaches this field, as in Fig. 2, it 'steals' some of the charge from the field by shunting it to ground through its own inherent capacitance path—reducing the steady-state C by some amount (ΔC).[1] For a human finger, this is typically on the order of $100\,\text{pF}$.

In a touch sensor on a display, these electrodes are typically made from a transparent conductor (such as indium tin oxide—ITO), and arranged as a layer of rows and a layer of columns, with the dielectric sandwiched between them [33, 59]. The locations where the electrodes overlap (the *cells*) are where ΔC is measured.

This matrix of electrodes has a much lower resolution than the pixel matrix of the underlying display—for example, the Google Pixel 4 has pixel density of roughly $20\,\text{px/mm}$, but a touch cell density of roughly $0.25\,\text{cells/mm}$. This discrepancy is resolved by a *touch controller* that performs several processing steps [38, 58]—

1. *Baselining* to remove the steady-state capacitance C when there are no touch contacts.
2. *Filtering* to remove analogue noise (e.g. from the components driving the display) and parasitic capacitance.
3. *Centroiding* to segment and interpolate the cell responses to a set of contacts and their precise locations.

Figure 3 (left) shows an example of a touch sensor's response to a $25\,\text{mm}$ metal coin after baselining and filtering. The touch sensor produces a signal that is concentrated at the centre of the coin, and with fringe fields that extend slightly beyond its bounds. The signal's high sensitivity to minute changes in an object's position allows a centroid to be resolved with sub-pixel precision.

---

[1] Sensing ΔC is known as sensing the *mutual capacitance* between electrodes. In a related (but more limited) technique, the *self capacitance* C of each electrode is measured individually [7, 55].

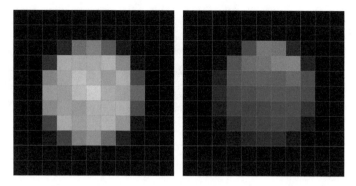

Fig. 3 A touch sensor's response to a 25 mm metal coin (left) and with a 0.5 mm plastic shim under its base (right). Each cell is 4.5 mm^2; brighter cells indicate higher ΔC values

Touch sensors are protected by a covering glass and are tuned to maximise their sensitivity to objects touching this glass—but they do not require an object to be in direct contact to produce a signal. Figure 3 (right) shows the sensor's response with a plastic shim lifting the coin at a small angle. The signal produced is a smooth gradient as the distance between the touch sensor and the coin increases. Some sensor designs can amplify this effect for sensing objects that are up to 30 cm from the sensor (e.g. [30]).

PCT does not inherently detect the force applied to a sensor as changes in force do not normally alter the capacitive properties of an object. That is, orthogonal forces applied to the finger in Fig. 2 will not change the ΔC.[2] Rather, the force on a touch surface is typically measured using a layer of Force Sensing Resistors (FSRs) or strain gauges that change their electrical resistance with forces upon them that deform the surface [45, 61].

2.2 Finger-Surface Biomechanics

A finger's contact with a touchscreen is not a rigid-body interaction. The fingertip is a soft, compliant object with complex dynamic properties. These properties produce consequential dynamic changes to the signal observed by a touch sensor when a fingertip is pressed against it.

The fingertip consists of a distal phalanx bone wrapped by a *fingertip pulp* that is mostly composed of subcutaneous fat, and a skin membrane (Fig. 4). The fingertip pulp has the properties of a viscoelastic material when it is pressed against a surface: responses are repeatable, but have hysteresis, rate-dependence, and non-linear effects [37, 39, 48, 50, 51].

---

[2] If the electrodes are allowed the 'float' with respect to each other, then changes in the distance between them from external forces can be detected by Eq. 1.

Fig. 4 The primary parts of
a fingertip

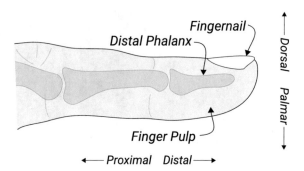

Serina and colleagues [48, 49] measured and modelled the vertical compression
and contact area responses of a fingertip pressing against a flat surface at different
angles and forces. They found the fingertip pulp was very responsive to changes at
force levels under 1 N, and quickly saturated at higher levels (e.g. 69% of the contact
area at 5.2 N of force was achieved by 1 N). The effects were robust across angles,
and were invariant to subjects' age and sex. In similar experiments, Birznieks et al.
[10] reported that most of the changes to the finger's structure occur in the fingertip
pulp, and not between the fingernail and the bone.

Sakai and Shimawaki [47] examined a finger's contact area at acute angles and
found that contact length (along the axis of the finger) increased non-linearly at force
levels under 3 N, and saturated thereafter. The change in contact length between force
levels was more pronounced as the angle of contact became more acute—caused by
a difference in dorsal and proximal pulp compliance.

Goguey et al. [19] characterised finger pitch, roll, and yaw in a series of fundamental touch operations (e.g. tapping, dragging, and flicking—see Sect. 2.3) with
each finger and the thumb. They found touch operations generally occurred at a low
pitch (less than 45°), but with significant effects for the digit used and the orientation
of the touch surface. Finger posture has also been studied in specific task contexts—
for example, Azenkot and Zhai [5] reported systematic shifts in touch distribution
patterns with different typing patterns, which were later used to improve text entry
performance [18, 62].

Even when force is not a parameter to an action, touch gestures necessarily convey
a certain force level and profile—particularly for gestures that involve extended
motion. Taher et al. [53] analysed these inherent force profiles (but explicitly not
the force level) for common interactions: tapping, typing, zooming, rotating, and
panning. They found typing and panning were generally characterised by a sharp
increase and decrease in force, with a slightly extended force plateau at the peak for
tapping actions (hypothesised to be a confirmation phase). For gestures that involved
extended interaction, force varied with the distance between the fingers (e.g. when
zooming), and with substantial variation in the profiles that included use of the thumb.

2.3 Touch Interaction Design

Touch, by its nature, encourages a direct-manipulation style of interaction. The absence of disparity in space or time (i.e. immediacy) elicits direct finger actions [34]. This is in contrast to desktop interaction, where a cursor separates an intended point of interest from an action invocation, and an input device separates the user's input from the movements of the cursor.

As a result, modern touch interactions adopt direct manipulation characterised by an instantaneous connection between the finger's action and its functional outcome: *tapping* an object activates or selects it; *dragging* or *sliding* over a distance moves an object, translates a view, or draws a stroke; and *pinching* or *spreading* adjusts a zoom factor.

An exception to direct touch interaction is the *touch and hold* (*long press*) gesture: a user first touches an object, and then holds their position for a predetermined time threshold (typically 400–500 ms). The temporal disparity from the time threshold creates a latency that separates the user's action from the system's response. That is, the system's response is triggered as a result of the user's *inaction*, rather than a parameter of their physical action. As reviewed below, this disparity has sometimes been remedied by using the force of the input as a triggering mechanism.

Direct interaction with a finger is not without costs: the finger's size (in comparison to a cursor or a stylus tip) and its necessary occlusion of targets on a touchscreen precludes very precise input—known as the *fat finger problem* [9, 28, 29, 54]. There has been substantial research on improving these accuracy problems, although typically by decreasing the directness of the interaction through intermediary devices or widgets (e.g. [1, 8, 40, 54])

2.3.1 Force-Based Interactions

Presuming that the force of a contact can be reliably measured (either with dedicated force sensors or a synthesised approximation using other available sensors), researchers have experimented with interaction use cases such as continuous input controls for scrolling [3, 6, 36], zooming [36, 52], selecting between modes of operation [13], context menus [20, 25, 60], and gesture operations [43, 44].

Researchers have also studied the benefits and limitations of 'pseudo-force' indicated by an overt 'rocking' or 'rolling' gesture [4, 8, 12, 16, 26].

Boceck et al. [11] used a neural network on individual touch sensor images to estimate static touch force. However, despite limiting their model to index-finger data at a fixed posture (with the device resting on a flat surface), their model suffered from substantial variance.

2.3.2   Developing a Deeper Touch Interaction

The touch and hold gesture is the weakest of the common touch gestures due to its indirectness: it is difficult for users to discover or perform if the time threshold is too long, or prone to misclassification as a tap gesture if the threshold is too short. These problems are particularly acute on mobile devices where there is strong demand for providing a wide range of interactive functionality within the limited physical bounds of the display and input space. Force sensing offers a possible mechanism for creating a direct *press* gesture, but has been challenged by the practical difficulties of providing it in commercial hardware.

The biomechanical interaction between the finger and a touch sensor reviewed in Sect. 2.2 suggests that there is an opportunity to use the dynamic properties of the finger to sense a more natural, direct *pressing* gesture. As touch sensor data does not inherently contain force information (Eq. 1), it is not possible to quantify the force at which a user is pressing. However, the temporal changes in the touch sensor data due to the biomechanical effects should reveal whether the force is qualitatively changing. The remainder of this chapter describes the design and development of a deep learning approach to sensing this change to provide a force-based direct *press* gesture.

3   Deep Touch Model

Deep touch aims to discriminate a user's touch intentions based on an understanding of the biomechanical interface between their finger and a capacitive touch sensor, and its temporal evolution as a gesture is performed. In particular, we aim to sense a force-based *press* gesture to create a direct means of interaction.

Instead of estimating the parameters of tap location, force level, or scroll distance, deep touch is explicitly focussed on the classification of a gesture (e.g. tapping, pressing, or scrolling). Deep touch takes a holistic and dynamic approach in processing the temporal changes in touch sensor data: rather than estimating a finger's force at each frame of data and applying a heuristic over the estimated force, the sequence of frames are considered together as to whether they represent increasing force. This is advantageous because a single touch sensor image of an arbitrary finger contact does not contain any force information, but through a sequence of such images the application of force can be observed.

We develop anticipated patterns of touch sensor signals from the reviewed biomechanical literature and apply them to specific touch-gesture designs. Each gesture is designed in terms of a finger's contact with a touch sensor: how that contact evolves over the course of the gesture and how that contact is realised in a temporal sequence of touch sensor images.

These patterns can be identified in data by a neural network that combines learned spatial features and learned temporal features. Rather than using an unconstrained deep neural network, we use the anticipated touch sensor signal patterns to limit the

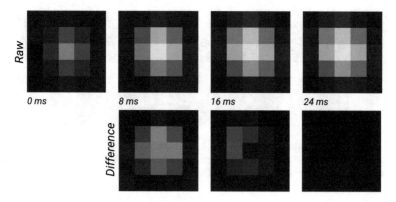

Fig. 5 A *tap* gesture observed by a touch sensor: the signal values (cell brightness) change symmetrically around the centre of mass. The top row shows the raw frames; the bottom row shows each frame's difference from the preceding frame

size of the model so that it is possible to use the network for real-time inference within the constraints of a production environment (see Sect. 4).

In the remainder of this section, we detail these biomechanical patterns of touch sensor signals and the design of the model. We then describe a data collection procedure for gathering labelled data to train the model and the results of an offline evaluation.

3.1 Touch Gesture Patterns

Although we aim to sense a force-based *press* gesture with our model, it must be able to reliably discriminate this gesture from other touch gestures, namely, *tapping* and *scrolling*. We therefore describe analyses for these three gestures in terms of the features that can be used to discriminate them.

A *tap* is conceptually the simplest touch interaction: a finger comes into symmetrical contact with a touch sensor, reaches a stable saturation point, and then disengages (lifts) from it. From the perspective of a touch sensor, the finger's contact expands symmetrically around its centre of mass (Fig. 5). There is little modulation of force after it saturates [53], and therefore the contact size or area will not further increase after the first few frames.

As a user evolves a contact into a *press* by applying more force behind their finger, the biomechanical literature informs us this will be conducive to an asymmetric contact expansion along the axis of the finger [10, 39, 47–49, 51]. This will be prominent since touch interactions generally occur at a low pitch [19]. The touch sensor will therefore observe an expansion of the contact mass in one direction, while remaining 'anchored' at one edge (Figs. 1 and 6).

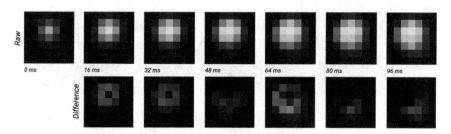

Fig. 6 A *press* gesture observed by a touch sensor: the signal values (cell brightness) change asymmetrically around the centre of mass. The top row shows the raw frames; the bottom row shows each frame's difference from the preceding frame

It is important to note this assumes that either tapping gestures will be performed with a force of less than 1 or 2 N (i.e. before the contact area saturates—[47–49]), or the speed of the force onset will be significantly different during a tap. However, an advantage of this design is its invariance to the finger used to make the contact—that is, although a thumb and little finger will have substantially different contact areas, the relative changes as force is applied will be similar.

Scrolling interactions—both *dragging* and *flicking* [42]—are primarily characterised by their contact displacement. This is facilitated in current systems by a 'touch slop' or hysteresis threshold to engage a scrolling mode (and exclude the possibility of tapping or pressing). Such a threshold is required because a contact point will rarely be stationary during tap and press interactions: jitter from the user's muscle tremor and from the unfolding contact area will retard the centroid location [56, 57].

This displacement is conveyed in the touch sensor image through changes at the fringes of a touch. If the image is held at the calculated centroid, then motion is conveyed through a consistent decrease in signal at one edge, with a matched increase in signal at the other.

3.2 Model Design

Classification of touch gestures must occur online, in real time, from continuous, variable-length time series data (i.e. without waiting for the finger to lift from the touch sensor). That is, the identification of a touch gesture should be made as soon as the user's intent is sufficiently expressed—without further perceptible delay in time (in the case of *tapping* or *pressing*) or in space (in the case of *scrolling*). The identification also needs to be incremental, and not based on the entire gesture after its completion. Such a task lends itself to classification with a recurrent neural network (RNN) (e.g. [21]): touch sensor images are input to the network as they are received, with the network's state preserved between each image. The output probability of each gesture class is updated and compared against a threshold after each image is

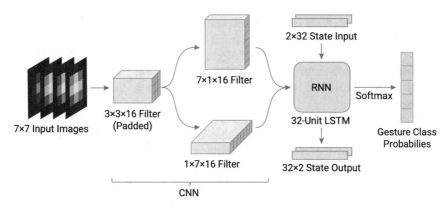

Fig. 7 An overview of the deep touch model's design

received—minimising classification latency. In particular, Long Short-Term Memory (LSTM) units allow for complex temporal patterns across the input to be identified [27].

Our model was designed to capture a learned sequence of the axial features described above, and is illustrated in Fig. 7. The input is a baselined 7×7 (16-bit; single-channel) image from the touch sensor, cropped around the calculated centroid. This image is large enough to cover all reasonable touch contacts while minimising bandwidth requirements (i.e. image data can be transmitted with centroid data at 120 Hz—the native frequency of the touch sensor).

Each touch sensor image is first passed through a convolutional neural network (CNN). The image is convolved with a 3×3 filter,[3] and is padded with zeros to produce a filtered image of the same height and width. This filtered image is processed separately by 1×7 and 7×1 filters to extract 'row' and 'column' features—reflecting the patterns of axial changes in contact mass and area. The concatenation of these features is passed into a recurrent layer (32 unit LSTM), which produces a gesture class output vector (softmax via linear activation) and a state vector. For each sequence of images the state vector is initialised with zeros, and is preserved between them.

3.3 Data Set Development

In many domains (e.g. computer vision or natural language processing), samples of natural phenomena can be collected into a corpus and used to train a model. However, interactive gestures are artificial—they are constructed by a designer that is expecting users to perform a particular set of inputs—and therefore, must be collected by eliciting them experimentally.

---

[3] All convolutional filters have a depth of 16, with ReLU activation between each operation [17].

We collected a data set of labelled capacitive touch sensor image sequences that were representative of tap, press, and scroll operations on mobile devices in three tasks: (1) a target selection task, (2) a dragging task, and (3) a search and select task. The first two tasks asked for mechanical performances of common interactions, while the third was indicative of actual interaction, and interleaved sequences of scrolling with tapping.

We collected data for both *long press* and *deep press* tasks separately: *long press* was defined using the system's standard time-based threshold of 400 ms, while *deep press* was a user-defined force gesture. Similarly, we divided *scroll* tasks into *flicking* and *dragging* tasks: *flicking* tasks were scrolling actions of medium-long distances, while *dragging* tasks were micro-scrolling movements. The data for each of these tasks were labelled with their respective categories: *tap, deep press, long press, flick*, and *drag*. The reason for these divisions was to separate different finger motions (e.g. drag and flick) that generate the same touch gesture (e.g. scroll), and ensure that the principal features of the underlying motions can be identified by the model.

3.3.1 Participants and Apparatus

Nineteen volunteers (11 male; 8 female) with an age range of 18–60 participated in the experiment and received a gift voucher for doing so. The experiment was run on a Google Pixel 4 device with a 144×67 mm display with a resolution of 3040×1440 px. The touch sensor had a resolution of 36×17 cells, and reported a 7×7 cell image centred on the cell that contained the calculated touch centroid 120 Hz.

3.3.2 Task Design

We used three interaction tasks—*target selection, dragging*, and *search-and-select*—to elicit the five classes of gestures identified earlier.

The *target selection* task (Fig. 8a) placed 12 circular targets of varying radii across the screen, and asked subjects to perform a particular touch gesture on each one (*tap, long press*, or *deep press*). Targets had their radius (105, 140 or 175 px), horizontal location (20, 50, or 80% of the screen width), and vertical location (9, 36, 64 or 91% of the screen height) randomly sampled to ensure interactions were distributed across the display. Only one target was visible at a time. Data from this task were labelled with the requested touch gesture.

Participants received haptic feedback when they were asked to long press (the system's default behaviour). However, no feedback was given for deep-press tasks in order to avoid biasing participants towards a particular biomechanical performance—any interaction on a target was recorded as a *deep press* sample.

The *dragging* task (Fig. 8b) simulated fine scrolling tasks (e.g. moving a cursor within a text field) by asking participants to drag a solid target to a hollow dock. The targets were created and displayed as with the target selection task, but with smaller target radii (70, 105 or 140 px) to simulate a fine-scrolling scenario like text

Fig. 8 The design of the
data collection tasks

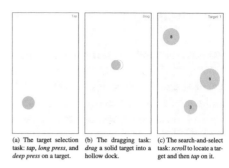

(a) The target selection task: *tap*, *long press*, and *deep press* on a target.   (b) The dragging task: *drag* a solid target into a hollow dock.   (c) The search-and-select task: *scroll* to locate a target and then *tap* on it.

selection. The dock was placed at varying distances (35, 53 or 70 px) and directions (up, down, left, right) from the target. Targets were initially blue, and turned orange with haptic feedback when they neared the dock—indicating that the task could be completed by lifting the finger. Data from this task were labelled as *drag* samples.

The *search-and-select* task (Fig. 8c) included tapping and flicking actions. Each task required participants to *scroll* and locate a circular target (using a combination of dragging and flicking), and perform a *tap* on the target. The 12 targets were created and displayed by random sampling their radius (140, 175 or 210 px), horizontal location (20, 50 or 80% of the screen width), and vertical location (25, 38 or 63% of the screen height between targets) to ensure interactions were distributed across the display. Each target had a randomly assigned label between 1 and 12, and the task proceeded sequentially through them (cued to participants in the top-right corner of the display). Data from this task were labelled as requested.

3.3.3 Procedure

Participants were encouraged to perform a deep press using their preferred force and duration (potentially shorter than the current long-press duration), and to perform the tap, long press, drag, and flick operations as usual.

Each task (one *target selection* task for each gesture, one *dragging* task, and one *search-and-select* task) was performed in a counter-balanced order, and repeated as three blocks. The tasks were repeated in each of four postures (counter-balanced): (1) one-handed using a thumb to interact, (2) two-handed using either thumb to interact, (3) one-handed using the opposing index finger to interact, and (4) in a landscape orientation with both hands, using either thumb to interact. In all postures the phone was hand-held. Participants could rest between blocks.

This procedure was repeated twice: once with a rubber case on the device, and once without a case. This ensured that touch sensor data were collected in both electrically grounded and ungrounded conditions—which have substantially different signal and noise characteristics.

3.4 Training

To train the model described above, the collected data were randomly divided into training (15 participants) and evaluation (4 participants) sets. No participant contributed samples to both sets. The model's output was configured to estimate probabilities for five classes: *tap*, *deep press*, *long press*, *flick*, and *drag*.

To isolate the portion of each sample that contained the gesture performance, the trailing 25% of each sequence was discarded. This effectively removed the portion where the participant's finger lifted from the touch sensor (i.e. after the gesture had been performed).

Each training sample was also extended to a minimum duration of 48 ms (6 frames) by linear interpolation, and truncated to a maximum duration of 120 ms (15 frames). This prevented certain touch gestures from being discriminable purely by their duration (in practice we expect to observe more variance in duration than captured in the laboratory). This processing was not applied to the samples used for evaluation.

We used the summed cross-entropy across each sequence as the loss function to minimise, with a linear temporal weight. That is, given a sequence of frames $t \in [1, T]$ with a true class distribution at each frame p_t, and a predicted class distribution at each frame q_t, the loss over the classes X was

$$\mathcal{L}(p, q, T) = -\sum_{t=1}^{T} \left[\frac{t}{T(1+T)/2} \sum_{x \in X} p_t(x) \log q_t(x) \right].$$

As with other weighted cross-entropy methods, this encourages the model to produce classifications with an increasing probability for the correct class as input is received [2, 35]. However, in our formulation the weights always summed to 1 in order to make the total loss invariant to the length of the sequence, and avoid a potential bias in the model towards classes with shorter sequences.

To reflect the temporal ambiguity in the sequence, the true class distribution was defined at each frame with a logistic function. As the first few frames of a sequence for all classes are likely to be substantially similar (i.e. at the moments a finger first contacts the touch sensor), it is unreasonable to claim there is a high likelihood in the sequence's ultimate classification for such frames (i.e. with a one-hot encoded probability distribution). Similarly, it is unreasonable to penalise the model with a high cross-entropy if it does not produce a confident prediction at these early frames. Therefore, the distribution p_t was defined to start at $1/|X|$ for all classes, and transition towards either 1 or 0, depending on the true label X for the sequence

$$p_t(x) = \begin{cases} \dfrac{1}{(|X| - 1)e^{-t+1} + 1} & x = X. \\[2ex] \dfrac{e^{-t+1}}{(|X| - 1)e^{-t+1} + 1} & x \neq X. \end{cases} \tag{2}$$

Table 1 Overall model accuracy and deep press precision/recall for the model component ablations

	Accuracy (%)	Deep press	
		Precision (%)	Recall (%)
Complete model	83	88	78
Without row/column filters	73	69	48
Without temporal labels	76	66	67

Table 2 The confusion matrix for the offline model evaluation

Actual	Predicted				
	Tap	Deep	Long	Flick	Drag
Tap	98%	–	–	–	2%
Deep	–	78%	14%	–	8%
Long	–	9%	60%	–	31%
Flick	1%	–	1%	95%	3%
Drag	2%	–	12%	7%	79%

Defining the true class distribution in this manner also helps calibrate the output probabilities and avoid spurious values in the first few frames during inference.

3.5 Results

To verify our patterns of axial change in sensor images and demonstrate the importance of using temporal weights in the loss function, we conducted ablation studies with three model variations: (1) the complete model, as described above; (2) the model trained without the 'row' and 'column' convolutional filters, (3) the model trained without the temporal labels (Eq. 2). Table 1 shows the overall accuracy and *deep press* precision/recall for these three models: the removal of the row/column filters or the temporal weights has a substantial negative effect on the model's performance.

Table 2 shows the confusion matrix for the evaluation data set, with an overall accuracy of 83%. When considering *deep press* as a binary class (i.e. *deep press* vs. *not-deep-press*), the overall accuracy is 95% with a precision of 89% and a recall of 75%.

In general, there is good separation between the classes, with the primary areas of confusion being between *deep press* and the *long press/drag* classes. However, a significant caveat with the reported *deep press* accuracy is the lack of feedback given to participants during the data collection procedure. The collected dataset was deliberately harder to classify than gestures with feedback will be in practice. That is, any action on the *deep press* targets were accepted and labelled as such, without constraint or validation. There are, likely to be poor samples in the data from either accidental touches or postures that do not produce a distinct 'press' (e.g. fingers approaching orthogonal to the display).

Creating a feedback loop would give users the opportunity to learn the distinguishing characteristics of the gesture, and drive them towards discriminating their own actions [31]. This issue is addressed in the following section.

4   System Integration and Evaluation

The prior section demonstrated that temporal changes in touch sensor images convey distinct signals that can be used to discern a force-based *press* gesture. However, the deep touch model does not eliminate the need for heuristic classification of touch gestures as not all touch intentions involve predictable finger-based interactions (e.g. a conductive stylus or certain finger postures would not exhibit the biomechanical properties described). Rather, the model provides a method for *accelerating* the recognition of a user's intentions when they are clear from the contact posture.

In this section we describe incorporating the deep touch model into the Android input system to enable its practical use [41]. This involves combining the neural deep touch model with the existing heuristic classification algorithm—allowing the neural model's signals to accelerate classification when they become manifest in the touch sensor data, but falling back to traditional classification for unusual postures or when there is ambiguity in the signal. We then describe a user study to examine the practical classification performance of this algorithm.

4.1   Gesture Classification Algorithm

The Android input system provides signals about touch gestures to applications in the three categories discussed: *tap*, *press*, and *scroll*.[4] Applications typically map *press* signals to secondary invocation functions (e.g. context menus or word selection), and so we decided to supplement this signal with our neural model classification—that is, allowing a *press* gesture to be triggered by either a *long press* or a *deep press*. This supports our goal of providing a direct touch gesture, but does not require existing applications to modify how they handle touch gestures in order to benefit from it.

Combining a probabilistic model with a heuristic algorithm also offers two benefits to users: (1) lower latency for interactions when the intention is clear from the touch expression, and (2) the certainty and reliability of a baseline in the presence of input

---

[4] https://developer.android.com/reference/android/view/GestureDetector.

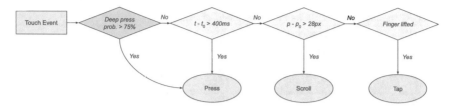

Fig. 9 An overview of the inference algorithm: the neural model is integrated into the heuristic classification pipeline to provide an acceleration for *press* gestures when the model's output indicates high confidence

ambiguity. We, therefore, prefaced the existing gesture detection algorithm (steps 2–4 below) with a decision point for the neural model's classification (Fig. 9):

1. If the neural model indicates the sequence is a 'deep press' with a probability greater than 75%, the gesture is classified as a *press*. (If the neural model indicates similar confidence in another gesture classification, then only the heuristics are used for the remainder of the sequence.)
2. If the duration since the initial contact exceeds a time threshold of 400 ms, the gesture is a *press*.
3. If the distance from the initial contact location exceeds a hysteresis threshold, the gesture is a *scroll*.
4. Otherwise, the gesture is a *tap* when the contact is lifted.

Once a sequence has been classified, it is never reconsidered.

The hysteresis threshold for *scroll* classification was dynamically set based on the output of the model: 56 px while the neural model's output was below the probability threshold of 75% for any of the gesture classes, and 28 px thereafter. That is, the threshold was doubled while the neural model expressed that the sequence was ambiguous—as it is common for some erroneous shift in the touch centroid as a finger's area expands into the touch sensor during a press.

This algorithm allows the heuristic criteria to identify *tap* and *long-press* gestures when the model is unable to confirm an interaction as a *press*. However, the model's training on five classes allows it to learn the discriminating characteristics of all possible interactions.

The neural model was implemented using TensorFlow Lite with an on-disk size of 167 kB, and a runtime memory load of less than 1 MB. When executing the model on a Google Pixel 4 device, inference time averages 50 µs per input frame. This allows the model to execute for each image received from the touch sensor (i.e. at 120 Hz) and report its results to applications without impacting touch latency or system performance.

Table 3 The confusion matrix for the online model evaluation

Actual	Predicted		
	Tap	Press	Scroll
Tap	99%	1%	–
Press	4%	88%	8%
Scroll	–	2%	98%

4.2 Evaluation

We conducted an evaluation of the algorithm to examine its performance. The evaluation followed a similar design and procedure as the data collection described earlier, but with two key differences: (1) haptic feedback was given to subjects when a *deep press* was detected (matching that for *long press*), and (2) the targets in the *search-and-select* task were either labelled *tap* or *press* (not just *tap*) to simulate realistic usage of the two touch expressions.

The gesture prompts to participants were the same as during data collection, and correctness was not enforced (e.g. a participant could perform a *tap* on a *press* target, which would be recorded as a failed classification).

Fourteen volunteers (10 male; 4 female) with an age range of 18–60 participated in the experiment and received a gift voucher. The experiment was run on the same type of device used for data collection. Due to time constraints, the use of a rubber phone case was a between-subjects condition.

Table 3 shows the confusion matrix across all data in the user study. As the gesture classification algorithm does not distinguish between the type of *press*—*long* or *deep*—we consider them together. This matches the experience that users will receive in practice, as the system response for all types of *press*—secondary invocation—is identical. The performance for binary *press* classification has a precision of 97% and a recall of 88%, with an average time to classify a *press* with the neural model of 235 ms (from the initial contact to the crossing of the probability threshold).

The largest source of confusion for *press* was with *scroll*. Much of this was due to a shift in the centroid caused by the expanding finger contact exceeding the hysteresis threshold before the model probability threshold. This occurred at approximately twice the rate for *deep press* than for *long press*, which is unsurprising given that *deep press* encourages an expanding contact area that may affect the centroid. The confusion between *press* and *tap* occurred at the same rate for *deep press* and *long press*, and was likely due to user error.

The rate of false-positive *scrolls* can be balanced against false-positive *presses* using the scroll hysteresis threshold, which is weighted by the cost of different types of classification errors. For instance, a false-positive press is likely to be more costly to a user than a false-positive scroll because a press typically invokes some action that may be difficult for a user to reverse or correct, whereas a scroll may only displace the content.

5 Discussion

The deep touch neural model uses biomechanical signals captured by a touch sensor to identify force-based *press* gestures from users without dedicated force-sensing hardware. By extracting spatial and temporal features in the touch image sequence, the deep touch neural network can enhance the modern touchscreen gesture experience beyond what conventional heuristics-based gesture classification algorithms could do alone. The model can be executed in a production environment (delivered with Google Pixel 4 and Pixel 5 devices) without increasing touch input latency or impairing system performance.

Instead of creating a new interaction modality, we focussed on improving the user experience of long press interactions by accelerating them with force-induced deep press in a unified *press* gesture. A press gesture has the same outcome as a long press gesture, whose time threshold remains effective, but provides a stronger connection between the outcome and the user's action when force is used. This allowed us to create a more natural and direct gesture to supplement the conventional, indirect *touch and hold* gesture.

Combining a neural model with the existing heuristic method of gesture detection allows biomechanical information to be identified and utilised when it is present, but without harming the usability of touch input for other finger postures. However, this means that the relationship between the heuristic criteria and the probabilistic output of a neural model needs to be carefully considered. Specifically, in cases of ambiguity the system may want to err towards the least costly or most consistent classification for the user, rather than the most accurate.

This is most visible in the confusion between a *press* and a *scroll*, where the expanding contact area of the *press* gesture erroneously induces a change in the touch centroid that triggers a heuristic *scroll* classification. There are further opportunities here to either tune the scroll hysteresis threshold, or to leverage the neural model to aid in classification of a *scroll* gesture as well.

While data curation and training are key to any successful neural network development, they are particularly important and challenging in solving low-level HCI problems with neural networks where the human actions and their effects and feedback are linked in a tight interaction loop. Lacking naturally existing datasets that can be labelled offline, we took a data-elicitation approach in developing the deep touch model by asking human participants to intuitively perform touch gestures as they expect and against a set of tasks. However, this data collection procedure for training samples lacked haptic feedback for the deep press gesture, which might have affected its offline classification performance (Table 2). Potentially, the training datasets and the network's performance can be further enhanced by a closed-loop data collection with haptic feedback for all touch gestures, with the feedback driven by the current deep touch model.

Neural models are also well-suited for touch interactions beyond those studied here—and the human–computer interaction literature has many examples. For example, finger rolling [46], 'pushing' and 'pulling' shear forces [23, 24, 26, 32], and 'positive' and 'negative' force gestures [43] might be supported with similar biomechanical patterns. This style of analysis may also provide insight into perceived input location issues [28] and improved touch contact location algorithms by capturing more information about the contact mass.

6 Conclusion

This work demonstrates that combining capacitive touch sensing with modern neural network algorithms is a practical direction to improve the usability and expressivity of touch-based user interfaces. The work was motivated by a *deep touch* hypothesis that (1) the human finger performs richer expressions on a touch surface than simple pointing; (2) such expressions are manifested in touch sensor image sequences due to finger-surface biomechanics; and (3) modern neural networks are capable of discriminating touch gestures using these sequences. In particular, a deep *press* gesture, accelerated from long press based on an increase in a finger's force could be sensed by a neural model in real time without additional hardware, and reliably discriminated from tap and scroll gestures. The *press* classification has a precision of 97% and a recall of 88%, with an average time reduced to 235 ms from the conventional 400–500 ms) long press.

More broadly, input sensors often capture rich streams of high-dimensionality data that are typically summarised to a few key metrics to simplify the development of heuristic analyses and classifications. Neural methods permit the analysis of the raw data stream to find more complex relationships than can be feasibly expressed with heuristics, and computational advances have made it feasible to operationalise these models in real time. This chapter has described a practical instance of this— *deep touch*—where a neural model has enhanced existing heuristic methods, and been deployed widely to enable a richer user experience.

Acknowledgements We thank many Google and Android colleagues in engineering, design, and product management for their direct and indirect contributions to the project.

References

1. Albinsson PA, Zhai S (2003) High precision touch screen interaction. In: Proceedings of the SIGCHI conference on human factors in computing systems, association for computing machinery, New York, NY, CHI '03, pp 105–112. https://doi.org/10.1145/642611.642631
2. Aliakbarian MS, Saleh FS, Salzmann M, Fernando B, Petersson L, Andersson L (2017) Encouraging LSTMs to anticipate actions very early. In: 2017 IEEE international conference on computer vision (ICCV), pp 280–289. https://doi.org/10.1109/ICCV.2017.39
3. Antoine A, Malacria S, Casiez G (2017) Forceedge: Controlling autoscroll on both desktop and mobile computers using the force. In: Proceedings of the 2017 CHI conference on human factors in computing systems, ACM, New York, NY, CHI '17, pp 3281–3292. https://doi.org/10.1145/3025453.3025605

4. Arif AS, Stuerzlinger W (2013) Pseudo-pressure detection and its use in predictive text entry on touchscreens. In: Proceedings of the 25th australian computer-human interaction conference: augmentation, application, innovation, collaboration, ACM, New York, NY, OzCHI '13, pp 383–392. https://doi.org/10.1145/2541016.2541024
5. Azenkot S, Zhai S (2012) Touch behavior with different postures on soft smartphone keyboards. In: Proceedings of the 14th international conference on Human-computer interaction with mobile devices and services, ACM, New York, NY, MobileHCI '12, pp 251–260. https://doi.org/10.1145/2371574.2371612
6. Baglioni M, Malacria S, Lecolinet E, Guiard Y (2011) Flick-and-Brake: Finger control over inertial/sustained scroll motion. In: CHI '11 Extended abstracts on human factors in computing systems, ACM, New York, NY, CHI EA '11, pp 2281–2286. https://doi.org/10.1145/1979742.1979853
7. Barrett G, Omote R (2010) Projected-capacitive touch technology. Inf Display 26(3):16–21
8. Benko H, Wilson AD, Baudisch P (2006) Precise selection techniques for multi-touch screens. In: CHI '06, ACM, New York, NY, pp 1263–1272. https://doi.org/10.1145/1124772.1124963
9. Bi X, Li Y, Zhai S (2013) FFitts law: Modeling finger touch with Fitts' law. In: Proceedings of the SIGCHI conference on human factors in computing systems, ACM, New York, NY, CHI '13, pp 1363–1372. https://doi.org/10.1145/2470654.2466180
10. Birznieks I, Jenmalm P, Goodwin AW, Johansson RS (2001) Encoding of direction of fingertip forces by human tactile afferents. J Neurosci 21(20):8222–8237. https://doi.org/10.1523/jneurosci.21-20-08222.2001
11. Boceck T, Le HV, Sprott S, Mayer S (2019) Force touch detection on capacitive sensors using deep neural networks. In: Proceedings of the 21st international conference on human-computer interaction with mobile devices and services. https://doi.org/10.1145/3338286.3344389
12. Boring S, Ledo D, Chen XA, Marquardt N, Tang A, Greenberg S (2012) The fat thumb: using the thumb's contact size for single-handed mobile interaction. In: Proceedings of the 14th international conference on human-computer interaction with mobile devices and services, ACM, New York, NY, MobileHCI '12, pp 39–48. https://doi.org/10.1145/2371574.2371582
13. Brewster SA, Hughes M (2009) Pressure-based text entry for mobile devices. In: Proceedings of the 11th international conference on human-computer interaction with mobile devices and services, ACM, New York, NY, MobileHCI '09, pp 9:1–9:4. https://doi.org/10.1145/1613858.1613870
14. Buxton W (1995) Touch, gesture, and marking. In: Baecker RM, Grudin J, Buxton W, Greenberg S (eds) Human-computer interaction: toward the year 2000, Morgan Kaufmann Publishers, San Francisco, CA, chap 7, pp 469–482
15. Buxton W, Hill R, Rowley P (1985) Issues and techniques in touch-sensitive tablet input. In: Proceedings of the 12th annual conference on Computer graphics and interactive techniques, ACM, New York, NY, SIGGRAPH '85, pp 215–224. https://doi.org/10.1145/325334.325239, http://doi.acm.org/10.1145/325334.325239
16. Forlines C, Wigdor D, Shen C, Balakrishnan R (2007) Direct-touch vs. mouse input for tabletop displays. In: Proceedings of the SIGCHI conference on human factors in computing systems, association for computing machinery, New York, NY, CHI '07, pp 647–656. https://doi.org/10.1145/1240624.1240726
17. Glorot X, Bordes A, Bengio Y (2011) Deep sparse rectifier neural networks. In: Gordon G, Dunson D, Dudík M (eds) Proceedings of the fourteenth international conference on artificial intelligence and statistics, PMLR, Fort Lauderdale, FL, Proceedings of machine learning research, vol 15, pp 315–323
18. Goel M, Jansen A, Mandel T, Patel SN, Wobbrock JO (2013) ContextType: using hand posture information to improve mobile touch screen text entr. In: Proceedings of the SIGCHI conference on human factors in computing systems, ACM, New York, NY, CHI '13, pp 2795–2798. https://doi.org/10.1145/2470654.2481386
19. Goguey A, Casiez G, Vogel D, Gutwin C (2018) Characterizing finger pitch and roll orientation during atomic touch actions. In: Proceedings of the 2018 CHI conference on human factors in computing systems, ACM, New York, NY, CHI '18, pp 589:1–589:12. https://doi.org/10.1145/3173574.3174163

20. Goguey A, Malacria S, Gutwin C (2018) Improving discoverability and expert performance in force-sensitive text selection for touch devices with mode gauges. In: Proceedings of the 2018 CHI conference on human factors in computing systems, ACM, New York, NY, CHI '18. https://doi.org/10.1145/3173574.3174051
21. Graves A (2012) Supervised sequence labelling with recurrent neural networks. Springer, Berlin. https://doi.org/10.1007/978-3-642-24797-2
22. Grosse-Puppendahl T, Holz C, Cohn G, Wimmer R, Bechtold O, Hodges S, Reynolds MS, Smith JR (2017) Finding common ground: A survey of capacitive sensing in human-computer interaction. In: Proceedings of the 2017 CHI conference on human factors in computing systems, ACM, New York, NY, CHI '17, pp 3293–3315. https://doi.org/10.1145/3025453.3025808
23. Harrison C, Hudson S (2012) Using shear as a supplemental two-dimensional input channel for rich touchscreen interaction. In: Proceedings of the sigchi conference on human factors in computing systems, ACM, New York, NY, CHI '12, pp 3149–3152. https://doi.org/10.1145/2207676.2208730
24. Heo S, Lee G (2011) Force gestures: augmenting touch screen gestures with normal and tangential forces. In: Proceedings of the 24th annual ACM symposium on User interface software and technology, ACM, New York, NY, UIST '11, pp 621–626. https://doi.org/10.1145/2047196.2047278
25. Heo S, Lee G (2011) ForceTap: extending the input vocabulary of mobile touch screens by adding tap gestures. In: Proceedings of the 13th international conference on human computer interaction with mobile devices and services, ACM, New York, NY, MobileHCI '11, pp 113–122. https://doi.org/10.1145/2037373.2037393
26. Heo S, Lee G (2013) Indirect shear force estimation for multi-point shear force operations. In: Proceedings of the SIGCHI Conference on human factors in computing systems, ACM, New York, NY, CHI '13, pp 281–284. https://doi.org/10.1145/2470654.2470693
27. Hochreiter S, Schmidhuber J (1997) Long short-term memory. Neural Comput 9(8):1735–1780. https://doi.org/10.1162/neco.1997.9.8.1735
28. Holz C, Baudisch P (2010) The generalized perceived input point model and how to double touch accuracy by extracting fingerprints. In: Proceedings of the 28th international conference on Human factors in computing systems, ACM, New York, NY, CHI '10, pp 581–590. https://doi.org/10.1145/1753326.1753413
29. Holz C, Baudisch P (2011) Understanding touch. In: Proceedings of the 2011 annual conference on Human factors in computing systems, ACM, New York, NY, CHI '11, pp 2501–2510. https://doi.org/10.1145/1978942.1979308
30. Hu Y, Huang L, Rieutort-Louis W, Sanz-Robinson J, Wagner S, Sturm JC, Verma N (2014) 3D gesture-sensing system for interactive displays based on extended-range capacitive sensing. In: 2014 IEEE international solid-state circuits conference digest of technical papers, ISSCC, pp 212–213. https://doi.org/10.1109/ISSCC.2014.6757404
31. Kaaresoja T, Brewster S, Lantz V (2014) Towards the temporally perfect virtual button: Touch-feedback simultaneity and perceived quality in mobile touchscreen press interactions. ACM Trans Appl Percep 11(2):9:1–9:25, https://doi.org/10.1145/2611387
32. Lee B, Lee H, Lim SC, Lee H, Han S, Park J (2012) Evaluation of human tangential force input performance. In: Proceedings of the SIGCHI conference on human factors in computing systems, ACM, New York, NY, CHI '12, pp 3121–3130. https://doi.org/10.1145/2207676.2208727
33. Lee J, Cole MT, Lai JCS, Nathan A (2014) An analysis of electrode patterns in capacitive touch screen panels. J Display Technol 10(5):362–366. https://doi.org/10.1109/JDT.2014.2303980
34. Lee S, Buxton W, Smith KC (1985) A multi-touch three dimensional touch-sensitive tablet. In: Proceedings of the SIGCHI conference on human factors in computing systems, ACM, New York, NY, CHI '85, pp 21–25. https://doi.org/10.1145/317456.317461
35. Ma S, Sigal L, Sclaroff S (2016) Learning activity progression in LSTMs for activity detection and early detection. In: 2016 IEEE conference on computer vision and pattern recognition (CVPR), pp 1942–1950. https://doi.org/10.1109/CVPR.2016.214

36. Miyaki T, Rekimoto J (2009) GraspZoom: Zooming and scrolling control model for single-handed mobile interaction. In: Proceedings of the 11th international conference on human-computer interaction with mobile devices and services, ACM, New York, NY, MobileHCI '09, pp 11:1–11:4. https://doi.org/10.1145/1613858.1613872
37. Miyata N, Yamaguchi K, Maeda Y (2007) Measuring and modeling active maximum fingertip forces of a human index finger. In: 2007 IEEE/RSJ international conference on intelligent robots and systems, pp 2156–2161. https://doi.org/10.1109/IROS.2007.4399243
38. O'Connor T (2010) mTouch projected capacitive touch screen sensing theory of operation. Technical Report, TB3064, Microchip Technology Inc
39. Pawluk DTV, Howe RD (1999) Dynamic contact of the human fingerpad against a flat surface. J Biomech Eng 121(6):605–611. https://doi.org/10.1115/1.2800860
40. Potter RL, Weldon LJ, Shneiderman B (1988) Improving the accuracy of touch screens: an experimental evaluation of three strategies. In: CHI '88, ACM, New York, NY, pp 27–32. https://doi.org/10.1145/57167.57171
41. Quinn P, Feng W (2020) Sensing force-based gestures on the Pixel 4. Google AI Blog, https://ai.googleblog.com/2020/06/sensing-force-based-gestures-on-pixel-4.html
42. Quinn P, Malacria S, Cockburn A (2013) Touch scrolling transfer functions. In: Proceedings of the 26th annual ACM symposium on user interface software and technology, ACM, New York, NY, UIST '13, pp 61–70, https://doi.org/10.1145/2501988.2501995
43. Rekimoto J, Schwesig C (2006) PreSenseII: Bi-directional touch and pressure sensing inter-actions with tactile feedback. In: CHI '06 extended abstracts on human factors in computing systems, ACM, New York, NY, CHI EA '06, pp 1253–1258. https://doi.org/10.1145/1125451.1125685
44. Rendl C, Greindl P, Probst K, Behrens M, Haller M (2014) Presstures: exploring pressure-sensitive multi-touch gestures on trackpads. In: Proceedings of the SIGCHI conference on human factors in computing systems, ACM, New York, NY, CHI '14, pp 431–434. https://doi.org/10.1145/2556288.2557146
45. Rosenberg I, Perlin K (2009) The unmousepad: an interpolating multi-touch force-sensing input pad. ACM Trans Graph 28(3):65:1–65:9. https://doi.org/10.1145/1531326.1531371
46. Roudaut A, Lecolinet E, Guiard Y (2009) Microrolls: expanding touch-screen input vocabulary by distinguishing rolls vs. slides of the thumb. In: Proceedings of the SIGCHI conference on human factors in computing systems, ACM, New York, NY, CHI '09, pp 927–936. https://doi.org/10.1145/1518701.1518843
47. Sakai N, Shimawaki S (2006) Mechanical responses and physical factors of the fingertip pulp. Appl Bionics Biomech 3(4):273–278. https://doi.org/10.1533/abbi.2006.0046
48. Serina ER, Mote CD Jr, Rempel D (1997) Force response of the fingertip pulp to repeated compression–effects of loading rate, loading angle and anthropometry. J Biomech 30(10):1035–1040. https://doi.org/10.1016/S0021-9290(97)00065-1
49. Serina ER, Mockensturm E, Mote CD Jr, Rempel D (1998) A structural model of the forced compression of the fingertip pulp. J Biomech 31(7):639–646. https://doi.org/10.1016/S0021-9290(98)00067-0
50. Srinivasan MA, LaMotte RH (1995) Tactual discrimination of softness. J Neurophysiol 73(1):88–101. https://doi.org/10.1152/jn.1995.73.1.88
51. Srinivasan MA, Gulati RJ, Dandekar K (1992) In vivo compressibility of the human fingertip. Adv Bioeng 22:573–576
52. Suzuki K, Sakamoto R, Sakamoto D, Ono T (2018) Pressure-sensitive zooming-out interfaces for one-handed mobile interaction. In: Proceedings of the 20th international conference on human-computer interaction with mobile devices and services, ACM, New York, NY, Mobile-HCI '18, pp 30:1–30:8. https://doi.org/10.1145/3229434.3229446
53. Taher F, Alexander J, Hardy J, Velloso E (2014) An empirical characterization of touch-gesture input-force on mobile devices. In: Proceedings of the ninth ACM international conference on interactive tabletops and surfaces, ACM, New York, NY, ITS '14, pp 195–204. https://doi.org/10.1145/2669485.2669515

54. Vogel D, Baudisch P (2007) Shift: a technique for operating pen-based interfaces using touchs. In: Proceedings of the SIGCHI conference on human factors in computing systems, ACM, New York, NY, CHI '07, pp 657–666. https://doi.org/10.1145/1240624.1240727

55. Walker G (2012) A review of technologies for sensing contact location on the surface of a display. J Soc Inf Display 20(8):413–440. https://doi.org/10.1002/jsid.100

56. Wang F, Ren X (2009) Empirical evaluation for finger input properties in multi-touch interaction. In: Proceedings of the SIGCHI conference on human factors in computing systems, ACM, New York, NY, CHI '09, pp 1063–1072. https://doi.org/10.1145/1518701.1518864

57. Wang F, Cao X, Ren X, Irani P (2009) Detecting and leveraging finger orientation for interaction with direct-touch surfaces. In: Proceedings of the 22nd annual ACM symposium on user interface software and technology, ACM, New York, NY, UIST '09, pp 23–32. https://doi.org/10.1145/1622176.1622182

58. Wang T, Blankenship T (2011) Projected-capacitive touch systems from the controller point of view. Inf Display 27(3):8–11

59. Westerman W (1999) Hand tracking, finger identification, and chordic manipulation on a multitouch surface. PhD thesis, University of Delaware

60. Wilson G, Stewart C, Brewster SA (2010) Pressure-based menu selection for mobile devices. In: Proceedings of the 12th international conference on human computer interaction with mobile devices and services, ACM, New York, NY, MobileHCI '10, pp 181–190. https://doi.org/10.1145/1851600.1851631

61. Yaniger SI (1991) Force sensing resistors: a review of the technology. In: Electro international, pp 666–668. https://doi.org/10.1109/ELECTR.1991.718294

62. Yin Y, Ouyang TY, Partridge K, Zhai S (2013) Making touchscreen keyboards adaptive to keys, hand postures, and individuals: a hierarchical spatial backoff model approach. In: Proceedings of the SIGCHI conference on human factors in computing systems, ACM, New York, NY, CHI '13, pp 2775–2784. https://doi.org/10.1145/2470654.2481384

63. Zimmerman TG, Smith JR, Paradiso JA, Allport D, Gershenfeld N (1995) Applying electric field sensing to human-computer interfaces. In: Proceedings of the SIGCHI conference on human factors in computing systems, ACM Press/Addison-Wesley Publishing Co., New York, NY, CHI '95, pp 280–287. https://doi.org/10.1145/223904.223940

Deep Learning-Based Hand Posture Recognition for Pen Interaction Enhancement

Fabrice Matulic and Daniel Vogel

Abstract This chapter examines how digital pen interaction can be expanded by detecting different hand postures formed primarily by the hand while it grips the pen. Three systems using different types of sensors are considered: an EMG armband, the raw capacitive image of the touchscreen, and a pen-top fisheye camera. In each case, deep neural networks are used to perform classification or regression to detect hand postures and gestures. Additional analyses are provided to demonstrate the benefit of deep learning over conventional machine-learning methods, as well as explore the impact on model accuracy resulting from the number of postures to be recognised, user-dependent versus user-independent models, and the amount of training data. Examples of posture-based pen interaction in applications are discussed and a number of usability aspects resulting from user evaluations are identified. The chapter concludes with perspectives on the recognition and design of posture-based pen interaction for future systems.

1 Introduction

Digital pens and styli are popular tools to write, sketch, and design on tablet-like devices. In many ways, the interaction experience can be like using a pen on paper, where touching the surface with the nib makes a "mark" on the digital canvas. However, pen-based systems are capable of much more than pen-on-paper marking, but using these capabilities requires different kinds of input. In a standard setting with a conventional graphical user interface (GUI), a pen can work like a mouse, where tapping or dragging on widgets can change input modes, adjust application parameters, or execute commands. If the pen device supports hover detection, then it is

F. Matulic (✉)
Preferred Networks Inc., Tokyo, Japan
e-mail: fmatulic@preferred.jp

D. Vogel
Cheriton School of Computer Science, University of Waterloo, Waterloo, ON, Canada
e-mail: dvogel@uwaterloo.ca

Y. Li and O. Hilliges (eds.), *Artificial Intelligence for Human Computer Interaction: A Modern Approach*, Human–Computer Interaction Series,
https://doi.org/10.1007/978-3-030-82681-9_7

almost identical to a single-button mouse in terms of input space. However, using a pen with a conventional GUI can be problematic due to poor precision when tapping and dragging, hand occlusion, and other issues [69]. For this reason, researchers have explored ways to increase the efficiency and expressivity of pen interaction by leveraging pen-specific sensing capabilities, such as hover [21], pressure [54], tilt [67, 76], rolling [6], and contact surface [15, 70].

A category of pen interaction enhancements that has received much attention in the research community, is combining touch with pen input to quickly trigger actions and mode switches. One popular approach is a bimanual interaction paradigm, where the non-dominant hand performs touch manipulations to set the context for the dominant pen-holding hand [7, 22, 28, 45, 70]. Touch-modified pen interaction has also been explored in the unimanual case, with touch sensors directly integrated into the barrel of the pen [27, 63, 65]. This allows commands to be triggered or modes to be activated when changing the pen grasp, such as switching from a normal tripod grip to an overhand or fist hold. These techniques are partially motivated by how artists hold their pens or brushes differently to create various stroking or painting styles for artistic effects.

Many of the techniques using additional sensing to expand pen interaction are in essence hand-posture estimation methods (for either the pen-holding hand, the other hand, or both). When a certain hand or finger posture is detected, an associated action is triggered, such as changing the input mode or issuing a system command. This detection and mapping can be coarse and event-based, like forming a fist to switch from pen drawing to erasing, or it can be fine-grained and time-based to support continuous actions, for instance, placing a hand flat on the touchscreen and extending or flexing the thumb to control a parameter [47]. Depending on the type of sensor data and how the posture is recognised, differentiating poses can be relatively straightforward, for example, counting how many fingers contact the tablet surface (called "chords" [74]) to set the pen mode [45]. Other techniques rely on less easily identifiable patterns, such as classifying pen-holding grips using raw touch images of capacitive sensors [27, 63]. In these cases, machine learning is often the only viable approach for detection. Simple methods such as k-nearest neighbours (k-NN) and support vector machines (SVMs) on hand-crafted features have been employed to distinguish between a few postures, but recent deep learning techniques now make it possible to recognise more poses with high accuracy. In computer vision, particularly, there are now models that can robustly estimate the position of finger joints from single monocular RGB images [18, 51]. With regard to pen interaction, deep learning has been used to track pen tips and recognise handwriting online [14, 35, 59], but it is not yet widely used to detect hand postures for the purpose of expanding digital pen input.

In this chapter, we describe three methods to detect hand poses using deep neural networks in order to enhance pen input in tablet applications. These examples span different sensing approaches: electromyography (EMG) signals from an armband [46], raw capacitive touch sensor images [8], and RGB images streamed from a small downward-facing wide-angle camera attached to the top of the pen [43]. Within these examples, we investigate considerations that often arise when creating machine-learning recognisers for HCI techniques: the benefit of deep learning compared to more traditional machine-learning techniques and how recognition accuracy is impacted by the vocabulary size (number of postures to be classified) and data quantity (fewer or more people contributing more or less data).

We show how posture-based interaction in these cases can be leveraged in pendriven applications and, informed by user evaluations, we discuss various usability aspects and limitations of such techniques. An outlook on future enhancements to hand-posture driven pen interaction concludes our discussion.

2 Background

Research on pen input and interaction is abundant. We focus on sensing methods for enhanced pen interaction and hand pose estimation techniques that could be used for pen input.

2.1 Hand Independent Pen Sensors

The pen itself offers numerous possibilities for extending input channels. This can be done using active pens with additional sensors or external tracking. Common approaches in commercial devices include nib pressure [54] and barrel or tip buttons [38]. The 3D orientation of the pen has been used for rolling and tilt-based input for menu operation while in contact with the screen [6, 24, 67] as well as in mid-air [26, 31]. A related approach is FlexStylus, a deformable pen that uses bend input to increase artistic expressivity [16]. In these cases, mappings between the angles and the associated interface action are direct, for instance, the rolling or bend angle determines which item of a marking menu is selected. The different pen grips or hand postures used to manipulate the pen are not detected by the system.

2.2 Capacitive Touch Sensors

Since pen input occurs on touch screens, one of the most straightforward methods to expand the vocabulary of pen interaction is by combining it with touch on the surface device. Differentiating pen and touch input enables hybrid interaction patterns that can be effectively leveraged with both hands. In this configuration, the non-dominant hand uses touch to support the task of the dominant-hand holding the pen, for instance, to set pen modes. These bimanual "pen+touch" scenarios have been extensively explored [7, 17, 22, 28, 44]. In these works, touch input mostly consists of classic single and two-finger touch operations, but a few utilise more complex postures such as multi-finger chords [22, 45] and contact-shape-based touch patterns to set modes and invoke menus [47]. In the latter example, seven postures are detected with 84% accuracy using Hu moments applied to templates from other users, a form of "user-independent" model.

In Sect. 4, we describe a method using raw capacitive data from the tablet surface to detect hand postures performed by the pen-gripping hand with a deep neural network.

2.3 Vision-Based Camera Sensing

Computer vision is perhaps the most common way to determine relative hand and finger positions. Markerless hand pose estimation using RGB and depth data (RGB-D) have improved considerably with deep learning [9], and current techniques are able to recover the full 3D shape of a hand using a single monocular RGB image [18, 62]. The majority of the proposed algorithms deal only with bare hands, but some approaches also consider hands manipulating objects such as cans and bottles [25, 64, 66]. None of these works are specifically designed or tested for a hand holding a pen or pen-like object. Capturing hands with external cameras can introduce mobility constraints since hands can only be detected within the camera viewing range, and detection accuracy can suffer from changing backgrounds and potential occlusions. Datasets and models using egocentric views have been proposed to enable more mobility [3]), but they typically require head-worn cameras, like smartglasses or a headset, which may not be practical for everyday pen activities. Similarly, systems using wrist-worn cameras such as Digits [36] and Back-Hand-Pose [75], while supporting mobility, require the user's hand to be instrumented and thus can be an impediment for pen tasks.

With regard to using the other hand to complement pen input, mid-air gestures detected by a depth camera have been proposed by Aslan et al. [2]. The technique only recognises gestures and no advanced posture recognition is performed.

In Sect. 5, we describe a method to use an RGB camera directly mounted on a pen, which supports mobile vision-based capturing without any wearable sensor.

2.4 Physiological Sensors

To avoid sensing range limitations and environmental influence, sensors can be directly placed on or near the hand. Perhaps the most direct way of capturing hand and finger movements is via a data glove [10, 37]. Given a glove with a dense array of stretch sensors, accurate 3D hand models that are robust to environmental conditions can be constructed with deep neural networks [20], but a glove can hinder finger movement and impedes the sense of direct touch. Slightly further away from the hand, but still close enough to enable sensing with little interference are the wrist and forearm. Perhaps the most readily available wrist-worn sensors are IMUs in smartwatches. These can be used to recognise gestures like hand and finger motions [73, 77], but do not produce sufficient information to recognise a large number of static postures. SmartGe detects correct and incorrect pen grips for handwriting using a CNN [5] and a classification accuracy of 98% for nine pen grips is reported. However, users have to write slowly for the system to work, and the model was trained on a fully random dataset split (without distinguishing between users and time occurrence) so the evaluation is not ecologically valid.

Several types of wrist or forearm biometric signal sensors have been proposed to detect postures and microgestures using machine learning. Detection techniques include force sensitive resistors [12], electrical impedance tomography [79], ultrasound [32, 49], intradermal infrared sensing [48], electromyography (EMG) [23, 33, 78], skin stretching [39], and thermal imaging [30]. These sensors do not suffer from external visual disturbances, but the models used for classification are typically very sensitive to sensor position on the arm and environmental factors like humidity (such as sweat [56]), so they are considerably user- and session-dependent. Combining different types of sensors increases recognition robustness [50], but also adds complexity, as well as weight and power demands, for the wearable sensing device. In Sect. 3, we describe a method using a commercial EMG armband to detect a moderate vocabulary of pen-holding postures.

In summary, pen input enhancement techniques have not used deep learning so they are limited to direct mappings between pen input channels and UI actions (tilt, roll, bend) and for posture-based approaches, detection is limited to a few poses. Deep learning has been used to recognise bare hand gestures and postures and the models could potentially be fine-tuned to detect pen-holding hands, but sensors considered so far are either fixed in the environment (external cameras), insufficiently precise (smartwatches) or use DIY hardware (biometric sensors), so these approaches have limited applicability in mobile pen tasks. The sensing environments in the three pen posture detection settings that we consider are based on commercial devices (touch screen and EMG armband) or require just a 3D-printed mount (pen-top camera) without any custom electronics. We apply deep learning techniques for the specific purpose of triggering application events based on detected postures, and therefore, we do not aim to fully reconstruct accurate 3D models of the hand.

3 Posture Recognition Using an EMG Armband

The first posture recognition technique we discuss uses surface electromyography (EMG), a technology that measures the electrical activity of muscles. Specifically, we use a commercial Myo EMG armband worn on the forearm of the pen-holding hand (Fig. 1). The five different pen grip postures we select for our analysis are shown in Fig. 3. They consist of the Dynamic Tripod, which is the most common handwriting grip [68], two pressure-based postures (Ring+Pinkie pressed against the Palm and Pen Squeezed Firmly), which we hypothesise EMG can detect well, and two grips

Fig. 1 EMG armband used
to recognise pen-holding
grips

with finger extensions (Extended Index finger and Extended Pinkie), which are just
slight variations of a normal pen grip (Fig. 2).

EMG data for each of these postures is collected from 30 participants (10 female,
20 female with 4 left-handed people) who perform a set of simple tracing, tapping,
sketching, and writing tasks on a Wacom Cintiq 22HD Touch tablet while wearing
the armband (Fig. 2). Please see [8, 46] for further detail about the tasks and data-
gathering procedure.

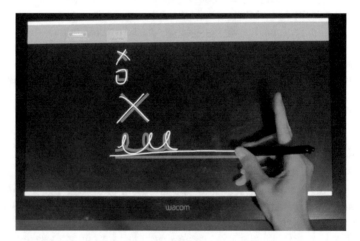

Fig. 2 Tracing tasks for data collection on Wacom Cintiq

(a) Dynamic Tripod   (b) Squeeze Pen   (c) Ring+Pinkie on Palm   (d) Extended Index   (e) Extended Pinkie

Fig. 3 Five pen grips considered for detection with EMG armband

3.1 Data Sampling

The different pen grips are intended as triggers for mode switches in applications where users form the desired posture just before touching the tablet with the pen. Since the contact of the pen with the tablet may affect the EMG response, we need to validate our posture recognition approach with windows of data captured around pen-down events. We choose a window of 1060 ms, with 1000 ms before pen-down event and 60 ms after the event to reflect possible system reaction time within acceptable latency. Since the Myo has a sampling rate of 250 Hz and 8 electrodes, this gives us 2120 raw sensor values per window. While these windows around pen-down events need to be used for validation to better reflect when postures are formed for mode switching, there is no such restriction regarding training data. Any data that may contribute to increasing model accuracy can be used. Since data was acquired while continuously maintaining postures, we can use as much of the collected sensor data as possible for model training. For consistency with validation and testing, we similarly sample 1060 ms windows of data, but we use sliding windows with 75% overlap over the entire data sequence for each posture.

We consider three machine-learning approaches to classify these postures. The first technique is based on a Convolutional Neural Network (CNN) applied to the data transformed into spectrograms and two methods using hand-crafted features of the data, Support Vector Machines (SVM) and Random Forests (RF). The latter two techniques represent baselines for "classic machine learning" used for similar scenarios in HCI [57, 58].

3.2 CNN Classification

We briefly describe the CNN approach. For full details, please refer to [46].

3.2.1 Spectrogram Pre-processing

EMG data is best converted into the frequency domain to use for classification, with spectrograms, in particular, exhibiting useful features for convolutional neural networks [11]. We convert our segmented raw EMG data into spectrograms using a

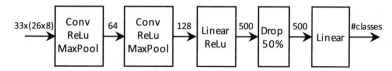

Fig. 4 CNN Architecture

Fast Fourier Transform (FFT) size of 64 samples (corresponding to 256 ms) and a hop distance of 8 samples (32 ms), which results in 33 frequency bins and 26 time slices. We further normalise the values using min-max scaling over all participants' data to ensure all features have equal range.

3.2.2 CNN Architecture

A spectrogram can be considered as an image of dimension 26×8 (time slices $\times$ electrodes) with 33 channels (frequency bins). We design a CNN to process such "images". Considering the low resolution of the data, we use a relatively shallow CNN architecture with just two convolutional layers and two fully-connected layers, with ReLU activations and dropout for regularisation (Fig. 4). This enables relatively fast training and inference.

3.3 Baseline SVM and RF Classification

We compare our CNN classifier with traditional machine-learning techniques, SVM and RF, trained on features derived from the input EMG data. We use the features used by Saponas et al. for their EMG-based gesture recognition [57, 58]. These are the root mean square (RMS) amplitude of each electrode (8 features), the RMS ratios between all electrodes (28 features), frequency energy (33 features), the ratio of high-frequency to low-frequency energy for each electrode (8 features), and the signal phase ratio between each pair of electrodes (28 features). This yields a feature vector of size 105. We use the same data selection and segmentation strategy as for the CNN to compute the features, i.e. 1060 ms windows around pen-down events divided into 26 data chunks.

We train SVMs and RFs with the obtained feature values. The SVM classifier uses a linear SVC model with default parameters in the Scikit-learn framework. Considering the high amount of input data (roughly 4000 samples per posture in the training set) and the quadratic fit time complexity for SVMs, approximate kernel maps using the Nystroem method with $\gamma = 0.2$ are used. RF are more scalable and no such optimisation scheme is needed with our data. We use 100 trees in our RF.

3.4   Model Evaluation

Large differences in classification accuracy can be observed for EMG-based detection, depending on whether *general models* (i.e. trained only with other people's data) or *user-specific models* (i.e. including training data from only that user) are used [34, 41]. Deploying a general model would require no user calibration, but detection would be less accurate, whereas user-specific models are more accurate but require each user to calibrate before using the system. Our evaluation reflects these two situations by considering within- and between-user analyses.

For our within-user evaluation, the data from all users is divided according to task type (tracing, tapping, sketching, or writing) to avoid ecologically invalid random partitioning. The tracing tasks provided the most data, so we use it for training. Sketching data is used for validating and the data for the writing and tapping tasks is used for testing. This gives an approximate 83%/4%/13% split between training, validation, and test sets.

The data split for the between-user evaluation is as follows: 17 people for training (57% of the total data), 6 people for validation (21%), and 6 people for testing (21%). To reduce variability, we perform 5 rounds of cross-validations with random splits and average the accuracy results to calculate the final score (repeated random sub-sampling).

In both cases, training data includes all the captured sensor data, whereas validating and testing sets include only data around pen-down events to remain ecologically valid.

3.5   Results

Table 1 shows classification accuracy for a variety of combinations of the five postures using the three classifiers.

Unsurprisingly, the CNN gives the best results overall with roughly a 19% higher accuracy compared to SVM and a 10% gain over RF on average. Interestingly, RF achieves significantly higher accuracy than SVM for the within-user analysis, but performs worse than SVM for between-user comparisons. This pattern was consistent even after trying to optimise model hyperparameters for both techniques. The between-user values are very low compared to within-users results. For the full five-posture set, classification accuracy is just slightly above 32% between-users versus 73% within-users. This confirms the high user-dependence of posture detection using the Myo and reflects why the commercial Myo gesture recogniser also requires users to calibrate before use. A three-posture set consisting of **Dynamic Tripod**, the pressure-based **Ring+Pinkie on Palm**, and the finger-extension posture **Ext. Pinkie** can be recognised with almost 86% accuracy with a user-dependent model. This potentially makes this set practical for some applications. Recognition can likely

Table 1 Posture recognition accuracy for different posture sets using within- and between-user datasets with CNN, SVM, and RF classifiers

Postures	CNN		SVM		RF	
	Within	Between	Within	Between	Within	Between
Tripod, Ring+Pinkie on Palm, Squeeze Pen, Ext. Index, Ext. Pinkie	73.0%	32.4%	47.9%	29.0%	68.2%	27.5%
Tripod, Ring+Pinkie on Palm, Squeeze Pen, Ext. Pinkie	77.1%	35.4%	56.0%	38.1%	74.8%	33.8%
Tripod, Ring+Pinkie on Palm, Ext. Pinkie	85.7%	53.1%	68.5%	49.7%	83.3%	44.1%
Tripod, Ring+Pinkie on Palm, Squeeze Pen	78.9%	56.3%	62.3%	42.6%	76.7%	38.1%
Tripod, Ring+Pinkie on Palm	88.5%	67.1%	77.4%	56.2%	87.6%	50.0%
Tripod, Ext. Pinkie	89.3%	68.0%	78.4%	67.9%	87.5%	59.3%

be made more robust by introducing temporal consistency between data frames and using mitigation strategies such as transfer learning and normalisation [11].

3.5.1 Sensor Limitations

We believe the relatively low classification accuracy is mainly due to limitations of the Myo device rather than EMG as a sensing method. The Myo is not able to capture distinguishable electrical activity patterns in forearm muscles to reliably detect different pen-holding grips when performing common tasks such as writing and sketching. This is especially the case when attempting to recognise postures for unknown users without calibration. The Myo is an old device (discontinued in 2018), which was optimised for mass market pricing. Future EMG and biosignal sensors might have the required sensitivity and precision to not only identify different pen grips, but also to fully determine the hand pose [53]. As with almost all sensitive biosensors, high user-dependence might still remain a problem.

Our comparison of a deep learning CNN with classic machine-learning methods demonstrates a clear advantage for robust hand-posture recognition with EMG. We believe this advantage also applies to most sensing technology, as long as considerable amounts of data are available. In the next section, we explore the impact of the vocabulary size (the number of postures to classify) when training models with deep CNNs.

4 Posture Recognition Using Raw Capacitive Images

The second hand-posture sensing system that we describe uses the tablet itself. Specifically, the raw capacitive sensors used to detect touch input in the form of a full image of the contact imprint of the hand against the tablet display (Fig. 5) [8]. Unlike the EMG armband, which could detect mid-air finger movements and pressure on the pen, the tablet can only detect direct touch. This means the pen grip posture variations in this context are limited to contact patterns, i.e. how the hand,

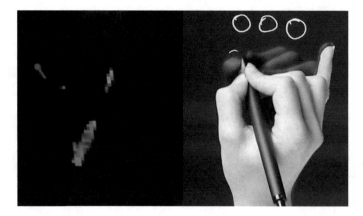

Fig. 5 Explicit "pinkie out" pen-gripping posture recognised by the pen and hand contact pattern on the screen. Raw image shown on the left

fingers, and pen touch the display. We consider pen interaction enhancements in the form of unimanual pen and touch interaction a complement to the bimanual pen and touch input design space explored in the HCI literature [7, 22, 28, 45].

4.1 Posture Set

To be able to easily distinguish postures based on their contact with the tablet display, we could choose postures that form clearly identifiable shapes or patterns in the raw capacitive images. For instance, the number of distinct areas (i.e. "blobs") created by the palm and fingers [45]. This would, however, limit the number of possible postures, as fingers have reduced mobility when simultaneously holding a pen. Deep learning, which excels at image classification, allows us to consider a broader range of postures that can also, to some extent, accommodate dexterity constraints and user preferences.

For our analysis, we consider postures gathered from 18 study participants performing tracing and sketching tasks on a Wacom Cintiq 22HD Touch tablet. The device and tasks are the same as those used for the EMG-based postures described above and illustrated in Fig. 2.

The potential design space of our unimanual postures is defined by how the palm and specific fingers touch the screen. The palm can contact at the heel, the side, or be "floating" with no touch. Fingers can contact outside the hand, such as when the pinkie is stretched out, contact inside the hand, such as when the pinkie is curled in, or contact near the nib, such as sliding the index down to touch the surface right beside the nib. Theoretically, there are many permutations of these palm and finger states, but manual dexterity and comfort limit the viable set to 34 potential postures. From these 34 different postures, we narrow down to the 12 postures shown in Fig. 6.

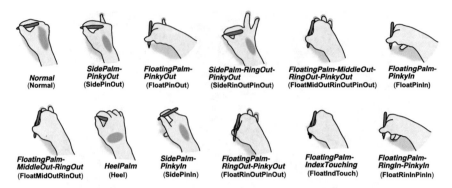

Fig. 6 Pen postures used for classification (shown in decreasing order of preference)

These were rated the most comfortable in our study and did not significantly overlap with a normal hand writing posture. More detail about the different postures and their subjective ratings is available in the original article [8].

4.2 Classification

Since we use posture changes mainly for pen mode switches, we again only consider touch data around pen-down events. Specifically, we select data 100 ms before and after pen down, giving a 200 ms capture window. From this data, we only take frames that include detected pen input (cursor coordinates), while the pen is in contact with the screen or hovering within 2 cm, as detected by the Wacom tablet.

The touch frames yield 120×77 single-channel (greyscale) raw images and pen data including x, y coordinates labelled with a hovering or touching state. We combine this information in a 3-channel (RGB) image. The first channel contains the raw touch image. A blob is drawn at the pen position either in the second channel if hovering or in the third if touching. Examples of resulting images are shown in Fig. 7.

4.3 Network Architecture

Instead of comparing deep learning with traditional machine-learning approaches as above, we evaluate recognition accuracy for classification of increasingly large posture sets using the same deep learning architecture, a VGG convolutional neural network with 16 layers (VGG-16) [61] with weights pre-trained on ImageNet.

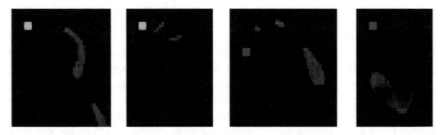

Fig. 7 Examples of images with combined pen and touch data for four postures. From left to right: **Normal**, **FloatRinInPinIn**, **SideRinOutPinOut**, **Heel** (Images cropped and colour saturation enhanced for better visibility)

4.4 Training and Validation

We train our VGG network with the RGB images combining pen and touch information in a pre-processing step and two training stages. First, images are resized to 224 × 224 squares, which is the standard input size for VGG. Since the network has pre-trained weights, we replace its final layer to match our desired output and train that layer while freezing the others for a single epoch. In a second training stage, the full network is trained for 10 epochs using discriminative learning rates (lower learning rates for first layers). A batch size of 64 is used in both stages. Training uses cross entropy as the loss function and recognition performance is measured using the error rate. For implementation, we use the *fastai* deep learning framework [29], which provides a direct function (`fine_tune`) with optimised default hyperparameters for this process.

For validation, we consider only between-user evaluations, since we anticipate that pen and touch traces are sufficiently similar between users and sufficiently different between postures to build robust general models. We use the data of 15 participants for training and the remaining 3 participants as the validation set (i.e. a "leave-3-out" scheme). There are three left-handed people among our participants, so we mirror their images for analysis. We use data augmentation techniques on the training set to artificially increase the amount of data, in the form of random affine transformations such as translations, scale, and rotations. This yields roughly 22,000 training and 2,400 validation images for each posture.

To evaluate the robustness of our VGG model with an increasingly large posture vocabulary (i.e. more classes), we perform successive training iterations. We start with the top two postures of our 12-posture set, then add the next preferred posture to train the next model, and continue until we reach the full 12-posture set for the final model. For each training iteration, we randomly subsample our dataset following our leave-3-out scheme to create 5 training and validation set splits for cross-validation. We use the same seeds for each posture set to keep the same partitions between iterations. We average the error rates in each of these 5 rounds to obtain a measure of classification accuracy for the given posture set.

4.5 Results

Figure 8 shows the classification accuracy for each iteration with increasing number of postures and Fig. 9 shows the confusion matrix of the final set with all 12 postures.

Starting at over 97% with two postures, the classification accuracy decreases approximately linearly as postures are added to the set to reach an average accuracy of 78.6% with the full 12-posture set. The confusion matrix shows that *Normal* has only a 51% recognition accuracy. "Normal" postures may vary among participants as each person has a different handwriting grip so lower recognition performance is not surprising. Furthermore, we observe it is often confused with *SidePinIn*, a relatively similar posture. Looking at the images that caused the highest losses, we notice that some *Heel* postures exhibited touch traces that are very similar to *Normal*, hinting at difficulties for some participants to maintain the *Heel* posture throughout the tracing tasks. Other errors with a high loss include images of float postures with fingers curled in mistaken for postures with fingers stretched out. The confusion matrix confirms that postures with fingers in have a lower accuracy than those with fingers out, which may be due to the former being more difficult to maintain and leaving a lighter or less consistent touch trace compared to the latter. Removing *FloatPinIn* and *SidePinIn*, two postures causing significant misclassifications, increases accuracy for 10 postures to 85%. Two postures that also enjoy relatively high recognition accuracy are *Heel* and *FloatIndexTouch* as they differ significantly from other poses.

In practice, people may only want to use up to five different postures in applications. These would be recognised with above 92% accuracy with even higher rates likely possible if using temporal consistency checks and training per-user models.

Fig. 8 Classification accuracy for increasing number of postures

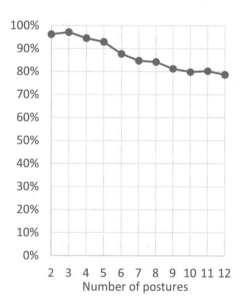

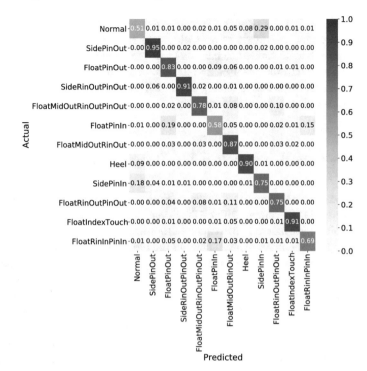

Fig. 9 Normalised confusion matrix for the full 12-posture set

The performance cost of adding a few more postures is relatively low, so this can be considered if needed.

4.6 Postures Using the Other Hand

While we only consider touch postures formed by the pen-holding hand in this analysis, it would also be possible to use a CNN classifier on the raw capacitive image to detect contact patterns of the other hand touching the screen. In this case, only the original grey image would be used, as added channels with pen data are not needed since the the pen moves independently from the other hand. If both hands can touch the screen simultaneously, it may be necessary to first isolate which touch blobs belong to which hand in the raw capacitive image. Our data was captured with only the pen-holding hand contacting the display and we did not consider the other hand resting on the tablet that could potentially cause interference. To support detection when both hands can touch the tablet screen, either hand segmentation or a completely data-driven approach covering resting hand cases would be required.

Raw capacitive images of touch screens provide reliable input data for hand-posture detection independently of physiological factors and without any wearable sensor, but postures are limited to hands and fingers contacting the display. In the next section, we consider postures and gestures captured by a small downward-facing RGB camera attached to the top of the pen and we examine how the amount of training data affects recognition accuracy.

5   Posture Detection with Pen-Top Camera

The third and the final example of hand-posture detection that we discuss uses a small downward-facing camera with a fisheye lens fixed to the top end of the pen [43] (Fig. 10a). This allows the camera to capture a top-down view of the pen-holding hand and the surrounding environment, including the other hand (Fig. 10b). Contrary to systems with cameras fixed to the environment, a pen-top camera preserves mobility and does not suffer from occlusions caused by objects in between the cameras and the hand. Cameras built into the tablet also maintain mobility, but they can only see hands placed directly in front or behind the device. Furthermore, hands moving on or just below the tablet plane are beyond capturing range.

While in an ideal mobile setting, the pen-top camera should be small and operate wirelessly (similar to so-called "spy pens" with cameras integrated in the barrel), our proof-of-concept prototype uses a tethered USB camera, which streams image data via a cable to a server. The camera needs to be elevated above the pen to have a sufficiently open view of the hands and the environment in order to properly capture different postures. However, any increased length also adds weight and moves the centre of gravity upwards, making the pen more unwieldy and uncomfortable to use. We create a 6.2 cm high mount as a compromise between these two considerations. The combined weight of the mount and camera without the cable is 18 g. The camera streams images at 30 fps in 1920 × 1080 resolution over USB2.

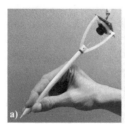

Fig. 10 Downward-facing fisheye camera attached to a pen via a 3D-printed mount (**a**) that can "see" hands and surrounding environment (**b**). This enables various posture-based interactions using both hands (**c**)

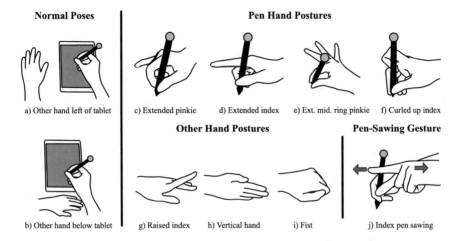

Fig. 11 Postures used to trigger discrete actions (classification) (**a–f**) and two-hand sawing gesture used for continuous parameter control (regression) (**j**)

5.1 Posture and Gesture Detection

For our analysis of deep learning-based posture detection models in this setting, we consider two different posture sets corresponding to poses formed by either the "pen hand" or the "other hand". These are both *classification* problems. We further include a two-hand "sawing" gesture consisting in placing the index finger orthogonally against the pen barrel and rubbing the finger towards or away. The distance between the pen (i.e. the centre of the image) and the index fingertip (blue circle in Fig. 18c) can be mapped to a continuous parameter used by the application. This is a *regression* problem.

Note that the sawing gesture's associated mode first needs to be activated so that the system knows when parameter mapping should occur. The trigger for mode activation is when the user hits the pen with their index finger. To correctly identify the moment when the mode should be engaged and disengaged, a classification network needs to be trained. Such a neural network needs to be exposed to multiple images showing the other hand approaching the pen just before touching it, so that it can distinguish "touch" from "no touch" images. In this analysis, we do not consider the classification of these two states for mode engagement and only focus on the regression problem once the sawing gesture mode is enabled. All postures and gesture are illustrated in Fig. 11.

We directly feed the images captured by the fisheye camera to our deep neural networks. As can be seen in Fig. 10b, three stripes belonging to the support blades of the mount appear in the images captured by the fisheye camera. Depending on how the pen is held, these stripes may overlap with hands and figures forming postures thereby causing partial occlusions. In the original article, we describe possible pen designs to deal with this problem [43].

5.2   Data Gathering

Image data is gathered from 11 participants seated at a table and randomly drawing on an iPad Pro with an Apple Pencil while performing each posture and gesture, one after the other. Participants are instructed to move their hands and continuously rotate and tilt the pen to cover multiple positions and angles as the networks need to recognise postures and gestures independently of these factors.

The location of the index fingertip in the images of the pen-sawing gesture is manually coded by human annotators. The distance between the fingertip and the centre of the image, corresponding to the location of the pen, is then computed to form the labelled continuous data.

5.3   Network Architecture

For both classification and regression on these natural RGB images, we use a ResNet-50 architecture. This is a deeper network than the VGG-16 used for the system described in the previous section, since classification is on natural images containing more complex detection patterns. Like the previous system, we start with a network that is pre-trained on ImageNet to bootstrap training.

5.4   Experiments with Training and Validation

Previously, we examined how gradually increasing the number of postures (i.e. number of classes) in the set affects recognition accuracy. In this setting, we instead analyse the impact of the amount of training data by training networks with the data of an increasing number of participants. Specifically, we train using data from one to nine participants (i.e. [P1], [P1, P2], [P1, P2, P3],…, [P1, P2, …, P9]) and always test with the last two participants [P10, P11]. P10 was left-handed so their images are mirrored. While this fixed partitioning does not fully account for potential feature interactions among our participants' data, it gives us an idea of how much data and how many people are required to achieve a certain level of recognition performance.

We create three different sets from the postures and gesture of Fig. 11:

- *Pen Hand* set, which includes the Pen Hand and Normal postures, i.e. classification among 5 postures.
- *Other Hand* set, which includes the Other Hand and Normal postures, i.e. classification among 4 postures.
- *Pen-Sawing* set, which includes the Pen-Sawing gesture and its associated fingertip distance used for regression.

Since participants contributed different amounts of data for each posture due to the nature of the task, we need to select an equal number of images per posture to ensure data balance for our analysis. Across all participants and postures, the minimum number of images contributed for one posture per participant was 587, so we select 587 images per posture per participant. For participants that contributed more images, we take 587 equally spaced images for each posture in the capturing sequence. For example, if the participant has 800 images for a posture, we select images 1, 3, 4, 5, 7, ..., and 800. This provides better data distribution compared to simply selecting the first 587 images in the set. We apply the same procedure for the sawing gesture, where the minimum number of images contributed by a participant is 924.

For regression, since we only consider a single gesture and the minimum number of images for it is larger, in addition to gradually increasing the number of participants, we also vary the number of images contributed by each person. This allows us to compare the impact of more data contributed by fewer participants vs more participants contributing less data. For instance, given 3696 training images per posture, we can compare the accuracy of the ResNet when those images come from four participants (4×924), six participants (6×616), and eight participants (8×462).

We train all networks using the same procedure and framework used in the previous section: With fastai's `fine_tune` function [29], we first fine-tune the final layer of the pre-trained network for one epoch and then unfreeze all layers to train further 10 epochs with discriminative learning rates. We perform three runs for each setting and average the results to smooth differences due to randomness in the training process. We use again a batch size of 64. For classification, we use cross entropy for the loss and the error rate as metric and for regression, mean squared error loss, and root mean square error (RMSE).

5.5   Results

We report results of experiments for varying training data size first for the two posture classification models, then the sawing gesture regression model.

5.5.1   Classification Models

Figure 12 shows the classification performance of the ResNet-50 model for the two posture datasets with increasing number of participants contributing training data. We observe that both sets start with accuracy just below 60% and significantly increase their performance with three to four participants. After four participants, classification performance only marginally increases and stagnates after 7 participants. The final rate for Pen Hand is roughly 90% and 78% for Other Hand. Pen Hand contains more postures, but exhibits a higher recognition accuracy likely because Pen Hand postures occupy a larger amount of pixel space and are centrally located in the images. The other hand is further away from the camera and appears less prominently, therefore, small differences in hand postures are harder to distinguish.

Confusion matrices for both sets (Figs. 13 and 16) reveal once again that the normal hand postures are the most error prone, no doubt due to the diversity of pen-holding and pen-resting poses. Networks likely need to see a large variety of these "normal" poses in order to robustly identify them.

Delving deeper into the data to analyse misrecognised cases, we again examine the images that caused the highest losses. We generate Grad-CAM heatmaps [60] using the final layer of the CNN to visualise class activations. These activation maps show which regions of the image the network focussed on to classify it. Three examples of misclassified postures for each of the two sets are shown in Fig. 14. As can be seen, five of these wrong predictions are likely due to fingers being occluded by the support blades ((a) and (e)), badly formed postures ((b)) and normal poses resembling input postures ((c), (d), and (f)). The activation map of the (f) case further reveals that the model mainly focussed on a spot on the forearm instead of the hand, which is placed on the top left corner of the tablet. The latter pattern is underrepresented in our data, which mostly consists of other hands resting at the side or below the device without touching it. This confirms the need to include more samples of other hands in different locations around and on the tablet in the training data to expose the network to these cases.

5.5.2 Regression Model

As can be seen in Fig. 15, with one and two participants the RMSE is around 160, regardless of the number of images per participant. With 924 images per person, the error rate starts improving with the third participant and decreases significantly until it reaches a plateau with 7 participants, achieving an RMSE between 15 and 20. Adding more participant data after that does not further lead to lower rates, suggesting that a limit has been attained. With lower amounts of images per participant, the inflexion point comes at a later stage with the start of the error rate dip occurring from the

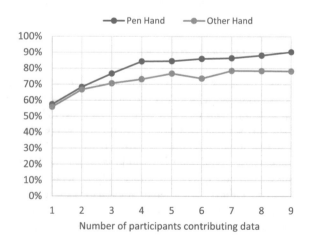

Fig. 12 Classification accuracy for Pen-Hand and Other-Hand posture sets with increasing number of participants contributing data. Each participant contributes 587 images

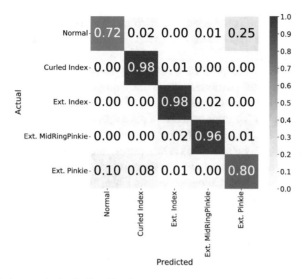

Fig. 13 Confusion matrix for the Pen Hand set

Pen Hand Postures

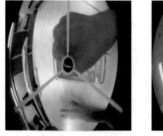

(a) Normal - Ext. index (b) Mid ring pinkie - Pinkie (c) Curled up index - Normal

Other Hand Postures

(d) Raised index - Normal (e) Normal - Fist (f) Fist - Normal

Fig. 14 Misclassified postures with Grad-CAM heatmaps applied to the final layer of the CNN. Posture pairs in each image caption are predicted and actual posture

sixth participant. There is not enough data to reach a plateau in these cases, but we presume that it would likely be similar to the previous case, with RMSE values just under 20.

Interestingly, there seems to be little effect whether a specific amount of data comes from few or many participants with this dataset. Comparing the RMSE within the major gains region of the curves, accuracy with four participants each contributing 924 images is roughly the same as with six participants contributing 616 images and with eight participants providing 462 images, i.e. the source of the 3696 images does not seem to significantly matter. This is interesting since there *is* some diversity in our participants, with male female representation, people with darker skin tones, hands of different sizes, with and without body hair. This suggests that the network is able to reliably capture general hand features with only a few different participants.

Fig. 15 Root Mean Square Error (RMSE) for regression on the Pen-Sawing gesture with increasing number of participants contributing data and different amounts of data per participant

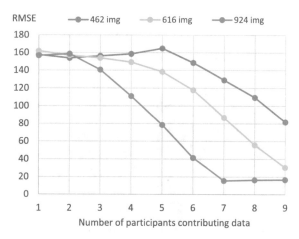

Fig. 16 Confusion matrix for the Other Hand set

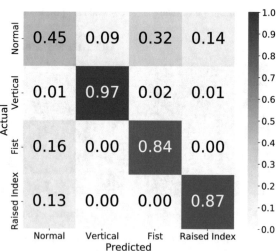

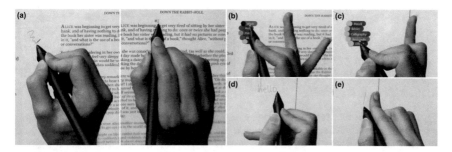

Fig. 17 Examples of unimanual pen and touch postures to perform various operations in vector drawing and PDF annotation applications: **a** switching from *Normal* posture for inking to *Heel* posture for highlighting (document annotation); **b** invoking a colour chooser with *SideRinOutPinOut* (document annotation); **c** invoking an object creation menu with *SidePinOut* (vector drawing); **d** creating a text object with handwriting recognition using *SidePinIn* (vector drawing); **e** making stroke gestures to issue commands with *FloatIndTouch* (vector drawing)

6 Hand Postures for Pen Interaction in an Application Context

The main purpose of detecting hand postures and gestures is to quickly switch pen modes, trigger actions, and modify parameters in applications. These interactions can function as expert shortcuts in addition to traditional UI widgets and tools, similar to keyboard shortcuts complementing widget-based selections in a traditional GUI. Figures 17 and 18 show a few examples of how hand postures and gestures can be used for such kinds of interactions in pen-driven applications.

Typical examples of pen applications are drawing, sketching, and note-taking, where the pen can take on multiple roles. For instance, when viewing a document, the pen creates annotations in its default mode, but the mode can be switched so that the pen can also highlight text, scroll, invoke menus, etc. These modes or commands can be activated by forming specific hand postures. Setting continuous parameters can be supported with hand gestures mapped to a continuous feature such as the sawing gesture, which uses the distance between the index finger and the pen.

If the tablet is placed on a support such as a table or the user's lap, the other hand can also be used to perform postures and gestures. Even if the other hand is subject to movement constraints, such as when holding the tablet, it can still be used to perform a limited number of mode-setting postures, for instance, holding up the index finger to switch to zooming mode in a map application (Fig. 18d). However, if that finger is used to support the tablet, lifting it can result in reduced grip stability.

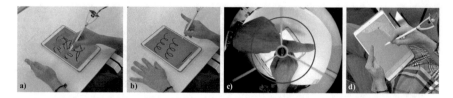

Fig. 18 Examples of interactions enabled by hand postures detected by a pen-top camera: **a** setting rectangle-input mode in a sketching application by forming a vertical flat hand with the other hand; **b** undoing an action by extending the index finger of the pen-holding hand; **c** pen "sawing" gesture with the distance between the index finger and the pen (blue circle) to set a continuous parameter like stroke width; **d** map application with raised finger of the tablet-gripping hand to enable zooming mode

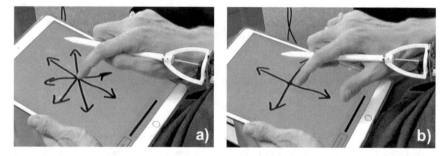

Fig. 19 Pen tucked in the hand to temporarily perform touch-drag panning. **a** All-direction panning with flexed thumb. **b** Axis-constrained panning with extended thumb

6.1 Pen-Grip Detection for Touch Input

The pen-holding hand can occasionally be used to perform finger touch interactions in between pen input actions, for example, when the user wants to scroll the canvas with panning finger gestures in between penning annotations. While the other hand could be used to perform these operations, it might not always be available because it may already be holding the device, or the user prefers to interact with the device using only one hand. The pen itself could be used after a mode switch, but panning with fingers is common on touchscreens. In these unimanual modality switches, the pen is temporarily tucked in the palm so that the index finger can be used for touch manipulations. We can support mode switching in these situations as well by distinguishing between different pen-stowing postures, such as triggering a different mode depending on whether the thumb is extended or not. This could be used, for example, to constrain scrolling or panning to specific directions (Fig. 19), similar to pressing a modifier key on the keyboard to apply constraints to a freeform operation.

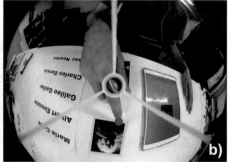

Fig. 20 Index finger pointing at off-tablet content to capture with camera. **a** External view of user pointing at photo near tablet while tilting the pen forward. **b** Camera view showing identified fingertip and object to capture

6.2 Pointing at and Capturing Off-Tablet Content

In the case of the pen-top camera sensor, off-tablet content, such as documents and photos around the tablet, can be captured for pick-and-drop operations [55] and to form search queries. The user can tilt the pen forward and point at elements to capture with their extended index finger (Fig. 20). The fingertip location in the camera image is detected using the same type of neural network as for the pen-sawing gesture, the output being two continuous values for the x,y coordinates (keypoint regression) instead of one. The system can then infer which element in the image is designated. In our proof-of-concept implementation of this feature, we use simple computer vision techniques, a Canny edge detector and contour finder, to locate objects in the vicinity of the detected fingertip [43]. We also support the capture and conversion of isolated text elements using the EAST detector [80] and Google's OCR engine. The obtained machine-readable text can then be used in the tablet applications, for example, to perform text searches.

6.3 Discrete and Continuous Actions

As described above, deep learning models can also detect finger movements for the control of continuous parameters, such as the pen-sawing gesture (Fig. 18c). The distance between the fingertip and the pen can be mapped to a continuous variable such as stroke thickness in a drawing application or zoom level in a map application. Other possible gestures for continuous parameter control include finger flexion and extension, with the flexion angle mapped to the desired variable [47]. However, these types of gestures might not achieve high precision using the sensing techniques above if captured from a distance (e.g. fingers of the other hand appearing too small) or when only partially visible (e.g. partially occluded fingers of the pen hand).

6.4 Posture Usability

For each system above, qualitative user studies were conducted to evaluate the comfort, suitability, and general usability of the proposed postures and gestures in example applications [8, 43, 46]. We summarise the main findings and their implications for the design of posture-based interactions in these contexts.

6.4.1 Posture Preferences

The choice of possible hand postures and interactions for a particular context depends on the sensing constraints, user preferences, and application functions to which the postures should be mapped. Our evaluations showed that user preferences for action-triggering postures can considerably vary, but some general trends can be identified.

Pressure-based postures were disliked if pressure has to be constantly applied to maintain a mode. However, brief squeezes to trigger quick actions were deemed acceptable. Similarly, postures requiring continuous contact with the surface were found unsuitable for maintained modes, especially when the hand needs to move, as dragging on the display causes friction. Touch-based postures are reasonable if the hand remains in the same position, such as a palm firmly planted while the pen is used locally, or if the postures consist of quick finger taps to invoke menus or execute commands.

Within contact-based postures, poses with the pinkie out, with or without the ring finger out as well, were preferred over others. Floating palm postures were also acceptable as long as precision was not required, since the palm is not planted on the display to afford stability.

Regarding raised fingers, preferences were mixed. People who adopt the dynamic quadrupod as a normal writing posture (four fingers gripping the pen) can easily raise their index finger while maintaining pen grip stability with their remaining three fingers. However, people who use a dynamic tripod grip (three fingers gripping the pen) cannot easily do this since lifting the index means that only two fingers remain to grip the pen. For these users, extending the pinkie is preferable, although that also implies a certain amount of dexterity.

Finally, pen tucking postures were considered comfortable overall, although a few people noted their pen grip became less stable when extending the thumb.

6.4.2 Pen Sawing Gesture

Participants generally found this kind of two-handed gesture to be very intuitive and easy to remember, but it also demands more effort as it requires moving the other hand which is resting next to the tablet towards the pen and back. Furthermore, many participants found it was difficult to find the precise location on the pen to place the index finger in order to obtain a specific value. This type of gesture might be more suitable for choosing among discrete, step-wise or coarse levels rather than setting a continuous parameter on a fine-grained spectrum.

6.4.3   Transitioning Between Postures

Transitioning from one pen hand posture to another can be difficult when the two postures are very different. For touch-based postures, the tablet surface can be an obstacle to finger movement. For example, when trying to extend the pinkie, sometimes the tablet is in the way so the hand needs to be raised. Another issue that can arise is when an unintentional posture is recognised midway during the action of forming the desired posture. For instance, when both pinkie out and pinkie out + ring out postures are included, if the user places the pinkie first to form the pinkie out + ring out posture, the action associated with pinkie out might be inadvertently triggered. Consideration for these conflicts and false activations should be given when designing posture sets.

6.4.4   Hand Choice for Postures

Switching modes using different pen grips requires only a single hand, which can be practical in case the other hand is busy, like when holding the tablet, or if the user does not want to interact with two hands [42, 43]. If the other hand is free and detectable, it is usually preferred for posture-based interaction as its movements are not constrained. In particular, it is a good option for the activation of maintained modes or quasimodes. A minority of people, however, do not want the other hand to participate in any action at all so they tend to prefer pen hand postures for everything.

If there are differences in pen-gripping styles, there is even more variability in ways people idly rest their hand on or near the tablet. In our experiments, we assumed that most people naturally rest their other hand more or less flatly on the table while engaged in a pen task (in the scenario where the tablet is placed on a table), but this is not necessarily the case for everybody. For example, some users who naturally curl their other hand when writing might accidentally trigger the action associated with the fist posture. Furthermore, hand position varies considerably while using pens and people naturally move their other hand to different locations, sometimes outside of detection range (e.g. when resting their head on it). Of course, users can change their habits if they are aware that their other hand is used for first-class input, but neural networks also need to be exposed to a large number of these various idle poses to be able to robustly distinguish them from explicit input postures.

6.4.5   Posture Memorisation

Similar to how stroke gestures are more easily memorised and recalled than keyboard shortcuts [1], it is helpful to try to semantically match certain types of postures to specific function categories. For instance, when using unimanual touch postures in a vector graphics editor, poses using the side of the palm can be assigned to creation modes such as sketching, erasing, and drawing shapes, while floating palm postures can be associated with "macro" interactions such as selecting and transforming shapes. Furthermore, dual actions can be assigned to two opposite positions of the same finger, such as a posture with a finger in for undo, and a finger out for redo.

Memorisation of the mode-to-posture mapping can further be helped if the shape of the posture roughly matches the associated input geometric shape, especially for the other hand, which is unconstrained. For example, associating a fist with circle input and a flat hand with rectangle input (Fig. 18a) was rated intuitive and easy to remember by our participants.

7 Conclusion

Pen-centric tablet applications can be enhanced by hand-posture interactions to quickly trigger shortcuts and UI actions. We examined three types of sensors that can detect different pen grips and other hand poses for this purpose: an EMG armband, the raw capacitive image of the touchscreen, and a pen-top fisheye camera facing downwards. We found that recognition accuracy differed based on sensor type, size of the posture sets, and amount of data. The least reliable sensor is the EMG armband, which can only identify a small number of postures and needs to be calibrated for each user. Raw touch data and pen-top camera images are more dependable sources, and it seems robust detection can be achieved given sufficient data with broad coverage of different posture variations, especially "normal" postures. Designers should make sure that input postures do not conflict with these cases.

Our evaluations showed that posture-based interaction is feasible, but there are usability issues to take into consideration. In particular, the relatively high variability in subjective posture preferences and hand dexterity for the pen-holding hand. The other hand is much less constrained for this type of interaction, but some users seem to prefer single handed interactions regardless, so flexibility regarding posture- and hand-action mappings is required.

Hand pose estimation, in general, is a very active research topic, especially now that deep learning has proven to be a robust tool to accurately track hands with common sensors. In computer vision, the latest models using only RGB images as input can track hands with high fidelity, even in the presence of occlusions and contacts with the other hand or objects [62]. These advances can no doubt be utilised for hand posture-based pen input given appropriate data. If finger joints can be tracked with millimetre precision, mapping hand and finger positions to specific postures and continuous parameters not only becomes straightforward, but also the possibility to choose which hand joints to map directly without retraining networks offers more flexibility.

Beyond tablets, we observe there is a growing interest in using pens in augmented reality [71] and virtual reality (VR) [13, 19], with vendors such as Logitech and

Wacom also recently releasing special digital pens for VR [40, 72]. When using the pen in mid-air, grip changes become easier to some degree as there is no screen underneath hindering finger extension. In this context, pens can not only be used for 3D drawing, but also as pointing instruments to select objects in 3D space [52]. Pen grip style has been shown to affect pointing precision [4], which suggests potential for grip detection not only to support mode switching, but also to make sure the user adopts the most efficient posture for a particular task. With hand tracking being an increasingly common feature of VR systems, the technical and practical hurdles for posture-based pen interaction in these contexts seem relatively low. We are hopeful that further novel and exciting research based on work for pen and tablet devices will emerge in this new space.

Acknowledgements We would like to acknowledge our co-authors on the three publications on which this article is based: Drini Cami, Brian Vogel, Richard G. Calland, Naoki Kimura and Riku Arakawa. While all evaluations of the neural networks presented in this article are new, we wish to recognise their contributions in the original publications.

References

1. Appert C, Zhai S (2009) Using strokes as command shortcuts: cognitive benefits and toolkit support. In: Proceedings of the SIGCHI conference on human factors in computing systems, pp 2289–2298
2. Aslan I, Buchwald I, Koytek P, André E (2016) Pen + Mid-Air: an exploration of mid-air gestures to complement pen input on tablets. In: Proceedings of the 9th Nordic conference on human-computer interaction, NordiCHI '16, pp 1:1-1:10, New York, NY, USA. ACM
3. Bandini A, Zariffa J (2020) Analysis of the hands in egocentric vision: a survey. IEEE Trans Pattern Anal Mach Intell
4. Batmaz AU, Mutasim AK, Stuerzlinger W (2020) Precision vs. power grip: a comparison of pen grip styles for selection in virtual reality. In: 2020 IEEE conference on virtual reality and 3D user interfaces abstracts and workshops (VRW), pp 23–28. IEEE
5. Hongliang B, Jian Z, Yanjiao C (2020) Smartge: identifying pen-holding gesture with smartwatch. IEEE Access 8:28820–28830
6. Bi X, Moscovich T, Ramos G, Balakrishnan R, Hinckley K (2008) An exploration of pen rolling for pen-based interaction. In: Proceedings of the 21st annual ACM symposium on User interface software and technology, pp 191–200
7. Brandl P, Forlines C, Wigdor D, Haller M, Shen C (2008) Combining and measuring the benefits of bimanual pen and direct-touch interaction on horizontal interfaces. In: Proceedings of the working conference on advanced visual interfaces, pp 154–161, Napoli, Italy. ACM
8. Cami D, Matulic F, Calland RG, Vogel B, Vogel D (2018) Unimanual Pen+Touch input using variations of precision grip postures. In: Proceedings of the 31st annual ACM symposium on user interface software and technology, UIST '18, pp 825–837, New York, NY, USA. ACM
9. Theocharis C, Andreas S, Dimitrios K, Kosmas D, Petros D (2020) A comprehensive study on deep learning-based 3d hand pose estimation methods. Appl Sci 10(19):6850
10. Weiya C, Yu C, Tu C, Zehua L, Jing T, Ou S, Fu Y, Zhidong X (2020) A survey on hand pose estimation with wearable sensors and computer-vision-based methods. Sensors 20(4):1074
11. Côté-Allard U, Fall CL, Drouin A, Campeau-Lecours A, Gosselin C, Glette K, Laviolette F, Gosselin B (2019) Deep learning for electromyographic hand gesture signal classification using transfer learning. IEEE Trans Neural Syst Rehab Eng 27(4):760–771

12. Dementyev A, Paradiso JA (2014) Wristflex: low-power gesture input with wrist-worn pressure sensors. In: Proceedings of the 27th annual ACM symposium on user interface software and technology, UIST '14, pp 161–166, New York, NY, USA. Association for Computing Machinery
13. Drey T, Gugenheimer J, Karlbauer J, Milo M, Rukzio E (2020) Vrsketchin: exploring the design space of pen and tablet interaction for 3d sketching in virtual reality. In: Proceedings of the 2020 CHI conference on human factors in computing systems, pp 1–14
14. Du H, Li P, Zhou H, Gong W, Luo G, Yang P (2018) Wordrecorder: accurate acoustic-based handwriting recognition using deep learning. In: IEEE INFOCOM 2018-IEEE conference on computer communications, pp 1448–1456. IEEE
15. Elkin LA, Beau J-B, Casiez G, Vogel D (2020) Manipulation, learning, and recall with tangible pen-like input. In: Proceedings of the 2020 CHI conference on human factors in computing systems, CHI '20, pp 1–12, New York, NY, USA. Association for Computing Machinery
16. Fellion N, Pietrzak T, Girouard A (2017) Flexstylus: leveraging bend input for pen interaction. In: Proceedings of the 30th annual ACM symposium on user interface software and technology, UIST '17, pages 375–385, New York, NY, USA. ACM
17. Frisch M, Heydekorn J, Dachselt R (2009) Investigating multi-touch and pen gestures for diagram editing on interactive surfaces. Proc ITS 2009:149–156
18. Ge L, Ren Z, Li Y, Xue Z, Wang Y, Cai J, Yuan J (2019) 3d hand shape and pose estimation from a single rgb image. In: Proceedings of the IEEE conference on computer vision and pattern recognition, pp 10833–10842
19. Gesslein T, Biener V, Gagel P, Schneider D, Kristensson PO, Ofek E, Pahud M, Grubert J (2020) Pen-based interaction with spreadsheets in mobile virtual reality. arXiv:2008.04543
20. Oliver G, Wu S, Daniele P, Otmar H, Olga S-H (2019) Interactive hand pose estimation using a stretch-sensing soft glove. ACM Trans Graph (TOG) 38(4):1–15
21. Grossman T, Hinckley K, Baudisch P, Agrawala M, Balakrishnan R (2006) Hover widgets: using the tracking state to extend the capabilities of pen-operated devices. In Proceedings of the SIGCHI conference on Human Factors in computing systems, pp 861–870, Montréal, Québec, Canada. ACM
22. Hamilton W, Kerne A, Robbins T (2012) High-performance pen+ touch modality interactions: a real-time strategy game esports context. In: Proceedings of the 25th annual ACM symposium on user interface software and technology, pp 309–318
23. Haque F, Nancel M, Vogel D (2015) Myopoint: pointing and clicking using forearm mounted electromyography and inertial motion sensors. In: Proceedings of the 33rd annual ACM conference on human factors in computing systems, CHI '15, pp 3653–3656, New York, NY, USA. Association for Computing Machinery
24. Hasan K, Yang X- D, Bunt A, Irani P (2012) A-coord input: coordinating auxiliary input streams for augmenting contextual pen-based interactions. In: Proceedings of the SIGCHI conference on human factors in computing systems, CHI '12, pp 805–814, New York, NY, USA. ACM
25. Hasson Y, Varol G, Tzionas D, Kalevatykh I, Black MJ, Laptev I, Schmid C (2019) Learning joint reconstruction of hands and manipulated objects. In: Proceedings of the IEEE conference on computer vision and pattern recognition, pp 11807–11816
26. Hinckley K, 'Anthony' Chen X, Benko H (2013) Motion and context sensing techniques for pen computing. In: Proceedings of graphics interface 2013, GI '13, pp 71–78, Toronto, Ont., Canada, Canada. Canadian Information Processing Society
27. Hinckley K, Pahud M, Benko H, Irani P, Guimbretière F, Gavriliu M, 'Anthony' Chen X, Matulic F, Buxton W, Wilson A (2014) Sensing techniques for tablet+stylus interaction. In: Proceedings of the 27th annual ACM symposium on user interface software and technology, UIST '14, pp 605–614, New York, NY, USA. ACM
28. Hinckley K, Yatani K, Pahud M, Coddington N, Rodenhouse J, Wilson A, Benko H, Buxton B (2010) Pen + touch = new tools. In: Proceedings of the 23nd annual ACM symposium on User interface software and technology, pp 27–36, New York, New York, USA. ACM
29. Howard J, Gugger S (2020) Fastai: a layered api for deep learning. Information 11(2):108

30. Hu F, He P, Xu S, Li Y, Zhang C (2020) Fingertrak: continuous 3d hand pose tracking by deep learning hand silhouettes captured by miniature thermal cameras on wrist. Proc ACM Interact Mob Wearable Ubiquitous Technol 4(2)

31. Hwang S, Bianchi A, Ahn M, Wohn K (2013) MagPen: magnetically driven pen interactions on and around conventional smartphones. In: Proceedings of the 15th international conference on human-computer interaction with mobile devices and services, MobileHCI '13, pp 412–415, New York, NY, USA. ACM

32. Iravantchi Y, Zhang Y, Bernitsas E, Goel M, Harrison C (2019) Interferi: gesture sensing using on-body acoustic interferometry. In: Proceedings of the 2019 CHI conference on human factors in computing systems, CHI '19, pp 1–13, New York, NY, USA. Association for Computing Machinery

33. Jiang S, Lv B, Guo W, Zhang C, Wang H, Sheng X, Shull PB (2017) Feasibility of wrist-worn, real-time hand, and surface gesture recognition via semg and imu sensing. IEEE Trans Ind Inf 14(8):3376–3385

34. Kefer K, Holzmann C, Findling RD (2017) Evaluating the placement of arm-worn devices for recognizing variations of dynamic hand gestures. J Mobile Multimedia 12(3&4):225–242

35. Kim C, Chiu P, Oda H (2017) Capturing handwritten ink strokes with a fast video camera. In: 2017 14th IAPR international conference on document analysis and recognition (ICDAR), vol 1, pp 1269–1274. IEEE

36. Kim D, Hilliges O, Izadi S, Butler AD, Chen J, Oikonomidis I, Olivier P (2012) Digits: freehand 3d interactions anywhere using a wrist-worn gloveless sensor. In: Proceedings of the 25th annual ACM symposium on user interface software and technology, UIST '12, pp 167–176, New York, NY, USA. Association for Computing Machinery

37. Kim J-H, Thang ND, Kim T-S (2009) 3-d hand motion tracking and gesture recognition using a data glove. In: 2009 IEEE international symposium on industrial electronics, pp 1013–1018. IEEE

38. Li Y, Hinckley K, Guan Z, Landay J (2005) Experimental analysis of mode switching techniques in pen-based user interfaces. CHI '05: proceedings of the sigchi conference on Human factors in computing systems, pp 461–470

39. Lin J-W, Wang C, Huang Y, Chou K-T, Chen H-Y, Tseng W-L, Chen MY (2015) Backhand: sensing hand gestures via back of the hand. In: Proceedings of the 28th annual ACM symposium on user interface software and technology, UIST '15, pp 557–564, New York, NY, USA. Association for Computing Machinery

40. Logitech vr ink pilot edition. https://www.logitech.com/en-roeu/promo/vr-ink.html. Accessed 17 Dec 2020

41. Matsubara T, Morimoto J (2013) Bilinear modeling of emg signals to extract user-independent features for multiuser myoelectric interface. IEEE Trans Biomed Eng 60(8):2205–2213

42. Matulic F (2018) Colouraize: Ai-driven colourisation of paper drawings with interactive projection system. In: Proceedings of the 2018 ACM international conference on interactive surfaces and spaces, pp 273–278

43. Matulic F, Arakawa R, Vogel B, Vogel D (2020) Pensight: enhanced interaction with a pen-top camera. In: Proceedings of the 2020 CHI conference on human factors in computing systems, pp 1–14

44. Matulic F, Norrie M (2012) Empirical evaluation of uni- and bimodal pen and touch interaction properties on digital tabletops. In: Proceedings of the 2012 ACM international conference on interactive tabletops and surfaces, ITS '12, pp 143–152, New York, NY, USA. ACM

45. Matulic F, Norrie MC (2013) Pen and touch gestural environment for document editing on interactive tabletops. In: Proceedings of the 2013 ACM international conference on interactive tabletops and surfaces, ITS '13, pp 41–50, New York, NY, USA. ACM

46. Matulic F, Vogel B, Kimura N, Vogel D (2019) Eliciting pen-holding postures for general input with suitability for emg armband detection. In: Proceedings of the 2019 ACM international conference on interactive surfaces and spaces, pp 89–100

47. Matulic F, Vogel D, Dachselt R (2017) Hand contact shape recognition for posture-based tabletop widgets and interaction. In: Proceedings of the 2017 ACM international conference on interactive surfaces and spaces, ISS '17, pp 3–11, New York, NY, USA. ACM

48. McIntosh J, Marzo A, Fraser M (2017) Sensir: detecting hand gestures with a wearable bracelet using infrared transmission and reflection. In: Proceedings of the 30th annual ACM symposium on user interface software and technology, UIST '17, pp 593–597, New York, NY, USA. Association for Computing Machinery

49. McIntosh J, Marzo A, Fraser M, Phillips C (2017) Echoflex: hand gesture recognition using ultrasound imaging. In: Proceedings of the 2017 CHI conference on human factors in computing systems, CHI '17, pp 1923–1934, New York, NY, USA. Association for Computing Machinery

50. McIntosh J, McNeill C, Fraser M, Kerber F, Löchtefeld M, Krüger A (2016) Empress: practical hand gesture classification with wrist-mounted emg and pressure sensing. In: Proceedings of the 2016 CHI conference on human factors in computing systems, CHI '16, pp 2332–2342, New York, NY, USA. Association for Computing Machinery

51. Panteleris P, Oikonomidis I, Argyros A (2018) Using a single rgb frame for real time 3d hand pose estimation in the wild. In: 2018 IEEE winter conference on applications of computer vision (WACV), pp 436–445. IEEE

52. Pham D-M, Stuerzlinger W (2019) Is the pen mightier than the controller? A comparison of input devices for selection in virtual and augmented reality. In: 25th ACM symposium on virtual reality software and technology, VRST '19, New York, NY, USA. Association for Computing Machinery

53. Protalinski E (2019) Ctrl-labs ceo: we'll have neural interfaces in less than 5 years. VentureBeat

54. Ramos G, Boulos M, Balakrishnan R (2004) Pressure widgets. In: Proceedings of the SIGCHI conference on Human factors in computing systems, pp 487–494, Vienna, Austria. ACM

55. Rekimoto J (1997) Pick-and-drop: a direct manipulation technique for multiple computer environments. In: Proceedings of the 10th annual ACM symposium on user interface software and technology, UIST '97, pp 31–39, New York, NY, USA. ACM

56. Roland T, Wimberger K, Amsuess S, Russold MF, Baumgartner W (2019) An insulated flexible sensor for stable electromyography detection: application to prosthesis control. Sensors 19(4):961

57. Saponas TS, Tan DS, Morris D, Balakrishnan R (2008) Demonstrating the feasibility of using forearm electromyography for muscle-computer interfaces. In: Proceedings of the SIGCHI conference on human factors in computing systems, CHI '08, pp 515–524, New York, NY, USA. Association for Computing Machinery

58. Saponas TS, Tan DS, Morris D, Turner J, Landay JA (2010) Making muscle-computer interfaces more practical. In: Proceedings of the SIGCHI conference on human factors in computing systems, CHI '10, pp 851–854, New York, NY, USA. Association for Computing Machinery

59. Schrapel M, Stadler M-L, Rohs M (2018) Pentelligence: combining pen tip motion and writing sounds for handwritten digit recognition. In: Proceedings of the 2018 CHI conference on human factors in computing systems, pp 1–11

60. Selvaraju RR, Cogswell M, Das A, Vedantam R, Parikh D, Batra D (2017) Grad-cam: Visual explanations from deep networks via gradient-based localization. In Proceedings of the IEEE international conference on computer vision, pp 618–626

61. Simonyan K, Zisserman A (2014) Very deep convolutional networks for large-scale image recognition. arXiv:1409.1556

62. Smith B, Wu C, Wen H, Peluse P, Sheikh Y, Hodgins JK, Shiratori T (2020) Constraining dense hand surface tracking with elasticity. ACM Trans Graph (TOG), 39(6):1–14

63. Song H, Benko H, Guimbretiere F, Izadi S, Cao X, Hinckley K (2011) Grips and gestures on a multi-touch pen. In: Proceedings of the SIGCHI conference on human factors in computing systems, CHI '11, pp 1323–1332, New York, NY, USA. ACM

64. Sridhar S, Mueller F, Zollhöfer M, Casas D, Oulasvirta A, Theobalt C (2016) Real-time joint tracking of a hand manipulating an object from rgb-d input. In: European conference on computer vision, pp 294–310. Springer

65. Suzuki Y, Misue K, Tanaka J (2009) Interaction technique for a pen-based interface using finger motions. In: Jacko JA (ed) Human-computer interaction. Novel interaction methods and techniques, pp 503–512. Springer, Berlin Heidelberg

66. Tekin B, Bogo F, Pollefeys M (2019) H+ o: unified egocentric recognition of 3d hand-object poses and interactions. In: Proceedings of the IEEE conference on computer vision and pattern recognition, pp 4511–4520
67. Tian F, Xu L, Wang H, Zhang X, Liu Y, Setlur V, Dai G (2008) Tilt menu: using the 3d orientation information of pen devices to extend the selection capability of pen-based user interfaces. In: Proceedings of the SIGCHI conference on human factors in computing systems, CHI '08, pp 1371–1380, New York, NY, USA. ACM
68. van Drempt N, McCluskey A, Lannin NA (2011) A review of factors that influence adult handwriting performance. Aust Occup Therapy J 58(5):321–328
69. Vogel D, Balakrishnan R (2010) Direct pen interaction with a conventional graphical user interface. Human-Comput Inter 25(4):324–388
70. Vogel D, Casiez G (2011) Conté: multimodal input inspired by an artist's crayon. In: Proceedings of the 24th annual ACM symposium on User interface software and technology, pp 357–366
71. Wacker P, Nowak O, Voelker S, Borchers J (2019) Arpen: mid-air object manipulation techniques for a bimanual ar system with pen & smartphone. In: Proceedings of the 2019 CHI conference on human factors in computing systems, pp 1–12
72. Wacom vr pen. https://developer.wacom.com/en-us/wacomvrpen. Accessed 17 Dec 2020
73. Wen H, Rojas JR, Dey AK (2016) Serendipity: finger gesture recognition using an off-the-shelf smartwatch. In: Proceedings of the 2016 CHI conference on human factors in computing systems, pp 3847–3851
74. Westerman W (1999) Hand tracking, finger identification, and chordic manipulation on a multi-touch surface. PhD thesis, University of Delaware
75. Wu E, Yuan Y, Yeo H-S, Quigley A, Koike H, Kitani KM (2020) Back-hand-pose: 3d hand pose estimation for a wrist-worn camera via dorsum deformation network. In: Proceedings of the 33rd annual ACM symposium on user interface software and technology, UIST '20, pp 1147–1160, New York, NY, USA. Association for Computing Machinery
76. Xin Y, Bi X, Ren X (2011) Acquiring and pointing: an empirical study of pen-tilt-based interaction. In: Proceedings of the SIGCHI conference on human factors in computing systems, CHI '11, pp 849–858, New York, NY, USA. ACM
77. Xu C, Pathak PH, Mohapatra P (2015) Finger-writing with smartwatch: a case for finger and hand gesture recognition using smartwatch. In: Proceedings of the 16th international workshop on mobile computing systems and applications, pp 9–14
78. Zhang X, Chen X, Li Y, Lantz V, Wang K, Yang J (2011) A framework for hand gesture recognition based on accelerometer and emg sensors. IEEE Trans Syst Man Cybernet-Part A: Syst Hum 41(6):1064–1076
79. Zhang Y, Harrison C (2015) Tomo: wearable, low-cost electrical impedance tomography for hand gesture recognition. In: Proceedings of the 28th annual ACM symposium on user interface software and technology, UIST '15, pp 167–173, New York, NY, USA. Association for Computing Machinery
80. Zhou X, Yao C, Wen H, Wang Y, Zhou S, He W, Liang J (2017) East: an efficient and accurate scene text detector. In: Proceedings of the IEEE conference on computer vision and pattern recognition, pp 5551–5560

Part III
Data and Tools

An Early Rico Retrospective: Three Years of Uses for a Mobile App Dataset

Biplab Deka, Bardia Doosti, Forrest Huang, Chad Franzen,
Joshua Hibschman, Daniel Afergan, Yang Li, Ranjitha Kumar, Tao Dong,
and Jeffrey Nichols

Abstract The Rico dataset, containing design data from more than 9.7 k Android apps spanning 27 categories, was released in 2017. It exposes visual, textual, structural, and interactive design properties of more than 72 k unique UI screens. Over the years since its release, the original paper has been cited nearly 100 times according to Google Scholar and the dataset has been used as the basis for numerous research

B. Deka
McKinsey, Chicago, IL, USA
e-mail: biplab.uiuc@gmail.com

B. Doosti · C. Franzen · D. Afergan · Y. Li · T. Dong
Google, Inc., Mountain View, CA, USA
e-mail: bardiad@google.com

C. Franzen
e-mail: cfranzen@google.com

D. Afergan
e-mail: afergan@google.com

Y. Li
e-mail: liyang@google.com

T. Dong
e-mail: taodong@google.com

F. Huang
University of California, Berkeley, CA, USA
e-mail: forrest_huang@berkeley.edu

J. Hibschman
Northwestern University, Evanston, IL, USA
e-mail: jh@u.northwestern.edu

R. Kumar
University of Illinois at Urbana-Champaign, Champaign, IL, USA
e-mail: ranjitha@illinois.edu

J. Nichols (✉)
Apple, Inc., Seattle, WA, USA
e-mail: jeff@jeffreynichols.com

© The Author(s), under exclusive license to Springer Nature Switzerland AG 2021   229
Y. Li and O. Hilliges (eds.), *Artificial Intelligence for Human Computer Interaction:
A Modern Approach*, Human–Computer Interaction Series,
https://doi.org/10.1007/978-3-030-82681-9_8

projects. In this chapter, we describe the creation of Rico using a system that combined crowdsourcing and automation to scalably mine design and interaction data from Android apps at runtime. We then describe two projects that we conducted using the dataset: the training of an autoencoder to identify similarity between UI designs, and an exploration of the use of Google's Material Design within the dataset using machine learned models. We conclude with an overview of other work that has used Rico to understand our mobile UI world and build data-driven models that assist users, designers, and developers.

1 Introduction

We created the Rico[1] dataset and released it publicly in 2017 [21]. We believe it is still the largest repository of Android mobile app designs, comprising visual, textual, structural, and interactive property data for 72,219 UIs from 9,772 apps, spanning 27 Google Play categories. For each app, Rico presents a collection of individual user interaction traces, as well as a collection of unique UIs determined by a novel *content-agnostic similarity heuristic*. In total, the dataset contains more than 72 k unique UI screens.

To download the Rico dataset and learn more about the project, please visit http://interactionmining.org/rico.

To understand what makes Rico unique, it is helpful to consider it in the context of other Android app datasets. Existing datasets expose different kinds of information: Google Play Store metadata (e.g., reviews, ratings) [2, 25], software engineering and security related information [24, 52], and design data [7, 22, 45]. Rico captures both design data and Google Play Store metadata.

Mobile app designs comprise several different components, including user interaction flows (e.g., search, login), UI layouts, visual styles, and motion details. These components can be computed by mining and combining different types of app data. For example, combining the structural representation of UIs—Android *view hierarchies* [3]—with the visual realization of those UIs—screenshots—can help explicate app layouts and their visual stylings. Similarly, combining *user interaction* details with view hierarchies and screenshots can help identify the user flows that apps are designed to support.

Figure 1 compares Rico with other popular datasets that expose app design information. Design datasets created by *statically* mining app packages contain view hierarchies, but cannot capture data created at runtime such as screenshots or interaction details [7, 45]. ERICA's dataset, on the other hand, is created by *dynamically* mining apps and captures view hierarchies, screenshots, and user interactions [22].

Like the ERICA dataset, Rico is created by mining design and interaction data from apps at runtime. Rico's data was collected via a combination of human-powered and programmatic exploration, as shown in Fig. 2. Also like ERICA, Rico's app

---

[1] Rico—a Spanish word meaning "rich".

	Year	# Apps	# UIs	Mining	View Hierarchies	Screenshots	User Interactions
Shirazi et al.	2013	400	29K	Static	●	○	○
Alharbi et al.	2015	24K	-	Static	●	○	○
ERICA	2016	2.4K	18.6K	Dynamic	●	●	●
Rico	2017	9.7K	72.2K	Dynamic	●	●	●

Fig. 1 A comparison of Rico with other popular app datasets

mining infrastructure requires no access to—or modification of—an app's source code. Apps are downloaded from the Google Play Store and served to crowd workers through a web interface. When crowd workers use an app, the system records a *user interaction trace* that captures the UIs visited and the interactions performed on them. Then, an automated agent replays the trace to "warm up" a new copy of the app and continues the exploration programmatically. By combining crowdsourcing and automation, Rico can achieve higher coverage over an app's UI states than either crawling strategy alone.

Rico is four times larger than the ERICA dataset and presents a superset of its design information. Rico also exposes an additional view of each app's design data: while ERICA provides a collection of individual user interaction traces for an app, Rico additionally provides a list of the unique UIs discovered by aggregating over user interaction traces and merging UIs based on a similarity measure. This representation is useful for training machine learning models over UIs that do not depend on the sequence in which they were seen. Lastly, Rico annotates each UI with a low-dimensional vector representation that encodes layout based on the distribution of text and images, which can be used to cluster and retrieve similar UIs from different apps.

We chose to release the Rico dataset publicly as we believed others in the research community might benefit from it, and we were especially optimistic that the dataset would find use because it is large enough to support deep learning applications. We envisioned that the dataset would be used for applications related to user interface design, such as UI layout generation and UI code generation, similar to the directions that we were pursuing when we created it. To our surprise, the community has found much broader use cases for the dataset than we could have imagined. Over the years since Rico's release, the original paper [21] has been cited nearly 100 times according to Google Scholar and the dataset has been used as the basis for numerous research projects, including explorations of the usage of specific features within the app ecosystem [39, 44], the creation of intelligent assistants [47], and mapping natural language to UI actions [34]. The dataset has also been extended by a number of research groups, who have added semantic metadata [37], language mappings [34], UI embeddings [38], and more. We will examine these use cases and develop a preliminary taxonomy later in the chapter.

In this chapter, we begin by describing the creation of Rico using a system that combined crowdsourcing and automation to scalably mine design and interaction data from Android apps at runtime. We then describe two projects that we conducted using the dataset: the training of an autoencoder to identify similarity between UI

Authors Suppressed Due to Excessive Length

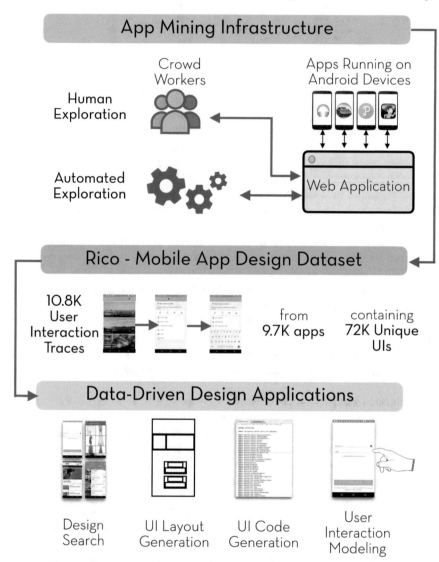

Fig. 2 Rico is a design dataset with 72 k UIs mined from 9.7 k free Android apps using a combination of human and automated exploration. The dataset can power a number of design applications, including ones that require training state-of-the-art machine learning models

designs, and an exploration of the use of Google's Material Design within the dataset using machine learned models. We conclude with an overview of other work that has used Rico to understand our mobile UI world and build data-driven models that assist users, designers, and developers.

2 Collecting Rico

To create Rico, we developed a platform that mines design data from Android apps at runtime by combining human-powered and programmatic exploration. Humans rely on prior knowledge and contextual information to effortlessly interact with a diverse array of apps. Apps, however, can have hundreds of UI states, and human exploration clusters around common use cases, achieving low coverage over UI states for many apps [10, 22]. Automated agents, on the other hand, can be used to exhaustively process the interactive elements on a UI screen [13, 50]; however, they can be stymied by UIs that require complex interaction sequences or human inputs (Fig. 3) [8].

We developed a hybrid approach for design mining mobile apps that combine the strengths of human-powered and programmatic exploration: leveraging humans to unlock app states that are hidden behind complex UIs and using automated agents to exhaustively process the interactive elements on the uncovered screens to discover new states. The automated agents leverage a novel *content-agnostic similarity heuristic* to efficiently explore the UI state space. Together, these approaches achieve higher coverage over an app's UI states than either technique alone.

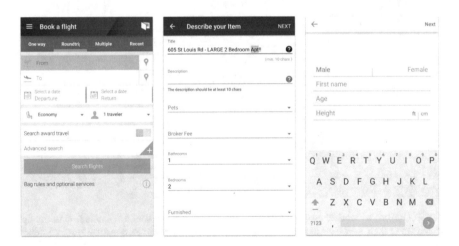

Fig. 3 Automated crawlers are often stymied by UIs that require complex interaction sequences, such as the three shown here

2.1   Crowdsourced Exploration

The crowdsourced mining system uses a web-based architecture similar to ERICA [22]. A crowd worker connects to the design mining platform through a web application, which establishes a dedicated connection between the worker and a phone in our mobile device farm. The system loads an app on the phone and starts continuously streaming images of the phone's screen to the worker's browser. As the worker interacts with the screen on his browser, these interactions are sent back to the phone, which performs the interactions on the app.

We extended the ERICA architecture to enable large-scale crowdsourcing over the Internet. We added an authorization system that supports both short- and long-term engagement models. For micro-task style crowdsourcing on platforms like Amazon Mechanical Turk, we generate URLs with tokens. When a worker clicks on a URL with a valid token, the system installs an app on a device and hands over control to the user for a limited time. To facilitate longer term engagements on platforms such as UpWork, we provide a separate interface through which workers can repeatedly request apps and use them. This interface is protected by a login wall, and each worker is provided separate login credentials.

We show the web interface in Fig. 4. To ensure that no personally identifiable information is captured, the web interface provides a name, email address, location, and phone number for crowd workers to use in the app. It also displays emails or text messages sent to the specified email addresses and phone numbers, letting crowd workers complete app verification steps with minimal effort.

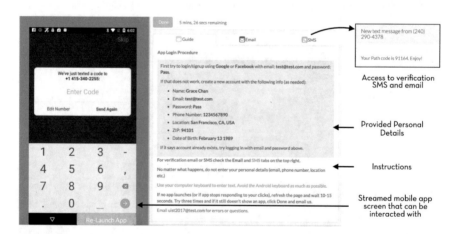

Fig. 4 Our crowd worker web interface. On the left, crowd workers can interact with the app screen using their keyboard and mouse. On the right, there are provided instructions and details such as the name, location, phone number, and email address to use in the app. The interface also allows workers to access SMS and email messages sent to the provided phone number and email to complete app verification processes

2.2 Automated Exploration

To move beyond the set of UI states uncovered by humans, Rico employs an automated mining system. Existing automated crawlers hard-code inputs for each app to unlock states hidden behind complex UIs [8, 33]. We achieve a similar result by leveraging the interaction data contained within the collected user traces: when the crawler encounters an interface requiring human input, it replays the interactions that a crowd worker performed on that screen to advance to the next UI state.

Similar to prior work [8, 33], the automated mining system uses a depth-first search strategy to crawl the state space of UIs in the app. For each unique UI, the crawler requests the view hierarchy to identify the set of interactive elements. The system programmatically interacts with these elements, creating an *interaction graph* that captures the unique UIs that have been visited as nodes and the connections between interactive elements and their resultant screens as edges. This data structure also maintains a queue of unexplored interactions for each visited UI state. The system programmatically crawls an app until it hits a specified time budget or has exhaustively explored all interactions contained within the discovered UI states.

2.3 Content-Agnostic Similarity Heuristic

After Rico's crawler interacts with a UI element, it must determine whether the interaction led to a new UI state or one that is already captured in the interaction graph. Database-backed applications can have thousands of views that represent the same semantic concept and differ only in their content (Fig. 5). Therefore, we employ a *content-agnostic similarity heuristic* to compare UIs.

Fig. 5 Pairs of UI screens from apps that are visually distinct but have the same design. Our content-agnostic similarity heuristic uses structural properties to identify these sorts of design collisions

This similarity heuristic compares two UIs based on their visual and structural composition. If the screenshots of two given UIs differ by fewer than α pixels, they are treated as equivalent states. Otherwise, the crawler compares the set of element resource-ids present on each screen. If these sets differ by more than β elements, the two screens are treated as different states.

We evaluated the heuristic with different values of α and β on 1,044 pairs of UIs from 12 apps. We found that $\alpha = 99.8\%$ and $\beta = 1$ produce a false positive rate of 6% and a false negative rate of 3%. We use these parameter values for automated crawling and computing the set of unique UIs for a given app.

2.4 Coverage Benefits of Hybrid Exploration

To measure the coverage benefits of our hybrid exploration approach, we compare Rico's crawling strategy to human and automated exploration alone. We selected 10 apps (Fig. 6) from the top 200 on the Google Play Store. Each app had an average rating higher than 4 stars (out of 5) and had been downloaded more than a million times. We recruited 5 participants for each app and instructed them to use the app until they believed they had discovered all its features. We then ran the automated explorer on each app for three hours, after warming it up with the collected human traces.

Prior work [1, 10, 22] measured coverage using Android activities, a way of organizing an Android app's codebase that can comprise multiple UI screens. While activities are a useful way of statically analyzing an Android app, developers do

Name	Description
Polyvore	Fashion social-network and marketplace
Fabulous	Goal-setting app
Issuu	Magazine browsing and collection
Foursquare	City guide and reviews
Yelp	Guide for local businesses
Newsrepublic	World news digest
Etsy	Homemade and Vintage goods marketplace
Todoist	To-do list and reminder
WeHeartIt	Photo-sharing social network
Weather Channel	Weather tracker
Evernote	Note-taking app for collaboration

Fig. 6 The Android apps used in our evaluation. Each had a rating higher than 4 stars (out of 5) and more than 1 M downloads on the Google Play store

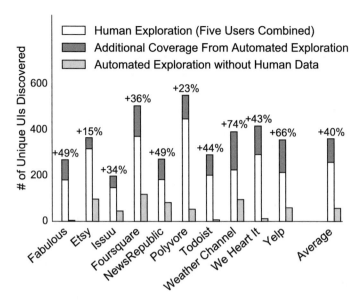

Fig. 7 The performance of our hybrid exploration system compared to human and automated exploration alone, measured across ten diverse Android apps

not use them consistently: in practice, complex apps can have the same number of activities as simple apps. In contrast, we use a coverage measure that correlates with app complexity: computing coverage as the number of unique UIs discovered under the similarity heuristic.

Figure 7 presents the coverage benefits of a hybrid system: combining human and automated exploration increases UI coverage by an average of 40% over human exploration alone and discovered several new Android activities for each app. For example, on the Etsy app, our hybrid system uncovered screens from 7 additional Activities beyond the 18 discovered by human exploration.

We also evaluated the coverage of the automated system in isolation, without bootstrapping it with a human trace. The automated system achieved 26% lower coverage across the tested apps than Rico's hybrid approach. This poor performance is largely attributable to experiences that are gated beyond a login screen or paywall that our pure, automated approach cannot handle. For instance, Todoist and WeHeartIt hide most of their features behind a login wall.

3   The Rico Dataset

The Rico dataset comprises 10,811 user interaction traces and 72,219 unique UIs from 9,772 Android apps spanning 27 categories (Fig. 8). We excluded from our crawl categories that primarily involve multimedia (such as video players and photo

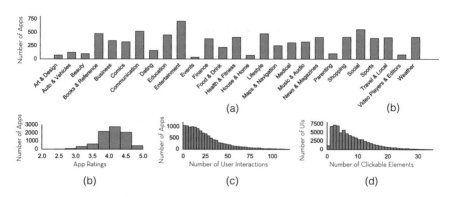

Fig. 8 Summary statistics of the Rico Dataset: app distribution by **a** category, **b** average rating, and **c** number of mined interactions. **d** The distribution of mined UIs by number of interactive elements

editors) as well as productivity and personalization apps. Apps in the Rico dataset have an average rating of 4.1 stars and data pertaining to 26 user interactions.

3.1 Data Collection

To create Rico, we downloaded 9,772 free apps from the Google Play Store and crowdsourced user traces for each app by recruiting 13 workers (10 from the US, 3 from the Philippines) on UpWork. We chose UpWork over other crowdsourcing platforms because it allows managers to directly communicate with workers: a capability that we used to resolve any technical issues that arose during crawling. We instructed workers to use each app as it was intended based on its Play Store description for no longer than 10 min.

In total, workers spent 2,450 h using apps on the platform over five months, producing 10,811 user interaction traces. We paid US $19, 200 in compensation or approximately two dollars to crowdsource usage data for each app. To ensure high-quality traces, we visually inspected a subset of each user's submissions. After collecting each user trace for an app, we ran the automated crawler on it for one hour.

3.2 Design Data Organization

For each app, Rico exposes Google Play Store metadata, a set of user interaction traces, and a list of all the unique discovered UIs through crowdsourced and automated exploration. The Play Store metadata includes an app's category, average rating, number of ratings, and number of downloads. Each user trace is composed of a sequence of UIs and user interactions that connect them. Each UI comprises a screenshot, an augmented view hierarchy, a set of explored user interactions, a set of animations capturing transition effects in response to user interactions, and a learned vector representation of the UI's layout.

View hierarchies capture all of the elements comprising a UI, their properties, and relationships between them. For each element, Rico exposes its *visual* properties such as screen position, dimensionality, and visibility; *textual* properties such as class name, id, and displayed text; *structural* properties such as a list of its children in the hierarchy; and *interactive* properties such as the ways a user can interact with it. Additionally, we annotate elements with any Android superclasses that they are derived from (e.g., `TextView`), which can help third-party applications reason about element types. Rico contains more than 3 M elements, of which approximately 500 k are interactive. On average, each UI comprises eight interactive elements.

4 Our Uses of Rico

Having created the Rico dataset, we then made use of it in several different projects. Two of these projects are described here: the training of a UI layout embedding using an autoencoder, and an investigation of the usage of Material Design. We also built a system called Swire [27], which allowed users to investigate the Rico dataset by sketching a full or partial user interface and using that sketch as a search query over the dataset. Swire is described in more detail in Chapter 12 of this book.

4.1 Training a UI Layout Embedding

The large size of the Rico dataset makes it difficult to browse comprehensively, so in this work, we set out to create a method that would allow users to search the dataset. As a starting point, we allow users to use a screenshot of a mobile UI as their query.

Since the Rico dataset is large and comprehensive enough to support deep learning applications, we trained a deep autoencoder to learn an embedding for UI layouts and used it to annotate each UI with a 64-dimensional vector representation encoding visual layout. This vector representation can be used to compute structurally—and often semantically—similar UIs, supporting example-based search over the dataset (see figures in the original Rico paper [21]).

An autoencoder is a neural network that involves two models—an encoder and a decoder—to support the *unsupervised* learning of lower-dimensional representations [12]. The encoder maps its input to a lower-dimensional vector, while the decoder maps this lower-dimensional vector back to the input's dimensions. Both models are trained together with a loss function based on the differences between inputs and their reconstructions. Once an autoencoder is trained, the encoder portion is used to produce lower-dimensional representations of the input vectors.

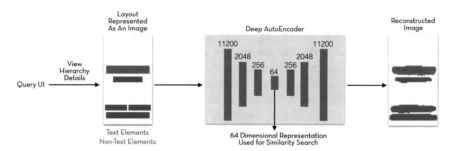

Fig. 9 We train an autoencoder to learn a 64-dimensional representation for each UI in the repository, encoding structural information about its layout. This is accomplished by creating training images that encode the positions and sizes of elements in each UI, differentiating between text and non-text elements

To create training inputs for the autoencoder that embed layout information, we constructed a new image for each UI encoding the bounding box regions of all leaf elements in its view hierarchy, differentiating between text and non-text elements (Fig. 9). Rico's view hierarchies obviate the need for noisy image processing or OCR techniques to create these inputs. In the future, we could incorporate more recent work on predicting functional semantic labels [37] for elements such as *search icon* or *login button* to train embeddings with even richer semantics.

The encoder has an input dimension of 11,200 and an output dimension of 64 and uses two hidden layers of dimension 2,048 and 256 with ReLU non-linearities [41]. The decoder has the reverse architecture. We trained the autoencoder with 90% of our data and used the rest as a validation set, and we found that the validation loss stabilized after 900 epochs or approximately 5 h on an Nvidia GTX 1060 GPU. Once the autoencoder was trained, we used the encoder to compute a 64-dimensional representation for each UI, which we expose as part of the Rico dataset.

Figure 10 shows several example query UIs and their nearest neighbors in the learned 64-dimensional space. The results demonstrate that the learned model is able to capture common mobile and Android UI patterns such as lists, login screens, dialog screens, and image grids. Moreover, the diversity of the dataset allows the model to distinguish between layout nuances, like lists composed of smaller and larger image thumbnails.

4.2   Understanding Material Design Usage in the Wild

Material Design[2] is a UI design pattern language introduced by Google in 2014, which can be applied to user interfaces on many types of computing devices. In this

---

[2] Material Design https://material.io/guidelines/.

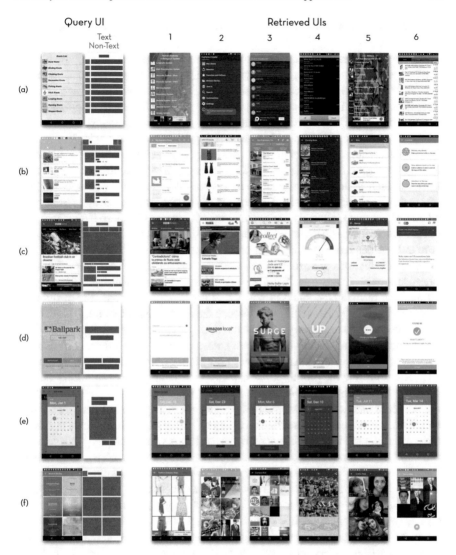

Fig. 10 The top six results obtained from querying the repository for UIs with similar layouts to those shown on the left, via a nearest-neighbor search in the learned 64-dimensional autoencoder space. The returned results share a common layout and even distinguish between layout nuances such as lists composed of smaller and larger image thumbnails (**a, b**)

work, we leverage the Rico dataset to understand how Material Design has been used on mobile devices.

Pattern languages have been long used in Human–Computer Interaction (HCI) for distilling and communicating design knowledge [14, 20]. According to Christopher Alexander [6], who introduced pattern-based design to architecture, "each pattern describes a problem which occurs over and over again in our environment, and then describes the core of the solution to that problem, in such a way that you can use this solution a million times over, without ever doing it the same way twice".

HCI researchers and design practitioners have documented and introduced pattern languages for general UI design (e.g., [42, 51]) as well as a wide variety of application domains, such as learning management systems [9], ubiquitous computing [30], information retrieval [53], and many more. Nonetheless, as Dearden and Finlay point out, there have been relatively few evaluations of how useful pattern languages are in user interface design [20]. Since Dearden and Finlay published their critical review, more evaluations have been done on pattern languages in HCI (e.g., [18, 46, 53]). But these evaluations are usually limited in at least one of several ways. First, the pattern languages in those evaluations were often developed in an academic research setting. Few have been applied to real-world applications. Second, the evaluations were usually done in lab settings and hence lacked ecological validity. Last, those evaluations were done at a very small scale (i.e., applying a pattern language to either one or no more than a handful of systems). As a result of the limitations of how the field has evaluated pattern languages, we know little about whether pattern languages in HCI are fulfilling the promise of Alexander—providing design solutions that can be reused "a million times over".

The recent success of commercial UI design pattern languages offers a rare opportunity for us to evaluate the usefulness of pattern languages in HCI at scale and in the wild. In particular, Material Design seems to have been widely adopted by developers who build applications for Google's Android operating system. *How can we understand the impact of a pattern language in one of the largest computing ecosystems in the world?* This is the first research question we seek to answer in this project.

In addition to developing a method for measuring a pattern language's overall impact, we also want to address questions about how and where certain patterns should be used when they get applied to new use cases. For Material Design, few patterns have been more controversial, yet at the same time iconic, than the Floating Action Button (aka, FAB) and the Navigation Drawer (i.e., the hamburger menu). Tens of thousands of words have been written about the merits and more often the downsides of these two patterns (e.g., [11, 28, 48] for FAB and [4, 19, 43] for Hamburger Menu). Sometimes, the conclusions are daunting. For example, one online critic said, "...in actual practice, widespread adoption of FABs might be detrimental to the overall UX of the app" [48]. Even when the criticisms are moderate and well-reasoned, they are based on the writer's examination of a limited number of examples. It is hard to know whether these criticisms reflect the full picture, since these patterns are likely to be used in a huge number of different apps. Thus, the second research question driving this work is: *How can we examine real-world use of design patterns to inform debates about UI design?*

We took a data-driven approach to shed light on these two questions, leveraging the app screenshots and view hierarchies in the Rico dataset and the app ratings and downloads data from Google Play. Using text mining and computer vision techniques, we built a computational model to detect six widely used UI components specified in Material Design, including the FAB, the Navigation Drawer, and four other components. We then used the metadata of the apps in the first dataset to measure the relationship between the use of certain patterns and the popularity of apps, as indicated by app ratings and the number of installs. Furthermore, we used app category data to examine in what domain a certain pattern might be more useful.

Our results show that the use of Material Design is positively correlated with both the app's average rating and the number of installs, which we believe is the first quantitative evidence for the value of a pattern language applied to a large ecosystem in the wild. Our data analysis further shows that, despite the criticisms the FAB and the Navigation Drawer have received from vocal writers in the design community, they are more popular among apps with higher ratings and higher number of installs than their less popular peers. Furthermore, we found that the use of UI components varies by app category, suggesting a more nuanced view needed in ongoing debates about UI design patterns.

4.2.1 Detecting Material Design Elements

There were two general stages in our data analysis. First, we detected Material Design elements in a large number of mobile apps. We focused on six elements in Material Design: App Bar, Floating Action Button, Bottom Navigation, Navigation Drawer, Snack Bar, and Tab Layout. Second, we looked for relationships between usage of Material Design elements and app popularity as well as app category.

The main challenge in our data analysis was to reliably detect Material Design elements, which lacked standardized names in the app view hierarchies. Therefore, to detect as many Material Design elements as possible from an app (either implemented with official or unofficial Material Design libraries), we leveraged the pixel data from the apps' screenshots in the Rico dataset.

Specifically, we used computer vision techniques such as deep Convolutional Neural Networks (CNNs) to detect Material Design elements from screenshots. To train these models, we needed positive and negative cropped snapshots of Material Design elements as training data. To collect the ground truth data, we turned to those apps that implemented their UIs using the official Material Design library. These elements were easy to find by class name in the view hierarchy JSON files. In order to train a good classifier, negative examples of each element also need to be collected from a relevant location and should not be cropped from a random part of the screen. To this end, we created a heatmap for each type of element based on the apps using the official library. With these heatmaps, we cropped the UI regions which did not use Material Design elements. Therefore, for the screenshots which did not include a Material Design element, we cropped the screenshot based on the most probable part

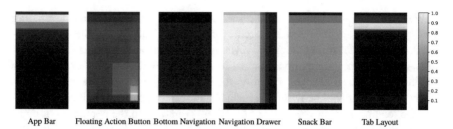

| App Bar | Floating Action Button | Bottom Navigation | Navigation Drawer | Snack Bar | Tab Layout |

Fig. 11 The heatmap of the frequency divided by maximum value of each Material Design element in *Rico* dataset

of the screen (heatmap) for that element to generate negative examples. Figure 11 shows the heatmaps of each Material Design element in *Rico* dataset.

After collecting a set of images for each Material Design element, we used deep Convolutional Neural Networks to detect Material Design elements in the apps. We trained a separate classifier for each Material Design element to detect that element in an app's screenshot. We selected the AlexNet [29] architecture for our Convolutional Neural Networks. We trained all the networks from scratch with a learning rate of 0.001 and 50,000 iterations. We split our data into 80% training, 10% validation, and 10% for testing the trained network and got at least 95% of accuracy on each component. We used Google's open-source machine learning platform TensorFlow [5] to implement all our machine learning models. For detailed information about our methodology, please refer to [23].

4.2.2 Results of Data Analysis

Our data analysis led to a number of interesting findings about Material Design's usage in the wild. We first report the usage of specific elements such as the Floating Action Button and the Navigation Drawer, two popular but somewhat controversial patterns in Material Design, and how the usage of these elements relate to app ratings, installs, and categories. We then report the usage of Material Design in general and examine its impact on app popularity.

4.2.3 Usage of Floating Action Buttons

If the drawbacks of FABs generally outweigh their benefits, as some design critics argued, one would assume that higher-rated apps would be less likely to use FABs than those lower-rated apps. To test this hypothesis, we split apps into two groups: a high-rating group and a low-rating group by the median average rating of all apps in the Play Store dataset, which was 4.16 at the time of this analysis. The two groups of apps were balanced and each group had 4673 number of apps.

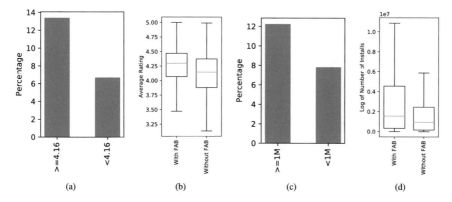

Fig. 12 **a** The percentage of apps using the Floating Action Button (FAB) in the high-rating group versus the low-rating group. **b** Box plots of the average ratings of apps using the FAB versus those not using the FAB. **c** The percentage of apps using the FAB in the more-installed group versus the less-installed group. **d** Box plots of the number of installs of apps using the FAB versus those not using the FAB

As Fig. 12a shows, there was actually a higher percentage of apps using FABs in the high-rating group than those in the low-rating group (13.4% vs. 6.6%). The box plots in Fig. 12b further shows that apps using the FAB were rated higher than those that did not use it. In fact, 66.6% of apps that used the FAB belonged to the higher-rating group.

We also used the number of installs as another measure of app popularity. Thus, we decided to split our apps into two groups: (1) apps with greater than or equal to 1 million installs, and (2) apps with less than 1 million installs. The two groups were nearly balanced after the split, with 4723 in the more-installed group and 4623 in the less-installed group. Similar to what we saw in the analysis of FAB usage and app ratings, apps in the more-installed group appeared to be more likely to feature FABs than those in the less-installed group (see Fig. 12c). Also, apps using the FAB had a larger number of installs in comparison to apps without the FAB (see Fig. 12d).

The results above suggest that many developers of popular apps consider the FAB to be a valuable design pattern. Nonetheless, it's still possible that the FAB is a more useful pattern in some situations than others.

To understand where the FAB might be more useful, we examined the usage of the FAB by app category. Figure 13 shows the top 11 app categories by the percentage of apps featuring the FAB, excluding categories for which there were too few apps in the *Rico* dataset (less than 0.05% of the apps of that category in Google Play). As it is obvious to see, FAB usage varied considerably among these 11 categories of apps. The *Food and Drink* category had the highest percentage of FAB usage among all the qualified categories. Figure 14 shows some of the FABs in the *Food and Drink* category. Each thumbnail belongs to a different app but there are FABs with similar icons in this category, suggesting common usage of the FAB such as suggesting recipes (the "folk" FAB), locating nearby restaurants (the "location" FAB). Note

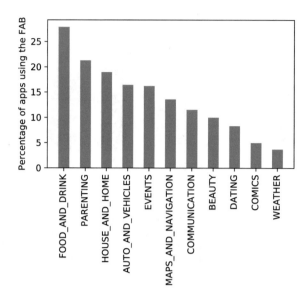

Fig. 13 The top category of apps which used the most FAB by percentage in their category

Fig. 14 Thumbnails of FABs in the Food and Drink category apps

that some of the thumbnails in this picture do not appear to include a FAB, because they are occluded by another UI component.

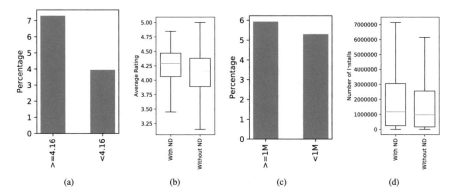

Fig. 15 **a** The percentage of apps using the Navigation Drawer in the high-rating group versus the low-rating group. **b** Box plots of the average ratings of apps using the Navigation Drawer versus those not using the Navigation Drawer. **c** The percentage of apps using the Navigation Drawer in the more-installed group versus the less-installed groups. **d** Box plots of the number of installs of apps using the Navigation Drawer versus those not using the Navigation Drawer

4.2.4 Usage of Navigation Drawers

We applied the same analysis to examine the usage of the Navigation Drawer in Material Design. As we can see in Fig. 15a, there were more apps in the high-rating group which had a Navigation Drawer than those in the low-rating group (7.3% vs. 3.9%). The box plots in Fig. 15b show that the average rating for apps using the Navigation Drawer was higher than those that did not use it. Among all the apps that used the Navigation Drawer, 65% of them belonged to the high-rating group.

Similar to our analysis of the FAB usage, we examined the usage of the Navigation Drawer and the number of app installs. As it is shown in Fig. 15b, apps in the high-rating group were slightly more likely to feature a Navigation Drawer than those in the low-rating group. Also, the box plots in Fig. 15d show that apps using Navigation Drawer had a slightly higher number of installs.

4.2.5 Material Design and App Popularity

We conducted an analysis to understand the usage of Material Design in general and its relationship to apps' average ratings and the number of installs. The first step was to determine if an app used Material Design. We adopted a relatively relaxed criterion: if an app used one of the six Material Design components our model could detect, we considered Material Design was used in that app.

First, we examined the relationship between the usage of Material Design and apps' average ratings. To this end, we sorted all the apps in the *Rico* dataset by their average ratings, split them into one hundred buckets, and calculated the percentage of apps that used Material Design for each percentile. We then plotted the percentage of

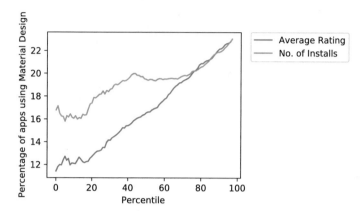

Fig. 16 Distribution of the percentage of apps using at least one of the six common Material Design elements over percentiles in average rating (blue) and number of installs (orange)

Material Design usage over average rating percentiles. As we can see in Fig. 16, the usage of Material Design was highly correlated with the average rating percentile (with the Pearson correlation coefficient $\rho = 0.99$ and p-value $= 3.1 \times 10^{-91}$). In other words, as the average rating increased, the percentage of apps using Material Design also increased.

Next, we examined the relationship of the usage of Material Design and the number of installs, an alternate measure of app popularity. As in the previous step, we sorted apps by their number of installs and split them into one hundred equal-sized buckets by percentile. As shown in Fig. 16, the percent of the apps using Material Design is also highly correlated to number of installs $\rho = 0.94$ and p-value $= 2.3 \times 10^{-47}$).

4.2.6 Summary

To sum up, we review the two research questions we set out to answer. Our first research question was *How can we understand the impact of a pattern language in one of the largest computing ecosystems in the world?* We developed a computational method to measure the relationship between Material Design, the pattern language in question, and app popularity in the Android ecosystem. We used Convolutional Neural Networks as a data mining tool to analyze big UI data. We trained multiple models to detect Material Design elements in apps' screenshots.

Our second research question was *How can we examine real-world use of design patterns to inform debates about UI design?* To answer this question, we examined the usage of the Floating Action Button and the Navigation Drawer, two frequently criticized patterns in online design discussions. While our results do not directly rebut specific arguments against these two patterns, they clearly show that many developers and designers found these two patterns valuable and use both patterns frequently in their highly rated and highly popular apps. Moreover, our results have suggested that evaluating the merit of a design pattern should consider the context it is applied to. For example, developers used the FAB more frequently in certain app categories such as *Food and Drink* and *Parenting* than others.

5 Rico in the World

Over the last three years since its release, Rico has been used by many research teams as the basis for their own projects. In this section, we attempt to categorize the uses that Rico has seen to date and highlight a few projects of interest.

We found in our exploration of these use cases that they could be broadly categorized into five areas: (a) mobile ecosystem explorations, (b) UI automation, (c) design assistance, (d) understanding UI semantics, and (e) automated design. In addition, efforts in many of these areas have additionally enhanced the Rico dataset itself, which we will discuss separately. We describe the research in these areas below.

5.1 Mobile Ecosystem Explorations

The research summarized in this section attempts to understand the Android app ecosystem by using the Rico dataset as a sample. Our own work described in Sect. 4.2 falls under this category, where we used Rico to explore the usage of the Material Design pattern language in the Android app ecosystem.

Micallef et al. used Rico to study the use of login functionality in Android apps [39]. They found that 32% of apps use at least one kind of login functionality and 9% provided at least one social login (e.g., Facebook, Google). They found no correlation between the usage of login features and the number of app downloads or app ratings.

Ross et al. investigated the state of mobile app accessibility using a subset of the Rico dataset [44]. They specifically focused on the accessibility of image-based buttons and studied the prevalence of accessibility issues due to missing labels, duplicate labels, or uninformative labels. They discovered a bi-modal distribution of missing labels in apps with 46% of apps having less than 10% (46%) of their image-based buttons labeled and 36% of apps having more than 90% labeled. The correlation between accessibility, as measured by missing labels, and app ratings was found to be weak.

5.2 UI Automation

Several works have used Rico to develop mobile UI automation tools and techniques. One popular use of UI automation is for helping end users. Li et al. look at task automation in which natural language instructions must be interpreted as a sequence of actions on a mobile touch-screen UI [34]. Toward that end, they used a subset of the Rico dataset, enhanced it with action commands, and created the RicoSCA dataset. This dataset, along with two other datasets, allowed them to develop models to map multi-step instructions into automatically executable actions given the screen information. Sereskeh et al. developed programming by demonstration system for smartphone task automation called VASTA[47]. They used the Rico dataset to train a detector for UI elements that powered the vision capabilities of their system.

Another popular use of UI automation is for testing. Li et al. developed Humanoid, a test input generator for Android apps [36]. They use the interactions traces from the Rico dataset to train a deep learning-based model of how humans interact with app screens. This model is then used to guide Humanoid's test input generation. Zhang et al. used Rico to train a deep learning-based model for identifying isomorphic GUIs, which are GUI's that may have different contents but represent the same screen semantically [55]. Although they intend to use such identification to enable robotic testing for mobile GUIs, this feature could also be useful for crawling mobile apps. Section 2.3 describes how we handled the identification of isomorphic GUIs during data collection for the Rico dataset.

5.3   Design Assistance

Another popular use of the Rico dataset is to develop data-driven tools to assist with mobile UI design. An example of such a tool is a search engine for finding example UIs of interest. Such search engines would enable designers to use relevant examples early on in the design process for inspiration and to guide their design process. Section 4.1 describes how we used Rico to train an autoencoder to learn an embedding for UI layouts and used it to demonstrate an example-based search for UIs which gives the user the ability to search for UIs similar to a UI of interest. Chen et al. collected an Android UI dataset similar to Rico and used it to train a CNN to enable searching UIs based on wireframes [15]. Huang et al. developed Swire, a UI retrieval system that can be queried by using hand-drawn sketches of UIs [27]. This was enabled by training a deep neural network to learn a sketch-screenshot embedding space for UIs in the Rico dataset and performing a nearest-neighbor search in that space. Swire is also described in Chapter XX in this book.

Another set of data-driven tools attempt to provide feedback and guide designers, especially novice designers, during the design process. Lee et al. developed GUIComp, a tool that provides real-time feedback to designers including showing other relevant examples, predicting user attention characteristics of the design, and showing design complexity metrics [31]. They used a subset of the Rico dataset as a basis for their tool and trained an autoencoder to find similar UIs following an approach similar to that described in Sect. 4.1. Wu et al. developed a tool to predict user engagement based on the types of animations used within the app [54]. Their approach was enabled by training a deep learning model on the animations released as part of the Rico dataset. Finally, Swearngin et al. built upon the Rico dataset to create a new dataset for mobile interface tappability using crowdsourcing and then computationally investigated a variety of signals that are used by typical users to distinguish tappable versus not-tappable elements [49].

5.4 Understanding UI Semantics

Several recent works have also used the Rico dataset to develop approaches for developing a taxonomy of UI elements and then building detectors for different UI element types found in mobile UIs. Liu et al. identified 25 semantic concepts that are commonly implemented by UI elements, such as next, create, and delete. They then trained a Convolutional Neural Network (CNN) to detect the corresponding UI elements in app screens and used it to annotate the elements in Rico dataset. These semantic annotations are now available for download as part of the Rico dataset.

Moran et al. mined a dataset of app screens similar to Rico and used the resulting dataset to develop an automated approach for converting GUI mockups to implemented code [40]. To do that, they too developed techniques to detect and classify different UI elements found in UIs. Chen et al. used the Rico dataset to perform a large-scale empirical study of seven representative GUI element detection methods on over 50 k GUI images [16].

Finally, Li et al. collected natural language descriptions, called *captions*, for elements in the Rico dataset and used it to train models that generate captions for UI elements (useful for accessibility and language-based interactions) [35]. In this work, they also augmented Rico with 12 K newly crawled UI screens.

5.5 Automated Design

Another area where a UI dataset is essential is for the development of methods for the automated generation of UIs. Lee et al. developed the Neural Design Network, an approach to generate a graphic design layout given a set of components with user-specified attributes and constraints [32]. Gupta et al. developed the Layout-Transformer, a technique that leverages a self-attention-based approach to learn contextual relationships between layout elements and generate new layouts [26]. Both these works use the Rico dataset to test their approaches for mobile UIs.

5.6 Enhancements to the Rico Approach and Dataset

Several of the research projects discussed above have also enhanced the Rico dataset with new annotations or additional screens. Liu et al. added semantic annotations for UI elements (e.g, delete, save, search, etc.) to the Rico dataset [37]. This was accomplished by (a) iterative open coding of 73 k UI elements and 720 screens, (b) training a convolutional neural network that distinguishes between icon classes, and (c) using that network to compute semantic annotations for the 72 k unique UIs in the Rico dataset, assigning labels for 78% of the total visible, non-redundant elements.

Leiva et al. released Enrico, a curated dataset of 1460 mobile UIs drawn from Rico that are tagged with one of 20 different semantic topics (e.g., gallery, chat, etc.) [38]. This was accomplished by using human annotators to (a) systematically identify *popular* UI screens that have consistent screenshots and view hierarchies in 10k randomly drawn screens from the Rico dataset, (b) create a taxonomy with 19 topics that accurately represented these popular UI screens, and (c) assign each UI to a topic.

For crowd crawling of apps, new tools are available to offer more support to crowd workers. For example, Chen et al. developed tools that offer guidance to crowd explorers that can reduce redundant exploration and increase coverage [17].

6 Discussion

To our knowledge, the Rico dataset remains the largest repository of Android mobile app designs, and it has been used by many research teams worldwide to facilitate our understanding of the Android mobile app ecosystem and to create tools and technologies that advance our use of mobile user interfaces. We are happy that we chose to release the dataset publicly and are impressed with the follow-on work that has been done as a result. We hope that others who augment Rico or create their own new datasets will likewise make them publicly available, as this helps the entire research community. One challenge for the future is how to aggregate these new additions and new datasets into a single accessible place, as today those that have been released are shared in a variety of locations with little standardization.

While Rico continues to be useful, it has weaknesses that we hope to address. The initial idea to create the dataset was born out of a need to train machine learned models that incorporated an understanding of the user interface. At the time, we were interested in creating generative models that could produce full or partial user interfaces designs. While we ended up not pursuing this direction, this initial use case is reflected in the type of data collected in the Rico dataset. Our goal was to collect a nearly complete picture of every app that we explored, including each of its screens, dialog boxes, etc. In our collection process, we intentionally did not try to capture data about how humans used these interfaces, and we disregarded the tasks for which the user interfaces might be used, common user behaviors with the interfaces, and other semantic information and metadata related to the user interfaces. Another omission in Rico is that it contains no task-related information nor any ecologically valid traces of human interaction on its UIs. Collecting such data will require new crowdsourcing techniques, especially at the scale needed for the data to be useful for deep learning, but would open up the possibility of many new applications that are not possible with the current dataset.

Another weakness in Rico is its lack of temporal data; Rico contains a snapshot of Android UIs collected at just one period of time in early 2017. Presumably many of the apps in the dataset have changed since they were originally collected, and certainly, new apps have been created that are not in the dataset. Although we see little evidence of it so far, models trained from the dataset could suffer from concept drift if present or future UIs change sufficiently from what was recorded in the dataset. To this end, we hope to capture an updated version of the dataset and release that publicly at some point in the future.

Finally, Rico contains just data from Android phone UIs in US English. Collecting data from other device types (e.g., tablets), other operating systems (e.g., iOS), and other internationalization and localization settings beyond US English would also open up new applications for the dataset. For example, being able to train design mappings between UIs that serve the same function but use different languages might create an opportunity to build automated or semi-automated tools for internationalizing UIs. Training mappings between phone and tablet interfaces could enable the creation of tools and techniques for improved responsive design.

7 Conclusion

In this chapter, we have:

- Presented the Rico dataset, the largest publicly released repository of Android mobile app designs, containing data for 72,219 user interfaces from 9,772 apps spanning 27 Google Play store categories.
- Described the hybrid human plus automation crawling process that was used to collect the dataset, which increased UI coverage by an average of 40% over human crawling alone.
- Shown a method of training a UI layout embedding with a deep autoencoder neural network architecture, which we demonstrated to be effective for searching for related screens within the Rico dataset.
- Explored the usage of the Material Design pattern language within the Rico dataset through machine learned techniques.
- Summarized the large body of work that others in the research community have undertaken using the Rico dataset.

While we are humbled by the many systems that have been built to date using Rico, applications of machine learning to the use and design of user interfaces are still very early. Further work in this area will continue to be enabled by the creation of datasets like Rico. We look forward to see what new datasets and applications that researchers create to make our user interfaces truly intelligent.

Acknowledgements We thank the reviewers for their helpful comments and suggestions and the crowd workers who helped build the Rico dataset. This work was supported in part by a Google Faculty Research Award.

References

1. Android Activities (2016). https://developer.android.com/guide/components/activities.html
2. Database of Android Apps on Kaggle (2016). https://www.kaggle.com/orgesleka/android-apps
3. UI Overview (2016). https://developer.android.com/guide/topics/ui/overview.html
4. A L (2014) Why and how to avoid hamburger menus
5. Abadi M, Agarwal A, Barham P, Brevdo E, Chen Z, Citro C, Corrado GS, Davis A, Dean J, Devin M, Ghemawat S, Goodfellow I, Harp A, Irving G, Isard M, Jia Y, Jozefowicz R, Kaiser L, Kudlur M, Levenberg J, Mané D, Monga R, Moore S, Murray D, Olah C, Schuster M, Shlens J, Steiner B, Sutskever I, Talwar K, Tucker P, Vanhoucke V, Vasudevan V, Viégas F, Vinyals O, Warden P, Wattenberg M, Wicke M, Yu Y, Zheng X (2015) TensorFlow: large-scale machine learning on heterogeneous systems. Software available from tensorflow.org
6. Alexander C (1977) A pattern language: towns, buildings, construction. Oxford University Press, Oxford
7. Alharbi K, Yeh T (2015) Collect, decompile, extract, stats, and diff: mining design pattern changes in Android apps. In: Proceedings of MobileHCI
8. Amini S (2014) Analyzing mobile app privacy using computation and crowdsourcing. PhD thesis, Carnegie Mellon University
9. Avgeriou P, Papasalouros A, Retalis S, Skordalakis M (2003) Towards a pattern language for learning management systems. Educ Technol & Soc 6(2):11–24
10. Azim T, Neamtiu I (2013) Targeted and depth-first exploration for systematic testing of android apps. In: ACM SIGPLAN Notices
11. Babich N (2017) Floating action button in ux design
12. Bengio Y (2009) Learning deep architectures for ai. Found Trends Mach Learn 2:1
13. Bhoraskar R, Han S, Jeon J, Azim T, Chen S, Jung J, Nath S, Wang R, Wetherall D (2014) Brahmastra: driving apps to test the security of third-party components. In: Proceeding of the SEC
14. Borchers JO (2000) A pattern approach to interaction design. In: Proceedings of the 3rd conference on designing interactive systems: processes, practices, methods, and techniques, DIS '00, ACM, New York, NY, USA, pp 369–378
15. Chen J, Chen C, Xing Z, Xia X, Zhu L, Grundy J, Wang J (2020) Wireframe-based ui design search through image autoencoder. ACM Trans Softw Eng Methodol 29:3
16. Chen J, Xie M, Xing Z, Chen C, Xu X, Zhu L, Li G (2020) Object detection for graphical user interface: old fashioned or deep learning or a combination? New York, NY, USA, Association for Computing Machinery, pp 1202–1214
17. Chen Y, Pandey M, Song JY, Lasecki WS, Oney S (2020) Improving crowd-supported gui testing with structural guidance. In: Proceedings of the 2020 CHI conference on human factors in computing systems, CHI '20, Association for Computing Machinery, New York, NY, USA, pp 1–13
18. Chung ES, Hong JI, Lin J, Prabaker MK, Landay JA, Liu AL (2004) Development and evaluation of emerging design patterns for ubiquitous computing. In: Proceedings of the 5th conference on designing interactive systems: processes, practices, methods, and techniques, ACM, pp 233–242
19. Constine J (2014) Kill the hamburger button
20. Dearden A, Finlay J (2006) Pattern languages in hci: a critical review. Human-Comput Inter 21(1):49–102
21. Deka B, Huang Z, Franzen C, Hibschman J, Afergan D, Li Y, Nichols J, Kumar R (2017) Rico: a mobile app dataset for building data-driven design applications. In: 30th annual symposium on user interface software and technology, UIST '17, ACM, New York, NY, USA
22. Deka B, Huang Z, Kumar R (2016) ERICA: Interaction mining mobile apps. In: Proceedings of the UIST
23. Doosti B, Dong T, Deka B, Nichols J (2018) A computational method for evaluating UI patterns. ArXiv e-prints

24. Frank M, Dong B, Felt AP, Song D (2012) Mining permission request patterns from android and facebook applications. In: Proceeding of the ICDM
25. Fu B, Lin J, Li L, Faloutsos C, Hong J, Sadeh N (2013) Why people hate your app: making sense of user feedback in a mobile app store. In: Proceedings of the KDD
26. Gupta K, Achille A, Lazarow J, Davis L, Mahadevan V, Shrivastava A (2020) Layout generation and completion with self-attention
27. Huang F, Canny JF, Nichols J (2019) Swire: sketch-based user interface retrieval. In: Proceedings of the 2019 CHI conference on human factors in computing systems, CHI '19, Association for Computing Machinery, New York, NY, USA, pp 1–10
28. Jager T (2017) Is the floating action button bad ui design?
29. Krizhevsky A, Sutskever I, Hinton GE (2012) Imagenet classification with deep convolutional neural networks. In: Pereira F, Burges CJC, Bottou L, Weinberger KQ (eds) Advances in neural information processing systems 25. Curran Associates Inc, Stateline, NV, USA, pp 1097–1105
30. Landay JA, Borriello G (2003) Design patterns for ubiquitous computing. Computer 36(8):93–95
31. Lee C, Kim S, Han D, Yang H, Park Y-W, Kwon BC, Ko S (2020) Guicomp: a gui design assistant with real-time, multi-faceted feedback. In: Proceedings of the 2020 CHI conference on human factors in computing systems, CHI '20, Association for Computing Machinery, New York, NY, USA, pp 1–13
32. Lee H-Y, Yang W, Jiang L, Le M, Essa I, Gong H, Yang M-H (2020) Neural design network: graphic layout generation with constraints. In: Proceedings of European conference on computer vision (ECCV)
33. Lee K, Flinn J, Giuli T, Noble B, Peplin C (2013) Amc: verifying user interface properties for vehicular applications. In: Proceeding of the Mobisys
34. Li Y, He J, Zhou X, Zhang Y, Baldridge J (2020) Mapping natural language instructions to mobile UI action sequences. In: Proceedings of the 58th annual meeting of the association for computational linguistics, Association for Computational Linguistics, pp 8198–8210
35. Li Y, Li G, He L, Zheng J, Li H, Guan Z (2020) Widget captioning: generating natural language description for mobile user interface elements. In: Proceedings of the 2020 conference on empirical methods in natural language processing (EMNLP), Association for Computational Linguistics, pp 5495–5510
36. Li Y, Yang Z, Guo Y, Chen X (2019) Humanoid: a deep learning-based approach to automated black-box android app testing. In: 2019 34th IEEE/ACM international conference on automated software engineering (ASE), pp 1070–1073
37. Liu TF, Craft M, Situ J, Yumer E, Mech R, Kumar R (2018) Learning design semantics for mobile apps. In: Proceedings of the 31st annual ACM symposium on user interface software and technology, UIST '18, Association for Computing Machinery, New York, NY, USA, pp 569–579
38. Luis AL, Asutosh Hota AO (2020) Enrico: a high-quality dataset for topic modeling of mobile ui designs. In: Proceedings of MobileHCI extended abstracts
39. Micallef N, Adi E, Misra G (2018) Investigating login features in smartphone apps. In: Proceedings of the 2018 ACM international joint conference and 2018 international symposium on pervasive and ubiquitous computing and wearable computers, UbiComp '18, Association for Computing Machinery, New York, NY, USA, pp 842–851
40. Moran K, Bernal-Cárdenas C, Curcio M, Bonett R, Poshyvanyk D (2020) Machine learning-based prototyping of graphical user interfaces for mobile apps. IEEE Trans Softw Eng 46(2):196–221
41. Nair V, Hinton GE (2010) Rectified linear units improve restricted boltzmann machines. In: Proceeding of the ICML, pp 807–814
42. Neil T (2014) Mobile design pattern gallery: UI patterns for smartphone apps. O'Reilly Media, Inc., Sebastopol
43. Pernice K, Budiu R (2016) Hamburger menus and hidden navigation hurt ux metrics
44. Ross AS, Zhang X, Fogarty J, Wobbrock JO (2018) Examining image-based button labeling for accessibility in android apps through large-scale analysis. In: Proceedings of the 20th

international ACM SIGACCESS conference on computers and accessibility, ASSETS '18, Association for Computing Machinery, New York, NY, USA, pp 119–130

45. Sahami Shirazi A, Henze N, Schmidt A, Goldberg R, Schmidt B, Schmauder H (2013) Insights into layout patterns of mobile user interfaces by an automatic analysis of Android apps. In: Proceeding of the EICS

46. Saponas TS, Prabaker MK, Abowd GD, Landay JA () The impact of pre-patterns on the design of digital home applications. In: Proceedings of the 6th conference on designing interactive systems, ACM (2006), pp 189–198

47. Sereshkeh AR, Leung G, Perumal K, Phillips C, Zhang M, Fazly A, Mohomed I (2020) Vasta: a vision and language-assisted smartphone task automation system. In: Proceedings of the 25th international conference on intelligent user interfaces, IUI '20, Association for Computing Machinery, New York, NY, USA, pp 22–32

48. Siang TY (2015) Material design: why the floating action button is bad ux design. https://medium.com/tech-in-asia/material-design-why-the-floating-action-button-is-bad-ux-design-acd5b32c5ef, https://medium.com/tech-in-asia/material-design-why-, https://medium.com/tech-in-asia/material-design-why-the-floating-action-button-is-bad-ux-design-acd5b32c5ef-the-floating-action-button-is-bad-ux-design-acd5b32c5ef

49. Swearngin A, Li Y (2019) Modeling mobile interface tappability using crowdsourcing and deep learning. In: Proceedings of the 2019 CHI conference on human factors in computing systems, CHI '19, Association for Computing Machinery, New York, NY, USA, pp 1–11

50. Szydlowski M, Egele M, Kruegel C, Vigna G (2012) Challenges for dynamic analysis of iOS applications. In: Open problems in network security. Springer, pp 65–77

51. Tidwell J (2010) Designing interfaces: patterns for effective interaction design. O'Reilly Media, Inc., Sebastopol

52. Viennot N, Garcia E, Nieh J (2014) A measurement study of google play. In: ACM SIGMETRICS performance evaluation review, vol. 42, ACM, pp 221–233

53. Wania CE, Atwood ME (2009) Pattern languages in the wild: exploring pattern languages in the laboratory and in the real world. In: Proceedings of the 4th international conference on design science research in information systems and technology, ACM, p 12

54. Wu Z, Jiang Y, Liu Y, Ma X (2020) Predicting and diagnosing user engagement with mobile ui animation via a data-driven approach. In: Proceedings of the 2020 CHI conference on human factors in computing systems, CHI '20, Association for Computing Machinery, New York, NY, USA, pp 1–13

55. Zhang T, Liu Y, Gao J, Gao LP, Cheng J (2020) Deep learning-based mobile application isomorphic gui identification for automated robotic testing. IEEE Softw 37(4):67–74

Visual Intelligence through Human Interaction

Ranjay Krishna, Mitchell Gordon, Li Fei-Fei, and Michael Bernstein

Abstract Over the last decade, Computer Vision, the branch of Artificial Intelligence aimed at understanding the visual world, has evolved from simply recognizing objects in images to describing pictures, answering questions about images, aiding robots maneuver around physical spaces, and even generating novel visual content. As these tasks and applications have modernized, so too has the reliance on more data, either for model training or for evaluation. In this chapter, we demonstrate that novel interaction strategies can enable new forms of data collection and evaluation for Computer Vision. First, we present a crowdsourcing interface for speeding up paid data collection by an order of magnitude, feeding the data-hungry nature of modern vision models. Second, we explore a method to increase volunteer contributions using automated social interventions. Third, we develop a system to ensure human evaluation of generative vision models are reliable, affordable, and grounded in psychophysics theory. We conclude with future opportunities for Human–Computer Interaction to aid Computer Vision.

1 Introduction

Today, Computer Vision applications are ubiquitous. They filter our pictures, control our car, aid medical experts in disease diagnosis, analyze sports games, and even generate complete new content. This recent emergence of Computer Vision tools

R. Krishna (✉) · M. Gordon · L. Fei-Fei · M. Bernstein
Stanford University, Stanford, CA, USA
e-mail: ranjaykrishna@cs.stanford.edu

M. Gordon
e-mail: mgord@cs.stanford.edu

L. Fei-Fei
e-mail: feifeili@cs.stanford.edu

M. Bernstein
e-mail: msb@cs.stanford.edu

© The Author(s), under exclusive license to Springer Nature Switzerland AG 2021   257
Y. Li and O. Hilliges (eds.), *Artificial Intelligence for Human Computer Interaction:*
A Modern Approach, Human–Computer Interaction Series,
https://doi.org/10.1007/978-3-030-82681-9_9

has been made possible because of a shift in the underlying techniques used to train models; this shift has transferred attention away from hand engineered features [41, 126] toward deep learning [43, 101]. With deep learning techniques, vision models have surpassed human performance on fundamental tasks, such as object recognition [159]. Today, vision models are capable of an entirely new host of applications, such as generating photo-realistic images [90] and 3D spaces [134]. These tasks have made possible numerous vision-powered applications [74, 107, 204, 206, 207].

This shift is also reflective of yet another change in Computer Vision: algorithms are becoming more generic and data has become the primary hurdle in performance. Today's vision models are data-hungry; they feed on large amounts of annotated training data. In some cases, data needs to be continuously annotated in order to evaluate models; for new tasks such as image generation, model-generated images can only be evaluated if people provide realism judgments. To support data needs, Computer Vision has relied on a specific pipeline for data collection—one that focuses on manual labeling using online crowdsourcing platforms such as Amazon Mechanical Turk [43, 98].

Unfortunately, this data collection pipeline has numerous limiting factors. First, crowdsourcing can be insufficiently scalable and it remains too expensive for use in the production of many industry-size datasets [84]. Cost is bound to the amount of work completed per minute of effort, and existing techniques for speeding up labeling are not scaling as quickly as the volume of data we are now producing that must be labeled [184]. Second, while cost issues may be mitigated by relying on volunteer contributions, it remains unclear how best to incentivize such contributions. Even though there has been a lot of work in Social Psychology exploring strategies to incentivize volunteer contributions to online communities [25, 42, 95, 131, 194, 205], it remains unclear how we can employ such strategies to develop automated mechanisms that incentivize volunteer data annotation useful for Computer Vision. Third, existing data annotation methods are ad hoc, each executed in idiosyncrasy without proof of reliability or grounding to theory, resulting in high variance in their estimates [45, 141, 164]. While high variance in labels might be tolerable when collecting training data, it becomes debilitating when such ad hoc methods are used to evaluate models.

Human–Computer Interaction's opportunity is to look to novel interaction strategies to break this away from traditional data collection pipeline. In this chapter, we showcase three projects [99, 144, 210], that have helped modern Computer Vision data needs. The first two projects introduce new training data collection interfaces [99] and interactions [144], while the third introduces a reliable system for evaluating vision models with humans [210]. Our contributions (1) speed up data collection by an order of magnitude in terms of speed and cost, (2) incentivize volunteer contributions to provide labels through conversational interactions over social media, and (3) capacitate reliable human evaluation of vision models.

In the first section, we highlight work that accelerates human interactions in microtask crowdsourcing, a core process through which computer vision and machine learning (ML) datasets are predominantly curated [99]. Microtask crowdsourcing has enabled dataset advances in social science and ML, but existing crowdsourcing schemes are too expensive to scale up with the expanding volume of data. To scale and widen the applicability of crowdsourcing, we present a technique that produces extremely rapid judgments for binary and categorical labels. Rather than punishing all errors, which causes workers to proceed slowly and deliberately, our technique speeds up workers' judgments to the point where errors are acceptable and even expected. We demonstrate that it is possible to rectify these errors by randomizing task order and modeling response latency. We evaluate our technique on a breadth of common labeling tasks such as image verification, word similarity, sentiment analysis, and topic classification. Where prior work typically achieves a $0.25\times$ to $1\times$ speedup over fixed majority vote, our approach often achieves an order of magnitude $(10\times)$ speedup.

In the second section, we turn our attention from paid crowdsourcing to volunteer contributions; we explore how to design social interventions to improve volunteer contributions when curating datasets [144]. To support the massive data requirements of modern supervised ML algorithms, crowdsourcing systems match volunteer contributors to appropriate tasks. Such systems learn *what* types of tasks contributors are interested to complete. In this paper, instead of focusing on *what* to ask, we focus on learning *how* to ask: how to make relevant and interesting requests to encourage crowdsourcing participation. We introduce a new technique that augments questions with learning-based request strategies drawn from social psychology. We also introduce a contextual bandit algorithm to select which strategy to apply for a given task and contributor. We deploy our approach to collect volunteer data from Instagram for the task of visual question answering, an important task in computer vision and natural language processing that has enabled numerous human–computer interaction applications. For example, when encountering a user's Instagram post that contains the ornate Trevi Fountain in Rome, our approach learns to augment its original raw question "Where is this place?" with image-relevant compliments such as "What a great statue!" or with travel-relevant justifications such as "I would like to visit this place," increasing the user's likelihood of answering the question and thus providing a label. We deploy our agent on Instagram to ask questions about social media images, finding that the response rate improves from 15.8% with unaugmented questions to 30.54% with baseline rule-based strategies and to 58.1% with learning-based strategies.

Finally, in the third section, we spotlight our work on constructing a reliable human evaluation system for generative computer vision models [210]. Generative models often use human evaluations to measure the perceived quality of their outputs. Automated metrics are noisy indirect proxies, because they rely on heuristics or pretrained embeddings. However, up until now, direct human evaluation strategies have been ad hoc, neither standardized nor validated. Our work establishes a gold standard human benchmark for generative realism. We construct HUMAN EYE PERCEPTUAL EVALUATION (HYPE), a human benchmark that is *grounded* in psychophysics research in perception, *reliable* across different sets of randomly sampled outputs from a model, able to produce *separable* model performances, and *efficient* in cost and time. We introduce two variants: one that measures visual perception under adaptive time constraints to determine the threshold at which a model's outputs appear real (e.g., 250 ms), and the other a less expensive variant that measures human error rate on fake and real images sans time constraints. We test HYPE across six state-of-the-art generative adversarial networks and two sampling techniques on conditional and unconditional image generation using four datasets: CelebA, FFHQ, CIFAR-10, and ImageNet. We find that HYPE can track the relative improvements between models, and we confirm via bootstrap sampling that these measurements are consistent and replicable.

2 Data Annotation by Speeding up Human Interactions

Social science [92, 133], interactive systems [50, 104], and ML [43, 122] are becoming more and more reliant on large-scale, human-annotated data. Increasingly large annotated datasets have unlocked a string of social scientific insights [26, 56] and ML performance improvements [58, 101, 187]. One of the main enablers of this growth has been microtask crowdsourcing [174]. Microtask crowdsourcing marketplaces such as Amazon Mechanical Turk offer a scale and cost that makes such annotation feasible. As a result, companies are now using crowd work to complete hundreds of thousands of tasks per day [130].

However, even microtask crowdsourcing can be insufficiently scalable, and it remains too expensive for use in the production of many industry-size datasets [84]. Cost is bound to the amount of work completed per minute of effort, and existing techniques for speeding up labeling (reducing the amount of required effort) are not scaling as quickly as the volume of data we are now producing that must be labeled [184]. To expand the applicability of crowdsourcing, the number of items annotated per minute of effort needs to increase substantially.

In this paper, we focus on one of the most common classes of crowdsourcing tasks [78]: binary annotation. These tasks are yes-or-no questions, typically identifying whether or not an input has a specific characteristic. Examples of these types of tasks are topic categorization (e.g., "Is this article about finance?") [166], image classification (e.g., "Is this a dog?") [43, 119, 122], audio styles [167], and emotion detection [119] in songs (e.g., "Is the music calm and soothing?"), word similarity (e.g., "Are *shipment* and *cargo* synonyms?") [135], and sentiment analysis (e.g., "Is this tweet positive?") [142].

Previous methods have sped up binary classification tasks by minimizing worker error. A central assumption behind this prior work has been that workers make errors because they are not trying hard enough (e.g., "a lack of expertise, dedication [or] interest" [168]). Platforms thus punish errors harshly, for example, by denying payment. Current methods calculate the minimum redundancy necessary to be confident that errors have been removed [168, 172, 173]. These methods typically result in a $0.25\times$ to $1\times$ speedup beyond a fixed majority vote [87, 146, 160, 168].

We take the opposite position: that designing the task to encourage some error, or even make errors inevitable, can produce far greater speedups. Because platforms strongly punish errors, workers carefully examine even straightforward tasks to make

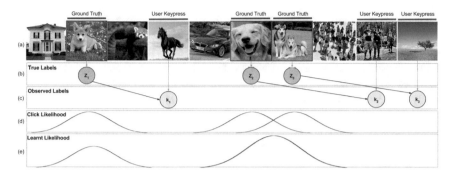

Fig. 1 a Images are shown to workers at 100 ms per image. Workers react whenever they see a dog. **b** The true labels are the ground truth dog images. **c** The workers' keypresses are slow and occur several images after the dog images have already passed. We record these keypresses as the observed labels. **d** Our technique models each keypress as a delayed Gaussian to predict **e** the probability of an image containing a dog from these observed labels

sure they do not represent edge cases [80, 132]. The result is slow, deliberate work. We suggest that there are cases where we can encourage workers to move quickly by telling them that making some errors is acceptable. Though individual worker accuracy decreases, we can recover from these mistakes post hoc algorithmically (Fig. 1).

We manifest this idea via a crowdsourcing technique in which workers label a rapidly advancing stream of inputs. Workers are given a binary question to answer, and they observe as the stream automatically advances via a method inspired by rapid serial visual presentation (RSVP) [51, 117]. Workers press a key whenever the answer is "yes" for one of the stream items. Because the stream is advancing rapidly, workers miss some items and have delayed responses. However, workers are reassured that the requester expects them to miss a few items. To recover the correct answers, the technique randomizes the item order for each worker and model workers' delays as a normal distribution whose variance depends on the stream's speed. For example, when labeling whether images have a "barking dog" in them, a self-paced worker on this task takes 1.7 s per image on average. With our technique, workers are shown a stream at 100 ms per image. The technique models the delays experienced at different input speeds and estimates the probability of intended labels from the key presses.

We evaluate our technique by comparing the total worker time necessary to achieve the same precision on an image labeling task as a standard setup with majority vote. The standard approach takes three workers an average of 1.7 s each for a total of 5.1 s. Our technique achieves identical precision (97%) with five workers at 100 ms each, for a total of 500 ms of work. The result is an order of magnitude speedup of 10×.

This relative improvement is robust across both simple tasks, such as identifying dogs, and complicated tasks, such as identifying "a person riding a motorcycle" (interactions between two objects) or "people eating breakfast" (understanding relationships among many objects). We generalize our technique to other tasks such as word similarity detection, topic classification, and sentiment analysis. Additionally, we extend our method to categorical classification tasks through a ranked cascade of binary classifications. Finally, we test workers' subjective mental workload and find no measurable increase.

Overall, we make the following contributions: (1) We introduce a rapid crowdsourcing technique that makes errors normal and even inevitable. We show that it can be used to effectively label large datasets by achieving a speedup of an order of magnitude on several binary labeling crowdsourcing tasks. (2) We demonstrate that our technique can be generalized to multi-label categorical labeling tasks, combined independently with existing optimization techniques, and deployed without increasing worker mental workload.

2.1 Related Work

The main motivation behind our work is to provide an environment where humans can make decisions quickly. We encourage a margin of human error in the interface that is then rectified by inferring the true labels algorithmically. In this section, we review prior work on crowdsourcing optimization and other methods for motivating contributions. Much of this work relies on artificial intelligence techniques: we complement this literature by changing the crowdsourcing interface rather than focusing on the underlying statistical model.

Our technique is inspired by rapid serial visual presentation (RSVP), a technique for consuming media rapidly by aligning it within the foveal region and advancing between items quickly [51, 117]. RSVP has already been proven to be effective at speeding up reading rates [203]. RSVP users can react to a single-target image in a sequence of images even at 125 ms per image with 75% accuracy [148]. However, when trying to recognize concepts in images, RSVP only achieves an accuracy of 10% at the same speed [149]. In our work, we integrate multiple workers' errors to successfully extract true labels.

Many previous papers have explored ways of modeling workers to remove bias or errors from ground truth labels [79, 146, 199, 200, 209]. For example, an unsupervised method for judging worker quality can be used as a prior to remove bias on binary verification labels [79]. Individual workers can also be modeled as projections into an open space representing their skills in labeling a particular image [200]. Workers may have unknown expertise that may in some cases prove adversarial to the task. Such adversarial workers can be detected by jointly learning the difficulty of labeling a particular datum along with the expertises of workers [199]. Finally, a generative model can be used to model workers' skills by minimizing the entropy of the distribution over their labels and the unknown true labels [209]. We draw inspiration from this literature, calibrating our model using a similar generative approach to understand worker reaction times. We model each worker's reaction as a delayed Gaussian distribution.

In an effort to reduce cost, many previous papers have studied the tradeoffs between speed (cost) and accuracy on a wide range of tasks [20, 159, 192, 193]. Some methods estimate human time with annotation accuracy to jointly model the errors in the annotation process [20, 192, 193]. Other methods vary both the labeling cost and annotation accuracy to calculate a tradeoff between the two [44, 81]. Similarly, some crowdsourcing systems optimize a budget to measure confidence in worker annotations [86, 87]. Models can also predict the redundancy of non-expert labels needed to match expert-level annotations [168]. Just like these methods, we show that non-experts can use our technique and provide expert-quality annotations; we also compare our methods to the conventional majority-voting annotation scheme.

Another perspective on rapid crowdsourcing is to return results in real time, often by using a retainer model to recall workers quickly [7, 109, 111]. Like our approach, real-time crowdsourcing can use algorithmic solutions to combine multiple in-progress contributions [110]. These systems' techniques could be fused with ours to create crowds that can react to bursty requests.

One common method for optimizing crowdsourcing is active learning, which involves learning algorithms that interactively query the user. Examples include training image recognition [175] and attribution recognition [145] with fewer examples. Comparative models for ranking attribute models have also optimized crowdsourcing using active learning [120]. Similar techniques have explored optimization of the "crowd kernel" by adaptively choosing the next questions asked of the crowd in order to build a similarity matrix between a given set of data points [180]. Active learning needs to decide on a new task after each new piece of data is gathered from the crowd. Such models tend to be quite expensive to compute. Other methods have been proposed to decide on a set of tasks instead of just one task [186]. We draw on this literature: in our technique, after all the images have been seen by at least one worker, we use active learning to decide the next set of tasks. We determine which images to discard and which images to group together and send this set to another worker to gather more information.

Finally, there is a group of techniques that attempt to optimize label collection by reducing the number of questions that must be answered by the crowd. For example, a hierarchy in label distribution can reduce the annotation search space [44], and information gain can reduce the number of labels necessary to build large taxonomies using a crowd [18, 35]. Methods have also been proposed to maximize accuracy of object localization in images [177] and videos [191]. Previous labels can also be used as a prior to optimize acquisition of new types of annotations [19]. One of the benefits of our technique is that it can be used independently of these others to jointly improve crowdsourcing schemes. We demonstrate the gains of such a combination in our evaluation.

2.2 Error-Embracing Crowdsourcing

Current microtask crowdsourcing platforms like Amazon Mechanical Turk incentivize workers to avoid rejections [80, 132], resulting in slow and meticulous work. But is such careful work necessary to build an accurate dataset? In this section, we detail our technique for rapid crowdsourcing by encouraging less accurate work.

The design space of such techniques must consider which tradeoffs are acceptable to make. The first relevant dimension is accuracy. When labeling a large dataset (e.g., building a dataset of ten thousand articles about housing), *precision* is often the highest priority: articles labeled as on-topic by the system must in fact be about housing. *Recall*, on the other hand, is often less important, because there is typically a large amount of available unlabeled data: even if the system misses some on-topic articles, the system can label more items until it reaches the desired dataset size. We thus develop an approach for producing high precision at high speed, sacrificing some recall if necessary.

The second design dimension involves the task characteristics. Many large-scale crowdsourcing tasks involve closed-ended responses such as binary or categorical classifications. These tasks have two useful properties. First, they are time-bound by users' perception and cognition speed rather than motor (e.g., pointing, typing) speed [33], since acting requires only a single button press. Second, it is possible to aggregate responses automatically, for example, with majority vote. Open-ended crowdsourcing tasks such as writing [8] or transcription are often time-bound by data entry motor speeds and cannot be automatically aggregated. Thus, with our technique, we focus on closed-ended tasks.

Rapid Crowdsourcing of Binary Decision Tasks

Binary questions are one of the most common classes of crowdsourcing tasks. Each yes-or-no question gathers a label on whether each item has a certain characteristic. In our technique, rather than letting workers focus on each item too carefully, we display each item for a specific period of time before moving on to the next one in a rapid slideshow. For example, in the context of an image verification task, we show workers a stream of images and ask them to press the spacebar whenever they see a specific class of image. In the example in Fig. 2, we ask them to react whenever they see a "dog."

The main parameter in this approach is the length of time each item is visible. To determine the best option, we begin by allowing workers to work at their own pace. This establishes an initial average time period, which we then slowly decrease in successive versions until workers start making mistakes [33]. Once we have identified this error point, we can algorithmically model workers' latency and errors to extract the true labels.

To avoid stressing out workers, it is important that the task instructions convey the nature of the rapid task and the fact that we expect them to make some errors. Workers are first shown a set of instructions (Fig. 2a) for the task. They are warned that reacting to every single correct image on time is not feasible and thus not expected. We also warn them that we have placed a small number of items in the set that we know to

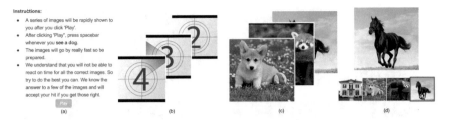

Instructions:

- A series of images will be rapidly shown to you after you click 'Play'.
- After clicking 'Play', press spacebar whenever you **see a dog**.
- The images will go by really fast so be prepared.
- We understand that you will not be able to react on time for all the correct images. So try to do the best you can. We know the answer to a few of the images and will accept your hit if you get those right.

Play

(a)   (b)   (c)   (d)

Fig. 2 **a** Task instructions inform workers that we expect them to make mistakes since the items will be displayed rapidly. **b** A string of countdown images prepares them for the rate at which items will be displayed. **c** An example image of a "dog" shown in the stream—the two images appearing behind it are included for clarity but are not displayed to workers. **d** When the worker presses a key, we show the last four images below the stream of images to indicate which images might have just been labeled

be positive items. These help us calibrate each worker's speed and also provide us with a mechanism to reject workers who do not react to any of the items.

Once workers start the stream (Fig. 2b), it is important to prepare them for pace of the task. We thus show a film-style countdown for the first few seconds that decrements to zero at the same interval as the main task. Without these countdown images, workers use up the first few seconds getting used to the pace and speed. Figure 2c shows an example "dog" image that is displayed in front of the user. The dimensions of all items (images) shown are held constant to avoid having to adjust to larger or smaller visual ranges.

When items are displayed for less than 400 ms, workers tend to react to all positive items with a delay. If the interface only reacts with a simple confirmation when workers press the spacebar, many workers worry that they are too late because another item is already on the screen. Our solution is to also briefly display the last four items previously shown when the spacebar is pressed, so that workers see the one they intended and also gather an intuition for how far back the model looks. For example, in Fig. 2d, we show a worker pressing the spacebar on an image of a horse. We anticipate that the worker was probably delayed, and we display the last four items to acknowledge that we have recorded the keypress. We ask all workers to first complete a qualification task in which they receive feedback on how quickly we expect them to react. They pass the qualification task only if they achieve a recall of 0.6 and precision of 0.9 on a stream of 200 items with 25 positives. We measure precision as the fraction of worker reactions that were within 500 ms of a positive cue.

In Fig. 3, we show two sample outputs from our interface. Workers were shown images for 100 ms each. They were asked to press the spacebar whenever they saw an image of "a person riding a motorcycle." The images with blue bars underneath them are ground truth images of "a person riding a motorcycle." The images with red bars show where workers reacted. The important element is that red labels are often delayed behind blue ground truth and occasionally missed entirely. Both Fig. 3a, b have 100 images each with 5 correct images.

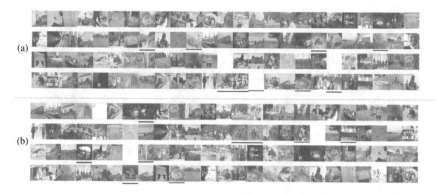

Fig. 3 Example raw worker outputs from our interface. Each image was displayed for 100 ms and workers were asked to react whenever they saw images of "a person riding a motorcycle." Images are shown in the same order they appeared in for the worker. Positive images are shown with a blue bar below them and users' keypresses are shown as red bars below the image to which they reacted

Because of workers' reaction delay, the data from one worker has considerable uncertainty. We thus show the same set of items to multiple workers in different random orders and collect independent sets of keypresses. This randomization will produce a cleaner signal in aggregate and later allow us to estimate the images to which each worker intended to react.

Given the speed of the images, workers are not able to detect every single positive image. For example, the last positive image in Fig. 3a and the first positive image in Fig. 3b are not detected. Previous work on RSVP found a phenomenon called "attention blink" [21], in which a worker is momentarily blind to successive positive images. However, we find that even if two images of "a person riding a motorcycle" occur consecutively, workers are able to detect both and react twice (Fig. 3a, b). If workers are forced to react in intervals of less than 400 ms, though, the signal we extract is too noisy for our model to estimate the positive items.

Multi-class Classification for Categorical Data

So far, we have described how rapid crowdsourcing can be used for binary verification tasks. Now we extend it to handle multi-class classification. Theoretically, all multi-class classification can be broken down into a series of binary verifications. For example, if there are N classes, we can ask N binary questions of whether an item is in each class. Given a list of items, we use our technique to classify them one class at a time. After every iteration, we remove all the positively classified items for a particular class. We use the rest of the items to detect the next class.

Assuming all the classes contain an equal number of items, the order in which we detect classes should not matter. A simple *baseline approach* would choose a class at random and attempt to detect all items for that class first. However, if the distribution of items is not equal among classes, this method would be inefficient. Consider the case where we are trying to classify items into ten classes, and one class has 1000 items, while all other classes have 10 items. In the worst case, if we classify the class with 1000 examples last, those 1000 images would go through our interface ten times (once for every class). Instead, if we had detected the large class first, we would be able to classify those 1000 images and they would only go through our interface once. With this intuition, we propose a *class-optimized approach* that classifies the most common class of items first. We maximize the number of items we classify at every iteration, reducing the total number of binary verifications required.

2.3 Model

To translate workers' delayed and potentially erroneous actions into identifications of the positive items, we need to model their behavior. We do this by calculating the probability that a particular item is in the positive class given that the user reacted a given period after the item was displayed. By combining these probabilities across several workers with different random orders of the same images, these probabilities sum up to identify the correct items.

We use maximum likelihood estimation to predict the probability of an item being a positive example. Given a set of items $\mathcal{I} = \{I_1, \ldots, I_n\}$, we send them to W workers in a different random order for each. From each worker w, we collect a set of keypresses $\mathcal{C}^w = \{c_1^w, \ldots, c_k^w\}$, where $w \in W$ and k is the total number of keypresses from w. Our aim is to calculate the probability of a given item $P(I_i)$ being a positive example. Given that we collect keypresses from W workers:

$$P(I_i) = \sum_w P(I_i | \mathcal{C}^w) P(\mathcal{C}^w), \tag{1}$$

where $P(\mathcal{C}) = \prod_k P(\mathcal{C}_k)$ is the probability of a particular set of items being keypresses. We set $P(\mathcal{C}_k)$ to be constant, assuming that it is equally likely that a worker might react to any item. Using Bayes' rule,

$$P(I_i | \mathcal{C}^w) = \frac{P(\mathcal{C}^w | I_i) P(I_i)}{P(\mathcal{C}^w)}. \tag{2}$$

$P(I_i)$ models our estimate of item I_i being positive. It can be a constant, or it can be an estimate from a domain-specific ML algorithm [85]. For example, to calculate $P(I_i)$, if we were trying to scale up a dataset of "dog" images, we would use a small set of known "dog" images to train a binary classifier and use that to calculate $P(I_i)$ for all the unknown images. With image tasks, we use a pretrained convolutional neural network to extract image features [171] and train a linear support vector machine to calculate $P(I_i)$.

We model $P(\mathcal{C}^w | I_i)$ as a set of independent keypresses:

$$P(\mathcal{C}^w | I_i) = P(c_1^w, \ldots, c_k^w | I_i) = \prod_k P(\mathcal{C}_k^w | I_i). \tag{3}$$

Finally, we model each keypress as a Gaussian distribution $\mathcal{N}(\mu, \sigma)$ given a positive item. We train the mean μ and variance σ by running rapid crowdsourcing on a small set of items for which we already know the positive items. Here, the mean and variance of the distribution are modeled to estimate the delays that a worker makes when reacting to a positive item.

Intuitively, the model works by treating each keypress as creating a Gaussian "footprint" of positive probability on the images about 400 ms before the keypress (Fig. 1). The model combines these probabilities across several workers to identify the images with the highest overall probability.

Now that we have a set of probabilities for each item, we need to decide which ones should be classified as positive. We order the set of items $\mathcal{I}$ according to likelihood of being in the positive class $P(I_i)$. We then set all items above a certain threshold as positive. This threshold is a hyperparameter that can be tuned to trade off precision vs. recall.

In total, this model has two hyperparameters: (1) the threshold above which we classify images as positive and (2) the speed at which items are displayed to the user. We model both hyperparameters in a per-task (image verification, sentiment analysis, etc.) basis. For a new task, we first estimate how long it takes to label each item in the conventional setting with a small set of items. Next, we continuously reduce the time each item is displayed until we reach a point where the model is unable to achieve the same precision as the untimed case.

2.4 Calibration: Baseline Worker Reaction Time

Our technique hypothesizes that guiding workers to work quickly and make errors can lead to results that are faster yet with similar precision. We begin evaluating our technique by first studying worker reaction times as we vary the length of time for which each item is displayed. If worker reaction times have a low variance, we accurately model them. Existing work on RSVP estimated that humans usually react about 400 ms after being presented with a cue [153, 197]. Similarly, the model human processor [27] estimated that humans perceive, understand, and react at least 240 ms after a cue. We first measure worker reaction times, then analyze how frequently positive items can be displayed before workers are unable to react to them in time.

Method. We recruited 1,000 workers on Amazon Mechanical Turk with 96% approval rating and over 10,000 tasks submitted. Workers were asked to work on one task at a time. Each task contained a stream of 100 images of polka dot patterns of two different colors. Workers were asked to react by pressing the spacebar whenever they saw an image with polka dots of one of the two colors. Tasks could vary by two variables: the *speed* at which images were displayed and the *percentage* of the positively colored images. For a given task, we held the display speed constant. Across multiple tasks, we displayed images for 100 ms–500 ms. We studied two variables: *reaction time* and *recall*. We measured the reaction time to the positive

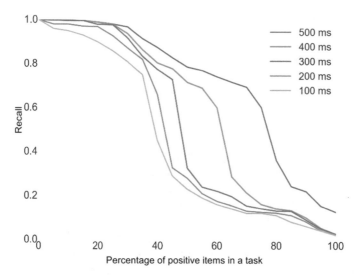

Fig. 4 We plot the change in recall as we vary percentage of positive items in a task. We experiment at varying display speeds ranging from 100 ms to 500 ms. We find that recall is inversely proportional to the rate of positive stimuli and not to the percentage of positive items

color across these speeds. To study recall (percentage of positively colored images detected by workers), we varied the ratio of positive images from 5% to 95%. We counted a keypress as a detection only if it occurred within 500 ms of displaying a positively colored image.

Results. Workers' reaction times corresponded well with estimates from previous studies. Workers tend to react an average of 378 ms ($\sigma = 92$ ms) after seeing a positive image. This consistency is an important result for our model because it assumes that workers have a consistent reaction delay.

As expected, recall is inversely proportional to the speed at which the images are shown. A worker is more likely to miss a positive image at very fast speeds. We also find that recall decreases as we increase the percentage of positive items in the task. To measure the effects of positive frequency on recall, we record the percentage threshold at which recall begins to drop significantly at different speeds and positive frequencies. From Fig. 4, at 100 ms, we see that recall drops when the percentage of positive images is more than 35%. As we increase the time for which an item is displayed, however, we notice that the drop in recall occurs at a much higher percentage. At 500 ms, the recall drops at a threshold of 85%. We thus infer that recall is inversely proportional to the *rate* of positive stimuli and not to the percentage of positive images. From these results, we conclude that, at faster speeds, it is important to maintain a smaller percentage of positive images, while at slower speeds, the percentage of positive images has a lesser impact on recall. Quantitatively, to maintain a recall higher than 0.7, it is necessary to limit the frequency of positive cues to one every 400 ms.

2.5 Study 1: Image Verification

In this study, we deploy our technique on image verification tasks and measure its speed relative to the conventional self-paced approach. Many crowdsourcing tasks in computer vision require verifying that a particular image contains a specific class or concept. We measure precision, recall, and cost (in seconds) by the conventional approach and compare against our technique.

Some visual concepts are easier to detect than others. For example, detecting an image of a "dog" is a lot easier than detecting an image of "a person riding a motorcycle" or "eating breakfast." While detecting a "dog" is a perceptual task, "a person riding a motorcycle" requires understanding of the interaction between the person and the motorcycle. Similarly, "eating breakfast" requires workers to fuse concepts of people eating a variety foods like eggs, cereal, or pancakes. We test our technique on detecting three concepts: "dog" (easy concept), "a person riding a motorcycle" (medium concept) and "eating breakfast" (hard concept). In this study, we compare how workers fare on each of these three levels of concepts.

Method. In this study, we compare the conventional approach with our technique on three (easy, medium, and hard) concepts. We evaluate each of these comparisons using precision scores, recall scores, and the speedup achieved. To test each of the three concepts, we labeled 10,000 images, where each concept had 500 examples. We divided the 10,000 images into streams of 100 images for each task. We paid workers $0.17 to label a stream of 100 images (resulting in a wage of $6 per hour [163]). We hired over 1,000 workers for this study satisfying the same qualifications as the calibration task.

The conventional method of collecting binary labels is to present a crowd worker with a set of items. The worker proceeds to label each item, one at a time. Most datasets employ multiple workers to label each task because majority voting [174] has been shown to improve the quality of crowd annotations. These datasets usually use a redundancy of 3–5 workers [169]. In all our experiments, we used a redundancy of three workers as our baseline.

When launching tasks using our technique, we tuned the image display speed to 100 ms. We used a redundancy of five workers when measuring precision and recall scores. To calculate *speedup*, we compare the total worker time taken by all the five workers using our technique with the total worker time taken by the three workers using the conventional method. Additionally, we vary redundancy on all the concepts to from one to ten workers to see its effects on precision and recall.

Results. Self-paced workers take 1.70 s on average to label each image with a concept in the conventional approach (Table 1). They are quicker at labeling the easy concept (1.50 s per worker), while taking longer on the medium (1.70 s) and hard (1.90 s) concepts.

Using our technique, even with a redundancy of five workers, we achieve a speedup of 10.20× across all concepts. We achieve *order of magnitude* speedups of 9.00×, 10.20×, and 11.40× on the easy, medium, and hard concepts, respectively. Overall,

Table 1 We compare the conventional approach for binary verification tasks (image verification, sentiment analysis, word similarity, and topic detection) with our technique and compute precision and recall scores. Precision scores, recall scores, and speedups are calculated using three workers in the conventional setting. Image verification, sentiment analysis, and word similarity used five workers using our technique, while topic detection used only two workers. We also show the time taken (in seconds) for one worker to do each task

Task		Conventional approach			Our technique			Speedup
		Time (s)	Precision	Recall	Time (s)	Precision	Recall	
Image verification	Easy	1.50	0.99	0.99	0.10	0.99	0.94	**9.00×**
	Medium	1.70	0.97	0.99	0.10	0.98	0.83	**10.20×**
	Hard	1.90	0.93	0.89	0.10	0.90	0.74	**11.40×**
	All concepts	1.70	0.97	0.96	0.10	0.97	0.81	**10.20×**
Sentiment analysis		4.25	0.93	0.97	0.25	0.94	0.84	**10.20×**
Word similarity		6.23	0.89	0.94	0.60	0.88	0.86	**6.23×**
Topic detection		14.33	0.96	0.94	2.00	0.95	0.81	**10.75×**

across all concepts, the precision and recall achieved by our technique are 0.97 and 0.81, respectively. Meanwhile, the precision and recall of the conventional method are 0.97 and 0.96, respectively. We thus achieve the same precision as the conventional method. As expected, recall is lower because workers are not able to detect every single true positive example. As argued previously, lower recall can be an acceptable tradeoff when it is easy to find more unlabeled images.

Now, let's compare precision and recall scores between the three concepts. We show precision and recall scores in Fig. 5 for the three concepts. Workers perform slightly better at finding "dog" images and find it the most difficult to detect the more challenging "eating breakfast" concept. With a redundancy of 5, the three concepts achieve a precision of 0.99, 0.98, and 0.90, respectively, at a recall of 0.94, 0.83, and 0.74 (Table 1). The precision for these three concepts are identical to the conventional approach, while the recall scores are slightly lower. The recall for a more difficult cognitive concept ("eating breakfast") is much lower, at 0.74, than for the other two concepts. More complex concepts usually tend to have a lot of contextual variance. For example, "eating breakfast" might include a person eating a "banana," a "bowl of cereal," "waffles," or "eggs." We find that while some workers react to one variety of the concept (e.g., "bowl of cereal"), others react to another variety (e.g., "eggs").

When we increase the redundancy of workers to ten (Fig. 6), our model is able to better approximate the positive images. We see diminishing increases in both recall and precision as redundancy increases. At a redundancy of 10, we increase recall to the same amount as the conventional approach (0.96), while maintaining a high precision (0.99) and still achieving a speedup of 5.1×.

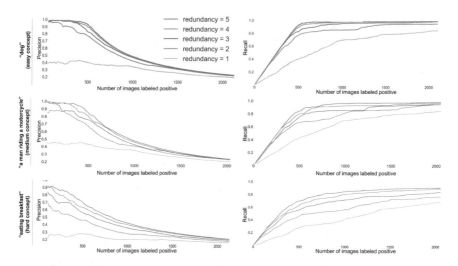

Fig. 5 We study the precision (left) and recall (right) curves for detecting "dog" (top), "a person on a motorcycle" (middle), and "eating breakfast" (bottom) images with a redundancy ranging from 1 to 5. There are 500 ground truth positive images in each experiment. We find that our technique works for simple as well as hard concepts

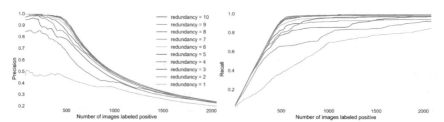

Fig. 6 We study the effects of redundancy on recall by plotting precision and recall curves for detecting "a person on a motorcycle" images with a redundancy ranging from 1 to 10. We see diminishing increases in precision and recall as we increase redundancy. We manage to achieve the same precision and recall scores as the conventional approach with a redundancy of 10 while still achieving a speedup of $5\times$

We conclude from this study that our technique (with a redundancy of 5) can speed up image verification with easy, medium, and hard concepts by an order of magnitude while still maintaining high precision. We also show that recall can be compensated by increasing redundancy.

2.6   Study 2: Non-visual Tasks

So far, we have shown that rapid crowdsourcing can be used to collect image verification labels. We next test the technique on a variety of other common crowdsourcing tasks: sentiment analysis [142], word similarity [174], and topic detection [116].

Method. In this study, we measure precision, recall, and speedup achieved by our technique over the conventional approach. To determine the stream speed for each task, we followed the prescribed method of running trials and speeding up the stream until the model starts losing precision. For sentiment analysis, workers were shown a stream of tweets and asked to react whenever they saw a positive tweet. We displayed tweets at 250 ms with a redundancy of five workers. For word similarity, workers were shown a word (e.g., "lad") for which we wanted synonyms. They were then rapidly shown other words at 600 ms and asked to react if they see a synonym (e.g., "boy"). Finally, for topic detection, we presented workers with a topic like "housing" or "gas" and presented articles of an average length of 105 words at a speed of 2 s per article. They reacted whenever they saw an article containing the topic we were looking for. For all three of these tasks, we compare precision, recall, and speed against the self-paced conventional approach with a redundancy of three workers. Every task, for both the conventional approach and our technique, contained 100 items.

To measure the cognitive load on workers for labeling so many items at once, we ran the widely used NASA Task Load Index (TLX) [37] on all tasks, including image verification. TLX measures the perceived workload of a task. We ran the survey on 100 workers who used the conventional approach and 100 workers who used our technique across all tasks.

Results. We present our results in Table 1 and Fig. 7. For sentiment analysis, we find that workers in the conventional approach classify tweets in 4.25 s. So, with a redundancy of three workers, the conventional approach would take 12.75 s with a precision of 0.93. Using our method and a redundancy of five workers, we complete the task in 1250 ms (250 ms per worker per item) and 0.94 precision. Therefore, our technique achieves a speedup of 10.2×.

Likewise, for word similarity, workers take around 6.23 s to complete the conventional task, while our technique succeeds at 600 ms. We manage to capture a comparable precision of 0.88 using five workers against a precision of 0.89 in the conventional method with three workers. Since finding synonyms is a higher level cognitive task, workers take longer to do word similarity tasks than image verification and sentiment analysis tasks. We manage a speedup of 6.23×.

Finally, for topic detection, workers spend significant time analyzing articles in the conventional setting (14.33 s on average). With three workers, the conventional approach takes 43 s. In comparison, our technique delegates 2 s for each article. With a redundancy of only two workers, we achieve a precision of 0.95, similar to the 0.96 achieved by the conventional approach. The total worker time to label one article using our technique is 4 s, a speedup of 10.75×.

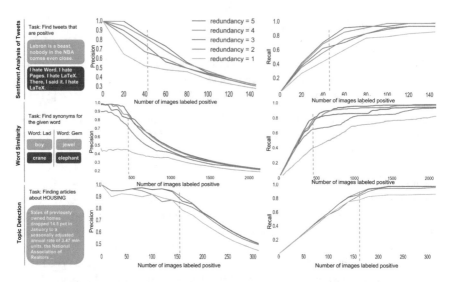

Fig. 7 Precision (left) and recall (right) curves for sentiment analysis (top), word similarity (middle), and topic detection (bottom) images with a redundancy ranging from 1 to 5. Vertical lines indicate the number of ground truth positive examples

The mean TLX workload for the control condition was 58.5 ($\sigma = 9.3$), and 62.4 ($\sigma = 18.5$) for our technique. Unexpectedly, the difference between conditions was not significant ($t(99) = -0.53$, $p = 0.59$). The "temporal demand" scale item appeared to be elevated for our technique (61.1 vs. 70.0), but this difference was not significant ($t(99) = -0.76$, $p = 0.45$). We conclude that our technique can be used to scale crowdsourcing on a variety of tasks without statistically increasing worker workload.

2.7 Study 3: Multi-class Classification

In this study, we extend our technique from binary to multi-class classification to capture an even larger set of crowdsourcing tasks. We use our technique to create a dataset where each image is classified into one category ("people," "dog," "horse," "cat," etc.). We compare our technique with a conventional technique [43] that collects binary labels for each image for every single possible class.

Method. Our aim is to classify a dataset of 2,000 images with ten categories where each category contains between 100 and 250 examples. We compared three methods of multi-class classification: (1) a *naive approach* that collected ten binary labels (one for each class) for each image, (2) a *baseline approach* that used our interface and classified images one class (chosen randomly) at a time, and (3) a *class-optimized approach* that used our interface to classify images starting from the class with the most examples. When using our interface, we broke tasks into streams of 100 images displayed for 100 ms each. We used a redundancy of three workers for the conventional interface and five workers for our interface. We calculated the precision and recall scores across each of these three methods as well as the cost (in seconds) of each method.

Results. (1) In the *naive approach*, we need to collect 20,000 binary labels that take 1.7 s each. With five workers, this takes 102,000 s ($170 at a wage rate of $6/hr) with an average precision of 0.99 and recall of 0.95. (2) Using the *baseline approach*, it takes 12,342 s ($20.57) with an average precision of 0.98 and recall of 0.83. This shows that the baseline approach achieves a speedup of 8.26× when compared with the naive approach. (3) Finally, the *class-optimized approach* is able to detect the most common class first and hence reduces the number of times an image is sent through our interface. It takes 11,700 s ($19.50) with an average precision of 0.98 and recall of 0.83. The class-optimized approach achieves a speedup of 8.7× when compared to the naive approach. While the speedup between the baseline and the class-optimized methods is small, it would be increased on a larger dataset with more classes.

2.8 Application: Building ImageNet

Our method can be combined with existing techniques [13, 44, 145, 175] that optimize binary verification and multi-class classification by preprocessing data or using active learning. One such method [44] annotated ImageNet (a popular large dataset for image classification) effectively with a useful insight: they realized that its classes could be grouped together into higher semantic concepts. For example, "dog," "rabbit," and "cat" could be grouped into the concept "animal." By utilizing the hierarchy of labels that is specific to this task, they were able to preprocess and reduce the number of labels needed to classify all images. As a case study, we combine our technique with their insight and evaluate the speedup in collecting a subset of ImageNet.

Method. We focused on a subset of the dataset with 20,000 images and classified them into 200 classes. We conducted this case study by comparing three ways of collecting labels: (1) The naive approach asked 200 binary questions for each image in the subset, where each question asked if the image belonged to one of the 200 classes. We used a redundancy of 3 workers for this task. (2) The optimal labeling method used the insight to reduce the number of labels by utilizing the hierarchy of image classes. (3) The combined approach used our technique for multi-class classification combined with the hierarchy insight to reduce the number of labels collected. We used a redundancy of five workers for this technique with tasks of 100 images displayed at 250 ms.

Results. (1) Using the naive approach, this would result in asking 4 million binary verification questions. Given that each binary label takes 1.7 s (Table 1), we estimate that the total time to label the entire dataset would take 6.8 million seconds ($11,333 at a wage rate of $6/hr). (2) The optimal labeling method is estimated to take 1.13 million seconds ($1,888) [44]. (3) Combining the hierarchical questions with our interface, we annotate the subset in 136,800 s ($228). We achieve a precision of 0.97 with a recall of 0.82. By combining our $8\times$ speedup with the $6\times$ speedup from intelligent question selection, we achieve a $50\times$ speedup in total.

2.9 Discussion

Absence of Concepts. We focused our technique on positively identifying concepts. We then also test its effectiveness at classifying the absence of a concept. Instead of asking workers to react when they see a "dog," if we ask them to react when they do *not* see a "dog," our technique performs poorly. At 100 ms, we find that workers achieve a recall of only 0.31, which is much lower than a recall of 0.94 when detecting the presence of "dogs." To improve recall to 0.90, we must slow down the feed to 500 ms. Our technique achieves a speedup of $2\times$ with this speed. We conclude that our technique performs poorly for anomaly detection tasks, where the presence of a concept is common but its absence, an anomaly, is rare. More generally, this exercise suggests that some cognitive tasks are less robust to rapid judgments. Preattentive processing can help us find "dogs," but ensuring that there is no "dog" requires a linear scan of the entire image.

Typicality. To better understand the active mechanism behind our technique, we turn to concept typicality. A recent study [77] used fMRIs to measure humans' recognition speed for different object categories, finding that images of most typical exemplars from a class were recognized faster than the least typical categories. They calculated typicality scores for a set of image classes based on how quickly humans recognized them. In our image verification task, 72% of false negatives were also atypical. Not detecting atypical images might lead to the curation of image datasets that are biased toward more common categories. For example, when curating a dataset of dogs, our technique would be more likely to find usual breeds like "dalmatians" and "labradors" and miss rare breeds like "romagnolos" and "otterhounds." More generally, this approach may amplify biases and minimize clarity on edge cases. Slowing down the feed reduces atypical false negatives, resulting in a smaller speedup but with a higher recall for atypical images.

Conclusion. We have suggested that crowdsourcing can speed up labeling by encouraging a small amount of error rather than forcing workers to avoid it. We introduce a rapid slideshow interface where items are shown too quickly for workers to get all items correct. We algorithmically model worker errors and recover their intended labels. This interface can be used for binary verification tasks like image verification, sentiment analysis, word similarity, and topic detection, achieving speedups of $10.2\times$, $10.2\times$, $6.23\times$, and $10.75\times$, respectively. It can also extend to multi-class classification and achieve a speedup of $8.26\times$. Our approach is only one possible interface instantiation of the concept of encouraging some error; we suggest that future work may investigate many others. Speeding up crowdsourcing enables us to build larger datasets to empower scientific insights and industry practice. For many labeling goals, this technique can be used to construct datasets that are an order of magnitude larger without increasing cost.

3   Data Acquisition Through Social Interactions

Modern supervised ML systems in domains such as computer vision are reliant on mountains of human-labeled training data. These labeled images, for example, the 14 million images in ImageNet [43], require basic human knowledge such as whether an image contains a chair. Unfortunately, this knowledge is both so simple that it is extremely tedious for humans to label, and also so tacit that the human annotators are required. In response, crowdsourcing efforts often recruit volunteers to help create labels via intrinsic interest, curiosity or gamification [113, 123, 189, 202].

The general approach of these crowdsourcing efforts is to focus on *what* to ask each contributor. Specifically, from a large set of possible tasks, many systems formalize an approach to route or recommend tasks to specific contributors [2, 47, 55, 121]. Unfortunately, many of these volunteer efforts are restricted to labels for which contributions can be motivated, leaving incomplete any task that is uninteresting to contributors [66, 69, 155, 196].

Our paper specifically studies an instantiation of this common ailment in the context of visual question answering (VQA). VQA generalizes numerous computer vision tasks, including object detection [43], relationship prediction [127], and action prediction [140]. Progress in VQA supports the development of many human–computer interaction systems, including VizWiz [10], TapTapSee, BeMyEyes, and CamFind.[1] VQA is a data-hungry ML task that is challenging to motivate contributors. Existing VQA crowdsourcing strategies have suggested using social media to incentivize online participants to answer visual questions for assistive users [10, 16], but many such questions remain unanswered [17].

To meet the needs of modern ML systems, we argue that crowdsourcing systems can automatically generate plans not just for *what* to ask about but also for *how* to make that request. Social psychology and social computing research have made clear that how a request is structured can have substantial effects on resulting contribution rates [95, 205]. However, while it is feasible to manually design a single request such as one email message to all users in an online community, or one motivational message on all web pages on Wikipedia, in real life (as in VQA), there exist a wide variety of situations that must each be approached differently. Supporting this variety in *how* a request is made has remained out of reach; in this paper, we contribute algorithms to achieve it.

---

[1] Applications can be found at https://taptapsee.com/, https://www.bemyeyes.com/, and https://camfindapp.com/.

Caption	Raw question	Social strategy augmentation
Modelling outdoors today.	Where is this place?	That's a great outfit! Where is this place?
	Where can I get that?	I love black too! Where can I get that?
Saw the meme dog finally.	Where is this place?	What a cute dog! Where is this place?
	What animal Is that?	You seem to know a lot about animals! What animal is that?

Fig. 8 We introduce an approach that increases crowdsourcing participation rates by learning to augment requests with image- and text-relevant question asking strategies drawn from social psychology. Given a social media image post and a question, our approach selects a strategy and generates a natural language phrase to augment the question

Consider, for example, that we are building a dataset of images with their tagged geolocations (Fig. 8). When we encounter an image of a person wearing a black shirt next to a beautiful scenery, existing ML systems can generate questions such as "where is this place?". However, prior work reports that such requests seem mechanical, resulting in lower response rates [17]. In our approach, requests might be augmented by content compliment strategies [156] reactive to the image content, such as "What a great statue!" or "That's a beautiful building!," or by interest matching strategies [36] reactive to the image content, such as "I love visiting statues!" or "I love seeing old buildings!"

Augmenting requests with social strategies requires (1) defining a set of possible social strategies, (2) developing a method to generate content for each strategy conditioned on an image, and (3) choosing the appropriate strategy to maximize response conditioned on the user and their post. In this paper, we tackle these three challenges. First, we adopt a set of social strategies that social psychologists have demonstrated to be successful in human–human communication [36, 72, 108, 156, 181]. While our set is not exhaustive, it represents a diverse list of strategies—some that augment questions conditioned on the image and others conditioned on the user's language. While previous work has explored the use of ML models to generate image-conditioned natural language fragments, for generating captions and questions, ours is the first method that employs these techniques to generate strategies that increase worker participation.

To test the efficacy of our approach, we deploy our system on Instagram, a social media image-sharing platform. We collect datasets and develop ML-based models that use a convolutional neural network (CNN) to encode the image contents and a long short-term memory network (LSTM) to generate each social strategy across a large set of different kinds of images. We compare our ML strategies against baseline rule-based strategies using linguistic features extracted from the user's post [118]. We show a sample of augmented questions in Fig. 9. We find that choosing appropriate strategies and augmenting requests leads to a significant absolute participation

Fig. 9 Our agent chooses appropriate social strategies and contextualizes questions to maximize crowdsourcing participation

increase of 42.36% over no strategy when using ML strategies and a 14.78% increase when using rule-based strategies. We also find that no specific strategy is the universal best choice, implying that knowing when to use a strategy is important. While we specifically focus on VQA and Instagram, our approach generalizes to other crowdsourcing systems that support language-based interaction with contributors.

3.1 Related Work

Our work is motivated by research in crowdsourcing, peer production, and social computing that increase contributors' levels of intrinsic motivation. We thread this work together with advances in natural language generation technologies to contribute generative algorithms that modulating the form of the requests to increase contribution rates.

Crowdsourcing strategies. The HCI community has investigated different ways to incentivize people to participate in data-labeling tasks [66, 69, 155]. Designing for curiosity, for example, increases crowdsourcing participation [113]. Citizen science projects like GalaxyZoo mobilize volunteers by motivating them to work on a domain that aligns with their interests [123]. Unlike the tasks typically explored by such methods, image labeling is not typically an intrinsically motivated task, and is instead completed by paid ghost work [60]. To improve image labeling, the ESP Game harnessed game design to solve annotation tasks as by-products of entertainment activities [190]. However, games result in limited kinds of labels, and need to be designed specifically to attain certain types of labels. Instead, we ask directed questions through conversations to label data and use social strategies to motive participation.

Interaction through conversations. The use of natural language as a medium for interaction has galvanized many systems [75, 112]. Natural language has been proposed as a medium to gather new data from online participants [10] or guide users through workflows [49]. Conversational agents have also been deployed through products like Apple's Siri, Amazon's Echo, and Microsoft's Cortana. Substantial effort has been placed on teaching people how to talk to such assistants. Noticing this limitation, more robust crowd-powered conversational systems have been created by hiring professionals, as in the case of Facebook M [67], or crowd workers [14, 112]. Unlike these approaches where people have a goal and invoke a passive conversational agent, we build active agents reach out to people with questions that increase humans participation.

Social interaction with machines. To design an agent capable of eliciting a user's help, we need to understand how a user views the interaction. The Media Equation proposes that people adhere to similar social norms in their interactions with computers as they do in interactions with other people [154]. It shoes that agents that seem more human-like, in terms of behavior and gestures, provoke users to treat them similar to a person [29, 30, 139]. Consistent with these observations, prior work has also shown that people are more likely to resolve misunderstandings with more human-like agents [39]. This leads us to question whether a human-like conversational agent can encourage more online participation from online contributors. Prior work on interactions with machines investigates social norms that a machine can mimic in a binary capacity—either it respects the norm correctly or violates it with negligence [34, 165]. Instead, we project social interaction on a spectrum—some social strategies are more successful than others in a given context—and learn a selection strategy that maximizes participation.

Structuring requests to enhance motivation. There have been many proposed social strategies to enhance the motivation to contribute in online communities [95]. For example, asking a specific question rather than making a statement or asking an open-ended question increases the likelihood of getting a response [25]. Requests succeed significantly more often when contributors are addressed by name [131]. Emergencies receive more responses than requests without time constraints [42]. Prior work has shown that factors that increase the contributor's affinity for the requester increase the persuasive power of the message on online crowdfunding sites [205]. It has also been observed that different behavior elicits different kind of support from online support groups with self disclosure eliciting emotional support and questioning resulting in informational support [194]. The severity of the outcome of responding to a request can also influence motivation [31]. Our work incorporates some of these established social strategies and leverages language generation algorithms to build an agent that can deploy them across a wide variety of different requests.

3.2   Social Strategies

The goal of our system is to draw on theories of how people ask other people for help and favors, then learn how to emulate those strategies. Drawing on prior work, we sampled a diverse set of nine social strategies. While the set of nine social strategies, we explore are not an exhaustive set, we believe it represents a wide enough range of possible strategies to demonstrate the method and effects of teaching social strategies to machines. The social strategies we explore are:

1. Content compliment: Compliment the image or an object in the image before asking the question. This increases the liking between the agent and the contributor, making them more likely to reciprocate with the request [156].
2. Expertise compliment: Compliment the knowledge of the contributor who posted the image. This commits the contributor as an "expert," resulting in a thoughtful response [156].
3. Interest matching: Show interest in the topic of the contributor's post. This creates a sense of unity between the agent and contributor [36].
4. Valence matching: Match the valence of the contributor based on their image's caption. People evolved to act kindly to others who exhibit behaviors from a similar culture [181].
5. Answer attempt: Guess an answer and ask for a validation. Recognizing whether a shown answer is correct or not is cognitively an easier task for the listener than recalling the correct answer [57].
6. Time scarcity: Specify an arbitrary deadline for the response. People are more likely to act if the opportunity is deemed to expire, even if they neither need nor want the opportunity [156].
7. Help request: Explicitly request the contributor's help. People are naturally inclined to help others when they are asked and able to do so [72].
8. Logical justification: Give a logical reason for asking the question to persuade the contributor at a cognitive level [108].
9. Random justification: Give a random reason for asking the question. People are more likely to help if a justification is provided, even if it does not actually entail the request [108].

3.3 System Design

In this section, we describe our approach for augmenting requests with social strategies. Our approach is divided into two components: generation and selection. A high-level system diagram is depicted in Fig. 10. Given a social media post, we featurize the post metadata, question, and caption, then send them to the selection component. The main goal of the selection component is to choose an effective social strategy to use for the given post. This strategy, along with a generated question to ask [96], and the social media post are sent to the generation component, which augments the question by generating a natural language phrase for the chosen social strategy. The augmented request is then shared with the contributor. The selection module gathers feedback, positive if the contributor responds in an informative manner. Uninformative responses or no response are counted as a negative feedback.

Selection: Choosing a Social Strategy
We model our selection component as a contextual bandit. Contextual bandits are a common reinforcement learning technique for efficiently exploring different options and exploiting the best choices over time, generalizing from previous trials to uncom-

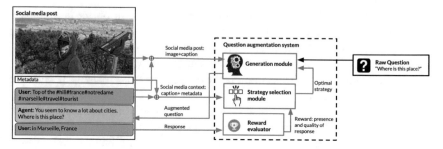

Fig. 10 Given a social media post and a question we want to ask, we augment the question with a social strategy. Our system contains two components. First, a selection component featurizes the post and user and chooses a social strategy. Second, a generation component creates a natural language augmentation for the question given the image and the chosen strategy. The contributor's response or silence is used to generate a feedback reward for the selection module

monly observed situations [118]. The component receives a feature vector and outputs its choice of an arm (option) that it expects to result in the highest expected reward.

Each social media post is represented as a feature vector that encodes information about the user, the post, and the caption. User features include—number of posts the user has posted, number of followers, number of accounts the user is following, number of other users tagged in their posts, filters, and AR effects the user uses frequently on the platform, user's engagement with videos, whether the user is a verified business or an influencer, user's privacy settings, the engagement with Instagram features such as highlight reels and resharing, and sentiment analysis on their biography. Post features include the number of users who like the post and the number of users who commented on the post. User and post features are drawn from Instagram's API and featurized as bag of words or one-hot vectors. Lastly, caption features are extracted from sentiment using Vader [76], and the hashtags extracted using regular expressions.

We train a contextual bandit model to choose a social strategy given the extracted features, conditioned on the success of each social strategy used on similar social media posts in the past. The arms that the contextual bandit considers represent each of the nine social strategies that the system can use. If a chosen social strategy receives a response, we parse and check if the response contains an answer [46]. If so, the model receives a positive reward for choosing the social strategy. If a chosen social strategy does not receive a response, or if the response does not contain an answer, the model receives a negative reward.

Our implementation of contextual bandit uses the adaptive greedy algorithm for balancing the tradeoff between exploration and exploitation. During training, the algorithm chooses an option that the model associates with a high uncertainty of reward. If there is no option with a high uncertainty, the algorithm chooses a random option to explore. The threshold for uncertainty decreases as the model is exposed to more data. During inference, the model predicts the social strategy with highest expected reward [208].

Generation: Augmenting Questions

The generation component receives the social media post (an image and a caption) and a raw question automatically generated by existing visual question generation algorithms (e.g., "Where is this place?"). It produces a natural language contextualization of the question using one of the nine social strategies chosen by the selection component.

We build nine independent natural language generation systems that each receive a social media post as input and produce a comment using the corresponding social strategy as output. Four of the social strategies require knowledge about the content of images, and are implemented using ML-based models. These strategies cannot be templatized, as there is substantial variation in the kinds of images found online and the approaches much be personalized to the content of the image. We use the other five social strategies as baseline strategies that only require knowledge about the speaking style of the social media user, and are implemented as rule-based expert systems in conjunction with natural language processing techniques. We discuss these two types of models below.

Machine learning-based social strategies. To generate sentences specific to the image of each post, we train one ML model for each of the four social strategies that require knowledge about the image: `expert compliment`, `content compliment`, `interest matching`, and `logical justification`.

We build a dataset of 10k social media posts alongside examples of questions that use each of the four social social strategies, with the help of crowd workers on Amazon Mechanical Turk. This process results in a dataset of 40k questions, each with social strategy augmentations. The posts are randomly selected by polling Instagram for images with one of the top 100 most popular hashtags on Instagram and filter for those that refer to visual content, such as #animal, #travel, #shopping, #food, etc. Crowdworkers are designated to one of the four strategy categories and trained using examples and a qualifying task, which we manually evaluate. Each task contains 10 social media posts (images and captions) and the generated questions. Workers are asked to submit a natural language sentence that can be pre- and post-pended to the question while adhering to the social strategy they are trained to emulate. The workers are paid a compensation that is equivalent to $12 an hour for their work.[2]

We adopt a traditional image-to-sequence ML model to generate the sentence for each strategy. Each model encodes the social media image using a convolutional neural network (CNN) [102] and generates a social strategy sentence, conditioned on image features, using a long short term memory (LSTM) network [71]. We train each model using the dataset of 10k posts dedicated to its assigned strategy using stochastic gradient descent with a learning rate of $1e - 3$ for 15 epochs.

Baseline Rule-Based Social Strategies.

To generate social strategy sentences that are relevant to the caption of each social media post, we create a rule-based expert system for each of the five social

---

[2] The dataset of social media posts and social strategies for training the reinforcement learning model, as well as the trained contextual bandit model, is publicly available at http://cs.stanford.edu/people/ranjaykrishna/socialstrategies.

Fig. 11 Example augmentations generated by each of our social strategies

strategies: `valence matching, answer attempt, help request, time scarcity,` and `random justification`. While these algorithms use statistical ML approaches for natural language processing, we call them rule-based systems to clarify that the generation, itself, is a deterministic process unlike the sentences generated by the LSTM networks.

`Valence matching` detects the emotional valence of the caption through punctuation parsing and sentiment analysis using an implementation of the Vader algorithm [76]. The algorithm generates a sentence with emotional valence that is approximately equal to valence of the caption by matching type and number of punctuations and adding appropriate exclamations like "Wow!" or "Aw."

`Answer attempt` guesses a probable answer for the input post based on the raw question and hashtags of the post. To guess a probable answer, we manually curate a set of likely answers for problem domains and words from caption and randomly choose one from the set. For example, when asking where we could buy the same item on a post that references the word "jean" in the "#shopping" domain, the set of probable answers are a list of brands that sell jeans to consumers. Deployments of this strategy does not have to rely on a curated list and can instead use existing answering models [3].

`Help request` augments the agent's question with variations of words and sentence structures that humans use to request help from one another. `Time scarcity` augments the agent's question with variations of a sentence that requests the answer to be provided within 24 hours. `Random justification` augments the agent's question with a justification that is chosen irrespective of the social media post. Specifically, we store a list of justification sentences generated from the logical justification system for other posts, and retrieve one at random. Figure 11 visualizes example augmentations generated by each of our nine strategies, conditioned on the post.

3.4 Experiments

We evaluate the utility of augmenting questions with social strategies through a real-world deploying on Instagram. Our aim is to increase online crowdsourcing participation from Instagram users when we ask them questions about their image contents. We begin our experiments by first describing the experimental setup, the metrics used, the baselines, and strategies surveyed. Next, we study how generated social strategies impact participation. Finally, we study the importance of selecting the correct social strategy.

Experimental Setup
We poll images from Instagram, featurize the post, select a social strategy, and generate the question augmentation. We post the augmented question and wait for a response.

Images and raw questions. We source images from Instagram across 4 domains: travel, animals, shopping and food. Images from each domain are polled by searching for posts with hashtags: #travel, #animals, #shopping, and #food. Images in these four domains constitute an upper bound of 7.06% of all images posted with one of the top 100 popular hashtags that represent visual content. Since we are studying the impact of using different social strategies by directly interacting with real users on Instagram, we can not post multiple questions, each augmented with a different strategy, to the same image post. Ideally, in online crowdsourcing deployments, the raw questions generated would be conditioned on the post or image. In our case, however, we use only one question per domain so that all users are exposed to the same basic question. For each domain, we hold the raw question constant. For example, "Where is this place?" for travel, "What animal is that?" for animals, "Where can I get that?" for shopping, and "What is this food?" for food.

Metrics. To measure the improvements in crowdsourcing participation, we report the percentage of informative responses. After a question is posted on Instagram, we wait 24 hours to check if a response was received. If the question results in no response or if the response doesn't answer the question or the user appears confused (e.g., "huh?" or "I don't understand"), the interaction is not counted as an informative response. To verify if a response is informative, we send all responses to Amazon Mechanical Turk (AMT) workers to report whether the question was actually answered with gold standard responses to guarantee quality.

Strategies surveyed. We use all nine strategies described earlier and add a baseline and an oracle strategy. The baseline case posts the raw question with no augmentation. The oracle method asks AMT workers to modify the question without any restrictions to maximize the chances of receiving the answer. They don't have to follow any of our outlined social strategies.

Dataset of online interactions. To study the impact of using social strategies, we collect a dataset of 10k posts for each of the 4 ML social strategies, resulting in a dataset of 40k questions with augmentations. The 5 rule strategies don't require any training data. Once trained, we post 100 questions per strategy to Instagram, resulting in 1100 total posts. To further study the scalability and transfer of strategies learned in one domain and applied to another, we train augmentation models using data from a "source" domain and test its effect on posts from "target" domains. For example, we train models using data collected from the #travel source domain and test on the rest as target domains.

To train the selection model, we gather 10k posts from Instagram and generate augmentations with each of the social strategies. Each post, with all the augmentated questions, is sent to AMT workers, who are asked to pick the strategies that would be appropriate to use. We choose to train the selection model using AMT instead of Instagram as it allows us to quickly collect large amounts of training data and negate the impact of other confounds. Each AMT task included 10 social media posts. One out of the ten posts contained an attention checker in the question to verify that the workers were actually reading the questions. Workers were compensated at a rate of $12 per hour.

Augmenting Questions with Social Strategies
Our goal in the first set of experiments is to study the effect of using social strategies to augment questions.

Informative responses. Before we inspect the effects of social strategies, we first report the quality of responses from Instagram users. We manually annotate all our responses and find that 93.01% of questions are both relevant as well as answerable. Out of the relevant questions, 95.52% of responses were informative, i.e. the responses contained the correct answer to the question. Figure 12 visualizes a set of example responses for different posts with different social strategies in the travel domain. While all social strategies outperformed the baseline in receiving responses, the quality of the responses differed across strategies.

Effect of social strategies. Table 2 reports the informative response rate across all the social strategies. We find that, compared to the baseline case, where no strategy is used, rule-based strategies improve participation by 14.78 percent points. An unpaired t-test confirms that participation increases by designing appropriate rule-based social strategies ($t(900) = 3.05$, $p < 0.01$). When social strategy data is collected and used to train ML strategies, performance increases by 42.36 percent points and 27.58 percent points when compared against un-augmented ($t(900) = 8.17$, $p < 0.001$) and rule-based strategies ($t(900) = 8.96$, $p < 0.001$) and confirmed by unpaired t-tests. Overall, we find that expertise compliment and logical justification performed strongly in shopping domain, but weakly in animals and food domains.

To test the scalability of our strategies across image domains, we train models on a source domain and deploy them on a target domain. We find that expertise compliment drops in performance while interest matching improves. The drop implies that ML models that heavily depend on example data points used in training process are not robust in new domains. Therefore, while ML strategies are the most effective, they require strategy data collected for the domain in which they

Fig. 12 Example responses to expertise compliment, help request, logical justification, content compliment and valence matching in the travel domain

Table 2 Response rates achieved by different strategies on posts in the source and target domains. The bottom of the table shows a comparison between average performance of ML based strategies, average performance of rule-based strategies and baseline un-augmented questions

	Source domain (%)	Target domain (%)
Expertise compliment	**72.90**	29.55
Content compliment	59.11	68.96
Interest matching	45.31	**85.38**
Logical justification	55.17	19.7
Answer attempt	41.37	42.69
Help request	31.52	32.84
Valence matching	37.43	36.12
Time scarcity	24.63	26.27
Random justification	17.73	32.84
ML based strategies	**58.12**	**50.89**
Rule based strategies	30.54	34.15
No strategy	15.76	13.13

are deployed. The drop in performance, however, still results in improvements in response rate, demonstrating that ML strategies scale across domains but their impact reduces as the distribution of image content increases from the source domain. The increase in performance of interest matching indicates that different domains might have different dominating social strategies, i.e. no single dominant strategy exists across all domains and that a selection component is necessary.

Agent versus human augmentations. We compare the augmentations generated by our agent against those created by crowdworkers. We report the difference in response rate between the agent and the human augmentations across the different strategies in Fig. 13. A two-way ANOVA finds that the strategy used has a significant effect on the response rate ($F(8, 900) = 12.99$, $p < 0.001$) but the poster has no significant effect on the response rate ($F(1, 900) = 1.82$, $p = 0.17$). The ANOVA also found a significant interaction effect between the strategy and the poster on response rate ($F(1, 900) = 2.09$, $p = 0.03$). A post hoc Tukey test indicates that the agent using the ML strategies is significantly increases response rate than the agent

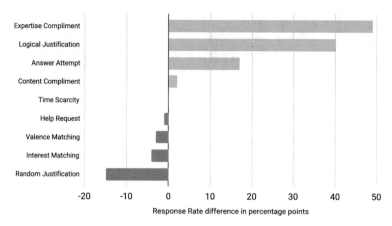

Fig. 13 Difference between response rate of the agent and humans for each social strategy. Green indicates the agent is better than people and red indicates the opposite

using rule-based ($p < 0.05$) or humans using rule-based strategies ($p < 0.05$). This demonstrates that a ML model that has witnessed examples of social strategies can outperform rule-based systems. However, there is no significant difference between the agent using ML strategies versus humans using the same social strategies.

Learning to Select a Social Strategy

In our previous experiment we established that different domains have different strategies that perform best. Now, we evaluate how well our selection component performs at selecting the most effective strategy. Specifically, we test how well our selection model performs (1) against a random strategy, (2) against the most effective strategy (expertise compliment) from the previous experiment, and (3) against the oracle strategy generated by crowdworkers. Recall that the oracle strategy does not constrain workers to use any particular strategy.

Since this test needs be able to test multiple strategies on the same post, we perform our evaluation on AMT. Workers are shown two strategies for a given post and asked to choose which strategy is most likely to receive a response. We perform pairwise comparisons between our selection model against a random strategy across 11k posts, against expertise compliment across 549 posts and against open-ended human questions across 689 posts.

Effect of selection. A binomial test indicates that our selection method was chosen 54.12% more often than a random strategy $B(N = 11, 844, p < 0.001)$. It was chosen 58.28% more often than expertise compliment $B(N = 549, p < 0.001)$. And finally, it was chosen 75.61% more often than the oracle human generated questions $B(N = 689, p < 0.001)$. We conclude that our selection model outperforms all existing baselines.

Qualitative analysis. Figure 14a shows that the agent can choose to focus on different aspects of the image even when the subject of the image is roughly the same: old

Fig. 14 Example strategy selection and augmentations in the travel domain. **a** Our system learns to focus on different aspects of the image. **b** The system is able to discern between very similar images and understand that the same objects can have different connotations. **c, d** Example failure case when objects were misclassified

traditional buildings. In one, the agent compliments the statue, which is the most salient feature of the old European building shown in the image. In the other, it shows appreciation for the overall architecture of the old Asian building, which does not have a single defining feature like a statue.

Figure 14b shows two images that are both contain water and has similar color composition. In one, the agent compliments the water seen on the beach as refreshing and in the other, the fish seen underwater as cute. Referring to a fish in a beach photo would have been incorrect as would have been describing water as refreshing in an underwater photo.

Though social strategies are useful, they can also lead to new errors. Figure 14c, d showcases an example questions where the agent fails to recognize mountains and food and generates phrases referring to beaches and flowers.

3.5 Discussion

Intended use. This work demonstrates that it is possible to train an AI agent to use social strategies that are found in human-to-human interaction contexts to increase the likelihood of a human crowdsourcing respondent. Such responses suggest a future in which supervised ML models can be trained on authentic online data that are provided by willing helpers than from paid workers. We expect that such strategies can lead to adaptive ML systems that can learn during their deployment, by asking their users whenever they are uncertain about their environment. Unlike existing paid crowdsourcing techniques that grow linearly in cost as the number of annotations increases, our method is a fixed cost solution where social strategies need to be collected for a specific domain and then deployed to encourage volunteers.

Negative usage. It is also important that we pause to note the potential negative implications of computing research, and how they can be addressed. The psychology techniques that our work relies on have been used in negotiations and marketing campaigns for decades. Automating such techniques can also lead to influencing emotions or behavior at a magnitude greater than single human–human interaction [53, 94]. When using natural language techniques, we advocate that agents continue to self-identify as bots for this reason. There is a need for online communities to establish a standard acceptable use of such techniques and how the contributors should be informed about the intentions behind an agent's request.

Limitations and future work. Our social strategies are inspired by social psychology research. Ours are by no means an exhaustive list of possible strategies. Future research could follow a more "bottom-up" approach of directly learning to emulate strategies by observing human–human interactions. Currently, our requests involve exactly one dialogue turn, and we do not yet explore multi-turn conversations. This can be important: for example, the answer attempt strategy may be more effective at getting an answer now, but might also decrease the probability that the contributor will want to continue cooperating in the long term. Future work can explore how to guide conversations to enable more complex labeling schemes.

Conclusion Our work: (1) identifies social strategies that can be repurposed to improve crowdsourcing requests for visual question answering, (2) trains and deploys ML- and rule-based models that deploy these strategies to increase crowdsourcing participation, and (3) demonstrates that these models significantly improve participation on Instagram, that no single strategy is optimal, and that a selection model can chooses the appropriate strategy.

4   Model Evaluation Using Human Perception

Generating realistic images is regarded as a focal task for measuring the progress of generative models. Automated metrics are either heuristic approximations [22, 45, 89, 150, 158, 164] or intractable density estimations, examined to be inaccurate on high dimensional problems [12, 70, 182]. Human evaluations, such as those given on Amazon Mechanical Turk [45, 158], remain ad hoc because "results change drastically" [164] based on details of the task design [92, 114, 124]. With both noisy automated and noisy human benchmarks, measuring progress over time has become akin to hill-climbing on noise. Even widely used metrics, such as Inception Score [164] and Fréchet Inception Distance [68], have been discredited for their application to non-ImageNet datasets [6, 15, 151, 157]. Thus, to monitor progress, generative models need a systematic gold standard benchmark. In this paper, we introduce a gold standard benchmark for realistic generation, demonstrating its effectiveness across four datasets, six models, and two sampling techniques, and using it to assess the progress of generative models over time (Fig. 15).

Realizing the constraints of available automated metrics, many generative modeling tasks resort to human evaluation and visual inspection [45, 158, 164]. These human measures are (1) ad hoc, each executed in idiosyncrasy without proof of reliability or grounding to theory, and (2) high variance in their estimates [45, 141, 164]. These characteristics combine to a lack of reliability, and downstream, (3) a lack of clear separability between models. Theoretically, given sufficiently large sample sizes of human evaluators and model outputs, the law of large numbers would smooth

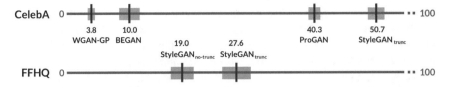

Fig. 15 Our human evaluation metric, HYPE, consistently distinguishes models from each other: here, we compare different generative models performance on FFHQ. A score of 50% represents indistinguishable results from real, while a score above 50% represents hyper-realism

out the variance and reach eventual convergence; but this would occur at (4) a high cost and a long delay.

We present HYPE (HUMAN EYE PERCEPTUAL EVALUATION) to address these criteria in turn. HYPE: (1) measures the perceptual realism of generative model outputs via a **grounded** method inspired by psychophysics methods in perceptual psychology, (2) is a **reliable** and consistent estimator, (3) is statistically **separable** to enable a comparative ranking, and (4) ensures a cost and time **efficient** method through modern crowdsourcing techniques such as training and aggregation. We present two methods of evaluation. The first, called $HYPE_{time}$, is inspired directly by the psychophysics literature [38, 93], and displays images using adaptive time constraints to determine the time-limited perceptual threshold a person needs to distinguish real from fake. The $HYPE_{time}$ score is understood as the minimum time, in milliseconds, that a person needs to see the model's output before they can distinguish it as real or fake. For example, a score of 500 ms on $HYPE_{time}$ indicates that humans can distinguish model outputs from real images at 500 ms exposure times or longer, but not under 500 ms. The second method, called $HYPE_\infty$, is derived from the first to make it simpler, faster, and cheaper while maintaining reliability. It is interpretable as the rate at which people mistake fake images and real images, given unlimited time to make their decisions. A score of 50% on $HYPE_\infty$ means that people differentiate generated results from real data at chance rate, while a score above 50% represents hyper-realism in which generated images appear more real than real images.

We run two large-scale experiments. First, we demonstrate HYPE's performance on unconditional human face generation using four popular generative adversarial networks (GANs) [9, 62, 88, 89] across CelebA-64 [125]. We also evaluate two newer GANs [22, 138] on FFHQ-1024 [89]. HYPE indicates that GANs have clear, measurable perceptual differences between them; this ranking is identical in both $HYPE_{time}$ and $HYPE_\infty$. The best performing model, StyleGAN trained on FFHQ and sampled with the truncation trick, only performs at 27.6% $HYPE_\infty$, suggesting substantial opportunity for improvement. We can reliably reproduce these results with 95% confidence intervals using 30 human evaluators at $60 in a task that takes 10 min.

Second, we demonstrate the performance of $HYPE_\infty$ beyond faces on conditional generation of five object classes in ImageNet [43] and unconditional generation of CIFAR-10 [100]. Early GANs such as BEGAN are not separable in $HYPE_\infty$ when generating CIFAR-10: none of them produce convincing results to humans, verifying that this is a harder task than face generation. The newer StyleGAN shows separable improvement, indicating progress over the previous models. With ImageNet-5, GANs have improved on classes considered "easier" to generate (e.g., lemons), but resulted in consistently low scores across all models for harder classes (e.g., French horns).

HYPE is a rapid solution for researchers to measure their generative models, requiring just a single click to produce reliable scores and measure progress. We deploy HYPE at https://hype.stanford.edu, where researchers can upload a model and retrieve a HYPE score. Future work will extend HYPE to additional generative tasks such as text, music, and video generation.

4.1 HYPE: A Benchmark for HUMAN EYE PERCEPTUAL EVALUATION

HYPE displays a series of images one by one to crowdsourced evaluators on Amazon Mechanical Turk and asks the evaluators to assess whether each image is real or fake. Half of the images are real images, drawn from the model's training set (e.g., FFHQ, CelebA, ImageNet, or CIFAR-10). The other half are drawn from the model's output. We use modern crowdsourcing training and quality control techniques [137] to ensure high-quality labels. Model creators can choose to perform two different evaluations: $HYPE_{time}$, which gathers time-limited perceptual thresholds to measure the psychometric function and report the minimum time people need to make accurate classifications, and $HYPE_\infty$, a simplified approach which assesses people's error rate under no time constraint (Fig. 16).

$HYPE_{time}$: Perceptual Fidelity Grounded in Psychophysics

Our first method, $HYPE_{time}$, measures time-limited perceptual thresholds. It is rooted in psychophysics literature, a field devoted to the study of how humans perceive stimuli, to evaluate human time thresholds upon perceiving an image. Our evaluation protocol follows the procedure known as the *adaptive staircase method* (Fig. 17) [38]. An image is flashed for a limited length of time, after which the evaluator is asked to judge whether it is real or fake. If the evaluator consistently answers correctly, the staircase descends and flashes the next image with less time. If the evaluator is incorrect, the staircase ascends and provides more time.

This process requires sufficient iterations to converge to the evaluator's perceptual threshold: the shortest exposure time at which they can maintain effective performance [38, 51, 61]. The process produces what is known as the *psychometric function* [201], the relationship of timed stimulus exposure to accuracy. For example, for an easily distinguishable set of generated images, a human evaluator would immediately drop to the lowest millisecond exposure.

$HYPE_{time}$ displays three blocks of staircases for each evaluator. An image evaluation begins with a 3-2-1 countdown clock, each number displaying for 500 ms [99]. The sampled image is then displayed for the current exposure time. Immediately

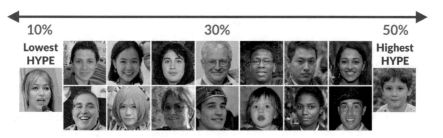

10%   30%   50%
Lowest   Highest
HYPE   HYPE

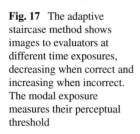

Fig. 16 Example images sampled with the truncation trick from StyleGAN trained on FFHQ. Images on the right exhibit the highest HYPE$_\infty$ scores, the highest human perceptual fidelity

Fig. 17 The adaptive staircase method shows images to evaluators at different time exposures, decreasing when correct and increasing when incorrect. The modal exposure measures their perceptual threshold

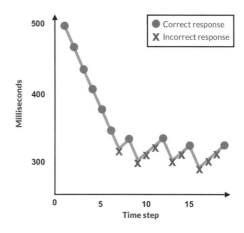

after each image, four perceptual mask images are rapidly displayed for 30 ms each. These noise masks are distorted to prevent retinal afterimages and further sensory processing after the image disappears [61]. We generate masks using an existing texture-synthesis algorithm [147]. Upon each submission, HYPE$_{time}$ reveals to the evaluator whether they were correct.

Image exposures are in the range [100 ms, 1000 ms], derived from the perception literature [54]. All blocks begin at 500 ms and last for 150 images (50% generated, 50% real), values empirically tuned from prior work [38, 40]. Exposure times are raised at 10 ms increments and reduced at 30 ms decrements, following the 3-up/1-down adaptive staircase approach, which theoretically leads to a 75% accuracy threshold that approximates the human perceptual threshold [38, 61, 115].

Every evaluator completes multiple staircases, called *blocks*, on different sets of images. As a result, we observe multiple measures for the model. We employ three blocks, to balance quality estimates against evaluators' fatigue [65, 103, 161]. We average the modal exposure times across blocks to calculate a final value for each evaluator. Higher scores indicate a better model, whose outputs take longer time exposures to discern from real.

HYPE$_\infty$: Cost-Effective Approximation

Building on the previous method, we introduce HYPE$_\infty$: a simpler, faster, and cheaper method after ablating HYPE$_{time}$ to optimize for speed, cost, and ease of interpretation. HYPE$_\infty$ shifts from a measure of perceptual time to a measure of human deception rate, given infinite evaluation time. The HYPE$_\infty$ score gauges total error on a task of 50 fake and 50 real images,[3] enabling the measure to capture errors on both fake and real images, and effects of hyperrealistic generation when fake images look even more realistic than real images.[4] HYPE$_\infty$ requires fewer images than HYPE$_{time}$ to find a stable value, empirically producing a 6x reduction in time and cost (10 min per evaluator instead of 60 min, at the same rate of $12 per hour). Higher scores are again better: 10% HYPE$_\infty$ indicates that only 10% of images deceive people, whereas 50% indicates that people are mistaking real and fake images at chance, rendering fake images indistinguishable from real. Scores above 50% suggest hyperrealistic images, as evaluators mistake images at a rate greater than chance.

HYPE$_\infty$ shows each evaluator a total of 100 images: 50 real and 50 fake. We calculate the proportion of images that were judged incorrectly, and aggregate the judgments over the n evaluators on k images to produce the final score for a given model.

4.2 Consistent and Reliable Design

To ensure that our reported scores are consistent and reliable, we need to sample sufficiently from the model as well as hire, qualify, and appropriately pay enough evaluators.

Sampling sufficient model outputs. The selection of K images to evaluate from a particular model is a critical component of a fair and useful evaluation. We must sample a large enough number of images that fully capture a model's generative diversity, yet balance that against tractable costs in the evaluation. We follow existing work on evaluating generative output by sampling $K = 5000$ generated images from each model [138, 164, 195] and $K = 5000$ real images from the training set. From these samples, we randomly select images to give to each evaluator.

Quality of evaluators. To obtain a high-quality pool of evaluators, each is required to pass a qualification task. Such a pre-task filtering approach, sometimes referred to as a person-oriented strategy, is known to outperform process-oriented strategies that perform post-task data filtering or processing [137]. Our qualification task displays

---

[3] We explicitly reveal this ratio to evaluators. Amazon Mechanical Turk forums would enable evaluators to discuss and learn about this distribution over time, thus altering how different evaluators would approach the task. By making this ratio explicit, evaluators would have the same prior entering the task.

[4] Hyper-realism is relative to the real dataset on which a model is trained. Some datasets already look less realistic because of lower resolution and/or lower diversity of images.

100 images (50 real and 50 fake) with no time limits. Evaluators must correctly classify 65% of both real and fake images. This threshold should be treated as a hyperparameter and may change depending upon the GANs used in the tutorial and the desired discernment ability of the chosen evaluators. We choose 65% based on the cumulative binomial probability of 65 binary choice answers out of 100 total answers: there is only a one in one-thousand chance that an evaluator will qualify by random guessing. Unlike in the task itself, fake qualification images are drawn equally from multiple different GANs to ensure an equitable qualification across all GANs. The qualification is designed to be taken occasionally, such that a pool of evaluators can assess new models on demand.

Payment. Evaluators are paid a base rate of $1 for working on the qualification task. To incentivize evaluators to remained engaged throughout the task, all further pay after the qualification comes from a bonus of $0.02 per correctly labeled image, typically totaling a wage of $12/hr.

4.3   Experimental Setup

Datasets. We evaluate on four datasets. (1) CelebA-64 [125] is popular dataset for unconditional image generation with 202k images of human faces, which we align and crop to be 64×64 px. (2) FFHQ-1024 [89] is a newer face dataset with 70k images of size 1024×1024 px. (3) CIFAR-10 consists of 60k images, sized 32×32 px, across 10 classes. (4) ImageNet-5 is a subset of 5 classes with 6.5k images at 128×128 px from the ImageNet dataset [43], which have been previously identified as easy (lemon, Samoyed, library) and hard (baseball player, French horn) [22].

Architectures. We evaluate on four state-of-the-art models trained on CelebA-64 and CIFAR-10: StyleGAN [89], ProGAN [88], BEGAN [9], and WGAN-GP [62]. We also evaluate on two models, SN-GAN [138] and BigGAN [22] trained on ImageNet, sampling conditionally on each class in ImageNet-5. We sample BigGAN with ($\sigma = 0.5$ [22]) and without the truncation trick.

We also evaluate on StyleGAN [89] trained on FFHQ-1024 with ($\psi = 0.7$ [89]) and without truncation trick sampling. For parity on our best models across datasets, StyleGAN instances trained on CelebA-64 and CIFAR-10 are also sampled with the truncation trick.

We sample noise vectors from the d-dimensional spherical Gaussian noise prior $z \in \mathbb{R}^d \sim \mathcal{N}(0, I)$ during training and test times. We specifically opted to use the same standard noise prior for comparison, yet are aware of other priors that optimize for FID and IS scores [22]. We select training hyperparameters published in the corresponding papers for each model.

Evaluator recruitment. We recruit 930 evaluators from Amazon Mechanical Turk, or 30 for each run of HYPE. To maintain a between-subjects study in this evaluation, we recruit independent evaluators across tasks and methods.

Metrics. For $HYPE_{time}$, we report the modal perceptual threshold in milliseconds. For $HYPE_\infty$, we report the error rate as a percentage of images, as well as the breakdown of this rate on real and fake images separately. To show that our results for each model are separable, we report a one-way ANOVA with Tukey pairwise post hoc tests to compare all models.

Reliability is a critical component of HYPE, as a benchmark is not useful if a researcher receives a different score when rerunning it. We use bootstrapping [52], repeated resampling from the empirical label distribution, to measure variation in scores across multiple samples with replacement from a set of labels. We report 95% bootstrapped confidence intervals (CIs), along with standard deviation of the bootstrap sample distribution, by randomly sampling 30 evaluators with replacement from the original set of evaluators across 10, 000 iterations.

Experiment 1: We run two large-scale experiments to validate HYPE. The first one focuses on the controlled evaluation and comparison of $HYPE_{time}$ against $HYPE_\infty$ on established human face datasets. We recorded responses totaling (4 CelebA-64 + 2 FFHQ-1024) models $\times$ 30 evaluators $\times$ 550 responses = 99k total responses for our $HYPE_{time}$ evaluation and (4 CelebA-64 + 2 FFHQ-1024) models $\times$ 30 evaluators $\times$ 100 responses = 18k, for our $HYPE_\infty$ evaluation.

Experiment 2: The second experiment evaluates $HYPE_\infty$ on general image datasets. We recorded (4 CIFAR-10 + 3 ImageNet-5) models $\times$ 30 evaluators $\times$ 100 responses = 57k total responses.

4.4   Experiment 1: $HYPE_{time}$ and $HYPE_\infty$ on Human Faces

We report results on $HYPE_{time}$ and demonstrate that the results of $HYPE_\infty$ approximates those from $HYPE_{time}$ at a fraction of the cost and time.

$HYPE_{time}$

CelebA-64 We find that $StyleGAN_{trunc}$ resulted in the highest $HYPE_{time}$ score (modal exposure time), at a mean of 439.3 ms, indicating that evaluators required nearly a half-second of exposure to accurately classify $StyleGAN_{trunc}$ images (Table 3). $StyleGAN_{trunc}$ is followed by ProGAN at 363.7 ms, a 17% drop in time. BEGAN and WGAN-GP are both easily identifiable as fake, tied in last place around the minimum available exposure time of 100 ms. Both BEGAN and WGAN-GP exhibit

Table 3 $HYPE_{time}$ on $StyleGAN_{trunc}$ and $StyleGAN_{no-trunc}$ trained on FFHQ-1024

Rank	GAN	$HYPE_{time}$ (ms)	Std.	95% CI
1	$StyleGAN_{trunc}$	363.2	32.1	300.0–424.3
2	$StyleGAN_{no-trunc}$	240.7	29.9	184.7–302.7

Table 4 $HYPE_\infty$ on four GANs trained on CelebA-64. Counterintuitively, real errors increase with the errors on fake images, because evaluators become more confused and distinguishing factors between the two distributions become harder to discern

Rank	GAN	$HYPE_\infty$ (%)	Fakes error	Reals error	Std.	95% CI	KID	FID	Precision
1	StyleGAN$_{trunc}$	50.7%	62.2%	39.3%	1.3	48.2–53.1	0.005	131.7	0.982
2	ProGAN	40.3%	46.2%	34.4%	0.9	38.5–42.0	0.001	2.5	0.990
3	BEGAN	10.0%	6.2%	13.8%	1.6	7.2–13.3	0.056	67.7	0.326
4	WGAN-GP	3.8%	1.7%	5.9%	0.6	3.2–5.7	0.046	43.6	0.654

a bottoming out effect—reaching the minimum time exposure of 100 ms quickly and consistently.

To demonstrate separability between models we report results from a one-way analysis of variance (ANOVA) test, where each model's input is the list of modes from each model's 30 evaluators. The ANOVA results confirm that there is a statistically significant omnibus difference ($F(3, 29) = 83.5$, $p < 0.0001$). Pairwise post hoc analysis using Tukey tests confirms that all pairs of models are separable (all $p < 0.05$) except BEGAN and WGAN-GP (*n.s.*).

FFHQ-1024. We find that StyleGAN$_{trunc}$ resulted in a higher exposure time than StyleGAN$_{no-trunc}$, at 363.2 ms and 240.7 ms, respectively (Table 3). While the 95% confidence intervals that represent a very conservative overlap of 2.7 ms, an unpaired t-test confirms that the difference between the two models is significant ($t(58) = 2.3$, $p = 0.02$).

$HYPE_\infty$

CelebA-64. Table 4 reports results for $HYPE_\infty$ on CelebA-64. We find that StyleGAN$_{trunc}$ resulted in the highest $HYPE_\infty$ score, fooling evaluators 50.7% of the time. StyleGAN$_{trunc}$ is followed by ProGAN at 40.3%, BEGAN at 10.0%, and WGAN-GP at 3.8%. No confidence intervals are overlapping and an ANOVA test is significant ($F(3, 29) = 404.4$, $p < 0.001$). Pairwise post hoc Tukey tests show that all pairs of models are separable (all $p < 0.05$). Notably, $HYPE_\infty$ results in separable results for BEGAN and WGAN-GP, unlike in $HYPE_{time}$ where they were not separable due to a bottoming-out effect.

FFHQ-1024. We observe a consistently separable difference between StyleGAN$_{trunc}$ and StyleGAN$_{no-trunc}$ and clear delineations between models (Table 5). $HYPE_\infty$ ranks StyleGAN$_{trunc}$ (27.6%) above StyleGAN$_{no-trunc}$ (19.0%) with no overlapping CIs. Separability is confirmed by an unpaired t-test ($t(58) = 8.3$, $p < 0.001$).

Cost Tradeoffs with Accuracy and Time

One of HYPE's goals is to be cost and time efficient. When running HYPE, there is an inherent tradeoff between accuracy and time, as well as between accuracy and cost. This is driven by the law of large numbers: recruiting additional evaluators in a crowdsourcing task often produces more consistent results, but at a higher cost (as

Table 5 HYPE$_\infty$ on StyleGAN$_{trunc}$ and StyleGAN$_{no\text{-}trunc}$ trained on FFHQ-1024. Evaluators were deceived most often by StyleGAN$_{trunc}$. Similar to CelebA-64, fake errors and real errors track each other as the line between real and fake distributions blurs

Rank	GAN	HYPE$_\infty$ (%)	Fakes error	Reals error	Std.	95% CI	KID	FID	Precision
1	StyleGAN$_{trunc}$	27.6%	28.4%	26.8%	2.4	22.9–32.4	0.007	13.8	0.976
2	StyleGAN$_{no\text{-}trunc}$	19.0%	18.5%	19.5%	1.8	15.5–22.4	0.001	4.4	0.983

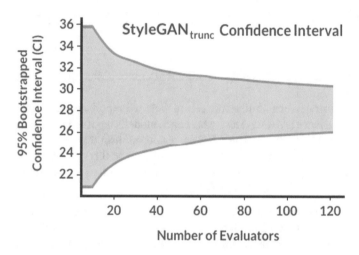

Fig. 18 Effect of more evaluators on CI

each evaluator is paid for their work) and a longer amount of time until completion (as more evaluators must be recruited and they must complete their work).

To manage this tradeoff, we run an experiment with HYPE$_\infty$ on StyleGAN$_{trunc}$. We completed an additional evaluation with 60 evaluators, and compute 95% bootstrapped confidence intervals, choosing from 10 to 120 evaluators (Fig. 18). We see that the CI begins to converge around 30 evaluators, our recommended number of evaluators to recruit.

At 30 evaluators, the cost of running HYPE$_{time}$ on one model was approximately $360, while the cost of running HYPE$_\infty$ on the same model was approximately $60. Payment per evaluator for both tasks was approximately $12/hr. Evaluators spent an average of one hour each on a HYPE$_{time}$ task and 10 min each on a HYPE$_\infty$ task. Thus, HYPE$_\infty$ achieves its goals of being significantly cheaper to run, while maintaining consistency.

Comparison to Automated Metrics

As FID [68] is one of the most frequently used evaluation methods for unconditional image generation, it is imperative to compare HYPE against FID on the same models. We also compare to two newer automated metrics: KID [11], an unbiased estimator independent of sample size, and $F_{1/8}$ (precision) [162], which captures fidelity independently. We show through Spearman rank-order correlation coefficients that HYPE scores are not correlated with FID ($\rho = -0.029$, $p = 0.96$), where a Spearman correlation of -1.0 is ideal because lower FID and higher HYPE scores indicate stronger models. We therefore find that FID is not highly correlated with human judgment. Meanwhile, $HYPE_{time}$ and $HYPE_\infty$ exhibit strong correlation ($\rho = 1.0$, $p = 0.0$), where 1.0 is ideal because they are directly related. We calculate FID across the standard protocol of 50K generated and 50K real images for both CelebA-64 and FFHQ-1024, reproducing scores for $StyleGAN_{no\text{-}trunc}$. KID ($\rho = -0.609$, $p = 0.20$) and precision ($\rho = 0.657$, $p = 0.16$) both show a statistically insignificant but medium level of correlation with humans.

$HYPE_\infty$ During Model Training

HYPE can also be used to evaluate progress during model training. We find that $HYPE_\infty$ scores increased as StyleGAN training progressed from 29.5% at 4k epochs, to 45.9% at 9k epochs, to 50.3% at 25k epochs ($F(2, 29) = 63.3$, $p < 0.001$).

4.5 Experiment 2: $HYPE_\infty$ Beyond Faces

We now turn to another popular image generation task: objects. As Experiment 1 showed $HYPE_\infty$ to be an efficient and cost effective variant of $HYPE_{time}$, here we focus exclusively on $HYPE_\infty$.

ImageNet-5

We evaluate conditional image generation on five ImageNet classes (Table 6). We also report FID [68], KID [11], and $F_{1/8}$ (precision) [162] scores. To evaluate the relative effectiveness of the three GANs within each object class, we compute five one-way ANOVAs, one for each of the object classes. We find that the $HYPE_\infty$ scores are separable for images from three easy classes: samoyeds (dogs) ($F(2, 29) = 15.0$, $p < 0.001$), lemons ($F(2, 29) = 4.2$, $p = 0.017$), and libraries ($F(2, 29) = 4.9$, $p = 0.009$). Pairwise Post hoc tests reveal that this difference is only significant between SN-GAN and the two BigGAN variants. We also observe that models have unequal strengths, e.g., SN-GAN is better suited to generating libraries than samoyeds.

Comparison to automated metrics. Spearman rank-order correlation coefficients on all three GANs across all five classes show that there is a low to moderate correlation between the $HYPE_\infty$ scores and KID ($\rho = -0.377$, $p = 0.02$), FID ($\rho = -0.282$, $p = 0.01$), and negligible correlation with precision ($\rho = -0.067$, $p = 0.81$). Some correlation for our ImageNet-5 task is expected, as these metrics use pretrained ImageNet embeddings to measure differences between generated and real data.

Interestingly, we find that this correlation depends upon the GAN: considering only SN-GAN, we find stronger coefficients for KID ($\rho = -0.500$, $p = 0.39$), FID ($\rho = -0.300$, $p = 0.62$), and precision ($\rho = -0.205$, $p = 0.74$). When considering

Table 6 HYPE$_\infty$ on three models trained on ImageNet and conditionally sampled on five classes. BigGAN routinely outperforms SN-GAN. BigGan$_{trunc}$ and BigGan$_{no\text{-}trunc}$ are not separable

	GAN	Class	HYPE$_\infty$ (%)	Fakes Error	Reals Error	Std.	95% CI	KID	FID	Precision
Easy	BigGan$_{trunc}$	Lemon	18.4%	21.9%	14.9%	2.3	14.2–23.1	0.043	94.22	0.784
	BigGan$_{no\text{-}trunc}$	Lemon	20.2%	22.2%	18.1%	2.2	16.0–24.8	0.036	87.54	0.774
	SN-GAN	Lemon	12.0%	10.8%	13.3%	1.6	9.0–15.3	0.053	117.90	0.656
Easy	BigGan$_{trunc}$	Samoyed	19.9%	23.5%	16.2%	2.6	15.0–25.1	0.027	56.94	0.794
	BigGan$_{no\text{-}trunc}$	Samoyed	19.7%	23.2%	16.1%	2.2	15.5–24.1	0.014	46.14	0.906
	SN-GAN	Samoyed	5.8%	3.4%	8.2%	0.9	4.1–7.8	0.046	88.68	0.785
Easy	BigGan$_{trunc}$	Library	17.4%	22.0%	12.8%	2.1	13.3–21.6	0.049	98.45	0.695
	BigGan$_{no\text{-}trunc}$	Library	22.9%	28.1%	17.6%	2.1	18.9–27.2	0.029	78.49	0.814
	SN-GAN	Library	13.6%	15.1%	12.1%	1.9	10.0–17.5	0.043	94.89	0.814
Hard	BigGan$_{trunc}$	French Horn	7.3%	9.0%	5.5%	1.8	4.0–11.2	0.031	78.21	0.732
	BigGan$_{no\text{-}trunc}$	French Horn	6.9%	8.6%	5.2%	1.4	4.3–9.9	0.042	96.18	0.757
	SN-GAN	French Horn	3.6%	5.0%	2.2%	1.0	1.8–5.9	0.156	196.12	0.674
Hard	BigGan$_{trunc}$	Baseball player	1.9%	1.9%	1.9%	0.7	0.8–3.5	0.049	91.31	0.853
	BigGan$_{no\text{-}trunc}$	Baseball player	2.2%	3.3%	1.2%	0.6	1.3–3.5	0.026	76.71	0.838
	SN-GAN	Baseball player	2.8%	3.6%	1.9%	1.5	0.8–6.2	0.052	105.82	0.785

Table 7 Four models on CIFAR-10. StyleGAN$_{trunc}$ can generate realistic images from CIFAR-10

GAN	HYPE$_\infty$ (%)	Fakes error	Reals error	Std.	95% CI	KID	FID	Precision
StyleGAN$_{trunc}$	23.3%	28.2%	18.5%	1.6	20.1–26.4	0.005	62.9	0.982
PROGAN	14.8%	18.5%	11.0%	1.6	11.9–18.0	0.001	53.2	0.990
BEGAN	14.5%	14.6%	14.5%	1.7	11.3–18.1	0.056	96.2	0.326
WGAN-GP	13.2%	15.3%	11.1%	2.3	9.1–18.1	0.046	104.0	0.654

only BigGAN, we find far weaker coefficients for KID ($\rho = -0.151$, $p = 0.68$), FID ($\rho = -0.067$, $p = .85$), and precision ($\rho = -0.164$, $p = 0.65$). This illustrates an important flaw with these automatic metrics: their ability to correlate with humans depends upon the generative model that the metrics are evaluating on, varying by model and by task.

CIFAR-10
For the difficult task of unconditional generation on CIFAR-10, we use the same four model architectures in Experiment 1: CelebA-64. Table 7 shows that HYPE$_\infty$ was able to separate StyleGAN$_{trunc}$ from the earlier BEGAN, WGAN-GP, and ProGAN, indicating that StyleGAN is the first among them to make human-perceptible progress on unconditional object generation with CIFAR-10.

Comparison to automated metrics. Spearman rank-order correlation coefficients on all four GANs show medium, yet statistically insignificant, correlations with KID ($\rho = -0.600$, $p = 0.40$) and FID ($\rho = 0.600$, $p = 0.40$) and precision ($\rho = -.800$, $p = 0.20$).

4.6 Related Work

Cognitive psychology. We leverage decades of cognitive psychology to motivate how we use stimulus timing to gauge the perceptual realism of generated images. It takes an average of 150 ms of focused visual attention for people to process and interpret an image, but only 120 ms to respond to faces because our inferotemporal cortex has dedicated neural resources for face detection [32, 152]. Perceptual masks are placed between a person's response to a stimulus and their perception of it to eliminate post-processing of the stimuli after the desired time exposure [176]. Prior work in determining human perceptual thresholds [61] generates masks from their test images using the texture-synthesis algorithm [147]. We leverage this literature to establish feasible lower bounds on the exposure time of images, the time between images, and the use of noise masks.

Success of automatic metrics. Common generative modeling tasks include realistic image generation [59], machine translation [4], image captioning [188], and abstract summarization [129], among others. These tasks often resort to automatic metrics like the Inception Score (IS) [164] and Fréchet Inception Distance (FID) [68] to evaluate images and BLEU [143], CIDEr [185] and METEOR [5] scores to evaluate text. While we focus on how realistic generated content appears, other automatic metrics also measure diversity of output, overfitting, entanglement, training stability, and computational and sample efficiency of the model [6, 15, 128]. Our metric may also capture one aspect of output diversity, insofar as human evaluators can detect similarities or patterns across images. Our evaluation is not meant to replace existing methods but to complement them.

Limitations of automatic metrics. Prior work has asserted that there exists coarse correlation of human judgment to FID [68] and IS [164], leading to their widespread adoption. Both metrics depend on the Inception-v3 Network [179], a pretrained ImageNet model, to calculate statistics on the generated output (for IS) and on the real and generated distributions (for FID). The validity of these metrics when applied to other datasets has been repeatedly called into question [6, 15, 151, 157]. Perturbations imperceptible to humans alter their values, similar to the behavior of adversarial examples [105]. Finally, similar to our metric, FID depends on a set of real examples and a set of generated examples to compute high-level differences between the distributions, and there is inherent variance to the metric depending on the number of images and which images were chosen—in fact, there exists a correlation between accuracy and budget (cost of computation) in improving FID scores, because spending a longer time and thus higher cost on compute will yield better FID scores [128]. Nevertheless, this cost is still lower than paid human annotators per image.

Human evaluations. Many human-based evaluations have been attempted to varying degrees of success in prior work, either to evaluate models directly [45, 141] or to motivate using automated metrics [68, 164]. Prior work also used people to evaluate GAN outputs on CIFAR-10 and MNIST and even provided immediate feedback after every judgment [164]. They found that generated MNIST samples have saturated human performance—i.e. people cannot distinguish generated numbers from real MNIST numbers, while still finding 21.3% error rate on CIFAR-10 with the same model [164]. This suggests that different datasets will have different levels of complexity for crossing realistic or hyper-realistic thresholds. The closest recent work to ours compares models using a tournament of discriminators [141]. Nevertheless, this comparison was not yet rigorously evaluated on humans nor were human discriminators presented experimentally. The framework we present would enable such a tournament evaluation to be performed reliably and easily.

4.7 Discussion

Envisioned Use. We created HYPE as a turnkey solution for human evaluation of generative models. Researchers can upload their model, receive a score, and compare progress via our online deployment. During periods of high usage, such as competitions, a retainer model [7] enables evaluation using $HYPE_\infty$ in 10 min, instead of the default 30 min.

Limitations. Extensions of HYPE may require different task designs. In the case of text generation (translation, caption generation), $HYPE_{time}$ will require much longer and much higher range adjustments to the perceptual time thresholds [97, 198]. In addition to measuring realism, other metrics like diversity, overfitting, entanglement, training stability, and computational and sample efficiency are additional benchmarks that can be incorporated but are outside the scope of this paper. Some may be better suited to a fully automated evaluation [15, 128]. Similar to related work in evaluating text generation [64], we suggest that diversity can be incorporated using the automated recall score measures diversity independently from precision $F_{1/8}$ [162].

Conclusion. HYPE provides two human evaluation benchmarks for generative models that (1) are **grounded** in psychophysics, (2) provide task designs that produce **reliable** results, (3) **separate** model performance, (4) are cost and time **efficient**. We introduce two benchmarks: $HYPE_{time}$, which uses time perceptual thresholds, and $HYPE_\infty$, which reports the error rate sans time constraints. We demonstrate the efficacy of our approach on image generation across six models {StyleGAN, SN-GAN, BigGAN, ProGAN, BEGAN, WGAN-GP}, four image datasets {CelebA-64, FFHQ-1024, CIFAR-10, ImageNet-5 }, and two types of sampling methods {with, without the truncation trick}.

5 Conclusion

Popular culture has long depicted vision as a primary interaction modality between people and machines; vision is a necessary sensing capability for humanoid robots such as *C-3PO* from "Star Wars," *Wall-E* from the eponymous film, and even disembodied Artificial Intelligence such as *Samantha* the smart operating system from the movie "Her." These fictional machines paint a potential real future where machines can tap into the expressive range of non-intrusive information that Computer Vision affords. Our expressions, gestures, and relative position to objects carry a wealth of information that intelligent interactive machines can use, enabling new applications in domains such as healthcare [63], sustainability [83], human-interpretable actions [48], and mixed-initiative interactions [73].

While Human–Computer Interaction (HCI) researchers have long discussed and debated what human–AI interaction should look like [73, 170], we have rarely provided concrete, immediately operational goals to Computer Vision researchers. Instead, we've largely left this job up to the vision community itself, which has produced a variety of immediately operational tasks to work on. These tasks play an important role in the AI community; some of them ultimately channel the efforts of thousands of AI researchers and set the direction of progress for years to come. The tasks range from object recognition [43], to scene understanding [98], to explainable AI [1], to interactive robot training [183]. And while many such tasks have been worthwhile endeavors, we often find that the models they produce don't work in practice or don't fit end-users' needs as hoped [24, 136].

If the tasks that guide the work of thousands of AI researchers do not reflect the HCI community's understanding of how humans can best interact with AI-powered systems, then the resulting AI-powered systems will not reflect it either. We therefore believe there is an important opportunity for HCI and Computer Vision researchers to begin closing this gap by collaborating to directly integrate HCI's insights and goals into immediately actionable vision tasks, model designs, data collection protocols, and evaluation schemes. One such example of this type of work is the HYPE benchmark mentioned earlier in this chapter [210], which aimed to push GAN researchers to focus directly on a high-quality measurement of human perception when creating their models. Another is the approach taken by the social strategies project mentioned earlier in this chapter [144], which aimed to push data collection protocols to consider social interventions designed to elicit volunteer contributions.

What kind of tasks might HCI researchers work to create? First, explainable AI aims to help people understand how computer vision models work, but methods are developed without real consideration of how humans will ultimately use explanations to interact with them. HCI researchers might propose design choices for how to introduce and explain vision models grounded in human subjects experiments [23, 91]. Second, perceptual robotics can learn to complete new tasks by incorporating human rewards, but do not consider how people actually want to provide feedback to robots [183]. If we want robots to incorporate an understanding of how humans want to give feedback when deployed, then HCI researchers might propose new training paradigms with ecologically valid human interactions. Third, multi-agent vision systems [82] are developed that ignore key aspects of human psyche, such as choosing to perform non-optimal behaviors, despite foundational work in HCI noting the perils of such assumptions in AI planning [178]. Without incorporating human behavioral priors, these multi-agents systems work well when collaborating between AI agents but fail when one of the agents is replaced by a human [28]. If we want multi-agent vision systems that understand biases that people have when performing actions, then HCI researchers might propose human–AI collaboration tasks and benchmarks in which agents are forced to encounter realistic human actors (indeed, non-vision work has begun to move in this direction [106]).

Acknowledgements The first project was supported by the National Science Foundation award 1351131. The second project was partially funded by the Brown Institute of Media Innovation and by Toyota Research Institute ("TRI"). The third project was partially funded by a Junglee Corporation Stanford Graduate Fellowship, an Alfred P. Sloan fellowship and by TRI. This chapter solely reflects the opinions and conclusions of its authors and not TRI or any other Toyota entity.

References

1. Adadi A, Berrada M (2018) Peeking inside the black-box: a survey on explainable artificial intelligence (xai). IEEE Access 6:52138–52160
2. Ambati V, Vogel S, Carbonell J (2011) Towards task recommendation in micro-task markets

3. Antol S, Agrawal A, Lu J, Mitchell M, Batra D, Lawrence Zitnick C, Parikh D (2015) Vqa: visual question answering. In: Proceedings of the IEEE international conference on computer vision, pp 2425–2433

4. Bahdanau D, Cho K, Bengio Y (2014) Neural machine translation by jointly learning to align and translate. arXiv:1409.0473

5. Banerjee S, Lavie A (2005) Meteor: an automatic metric for mt evaluation with improved correlation with human judgments. In: Proceedings of the acl workshop on intrinsic and extrinsic evaluation measures for machine translation and/or summarization, pp 65–72

6. Barratt S, Sharma R (2018) A note on the inception score. arXiv:1801.01973

7. Bernstein MS, Brandt J, Miller RC, Karger DR (2011) Crowds in two seconds: enabling realtime crowd-powered interfaces. In: Proceedings of the 24th annual ACM symposium on User interface software and technology. ACM, pp 33–42

8. Bernstein MS, Little G, Miller RC, Hartmann B, Ackerman MS, Karger DR, Crowell D, Panovich K (2010) Soylent: a word processor with a crowd inside. In: Proceedings of the 23nd annual ACM symposium on user interface software and technology. ACM, pp 313–322

9. Berthelot D, Schumm T, Metz L (2017) Began: boundary equilibrium generative adversarial networks. arXiv:1703.10717

10. Bigham JP, Jayant C, Ji H, Little G, Miller A, Miller RC, Miller R, Tatarowicz A, White B, White S, et al (2010) Vizwiz: nearly real-time answers to visual questions. In: Proceedings of the 23nd annual ACM symposium on User interface software and technology. ACM, pp 333–342

11. Bińkowski M, Sutherland DJ, Arbel M, Gretton A (2018) Demystifying mmd gans. arXiv:1801.01401

12. Bishop CM (2006) Pattern recognition and machine learning. Springer

13. Biswas A, Parikh D (2013) Simultaneous active learning of classifiers & attributes via relative feedback. In: 2013 Ieee conference on computer vision and pattern recognition (CVPR). IEEE, pp 644–651

14. Bohus D, Rudnicky AI (2009) The ravenclaw dialog management framework: architecture and systems. Comput Speech Lang 23(3):332–361

15. Borji A (2018) Pros and cons of gan evaluation measures. In: Computer vision and image understanding

16. Brady E, Morris MR, Bigham JP (2015) Gauging receptiveness to social microvolunteering. In: Proceedings of the 33rd annual ACM conference on human factors in computing systems, CHI '15. ACM, New York, NY, USA, pp 1055–1064

17. Brady EL, Zhong Y, Morris MR, Bigham JP (2013) Investigating the appropriateness of social network question asking as a resource for blind users. In: Proceedings of the 2013 conference on computer supported cooperative work. ACM, pp 1225–1236

18. Bragg J, Daniel M, Weld DS (2013) Crowdsourcing multi-label classification for taxonomy creation. In: First AAAI conference on human computation and crowdsourcing

19. Branson S, Hjorleifsson KE, Perona P (2014) Active annotation translation. In: 2014 IEEE conference on computer vision and pattern recognition (CVPR). IEEE, pp 3702–3709

20. Branson S, Wah C, Schroff F, Babenko B, Welinder P, Perona P, Belongie S (2010) Visual recognition with humans in the loop. In: Computer vision–ECCV 2010. Springer, pp 438–451

21. Broadbent DE, Broadbent MHP (1987) From detection to identification: response to multiple targets in rapid serial visual presentation. Percept Psychophys 42(2):105–113

22. Brock A, Donahue J, Simonyan K (2018) Large scale gan training for high fidelity natural image synthesis. arXiv:1809.11096

23. Buçinca Z, Lin P, Gajos KZ, Glassman EL (2020) Proxy tasks and subjective measures can be misleading in evaluating explainable ai systems. In: Proceedings of the 25th international conference on intelligent user interfaces, pp 454–464

24. Buolamwini J, Gebru T (2018) Gender shades: intersectional accuracy disparities in commercial gender classification. In: Conference on fairness, accountability and transparency, pp 77–91

25. Burke M, Kraut RE, Joyce E (2014) Membership claims and requests: some newcomer socialization strategies in online communities. Small Group Research
26. Burke M, Kraut R (2013) Using facebook after losing a job: Differential benefits of strong and weak ties. In: Proceedings of the 2013 conference on computer supported cooperative work. ACM, pp 1419–1430
27. Card SK, Newell A, Moran TP (1983) The psychology of human-computer interaction
28. Carroll M, Shah R, Ho MK, Griffiths T, Seshia S, Abbeel P, Dragan A (2019) On the utility of learning about humans for human-ai coordination. In: Advances in neural information processing systems, pp 5174–5185
29. Cassell J, Thórisson KR (1999) The power of a nod and a glance: envelope vs. emotional feedback in animated conversational agents. Appl Artif Intell 13:519–538
30. Cerrato L, Ekeklint S (2002) Different ways of ending human-machine dialogues
31. Chaiken S (1989) Heuristic and systematic information processing within and beyond the persuasion context. In: Unintended thought, pp 212–252
32. Chellappa R, Sinha P, Jonathon Phillips P (2010) Face recognition by computers and humans. Computer 43(2):46–55
33. Cheng J, Teevan J, Bernstein MS (2015) Measuring crowdsourcing effort with error-time curves. In: Proceedings of the 33rd annual ACM conference on human factors in computing systems. ACM, pp 1365–1374
34. Chidambaram V, Chiang Y-H, Mutlu B (2012) Designing persuasive robots: how robots might persuade people using vocal and nonverbal cues. In: Proceedings of the seventh annual ACM/IEEE international conference on human-robot interaction. ACM, pp 293–300
35. Chilton LB, Little G, Edge D, Weld DS, Landay JA (2013) Cascade: crowdsourcing taxonomy creation. In: Proceedings of the SIGCHI conference on human factors in computing systems. ACM, pp 1999–2008
36. Cialdini R (2016) Pre-suasion: a revolutionary way to influence and persuade. Simon and Schuster
37. Colligan L, Potts HWW, Finn CT, Sinkin RA (2015) Cognitive workload changes for nurses transitioning from a legacy system with paper documentation to a commercial electronic health record. Int J Med Inform 84(7):469–476
38. Cornsweet TN (1962) The staircrase-method in psychophysics
39. Corti K, Gillespie A (2016) Co-constructing intersubjectivity with artificial conversational agents: people are more likely to initiate repairs of misunderstandings with agents represented as human. Comput Hum Behav 58:431–442
40. Dakin SC, Omigie D (2009) Psychophysical evidence for a non-linear representation of facial identity. Vis Res 49(18):2285–2296
41. Dalal N, Triggs B (2005) Histograms of oriented gradients for human detection. In: 2005 IEEE computer society conference on computer vision and pattern recognition (CVPR'05), vol 1, pp 886–893
42. Darley JM, Latané B (1968) Bystander intervention in emergencies: diffusion of responsibility. J Personal Soc Psychol 8(4p1):377
43. Deng J, Dong W, Socher R, Li L-J, Li K, Fei-Fei L (2009) Imagenet: a large-scale hierarchical image database. In: 2009 IEEE conference on computer vision and pattern recognition. Ieee, pp 248–255
44. Deng J, Russakovsky O, Krause J, Bernstein MS, Berg A, Fei-Fei L (2014) Scalable multi-label annotation. In: Proceedings of the SIGCHI conference on human factors in computing systems. ACM, pp 3099–3102
45. Denton EL, Chintala S, Fergus R, et al (2015) Deep generative image models using a laplacian pyramid of adversarial networks. In: Advances in neural information processing systems, pp 1486–1494
46. Devlin J, Chang M-W, Lee K, Toutanova K (2018) Bert: pre-training of deep bidirectional transformers for language understanding. arXiv:1810.04805
47. Difallah DE, Demartini G, Cudré-Mauroux P (2013) Pick-a-crowd: tell me what you like, and i'll tell you what to do. In: Proceedings of the 22nd international conference on world wide web, WWW '13. ACM, New York, NY, USA, pp 367–374

48. Dragan AD, Lee KCT, Srinivasa SS (2013) Legibility and predictability of robot motion. In: 2013 8th ACM/IEEE international conference on human-robot interaction (HRI). IEEE, pp 301–308

49. Fast E, Chen B, Mendelsohn J, Bassen J, Bernstein MS (2018) Iris: a conversational agent for complex tasks. In: Proceedings of the 2018 CHI conference on human factors in computing systems. ACM, p 473

50. Fast E, Steffee D, Wang L, Brandt JR, Bernstein MS (2014) Emergent, crowd-scale programming practice in the ide. In: Proceedings of the 32nd annual ACM conference on Human factors in computing systems. ACM, pp 2491–2500

51. Fei-Fei L, Iyer A, Koch C, Perona P (2007) What do we perceive in a glance of a real-world scene? J Vis 7(1):10

52. Felsenstein J (1985) Confidence limits on phylogenies: an approach using the bootstrap. Evolution 39(4):783–791

53. Ferrara E, Varol O, Davis C, Menczer F, Flammini A (2016) The rise of social bots. Commun ACM 59(7):96–104

54. Fraisse P (1984) Perception and estimation of time. Ann Rev Psychol 35(1):1–37

55. Geiger D, Schader M (2014) Personalized task recommendation in crowdsourcing information systems – current state of the art. Decis Support Syst 65:3–16. Crowdsourcing and Social Networks Analysis

56. Gilbert E, Karahalios K (2009) Predicting tie strength with social media. In: Proceedings of the SIGCHI conference on human factors in computing systems. ACM, pp 211–220

57. Gillund G, Shiffrin RM (1984) A retrieval model for both recognition and recall. Psychol Rev 91(1):1

58. Girshick R, Donahue J, Darrell T, Malik J (2014) Rich feature hierarchies for accurate object detection and semantic segmentation. In: 2014 IEEE conference on computer vision and pattern recognition (CVPR). IEEE, pp 580–587

59. Goodfellow I, Pouget-Abadie J, Mirza M, Xu B, Warde-Farley D, Ozair S, Courville A, Bengio Y (2014) Generative adversarial nets. In: Advances in neural information processing systems, pp 2672–2680

60. Gray M, Suri S (2019) Ghost work: how to stop silicon valley from building a new global underclass. Eamon Dolan

61. Greene MR, Oliva A (2009) The briefest of glances: the time course of natural scene understanding. Psychol Sci 20(4):464–472

62. Gulrajani I, Ahmed F, Arjovsky M, Dumoulin V, Courville AC (2017) Improved training of wasserstein gans. In: Advances in neural information processing systems, pp 5767–5777

63. Haque A, Milstein A, Fei-Fei L (2020) Illuminating the dark spaces of healthcare with ambient intelligence. Nature 585(7824):193–202

64. Hashimoto TB, Zhang H, Liang P (2019) Unifying human and statistical evaluation for natural language generation. arXiv:1904.02792

65. Hata K, Krishna R, Fei-Fei L, Bernstein MS (2017) A glimpse far into the future: understanding long-term crowd worker quality. In: Proceedings of the 2017 ACM conference on computer supported cooperative work and social computing. ACM, pp 889–901

66. Healy K, Schussman A (2003) The ecology of open-source software development. Technical report, Technical report, University of Arizona, USA

67. Hempel J (2015) Facebook launches m, its bold answer to siri and cortana. In: Wired. Retrieved January 1:2017

68. Heusel M, Ramsauer H, Unterthiner T, Nessler B, Hochreiter S (2017) Gans trained by a two time-scale update rule converge to a local nash equilibrium. In: Advances in neural information processing systems, pp 6626–6637

69. Hill BM (2013) Almost wikipedia: eight early encyclopedia projects and the mechanisms of collective action. Massachusetts institute of technology, pp 1–38

70. Hinton GE (2002) Training products of experts by minimizing contrastive divergence. Neural Comput 14(8):1771–1800

71. Hochreiter S, Schmidhuber J (1997) Long short-term memory. Neural Comput 9(8):1735–1780
72. Hoffman ML (1981) Is altruism part of human nature? J Personal Soc Psychol 40(1):121
73. Horvitz E (1999) Principles of mixed-initiative user interfaces. In: Proceedings of the SIGCHI conference on human factors in computing systems. ACM, pp 159–166
74. Huang F, Canny JF (2019) Sketchforme: composing sketched scenes from text descriptions for interactive applications. In: Proceedings of the 32nd annual ACM symposium on user interface software and technology, pp 209–220
75. Huang T-HK, Chang J, Bigham J (2018) Evorus: a crowd-powered conversational assistant built to automate itself over time. In: Proceedings of the 2018 CHI conference on human factors in computing systems. ACM, p 295
76. Hutto CJ, Gilbert E (2014) Vader: a parsimonious rule-based model for sentiment analysis of social media text. In: Eighth international AAAI conference on weblogs and social media
77. Iordan MC, Greene MR, Beck DM, Fei-Fei L (2015) Basic level category structure emerges gradually across human ventral visual cortex. In: Journal of cognitive neuroscience
78. Ipeirotis PG (2010) Analyzing the amazon mechanical turk marketplace. XRDS: Crossroads. The ACM Mag Stud 17(2):16–21
79. Ipeirotis PG, Provost F, Wang J (2010) Quality management on amazon mechanical turk. In: Proceedings of the ACM SIGKDD workshop on human computation. ACM, pp 64–67
80. Irani LC, Silberman M (2013) Turkopticon: interrupting worker invisibility in amazon mechanical turk. In: Proceedings of the SIGCHI conference on human factors in computing systems. ACM, pp 611–620
81. Jain SD, Grauman K (2013) Predicting sufficient annotation strength for interactive foreground segmentation. In: 2013 IEEE international conference on computer vision (ICCV). IEEE, pp 1313–1320
82. Jain U, Weihs L, Kolve E, Farhadi A, Lazebnik S, Kembhavi A, Schwing A (2020) A cordial sync: Going beyond marginal policies for multi-agent embodied tasks. In: European conference on computer vision. Springer, pp 471–490
83. Jean N, Burke M, Xie M, Davis WM, Lobell DB, Ermon S (2016) Combining satellite imagery and machine learning to predict poverty. Science 353(6301):790–794
84. Josephy T, Lease M, Paritosh P (2013) Crowdscale 2013: crowdsourcing at scale workshop report
85. Kamar E, Hacker S, Horvitz E (2012) Combining human and machine intelligence in large-scale crowdsourcing. In: Proceedings of the 11th international conference on autonomous agents and multiagent systems-volume 1. International Foundation for Autonomous Agents and Multiagent Systems, pp 467–474
86. Karger DR, Oh S, Shah D (2011) Budget-optimal crowdsourcing using low-rank matrix approximations. In: 2011 49th annual allerton conference on communication, control, and computing (allerton). IEEE, pp 284–291
87. Karger DR, Oh S (2014) Shah D Budget-optimal task allocation for reliable crowdsourcing systems. Oper Res 62(1):1–24
88. Karras T, Aila T, Laine S, Lehtinen J (2017) Progressive growing of gans for improved quality, stability, and variation. arXiv:1710.10196
89. Karras T, Laine S, Aila T (2018) A style-based generator architecture for generative adversarial networks. arXiv:1812.04948
90. Karras T, Laine S, Aila T (2019) A style-based generator architecture for generative adversarial networks. In: Proceedings of the IEEE conference on computer vision and pattern recognition, pp 4401–4410
91. Khadpe P, Krishna R, Fei-Fei L, Hancock JT, Bernstein MS (2020) Conceptual metaphors impact perceptions of human-ai collaboration. Proc ACM Hum-Comput Interact 4(CSCW2):1–26
92. Kittur A, Chi EH, Suh B (2008) Crowdsourcing user studies with mechanical turk. In: Proceedings of the SIGCHI conference on human factors in computing systems. ACM, pp 453–456

93. Klein SA (2001) Measuring, estimating, and understanding the psychometric function: a commentary. Percept Psychophys 63(8):1421–1455

94. Kramer ADI, Guillory JE, Hancock JT (2014) Experimental evidence of massive-scale emotional contagion through social networks. Proc Natl Acad Sci 111(24):8788–8790

95. Kraut RE, Resnick P (2011) Encouraging contribution to online communities. Building successful online communities: evidence-based social design, pp 21–76

96. Krishna R, Bernstein M, Fei-Fei L (2019) Information maximizing visual question generation. In: IEEE conference on computer vision and pattern recognition

97. Krishna R, Hata K, Ren F, Fei-Fei L, Niebles JC (2017) Dense-captioning events in videos. In: Proceedings of the IEEE international conference on computer vision, pp 706–715

98. Krishna R, Zhu Y, Groth O, Johnson J, Hata K, Kravitz J, Chen S, Kalantidis Y, Li L-J, Shamma DA et al (2017) Visual genome: connecting language and vision using crowdsourced dense image annotations. Int J Comput Vis 123(1):32–73

99. Krishna RA, Hata K, Chen S, Kravitz J, Shamma DA, Fei-Fei L, Bernstein MS (2016) Embracing error to enable rapid crowdsourcing. In: Proceedings of the 2016 CHI conference on human factors in computing systems. ACM, pp 3167–3179

100. Krizhevsky A, Hinton G (2009) Learning multiple layers of features from tiny images. Technical report, Citeseer

101. Krizhevsky A, Sutskever I, Hinton GE (2012) Imagenet classification with deep convolutional neural networks. In: Advances in neural information processing systems, pp 1097–1105

102. Krizhevsky A, Sutskever I, Hinton GE (2012) Imagenet classification with deep convolutional neural networks. In: Pereira F, Burges CJC, Bottou L, Weinberger KQ (eds) Advances in neural information processing systems 25. Curran Associates, Inc., pp 1097–1105

103. Krueger GP (1989) Sustained work, fatigue, sleep loss and performance: a review of the issues. Work Stress 3(2):129–141

104. Kumar R, Satyanarayan A, Torres C, Lim M, Ahmad S, Klemmer SR, Talton JO (2013) Webzeitgeist: design mining the web. In: Proceedings of the SIGCHI conference on human factors in computing systems. ACM, pp 3083–3092

105. Kurakin A, Goodfellow I, Bengio S (2016) Adversarial examples in the physical world. arXiv:1607.02533

106. Kwon M, Biyik E, Talati A, Bhasin K, Losey DP, Sadigh D (2020) When humans aren't optimal: robots that collaborate with risk-aware humans. In: Proceedings of the 2020 ACM/IEEE international conference on human-robot interaction, pp 43–52

107. Laielli M, Smith J, Biamby G, Darrell T, Hartmann B (2019) Labelar: a spatial guidance interface for fast computer vision image collection. In: Proceedings of the 32nd annual ACM symposium on user interface software and technology, pp 987–998

108. Langer EJ, Blank A, Chanowitz B (1978) The mindlessness of ostensibly thoughtful action: the role of "placebic" information in interpersonal interaction. J Personal Soc Psychol 36(6):635

109. Laput G, Lasecki WS, Wiese J, Xiao R, Bigham JP, Harrison C (2015) Zensors: adaptive, rapidly deployable, human-intelligent sensor feeds. In: Proceedings of the 33rd annual ACM conference on human factors in computing systems. ACM, pp 1935–1944

110. Lasecki W, Miller C, Sadilek A, Abumoussa A, Borrello D, Kushalnagar R, Bigham J (2012) Real-time captioning by groups of non-experts. In: Proceedings of the 25th annual ACM symposium on user interface software and technology. ACM, pp 23–34

111. Lasecki WS, Murray KI, White S, Miller RC, Bigham JP (2011) Real-time crowd control of existing interfaces. In: Proceedings of the 24th annual ACM symposium on User interface software and technology. ACM, pp 23–32

112. Lasecki WS, Wesley R, Nichols J, Kulkarni A, Allen JF, Bigham JP (2013) Chorus: a crowd-powered conversational assistant. In: Proceedings of the 26th annual ACM symposium on User interface software and technology. ACM, pp 151–162

113. Law E, Yin M, Goh J, Chen K, Terry MA, Gajos KZ (2016) Curiosity killed the cat, but makes crowdwork better. In: Proceedings of the 2016 CHI conference on human factors in computing systems. ACM, pp 4098–4110

114. Le J, Edmonds A, Hester V, Biewald L (2010) Ensuring quality in crowdsourced search relevance evaluation: the effects of training question distribution. In: SIGIR 2010 workshop on crowdsourcing for search evaluation, vol 2126, pp 22–32
115. Levitt HCCH (1971) Transformed up-down methods in psychoacoustics. J Acoust Soc Am 49(2B):467–477
116. Lewis DD, Hayes PJ (1994) Guest editorial. ACM Trans Inf Syst 12(3):231 July
117. Li FF, VanRullen R, Koch C, Perona P (2002) Rapid natural scene categorization in the near absence of attention. Proc Natl Acad Sci 99(14):9596–9601
118. Li L, Chu W, Langford J, Schapire RE (2010) A contextual-bandit approach to personalized news article recommendation. In: Proceedings of the 19th international conference on world wide web. ACM, pp 661–670
119. Li T, Ogihara M (2003) Detecting emotion in music. In: ISMIR, vol 3, pp 239–240
120. Liang L, Grauman K (2014) Beyond comparing image pairs: setwise active learning for relative attributes. In: 2014 IEEE conference on computer vision and pattern recognition (CVPR). IEEE, pp 208–215
121. Lin C, Kamar E, Horvitz E (2014) Signals in the silence: models of implicit feedback in a recommendation system for crowdsourcing
122. Lin T-Y, Maire M, Belongie S, Hays J, Perona P, Ramanan D, Dollár P, Lawrence Zitnick C (2014) Microsoft coco: common objects in context. In: Computer vision–ECCV 2014. Springer, pp 740–755
123. Lintott CJ, Schawinski K, Slosar A, Land K, Bamford S, Thomas D, Raddick MJ, Nichol RC, Szalay A, Andreescu D et al (2008) Galaxy zoo: morphologies derived from visual inspection of galaxies from the sloan digital sky survey. Mon Not R Astron Soc 389(3):1179–1189
124. Liu A, Soderland S, Bragg J, Lin CH, Ling X, Weld DS (2016) Effective crowd annotation for relation extraction. In: Proceedings of the 2016 conference of the North American chapter of the association for computational linguistics: human language technologies, pp 897–906
125. Liu Z, Luo P, Wang X, Tang X (2015) Deep learning face attributes in the wild. In: Proceedings of international conference on computer vision (ICCV)
126. Lowe DG (1999) Object recognition from local scale-invariant features. In: Proceedings of the seventh IEEE international conference on computer vision. Ieee, vol 2, pp 1150–1157
127. Lu C, Krishna R, Bernstein M, Fei-Fei L (2016) Visual relationship detection with language priors. In: European conference on computer vision. Springer, pp 852–869
128. Lucic M, Kurach K, Michalski M, Gelly S, Bousquet O (2018) Are gans created equal? a large-scale study. In: Advances in neural information processing systems, pp 698–707
129. Mani I (1999) Advances in automatic text summarization. MIT press
130. Marcus A, Parameswaran A (2015) Crowdsourced data management: industry and academic perspectives. Foundations and Trends in Databases
131. Markey PM (2000) Bystander intervention in computer-mediated communication. Comput Hum Behav 16(2):183–188
132. Martin D, Hanrahan BV, O'Neill J, Gupta N (2014) Being a turker. In: Proceedings of the 17th ACM conference on computer supported cooperative work & social computing. ACM, pp 224–235
133. Mason W, Suri S (2012) Conducting behavioral research on amazon's mechanical turk. Behav Res Methods 44(1):1–23
134. Mildenhall B, Srinivasan PP, Tancik M, Barron JT, Ramamoorthi R, Ng R (2020) Nerf: representing scenes as neural radiance fields for view synthesis. arXiv:2003.08934
135. Miller GA, Charles WG (1991) Contextual correlates of semantic similarity. Lang Cogn Process 6(1):1–28
136. Mitchell M, Wu S, Zaldivar A, Barnes P, Vasserman L, Hutchinson B, Spitzer E, Raji ID, Gebru T (2019) Model cards for model reporting. In: Proceedings of the conference on fairness, accountability, and transparency, pp 220–229
137. Mitra T, Hutto CJ, Gilbert E (2015) Comparing person-and process-centric strategies for obtaining quality data on amazon mechanical turk. In: Proceedings of the 33rd annual ACM conference on human factors in computing systems. ACM, pp 1345–1354

138. Miyato T, Kataoka T, Koyama M, Yoshida Y (2018) Spectral normalization for generative adversarial networks. arXiv:1802.05957
139. Nass C, Brave S (2007) Wired for speech: how voice activates and advances the human-computer relationship. The MIT Press
140. Niebles JC, Wang H, Fei-Fei L (2008) Unsupervised learning of human action categories using spatial-temporal words. Int J Comput Vis 79(3):299–318
141. Olsson C, Bhupatiraju S, Brown T, Odena A, Goodfellow I (2018) Skill rating for generative models. arXiv:1808.04888
142. Pang B, Lee L (2008) Opinion mining and sentiment analysis. Found Trends Inf Retr 2(1–2):1–135
143. Papineni K, Roukos S, Ward T, Zhu W-J (2002) Bleu: a method for automatic evaluation of machine translation. In: Proceedings of the 40th annual meeting on association for computational linguistics. Association for Computational Linguistics, pp 311–318
144. Park J, Krishna R, Khadpe P, Fei-Fei L, Bernstein M (2019) Ai-based request augmentation to increase crowdsourcing participation. Proc AAAI Conf Hum Comput Crowdsourcing 7:115–124
145. Parkash A, Parikh D (2012) Attributes for classifier feedback. In: Computer vision–ECCV 2012. Springer, pp 354–368
146. Peng Dai MD, Weld S (2010) Decision-theoretic control of crowd-sourced workflows. In: In the 24th AAAI conference on artificial intelligence (AAAI'10. Citeseer
147. Portilla J, Simoncelli EP (2000) A parametric texture model based on joint statistics of complex wavelet coefficients. Int J Comput Vis 40(1):49–70
148. Potter MC (1976) Short-term conceptual memory for pictures. J Exp Psychol Hum Learn Mem 2(5):509
149. Potter MC, Levy EI (1969) Recognition memory for a rapid sequence of pictures. J Exp Psychol 81(1):10
150. Radford A, Metz L, Chintala S (2015) Unsupervised representation learning with deep convolutional generative adversarial networks. arXiv:1511.06434
151. Ravuri S, Mohamed S, Rosca M, Vinyals O (2018) Learning implicit generative models with the method of learned moments. arXiv:1806.11006
152. Rayner K, Smith TJ, Malcolm GL, Henderson JM (2009) Eye movements and visual encoding during scene perception. Psychol Sci 20(1):6–10
153. Reeves A, Sperling G (1986) Attention gating in short-term visual memory. Psychol Rev 93(2):180
154. Reeves B, Nass CI (1996) The media equation: how people treat computers, television, and new media like real people and places. Cambridge university press
155. Reich J, Murnane R, Willett J (2012) The state of wiki usage in us k–12 schools: Leveraging web 2.0 data warehouses to assess quality and equity in online learning environments. Educ Res 41(1):7–15
156. Robert C (1984) Influence: the psychology of persuasion. William Morrow and Company, Nowy Jork
157. Rosca M, Lakshminarayanan B, Warde-Farley D, Mohamed S (2017) Variational approaches for auto-encoding generative adversarial networks. arXiv:1706.04987
158. Rössler A, Cozzolino D, Verdoliva L, Riess C, Thies J, Nießner M (2019) Faceforensics++: learning to detect manipulated facial images. arXiv:1901.08971
159. Russakovsky O, Deng J, Su H, Krause J, Satheesh S, Ma S, Huang Z, Karpathy A, Khosla A, Bernstein M, Berg AC, Li F-F (2014) Imagenet large scale visual recognition challenge. In: International Journal of Computer Vision, pp 1–42
160. Russakovsky O, Li L-J, Fei-Fei L (2015) Best of both worlds: human-machine collaboration for object annotation. In: Proceedings of the IEEE conference on computer vision and pattern recognition, pp 2121–2131
161. Rzeszotarski JM, Chi E, Paritosh P, Dai P (2013) Inserting micro-breaks into crowdsourcing workflows. In: First AAAI conference on human computation and crowdsourcing

162. Sajjadi MSM, Bachem O, Lucic M, Bousquet O, Gelly S (2018) Assessing generative models via precision and recall. In: Advances in neural information processing systems, pp 5228–5237

163. Salehi N, Irani LC, Bernstein MS (2015) We are dynamo: overcoming stalling and friction in collective action for crowd workers. In: Proceedings of the 33rd annual ACM conference on human factors in computing systems. ACM, pp 1621–1630

164. Salimans T, Goodfellow I, Zaremba W, Cheung V, Radford A, Chen X (2016) Improved techniques for training gans. In: Advances in neural information processing systems, pp 2234–2242

165. Sardar A, Joosse M, Weiss A, Evers V (2012) Don't stand so close to me: users' attitudinal and behavioral responses to personal space invasion by robots. In: Proceedings of the seventh annual ACM/IEEE international conference on human-robot interaction. ACM, pp 229–230

166. Schapire RE, Singer Y (2000) Boostexter: a boosting-based system for text categorization. Mach Learn 39(2):135–168

167. Seetharaman P, Pardo B (2014) Crowdsourcing a reverberation descriptor map. In: Proceedings of the ACM international conference on multimedia. ACM, pp 587–596

168. Sheng VS, Provost F, Ipeirotis PG (2008) Get another label? improving data quality and data mining using multiple, noisy labelers. In: Proceedings of the 14th ACM SIGKDD international conference on Knowledge discovery and data mining. ACM, pp 614–622

169. Sheshadri A, Lease M (2013) Square: a benchmark for research on computing crowd consensus. In: First AAAI conference on human computation and crowdsourcing

170. Shneiderman B, Maes P (1997) Direct manipulation vs. interface agents. Interactions 4(6):42–61 November

171. Simonyan K, Zisserman A (2014) Very deep convolutional networks for large-scale image recognition. CoRR, abs/1409.1556

172. Smyth P, Burl MC, Fayyad UM, Perona P (1994) Knowledge discovery in large image databases: dealing with uncertainties in ground truth. In: KDD workshop, pp 109–120

173. Smyth P, Fayyad U, Burl M, Perona P, Baldi P (1995) Inferring ground truth from subjective labelling of venus images

174. Snow R, O'Connor B, Jurafsky D, Ng AY (2008) Cheap and fast—but is it good?: evaluating non-expert annotations for natural language tasks. In: Proceedings of the conference on empirical methods in natural language processing. Association for Computational Linguistics, pp 254–263

175. Song Z, Chen Q, Huang Z, Hua Y, Yan S (2011) Contextualizing object detection and classification. In: 2011 IEEE conference on computer vision and pattern recognition (CVPR). IEEE, pp 1585–1592

176. Sperling G (1963) A model for visual memory tasks. Hum Factors 5(1):19–31

177. Su H, Deng J, Fei-Fei L (2012) Crowdsourcing annotations for visual object detection. In: Workshops at the twenty-sixth AAAI conference on artificial intelligence

178. Suchman LA (1987) Plans and situated actions: the problem of human-machine communication. Cambridge University Press, Cambridge

179. Szegedy C, Vanhoucke V, Ioffe S, Shlens J, Wojna Z (2016) Rethinking the inception architecture for computer vision. In: Proceedings of the IEEE conference on computer vision and pattern recognition, pp 2818–2826

180. Tamuz O, Liu C, Belongie S, Shamir O, Kalai AT (2011) Adaptively learning the crowd kernel. arXiv:1105.1033

181. Taylor PJ, Thomas S (2008) Linguistic style matching and negotiation outcome. Negot Confl Manag Res 1(3):263–281

182. Theis L, van den Oord A, Bethge M (2015) A note on the evaluation of generative models. arXiv:1511.01844

183. Thomaz AL, Breazeal C (2008) Teachable robots: understanding human teaching behavior to build more effective robot learners. Artif Intell 172(6–7):716–737

184. Thomee B, Shamma DA, Friedland G, Elizalde B, Ni K, Poland D, Borth D, Li L-J (2016) Yfcc100m: the new data in multimedia research. Commun ACM 59(2). To Appear

185. Vedantam R, Zitnick CL, Parikh D (2015) Cider: consensus-based image description evaluation. In: Proceedings of the IEEE conference on computer vision and pattern recognition, pp 4566–4575
186. Vijayanarasimhan S, Jain P, Grauman K (2010) Far-sighted active learning on a budget for image and video recognition. In: 2010 IEEE conference on computer vision and pattern recognition (CVPR). IEEE, pp 3035–3042
187. Vinyals O, Toshev A, Bengio S, Erhan D (2014) Show and tell: a neural image caption generator. arXiv:1411.4555
188. Vinyals O, Toshev A, Bengio S, Erhan D (2015) Show and tell: a neural image caption generator. In: Proceedings of the IEEE conference on computer vision and pattern recognition, pp 3156–3164
189. von Ahn L, Dabbish L (2004) Labeling images with a computer game. In: Proceedings of the SIGCHI conference on Human factors in computing systems. ACM, pp 319–326
190. von Ahn L, Dabbish L (2004) Labeling images with a computer game, pp 319–326
191. Vondrick C, Patterson D, Ramanan D (2013) Efficiently scaling up crowdsourced video annotation. Int J Comput Vis 101(1):184–204
192. Wah C, Branson S, Perona P, Belongie S (2011) Multiclass recognition and part localization with humans in the loop. In: 2011 IEEE international conference on computer vision (ICCV). IEEE, pp 2524–2531
193. Wah C, Van Horn G, Branson S, Maji S, Perona P, Belongie S (2014) Similarity comparisons for interactive fine-grained categorization. In: 2014 IEEE conference on computer vision and pattern recognition (CVPR). IEEE, pp 859–866
194. Wang Y-C, Kraut RE, Levine JM (2015) Eliciting and receiving online support: using computer-aided content analysis to examine the dynamics of online social support. J Med Internet Res 17(4):e99
195. Warde-Farley D, Bengio Y (2016) Improving generative adversarial networks with denoising feature matching
196. Warncke-Wang M, Ranjan V, Terveen L, Hecht B (2015) Misalignment between supply and demand of quality content in peer production communities. In: Ninth international AAAI conference on web and social media
197. Weichselgartner E, Sperling G (1987) Dynamics of automatic and controlled visual attention. Science 238(4828):778–780
198. Weld DS, Lin CH, Bragg J (2015) Artificial intelligence and collective intelligence. In: Handbook of collective intelligence, pp. 89–114
199. Welinder P, Branson S, Perona P, Belongie SJ (2010) The multidimensional wisdom of crowds. In: Advances in neural information processing systems, pp 2424–2432
200. Whitehill J, Wu T-f, Bergsma J, Movellan JR, Ruvolo PL (2009) Whose vote should count more: optimal integration of labels from labelers of unknown expertise. In: Advances in neural information processing systems, pp 2035–2043
201. Wichmann FA, Jeremy Hill N (2001) The psychometric function: I. Fitting, sampling, and goodness of fit. Percept Psychophys 63(8):1293–1313
202. Willis CG, Law E, Williams AC, Franzone BF, Bernardos R, Bruno L, Hopkins C, Schorn C, Weber E, Park DS et al (2017) Crowdcurio: an online crowdsourcing platform to facilitate climate change studies using herbarium specimens. New Phytol 215(1):479–488
203. Wobbrock JO, Forlizzi J, Hudson SE, Myers BA (2002) Webthumb: interaction techniques for small-screen browsers. In: Proceedings of the 15th annual ACM symposium on User interface software and technology. ACM, pp 205–208
204. Xia H, Jacobs J, Agrawala M (2020) Crosscast: adding visuals to audio travel podcasts. In: Proceedings of the 33rd annual ACM symposium on user interface software and technology, pp 735–746
205. Yang D, Kraut RE (2017) Persuading teammates to give: systematic versus heuristic cues for soliciting loans. Proc. ACM Hum-Comput Interact 1(CSCW):114:1–114:21
206. Yue Y-T, Yang Y-L, Ren G, Wang W (2017) Scenectrl: mixed reality enhancement via efficient scene editing. In: Proceedings of the 30th annual ACM symposium on user interface software and technology, pp 427–436

207. Zhang H, Sciutto C, Agrawala M, Fatahalian K (2020) Vid2player: controllable video sprites that behave and appear like professional tennis players. arXiv:2008.04524
208. Zhang T (2004) Solving large scale linear prediction problems using stochastic gradient descent algorithms. In: Proceedings of the twenty-first international conference on Machine learning. ACM, p 116
209. Zhou D, Basu S, Mao Y, Platt JC (2012) Learning from the wisdom of crowds by minimax entropy. In: Advances in neural information processing systems, pp 2195–2203
210. Zhou S, Gordon M, Krishna R, Narcomey A, Fei-Fei LF, Bernstein M (2019) Hype: a benchmark for human eye perceptual evaluation of generative models. In: Advances in neural information processing systems, pp 3449–3461

ML Tools for the Web: A Way for Rapid Prototyping and HCI Research

Na Li, Jason Mayes, and Ping Yu

Abstract Machine learning (ML) has become a powerful tool with the potential to enable new interactions and user experiences. Although the use of ML in HCI research is growing, the process of prototyping and deploying ML remains challenging. We claim that ML tools designed to be used on the Web are suitable for fast prototyping and HCI research. In this chapter, we review literature, current technologies, and use cases of ML tools for the Web. We also provide a case study, using TensorFlow.js—a major Web ML library, to demonstrate how to prototype with Web ML tools in different prototyping scenarios. At the end, we discuss challenges and future directions of designing tools for fast prototyping and research.

1 Introduction

Machine learning (ML) is becoming increasingly powerful. ML usage has grown exponentially over the past few years; thanks to increased hardware performance at lower costs and growing research in the ML field. Convenient ML tools have now emerged for fast model development and experimentation. This includes core ML libraries such as TensorFlow[1] and PyTorch[2] (both released around 2016), along with supportive tooling such as Pandas,[3] NumPy[4] and more to reduce complexity or deal with common tasks.

In the HCI community, applied ML models have been used in prototypes to study augmented and new interactions. The problem space of ML applications ranges from

---

[1] https://www.tensorflow.org/.
[2] https://pytorch.org/.
[3] https://pandas.pydata.org/.
[4] https://numpy.org/.

N. Li, J. Mayes and P. Yu—have equal contributions to this chapter.

N. Li (✉) · J. Mayes · P. Yu
Google, TensorFlow.js Team, Mountain View, CA, USA
e-mail: linazhao@google.com

315

Table 1 Platforms where TensorFlow.js, an ML library, can run on

Browser	Server	Mobile	Desktop	IoT
Chrome	Node.js	React Native	Electron	RaspberryPi
Safari		WeChat		
FireFox		PWA		

understanding images, sounds, and texts, as well as understanding temporal or spatial signals, or even using ML to generate new contents. There are many examples, such as predicting gestures on touchscreens [18], generating responses on social media [35], predicting visual attention on a web page [38], just to name a few.

At the same time, ML usage in real applications is also growing fast. For web applications in particular, the TensorFlow.js library, one of the most popular Web ML tools, has been used by more than 13,000 projects on GitHub[5] as of March 2021. We think that Web ML tools create huge opportunities for prototyping and experimenting with ML ideas. First of all, Web ML tools are written in Javascript. JavaScript is the most popular language (JavaScript developers account for over 69.7% of professional developers according to the 2020 StackOverflow developer survey [32]). Many HCI researchers, designers, and a large portion of application developers have already been familiar with the language. So development and debugging will be easier. Secondly, because the Web ML tools can run models directly on the client side, it simplifies the process to use ML in the application. The application can directly take inputs from available sensors such as the camera, mic, and keyboards and feed the data to the ML model to run prediction. This saves round trip time to send and receive data from a remote server. It also eliminates the need and cost to setup the remote server. Thirdly, because Web ML tools take advantage of using native browsers or JS environments to accelerate computation, which doesn't need additional driver installation, it is easy to deploy the model across platforms. Table 1 shows the platforms that TensorFlow.js can readily be deployed and run. Fourthly, compared to running models in native apps, running in a Web browser allows easy sharing of prototypes. With just a hyperlink, users can open the ML-powered application in any browser on almost any device and start experiencing it right away.

There are, however, some remaining challenges for consideration. Running ML models efficiently on user devices needs careful thought for criteria that may be overlooked for a typical server side implementation where compute resources are known and fixed. Compared to dedicated ML infrastructure, user devices often have limited resources in terms of computation power, hardware acceleration options, storage capacity, and battery life, which is of concern to the user of the device. These are some of the key design challenges for ML engineers and library developers who want to support running models client side on device. There are various efforts to tackle this challenge, ranging from developing lightweight model architectures specifically for deploying on the client side [11], to distilling smaller models from

---

[5] https://github.com/tensorflow/tfjs.

large models [10]. There are also techniques to quantize model weights to make the model size smaller [13] or to prune and optimize model architecture for inference. We can even leverage device hardware acceleration such as the GPU to speed things further.

ML is still relatively new to many HCI researchers, designers, and application developers. We think that there is also a lack of understanding of ML, educational materials, and prototyping tools to bridge the gap between ML research and the rest of the world. The HCI community is now starting to study how to apply ML in design [7], and software development [4]. In the developer community, there have been a number of emerging supporting libraries such as Danfo.js[6] that replicates Pandas, and other common utilities. Books and courses teaching how to use ML tools in JavaScript are also now being published,[7,8] but there is room for improvement in helping people understand, discover, and share models, which we will discuss later in the chapter.

2 Related Work

There has been growing interest in designing ML libraries for on-device learning as seen in the number of ML system papers [6, 14, 30]. There has also been growing interest in applying ML in HCI and research as seen in recent CHI workshops [12, 17, 19]. To gain a full picture of what ML libraries for Web can do and how they can address the need for fast prototyping and research in HCI, we undertook a review of the following areas:

- ML use cases in HCI research.
- ML libraries for the Web.
- Task-specific libraries and User-friendly libraries for non-ML experts.
- Challenges for non-ML experts.

2.1 ML Use Cases in HCI

The technical side of the HCI community has been working on applying ML to improve interactions. We describe some common themes, categorized by input types; see Table 2.

Current state-of-the-art computer vision models are capable of capturing eye, face, body, and hand movement using webcams, therefore, reducing the need for special sensors and equipment.

---

[6] https://danfo.jsdata.org/.

[7] https://www.manning.com/books/deep-learning-with-javascript.

[8] https://www.coursera.org/learn/browser-based-models-tensorflow.

Table 2 Inputs, Data formats, TensorFlow.js models, and HCI use cases

Input	Data format	Model	Use case
Face,Eye,Iris	Video	FaceMesh	Eye tracking
Body	Video	BodyPix, PoseNet	Video conferencing, VR, health
Hand	Video	Handtracking	Art and design
Speech	Audio	Speech-command model	Dialog interface, Accessibility
Text	Text	MobileBERT	Chat bot

Face and eye tracking. Sewell and Komogortsev [29] demonstrate how to train a neural network to track eye gaze with only a standard webcam. Facial expressions can be used in many scenarios, one application area is affect detection. For example, Bosch et al. studied how ML-powered affect detection can be used to inform learning states in the classroom [3].

Body segmentation. Body-centric design relies on body segmentation techniques in designing a body-aware experience. In video conferencing, body segments of participants can be inserted into a co-located virtual space (see example research [26]), so that they can accomplish tasks that normally require pointing to or working on a shared artifact. Body segmentation can also be used to enhance a person's virtual presentation [15]. In health research, images or videos of body movements can be used to capture early symptoms [27].

Hand tracking. Hand or gesture tracking also has wide application, such as using virtual hands to accomplish complex tasks [34]. In another study, hand and body are used to recognize gestures of aircraft handling [31].

Speech recognition. Speech or command recognition has gained increasing attention as assistant agents popularize. It is also an important topic in accessibility research [28].

NLP. Language models can power many text-based research, such as chat bot [1]. NLP is also used to help diagnose mental health [33], machine translation [36], and spoken language interaction [22], just to name a few.

2.2 ML Libraries

Ma et al. [20] provided a comprehensive review of ML libraries for the web in 2019. There have been a lot of changes in this fast growing field, so we summarize the findings and provide an updated review here. The 2019 review examined 7 libraries, just 3 of them are still in active development as of Dec. 2020, including Tensor-

Flow.js,[9] brain.js[10] and WebDNN.[11] The other 4 libraries have not had code changes for 2 years. Concurrently to this, new ML libraries for the web emerged, such as ONNX.js[12] and Paddle.js.[13] These libraries can load a model and execute the model reasonably fast in the browser. Some of these libraries can also train new models directly in the web browser.

The primary challenge in model loading is to be able to load different model formats generated from different training libraries. Taking the MobileNet model as an example, the TensorFlow model format will be different from the PyTorch model format. By far, ONNX.js has the best coverage of different model formats. It can convert PyTorch, TensorFlow, Keras, and, of course, its own format enabling other libraries to use ONNX.js as a bridge to convert models to a desired format. The TensorFlow.js converter only supports TensorFlow and Keras models, but through ONNX.js, it can also convert a PyTorch model.

The primary challenge in model execution is computational efficiency. There are a number of different web technologies that can be used to accelerate computation. One method of acceleration is parallel computing. By far, TensorFlow.js has the largest parallel computing options for JS based ML. It can use the GPU to run the computation, which not only frees up the resource in CPU, but also further takes advantage of the GPU's architecture. On the GPU, a matrix can be stored in 2D space where each number in the matrix can be thought of as a point on the 2D space. The GPU can then apply any function to these points in parallel. This means that a large matrix multiplication can be just as fast as small matrix multiplication because the large matrix simply takes a larger space on GPU but the time taken to do the computation for all points in parallel is the same.

TensorFlow.js re-purposes the 2D GPU graphic API WebGL[14] for model computation. This means for an N-dimensional tensor, it would be flattened and stored in a 2D space, where each number is a point in the 2D space. Operations on each point can be run in parallel as previously described.

Alternatively, TensorFlow.js can also use a relatively new CPU computing technology, called WebAssembly (WASM).[15] WASM is a cross-browser, portable assembly and binary format for the web. Developers don't write WASM directly. Instead, existing C/C++/Rust code is compiled to WASM via tool chains such as Emscripten. Its SIMD[16] and Multithread[17] feature allows WASM code to be run in the browser on multiple cores. Currently, Multithreading is supported in Chrome and Firefox, while SIMD is supported in Chrome and Firefox behind a flag the user must set to enable.

---

[9] https://github.com/tensorflow/tfjs.

[10] https://github.com/BrainJS/brain.js.

[11] https://github.com/mil-tokyo/webdnn.

[12] https://github.com/microsoft/onnxjs.

[13] https://github.com/PaddlePaddle/Paddle.js.

[14] https://www.khronos.org/webgl/.

[15] https://webassembly.org/.

[16] https://v8.dev/features/simd.

[17] https://developers.google.com/web/updates/2018/10/wasm-threads.

TensorFlow.js is the only library that has SIMD and MultiThreading acceleration at the time of writing.

It is also worth-noting that on-device computation efficiency is studied extensively and an active field in mobile-based ML system design. As we know, existing C/C++ code can be compiled to WASM and run in the browser. Mobile-based frameworks for iOS are mostly written in C/C++, so that their solutions that run on the CPU can be easily migrated to the web through WASM. The problems mobile developers face when trying to run ML on device, i.e., model conversion and optimization, acceleration for different device hardware, lightweight in bundle size [14] are very similar to running ML in the web, therefore, these mobile-based libraries are very suitable to be adapted for web solutions too. This effectively brings a lot of mature optimization solutions to the web, which can expedite ML tool development for the web. There are several mobile-based libraries, including TensorFlow Lite,[18] Caffe2,[19] NCNN,[20] MNN,[21] and many more.

2.3   Task-Specific Libraries

Task-specific libraries provide simpler APIs for a specific task, such as face landmark recognition, pose recognition, command recognition, etc. These ML tasks usually require additional steps to pre/post-process data or feed the data through a pipeline of multiple models. These steps are hidden from users, so that they can just focus on the input and output for their application. There are many task-specific libraries for web usage. One example is face-api.js.[22] It takes a HTML image or video as input and output key points and bounding box coordinates from one of its high-level APIs, such as face detection, face landmark detection, face expression recognition, age estimation, and gender recognition. Another example is ml5.js.[23] It provides a collection of high-level APIs for input types like image, video, sound, and text, and can accomplish tasks such as face landmark recognition, style transfer, pitch detection, text generation, and more. These task-specific libraries are often designed to be very easy to integrate and use within existing web applications, usually only adding 2 to 3 lines to the application code.

---

[18] https://www.tensorflow.org/lite.

[19] https://caffe2.ai/.

[20] https://github.com/Tencent/ncnn.

[21] https://github.com/alibaba/MNN.

[22] https://github.com/justadudewhohacks/face-api.js/.

[23] https://ml5js.org/.

2.4   ML Systems with a Graphical Interface

User-friendly ML systems are also built on top of ML libraries, they provide end to end user experience to custom train a model with new data or to try an existing pre-trained model. These systems often provide GUIs to guide users through the workflow. Users can choose from many options, such as what model to load, set hyperparameters, preprocessing methods, and more. The tools will then take care of the rest to train and output a model.

One example of a user friendly ML system is Runway ML.[24] It allows you to download many pre-trained models from the cloud and run on your local machine in minutes. From image classifiers to generative networks, you can try pretty much all types of ML models that are popular right now. It even exposes a web server that acts like a local API you can call with your own custom data from web browsers to build ML enabled web apps in minutes. Runway ML aims to build the next generation of creative tools that are powered by machine learning to enable more than just researchers to be able to use these advanced models at scale.

Another representative example is Weka [9]. It is a popular choice among the data scientist community. The system provides a GUI interface for training classifiers. The UI guides users to go through the components of the training process, including uploading and preprocessing inputs, setting up training and testing data, setting up validation methods, choosing classifiers, training and seeing the results with accuracy analysis. The data is mostly presented in tabulated format.

Another great example would be AutoML systems. These systems hide even more of the steps by automating a lot of the above described processes. In a nutshell, they are systems that train many models concurrently, automatically selecting hyperparameters, comparing model accuracy, and then selects the best resulting model for use with a given input data set. This automatic compare-and-choose process is formally defined as a Combined Algorithm Selection and Hyperparameter optimization problem in Feurer et al. paper [8], in which they detailed AutoML system design. There is an emerging number of AutoML systems out there. The Auto-Weka system is built on top of Weka [16]. The Google AutoML system[25] [2] is a cloud-based service that provides classifiers specifically for images, video, and text.

Another example is Teachable Machine,[26] which makes the training process even easier by simplifying the two ends of the training process. On the input end, it allows data collection on the fly using inputs from camera and mic entirely in the web browser. On the output end, it allows users to use the just trained model right away in the browser, so that they can validate the accuracy of the output and retrain immediately. This simplified process immensely expedites the iterative training process and allows anyone (no matter what their background in ML or even programming) to make a working ML prototype in under 5 min.

---

[24] https://runwayml.com/.

[25] https://cloud.google.com/automl.

[26] https://teachablemachine.withgoogle.com/.

2.5 Challenges for Non-ML Expert

There's a large body of research on end-user programming [23], but few studies on programming with ML. This problem is different from traditional programming, as pointed out by Patel et al. [24], "Despite the widespread impact in research, ML algorithms are seldom applied in practice by ordinary software engineers. One reason is that applying machine learning is different from traditional programming. Traditional programming is often discrete and deterministic, but most machine learning is stochastic.... Traditional programming is often debugged with print statements and breakpoints, but machine learning requires analysis with visualizations and statistics." And Patel asserts that "Developers need new methods and tools to support the task of applying machine learning to their everyday problems."

We synthesize several pioneer works in this area. Patel et al. studied the difficulties software developers encountered in using statistical ML [25]. Yang et al. studied how non-experts build ML models [37]. Cai et al. studied the challenges software developers encounter in using deep learning ML [4]. From these studies, we found several themes for non-ML experts programming with ML.

2.5.1 Expertise in Problem Understanding but Not in ML

A lot of non-ML experts came to ML because they have a data set at hand with a real-world problem to solve. They see ML as "black boxes", with which given an input, it will output a result. They describe the problem as real-world situations and desired outcomes not as formalized ML problems. For example, they want to use ML to solve problems like: "Does my houseplant need watering? Is there any coffee left in the pot? What is the weather like outside? Are there any eggs in my refrigerator? Who left those dirty dishes in the sink? Has the mail been delivered yet? How many police cars pass by my window on a typical day?" [21], or alert when microwave finished, estimate emotion from wearables, predict machine maintenance, answer HR Policy questions [37]. Under this mindset, they often search for publicly-available working ML examples that solve similar problems [37]. They evaluate the models by visually examining the results or trying it in their applications [25, 37].

2.5.2 Rapid Trial-and-Error

Another common behavior seen in non-ML experts is that they select and debug models through rapid trial-and-error. Lacking sufficient ML knowledge, they seldom base their decision on model architecture, rather they often just "tried all algorithms" that they can get and choose the one that shows the best outcome [37]. Or as reflected in Patel et al. paper [25], "We basically tried a whole bunch of Weka experimentation and different algorithms."

2.5.3 Lack of Understanding of ML

Another common barrier for non-ML experts when applying ML is difficulties in understanding what ML is and what it can/can't do. Dove et al. argued that the next generation designers should be able to design new user experiences around ML [7]. However, they found out that the current state is that projects often use ML in ways that are totally familiar to ML researchers to solve classic ML problems, and the use cases described are quite typical, such as object classification, personal recommendation, etc. It is hard for UX designers to "apply their strength in problem re-framing and opportunity finding to envision new forms for ML to take, and the many new ways it might deliver value to people". In their survey of 43 UX designers, the respondents repeatedly expressed difficulties in understanding ML, and therefore, ideating and innovating with ML also became hard. It is also the most frequently mentioned hurdle for software developers (42%) to use ML in Cai et al.'s [4] survey with 421 responses.

3 The Positive Spiral Effect of Fast Prototyping and Research

We propose that fast prototyping and deploying ML models on the Web can have a positive spiral effect for the whole research cycle. Figure 1 depicts a general research workflow involving applied ML. It starts from a new model. We will take the new model, use ML web tools to convert the models to web format, and deploy with JavaScript code. Once deployed, we can study the experience. Feedback on experience about the application or bugs and biases about the models are exposed and collected. The model and/or the application is modified and redeployed taking this feedback into account, thus beginning the cycle again to further refine.

By easily deploying the model and sharing with users online, we are likely to get feedback faster, which, in turn, improves the model/application to produce more (and better) results in the future, creating a positive spiral of research and innovation at scale. Let's dive into each of these parts of the life cycle in more detail.

3.1 Releasing a New Research Model

Traditionally some research papers are accompanied by a link to a GitHub repo where you can clone the code to be set up in your own environment for testing/expanding upon. As the expectation is to clone the researcher's environment server side there are some rather large blocks for people adopting code in this form due to the assumptions and dependencies made. Let's take a look at a typical developer flow if someone is

Fig. 1 Positive spiral effect

new to machine learning (most people are new to ML right now at time of writing) and want to run your example Python code:

1. Find your code from a research paper/publication/video.
2. Clone your GitHub repository to their server (if they have one - else they need to set up a suitable environment and understand Linux/terminal usage etc. too).
3. Install ML library of choice and other dependencies you may have used.
4. Install CUDA (not trivial) to ensure GPU acceleration for training/inference on NVIDIA GPUs.
5. Read instructions on how to use the model (often these are not very detailed and have many assumptions on prior knowledge about said research).
6. If all previous 5 steps work out perfectly and the user understands your explanations to get the code running, they can finally try out your model. Majority of people have probably bailed by step 4 or 5.

Contrast this to the web ML experience:

1. Interested users visit a website which they found via a share/video/research paper.
2. The machine Learning model executes without needing to install any dependencies and automatically selects the best hardware to execute based on what is available on the client device.
3. Easy to adapt JavaScript code (as the web page itself is a live working demo whose source can be viewed with ease) showing how to send data to the model in the web environment which is easy to replicate (simply view source).

3.2   Using the Model

Now that we can easily access and deploy the model in web applications, it allows us to reach even more participants online. With the broadened user base, it is more likely that we find people interacting with the application in ways that may even surprise us as people may see a different vision to the one we had in mind for their unique experience.

3.3   Feedback

Now that we have more people using the model, we are likely to find potential bugs and biases in the model or design that we may have overlooked. Maybe we had created a speech recognition model trained with a US English data set. But when the application is tested with users in the UK (or other countries), issues with accuracy are discovered. We can then iterate on the model to produce a better model that takes into account these new considerations.

4   TensorFlow.js—An ML Tool for the Web

TensorFlow.js[27] is a comprehensive open source machine learning library that supports ML for the Web. It is written in JavaScript, allows converting models from TensorFlow to a web compatible format, runs in any browser, and uses native browser technology for computation acceleration. TensorFlow.js has the largest number of op support among all Web ML libraries [20], so it can enable more models than other libraries. As reviewed in the related work, its performance optimization and acceleration options are also among the best in the field. In the following several sections, we provide practical guidance on how to use TensorFlow.js for fast prototyping.

4.1   TensorFlow.js Models - Example: Body Segmentation

Related work has revealed that the task-specific APIs and user friendly interfaces are easier to adopt for non-ML experts. TensorFlow.js has a model garden[28] with carefully curated high-level APIs. These APIs are all task-oriented, including object detection, face-landmarks-detection, hand pose, body segmentation, toxicity detection, etc.

---

[27] https://www.tensorflow.org/js.

[28] https://github.com/tensorflow/tfjs-models.

In this section, we use body segmentation API as an example to illustrate how it can be used for fast prototyping.

4.1.1   Load API

There are two ways to load the body segmentation API in your application: through a HTML script tag, or via npm.

Below snippet shows the HTML script tag approach

HTML

```
<!-- Load TensorFlow.js -->
<script src="https://cdn.jsdelivr.net/npm/@tensorflow/
tfjs@3.3.0"></script>
<!-- Load BodyPix -->
<script src="https://cdn.jsdelivr.net/npm/@tensorflow-models/
body-pix@2.1.0"></script>
```

Below snippet shows how to install via npm

Terminal

```
npm install @tensorflow-models/body-pix
```

4.1.2   Feed Input and Run Model in Browser

Now the model's API is available to use, use the API to load the body segmentation model, this has to be done only once

Javascript

```
const model = await bodyPix.load();
```

This is an asynchronous operation, so we await this to load, and then we can run the model on any image or video input. Any element in a HTML page can be obtained through the standard JavaScript DOM API as shown below, and then the element (i.e., image or video) is fed to the API's segmentation function.

Javascript

```
const image = document.getElementById('image');
const result = await model.segmentPersonParts(image);
```

The result here will contain a JSON object we can parse through to then do with as we wish in our application.

4.1.3 Use Output in an Application

Given an image with one or more people, the API's segmentPersonParts method predicts the 24 body part segmentations for all people in a given image. It returns a PartSegmentation object corresponding to body parts for each pixel for all people found as one array of objects.

The PartSegmentation object returned contains a width, height, allPoses, and an Int32Array with each value in the array representing one pixel passed to the function, the value is one of −1 to 24, representing whether this pixel is one of 24 body parts or background (represented by −1). The allPoses array contains key points of the body, such as left_upper_arm_front, torso_front, left_hand, etc. For details; see the api documentation.[29]

Figure 2 shows the outputs of the model visualized. Figure 2a is the original image. Figure 2b renders different body parts in different colors (using the pixel level Int32Array that is returned). Figure 2c shows the key points of the body from "allPoses" object. The API also provides utility functions for rendering.

4.1.4 Example Use Cases

In this example, we have shown that ML can be integrated into a web application with just a few lines of code. With the output from the model, we can create many new experiences. For inspiration, we describe a few examples below (demos are available in the footnote):

---

[29] https://github.com/tensorflow/tfjs-models/tree/master/body-pix.

(a) Original   (b) Colored parts   (c) Key points

Fig. 2 Body-pix example

1. Real-time clothing size estimation[30]: A web-based prototype that can estimate your body size in under 15 s to automatically select the correct size for you at check out on a fashion website.
2. Real-time motion capture for character animation[31]: An app that recognizes key facial landmarks and body pose, allowing us to animate 2D SVG characters instantly.
3. Real-time teleportation[32]: An app that segments your body in real time and renders it in another scene.

4.2 TensorFlow Models - Example: Converting an Existing ML Model

The opportunities to use ML in web applications is far beyond what existing Tensor-Flow.js models can offer. As depicted in the positive spiral effect diagram, if any new model developed by the ML community can be converted to web format, it opens up many opportunities for non-ML experts to adopt and adapt ML in applications of their own. In this section, we provide an example of the workflow.

4.2.1 Convert Model

First, we need to convert a model developed in other libraries (e.g., TensorFlow or PyTorch) to a web format that TensorFlow.js can read. We focus on models created by TensorFlow because it has direct support from TensorFlow.js. For PyTorch models, they need other adapters to convert to TensorFlow models first. There are several sources to find TensorFlow models, we will detail them in the model discovery section. Here, we assume we already have a TensorFlow model in SavedModel format. Below steps shows how to convert it to TensorFlow.js format.

---

[30] https://www.youtube.com/watch?v=kFtIddNLcuM.

[31] https://github.com/yemount/pose-animator.

[32] https://www.youtube.com/watch?v=x1JYnsvvaJs.

Step 1: Install tensorflowjs converter python package.

Terminal

```
pip install tensorflowjs[wizard]
```

Step 2: Invoke the converter in the terminal and follow the instructions, it will ask for the location of the saved model and optional conversion configurations. After this step, it will output a model.json file and several model weights binaries. The model.json file specifies the model architecture as a graph. And the model weights binaries contain weights for each edge in the graph.

Terminal

```
tensorflowjs_wizard
```

4.2.2   Load Library

Similar to the example in the last section, you need to load the library either through a HTML script tag or npm. Below snippet shows how to use HTML script tag to load the library

HTML

```
<!-- Load TensorFlow.js -->
<script src="https://cdn.jsdelivr.net/npm/@tensorflow/
tfjs@3.3.0"></script>
```

4.2.3   Load Model

You need to host the model.json and weights files somewhere such as on a CDN or your web server that you can access. The below snippet shows how to use the TensorFlow.js library to load the model

Javascript

```
<!-- Load TensorFlow.js -->
import * as tf from '@tensorflow/tfjs';
const model = await tf.loadGraphModel(MODEL_URL);
```

4.2.4   Feed Input and Run Model in Browser

Now you have loaded the model, you can feed inputs to it and run the model. Below snippet shows the API to run the model.

Javascript

```
const inputs = {feature1, feature2, feature3};
const result = await model.executeAsync(inputs);
```

In this example, we have shown that with a few steps you can use any model in a web application so long as the ops used by that model are also supported in TensorFlow.js. We will be notified about not supported ops when converting the model.

5   Transfer Learning Made Simple

Transfer learning is very useful and common in classification models. In practice, we often have limited amount of data, not enough to train a high quality model from scratch. Using transfer learning, we can start with a previously trained model with another larger dataset for a similar problem, fine tune that model by optimizing only the last few layers of the model with our data. This way, we can efficiently just custom train an existing model for a new task. Transfer learning is very useful in

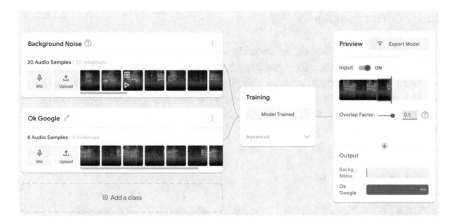

Fig. 3 Teachable machine example

two scenarios: (1) If an existing model is trained with one classification task, for example, to recognize sunflower vs. tulip, but your requirement is to recognize dog vs. cat, you can just redefine the classes and custom train the sunflower vs. tulip model to recognize dog vs. cat. (2) If you want to provide personalized results to each of your users, you can distribute the same original model to each user, have the user custom train their own model on their own devices. Then users can use their own model. We provide examples of two ML tools for transfer learning, they require little to no coding, therefore, allowing users, especially non programmers, to focus on ideas rather than coding.

5.1 Teachable Machine

Teachable Machine[33] is a web-based GUI tool for custom training classification models without writing any code. The GUI supports an end to end workflow of custom training a model, from collecting samples to training, and then evaluation and retrain. This iterative process can all be accomplished in one UI, allowing users to focus on ideas instead of the implementation of the underlying models. It has proved to be an effective way for generating new ideas with ML. According to the team developing Teachable Machine, users in 201 countries have created over 125,000 classification models with it [5]. Teachable Machine currently supports three classification tasks: image, audio, and pose. Figure 3 shows an example of using Teachable Machine to train a model that recognizes 'OK Google' sound.

---

[33] https://teachablemachine.withgoogle.com/.

5.1.1 Collect Samples

Users need to define classes and provide some samples for each class. The samples can be uploaded from the file system or collected in real time with microphone (for audio) or camera (for images). In this example, we use the microphone to collect sound in real time. We record 20 s of audio for the 'Background Noise' class, and record 8 s of audio for the 'Ok Google' class. For the second class, we just say 'Ok, Google.' several times.

5.1.2 Train the Model

Click the 'Train Model' button in the middle and wait for a few seconds.

5.1.3 Real-Time Evaluation

Once the model is trained, it will be available to test in real time on the right. Keep saying words to the microphone and see the model outputs confidence level for each class in real time. As seen in this example, when we say 'Ok, Google', the confidence score for the 'Ok Google' class is 99%. So within a few minutes, we are able to custom train a sound recognition model that can recognize hot words 'Ok, Google' with very high accuracy. Note that, if the accuracy is not satisfactory, we can add more samples and retrain the model again.

5.1.4 Deployment

Once you are satisfied with the model performance, download the model and run it with TensorFlow.js in the browser. The code to load and execute the model is the same as the above two examples.

5.2 Cloud AutoML

Cloud AutoML[34] allows you to train production quality models for computer vision and more by automatically trying different models and hyperparameters to figure out the best combination that works well with your dataset. Compared to Teachable Machine, Cloud AutoML provides more customization and typically is suitable when working with larger amounts of training data (think Gigabytes or more) for more advanced usage.

---

[34] https://cloud.google.com/automl.

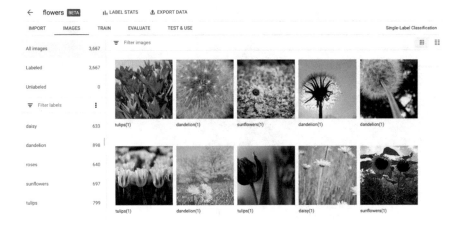

Fig. 4 Cloud AutoML example

5.2.1 Upload Images to Google Cloud Storage

First, you need to upload your training data to a cloud storage bucket that can be accessed by Cloud AutoML. In the example Fig. 4, we have uploaded several folders of flowers that we would like to recognize and train a model for

5.2.2 Specify Optimization

We can choose whether we would prefer the model training to optimize for higher accuracy or faster prediction time. Depending on the use case, you may have a preference for one over the other. Finally, set a budget to define the upper bounds of how long the exhaustive search is allowed to take and click on start training. See Fig. 5.

5.2.3 Export to TensorFlow.js

Once the model has finished training, we will be notified and we can log in and export the model to TensorFlow.js format. Then we can download the model.json and binary files required to run in the web browser; see Fig. 6

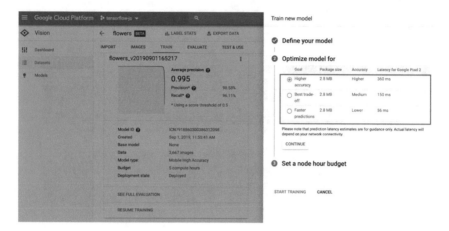

Fig. 5 Cloud AutoML example

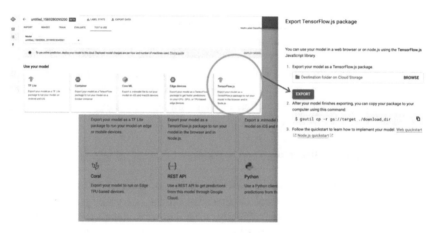

Fig. 6 Cloud AutoML example

5.2.4 Deployment

Similar to the previous examples, we use TensorFlow.js to deploy and run the model on the client side. For Google Cloud AutoML, it needs to load an additional library as shown below

HTML

```
<script src="//cdn.jsdelivr.net/npm/@tensorflow/tfjs/
dist/tf.min.js"></script>
<script src="//cdn.jsdelivr.net/npm/@tensorflow/tfjs-automl/
```

```
dist/tf-automl.min.js"></script>

<img id="daisy" crossorigin="anonymous" src="//path_to/daisy.jpg">

<script>
async function run() {
const model = await tf.automl.loadImageClassification('model.json');
const image = document.getElementById('daisy');
const predictions = await model.classify(image);
}
run();
</script>
```

6 Deployment Considerations

6.1 Model Optimization

The web allows us to reach a variety of devices: desktop, laptops, mobile phones, tablets, and even IoT devices like Raspberry Pi. Hardware support (CPU/GPU) has been improved dramatically for these devices in recent years, but resources such as memory, battery power, and network bandwidth need to be kept top of mind when deploying to such devices as they can vary from device to device and is not fixed. Therefore, there are several key aspects we need to consider when deploying models to the web.

Model size is an important performance factor, it is mainly affected by the number of nodes and the weights of a model. For example, a well-known image classification model—MobileNetV2—whose size is around 8MB.[35] Another example is Mobile-BERT, an NLP Model for question and answer finding from a piece of text, its size is around 95MB, and on average takes 10 s to download on a 4G network.[36]

Reducing model size will generally lead to better performance. One way of reducing model training parameters is to reduce layers or size of a layer, which usually leads to loss of accuracy, but it can work for applications that can tolerate accuracy loss. Another way is to quantize the model weights. By default, weights uses float32 as data type, which takes 32-bit to represent a number. If we use int16 to represent the number, then it will take 16-bit, half of the previous size. Converting from float32 to int16 or int8 can lead to 2–4 times size reduction. A caveat of quantization is that the precision loss will also result in slight model accuracy loss.

Besides reducing model size, there are also techniques to optimize the graph architecture for inference. For example, some of the graph architectures that are

---

[35] This model contains 3.47M parameters, which results in 300 million multiply-accumulate operations in every model execution.

[36] This model contains around 15.1M parameters.

useful in training but are unnecessary for inference can be pruned. We list some common optimization techniques here[37]:

- Constant Folding: Statically infers the value of tensors when possible by folding constant nodes in the graph and materializes the result using constants.
- Arithmetic: Eliminating common subexpressions and simplifying arithmetic statements.
- Op Fusing: Fuse subgraphs onto more efficient implementations by replacing commonly occurring subgraphs with optimized fused monolithic kernels.

6.2 Hardware Acceleration

TensorFlow.js provides options to use different acceleration techniques through its back ends: CPU, WebGL, WASM, and Node. Which backend to choose depends on the model size, target device capabilities, and speed requirements. For convolutional neural networks, WebGL generally provides better performance because it can use large amounts of GPU cores for parallel computing. On the other hand, WASM or CPU backends give more consistent performance for serialized models like recurrent neural networks.

There are several upcoming standards that can provide further performance boosts but are still in an early stage. For example, WebGPU[38] is a newer GPU API. It provides several key advantages over WebGL for using GPU as general purpose computation, such as faster local cache and better abstraction layer for manipulating data. In addition, WebML[39] is another W3C effort in bringing hardware acceleration for the Web. It is aiming to expose OS level ML API to the browser as a native browser offering.

6.3 Benchmarking

The model inference speed can vary by the type of device, its underlying hardware, the acceleration options, the model specific architecture, and even input size. As such there is no golden rule of when to choose what. We need to always benchmark a model to gauge its performance on a target device before deployment. TensorFlow.js provides a benchmarking tool[40] that allows users to benchmark their models against different back ends, acceleration options, and input sizes.

---

[37] https://www.tensorflow.org/guide/graph_optimization.

[38] https://gpuweb.github.io/gpuweb/.

[39] https://www.w3.org/groups/cg/webmachinelearning.

[40] https://tensorflow.github.io/tfjs/e2e/benchmarks/local-benchmark/index.html.

7 Discussion

In this chapter, we started a discussion of using Web ML tools for fast prototyping and research for non-ML experts, especially designers, web developers and HCI researchers. Throughout the chapter, we have demonstrated how Web ML tools can be used to quickly experiment with ML ideas in web applications.

7.1 Limitations

Admittedly, ML tools for the Web is only one way of supporting fast prototyping and research. Also, it still requires some level of programming skills, so it doesn't help designers without those skills, however, tools like Teachable Machine and Runway ML show that, in the future, there may be more tools aimed at designers allowing them to prototype in a way that is meaningful with limited technical knowledge of this domain. We briefly discuss the possible solutions for these other needs.

For mobile and IoT innovations, users can still use web tools like TensorFlow.js to deploy to those platforms. For mobile devices, TensorFlow.js can be deployed in mobile browsers, PWA apps, mini programs such as weChat, and native apps through WebView via frameworks like React Native. For IoT devices, TensorFlow.js can be deployed on Raspberry Pi through Node.

If the use case specifically requires a native app experience beyond what one can achieve with the above tooling, there are also several popular mobile ML libraries specifically for this purpose, such as TensorFlow Lite[41] and MNN.[42] To run models on IoT devices efficiently, the TensorFlow Lite for MicroController library[43] is specifically designed to be run on small, low-powered computing devices. There are high-level APIs for native development too, for example, TensorFlow Lite recently launched a Task Library,[44] which provides high- level APIs for vision and natural language processing.

For designers and HCI researchers, who need to design or study ML ideas in early stages, such as in low fidelity prototypes, we are not aware of any mainstream tools for this type of work. Dove et al. [7] conducted an in-depth study on challenges for designers working with ML and they found that prototyping with ML was difficult for designers because current prototyping tools can't support them. The unique challenges lie in that, (1) ML system has high degree of uncertainty, so is hard to prototype without the actual model and the data; (2) It is hard to prototype unexpected system behavior such as false positive and false negative; (3)Technical complexity of using ML system for designers are too high. While we need to consider new tools to overcome the above challenges, we have also shown the potential to adapt current

---

[41] https://www.tensorflow.org/lite.

[42] https://github.com/alibaba/MNN.

[43] https://www.tensorflow.org/lite/microcontrollers.

[44] https://www.tensorflow.org/lite/inference_with_metadata/task_library/overview.

available ML web tools for fast prototyping in some areas. The Teachable Machine and Cloud AutoML vision examples require no coding at all to train a new model for common detection tasks. High- level APIs exist to be directly used in HTML pages for common tasks, such as hand, face, pose detection, body segmentation, and more. A lot of interactions can be easily built with these available tools. This can be a starting point for designers to take the lead to innovate new design concepts with ML.

7.2   Advantages of Web-Based Machine Learning

We have proposed to use ML tools for the web as a way for fast prototyping and research. Throughout the chapter, we have demonstrated with examples and practical guides how to use those tools for prototyping. We summarize key points on why we think web ML tools are a suitable set for fast prototyping and research.

7.2.1   Privacy

We can both train and classify data on the client machine without ever sending data to a 3rd party web server. There may be times where this may be a requirement to comply with local laws and policies or when processing any data that the user may want to keep on their machine and not sent to a 3rd party, for example, in a medical application.

7.2.2   Speed

As we are not having to send data to a remote server, running the model can be faster as there is no round trip time from client to server and back to the client again. Even better, we have direct access to the device's sensors such as the camera, microphone, GPS, accelerometer, and more should the user grant us access opening up many opportunities for real-time applications.

7.2.3   Reach and Scale

With one click, anyone in the world can click a link we send them, open the web page in their browser, and utilize what we have made - a zero install frictionless experience. No need for a complex server side Linux setup with CUDA drivers and much more just to use the machine learning system. Anyone in the world can try our model with ease, no matter what their background is.

7.2.4 Cost

No servers means the only thing we need to pay for is a cloud storage to host the HTML, CSS, JavaScript, and model files. The cost of cloud storage is much cheaper than keeping a server (potentially with a graphics card attached) running 24/7.

7.2.5 Ecosystem

JavaScript is a popular language in college education, and is used by over 69.7% of professional developers [32]. The language itself has been developed for several decades already. As such the JS ecosystem is battlehardended for production environments and enables rapid prototyping via the numerous mature libraries available to JavaScript developers, for example, in 2D/3D graphics, data visualization, and much more with emerging web standards for virtual/augmented reality and beyond.

7.3 Challenges for Web-Based ML and Future Work

Machine Learning for the web is new. While this presents a great opportunity for those helping to shape its future, there are also a few challenges due to its young age. A few points to consider are as follows.

7.3.1 WebML Ecosystem

Supporting libraries may not yet be available in the JavaScript ecosystem that are common in Python, for example NumPy. However, this is changing fast, such as Danfo.js[45] that replicates Pandas. So with time, we will gain parity here as more JavaScript developers adopt ML into their workflows and find the need to recreate some of these popular tools and libraries to increase efficiency of using ML in their applications.

7.3.2 Educational Resources

Educational resources are also not as mature as Python equivalents. Once again this is changing fast although early adopters may need to spend some time to find the educational materials. We are already seeing a number of great books and courses come out for TensorFlow.js. A few are listed here for further reading:

---

[45] https://danfo.jsdata.org/.

- Learning TensorFlow.js (O'Reilly)[46]
- Deep Learning with JavaScript (Manning)[47]
- Practical TensorFlow.js (Apress)[48]
- Practical ML in JS (Apres)[49]
- Browser-based models with TensorFlow.js (Coursera)[50]
- Building ML Solutions with TensorFlow.js (PluralSight)[51]

7.3.3 Feature Parity

Supported ML ops in JavaScript are currently a subset of what is available in Python. Again, this will get better with time. Currently, TensorFlow.js supports the most common ones (about 240 at time of writing), meaning many models will convert without issue, and more are being added constantly.

7.3.4 Model Discovery and Sharing

Searching for ML models suitable for web applications can be hard, especially for non-ML experts. There are a number of starting points to find new models produced by the TensorFlow.js team and the community:

- tfjs-models[52]: Task-oriented APIs with premade models for many common use cases.
- TF Hub[53]: A site that hosts many open sourced models and allow model discovery through browsing, searching, and filtering.

8   Conclusion

ML tooling for web engineering provides opportunities for non-ML experts, e.g., software engineers, web developers, designers, and HCI researchers, to quickly prototype and research new ML-powered ideas. In this chapter, we reviewed the history of web-based ML tooling, presented examples and practical guides, showing how to use those tools for fast prototyping. We also presented limitations to consider. While

---

[46] https://www.oreilly.com/library/view/learning-tensorflowjs/9781492090786/.

[47] https://www.manning.com/books/deep-learning-with-javascript.

[48] https://www.apress.com/gp/book/9781484262726.

[49] https://www.apress.com/gp/book/9781484264171.

[50] https://www.coursera.org/learn/browser-based-models-tensorflow.

[51] https://www.pluralsight.com/courses/building-machine-learning-solutions-tensorflow-js-tfjs.

[52] https://github.com/tensorflow/tfjs-models.

[53] https://tfhub.dev/.

ML on Web is a new frontier for many right now, it can open great opportunities to deploy at scale both for production and HCI research. Now it is a great time to take your first step and join the fast growing Web ML community for your projects, applications, or ideas too.

Acknowledgements We would like to thank Sandeep Gupta and Daniel Smilkov for their contributions and valuable feedback.

References

1. Ashktorab Z, Jain M, Vera Liao Q, Weisz JD (2019) Resilient chatbots: repair strategy preferences for conversational breakdowns. In: Proceedings of the 2019 CHI conference on human factors in computing systems (CHI '19). Association for Computing Machinery, New York, NY, USA, Article Paper 254, 12 pp. ISBN 9781450359702. https://doi.org/10.1145/3290605.3300484
2. Bisong E (2019) Google AutoML: cloud vision. In: Building machine learning and deep learning models on google cloud platform. Apress, Berkeley, CA, pp 581–598
3. Bosch N, D'Mello S, Baker R, Ocumpaugh J, Shute V, Ventura M, Wang L, Zhao W (2015) Automatic detection of learning-centered affective states in the wild. In: Proceedings of the 20th international conference on intelligent user interfaces (IUI '15). Association for Computing Machinery, New York, NY, USA, pp 379–388. ISBN 9781450333061. https://doi.org/10.1145/2678025.2701397
4. Cai CJ, Guo PJ (2019) Software developers learning machine learning: motivations, hurdles, and desires. In: 2019 IEEE symposium on visual languages and human-centric computing (VL/HCC), pp 25–34. https://doi.org/10.1109/VLHCC.2019.8818751
5. Carney M, Webster B, Alvarado I, Phillips K, Howell N, Griffith J, Jongejan J, Pitaru A, Chen A (2020) Teachable machine: approachable web-based tool for exploring machine learning classification. In: Extended abstracts of the 2020 CHI conference on human factors in computing systems (CHI EA '20). Association for Computing Machinery, New York, NY, USA, pp 1–8. ISBN 9781450368193. https://doi.org/10.1145/3334480.3382839
6. David R, Duke J, Jain A, Janapa Reddi V, Jeffries N, Li J, Kreeger N, Nappier I, Natraj M, Regev S, Rhodes R, Wang T, Warden P (2021) TensorFlow lite micro: embedded machine learning on TinyML systems
7. Dove G, Halskov K, Forlizzi J, Zimmerman J (2017) UX design innovation: challenges for working with machine learning as a design material. In: Proceedings of the 2017 CHI conference on human factors in computing systems (CHI '17). Association for Computing Machinery, New York, NY, USA, pp 278–288. ISBN 9781450346559. https://doi.org/10.1145/3025453.3025739
8. Feurer M, Klein A, Eggensperger K, Springenberg J, Blum M, Hutter F (2015) Efficient and robust automated machine learning. In: Cortes C, Lawrence N, Lee D, Sugiyama M, Garnett R (eds) Advances in neural information processing systems, vol. 28. Curran Associates, Inc. https://proceedings.neurips.cc/paper/2015/file/11d0e6287202fced83f79975ec59a3a6-Paper.pdf
9. Hall M, Frank E, Holmes G, Pfahringer B, Reutemann P, Witten IH (2009) The WEKA data mining software: an update. 11, 1. ISSN1931-0145. https://doi.org/10.1145/1656274.1656278
10. Hinton G, Vinyals O, Dean J (2015) Distilling the knowledge in a neural network
11. Howard AG, Zhu M, Chen B, Kalenichenko D, Wang W, Weyand T, Andreetto M, Adam H (2017) MobileNets: efficient convolutional neural networks for mobile vision applications
12. Inkpen K, Chancellor S, De Choudhury M, Veale M, Baumer EPS (2019) Where is the human? Bridging the gap between AI and HCI (CHI EA '19). Association for Computing Machin-

ery, New York, NY, USA, pp 1–9. ISBN 9781450359719. https://doi.org/10.1145/3290607.
3299002

13. Jacob B, Kligys S, Chen B, Zhu M, Tang M, Howard A, Adam H, Kalenichenko D (2017)
    Quantization and training of neural networks for efficient integer-arithmetic-only inference

14. Jiang X, Wang H, Chen Y, Wu Z, Wang L, Zou B, Yang Y, Cui Z, Cai Y, Yu T, Lv C, Wu Z
    (2020) MNN: a universal and efficient inference engine

15. Jun J, Jung M, Kim S-Y, (Kenny) Kim K (2018) Full-body ownership illusion can change our
    emotion. In: Proceedings of the 2018 CHI conference on human factors in computing systems
    (CHI '18). Association for Computing Machinery, New York, NY, USA, Article Paper 601, 11
    pp ISBN 9781450356206. https://doi.org/10.1145/3173574.3174175

16. Kotthoff L, Thornton C, Hoos HH, Hutter F, Kevin L-B (2019) Auto-WEKA: automatic model
    selection and hyperparameter optimization in WEKA. Automated machine learning. Springer,
    Cham, pp 81–95

17. Lee MK, Grgić-Hlača N, Carl Tschantz M, Binns R, Weller A, Carney M, Inkpen K (2020)
    Human-centered approaches to fair and responsible AI. In: Extended abstracts of the 2020 CHI
    conference on human factors in computing systems (CHI EA '20). Association for Computing
    Machinery, New York, NY, USA, pp 1–8. ISBN 9781450368193. https://doi.org/10.1145/
    3334480.3375158

18. Li Y (2010) Protractor: a fast and accurate gesture recognizer. In: Proceedings of the SIGCHI
    conference on human factors in computing systems (CHI '10). Association for Computing
    Machinery, New York, NY, USA, pp 2169–2172. ISBN 9781605589299. https://doi.org/10.
    1145/1753326.1753654

19. Li Y, Kumar R, Lasecki WS, Hilliges O (2020) Artificial intelligence for HCI: a modern
    approach. In: Extended abstracts of the 2020 CHI conference on human factors in computing
    systems (CHI EA '20). Association for Computing Machinery, New York, NY, USA, pp 1–8.
    ISBN 9781450368193. https://doi.org/10.1145/3334480.3375147

20. Ma Y, Xiang D, Zheng S, Tian D, Liu X (2019) Moving deep learning into web browser: how
    far can we go?

21. Maynes-Aminzade D, Winograd T, Igarashi T (2007) Eyepatch: prototyping camera-based
    interaction through examples. In: Proceedings of the 20th annual ACM symposium on user
    interface software and technology (UIST '07). Association for Computing Machinery, New
    York, NY, USA, pp 33–42. ISBN 9781595936790. https://doi.org/10.1145/1294211.1294219

22. Munteanu C, Jones M, Oviatt S, Brewster S, Penn G, Whittaker S, Rajput N, Nanavati A
    (2013) We need to talk: HCI and the delicate topic of spoken language interaction. In: CHI
    '13 extended abstracts on human factors in computing systems (CHI EA '13). Association for
    Computing Machinery, New York, NY, USA, pp 2459–2464. ISBN 9781450319522. https://
    doi.org/10.1145/2468356.2468803

23. Myers BA, Ko AJ, Burnett MM (2006) Invited research overview: end-user programming. In:
    CHI '06 extended abstracts on human factors in computing systems (CHI EA '06). Association
    for Computing Machinery, New York, NY, USA, pp 75–80. ISBN 1595932984. https://doi.org/
    10.1145/1125451.1125472

24. Patel K, Bancroft N, Drucker SM, Fogarty J, Ko AJ, Landay J (2010) Gestalt: integrated support
    for implementation and analysis in machine learning. In: Proceedings of the 23nd annual ACM
    symposium on user interface software and technology (UIST '10). Association for Computing
    Machinery, New York, NY, USA, pp 37–46. ISBN 9781450302715. https://doi.org/10.1145/
    1866029.1866038

25. Patel K, Fogarty J, Landay JA, Harrison B (2008) Examining difficulties software developers
    encounter in the adoption of statistical machine learning. In: Proceedings of the 23rd national
    conference on artificial intelligence - volume 3 (AAAI'08). AAAI Press, pp 1563–1566. ISBN
    9781577353683

26. Pece F, Steptoe W, Wanner F, Julier S, Weyrich T, Kautz J, Steed A (2013) Panoinserts:
    mobile spatial teleconferencing. In: Proceedings of the SIGCHI conference on human factors
    in computing systems (CHI '13). Association for Computing Machinery, New York, NY, USA,
    pp 1319–1328. ISBN 9781450318990. https://doi.org/10.1145/2470654.2466173

27. Rick SR, Bhaskaran S, Sun Y, McEwen S, Weibel N (2019) NeuroPose: geriatric rehabilitation in the home using a webcam and pose estimation. In: Proceedings of the 24th international conference on intelligent user interfaces: companion (IUI '19). Association for Computing Machinery, New York, NY, USA, pp 105–106. ISBN 9781450366731. https://doi.org/10.1145/3308557.3308682

28. Rubin Z, Kurniawan S, Gotfrid T, Pugliese A (2016) Motivating individuals with spastic cerebral palsy to speak using mobile speech recognition. In: Proceedings of the 18th international ACM SIGACCESS conference on computers and accessibility (ASSETS '16). Association for Computing Machinery, New York, NY, USA, pp 325–326. ISBN 9781450341240. https://doi.org/10.1145/2982142.2982203

29. Sewell W, Komogortsev O (2010) Real-time eye gaze tracking with an unmodified commodity webcam employing a neural network. In: CHI '10 extended abstracts on human factors in computing systems (CHI EA '10). Association for Computing Machinery, New York, NY, USA, pp 3739–3744. ISBN 9781605589305. https://doi.org/10.1145/1753846.1754048

30. Smilkov D, Thorat N, Assogba Y, Yuan A, Kreeger N, Yu P, Zhang K, Cai S, Nielsen E, Soergel D et al (2019) Tensorflow. js: machine learning for the web and beyond. arXiv:1901.05350

31. Song Y, Demirdjian D, Davis R (2012) Continuous body and hand gesture recognition for natural human-computer interaction. *ACM Trans Interact Intell Syst* 2, 1, Article 5, 28 pp. ISSN2160-6455. https://doi.org/10.1145/2133366.2133371

32. Stackoverflow (2020) 2020 StackOverflow developer survey. https://insights.stackoverflow.com/survey/2020#technology-programming-scripting-and-markup-languages-professional-developers

33. Thieme A, Belgrave D, Doherty G (2020) Machine learning in mental health: a systematic review of the HCI literature to support the development of effective and implementable ML systems. ACM Trans Comput-Hum Interact 27, 5, Article 34, 53 pp. ISSN1073-0516. https://doi.org/10.1145/3398069

34. Wang R, Paris S, Popoviundefined J (2011) 6D hands: markerless hand-tracking for computer aided design. In: Proceedings of the 24th annual ACM symposium on user interface software and technology (UIST '11). Association for Computing Machinery, New York, NY, USA, pp 549–558. ISBN 9781450307161. https://doi.org/10.1145/2047196.2047269

35. Xu A, Liu Z, Guo Y, Sinha V, Akkiraju R (2017) A new chatbot for customer service on social media. In: Proceedings of the 2017 CHI conference on human factors in computing systems (CHI '17). Association for Computing Machinery, New York, NY, USA, pp 3506–3510. ISBN 9781450346559. https://doi.org/10.1145/3025453.3025496

36. Yamashita N, Ishida T (2006) Effects of machine translation on collaborative work. In: Proceedings of the 2006 20th anniversary conference on computer supported cooperative work (CSCW '06). Association for Computing Machinery, New York, NY, USA, pp 515–524. ISBN 1595932496. https://doi.org/10.1145/1180875.1180955

37. Yang Q, Suh J, Chen N-C, Ramos G (2018) Grounding interactive machine learning tool design in how non-experts actually build models. In: Proceedings of the 2018 designing interactive systems conference (DIS '18). Association for Computing Machinery, New York, NY, USA, pp 573–584. ISBN 9781450351980. https://doi.org/10.1145/3196709.3196729

38. Yuan A, Li Y (2020) Modeling human visual search performance on realistic webpages using analytical and deep learning methods. In: Proceedings of the 2020 CHI conference on human factors in computing systems (CHI '20). Association for Computing Machinery, New York, NY, USA, pp 1–12. ISBN 9781450367080. https://doi.org/10.1145/3313831.3376870

Interactive Reinforcement Learning for Autonomous Behavior Design

Christian Arzate Cruz and Takeo Igarashi

Abstract Reinforcement Learning (RL) is a machine learning approach based on how humans and animals learn new behaviors by actively exploring their environment that provides them positive and negative rewards. The interactive RL approach incorporates a human-in-the-loop that can guide a learning RL-based agent to personalize its behavior and/or speed up its learning process. To enable HCI researchers to make advances in this area, we introduce an interactive RL framework that outlines HCI challenges in the domain. By following this taxonomy, HCI researchers can (1) design new interaction techniques and (2) propose new applications. To help the role (1) researchers, we describe how different types of human feedback can adapt an RL model to perform as the users intend. We help researchers perform the role (2) by proposing generic design principles to create effective RL applications. Finally, we list current open challenges in interactive RL and what we consider the most promising research directions in this research area.

1 Introduction

The **reinforcement learning** (RL) paradigm is based on the idea of an agent that learns by interacting with its environment [40, 96]. The learning process is achieved by an exchange of signals between the agent and its environment; the agent can perform actions that affect the environment, while the environment informs the agent about the effects of its actions. Additionally, it is assumed that the agent has at least one goal to pursue and—by observing how its interactions affect its dynamic environment—it learns how to behave to achieve its goal. However, standard RL methods that learn models automatically are inconvenient for applications that could have a great impact on our everyday life, such as autonomous companion robots or medical applications. Generally speaking, to enable the use of RL in these types of environments, we need to overcome the next shortcomings: how to correctly specify

C. Arzate Cruz (✉) · T. Igarashi
The University of Tokyo, Tokyo, Japan
e-mail: takeo@acm.org

© The Author(s), under exclusive license to Springer Nature Switzerland AG 2021
Y. Li and O. Hilliges (eds.), *Artificial Intelligence for Human Computer Interaction: A Modern Approach*, Human–Computer Interaction Series,
https://doi.org/10.1007/978-3-030-82681-9_11

the problem, speed up the learning procedure, and personalize the model to the particular user preferences. One way to tackle these problems is through the use of interactive RL.

The interactive RL approach adds a human-in-the-loop that can adapt the underlying learning agent to facilitate its learning or make it solve a problem in a particular manner. In this chapter, we introduce the interactive RL framework and how HCI researchers can use it. In particular, we help researchers to play two main roles: (1) designing new interaction techniques and (2) proposing new applications.

To help researchers perform the role (1), in Sect. 2.1 we describe how different types of feedback can leverage an RL model for different purposes. Additionally, in Sect. 4 we provide an analysis of recent research in interactive RL to give the audience an overview of the state of the art. Then, in Sect. 5 we help researchers perform the role (2) by proposing generic design principles that will provide a guide to effectively implement interactive RL applications. Finally, in Sect. 6 we present what we consider the most promising research directions in interactive RL.

This chapter is an extension of our survey paper in [11], with changes to give it a more educational form, additional sections that give a broader view of RL and its interactive counterpart, and the inclusion of new papers in our analysis of recent research in interactive RL.

1.1 Reinforcement Learning Basics

One of the main advantages of the RL paradigm is that it let us define problems by assigning numeric rewards to certain situations in the environment. For instance, if our agent is learning how to drive a car, we need to specify (with a numeric reward) that crossing red lights is bad while advancing when the light is green is a positive behavior. It can be difficult to frame real-world problems using RL (like designing the rewards for an autonomous car), but once we have a good representation of the problem, we can create effective behaviors even for previously unseen situations. That is, RL designers don't need to manually code a behavior for every single situation the agent might face.

Some of the most complex applications where RL-based agents have been successful are playing most Atari games better than humans [72], defeating the world champion in Go [92], playing Dota 2 better than professional players [80], a human-like robot hand that manipulates physical objects [78], and automatically cooling a real-world data center [53]. These success stories have shown that RL-based applications can achieve high performance in real-world applications where historically, other (classic) machine learning techniques had been better.

The most common approach to model RL agents is the **Markov decision process** (MDP) formalism. An MDP is an optimization model for an agent acting in a stochastic environment [83], which is defined by the tuple $\langle S, A, T, R, \gamma \rangle$, where

- S is a set of states.

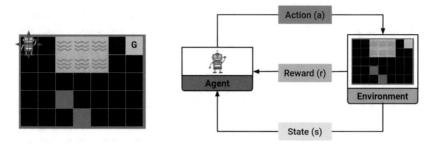

Fig. 1 A reinforcement learning example

- A is a set of actions.
- $T: S \times A \times S \rightarrow [0, 1]$ is the **transition function** that assigns the probability of reaching state s' when executing action a in state s, that is, $T(s' \mid s, a) = P(s' \mid a, s)$, and it follows the **Markov property** which implies that the future states of this process depend only upon the current state s.
- $R: S \times A \rightarrow \mathbb{R}$ is the **reward function**, with $R(s, a)$ denoting the immediate numeric reward value obtained when the agent performs action a in state s.
- $\gamma \in [0, 1]$ is the discount factor that defines the preference of the agent to seek immediate or more distant rewards.

The reward function defines the goals of the agent in the environment, while the transition function captures the effect of the agent's actions for each particular state. Although in many RL problems, it is assumed that the agent has access to a reward and transition function, for real-world problems the reward function is usually designed by an expert on the task at hand, and the transition function is learned by the agent exploring its environment.

We present an example of a problem defined by the reinforcement learning framework in Fig. 1. In this problem, the agent (triangle) starts in the top-left corner and must reach the goal G in the top-right corner by taking an action $a \in A$ in each state s that it encounters. The agent receives from the environment an immediate reward $r \in R$ and a state update after it executes an action. In our example, the agent receives a positive reward if it gets closer to the goal G, and a negative reward if it steps into lava. Therefore, the agent's objective is to find the optimal policy $\pi*$ that defines the best strategy to follow in each state s in the environment. The policy $\pi*$ is a function that characterizes the expected cumulative reward for selecting a given action in a particular state.

To compute a policy π, we can use different types of algorithms, such as dynamic programming, evolutionary algorithms (neuroevolution), Monte Carlo methods (e.g., MCTS), and other methods or combinations. For example, one of the limitations of dynamic programming is handling large action-state representations in a tabular form.

One way to overcome this obstacle is implementing a function approximation (e.g., using a deep neural network) to compact the action-state into a more manageable representation.

1.2 Why Use Interactive Reinforcement Learning?

In contrast to a typical RL setting, an interactive RL approach involves a human-in-the-loop that tailors specific elements of the underlying RL algorithm to improve its performance or produce a policy to solve a problem in a particular manner. As we show in Fig. 2, the foundation of an interactive RL approach is an RL-based agent that learns by interacting with its environment and a human user who evaluates and provides feedback to a (learning) agent.

One of the advantages of using the interactive RL framework is that we can model and solve problems in an unsupervised manner by using a reward function that captures the desired agent's behavior. We can have the reward signal from either the environment, human feedback, or a combination of both. For instance, the environment's reward signal could give feedback to the agent about its performance, while users can give a reward signal based on objective measures, or subjective preferences. An objective measure can be how good (or bad) an action is to help the agent get closer to the goal. On the other hand, we can also code as a reward signal more abstract and subjective user preferences (e.g., make the agent play a game with a particular play style).

Another way to take advantage of the interactive RL paradigm is by integrating previous experience in an offline manner. That is, we can use the previous experience of other agents to build a model offline (i.e., before the agent starts to explore the environment). Furthermore, we can refine this model in an online manner (at runtime) or combine it with the user's feedback.

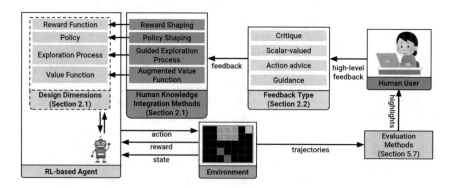

Fig. 2 The interactive reinforcement learning architecture

Regarding the performance of the RL models, it's been proven that integrating expert knowledge improves the accuracy of the models [31, 45]. Moreover, human feedback includes prior knowledge about the world that can significantly improve learning rates [27].

In short, the interactive RL approach provides HCI researchers with multiple options to personalize and/or improve the performance of agents by integrating knowledge about a task from different sources (other agents or human users), interpreting high-level feedback (e.g., voice, sketches, text, and eye gaze), and understanding high-level goals (e.g., a personal preference over particular actions). For instance, an interactive RL method can take as input voice commands or facial expressions to teach a robot how to navigate [9], or use play traces of the user as input to personalize the play style of a bot that plays Mario Bros [12]. Another possibility is focusing on improving the performance of training dialogue agents using as input crowd-sourced dialogue rewrites [91]. The (human) feedback for interactive RL methods comes in varied forms, and we can use it to tailor different aspects of the agent's behavior.

Finally, we can find a broad type of applications that use the interactive RL framework, such as teaching robots how to dance [69], creating adaptable task-oriented dialogue systems [90], learning the generation of dialogue [60], and an intelligent tutor that suggests courses to students so that their skills match the necessities of the industry [108]. Furthermore, there is the opportunity to adapt current automatic RL applications to an interactive setting, such as procedural content generation for video games [43], generating music [38], and modeling social influences in bots [39].

1.3   Interactive Reinforcement Learning Testbeds

In Fig. 3, we present examples of the most common testbeds in interactive RL research. The Gridworld platform (Fig. 3a) is a classic environment for testing RL algorithms. The small state-space size of this testbed allows for fast experiments, and its simplicity does not demand specialized knowledge from the users. Also, it's easy to develop oracles that simulate human feedback. These characteristics make Gridworld popular among researchers in the HCI field [50–52].

We can also find video games as testbeds such as the Mario AI benchmark (Fig. 3b) [42] and Pac-Man (Fig. 3c). Video games in general are complex testbeds because their action-state size is usually vast. This complexity makes games a good testbed for methods aimed at creating fast evaluation cycles. Furthermore, computer games offer arguably the richest HCI interaction in terms of the available options a player has at any given time [115]. The available expressiveness for players makes video games the perfect testbed for evaluating interactive RL algorithms to design bots with varied play styles. Another advantage of using games as testbeds is that they elicit a strong player experience and player emotional manifestations. Therefore, the study of human-game interaction can contribute to both a better understanding of human behavior and a better design of HCI experiences.

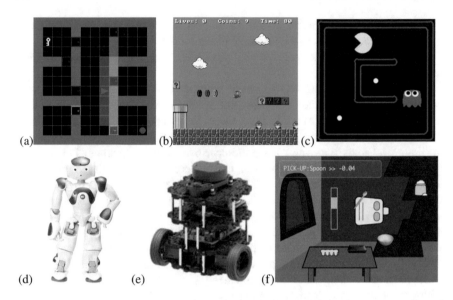

Fig. 3 Selected testbeds for interactive RL. **a** Gridworld. **b** Mario AI benchmark. **c** Pac-Man. **d** Nao Robot. **e** TurtleBot. **f** Sophie's Kitchen

The Nao robot (Fig. 3d) and the TurtleBot (Fig. 3e) are popular platforms in robotics that are perfect for testing natural ways to interact with human users. The main disadvantage of using robots as a testbed is that usually, RL algorithms require long periods of learning to achieve good results, which can be prohibitive in physical platforms such as robots. On the other hand, Sophie's kitchen (Fig. 3f) is designed as an online tool for interactive RL that explores the impact of demonstrating uncertainty to the users [103]. Finally, the main focus of the OpenAI Gym platform [16] is designing and comparing RL algorithms.

2 Design Guides for Interactive Reinforcement Learning

Choosing the right way for users to communicate their needs and preferences to a computer is key to achieve an effective human-computer interaction. The high-level input modalities for HCI extend from a keyboard, eye gaze, and sketches to natural language. We can use any of these high-level input modalities for interactive RL applications if we code their output with a format that an RL algorithm can use. In this section, we provide HCI researchers with the foundations to adapt the output of high-level input modalities to data that can tailor an RL algorithm (see Fig. 2). This knowledge is essential to design novel interaction techniques for interactive RL.

2.1 Design Dimensions

In this section, we analyze how human feedback is used to tailor the low-level modules of diverse RL algorithms; we call this form of interaction between users and RL algorithms **design dimensions**. Furthermore, the summary of selected works in Table 1 presents a concise and precise classification that helps to compare different design dimensions. For this summary, we focus on works that have been successfully applied to RL methods that use a human-in-the-loop. We further narrow the reach of this survey by considering only works published between 2010 and 2020.

2.1.1 Reward Function

All works classified in this design dimension tailor the reward function of the RL-based algorithm using human feedback. The main objectives of this feedback are to speed up learning, customize the behavior of the agent to fit the user's intentions, or teach the agent new skills or behaviors.

Designing a reward function by hand is trivial for simple problems where it is enough to assign rewards as 1 for winning and 0 otherwise. For example, in the simplest setup of a Gridworld environment, the agent receives -1 for each time-step and 1 if it reaches the goal state. However, for most problems that an agent can face in a real-world environment (e.g., with multiple and contradictory goals), encoding the desired behaviors in a reward function can be challenging.

The reward design problem is therefore complex because the RL designer has to define the agent's behaviors as goals that are explicitly represented as rewards. This approach can cause difficulties in complex applications where the designer has to foresee every obstacle the agent could possibly encounter. Furthermore, an effective reward function has to handle well trade-offs between goals. These reward design challenges make the process an iterative task: RL designers alternate between evaluating the reward function and optimizing it until they find it acceptable. This alternating process is called **reward shaping** [79].

Reward shaping (RS) is a popular method of guiding RL algorithms by human feedback [79, 111]. In what is arguably the most common version of RS, the user adds extra rewards that enhance the environmental reward function [9, 45, 102] as $R' = R + F$, where $F : S \times A \times S \to \mathbb{R}$ is the **shaping reward function** [79]. A hand-engineered reward function has been demonstrated to increase learning rates [7, 9, 26, 28–30, 32, 49, 59, 68, 79, 86, 102, 109]. A similar approach consists of only using human feedback as a reward signal for the agent [10, 46, 110].

Using RS is also beneficial in sparse reward environments: the user can provide the agent with useful information in states where there are no reward signals from the environment or in highly stochastic environments [111]. Another advantage of RS is that it gives researchers a tool with which to better specify, in a granular manner, the goals in the current environment. That is, the computational problem is specified via a reward function [95].

Table 1 Selected works for each design dimension. DD = design dimension, HKI = human knowledge integration, RS = reward shaping, PS = policy shaping, AcAd = action advice, VF = value function, SV = Scalar-valued, HeuFun = heuristic function, Dem = demonstration, Cri = critique, GUI = grafical user interface, FE = facial expression, VC = voice command, GC = game controller, AT = artifact, CT = controller, HF = human feedback, ER = environmental reward, GEP = guided exploration process, PBRS = potential-based reward shaping, ACTG = actions containing the target goal, Mario = Super Mario Bros

DD	Testbed	Interaction	Initiative	HKI	Feedback
Reward function	Robot in maze-like environment [9]	FE	Passive	RS using HF + ER	Cri
	Navigation simulation [10]	GUI	Passive	Advantage Function	Cri
	Sophie's Kitchen game [103, 105]	GUI	Passive, Active	RS using HF + EF	Cri
	Bowling game [110]	GUI	Passive	RS + HF	SV
	Shopping assistant, Gridworld [71]	GUI	Active	Active IRD	Queries
	Mario, Gridworld, Soccer simulation [86]	Coding	Passive	PBRS	HeuFun
	Navigation simulation [102]	VC	Passive	RS using HF + ER	
	Atari, robotics simulation [19]	GUI	Active	RS using HF	Queries
Policy	Gridworld, TurtleBot robot [66]	GUI, GC	Passive	PS	AcAd
	Gridworld [51]	VC	Passive	PS	Cri, AcAd
	Pac-Man, Frogger [32]	GUI	Passive	PS	Cri
	Mario [12]	GUI	Active	PS	Dem, Cri
Exploration process	Pac-Man, Cart-Pole simulation [116]	GUI	Passive	GEP	
	Simulated cleaning Robot [22, 23]	VC	Passive	GEP	AcAd
	Pac-Man [7]	GUI	Active	GEP	AcAd
	Pac-Man [30]	GUI	Active	Myopic Agent	AcAd
	Sophie's Kitchen game [103]	GUI	Active	ACTG	Guidence
	Street Fighter game [13]	Not apply	Passive	EB using Safe RL	Dem
	Nao Robot [94]	GUI	Passive	ACTG	Guidence
	Nexi robot [46]	AT + CT	Passive	Myopic Agent	AcAd
Value function	Mountain Car simulation [44]	GUI	Passive	Weighted VF	Dem
	Keepaway simulation [101]	GUI	Passive	Weighted VF	Dem
	Mario, Cart Pole [17]	Not apply	Passive	Initialization of VF	Dem

On the other hand, we need to consider the **credit assignment problem** [3, 97]. This difficulty emerges from the fact that when a human provides feedback, it is applied to actions that happened sometime in the past—there is always a delay between the action's occurrence and the human response. Furthermore, the human's feedback might refer to one specific state or an entire sequence of states the bot visited.

Reward hacking is another negative side effect resulting from a deficient reward design [8, 35, 47, 87]. This side effect can cause non-optimal behaviors that fail to achieve the goals or intentions of the designers. Usually, these kinds of failure behaviors arise from reward functions that do not anticipate all trade-offs between goals. For example, in [20] the authors present an agent that drives a boat in a race but instead of moving forward to reach the goal, the agent learned that the policy with the highest reward was to hit special targets along the track.

2.1.2 Policy

In the policy design dimension, we include interactive RL methods that augment the policy of an agent using human knowledge. This process is called **policy shaping** (PS) [33].

The PS approach consists of formulating human feedback as action advice that directly updates the agent's behavior. The user can interact with the RL algorithm using an action advice type of human feedback. For this design dimension, we need access to the (partial) policy of an (expert) user in the task the agent is learning to perform. Then, we use this feedback to directly update the policy of the agent at the corresponding states. In the RL example we present in Fig. 1, we could use a PS approach to show the agent the best strategy to avoid stepping on lava in a particular maze.

One advantage of the PS approach is that it does not rely on the representation of the problem using a reward function. In real-life scenarios with many conflicting objectives, the PS approach might make it easier for the agent to indicate if its policy is correct, rather than trying to explain it through a reward-shaping method. Nevertheless, the user should know a near-optimal policy to improve the agent's learning process. Even though the effect of the feedback's quality has been investigated in interactive RL [30], more research on this topic is needed to better understand which design dimension is least sensitive to the quality of feedback.

It's worth mentioning that some authors consider approaches that use a binary critique on the actions as PS [33]. In general, these methods prune the actions labeled as "bad" from the action set at the corresponding action-state. This pruning process creates a bias in the action selection of the agent, not its policy. Consequently, we categorize this method as a guided exploration process.

2.1.3 Exploration Process

RL is an ML paradigm based on learning by interaction [98]. To learn a given task, the agent aims to maximize the accumulated reward signal from the environment. This is achieved by performing the actions that have been effective in the past—a learning step called **exploitation**. However, to discover the best actions to achieve its goal, the agent needs to perform actions that have not been previously tried—a learning step called **exploration**. To learn an effective policy, the agent has to compromise between exploration and exploitation.

The **guided exploration process** aims to minimize the learning procedure by injecting human knowledge that guides the agent's exploration process to states with a high reward [7, 13, 22, 116]. This method biases the exploration process such that the agent avoids trying actions that do not correspond to an optimal policy. This design dimension also assumes that the user understands the task well enough to identify at least one near-optimal policy. Despite this assumption, there is empirical evidence indicating that using human feedback (i.e., guidance) to direct the exploration process is the most natural and sample-efficient interactive RL approach [94].

For example, in [94, 103], users direct the agent's attention by pointing out an object on the screen. Exploration is driven by performing actions that lead the agent to the suggested object. This interaction procedure thus requires access to a model of the environment, so the agent can determine what actions to perform to get to the suggested object.

Another popular approach to guiding the exploration process consists of creating myopic agents. This kind of shortsighted agent constructs its policy by choosing at every time-step to perform the action that maximizes the immediate reward, according to the action suggested by the user; that is, the action's long-term effects are not considered. Although this guiding approach creates agents that tend to overfit, it has been successfully used in different applications [7, 30, 46, 48].

2.1.4 Value Function

In general, the idea behind the value function design dimension is creating **augmented value functions**. We can perform this augmentation by combining two or more value functions. To integrate expert knowledge, at least one of those value functions must come from the expert's feedback (i.e., a value function that describes the expert's optimal behavior).

Using the value function design dimension is an effective strategy to personalize and accelerate the learning process of agents [17, 48, 101]. However, there are too few studies on this design dimension to conclusively compare its performance to other design dimensions [44].

The main advantage that this design dimension presents over the rest is that we can reuse expert's value functions in multiple scenarios that share similar state-action spaces. In this manner, we can transfer the expert's knowledge in a form (value function) that includes information about the long-term effects of taking an action at a given state.

2.1.5 Design Dimension Alternatives

So far, we have explained how RL experts can inject human knowledge through the main components of a basic RL algorithm. There are other ways, however, to interact with low-level features of particular RL approaches. Next, we will explain the two main design dimension alternatives for an interactive RL setting.

Function Approximation (FA) allows us to estimate continuous state spaces rather than tabular approaches such as tabular Q-learning in a Gridworld domain. For any complex domain with a continuous state space (especially for robotics), we need to represent the value function continuously rather than in discrete tables; this is a scalability issue. The idea behind FA is that RL engineers can identify patterns in the state space; that is, the RL expert is capable of designing a function that can measure the similarity between different states.

FA presents an alternative design dimension that can work together with any other type of interaction channel, which means the implementation of an FA in an interactive RL algorithm does not obstruct interaction with other design dimensions. For example, the authors of [110] proposed a reward-shaping algorithm that also uses an FA to enable their method to use raw pixels as input from the video game they used as a testbed. However, their FA is created automatically.

As far as we know, the paper in [86] is the only work that has performed user-experience experiments for an interactive RL that uses hand-engineered FAs to accelerate the base RL algorithm. Their authors asked the participants of the experiment to program an FA for a soccer simulation environment. The FAs proposed by the participants were successful: they accelerated the learning process of the base RL algorithm. The same experiment was performed again, this time using the game Super Mario Bros. [42] as a testbed. In the second experiment, the RL's performance worsened when using the FAs. This evidence suggests that designing an effective FA is more challenging than simply using an RS technique in complex environments.

Hierarchical Decomposition (HRL) is an effective approach to tackle high-dimensional state-action spaces by decomposing them into smaller sub-problems or temporarily extended actions [25, 54, 99, 106]. In an HRL setting, an expert can define a hierarchy of sub-problems that can be reused as skills in different applications. Although HRL has been successfully tested in different research areas [13, 14, 54], there are no studies from the user-experience perspective in an interactive RL application.

2.2   Feedback Types

In the previous subsection, we introduced the design dimensions to interact with RL algorithms. In this section, we focus on concrete ways to code high-level human feedback to something that an RL algorithm can understand and use to improve/personalize its model. In particular, we will describe how each type of feedback delivers the user's expertise to the different design dimensions.

2.2.1   Binary Critique

The use of **binary critique** to evaluate an RL model's policy refers to binary feedback (positive or negative) that indicates if the last chosen action by the agent was satisfactory. This signal of human feedback was initially the only source of reward used [37]. This type of feedback was shown to be less than optimal because people provide an unpredictable signal and stop providing critiques once the agent learns the task [36].

One task for the RL designer is to determine whether a type of reward will be effective in a given application. For example, it was shown that using binary critique as policy information is more efficient than using a reward signal [44, 104]. Similarly, in [33] the authors propose an algorithm that incorporates the binary critique signal as policy information. From a user-experience perspective, it has been shown that using critique to shape policy is unfavorable [51].

It is also worth noting that learning from binary critique is popular because it is an easy and versatile method of using non-expert feedback; the user is required to click only "+" and "−" buttons.

The **heuristic function** approach [15, 67] is another example of the critique feedback category. Instead of receiving binary feedback directly from the user, in this approach, the critique signal comes from a hand-engineered function. This function encodes heuristics that map state-action pairs to positive or negative critiques. The aim of the heuristic function method is to reduce the amount of human feedback. Empirical evidence suggests that this type of feedback can accelerate RL algorithms; however, more research is needed to test its viability in complex environments such as video games [86].

The authors of the **active inverse reward design** approach [71] present a query-based procedure for inverse reward design [34]. A **query** is presented to the user with a set of sub-rewards, and the user then has to choose the best among the set. The sub-rewards are constructed to include as much information as possible about unknown rewards in the environment, and the set of sub-rewards is selected to maximize the understanding of different sub-optimal rewards.

2.2.2   Scalar-Valued Critique

In a manner similar to binary critique, with the **scalar-valued critique** feedback, users evaluate the performance of a policy. In this case, the magnitude of the scalar-valued feedback determines how good or bad a policy is. This method can be used on its own to learn a reward function of the environment purely through human feedback. However, it has been shown that humans usually provide non-optimal numerical reward signals with this approach [55].

2.2.3   Action Advice

In the **action advice** type of feedback, the human user provides the agent with the action they believe is optimal at a given state, the agent executes the advised action, and the base RL algorithm continues as usual. From the standpoint of user experience, the immediate effect of the user's advice on the agent's policy makes this feedback procedure less frustrating [50, 51].

There are other ways to provide action advice to the agent, such as learning from demonstration [101], inverse RL [79, 120, 121], apprentice learning [1], and imitation learning [19]. All these techniques share the characteristic that the base RL algorithm receives as input an expert demonstration of the task the agent is supposed to learn, which is ideal, as people enjoy demonstrating how agents should behave [5, 41, 104].

2.2.4   Guidance

The last type of feedback, **guidance**, is based on the premise that humans find it more natural to describe goals in an environment by specifying the object(s) of interest at a given time-step [94, 103]. This human knowledge leverages the base RL algorithm because the focus is on executing actions that might lead it to a goal specified by the user, which means that the RL algorithm needs to have access to a transition function of the dynamics in the environment. If the transition function is available, or we can construct it, this can be an effective way to communicate which goal is the best to follow at any given state.

2.3   Typical Use of Feedback Input for the Design Dimensions

We began this section by describing the main components of the RL framework (design dimensions) and which interactive RL methods we can use to create autonomous behaviors that align with the user intentions (e.g., reward shaping, policy shaping, and guided exploration). Next, we presented the different usual types of low-level feedback (e.g., critique, action advice, and guidance) that each interactive

Table 2 Interactive RL methods and the usual types of feedback they can use as input

	Reward shaping	Policy shaping	Guided exploration	Augmented value functions
Critique	●			
Action advice		●	●	●
Guidance		●	●	
Demonstration	●	●		●
Inverse RL	●			

RL method can use as input. In Table 2, we summarize the typical feedback each interactive RL method can use.

For HCI researcher, playing the role of designing new interaction techniques can start a new project from the high-level feedback (e.g., voice, text, and sketches) they want to use. Then, by following our proposed design guides for interactive RL, they can choose which technique to use and its most common type of input. In this manner, it's easier to find out how to interpret high-level feedback and which elements of it are more useful to translate into low-level feedback for the underlying RL algorithm.

3 Design Example Using Interactive Reinforcement Learning

In this section, we present an example of an HCI researcher, named Emily, using our interactive RL architecture to design a novel application.

Emily has been thinking about creating a novel interactive machine learning application but she's not sure yet on which subject to focus on. Suddenly, she remembers that in Sect. 5 she read about different *design principles* and the importance of creating interactive RL applications that require as little human feedback as possible. These constraints help Emily to come up with the idea of implementing an interface that lets her communicate using natural language with a bot that plays Mario Bros. That is, she has decided the testbed (one from those presented in Sect. 1.3) and the type of *high-level feedback* she wants to use. Then, she decides to use RL to learn the policy for the bot because this paradigm gives her a wide range of *human integration methods* (see Sect. 2.1) from which she can choose. In particular, she codes the Super Mario Bros. game as a Markov Decision Process (MDP) and then uses a genetic algorithm (she found this implementation on the Internet) to find a policy and, at the same time, she codes an algorithm that computes the transition function.

Now Emily has an RL-based bot that is good at playing Super Mario Bros.; the next step is choosing the human integration methods that fit what she wants to. After

Fig. 4 A design example using interactive reinforcement learning

thinking for a few days (and playing a lot of Super Mario Bros.), she decides that it's important for her to adapt the play style of Mario to fit her preferences. Also, she thinks that specifying the right goal to achieve at a given time is a good communication method. After reading about the different *feedback types* in Sect. 2.2, she decides that *guidance* is the way to go. Then, she checks Table 2 and sees that the most common human integration methods that use guidance as input are *policy shaping* and *guided exploration*. After reading Sect. 2.1, she decides that using a guided exploration method is better because she has a transition model of the environment.

After spending a few days/weeks (and drinking a lot of coffee), she completes the implementation of the interface and an interactive RL algorithm that exposes some parts of the underlying MDP so Mario can express the current goal he's pursuing and Emily can use it as an input method to guide him to the right goal (see Fig. 4). Now, Emily can change the behavior of Mario by writing the appropriate goal and then pressing the button "Submit Feedback".

4 Recent Research Results

In this section, we present research in interactive RL for studies using each of the human knowledge integration methods. Given the vast amount of work in this research area, we focus on the methods we believe to be the most influential.

4.1 Reward Shaping

The reward shaping (RS) method aims to mold the behavior of a learning agent by modifying its reward function to encourage the behavior the RL designer wants.

Most research on interactive RL only focuses on the performance of the algorithms as the evaluation metric, which leaves unclear what type of feedback and

RL algorithm are better from an HCI perspective. On the other hand, in [103] its authors analyzed the teaching style of non-expert users depending on the reward channel they had at their disposal. Users were able to use two types of RS: positive numerical reward and negative numerical reward. These types of feedback directly modify the value function of the RL model. However, when the user gives negative feedback, the agent tries to undo the last action it performed; this reveals the learning progress to the user and motivates them to use more negative feedback, which achieves good performance with less feedback. They also found that some users give anticipatory feedback to the bot; that is, users assume that their feedback is meant to direct the bot in future states. This analysis displays the importance of studying users' teaching strategies in interactive RL. We need to better understand the user's preferences to teach agents, as well as how agents should provide better feedback about their learning mechanism to foster trust and improve the quality and quantity of users' feedback. Doing this type of user-experience evaluation is important to get a better idea of how humans prefer to communicate to RL-based algorithms and how exposing the behavior of the agent can help users on giving better feedback.

Another RS strategy is to manually create heuristic functions that encourage the agent to perform particular actions in certain states of the environment [15, 86]. This way, the agent automatically receives feedback from the hand-engineered heuristic function. The type of feedback is defined by the RL designer, and it can be given using any of the feedback types reviewed in this paper (i.e., critique or scalar value). The experiments conducted in [86] demonstrate that using heuristic functions as input for an interactive RL algorithm can be a natural approach to injecting human knowledge in an RL method. The main shortcoming of heuristic functions is that they are difficult to build and require programming skills. Although it has been investigated how non-experts build ML models in real life [114], there are not many studies on the use of more natural modes of communication to empower non-experts in ML to build effective heuristic functions that generalize well. Furthermore, users found challenging to design effective heuristic functions for a clone of Super Mario Bros. In this particular case, users found it more comfortable using a combination of vanilla RS and heuristic functions. It's important to notice that, in most interactive RL research, the results in small testbeds (e.g., Gridworld) are not representative in testbeds with a bigger state-action space.

The Evaluative Reinforcement (TAMER) algorithm [48] uses traces of demonstrations as input to build a model of the user that is later used to automatically guide the RL algorithm. Later, the authors of [9] proposed an algorithm called DQN-TAMER that combines the TAMER and Deep TAMER algorithms. This novel combination of techniques aims to improve the performance of the learning agent using both environment and human binary feedback to shape the reward function of the model. Furthermore, they experimented in a maze-like environment with a robot that receives implicit feedback; in this scenario, the RS method was driven by the facial expression of the user. Since human feedback can be imprecise and intermittent, mechanisms were developed to handle these problems. This work is one of the few examples that use high-level feedback (facial expressions) for RS. Furthermore, deep versions of interactive RL methods benefit mostly from function approximation, as the use of this technique minimizes the feedback needed to get good results. This advantage is due to the generalization of user feedback among all similar states—human knowledge is injected into multiple similar states instead of only one.

4.2 Policy Shaping

The policy shaping (PS) approach consists of directly molding the policy of a learning agent to fit its behavior to what the RL designer envisions.

The authors of [32] introduced an approach that directly infers the user's policy from critique feedback. In particular, they proposed a Bayesian approach that computes the optimal policy from human feedback, taking as input the critiques for each state-action pair. The results of this approach are promising, as it outperforms other methods, such as RS. However, PS experiments were carried out using a simulated oracle instead of human users. Further experiments with human users should be conducted to validate the performance of this interactive RL method from a user-experience perspective.

On the other hand, in [51] are conducted experiments to determine which type of feedback, critique, or action advice creates a better user experience in an interactive RL setting. Specifically, they compared the critique approach in [32] to the proposed Newtonian action advice in [52]. Compared to the critique approach, the action advice type of feedback got better overall results: it required less training time, it performed objectively better, and it produced a better user experience with it.

In [66], the Convergent Actor-Critic by Humans (COACH) interactive RL algorithm is introduced. Later, in [10] a deep version, named deep COACH, uses a deep neural network coupled with a replay memory buffer and an autoencoder. Unlike the COACH implementation, deep COACH uses raw pixels from the testbed as input. The authors argue that using this high-level representation as input means their implementation is better suited for real scenarios. However, the testbed consists of simplistic toy problems, and a recent effort demonstrated that deep neural networks using raw pixels as input spend most of their learning capacity extracting useful information from the scene and just a tiny part on the actual behaviors [24].

MarioMix [12] is an interactive RL method that uses as input high-level feedback to create varied bot behaviors for a clone of the Super Mario Bros. game in real-time. The user feedback is in the form of behavior demonstration from either the users playing the game or a particular play style of a pre-computed bot in the database of MarioMix. MarioMix uses this demonstration input to find in its behavior database bots that play in a way that resembles what the users want (the behavior used as input). Then, MarioMix presents to the user two different play styles from which the user can choose and assign to a particular segment of the game stage. In this manner, users can mix multiple policies that activate in particular segments of the stage. Since most of the computation is made offline, users can create play styles that align with their preferences in real-time. The main disadvantage of this approach is that users might want a particular play style that is not part of the pre-computed dataset. However, this approach allows short interaction cycles.

4.3 Guided Exploration Process

Guided exploration process methods aim to minimize the learning procedure by injecting human knowledge to guide the agent's exploration to states with a high reward.

The authors of [103] conducted human-subject experiments in the Sophie's Kitchen platform to evaluate the performance of diverse human knowledge integration methods. Their results suggest that using guidance feedback is more effective than using scalar reward feedback.

Based upon the algorithm in [103], in [94] is proposed a variation in which the user can guide exploration by pointing out goal states in the environment; the bot then biases its policy to choose actions that lead to the indicated goal. These experiments were generally successful, but their highlight is their finding that using only exploration guides from the user produces the best results and reduces the amount of user feedback needed.

There have been efforts to create adaptive shaping algorithms that learn to choose the best feedback channels based on the user's preferred strategies for a given problem. For instance, in [116] its authors defined an adaptive algorithm with four different feedback methods at its disposal that use the exploration bias and reward shaping techniques. To measure the effectiveness of the feedback methods, at every time-step they ask users for feedback and use it to check the similarity between the policy of each shaping algorithm and the policy of the user. Then, according to the similarity metric, the best method is selected using a softmax function, and the value function for the selected method is updated using q-learning. Once the adaptive algorithm has enough samples, it considers the cumulative rewards to determine which feedback methodology is the best. Overall, one of the exploration bias-based algorithms produced better results and was chosen most often by the adaptive algorithm, as well as demonstrating good performance on its own. They call this algorithm action biasing, which uses user feedback to guide the exploration process of the agent. The human feedback is incorporated into the RL model using the sum of the agent and the user value functions as value functions.

In general, using human feedback as guidance for interactive RL algorithms appears to be the most effective in terms of performance and user experience. However, to make human feedback work, it is necessary to have a model of the environment, so the interactive RL algorithm knows which actions to perform to reach the state proposed by the user. This can be a strong limitation in complex environments where precise models are difficult to create.

4.4 Augmented Value Function

The procedure to augment a value function consists of combining the value function of the agent with one created from human feedback.

Studies have proposed combining the human and agent value functions to accelerate learning [44, 101]. In [101], the authors introduce the Human-Agent Transfer (HAT) algorithm, which is based on the rule transfer method [100]. The HAT algorithm generates a policy from the recorded human traces. This policy is then used to shape the q-value function of the agent. This shaping procedure gives a constant bonus to state-action pairs of the agent q-learning function that aligns with the action proposed by the previously computed human policy.

In [17], its authors present an interactive RL algorithm named RLfD^2 that uses demonstrations by an expert as input. With these demonstrations, they create a potential-based piece-wise Gaussian function. This function has high values in state-action pairs that have been demonstrated by the expert and 0 values where no demonstrations were given. This function is used to bias the exploration process of a Q(λ)-learning algorithm in two different ways. First, the Q-function of the RL algorithm is initialized with the potential-based function values. Second, the potential-based function is treated as a shaping function that complements the reward function from the environment. The combination of these two bias mechanisms is meant to leverage human knowledge from the expert throughout the entire learning process.

From the user-experience standpoint, the augmented value function design dimension has the advantage of **transfer learning**. For instance, a value function constructed by one user can be used as a baseline to bias the model of another user trying to solve the same task—the learned knowledge from one user is transferred to another. Multiple sources of feedback (coded as value functions) can be combined to obtain more complete feedback in a wider range of states. It is also convenient that a model of the environment is not essential for this approach.

4.5 Inverse Reward Design

Inverse reward design (IRD) is the process of inferring a true reward function from a proxy reward function.

IRD [34, 71] is used to reduce reward hacking failures. According to the proposed terminology in [34], the hand-engineered reward function named the **proxy reward function** is just an approximation of the true reward function, which is one that perfectly models real-world scenarios. The process of inferring a true reward function from a proxy reward function is IRD.

To infer the true reward function, the IRD method takes as input a proxy reward function, the model of the test environment, and the behavior of the RL designer who created it. Then, using Bayesian approaches, a distribution function that maps the proxy reward function to the true reward function is inferred. This distribution of the true reward function makes the agent aware of uncertainty when approaching previously unseen states, so it behaves in a risk-averse manner in new scenarios. The results of the experiments in [34] reveal that reward hacking problems lessen with an IRD approach.

The main interaction procedure of IRD starts as regular RS, and the system then queries the user to provide more information about their preference for states with high uncertainty. This kind of procedure can benefit from interaction techniques to better explain uncertainty to humans and from compelling techniques to debug and fix problems in the model.

5   Design Principles for Interactive RL

The design of RL techniques with a human-in-the-loop requires consideration of how human factors impact the design of and interaction with these machine learning algorithms. To produce behaviors that align with the user's intention, clear communication between the human and the RL algorithm is key. In this section, we will introduce general design principles for interactive RL meant to guide HCI researchers to create capable and economical interactive RL applications that users can understand and trust.

5.1   Feedback

Delay of human feedback has a great impact on the performance of interactive RL applications. Delay refers to the time that a human user needs to evaluate and deliver their feedback to the interactive RL algorithm. Many examples propose different strategies to deal with feedback delay [9, 10, 37, 82, 103, 105, 110].

The most common approach consists of a delay parameter that expresses how many past time-steps the current feedback will be applied; this parameter is usually found in practice [10]. Warnell et al. conducted an experiment to quantify the effect of different reward distribution delays on the effectiveness of their algorithm Deep TAMER [110]. This experiment revealed that a small change in the parameters of the expected user feedback timing distribution can have a great impact on performance; expert knowledge on this timing distribution is key to achieving good results.

A different approach to deal with feedback delay is proposed in [94]. In this case, the interactive RL algorithm pauses the agent exploration process in every time-step to give the user time to give feedback. More elaborated approaches assume that the feedback delay follows a probability distribution [9]. Likewise, it has been found that less avid users need more time to think and decide on their feedback [82]. It is therefore important to adapt the feedback delay depending on users' level of knowledge.

Fatigue of users and its effects on the quantity and quality of feedback should be considered. It has been observed that humans tend to reduce the quantity of feedback they give over time [35, 37, 47]. The quality also diminishes, as humans tend to give less positive feedback over time. According to [66], this degradation of the quantity and quality of human feedback also depends on the behavior exhibited by the agent. The authors of [66] found that humans tend to give more positive feedback when they notice that the agent is improving its policy over time: feedback is therefore policy-dependent [70]. On the other hand, the experiments of [19] offer evidence to support that human users gradually diminish their positive feedback when the agent shows that it is adopting the proposed strategies. Fachantidis et al. performed experiments to determine the impact of the quality and distribution of feedback on the performance of their interactive RL algorithm [30].

Motivating users to give feedback—elements of gamification have been adopted with good results; gamification strategies have been shown to improve the quantity and quality of human feedback [57, 58].

Some studies focus on improving the quality and quantity of human feedback by incorporating an active question procedure in the learning agent [7, 30, 32, 59]; that is, the agent can ask the user to give feedback in particular states. In [7], its authors present an active interactive RL algorithm in which both the agent and the demonstrator (another agent) work together to decide when to make use of feedback in a setting with a limited advice budget. First, the agent determines if it needs help in a particular state and asks the demonstrator for attention. Depending on the situation of the agent, the demonstrator determines if it will help or not. The results of these experiments are promising because they achieve a good level of performance while requiring less attention from the demonstrator.

Maximizing the use of feedback is necessary because interactive RL in complex environments might require up to millions of interaction cycles to get good results [19, 73]. It has been demonstrated that the inclusion of an approximation function that propagates human feedback to all similar states is effective to tackle the sample inefficiency of interactive RL in complex environments such as video games [110].

5.2 Typification of the End-User

We found that the most important features to typify an end-user in interactive RL involve the following:

Knowledge level in the task at hand—this has an impact on the quality, quantity, and delay of feedback, and could limit the use of some feedback types that require more precise information, such as demonstrations or action advice.

Preferred teaching strategy—this is essential to select the feedback type appropriate for a given application (see Fig. 2).

Safety concerns—this refers to the severity of the effects of the agent's actions if an error in its behavior occurs. If the severity of the errors is high (e.g., property damage, personal harm, and politically incorrect behavior), end-users' perception and willingness to interact with the agent will diminish [74]. The quality and quantity of feedback are therefore also affected.

An end-user typification using these features would help researchers to select the best combination of feedback type and design dimension for a particular interactive RL and for the expected type of end-user. For instance, although all design dimensions assume that the user knows a policy that is at least good enough to solve the task, some design dimensions can better handle non-optimal policies from human feedback [32]. Empirical evidence suggests that the exploration process is the most economical design dimension for interactive RL applications [32, 51, 103]. Nonetheless, myopic agents—which use the policy design dimension—have demonstrated great success in some tasks [30, 55].

The hierarchical decomposition and function approximation design dimensions require human users with a deep understanding of the problem to make effective use of them. Another possibility is combining different design dimensions in the same interactive RL method. It would also be useful to design an active interactive RL that learns which design dimension best suits the application and type of use; in this way, the interactive RL algorithm can minimize the feedback needed from the user [32]. For example, a combination of function approximation and policy design dimensions would enable the use in a video game environment of an interactive RL that needs only 15 min of human feedback to get positive results [110].

5.3   Fast Interaction Cycles

In an iterative procedure, such as an interactive RL algorithm, a fast evaluation of the agent's behavior can substantially reduce the time needed for each teaching loop. Some of the approaches meant to lessen the evaluation process consist of evaluation, visualization, and explanatory techniques.

Evaluation techniques, such as queries, are those in which the user selects the best reward function among a set [34, 93], the presentation of multiple trajectories by the agent that then summarizes its behavior [112], or crowd evaluations that distribute the evaluation task among various users [56].

Visualization techniques, such as the HIGHLIGHTS algorithm [6], focus on creating summaries of agents so people can better understand an agent's behavior in crucial situations. These summaries are sets of trajectories that provide an overview of the agent's behavior in key states. It is therefore fundamental to define a metric that measures the importance of states. This is calculated as the difference between the highest and lowest expected returns for a given state. That is, a state in which taking a particular action that leads to a significant decrease in the expected reward is considered important.

Explanatory techniques are a different way to address the evaluation problem by explaining the agent's decision process to the human user. This approach enhances the user's understanding of how the agent learns, interprets, and determines the best action to take in a given state.

One example of uncertainty explanation is introduced in [103]. The authors use the gaze of the agent in their experiments as an indicator of its level of uncertainty in any given state.

The main idea of the gaze mechanism is to make the agent explicitly express at every time-step the options it considers most promising by staring at the object of interest. If there is more than one promising action in a given state, the agent will have to focus its gaze on different objects in the environment, communicating indecision to the user and giving the user time to give feedback to the agent. The authors also found that users tend to give more feedback when the agent displays uncertainty, which optimizes the exploration process of the robot.

5.4 Design Implications

Our analysis has found some design factors that need more exploration to better understand their impact on interactive RL. These include adaptive systems that can choose between different design dimensions, enabling the use of demonstration as feedback in complex robot environments where it is difficult for the user to show the agent how to perform the task it has to learn. This makes interactive RL-based applications accessible to more types of users (e.g., non-experts in RL, non-experts in the task at hand, and those with physical limitations), so this design dimension is better for non-experts in the task at hand.

6 Open Challenges

Below, we list what we consider the most promising research directions in interactive RL.

6.1 Making Interactive RL Usable in High-Dimensional Environments

Broadening the domains and applications in which interactive RL is useful is key to extending the impact of ML in people's life. HCI researchers can contribute to making interactive RL feasible for real-world applications with high-dimensional environments which is still a challenge.

One under-exploited approach is applying a crowd-sourced approach to interactive reinforcement learning [37]. The main obstacles in this particular setting are that the human feedback depends on the exhibited policy of the learning agent, and the global policy that the users have in mind [66]. These dependencies make it difficult to design a way to organize the workers and tasks that minimizes noise, incorrect feedback, and bias. Furthermore, there are no user-experience studies to better understand which interactive RL dimension works best for a crowd-sourced environment.

Another related setting is a framework that enables an agent to learn from both humans and other agents (through action advice) that know the current task [113]. This approach can help on reducing the needed human feedback in interactive RL. In the same vein, the use of simulated oracles in the early implementation stages of interactive RL applications is useful to save time and human feedback [22, 32, 116]. However, it has been found that results with simulated oracles can differ from those with human users [51, 116]. More studies are needed to determine what features make human feedback a better fit for those coming from simulated oracles or agents.

Besides action advice, humans can provide feedback to agents using more abstract information. For instance, eye gaze is an indicator of engagement, attention, and internal cognitive state [119] in tasks such as playing video games [118], watching pictures [18], and in human-robot social interactions [89]. Existing works have proposed to learn gaze prediction models to guide learning agents [62, 117]. Using this approach, we do not need to learn a human-like policy which can be more challenging in real-world environments. The HCI community can contribute to this direction by proposing other types of high-level feedback (e.g., facial expressions) that is natural, rich in information, and machine learning models can learn to predict.

One shortcoming of RL is that it tends to overfit; it is hard to create an RL-based agent that generalizes well to previously unseen states. On the other hand, we can partially overcome this by creating diverse testbeds for the learning agents [85]. Although there are RL-based procedural content generation (PCG) algorithms [43], there is not an interactive version that takes advantage of having a human-in-the-loop. The human user working together with the PCG algorithm could create more varied and complex challenges for the learning agent.

6.2 Lack of User-Experience Evaluation

The evaluation of interactive RL applications from the HCI perspective is limited; most studies focus on improving the performance of algorithms rather than the user experience, but proper evaluation is essential to create practical applications for different types of end-users. For instance, the studies in [50, 51] present an adequate evaluation of the user experience in an interactive RL setting.

In the same context, the *problem of generalization from simple testbeds* (e.g., Gridworld) exists, as the results are not consistent when using more complex testbeds. For example, even though RS has been demonstrated to be effective and easy to use by all types of users in a Gridworld environment [9, 10], using the same human knowledge integration method to train agents for the Infinite Mario platform is challenging and ineffective, even for expert users [86].

The type of feedback depends on the policy of the bot [66] (whether human trainers give a positive or negative feedback for a decision is influenced by the learner's current policy.), but there are not many studies on the type of feedback depending on the design dimension or depending on the feedback the bot gives to the user.

6.3   Modeling Users Preferences

As far as we know, a formal model of users for interactive RL (or IML in general) has not been proposed. Such a model could be used to create interactive RL applications with an active initiative that avoids user fatigue by detecting and predicting user behavior. That is, the interactive RL system would ask for help from the user with the correct frequency to avoid user fatigue. Another possibility is implementing RL-based applications that adapt the interaction channel and feedback type according to the user's preferences. This would require empirical studies to find a way to map between user types and their preferred interaction channels (see next subsection).

A better understanding of the strengths and weaknesses of each design dimension and feedback type in interactive RL would lead the community to develop effective *combinations of interactive RL approaches*. Achieving this would require extensive user-experience studies with all different combinations of design dimensions and feedback types in testbeds with small and big state spaces. Furthermore, it would be favorable to find a mapping that considers the type of end-user. Using this type of mapping and a model of the end-user would enable the design of interactive RL applications that adapt to the current end-user.

The crowd-sourced approach in interactive RL has the potential to enable the use of RL in real-world environments. However, there is not a model that typifies users (e.g., preferred teaching strategies and feedback accuracy) and key aspects of crowd-sourced settings such as division of work (e.g., partitioning a task into subtasks).

Finally, high-level behaviors such as facial expressions, gestures, eye gaze, and posture are useful to express the internal cognitive state of humans while interacting with physical robots [4]. However, there are no user-experience studies aimed at modeling these human-robot interactions for interactive RL applications.

6.4   Debugging Interactive RL

RL-based agents have a particular way of representing their environment, depending on the sensors at their disposal and how they interpret the incoming signals. It can be complicated for humans to elicit the state representation of agents which can lead to giving incorrect feedback to agents or debugging its model.

We can take advantage of explainable RL methods to help people understand how agents see the environment and their reasoning procedure for computing policies [2, 50, 64, 65]. With more transparency in an agent model, people could find better ways to teach agents or find errors or unwanted bias in the model [77]. This type of interaction is essential in applications that can have a substantial impact on people's lives [21]. The HCI community can contribute to this research sub-area by proposing novel interaction channels for agents to communicate their internal state.

One effective way to communicate the internal state of agents is through visualization techniques that users can interact with to trigger adaptations in the model (to fix errors) [88]. We can expose elements of a Markov Decision Process, such as the uncertainty of performing a given action or the main goal the agent is pursuing at a given time. As far as we know, there are no works on this subject that evaluate the user experience.

Another effective communication method consists of natural language [61, 63]. The main challenge here is creating explanations that provide users relevant information to diagnose the agent's policy. Then, to repair the policy, we would need to design an input method based on natural language.

Similar to the previous challenges, a crowd-sourced setting for debugging is relevant to have a broad understanding of human-AI interaction [107]. This setting has been applied to evaluate the interpretability of explanations of predictions in supervised learning settings [84] and to debug the components of a pipeline in a complex computer vision system [75, 76, 81]. Nevertheless, more advances in techniques to speed up the evaluation of behaviors are needed.

7 Conclusion

Reinforcement learning applications are starting to have a major effect on everybody's life, and the HCI community has an important role in spreading their use and impact on society. HCI researchers and practitioners can make advances in RL research by designing novel interaction techniques and applications for autonomous behaviors that users can personalize and understand.

Acknowledgements This work was supported by JST CREST Grant Number JPMJCR17A1, Japan. Additionally, we would like to thank the reviewers of our original DIS paper. Their kind suggestions helped to improve and clarify this manuscript.

References

1. Abbeel P, Ng AY (2004) Apprenticeship learning via inverse reinforcement learning. In: Proceedings of the twenty-first international conference on Machine learning. ACM, p 1
2. Adadi A, Berrada M (2018) Peeking inside the black-box: a survey on Explainable Artificial Intelligence (XAI). IEEE Access 6:52138–52160
3. Agogino AK, Tumer K (2004) Unifying temporal and structural credit assignment problems. In: Proceedings of the third international joint conference on autonomous agents and multiagent systems-vol 2. IEEE Computer Society, pp 980–987
4. Akalin N, Loutfi A (2021) Reinforcement learning approaches in social robotics. In: Sensors 21.4, p 1292

5. Amershi S et al (2014) Power to the people: the role of humans in interactive machine learning. AI Mag 35(4):105–120
6. Amir D, Amir O (2018) Highlights: summarizing agent behavior to people. In: Proceedings of the 17th international conference on autonomous agents and multiagent systems. International Foundation for Autonomous Agents and Multiagent Systems, pp 1168–1176
7. Amir O et al (2016) Interactive teaching strategies for agent training. In: In Proceedings of CAI 2016. https://www.microsoft.com/en-us/research/publication/interactive-teaching-strategies-agent-training/
8. Amodei D et al (2016) Concrete problems in AI safety. arXiv:1606.06565
9. Arakawa R et al (2018) DQN-TAMER: human-in-the-loop reinforcement learning with intractable feedback. arXiv:1810.11748
10. Arumugam D et al (2019) Deep reinforcement learning from policy-dependent human feedback. arXiv:1902.04257
11. Arzate Cruz C, Igarashi T (2020) A survey on interactive reinforcement learning: design principles and open challenges. In: Proceedings of the 2020 ACM designing interactive systems conference, pp 1195–1209
12. Arzate Cruz C, Igarashi T (2020) MarioMix: creating aligned playstyles for bots with interactive reinforcement learning. In: Extended abstracts of the 2020 annual symposium on computer-human interaction in play, pp 134–139
13. Arzate Cruz C, Ramirez Uresti J (2018) HRLB∧2: a reinforcement learning based framework for believable bots. Appl Sci 8(12):2453
14. Bai A, Wu F, Chen X (2015) Online planning for large markov decision processes with hierarchical decomposition. ACM Trans Intell Syst Technol (TIST) 6(4):45
15. Bianchi RAC et al (2013) Heuristically accelerated multiagent reinforcement learning. IEEE Trans Cybern 44(2):252–265
16. Brockman G et al (2016) OpenAI Gym. arXiv:1606.01540
17. Brys T et al (2015) Reinforcement learning from demonstration through shaping. In: Proceedings of the 24th international conference on artificial intelligence. CAI'15. Buenos Aires, Argentina: AAAI Press, pp 3352–3358. isbn: 978-1-57735-738-4. http://dl.acm.org/citation.cfm?id=2832581.2832716
18. Cerf M et al (2008) Predicting human gaze using low-level saliency combined with face detection. Adv Neural Inf Process Syst 20:1–7
19. Christiano PF et al (2017) Deep reinforcement learning from human preferences. In: Advances in neural information processing systems, pp 4299–4307
20. Clark J, Amodei D (2016) Faulty reward functions in the wild. Accessed: 2019–08-21. https://openai.com/blog/faulty-reward-functions/
21. European Commission (2018) 2018 reform of EU data protection rules. Accessed: 2019–06-17. https://ec.europa.eu/commission/sites/beta-political/files/data-protection-factsheet-changes_en.pdf
22. Cruz F et al (2015) Interactive reinforcement learning through speech guidance in a domestic scenario. In: 2015 international joint conference on neural networks (IJCNN). IEEE, pp 1–8
23. Cruz F et al (2016) Training agents with interactive reinforcement learning and contextual affordances. IEEE Trans Cogn Dev Syst 8(4):271–284
24. Cuccu G, Togelius J, Cudré-Mauroux P (2019) Playing atari with six neurons. In: Proceedings of the 18th international conference on autonomous agents and multiagent systems. International Foundation for Autonomous Agents and Multiagent Systems, pp 998–1006
25. Dieterich TG (2000) Hierarchical reinforcement learning with the MAXQ value function decomposition. J Artif Intell Res 13:227–303
26. Dodson T, Mattei N, Goldsmith J (2011) A natural language argumentation interface for explanation generation in Markov decision processes. In: International conference on algorithmic decision theory. Springer, pp 42–55
27. Dubey R et al (2018) Investigating human priors for playing video games. arXiv:1802.10217
28. Elizalde F, Enrique Sucar L (2009) Expert evaluation of probabilistic explanations. In: ExaCt, pp 1–12

29. Elizalde F et al (2008) Policy explanation in factored Markov decision processes. In: Proceedings of the 4th European workshop on probabilistic graphical models (PGM 2008), pp 97–104
30. Fachantidis A, Taylor ME, Vlahavas I (2018) Learning to teach reinforcement learning agents. Mach Learn Knowl Extr 1(1):21–42. issn: 2504–4990. https://www.mdpi.com/2504-4990/1/1/2. https://doi.org/10.3390/make1010002
31. Fails JA, Olsen Jr DR (2003) Interactive machine learning. In: Proceedings of the 8th international conference on intelligent user interfaces. ACM, pp 39–45
32. Griffith S et al (2013) Policy shaping: integrating human feedback with reinforcement learning. In: Advances in neural information processing systems, pp 2625–2633
33. Griffith S et al (2013) Policy shaping: integrating human feedback with reinforcement learning. In: Proceedings of the international conference on neural information processing systems (NIPS)
34. Hadfield-Menell D et al (2017) Inverse reward design. In: Guyon I et al (eds) Advances in neural information processing systems, vol 30. Curran Associates Inc, pp 6765–6774. http://papers.nips.cc/paper/7253-inverse-reward-design.pdf
35. Ho MK et al (2015) Teaching with rewards and punishments: reinforcement or communication? In: CogSci
36. Isbell CL et al (2006) Cobot in LambdaMOO: an adaptive social statistics agent. Auton Agents Multi-Agent Syst 13(3):327–354
37. Isbell Jr CL, Shelton CR (2002) Cobot: asocial reinforcement learning agent. In: Advances in neural information processing systems, pp 1393–1400
38. Jaques N et al (2016) Generating music by fine-tuning recurrent neural networks with reinforcement learning
39. Jaques N et al (2018) Social influence as intrinsic motivation for multi-agent deep reinforcement learning. arXiv:1810.08647
40. Kaelbling LP, Littman ML, Moore AW (1996) Reinforcement learning: a survey. J Artif Intell Res 4:237–285
41. Kaochar T et al (2011) Towards understanding how humans teach robots. In: International conference on user modeling, adaptation, and personalization. Springer, pp 347–352
42. Karakovskiy S, Togelius J (2012) The mario ai benchmark and competitions. IEEE Trans Comput Intell AI Games 4(1):55–67
43. Khalifa A et al (2020) Pcgrl: procedural content generation via reinforcement learning. arXiv:2001.09212
44. Knox WB, Stone P (2010) Combining manual feedback with subsequent MDP reward signals for reinforcement learning. In: Proceedings of the 9th international conference on autonomous agents and multiagent systems: volume 1-Volume 1. International Foundation for Autonomous Agents and Multiagent Systems, pp 5–12
45. Knox WB, Stone P (2012) Reinforcement learning from simultaneous human and MDP reward. In: Proceedings of the 11th international conference on autonomous agents and multiagent systems-volume 1. International Foundation for Autonomous Agents and Multiagent Systems, pp 475–482
46. Knox WB, Stone P, Breazeal C (2013) Training a robot via human feedback: a case study. In: International conference on social robotics. Springer, pp 460–470
47. Knox WB et al (2012) How humans teach agents. Int J Soc Robot 4(4):409–421
48. Knox WB, Stone P (2009) Interactively shaping agents via human reinforcement: the TAMER framework. In: The fifth international conference on knowledge capture. http://www.cs.utexas.edu/users/ai-lab/?KCAP09-knox
49. Korpan R et al (2017) Why: natural explanations from a robot navigator. arXiv:1709.09741
50. Krening S, Feigh KM (2019) Effect of interaction design on the human experience with interactive reinforcement learning. In: Proceedings of the 2019 on designing interactive systems conference. ACM, pp 1089–1100
51. Krening S, Feigh KM (2018) Interaction algorithm effect on human experience with reinforcement learning. ACM Trans Hum-Robot Interact (THRI) 7(2):16

52. Krening S, Feigh KM (2019) Newtonian action advice: integrating human verbal instruction with reinforcement learning. In: Proceedings of the 18th international conference on autonomous agents and multiagent systems. International Foundation for Autonomous Agents and Multiagent Systems, pp 720–727

53. Lazic N et al (2018) Data center cooling using model-predictive control

54. Lee Y-S, Cho S-B (2011) Activity recognition using hierarchical hidden markov models on a smartphone with 3D accelerometer. In: International conference on hybrid artificial intelligence systems. Springer, pp 460–467

55. Leike J et al (2018) Scalable agent alignment via reward modeling: a research direction. arXiv:1811.07871

56. Lelis LHS, Reis WMP, Gal Y (2017) Procedural generation of game maps with human-in-the-loop algorithms. IEEE Trans Games 10(3):271–280

57. Lessel P et al (2019) "Enable or disable gamification" analyzing the impact of choice in a gamified image tagging task. In: Proceedings of the 2019 CHI conference on human factors in computing systems. CHI '19. ACM, Glasgow, Scotland Uk , 150:1–150:12. isbn: 978-1-4503-5970-2. https://doi.org/10.1145/3290605.3300380

58. Li G et al (2018) Social interaction for efficient agent learning from human reward. Auton Agents Multi-Agent Syst 32(1):1–25. issn: 1573–7454. https://doi.org/10.1007/s10458-017-9374-8

59. Li G et al (2013) Using informative behavior to increase engagement in the tamer framework. In: Proceedings of the 2013 international conference on autonomous agents and multi-agent systems. AAMAS '13. International Foundation for Autonomous Agents and Multiagent Systems, St. Paul, MN, USA, pp 909–916. isbn: 978-1-4503-1993-5. https://dl.acm.org/citation.cfm?id=2484920.2485064

60. Li J et al (2016) Deep reinforcement learning for dialogue generation. arXiv:1606.01541

61. Li TJ-J et al (2019) Pumice: a multi-modal agent that learns concepts and conditionals from natural language and demonstrations. In: Proceedings of the 32nd annual ACM symposium on user interface software and technology, pp 577–589

62. Li Y, Liu M, Rehg JM (2018) In the eye of beholder: joint learning of gaze and actions in first person video. In: Proceedings of the European conference on computer vision (ECCV), pp 619–635

63. Little G, Miller RC (2006) Translating keyword commands into executable code. In: Proceedings of the 19th annual ACM symposium on User interface software and technology, pp 135–144

64. Liu Y et al (2019) Experience-based causality learning for intelligent agents. ACM Trans Asian Low-Resour Lang Inf Process (TALLIP) 18(4):45

65. Liu Y et al (2019) Experience-based causality learning for intelligent agents. ACM Trans Asian Low-Resour Lang Inf Process 18(4):45:1–45:22. issn: 2375–4699. https://doi.org/10.1145/3314943

66. MacGlashan J et al (2017) Interactive learning from policy-dependent human feedback. In: Proceedings of the 34th international conference on machine learning-volume 70. JMLR. org, pp 2285–2294

67. Martins MF, Bianchi RAC (2013) Heuristically accelerated reinforcement learning: a comparative analysis of performance. In: Conference towards autonomous robotic systems. Springer, pp 15–27

68. McGregor S et al (2017) Interactive visualization for testing markov decision processes: MDPVIS. J Vis Lang Comput 39:93–106

69. Meng Q, Tholley I, Chung PWH (2014) Robots learn to dance through interaction with humans. Neural Comput Appl 24(1):117–124

70. Miltenberger RG (2011) Behavior modification: principles and procedures. Cengage Learning

71. Mindermann S et al (2018) Active inverse reward design. arXiv:1809.03060

72. Mnih V et al (2015) Human-level control through deep reinforcement learning. Nature 518(7540):529–533

73. Mnih V et al (2015) Human-level control through deep reinforcement learning. Nature 518(7540):529
74. Morales CG et al (2019) Interaction needs and opportunities for failing robots. In: Proceedings of the 2019 on designing interactive systems conference, pp 659–670
75. Mottaghi R et al (2013) Analyzing semantic segmentation using hybrid human-machine crfs. In: Proceedings of the IEEE conference on computer vision and pattern recognition, pp 3143–3150
76. Mottaghi R et al (2015) Human-machine CRFs for identifying bottlenecks in scene understanding. IEEE Trans Pattern Anal Mach Intell 38(1):74–87
77. Myers CM et al (2020) Revealing neural network bias to non-experts through interactive counterfactual examples. arXiv:2001.02271
78. Nagabandi A et al (2020) Deep dynamics models for learning dexterous manipulation. In: Conference on robot learning. PMLR, pp 1101–1112
79. Ng AY, Harada D, Russell S (1999) Policy invariance under reward transformations: theory and application to reward shaping. In: ICML, vol. 99, pp 278–287
80. OpenAI et al (2019) Dota 2 with large scale deep reinforcement learning. arXiv: 1912.06680
81. Parikh D, Zitnick C (2011) Human-debugging of machines. NIPS WCSSWC 2(7):3
82. Peng B et al (2016) A need for speed: adapting agent action speed to improve task learning from non-expert humans. In: Proceedings of the 2016 international conference on autonomous agents & multiagent systems. International Foundation for Autonomous Agents and Multiagent Systems, pp 957–965
83. Puterman ML (2014) Markov decision processes: discrete stochastic dynamic programming. Wiley
84. Ribeiro MT, Singh S, Guestrin C (2016) Why should i trust you? Explaining the predictions of any classifier. In: Proceedings of the 22nd ACM SIGKDD international conference on knowledge discovery and data mining, pp 1135–1144
85. Risi S, Togelius J (2020) Increasing generality in machine learning through procedural content generation. Nat Mach Intell 2(8):428–436
86. Rosenfeld A et al (2018) Leveraging human knowledge in tabular reinforcement learning: a study of human subjects. In: The knowledge engineering review 33
87. Russell SJ, Norvig P (2016) Artificial intelligence: a modern approach. Pearson Education Limited, Malaysia
88. Sacha D et al (2017) What you see is what you can change: human-centered machine learning by interactive visualization. Neurocomputing 268:164–175
89. Saran A et al (2018) Human gaze following for human-robot interaction. In: 2018 IEEE/RSJ international conference on intelligent robots and systems (IROS). IEEE, pp 8615–8621
90. Shah P, Hakkani-Tur D, Heck L (2016) Interactive reinforcement learning for task-oriented dialogue management
91. Shah P et al (2018) Bootstrapping a neural conversational agent with dialogue self-play, crowdsourcing and on-line reinforcement learning. In: Proceedings of the 2018 conference of the North American chapter of the association for computational linguistics: human language technologies, volume 3 (Industry Papers), pp 41–51
92. Silver D et al (2017) Mastering the game of go without human knowledge. Nature 550(7676):354–359
93. Sørensen PD, Olsen JM, Risi S (2016) Breeding a diversity of super mario behaviors through interactive evolution. In: 2016 IEEE conference on computational intelligence and games (CIG). IEEE, pp 1–7
94. Suay HB, Chernova S (2011) Effect of human guidance and state space size on interactive reinforcement learning. In: 2011 Ro-Man. IEEE, pp 1–6
95. Sutton R, Littman M, Paris A (2019) The reward hypothesis. Accessed: 2019–08-21. http://incompleteideas.net/rlai.cs.ualberta.ca/RLAI/rewardhypothesis.html
96. Sutton RS (1996) Generalization in reinforcement learning: successful examples using sparse coarse coding. In: Advances in neural information processing systems, pp 1038–1044
97. Sutton RS (1985) Temporal credit assignment in reinforcement learning

98. Sutton RS, Barto AG (2011) Reinforcement learning: an introduction
99. Sutton RS, Precup D, Singh S (1999) Between MDPs and semi-MDPs: a framework for temporal abstraction in reinforcement learning. Artif Intell 112(1-2):181–211
100. Taylor ME, Stone P (2007) Cross-domain transfer for reinforcement learning. In: Proceedings of the 24th international conference on Machine learning. ACM, pp 879–886
101. Taylor ME, Bener Suay H, Chernova S (2011) Integrating reinforcement learning with human demonstrations of varying ability. In: The 10th international conference on autonomous agents and multiagent systems-volume 2. International Foundation for Autonomous Agents and Multiagent Systems, pp 617–624
102. Tenorio-González A, Morales E, Villaseñor-Pineda L (2010) Dynamic reward shaping: training a robot by voice, pp 483–492. https://doi.org/10.1007/978-3-642-16952-6_49
103. Thomaz AL, Breazeal C (2006) Adding guidance to interactive reinforcement learning. In: Proceedings of the twentieth conference on artificial intelligence (AAAI)
104. Thomaz AL, Breazeal C (2008) Teachable robots: understanding human teaching behavior to build more effective robot learners. Artif Intell 172(6–7), 716–737
105. Thomaz AL, Hoffman G, Breazeal C (2005) Real-time interactive reinforcement learning for robots. In: AAAI 2005 workshop on human comprehensible machine learning
106. Usunier N et al (2016) Episodic exploration for deep deterministic policies: an application to starcraft micromanagement tasks. arXiv:1609.02993
107. Vaughan JW (2017) Making better use of the crowd: how crowdsourcing can advance machine learning research. J Mach Learn Res 18(1):7026–7071
108. Velavan P, Jacob B, Kaushik A (2020) Skills gap is a reflection of what we value: a reinforcement learning interactive conceptual skill development framework for Indian university. In: International conference on intelligent human computer interaction. Springer, pp 262–273
109. Wang N et al (2018) Is it my looks? Or something i said? The impact of explanations, embodiment, and expectations on trust and performance in human-robot teams. In: International conference on persuasive technology. Springer, pp 56–69
110. Warnell G et al (2018) Deep tamer: interactive agent shaping in high dimensional state spaces. In: Thirty-second AAAI conference on artificial intelligence
111. Wiewiora E, Cottrell GW, Elkan C (2003) Principled methods for advising reinforcement learning agents. In: Proceedings of the 20th international conference on machine learning (ICML-03), pp 792–799
112. Wilson A, Fern A, Tadepalli P (2012) A bayesian approach for policy learning from trajectory preference queries. In: Advances in neural information processing systems, pp 1133–1141
113. Woodward M, Finn C, Hausman K (2020) Learning to interactively learn and assist. Proc AAAI Conf Artif Intell 34(03):2535–2543
114. Yang Q et al (2018) Grounding interactive machine learning tool design in how non-experts actually build models. In: Proceedings of the 2018 designing interactive systems conference, pp 573–584
115. Yannakakis GN, Togelius J (2018) Artificial intelligence and games, vol. 2. Springer
116. Yu C et al (2018) Learning shaping strategies in human-in-the-loop interactive reinforcement learning. arXiv:1811.04272
117. Zhang R et al (2018) Agil: learning attention from human for visuomotor tasks. In: Proceedings of the European conference on computer vision (eccv), pp 663–679
118. Zhang R et al (2020) Atari-head: atari human eye-tracking and demonstration dataset. Proc AAAI Conf Artif Intell 34(04):6811–6820
119. Zhang R et al (2020) Human gaze assisted artificial intelligence: a review. In: CAI: proceedings of the conference, vol 2020. NIH Public Access, p 4951
120. Ziebart BD et al (2009) Human behavior modeling with maximum entropy inverse optimal control. In: AAAI spring symposium: human behavior modeling, p 92
121. Ziebart BD et al (2008) Maximum entropy inverse reinforcement learning

Part IV
Specific Domains

Sketch-Based Creativity Support Tools Using Deep Learning

Forrest Huang, Eldon Schoop, David Ha, Jeffrey Nichols, and John Canny

Abstract Sketching is a natural and effective visual communication medium commonly used in creative processes. Recent developments in deep-learning models drastically improved machines' ability in understanding and generating visual content. An exciting area of development explores deep-learning approaches used to model human sketches, opening opportunities for creative applications. This chapter describes three fundamental steps in developing deep-learning-driven creativity support tools that consume and generate sketches: (1) a data collection effort that generated a new paired dataset between sketches and mobile user interfaces; (2) a sketch-based user interface retrieval system adapted from state-of-the-art computer vision techniques; and, (3) a conversational sketching system that supports the novel interaction of a natural-language-based sketch/critique authoring process. In this chapter, we survey relevant prior work in both the deep-learning and human-computer interaction communities, document the data collection process and the systems' architectures in detail, present qualitative and quantitative results, and paint the landscape of several future research directions in this exciting area.

F. Huang (✉) · E. Schoop · J. Canny
University of California, Berkeley, USA
e-mail: forrest_huang@berkeley.edu

E. Schoop
e-mail: eschoop@berkeley.edu

J. Canny
e-mail: canny@berkeley.edu

D. Ha
Google Brain, Tokyo, Japan
e-mail: hadavid@google.com

J. Nichols
Apple, Inc., Cupertino, USA
e-mail: jeff@jeffreynichols.com

© The Author(s), under exclusive license to Springer Nature Switzerland AG 2021
Y. Li and O. Hilliges (eds.), *Artificial Intelligence for Human Computer Interaction: A Modern Approach*, Human–Computer Interaction Series,
https://doi.org/10.1007/978-3-030-82681-9_12

379

1   Introduction

Sketching is a natural and effective means to express novel artistic and functional concepts. It is an integral part of the creative process for many artists, engineers, and educators. The abstract yet expressive nature of sketches enables sketchers to quickly communicate conceptual and high-level ideas visually while leaving out unnecessary details. These characteristics are most notably manifested in the use of sketches in design processes, where sketches are used by designers to iteratively discuss and critique high-level design concepts and ideas.

Recent advances in deep-learning (DL) models greatly improved machines' abilities to perform Computer Vision tasks. In particular, convolutional neural networks, recurrent neural networks, and attention mechanisms dramatically outperform prior state-of-the-art methods in comprehending and generating visual content. They can perform these tasks even conditioned on user-specified natural language or other accompanying semantic information. These architectures provide great opportunities for developing creativity support applications of the type we have argued for. They support sketch inputs and outputs for applications such as sketch-based image retrieval and sketch generation systems.

This chapter explores and surveys multiple facets of research in deep-learning-based sketching systems that support creative processes. We describe three research projects spanning design and artistic applications, targeting amateur and professional users, and using sketches as inputs and outputs. We outline three important aspects in this area of research: (1) collecting appropriate sketch-based data; (2) adapting existing architectures and tasks to the sketch domain; and, (3) formulating new tasks that support novel interactions using state-of-the-art model architectures and deploying and evaluating these novel systems.

The key projects that we will include in this chapter are as follows:

1. a new dataset consisting of paired sketches and UI designs produced by UI/UX designers.
2. a new system that retrieves relevant UI designs based on user-specified sketches that can support various design applications.
3. a novel formulation of an iterative sketch-authoring process based on user-specified natural language inputs.

We begin the chapter by reviewing relevant prior literature on sketch-based applications in both the Deep-Learning (DL) community and Human-Computer-Interaction (HCI) community. We then describe the three aforementioned projects in detail and present qualitative and quantitative experimental results on existing and novel tasks. Finally, we conclude the chapter with a discussion of several avenues of further research in sketch-based deep-learning systems. We hope to provide a guide to aid the research and development of newer systems that work with sketches and sketch-based tasks. We aim to push the frontier of future sketch-based systems research to allow machines to support sketch-based creativity in various domains for users with all levels of expertise.

2 Role of Sketching in Supporting Creative Activities

Sketching plays a pivotal role in many types of creative activities because of its highly visual nature and its flexibility for creation and manipulation: users can create and imagine any kind of visual content, and continuously revise it without being constrained by unnecessary details. Sketches are an independent art form, but are also extensively used to draft and guide other forms of artistic expression such as oil painting, or storyboarding in films and motion graphics. Moreover, because sketches effectively communicate visual ideas, they are well-suited for design processes such as User Interface (UI) or User Experience (UX) Design.

For these reasons, a plethora of research systems and tools that use sketches have been developed by the HCI community. We survey several notable systems in the domains of artistic sketches and design sketches in this section.

2.1 Sketch-Based Applications Supporting Artistic Expressions

Prior works that aim to support artistic sketches have mostly taken the form of real-time assistance to directly improve the final sketching product, or to generate sketching tutorials for improving users' sketching proficiency. A number of sketching assistants use automatically-generated and crowd-sourced drawing guidance. ShadowDraw [23] and EZ-sketching [36] use edge images traced from natural images to suggest realistic sketch strokes to users. PortraitSketch provides sketching assistance specifically on facial sketches by adjusting geometry and stroke parameters [39]. Real-time, crowd-sourced feedback have also been used to correct and improve users' sketched strokes [25].

In addition to assisted sketching tools, researchers have developed tutorial systems to improve users' sketching proficiency. How2Sketch automatically generates multi-step tutorials for sketching 3D objects [14]. Sketch-sketch revolution provides first-hand experiences created by sketch experts for novice sketchers [10].

2.2 Sketch-Based Applications Supporting Design in Various Domains

Designers use sketches to expand novel ideas, visualize abstract concepts, and rapidly compare alternatives [4]. They are commonplace in the modern design workspace and typically require minimal effort for designers to produce. They are also sometimes preferred over high-fidelity artifacts because the details left out by abstract sketches imply and indicate incompleteness of designs. They encourage designers to more freely imagine and provide alternatives based on current designs without being concerned about committed to an existing designs. From some of our informal conversations with designers, it is observed that designers will trace high-fidelity design renderings using rough sketch strokes for soliciting higher-level, creative feedback.

Research in the HCI community has produced interfaces that use drawing input for creating interactive design prototypes. SILK is the first system that allows designers to author interactive, low-fidelity UI prototypes by sketching [21]. DENIM allows web designers to prototype with sketches at multiple detail levels [26]. More recently, Apparition uniquely allows users to sketch their desired interfaces while having crowdworkers translate sketches into workable prototypes in near real time [22].

3 Large-Scale Sketch Datasets and Sketch-Based Deep-Learning Applications

With the widespread use of DL approaches in Computer Vision, researchers have collected large-scale sketch datasets to train and evaluate these models. We describe several projects in the DL community that enable sketch-based retrieval and sketch generation tasks using recently collected sketch datasets. The capabilities of these models allow us to create novel interactive systems that were difficult prior to the introduction of deep-learning.

3.1 Large-Scale Sketch Datasets

To support DL-based approaches toward sketch comprehension and generation, which rely heavily on large-scale datasets, researchers have crowdsourced sketch datasets of individual objects. Most of these datasets have focused on individual instances that either correspond to natural language or a general semantic class. The Quick, Draw! [18] and TU-Berlin [9] datasets consist of human-drawn sketches for 345 and 250 object classes, respectively. SketchyDB provides paired images and simple sketches for retrieval tasks [33].

More recently, researchers have explored beyond individual sketched instances to compile datasets of sketched multi-object scenes. The SketchyScene dataset consists of sketched scenes of pre-drawn objects transformed and resized by humans, as scene sketches are highly demanding for users to create from scratch [42]. Sketchy-COCO starts with the MSCOCO dataset and retrieves relevant instances from the Sketchy dataset, compiling them into complex scenes [11]. Nevertheless, none of these datasets consist of sketched scenes drawn by humans entirely from scratch. This is mainly due to the high skill barrier of generating these sketches that make large-scale crowd-sourcing difficult [42].

Related to complex sketches of multiple artistic objects, the DiDi dataset introduced drawings of flow-charts and functional diagrams traced entirely by human users [12]. While users did not design the diagrams from scratch, they generated each individual sketch stroke based on the procedurally generated templates.

3.2 Sketch-Based Image and 3D Model Retrieval

Sketch-based Image Retrieval is a frequently studied problem in the Computer Vision community. The current state-of-the-art solution to an instance of this problem is deep-learning-based [32]. A typical DL-based approach involves training an encoder network to produce meaningful representations in a low-dimensional embedding space based on high-dimensional image inputs. To learn this embedding space, the network is trained on 'triplets' of data samples: one 'anchor' image as the reference, one 'positive' image that is either directly paired with the 'anchor' image or is semantically relevant to the 'anchor' image, and another 'negative' image that is irrelevant to the 'anchor' image. The network is trained to produce similar embeddings (with a low analytical distance in the embedding space) for the 'positive' and 'anchor' images and dissimilar embeddings for the 'negative' and 'anchor' images. When retrieving images with a sketch query, the natural images are ranked by the distance (e.g., Euclidean Distance) between their embedding outputs and the sketch query's embedding outputs. A few of the recently introduced datasets mentioned in Sect. 3.1 have introduced DL-based architectures that establish state-of-the-art performance over non-neural baselines.

3.3 Neural Sketch Generation

Recent advancements in the DL community have introduced deep-neural-networks capable of recognizing and generating sketches. Sketch-RNN [13] is one of the first RNN-based models that can generate sequential sketch strokes through supervised learning on sketch datasets. We will describe this architecture in detail in Sect. 6 due to its high relevance to our work. Transformer networks [38] have shown superior performance in natural language modeling/generation tasks and have recently been applied to model sketch strokes and SVG graphics. These approaches have been shown to improve sketch generation performance over Sketch-RNN. Most recently,

CoSE is a hierarchical architecture that aims to improve the performance of DL models in generating structured sketches previously difficult for flat models [2]. In particular, this approach targets the generation of structured diagrams in the DiDi dataset.

Another highly relevant model architecture is Generative Adversarial Networks (GANs). GANs have also been used to translate realistic images into sketches (or edges) at the pixel level by training on paired [24] and unpaired [41] sketch and image data. While the pixel-based architectures have been effective when handling natural image data, it does not naturally couple with humans' sketching processes, which are inherently sequential.

4 Developing a Paired Sketch/User Interface Dataset

In this section, we explore the first step toward developing a novel deep-learning-driven creativity support application: collecting a large-scale sketch dataset. We specifically target the task of drawing correspondence between two types of visual artifacts commonly used in the early stage of UI design: low-fidelity design sketches and high-fidelity UI examples.

Both Sketches and UI design examples are commonly used in the UI design process as reported by a variety of prior studies [15, 28] and our informal conversation with designers. Designers search, consult and curate design examples to gain inspiration, explore viable alternatives and form the basis for comparative evaluations [3, 15]. Similarly, designers frequently use sketches to expand novel ideas, visualize abstract concepts, and rapidly compare alternatives [4]. As such, understanding correspondences between these two modalities would allow machines to rapidly retrieve popular visual illustrations, common flow patterns, and high-fidelity layout implementations [6] from large corpuses, which can greatly augment various design tasks [20, 29, 37].

To solve this task using deep-learning-based approaches, we decided to collect a dataset of actual sketches stylistically and semantically similar to designers' sketches of UIs. This also allows us to leverage large-scale UI datasets recently introduced by mobile-interaction mining applications [6], such that we would only need to collect sketches newly created by designers based on screenshots of original UIs in the Rico dataset [7]. The dataset is now publicly available at https://github.com/huang4fstudio/swire.

4.1 Designer Recruitment and Compensation

We recruited 4 designers through the freelancing platform Upwork. All designers reported having at least occasional UI/UX design experience and substantial sketching experience. In addition, all designers reported receiving formal training in UI design and degrees in design-related fields. They were compensated 20 USD per hour and worked for 60–73 h.

4.2 Dataset Statistics

We collected 3702 sketches[1] of 2201 UI examples from 167 popular apps in the Rico dataset. Each sketch was created with pen and paper in 4.1 min on average. Many UI examples were sketched by multiple designers. 66.5% of the examples were sketched by 2 designers, 32.7% of the examples were sketched by 1 designer and the remaining examples (<1%) were sketched by 3 designers in our dataset. Our 4 designers sketched 455/1017/1222/1008 UIs, respectively, based on their availability. We allocated batches of examples to different combinations of designers to ensure the generality of the dataset.

We did not have the resources to generate sketches for every UI in the Rico dataset, so we curated a diverse subset of well-designed UI examples that cover 23 app categories in the Google Play Store and were of average to high design quality. We omitted poorly designed UIs from the dataset because of the relatively small size of the dataset for neural network training. Noise introduced into training by poor designs would have the potential to negatively impact the training time and quality of our model.

4.3 Data Collection and Postprocessing Procedure

We supplied the screenshots of our curated UI examples to the recruited designers and asked them to create sketches corresponding to the screenshots with pen and paper. They were prompted to reconstruct a low-fidelity sketch from each screenshot as if they were the designers of the interfaces. We instructed them to replace all actual image content with a sketched placeholder (a square with a cross or a mountain) and replace dynamic text with template text in each screenshot as shown in Fig. 1. We added these instructions to obtain sketches with a more unified representation focused on the design layout of various UIs. These instructions also make it easier for the neural network to learn the concepts of images and text within the constraints of our small dataset.

In order to efficiently collect and calibrate sketches created by multiple designers in various formats of photos and scans, we supplied them with paper templates with frames for them to sketch on as shown in Fig. 1. These frames are annotated with four ArUco codes [27] at the corners to allow perspective correction. All photos and

---

[1] This total of 3702 sketches differs from original Swire publication [17]. We discovered that 100 trial sketches from a pilot study were accidentally included in the original stated total and we have corrected the numbers in this chapter.

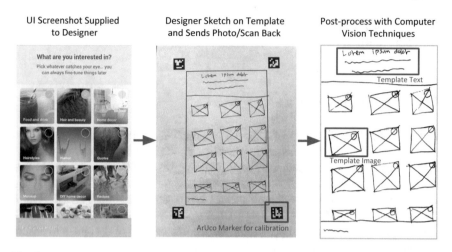

UI Screenshot Supplied to Designer   Designer Sketch on Template and Sends Photo/Scan Back   Post-process with Computer Vision Techniques

Fig. 1 Data collection procedure. We first send a UI screenshot (left) and paper templates with ArUco markers to designers. Designers then sketch on the template and send back a photo or a scan of the completed sketch (middle). We then post-process the photo using computer vision techniques to obtain the final clean sketch dataset (right)

scans of the sketches are corrected with affine transformation and thresholded to obtain binary sketches as final examples in the dataset.

5 Developing Swire: A Sketch-Based User Interface Retrieval System

After collecting a dataset of corresponding UIs and screenshots, we proceed to develop Swire, a sketch-based user interface retrieval system that learns correspondences between UIs and sketches in the dataset. In developing Swire, we adapted a commonly used DL architecture, training paradigm, and loss function that is able to retrieve relevant visual content given input sketches. Similar to prior work in sketch-based image retrieval, we used a convolutional neural network architecture and adopt the cross-modal embedding training scheme using a triplet loss. This allows us to take advantage of a convolutional neural network's strong capability to understand high-dimensional visual features while creating a unified embedding space for both sketches and UIs with learned concepts based on their correspondences. This means Swire can be used to search a dataset of UIs using either sketches or UI screenshots as the querying modality.

The development of Swire consists of a training phase and a querying phase. During the training phase, we train Swire's deep neural network to generate similar low-dimensional outputs (64-dimensional) for matching pairs of screenshots and sketches, and dissimilar outputs for non-matching pairs of screenshots and sketches.

This training scheme is shown to be useful for sketch-based image retrieval [33]. In the querying phase, we use Swire's trained neural network to encode a user's sketch query and retrieve UIs with the closest output to the sketch query's output.

5.1 Network Architecture

We used two convolutional sub-networks to handle the two inputs of sketch-screenshot pairs, these two sub-networks are similar to VGG-A [35], a shallow variant of the state-of-the-art network that won the ILSVRC2014 image recognition challenge [31]. Our network consists of 11 layers, with five convolutional blocks and three fully connected layers. Each convolutional block contains two (one for the first two blocks) convolutional layers with 3×3 kernels and one max-pooling layer. The convolutional layers in the five blocks have 64, 128, 256, 512, and 512 filters respectively. The first two fully connected layers have 4096 hidden units. The last layer has 64 hidden units and outputs the 64-dimensional embedding used for querying. The activation functions of all layers except the last layer are ReLU. The network architecture is described in detail in Fig. 2.

The final 64-dimensional output embeddings of the sub-networks are trained to produce adequate embeddings represented as codes in their respective final layers. The model is trained with a pairwise sampling scheme described in the following subsection.

5.2 Triplet Loss

The model is trained with a Triplet Loss function [34, 40] that involves the neural-network outputs of three inputs: an 'anchor' sketch s, a 'positive' matching screenshot i and a 'negative' mismatched screenshot i'. This forms two pairs of input during

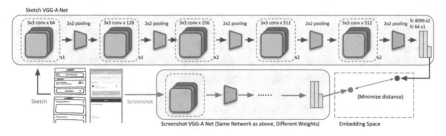

Fig. 2 Network architecture of Swire's neural network. Swire's neural network consists of two identical sub-networks similar to the VGG-A deep convolutional neural network. These networks have different weights and attempt to encode matching pairs of screenshots and sketches with similar values

training. The positive pair $p(s, i)^+$ consists of a sketch-screenshot pair that correspond to each other. The negative pair $p(s, i')^-$ consists of a sketch-screenshot pair that does not correspond. The negative pair is obtained with the same sketch from the positive pair and a random screenshot sampled from the mini-batch.

During training, each pair $p(s, i)$ is passed through two sub-networks such that the sketch sample s is passed through the sketch sub-network and outputs an embedding $f_s(s)$, and we similarly obtain the neural-network output of the screenshot $f_i(i)$ from the screenshot sub-network. We compute the Euclidean distance D between the neural network outputs. For the positive pair,

$$D(p(s, i)^+) = ||f_s(s) - f_i(i)||_2.$$

Similarly, for the distance of the negative pair,

$$D(p(s, i')^-) = ||f_s(s) - f_i(i')||_2$$

With these distances, we formulate a triplet loss function,

$$L = D(p(s, i)^+) + \max(0, m - D(p(s, i')^-))$$

$$m = \text{margin between positive and negative pairs.}$$

We maintain a margin m between the positive and negative pairs to prevent the network from learning trivial solutions (zero embeddings for all examples).

5.3 Data and Training Procedure

We train our network using the dataset described in Sect. 4. Since the sketches are created by four separate designers, we split the data and used data collected from three designers for training and from one designer for testing. This is to ensure that the model generalizes across sketches produced by different designers. In addition, we do not repeat interfaces from the same apps between the training and test sets. This creates 1722 matching sketch-screenshot pairs for training and 276 pairs for testing.

During training, the sketches and screenshots are resized to 224×224 pixels, and the pixel values are normalized between $(-1, 1)$ centered at 0. The network is trained using a Stochastic Gradient Descent Optimizer with a mini-batch size of 32. The learning rate is 1×10^{-2}. The margin is 0.2 in all models. All hyper-parameters listed above were determined by empirical experiments on the training set.

5.4 Querying

When a user makes a query with a drawn sketch, the model computes an output by passing the sketch through the sketch sub-network. This output is then compared with all neural-network outputs of the screenshots of UI examples in the dataset using a nearest neighbor search. The UI results are ranked by the distance between their outputs and the user's sketch's output.

5.5 Results

5.5.1 Baselines

We implement competitive non-neural baselines to evaluate the performance of our method. As described in Sect. 3.2, typical methods of sketch-based image retrieval involve two steps: (1) extract an edge-map from the original image to be queried, and (2) match the edge-map using a specific similarity metric. Using this framework, we first extracted the edges of the screenshots using the Canny Edge detector [5]. We then extracted features from the edges using Bag-of-words (BoW) Histogram of Oriented Gradients (HOG) filters. BoW-HOG filters are an advanced method of computing similarity between images. They capture edge features in an image by computing the magnitude of gradients across the entire image with respect to multiple orientations. This method summarizes image features with fixed-length vectors that describe the occurrences and characteristics of edges in images. This method is highly effective for sketch-based image retrieval as it focuses on the characteristics of edges while being insensitive to local translations and rotations.

After obtaining these fixed-length vectors for screenshots and sketch queries, we compare them using Euclidean distance as a simple metric to query for closest matching images (design screenshots in our case) to the sketch queries.

5.5.2 Quantitative Results

We use a test set that consists of 276 UI examples to compare Top-1 and Top-10 performances of BoW-HOG filters and Swire. The results are summarized in Table 1. We observe that Swire significantly outperform BoW-HOG filters for Top-10 performance at 60.9%. For Top-1 accuracy, Swire achieves an accuracy of 15.9% which only slightly outperformed the strong baseline of BoW-HOG filters at 15.6%. This shows Swire to be particularly effective for retrieving complex examples from the dataset compared to the BoW-HOG filters. We believe deep-learning-based Swire is advantageous compared to BoW-HOG filters that rely on matching edge-maps because UI sketches have semantic complexities that are not captured by edge-maps of screenshots.

Table 1 Top-k accuracy of various models on the test set. Swire significantly outperforms BoW-HOG filters

Technique	Top-1 (%)	Top-10 (%)
(Chance)	0.362	3.62
BoW-HOG filters	15.6	38.8
Swire	**15.9**	**60.9**

5.5.3   Qualitative Results

We visualize query results from the test set to qualitatively understand the performance of Swire in Fig. 3. Swire is able to retrieve relevant menu-based interfaces (Example a) despite the difference in visual appearance of the menu items. Swire is also able to retrieve pop-up windows (Example b) implemented in various ways despite the drastic difference in the dimensions of the pop-up windows. We observe similar efficacy in retrieving settings (Example c), list-based layouts (Example f), and login layouts (Example e). Nevertheless, we observe that Swire sometimes ignores smaller details of the interfaces described by sketched elements. This limitation will be further discussed in Sect. 7.1.

5.5.4   Expert Evaluation

To better evaluate Swire's performance from professional users' perspectives, we recruited 5 designers on Upwork with substantial experience in mobile UI/UX design to evaluate selected results from the test set. There was no overlap between these designers and those recruited for creating the dataset. We provided them with 9 sets of query sketches and the corresponding Top-10 retrieved results for each query from the test set. The 9 sets consist of 3 'best' results (the corresponding screenshot of the sketch query is retrieved as the Top-1 result), 3 'mediocre' results (the corresponding screenshot of the sketch query is retrieved within the Top-10 results, but not Top-1), and 3 'poor' results (the corresponding screenshot of the sketch query is not retrieved within the Top-10 results). We asked the designers to provide comments on each set of results regarding the relevance between the sketches and the screenshots, and to comment on the potential integration of this tool into their design workflows.

Most designers agreed that all retrieved results in the 'best' result sets are relevant to the query, and they would be satisfied with the results. They were especially satisfied with a result set of sliding menus (also shown in Fig. 3a). They were able to identify the results as 'variations on the theme of navigation drawers' (D3) or 'slide out modal pattern.' (D2) Moreover, the designers also expressed satisfaction toward some sets of 'mediocre' results. Most were satisfied with a set of results that 'show variations of the top tabbed navigation' (D5) which is a common design pattern.

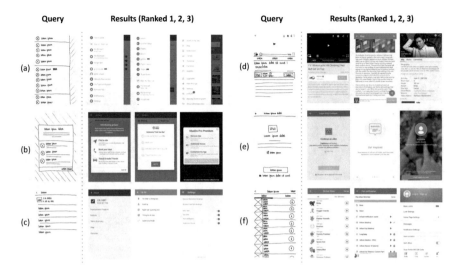

Fig. 3 Query results for complete sketches. Swire is able to retrieve common types of UIs such as sliding menus (**a**), settings (**c**), and login (**e**) layouts

On the other hand, some designers considered the 'poor' results unsatisfactory. For example, designers were less satisfied with the model's performance on a sign-up sketch, commenting that the model only gathered screens with similar element layouts while ignoring the true nature of the input fields and buttons in the query (D3). However, D4 considered 'rows of design elements' common in the results relevant to the sketch, and D1 considered two similar sign-up screens retrieved by the model as strong results even they did not match up perfectly with the sketch.

In general, we observed that designers were more satisfied with the results when the model was able to retrieve results that are semantically similar at a high-level instead of those with matching low-level element layouts. Notably, D1 commented that we 'probably already considered the common UI sketch patterns and train[ed] [our] system to match it up with image results,' which reflects the effectiveness of Swire in detecting common UI patterns in some instances provided that it was not specifically trained to recognize these patterns. All designers also considered Swire to be potentially useful in their workflows for researching, ideating, and implementing novel designs.

5.6 Applications

In Sect. 5.5, we evaluated and validated Swire's effectiveness for generally finding design examples through sketch-based queries. Since both sketches and UI design examples are commonly used in the early stages of the UI design process as reported

Query   **Results (Ranked 1, 2, 3)**

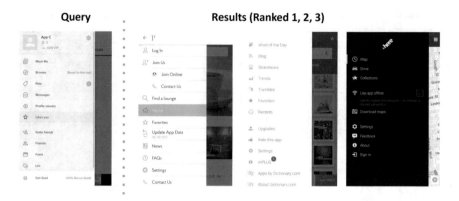

Fig. 4 Alternative design query results. Swire is able to retrieve similar UIs in the dataset from queries of complete, high-fidelity UI screenshots

by a variety of prior studies [15, 28], we explore the potential usage of Swire through several design applications in this section. Prototypes of these applications implemented with Jupyter Notebook are available at https://github.com/huang4fstudio/swire.

5.6.1 Evaluation with Alternative Designs

Designers often explore alternative design examples to support the implementation and comparative evaluation [15] of their own designs. HCI research literature also recommends the use of parallel prototyping techniques to obtain better final products through extensive comparison [8]. Swire is able to support design comparisons because it enables querying for similar UIs with high-fidelity UI prototypes.

Swire is effective in retrieving similar UIs because the visual content of UI screenshots is reinforced with the semantic structure of sketches in the embedding space during training. Swire can thus be used as a semantically aware similarity metric between interfaces.

Figure 4 shows an example of Swire retrieving similar menus using a high-fidelity screenshot. We similarly observe that it is able to retrieve design patterns such as login screens, list-based UIs, and grid-based UIs when querying with screenshots (please see the original Swire paper [17] for a complete figure illustrating these patterns). This enables effective comparison between similar designs with slight variations.

5.6.2 Auto-completing Partial Designs

Sketches are often used for rapid exploration of potential design solutions [4]. Designers use partial sketches to express core ideas, while leaving out parts of the interface in

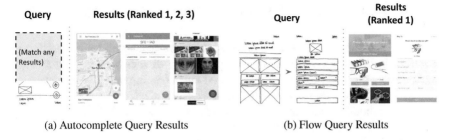

(a) Autocomplete Query Results   (b) Flow Query Results

Fig. 5 Query results for **a** incomplete sketches and **b** flow queries. Swire is able to retrieve interfaces only based on parts specified by users' sketches while remaining agnostic to other parts of the UIs. Swire is also able to retrieve user flows by querying multiple UIs in sequences concurrently

sketches for considering viable design alternatives. We trained an alternative model *Swire-segments* on partial sketches of UIs, which allows us to 'auto-complete' the remaining UI by retrieving a variety of examples that are only required to match parts of the UI sketched by the user. This model allows designers to quickly gain design inspirations that are relevant to the key UI elements desired by them.

In the training and querying phases of *Swire-segments*, UI examples are split into small parts. Designers can thus specify one-or-more parts of the UIs to be matched by the model with examples in the dataset. We compute an embedding for each part of the interface and match only the embeddings of the parts specified by the users for retrieval. Figure 5a shows that Swire-segments is able to retrieve multiple designs that all contain the Floating Action Button (FAB, a popular Android design paradigm) but with diverse layouts. Swire-segments is also able to retrieve interfaces with only tab-based top bars in common. In these examples, Swire-segments is able to remain agnostic to the unspecified part of the sketch queries.

5.6.3 User Flow Examples

Beyond querying for single UIs, designers also use sketches to illustrate user experience at multiple scales [28], such as conveying transitions and animations between multiple interfaces. Since the Rico dataset also includes user interaction data, we use this data to enable flow querying with Swire. Designers can use this application to interact with interaction design examples that can accelerate the design of effective user flows.

To query flow examples in the dataset, since Swire creates a single embedding for each UI, we can match an arbitrary number of interfaces in arbitrary order by concatenating the embedding values during the ranking process of querying. We qualitatively observe that Swire is able to retrieve registration (Fig. 5b) and 'closing menu' flows that are commonly implemented by designers. Since Rico also contains transition details between consequent UIs, these examples can demonstrate popular animation patterns [6] that provide inspiration to interaction and animation designers.

6 Developing Scones: A Conversational Sketching System

Beyond comprehending and understanding the correspondences between UIs and sketches, in this section we explore the possibility of sketch generation through another more abstract input modality: natural language. In particular we develop a system that supports *iterative generation* of sketches given users' text instructions to support refinement and critique. The goal is to mimic a user trying to verbally convey a visual idea to an expert sketcher.

While sketching is a powerful communication medium, creating sketches that effectively communicate ideas visually requires significant training. The use of sketches in an iterative design and/or artistic process, where the sketch itself is annotated or refined, requires additional, specialized expertise. Inspired by recent development of deep-learning-driven QA systems and generative sketching models, we develop Scones, a deep-learning-based sketching system that can progressively construct a sketched scene based on multiple natural language instructions across multiple turns, an interaction analogous to an iterative sketch/critique process. This system must unify knowledge of the *low-level* mechanics for generating sketch strokes and natural language modification instructions with a *high-level* understanding of composition and object relationships in scenes.

We formulate the novel task of iteratively generating and refining sketches with text instructions and present a web-deployable implementation of Scones. Scones contains a scene composition proposer that takes a novel approach in creating and editing scenes of objects using natural language. It adapts a recent neural network architecture and improves state-of-the-art performance on the scene modification task. We also introduce in Scones a novel method for specifying high-level scene semantics within individual object sketches by conditioning sketch generation with mask outlines of target sketches. Using Scones, we hope to enable users of all levels of sketch expertise to freely express their intent using abstract, text-based instructions, together with concrete visual media.

6.1 System Architecture

The creation of complex sketches often begins with semantic planning of scene objects. Sketchers often construct high-level scene layouts before filling in low-level details. Modeling ML systems after this high-to-low-level workflow has been shown to be beneficial for transfer learning from other visual domains and for supporting interactive interfaces for human users [16]. Inspired by this high-to-low-level process, Scones adopts a hierarchical workflow that first proposes a scene-level composition layout of objects using its *Composition Proposer*, then generates individual object sketches, conditioned on the scene-level information, using its *Object Generators* (Fig. 6).

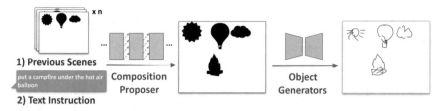

Fig. 6 Overall architecture of Scones. Scones take a two-stage approach toward generating and modifying sketched scenes based on users' instructions

6.1.1 Composition Proposer

The Composition Proposer in Scones uses text instructions to place and configure objects in the scene. It also considers recent past iterations of text instructions and scene *context* at each conversation turn. As text instructions and sketch components occur sequentially in time, each with a variable length of tokens and objects, respectively, we formulate composition proposal as a sequence modeling task. We use a self-attention-only decoder component of the Transformer [38], a recent deep-learning model architecture with high performance for this task.

To produce the output scene S_i at turn i, the Composition Proposer takes inputs of $n = 10$ previous scenes $S_{(i-n),...,(i-1)}$ and text instructions $C_{(i-n),...,(i-1)}$ as recent *context* of the conversation. Each output scene S_i contains l_i objects $o_{(i,1),...,(i,l_i)} \in S_i$ and special tokens o_s marking the beginning and o_e marking the end of the scene. Each text instruction C_i contains m_i text tokens $t_{(i,1),...,(i,m_i)} \in C_i$ that consist of words and punctuation marks.

We represent each object o as a 102-dimensional vector o:

$$o = [\mathbb{1}_s, \mathbb{1}_e, e^{(o)}, e^{(u)}, e^{(s)}, e^{(f)}, x, y]$$

The first two dimensions $\mathbb{1}_s$, $\mathbb{1}_e$ are Boolean attributes reserved for the start and end of the scene object sequences. $e^{(o)}$ is a 58-dimensional one-hot vector[2] representing one of 58 classes of the scene object. $e^{(u)}$ is a 35-dimensional one-hot vector representing one of 35 sub-types (minor variants) of the scene objects. $e^{(s)}$ is a three-dimensional one-hot vector representing one of three sizes of the scene objects. $e^{(f)}$ is a two-dimensional one-hot vector representing the horizontal orientation of whether the object is flipped in the x-direction. The last two dimensions $x, y \in [0, 1]$ represents the x- and y-position of the center of the object. This representation is very similar to that of the CoDraw dataset the model was trained on, which is described in detail in Sect. 6.2.1. For each text token t, we use a 300-dimensional GLoVe vector trained on 42B tokens from the Common Crawl dataset [30] to semantically represent these words in the instructions.

---

[2] An encoding of class information that is an array of bits where only the corresponding position for the class to be encoded is 1, and all other bits are 0s.

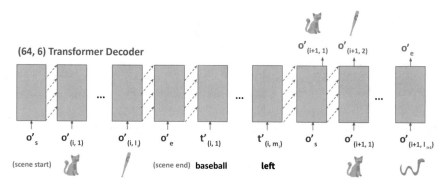

Fig. 7 The scene layout generation process using the Transformer model of the *Composition Proposer*

To train the Transformer network with the heterogeneous inputs of o and t across the two modalities, we create a unified representation of cardinality $|o| + |t| = 402$ and adapt o and t to this representation by simply padding additional dimensions in the representations with zeros as shown in Eq. 1.

$$o'_{i,j} = [o_{i,j}, \mathbf{0}_{(300)}] \quad t'_{i,j} = [\mathbf{0}_{(102)}, t_{i,j}]. \tag{1}$$

We interleave text instructions and scene objects chronologically to form a long sequence $[C_{(i-n)}, S_{(i-n)}, \ldots, C_{(i-1)}, S_{(i-1)}, C_i]$ as input to the model for generating an output scene representation S_i. We expand the sequential elements within C and S, and add separators to them to obtain the full input sequence to a single Transformer Decoder. To adapt the Transformer model to our multi-modal inputs t' and o' and produce new scene objects o, we employ a 402-dimensional input embedding layer and 102-dimensional output embedding layer in the Transformer model. The outputs from the network are then passed to sigmoid and softmax activations for object position and other properties respectively. We show this generation process in Eq. 2 and in Fig. 7.

$$S_i = [o_{(i,1),\ldots,(i,l)}] = \textbf{Transformer}([o'_s, o'_{(i-n,1)}, \ldots, o'_{(i-n,l_{(i-n)})},$$
$$o'_e, t'_{(i-n,1)}, \ldots, t'_{(i-n,m_{(i-n)})}, \ldots, t'_{(i,1)}, \ldots, t'_{(i,l_i)}, o'_s]) \tag{2}$$

6.1.2 Object Generators

Since the outputs of the Composition Proposer are scene layouts consisting of high-level object specifications, we generate the final raw sketch strokes for each of these objects based on their specifications with *Object Generators*. We adapt Sketch-RNN to generate sketches of individual object classes to present to users for evaluation and revision in the next conversation turn. Each sketched object Q consists of h strokes $q_{1...h}$. The strokes are encoded using the *Stroke-5* format [13]. Each stroke $q = [\Delta x, \Delta y, p_d, p_u, p_e]$ represents states of a pen performing the sketching process. The first two properties Δx and Δy are offsets from the previous point that the pen moved from. The last three elements $[p_d, p_u, p_e]$ are a one-hot vector representing the state of the pen after the current point (pen down, pen up, end of sketch, respectively). All sketches begin with the initial stroke $q_1 = [0, 0, 1, 0, 0]$.

Since Sketch-RNN does not constrain aspect ratios, directions and poses of its output sketches, we introduce two additional conditions for the sketch generation process: masks m and aspect ratios r. These conditions ensure our Object Generators generate sketches with appearances that follow the object specifications generated by the Composition Proposer. For each object sketch, we compute the aspect ratio $r = \dfrac{\Delta y}{\Delta x}$ by taking the distance between the leftmost and rightmost stroke as Δx and the distance between topmost and bottommost stroke as Δy. To compute the object mask m, we first render the strokes into a pixel bitmap, then mark all pixels as 1 if they are in between the leftmost pixel py_{xmin} and rightmost pixel py_{xmax} that are passed through by any strokes for each row y, or if they are in between the bottommost pixel px_{ymin} and topmost pixel px_{ymax} that are passed through by any strokes for each column x (Eq. 3). As this mask-building algorithm only involves pixel computations, we can use the same method to build masks for clip art objects (used to train the Composition Proposer) to generate sketches with poses matching the Composition Proposer's object representations.

$$m_{(x,y)} = \begin{cases} 1 \text{ if } py_{xmax} \geq x \geq py_{xmin}, \text{or;} \\ 1 \text{ if } px_{ymax} \geq y \geq px_{ymin} \\ 0 \text{ otherwise} \end{cases} \quad (3)$$

We adapt the Variational-Autoencoder (VAE)-based conditional variant of Sketch-RNN to enable generating and editing of sketch objects. Our adapted conditional Sketch-RNN encodes input sketches with a Bi-directional LSTM to a latent vector z. The Hyper-LSTM decoder then recreates sketch strokes $q'_{1...h}$ from z, and m, r described above during training, as defined in Eq. 4 and shown in Fig. 8. Since the latent space is also trained to match a multivariate Gaussian distribution, the Object Generators can support sketch generation when the objects are first added to the scene by randomly sampling $z \sim N(0, 1)^{128}$.

$$q'_{1...h} = \textbf{Sketch-RNN Decoder}([m, r, z]), z \sim N(0, 1)^{128}$$
$$z = \textbf{Sketch-RNN Encoder}(q_{1...h}). \quad (4)$$

As m is a two-dimensional mask, we encode m using a small convolutional neural network into a flattened embedding to be concatenated with z, r, and q_i as inputs to the decoder. The decoder then outputs parameters for a Gaussian Mixture Model

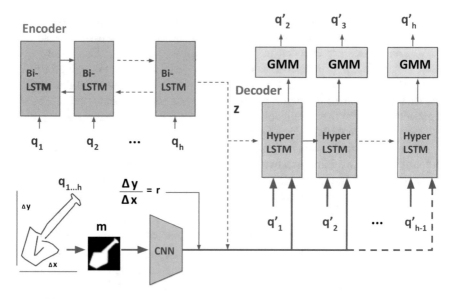

Fig. 8 Sketch-RNN model architecture of the Object Generators

(GMM) which will be sampled to obtain Δx and Δy. It also outputs probabilities for a categorical distribution that will be sampled to obtain p_d, p_u and p_e. This generation process and the architecture of the model are illustrated in Fig. 8, and are described in the Sketch-RNN paper [13].

6.2   Datasets and Model Training

As Scones uses two components to generate scenes of sketched objects, it is trained on two datasets that correspond to the tasks these components perform.

6.2.1   CoDraw Dataset

We used the CoDraw dataset [19] to train the Composition Proposer to generate high-level scene layout proposals from text instructions. The task used to collect this data involves two human users taking on the roles of *Drawer* and *Teller* in each session. First, the Teller is presented with an abstract scene containing multiple clip art objects in certain configurations, and the Drawer is given a blank canvas. The Teller provides instructions using only text in a chat interface to instruct the Drawer on how to modify clip art objects in the scene. The Teller has no access to the Drawer's canvas in most conversation turns, except in one of the turns when they can decide to 'peek' at the Drawer's canvas. The dataset consists of 9993 sessions of conversation records, scene modifications, and ground-truth scenes.

Using this dataset, we trained the Composition Proposer to respond to users' instructions given past instructions and scenes. We used the same training/validation/ test split as the original dataset. Our model is trained to optimize the loss function L_{cm} that corresponds to various attributes of the scene objects in the training set:

$$L_{cm} = L_c + \lambda_{\text{sub}} L_{\text{sub}} + \lambda_{\text{flip}} L_{\text{flip}} + \lambda_{\text{size}} L_{\text{size}} + \lambda_{xy} L_{xy}. \qquad (5)$$

L_c is the cross-entropy loss between the one-hot vector of the true class label and the predicted output probabilities by the model. Similarly L_{flip} and L_{size} are cross-entropy losses for the horizontal orientation and size of the object. L_{xy} is the Euclidean Distance between predicted position and true position of the scene object. We trained the model using an Adam Optimizer with the learning rate of $lr = 1 \times 10^{-4}$ for 200 epochs. We set $\lambda_{\text{sub}} = 5.0 \times 10^{-2}$, $\lambda_{\text{flip}} = 5.0 \times 10^{-2}$, $\lambda_{\text{size}} = 5.0 \times 10^{-2}$, $\lambda_{xy} = 1.0$. These hyper-parameters were tuned based on empirical experiments on the validation split of the dataset.

6.2.2 Quick, Draw! Dataset

The Quick, Draw! dataset consists of sketch strokes of 345 concept categories created by human users in a game in 20 s [18]. We trained our 34 Object Generators on 34 categories of Quick, Draw! data to create sketches of individual objects.

Each sketch stroke in Quick, Draw! was first converted to the Stroke-5 format. Δxs and Δys of the sketch strokes were normalized with their standard deviations for all sketches in their respective categories. Each category consists of 75000/2500/2500 sketches in the training/validation/test set.

The loss function of the conditional Sketch-RNN L_s consists of the reconstruction loss L_R and KL loss L_{KL}:

$$L_s = \lambda_{KL} L_{KL} + L_R \qquad (6)$$

The KL loss L_{KL} is the Kullback-Leibler divergence between the encoded z from the encoder and $N(0, 1)^{128}$. The reconstruction loss L_R is the negative log-likelihood of the ground-truth strokes under the GMM and a categorical distribution parametrized by the model. We refer interested readers to a detailed description of L_s in the original Sketch-RNN paper [13]. The initial learning rate of the training procedure was $lr = 1.0 \times 10^{-3}$ and exponentially decayed to 1.0×10^{-5} at a rate of 0.9999. λ_{KL} was initially 0.01 and exponentially increased to 0.5^3 at a rate of 0.99995. The models were also trained with gradient clipping of 1.0.

---

[3] For some object categories, we found that increasing the KL weight to 1.0 improves the authors' perceived quality of generated sketches.

6.3 Results

To compare the effectiveness of Scones at generating scene sketches with existing models and human-level performance, we quantitatively evaluated its performance in an iterative scene authoring task. Moreover, as Scones uses generative models to produce object sketches, we qualitatively evaluated a large number of examples generated by the two components of Scones.

6.3.1 Composition Modification State of the Art

To evaluate the output of the Composition Proposer against the models introduced with the CoDraw dataset, we adapted its output to match that expected by the well-defined evaluation metrics proposed by the original CoDraw paper [19]. The original task described in the CoDraw paper involves only proposing and modifying high-level object representations in scenes agnostic to their appearance. The performance of a 'Drawer' (a human or machine which generates scene compositions) can be quantified by a similarity metric constrained between 0 and 5 (higher is more similar) by comparing properties of and relations between objects in the generated scene and objects in the ground truth from the dataset.

Running our Composition Proposer on the CoDraw test set, we achieved an average similarity metric of 3.55. This exceeded existing state-of-the-art performance (Table 2) on the iterative scene authoring task using replayed text instructions (script) from CoDraw.

To provide an illustrative example of our Composition Proposer's output on this task, we visualize two example scenes generated from the CoDraw validation set in Fig. 9. In scene (a), the Composition Proposer extracted the class (slide), direction (faces right), and position relative to parts of the object (ladder along left edge) from the text instruction, to place a slide in the scene. Similarly, it was able to place the bear in between the oak and pine trees in scene (b), with the bear touching the left edge of the pine tree. It is important to note the Composition Proposer completely regenerates the entire scene at each conversation turn. This means it correctly preserved object attributes from previous scenes while making the requested modifications from the current turn. In these instances, the sun in scene (a) and the trees in scene (b) were left mostly unchanged while other attributes of the scenes were modified.

Table 2 Test set performance of various models on the CoDraw task

Teller	Drawer	Similarity ↑ (out of 5)
Script	**Scones**	**3.55**
Script	Neural network [19]	3.39
Script	Nearest-neighbor [19]	0.94
Script	Human	**3.83**

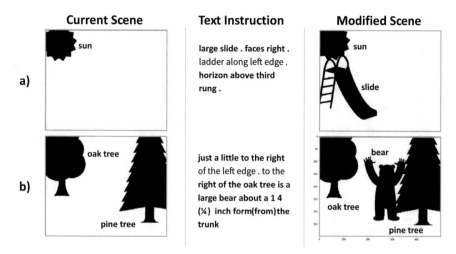

Fig. 9 Example scenes for the scene layout modification task. The Composition Proposer was able to improve state-of-the-art performance for modifying object representations in scene compositions

6.3.2 Sketches with Clip Art Objects as Mask and Ratio Guidance

The Object Generators are designed to generate sketches which respect high-level scene layout information under the guidance of the mask and aspect ratio conditions. To inform generated object sketches with pose suggestions from scene composition layouts, we built outline masks from clip art objects and computed aspect ratios using the same method as building them for training sketches described in Sect. 6.1.2. We demonstrate the Object Generators' performance in two important scenarios that allow Scones to adapt to specific subclass and pose contexts.

Generating Objects for Closely Related Classes
While the Composition Proposer classifies objects as one distinct class out of 58, some of these classes are closely related and are not differentiated by the Object Generators. In these cases, object masks can be used by an Object Generator to effectively disambiguate the desired output subclass. For instance, the Composition Proposer generates trees as one of three classes: Oak tree (tall and with curly edges), Apple tree (round and short), and Pine tree (tall and pointy); while there is only a single Object Generator trained on a general class of all types of tree objects. We generated three different masks and aspect ratios based on three clip art images and used them as inputs to a single tree-based Object Generator to generate appropriate tree objects (by sampling $z \sim N(0, 1)^{128}$). The Object Generator was able to sketch trees with configurations corresponding to input masks from clip art objects (Fig. 10). The generated sketches for pine trees were pointy; for apple trees, had round leaves; and for oak trees, had curvy edges.

Clip Art   **Mask**   **Generated Sketches**

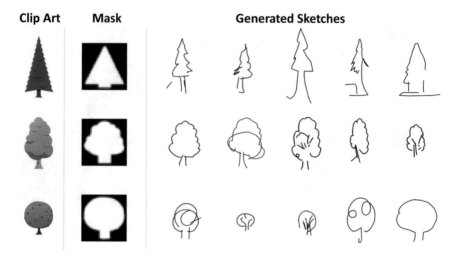

Fig. 10 Sketch generation results of trees conditioned on masks. The Object Generator was able to sketch trees of three different classes based on mask and aspect ratio inputs

Clip Art   **Mask**   **Generated Sketches**

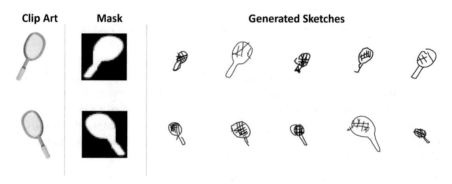

Fig. 11 Sketch generation results of racquets conditioned on masks. The Object Generator was able to sketch racquets at two orientations consistent with the masks

Generating Objects with Direction-Specific Poses

The Composition Proposer can specify the horizontal orientation of the objects (pointing left or right). As such, the Object Generators are required to sketch horizontally asymmetric objects (e.g., racquets, airplanes) with specific poses to follow users' instructions. We show the ability of an Object Generator to produce racquets at various orientations in Fig. 11. The generated racquet sketches conformed to the orientation of the mask, facing the specified direction at similar angles.

6.3.3 Complete Sessions with Composition Layouts and Sketches

We show the usage of Scones in six turns of conversation from multiple sessions in Fig. 12. We curated these sessions by interacting with the system ourselves to demonstrate various capabilities of Scones. In session (a), Scones was able to draw and move the duck to the left, sketch a cloud in the middle, and place and enlarge the tree on the right, following instructions issued by the user. In session (b), Scones was similarly able to place and move a cat, a tree, a basketball and an airplane, but at different positions from session (a). For instance, the tree was placed on the left as opposed to the right, and the basketball was moved to the bottom. We also show the ability of Scones to flip objects horizontally in session (b), such that the plane was flipped horizontally and regenerated given the instructions of 'flip the plane to point to the right instead'. This flipping action demonstrates the Object Generator's ability to generate objects with the require poses by only sharing the latent vectors z, such that the flipped airplane exhibits similar characteristics as the original airplane. In both sessions, Scones was able to correlate multiple scene objects, such as placing the owl on the tree in session (a), and basketball under the tree in session (b).

6.3.4 Interpreting Transformer's Attention Maps

We can further verify the relationships between text and object representations learned by the model by visualizing attention weights computed by the Transformer model of the Composition Proposer. These weights also create the unique possibility of generalizing and prompting for sketches of new objects specified by users.

The Transformer model in the Composition Proposer uses masked self-attention to attend to scene objects and instructions from previous time steps most relevant to generating the object specification at the current time step. We explore the attention weights of the first two turns of a conversation from the CoDraw validation set. In the first turn, the user instructed the system, 'top left is an airplane medium size pointing left'. When the model generated the first object, it attended to the 'airplane' and 'medium' text tokens to select class and output size. In the second turn, the user instructed the model to place a slide facing right under the airplane. The model similarly attended to the 'slide' token the most. It also significantly attended to the 'under' and 'plane' text tokens, and the airplane object. These objects and tokens are important for situating the slide object at the desired location relative to the existing airplane object (Figs. 13 and 14).

These attention weights could potentially be used to handle unknown scene objects encountered in instructions. When the model does not output any scene objects, but only a o_e (scene end) token, we can inspect the attention weights for generating this token to identify a potentially unknown object class, and ask the user for clarification. For example, when a user requests an unsupported class, such as a 'sandwich' or 'parrot' (Fig. 15), Scones could identify this unknown object by taking the text token with the highest attention weight, and prompting the user to sketch it by name.

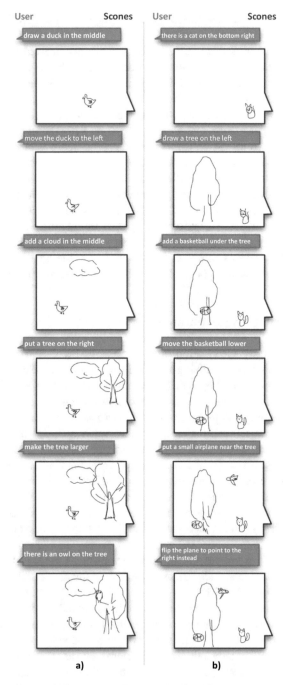

Fig. 12 Complete sketching sessions with Scones curated by the authors

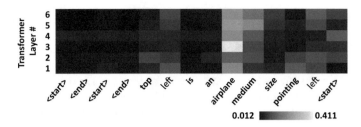

Fig. 13 Attention map of the Transformer across object and text tokens for the generation of an airplane, the first object in the scene

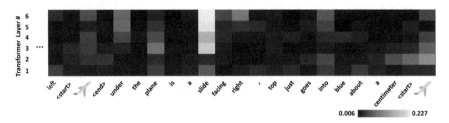

Fig. 14 Attention map of the Transformer across object and text tokens for the generation of slide in the second turn of conversation. We observed that the Transformer model attended to the corresponding words and objects related to the newly generated 'slide' object

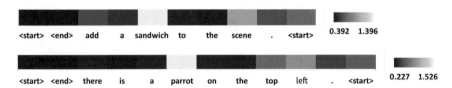

Fig. 15 Attention map of the Transformer for text instructions that specify unseen objects

6.4 Exploratory User Evaluation

To determine how effectively Scones can assist users in creating sketches from natural language, we conducted an exploratory evaluation of Scones. We recruited 50 participants from English-speaking countries on Amazon Mechanical Turk (AMT) for our study. We collected quantitative and qualitative results from user trials with Scones, as well as suggestions for improving Scones. Participants were given a maximum of 20 min to complete the study and were compensated $3.00 USD. Participants were only allowed to complete the task once.

6.4.1   Method

The participants were asked to recreate one of five randomly chosen target scene sketches by providing text instructions to Scones in the chat window. Each target scene had between four and five target objects from a set of 17 possible scene objects. Participants were informed that the final result did not have to be pixel perfect to the target scene, and to mark the sketch as complete once they were happy with the result. Instructions supplied in the chat window were limited to 500 characters, and submitting an instruction was considered as taking a 'turn'. The participants were only given the sketch strokes of the target scene without class labels, to elicit natural instructions.

Participants were first shown a short tutorial describing the canvas, chat interface, and target scene in the Scones interface (Fig. 16), and were asked to give simple instructions in the chat window to recreate the target scene. Only two sample instructions were given in the tutorial: 'add a tree', and 'add a cat next to the table'. At each turn, participants were given the option to redraw objects which remained in the scene for over three turns using a paintbrush-based interface. After completing the sketch, participants filled out an exit survey with likert-scale questions on their satisfaction at the sketch and enjoyment of the system, and open-ended feedback on the system.

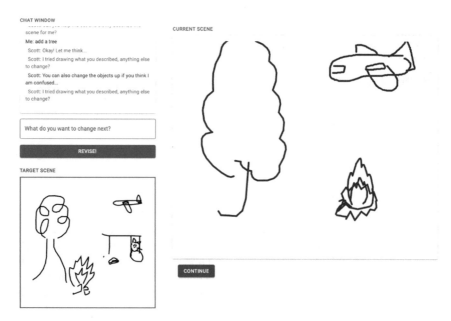

Fig. 16 Screenshot of Scones's evaluation user interface

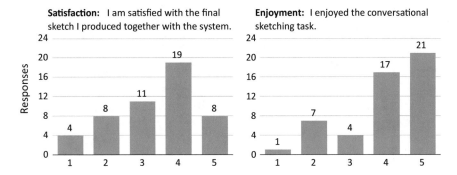

Fig. 17 Survey results from user sessions with Scones

6.4.2 Results

Participants Satisfied with Sketches, Enjoyment Was Bimodal
Participants were generally satisfied with their final sketches ($\mu = 3.38$, $\sigma = 1.18$), and enjoyed the task ($\mu = 4.0$, $\sigma = 1.12$). In open-ended feedback, participants praised Scones's ability to parse their instructions: *'it was able to similarly recreate the image with commands that I typed'* (P25); *'I liked that it would draw what I said. it was simple and fun to use'* (P40). Some participants even felt Scones was able to *intuitively* understand their instructions. P15 remarked, *'I thought it was cool how quickly and intuitively it responded'*, while P35 said, *'It had an intuitive sense of what to draw, and I did not feel constrained in the language I used'*.

While enjoyment was high on average, we found responses to enjoyment followed a bimodal distribution (Fig. 17). By reviewing qualitative feedback and instructions to Scones, we observe that many instances of low enjoyment (score ≤ 2) come from class confusion in target scene sketches. Some participants confused the tent in a target scene as a 'pyramid' in their instructions, which Scones does not support: *'There is a pyramid on the left side a little ways up from the bottom'* (P44). P49 tried five times to add a 'pyramid' to the scene.

P17, who strongly disagreed with enjoying the task (1/5), faced repeated class confusion issues, mentioning, *'it was very frustrating that it wouldn't draw the circle by the cloud …It wouldn't draw anything besides the plane, cloud, tent, and fire. Was that not a person up by the cloud?'* Scones does not support 'circle' or 'person' classes—the target sketch had the sun next to the cloud. When Scones is asked to draw an unsupported object, the canvas will be left unchanged. Providing participants with an explicit list of classes in the target image or adding error messages could mitigate these frustrations. Furthermore, attention-based methods mentioned in Sect. 6.3.4 could be used when an unrecognized class is detected to prompt users to provide sketch strokes with corresponding labels.

Fig. 18 Recreated scenes during the user study. Users combined Scones-generated outputs with their own sketch strokes to reproduce the target scenes presented to them

Participants Communicate with Scones at Varying Concept Abstraction Levels

On average, participants completed the sketching task in under 8 turns ($\mu = 7.56$, $\sigma = 3.42$), with a varied number of tokens (words in instructions) per turn ($\mu = 7.66$, $\sigma = 3.35$). Several participants only asked for the objects themselves (turns delimited by commas): *'helicopter, cloud, swing, add basketball' (P25).* Other participants made highly detailed requests: *'There is a sun in the top left, There is an airplane flying to the right in the top right corner, There is a cat standing on it's hind legs in the bottom right corner, Move the cat a little to the right, please, ...' (P14).* Participants who gave instructions at the expected high-level detail produced satisfying results, *'draw a tree in the middle, Draw a sun in the top left corner, A plane in the top right, A cat with a pizza under the tree' (P32).* The recreation of this participant is shown on the top right of Fig. 18.

The longest conversations were often from participants with mismatched expectations for Scones, who repeated commands: *'Draw a cloud in the upper left corner with three round edges, Change the cloud to have 3 round edges., Draw only 3 round waves around the edge of the cloud., ...Draw a snowman to the left of the table., ...Draw a circle touching the middle circle., ...' (P23).* This trial reflects the need for Scones to make clearer expectations of input to users. P23's 16-instruction session contains expectations for the system to modify low-level aspects of the sketches (changing the number of edges in the cloud), exhibits class confusion (snowman and circles with shovel), and has mismatched concept abstraction levels (drawing a shovel versus constructing a shovel from visual primitives, i.e., circles). A potentially simple mitigation for these hurdles would be to introduce more detailed tutorial content for a wider deployment of Scones.

Scones as a Tool for Collecting Iterative Sketching Data

The results of our study show significant potential for Scones to be used as a Game With a Purpose (GWAP) [1] to collect sketch critiques (natural language specified modifications to an input sketch to match a target sketch) and user-generated sketch strokes. 26 (52% of) participants redrew objects in their sketches when prompted ($\mu = 0.98$, $\sigma = 1.19$), and participants who redrew objects expressed their appreciation for this feature: *'I liked that I could redraw the image' (P48); 'I liked being able to draw parts myself because it was relaxing and I felt I was more accurate' (P11)*. Most participants who redrew objects also kept output from Scones in their final sketches, reflecting Scones's potential as a mixed-initiative design tool. Redrawing was voluntary in our task, and these results suggest Scones may be useful for collecting user-generated sketches in addition to natural language critique in a GWAP. Further motivating this application, 14 participants described the task as 'fun' in open-ended feedback, e.g., *'This was a very fun task' (P23); '[I liked] Playing the game and describing the drawing. It was fun!' (P42)*.

6.4.3 Participants' Feedback for Improving Scones

Participants offered suggestions for how they would improve Scones, providing avenues for future work.

Object Translations and Spatial Relationships
A major theme of dissatisfaction came from the limited ability of our system to respond to spatial relationships and translation-related instructions at times: *'It does not appear to understand spatial relationships that well' (P35); 'you are not able to use directional commands very easily' (P11)*. These situations largely originate from the CoDraw dataset [19], in which users had a restricted view of the canvas, resulting in limited relative spatial instructions. This limitation is discussed further in Sect. 7.1.

To improve the usability of Scones, participants suggest its interface could benefit from the addition of direct manipulation features, such as selecting and manually transforming objects in the scene: *'I think that I would maybe change how different items are selected in order to change of modify an object in the picture' (P33); 'maybe there should be a move function, where we keep the drawing the same but move it' (P40)*. Moreover, some participants also recommended adding an undo feature, *'Maybe a separate button to get back' (P31)*, or the ability to manually invoke Scones to redraw an object, *'I'd like a way to ask the computer to redraw a specific object' (P3)*. These features could help participants express corrective feedback to Scones, potentially creating sketches that better match their intent.

More Communicative Output
Some participants expected Scones to provide natural language output and feedback to their instructions. Some participants asked questions directly to elicit Scones's capabilities: *'In the foreground is a table, with a salad bowl and a jug of what may be lemonade. In the upper left is a roughly-sketched sun. Drifting down from the top-center is a box, tethered to a parachute, Did you need me to feed you smaller sentences? ...' (P38)*. P23 explicitly suggested users should be able to ask Scones questions to refine their intentions: *'I would like the system to ask more questions if it*

does not understand or if I asked for several revisions. I feel that could help narrow down what I am asking to be drawn'. Other participants used praise between their sketching instructions, which could be used as a cue to preserve the sketch output and guide further iteration: *'...Draw an airplane, Good try, Draw a table ...' (P1); 'Draw a sun in the upper left corner, The sun looks good! Can you draw a hot air balloon in the middle of the page, near the top? ...' (P15).* Providing additional natural language output and prompts from Scones could enable users to refine Scones's understanding of their intent and understand the system's capabilities. A truly *conversational* interface with a sketching support tool could pave the way for advanced mixed-initiative collaborative design tools.

7   Limitations and Future Research Opportunities

Through the development of a sketch dataset and two sketch-based creativity support systems, we identified some limitations of our work to date and opportunities for future work in this area.

7.1   Dataset Scale and Match

One crucial area for improvement for sketch-based application is the scale and quality of the datasets. Although the dataset we described in Sect. 4 can be used to train a sketch-based UI retrieval model described in Sect. 5, we observed that the performance of the system has been limited by the diversity and complexity of sketches and UIs in the dataset. This is demonstrated by two major modes of failure in Swire when it struggles to handle rare, custom UI elements as exhibited by Example a in Fig. 19, and fails to understand UIs with diverse colors, such as those with image backgrounds in Example b in Fig. 19. We believe with increased amount of training data, Swire can better generalize to more complex and colorful UIs.

Similarly, we observe that Scones (Sect. 6) has been constrained by the differences between the task protocol used to collect the CoDraw dataset (the dataset Scones was trained on) and the user interactions in Scones. Each conversation in CoDraw only offers the Teller one chance to 'peek' at the Drawer's canvas, which significantly decreases the number of modifications made to existing scene objects. As a result, Scones performs well at adding objects of correct classes at appropriate locations and sizes, but is not as advanced at modifying or removing objects. Moreover, the current dataset isn't end-to-end such that there is only a small, fixed number of styles of sketched objects, which reduces Scones' ability in handling stylistic instructions. The ideal data to train this system on shall directly record iterative master-apprentice interactions in creating, critiquing, modifying, and removing highly variable sketched scene objects at a large scale. Nevertheless, these datasets are considered to be difficult to collect due to the high sketching skill requirement for crowdworkers [42], such

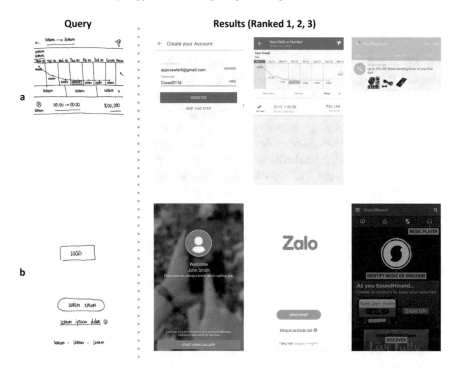

Fig. 19 Failure modes of UI retrieval using Swire. Swire failed to understand a) custom and b) colorful UI elements

that even single-turn multi-object sketched scenes are difficult for crowdworkers to create.

We believe a significant research direction is to enable the collection of legitimate sketching data at a large scale, especially in domains that require prior expertise such as UI and mechanical design. This can be achieved by either lowering the skill barrier, or by using tools like Scones and Swire to support parts of joint tasks. For example in the case of Scones, we can lower the skill barrier by decomposing each scene into object components allowing crowdworkers to only sketch a single object at a time in context. Alternatively, future research could explore other means of data collection beyond the crowd. Tools that are used for joint tasks provide natural incentives for designers during realistic design use-cases, and can allow the live collection of realistic design data from professional users. Researchers can also investigate sourcing sketches from students of sketching courses at various institutions offering design education who would possess higher sketching expertise.

7.2   Integration with Applications in Real Usage Scenarios

Another significant area of research is to create systems that tightly integrate with design and artistic applications in realistic use-cases. While many current research projects (including those described in this book chapter) demonstrate deep-neural-networks' capability and potential in supporting design applications, these applications are currently rough prototypes that are not yet suitable for everyday use by designers and artists. Further developing these applications and exploring how they integrate into design and artistic processes will reveal important usability issues and inform future design and implementation choices of similar tools. For instance, to successfully support UI design processes with Swire, we need to carefully consider the visual representation of UI examples in the application and the underlying datasets to be queried.

Moreover, some of the capabilities of these tools can be best demonstrated when applied to professional domains. For instance, Scones could participate in the UI/UX design process by iteratively suggesting multiple possible modifications of UI design sketches according to design critique. To enable this interaction, we could consider complete UI sketches as 'scenes' and UI components as 'scene objects'. Scones could be trained on this data along with text critiques of UI designs to iteratively generate and modify UI mockups from text. To allow Scones to generate multiple design candidates, we can modify the current architecture to model probabilistic outputs for both sketch strokes (which is currently probabilistic) and scene object locations. While datasets of UI layouts and components, such as those presented in Sect. 4, suggest this as a near possibility, this approach may generalize to other domains as well, such as industrial design. Nevertheless, this requires significant data support by solving the issues mentioned in Sect. 7.1.

8   Conclusion

This chapter presented three key aspects of developing deep-learning-driven, sketch-based creativity support tools. First, we collect the first large-scale dataset of sketches corresponding to UIs. Second, we develop a sketch-based UI retrieval technique that enables designers to interact with large-scale UI datasets using sketches. Third, we built a deep-learning-driven system that supports the novel interaction of generating scenes of sketched objects from text instructions. The dataset we collected supported our deep-learning-based tools, and we showed qualitatively and quantitatively that our systems can support targeted design and artistic applications. We further outlined several areas of future research opportunities and hope the documentation of our development experience and the release of our dataset can spur future research in this area.

Our ultimate goal in pursuing this line of research is to provide users of all levels of sketching expertise with relevant materials and computational resources to focus on creative and innovative tasks in creative processes. We also hope these projects can provide entirely new means for creative expression and rapid ideation. We are excited to continue designing for this future of design, art, and engineering.

References

1. von Ahn L, Dabbish L (2008) Designing games with a purpose. Commun ACM 51(8):58–67. https://doi.org/10.1145/1378704.1378719
2. Aksan E, Deselaers T, Tagliasacchi A, Hilliges O (2020) CoSE: compositional stroke embeddings. Adv Neural Inf Process Syst 33
3. Bonnardel N (1999) Creativity in design activities: the role of analogies in a constrained cognitive environment. In: Proceedings of the 3rd conference on creativity & cognition, C&C '99. ACM, New York, NY, USA, pp 158–165. https://doi.org/10.1145/317561.317589
4. Buxton B (2007) Sketching user experiences: getting the design right and the right design. Morgan Kaufmann Publishers Inc., San Francisco
5. Canny J (1986) A computational approach to edge detection. IEEE Trans Pattern Anal Mach Intell 6:679–698
6. Deka B, Huang Z, Kumar R (2016) ERICA: interaction mining mobile apps. In: Proceedings of the 29th annual symposium on user interface software and technology, UIST'16. ACM, New York, NY, USA, pp 767–776. https://doi.org/10.1145/2984511.2984581
7. Deka B, Huang Z, Franzen C, Hibschman J, Afergan D, Li Y, Nichols J, Kumar R (2017) Rico: a mobile app dataset for building data-driven design applications. In: Proceedings of the 30th annual ACM symposium on user interface software and technology, UIST'17. ACM, New York, NY, USA, pp 845–854. https://doi.org/10.1145/3126594.3126651
8. Dow SP, Glassco A, Kass J, Schwarz M, Schwartz DL, Klemmer SR (2010) Parallel prototyping leads to better design results, more divergence, and increased self-efficacy. ACM Trans Comput-Hum Interact 17(4):18:1–18:24. https://doi.org/10.1145/1879831.1879836
9. Eitz M, Hays J, Alexa M (2012) How do humans sketch objects? ACM Trans Graph (Proc SIGGRAPH) 31(4):44:1–44:10
10. Fernquist J, Grossman T, Fitzmaurice G (2011) Sketch-sketch revolution: an engaging tutorial system for guided sketching and application learning. In: Proceedings of the 24th annual ACM symposium on user interface software and technology, UIST'11. ACM, New York, NY, USA, pp 373–382. https://doi.org/10.1145/2047196.2047245
11. Gao C, Liu Q, Xu Q, Wang L, Liu J, Zou C (2020) SketchyCOCO: image generation from freehand scene sketches. In: Proceedings of the IEEE/CVF conference on computer vision and pattern recognition, pp 5174–5183
12. Gervais P, Deselaers T, Aksan E, Hilliges O (2020) The DIDI dataset: digital ink diagram data. arXiv:200209303
13. Ha D, Eck D (2018) A neural representation of sketch drawings. In: 6th international conference on learning representations, ICLR 2018, conference track proceedings, Vancouver, BC, Canada, April 30–May 3, 2018. https://openreview.net/forum?id=Hy6GHpkCW
14. Hennessey JW, Liu H, Winnemöller H, Dontcheva M, Mitra NJ (2017) How2Sketch: generating easy-to-follow tutorials for sketching 3D objects. In: Symposium on interactive 3D graphics and games
15. Herring SR, Chang CC, Krantzler J, Bailey BP (2009) Getting inspired!: understanding how and why examples are used in creative design practice. In: Proceedings of the SIGCHI conference on human factors in computing systems, CHI'09. ACM, New York, NY, USA, pp 87–96. https://doi.org/10.1145/1518701.1518717
16. Huang F, Canny JF (2019) Sketchforme: composing sketched scenes from text descriptions for interactive applications. In: Proceedings of the 32nd annual ACM symposium on user interface

software and technology, UIST'19. Association for Computing Machinery, New York, NY, USA, pp 209–220. https://doi.org/10.1145/3332165.3347878

17. Huang F, Canny JF, Nichols J (2019) Swire: sketch-based user interface retrieval. In: Proceedings of the 2019 CHI conference on human factors in computing systems, CHI'19. Association for Computing Machinery, New York, NY, USA. https://doi.org/10.1145/3290605.3300334

18. Jongejan J, Rowley H, Kawashima T, Kim J, Fox-Gieg N (2016) The quick, draw! - AI experiment. https://quickdraw.withgoogle.com/

19. Kim JH, Kitaev N, Chen X, Rohrbach M, Zhang BT, Tian Y, Batra D, Parikh D (2019) CoDraw: collaborative drawing as a testbed for grounded goal-driven communication. In: Proceedings of the 57th annual meeting of the association for computational linguistics. Association for Computational Linguistics, Florence, Italy, pp 6495–6513. https://doi.org/10.18653/v1/P19-1651

20. Kumar R, Talton JO, Ahmad S, Klemmer SR (2011) Bricolage: example-based retargeting for web design. In: Proceedings of the SIGCHI conference on human factors in computing systems, CHI'11. ACM, New York, NY, USA, pp 2197–2206. https://doi.org/10.1145/1978942.1979262

21. Landay JA (1996) SILK: sketching interfaces like krazy. In: Conference companion on human factors in computing systems, CHI'96. ACM, New York, NY, USA, pp 398–399. https://doi.org/10.1145/257089.257396

22. Lasecki WS, Kim J, Rafter N, Sen O, Bigham JP, Bernstein MS (2015) Apparition: crowdsourced user interfaces that come to life as you sketch them. In: Proceedings of the 33rd annual ACM conference on human factors in computing systems, CHI'15. ACM, New York, NY, USA, pp 1925–1934. https://doi.org/10.1145/2702123.2702565

23. Lee YJ, Zitnick CL, Cohen MF (2011) ShadowDraw: real-time user guidance for freehand drawing. ACM Trans Graph 30(4):27:1–27:10. https://doi.org/10.1145/2010324.1964922

24. Li M, Lin Z, Mech R, Yumer E, Ramanan D (2019) Photo-sketching: inferring contour drawings from images. In: 2019 IEEE winter conference on applications of computer vision (WACV). IEEE, pp 1403–1412

25. Limpaecher A, Feltman N, Treuille A, Cohen M (2013) Real-time drawing assistance through crowdsourcing. ACM Trans Graph 32(4):54:1–54:8. https://doi.org/10.1145/2461912.2462016

26. Lin J, Newman MW, Hong JI, Landay JA (2000) DENIM: finding a tighter fit between tools and practice for web site design. In: Proceedings of the SIGCHI conference on human factors in computing systems, CHI'00. ACM, New York, NY, USA, pp 510–517. https://doi.org/10.1145/332040.332486

27. Munoz-Salinas R (2012) ArUco: a minimal library for augmented reality applications based on OpenCV. Universidad de Córdoba

28. Newman MW, Landay JA (2000) Sitemaps, storyboards, and specifications: a sketch of web site design practice. In: Proceedings of the 3rd conference on designing interactive systems: processes, practices, methods, and techniques, DIS'00. ACM, New York, NY, USA, pp 263–274. https://doi.org/10.1145/347642.347758

29. Nguyen TA, Csallner C (2015) Reverse engineering mobile application user interfaces with REMAUI (T). In: 2015 30th IEEE/ACM international conference on automated software engineering (ASE), pp 248–259. https://doi.org/10.1109/ASE.2015.32

30. Pennington J, Socher R, Manning CD (2014) GloVe: global vectors for word representation. In: Empirical methods in natural language processing (EMNLP), pp 1532–1543. http://www.aclweb.org/anthology/D14-1162

31. Russakovsky O, Deng J, Su H, Krause J, Satheesh S, Ma S, Huang Z, Karpathy A, Khosla A, Bernstein MS, Berg AC, Li F (2014) ImageNet large scale visual recognition challenge. CoRR abs/1409.0575. arXiv:1409.0575

32. Sain A, Bhunia AK, Yang Y, Xiang T, Song YZ (2020) Cross-modal hierarchical modelling for fine-grained sketch based image retrieval. In: Proceedings of the 31st British machine vision virtual conference (BMVC 2020). British Machine Vision Association, pp 1–14

33. Sangkloy P, Burnell N, Ham C, Hays J (2016) The sketchy database: learning to retrieve badly drawn bunnies. ACM Trans Graph 35(4):119:1–119:12. https://doi.org/10.1145/2897824. 2925954

34. Schroff F, Kalenichenko D, Philbin J (2015) FaceNet: a unified embedding for face recognition and clustering. In: Proceedings of the IEEE conference on computer vision and pattern recognition, pp 815–823

35. Simonyan K, Zisserman A (2015) Very deep convolutional networks for large-scale image recognition. In: International conference on learning representations

36. Su Q, Li WHA, Wang J, Fu H (2014) EZ-sketching: three-level optimization for error-tolerant image tracing. ACM Trans Graph 33(4):54:1–54:9. https://doi.org/10.1145/2601097.2601202

37. Swearngin A, Dontcheva M, Li W, Brandt J, Dixon M, Ko AJ (2018) Rewire: interface design assistance from examples. In: Proceedings of the 2018 CHI conference on human factors in computing systems, CHI'18. ACM, New York, NY, USA, pp 504:1–504:12. https://doi.org/10.1145/3173574.3174078

38. Vaswani A, Shazeer N, Parmar N, Uszkoreit J, Jones L, Gomez AN, Kaiser L, Polosukhin I (2017) Attention is all you need. In: Guyon I, Luxburg UV, Bengio S, Wallach H, Fergus R, Vishwanathan S, Garnett R (eds) Advances in neural information processing systems, vol 30. Curran Associates, Inc., pp 5998–6008. http://papers.nips.cc/paper/7181-attention-is-all-you-need.pdf

39. Xie J, Hertzmann A, Li W, Winnemöller H (2014) PortraitSketch: face sketching assistance for novices. In: Proceedings of the 27th annual ACM symposium on user interface software and technology, UIST'14. ACM, New York, NY, USA, pp 407–417. https://doi.org/10.1145/2642918.2647399

40. Yu Q, Liu F, Song YZ, Xiang T, Hospedales T, Loy CC (2016) Sketch me that shoe. In: Computer vision and pattern recognition

41. Zhu JY, Park T, Isola P, Efros AA (2017) Unpaired image-to-image translation using cycle-consistent adversarial networks. In: 2017 IEEE international conference on computer vision (ICCV)

42. Zou C, Yu Q, Du R, Mo H, Song YZ, Xiang T, Gao C, Chen B, Zhang H (2018) SketchyScene: richly-annotated scene sketches. In: ECCV. Springer International Publishing, pp 438–454. https://doi.org/10.1007/978-3-030-01267-0_26, https://github.com/SketchyScene/SketchyScene

Generative Ink: Data-Driven Computational Models for Digital Ink

Emre Aksan and Otmar Hilliges

Abstract Digital ink promises to combine the flexibility of pen and paper interaction and the versatility of digital devices. Computational models of digital ink often focus on recognition of the content by following discriminative techniques such as classification, albeit at the cost of ignoring or losing personalized style. In this chapter, we propose augmenting the digital ink framework via generative modeling to achieve a holistic understanding of the ink content. Our focus particularly lies in developing novel generative models to gain fine-grained control by preserving user style. To this end, we model the inking process and learn to create ink samples similar to users. We first present how digital handwriting can be disentangled into style and content to implement editable digital ink, enabling content synthesis and editing. Second, we address a more complex setup of free-form sketching and propose a novel approach for modeling stroke-based data efficiently. *Generative ink* promises novel functionalities, leading to compelling applications to enhance the inking experience for users in an interactive and collaborative manner.

1 Introduction

Writing and drawing have served for centuries as our primary mean of communication and cornerstone of our education and culture, and often is considered a form of art [77] as being one of the most expressive ways of reflecting personal style. It has been shown to be beneficial in tasks such as note-taking [63], reading in conjunction with writing [79] and may have a positive impact on short- and long-term memory [7]. Handwriting and sketching have also been effective drafting tools to ideate and design [28, 76].

E. Aksan (✉) · O. Hilliges
Department of Computer Science, ETH Zürich, Stampfenbachstrasse 48, 8092 Zürich, Switzerland
e-mail: Emre.Aksan@inf.ethz.ch

O. Hilliges
e-mail: Otmar.Hilliges@inf.ethz.ch

As being one of the most natural communication mediums inking has taken place in digital devices. Digital pen, i.e., stylus, has been a versatile alternative to keyboard and mouse in digital content creation. However, the traditional note-taking with pen and paper has yet to be fully replaced by the digital counterparts albeit the flexibility and versatility provided by digital platforms [3]. The discrepancy between the analog and digital ink could be attributed to aesthetics or mechanical limitations such as stylus accuracy, latency, and texture [4]. Though there is more to do to meet or exceed the pen and paper experience, digital ink offers unique affordances otherwise not possible with the analog inking such as dynamic editing, annotations [76], and sketch-based content retrieval [55, 97].

Digital ink is arguably the most convenient for interacting with a reference material. It allows us to take notes, highlight content and organize the information swiftly and effectively. Consider Fig. 1 illustrating a user taking notes on an image, augmenting the content via sketches and organizing the semantic groups by relating them via arrows. A holistic experience is not always limited to a single type of digital ink such as handwriting or drawings only. Instead, a more natural experience often involves various inking modalities and digital media. We envision a system that is capable of controlling the ink content semantically (i.e., segmentation and editing of entities), modeling the digital ink environment holistically (i.e., relating different contents) and even parsing the reference material to understand the user's mental state and construct a context internally, allowing for collaboration between the model and the user. This vision motivates us to explore novel computational modeling techniques for digital ink. Current state of the digital ink framework consists of the hardware layer involving the sensory and a software layer providing the basic functionality of editing, coloring, and beautification. Our goal is to extend this framework with a new layer promising semantic understanding and fine-grained control of digital ink.

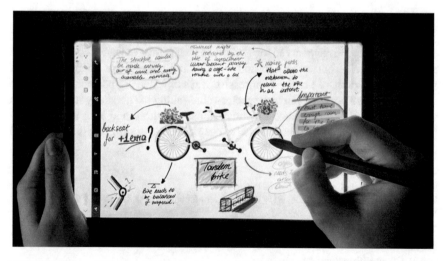

Fig. 1 Digital note taking involves handwritten text, sketching, and interaction with digital context

Our focus lies on the generative modeling of ink that is able to learn the data creation process (i.e., how we actually write and draw), dubbed as the generative ink. Deep generative models have shown to be powerful for content creation and manipulation in various domains such as speech synthesis [67], image editing [56, 68], and music creation [44]. First Graves [35], then Ha and Eck [38] pioneered generative modeling of the ink data on handwriting and doodle drawings, respectively, and have shown the potential it bears. Generative ink presents new opportunities for both the developers and the users and has potential for compelling applications. Learning to create the content enables editing of the available user data and synthesizing novel content to support the users in a collaborative manner.

In this chapter, we present two techniques addressing the computational challenges of digital ink. We show how to develop generative models tailored for the underlying problems by leveraging the domain priors. We particularly focus on modeling the data in time-series representation rather than the images, allowing us to operate on the raw ink representation. This enables interfacing the models with the applications directly.

In the first part, we focus on *editable* digital ink. Our goal is to develop a system for handwritten text that allows for editing the content while preserving the user's handwriting style. To process digital handwriting one has typically to resort to character recognition techniques (e.g., [30]) thus invariably losing the personalized aspect of written text. As the digital ink and the character recognition systems [17, 58] are decoupled and requiring a faithful integration, fully digital text remains easier to process, search, and manipulate than handwritten text which has lead to a dominance of typed text. To enhance the user experience with the digital ink, we propose a generative model that is capable of maintaining the author's original style, thus allowing for a seamless transition between handwritten and digital text. This is a challenging problem: while each user has a unique handwriting style [82, 103], the parameters that determine style are not well defined. Moreover, handwriting style is not fixed but changes temporally based on context, writing speed, and other factors [82]. Hence so far it has been elusive to algorithmically recreate style faithfully, while being able to control content.

In the second part, we explore a novel approach in a more complex setup; freeform sketching including flowchart diagrams, objects, and handwriting. We raised the question of how a model could complete a drawing in a collaborative manner. The answer to this question is highly context-sensitive and requires reasoning at the local (i.e., stroke) and global (i.e., the drawing) level. To this end, we focus on learning the compositional structure of the strokes where we model the local appearance of the strokes and the global structure explicitly. We consider it as the first step toward a holistic approach.

Before diving into generative model examples, we present the related work covering the computational ink models, provide a formal definition of the digital ink data, and introduce the datasets we use in our works.

2 Related Work

Our work touches the research areas of human–computer interaction and machine learning. In the following, we mention the previous work focusing on computational models for digital ink and relevant machine learning studies.

2.1 Understanding Handwriting

Research into the recognition of handwritten text has led to drastic accuracy improvements [27, 71] and such technology can now be found in mainstream UIs (e.g., Windows, Android, iOS). However, converting digital ink into ASCII characters removes individual style. Understanding what exactly constitutes style has been the subject of much research to inform font design [16, 26, 66] and the related understanding of human reading has served as a source of inspiration for the modern parametric-font systems [45, 50, 80]. Nonetheless no equivalent parametric model of handwritten style exists and analysis and description of style remains an inexact science [66, 73]. The variety of styles also poses a challenge for the handwriting recognition systems. Bhunia et al. [9] presents a few-shot learning approach to adapt the handwritten text recognition models to novel user styles at test time.

2.2 Pen-Based Interaction

Given the naturalness of the medium [21, 79], pen-based interfaces have seen enduring interest in both the graphics and HCI literature [84]. Ever since Ivan Sutherland's Sketchpad [85] researchers have explored sensing and input techniques for small screens [47, 99], tablets [41, 70] and whiteboards [64, 69, 96] and have proposed ways of integrating paper with digital media [12, 40]. Furthermore many domain specific applications have been proposed. For instance, manipulation of hand-drawn diagrams [6] and geometric shapes [5], note-taking (e.g., NiCEBook [12]), sharing of notes (e.g., NotePals [25]), browsing and annotation of multimedia content [91], including digital documents [100] using a stylus. Others have explored creation, management and annotation of handwritten notes on large screen displays [69, 96]. Typically such approaches do not convert ink into characters to preserve individual style.

2.3 Handwriting Beautification

Zitnick [104] proposes a method for beautification of digital ink by exploiting the smoothing effect of geometric averaging of multiple instances of the same stroke. While generating convincing results, this method requires several samples of the same text for a single user. A supervised machine learning method to remove slope and slant from handwritten text and to normalize it's size [29] has been proposed. Zanibbi et al. [102] introduce a tool to improve legibility of handwritten equations by applying style-preserving morphs on user-drawn symbols. Lu et al. [60] propose to learn style features from trained artist, and to subsequently transfer the strokes of a different writer to the learnt style and therefore inherently remove the original style.

2.4 Handwriting Synthesis

A large body of work is dedicated to the synthesis of handwritten text (for a comprehensive survey see [27]). Attempts have been made to formalize plausible biological models of the processes underlying handwriting [42] or by learning sequences of motion primitives [92]. Such approaches primarily validate bio-inspired models but do not produce convincing sequences. In [8, 72] sigma-lognormal models are proposed to synthesize handwriting samples by parameterizing rapid human movements and hence reflecting writer's fine motor control capability. The model can naturally synthesize variances of a given sample, but it lacks control of the content.

Realistic handwritten characters such as Japanese Kanji or individual digits can be synthesized from learned statistical models of stroke similarity [18] or control point positions (requiring characters to be converted to splines) [89]. Follow-up work has proposed methods that connect such synthetic characters [19, 90] using a ligature model. Haines et al. [39] take character-segmented images of a single author's writing and attempts to replicate the style via dynamic programming. These approaches either ignore style entirely or learn to imitate a single reference style from a large corpus of data. With the introduction of neural networks to handwriting synthesis task, the models have achieved generalization across various user styles. The works [10, 24] present approaches for offline handwritten text synthesis. The proposed models generate images of handwritten characters and text by imitating a given user style. In [31], the authors use handwriting synthesis to augment and increase the amount of training data for handwritten text recognition systems.

Graves [35] proposes an autoregressive model with long short-term memory recurrent (LSTM) neural networks to generate complex sequences with long-range structure such as handwritten text. The work demonstrates synthesis of handwritten text in specific styles, however lacking a notion of disentangling content from style. In our work [1], we decouple the content from style and represent them via separate random variables to achieve fine-grained control over the written text and the style. In [51], our disentanglement assumption is further applied to style component itself via decoupled style descriptors for character- and writer-level styles. This approach considers writer-independent and writer-dependent character representations as well as global writer styles, mitigating the loss of fine-grained style attributes in the synthesized text.

2.5 Free-Form Sketches

Free-form sketching includes a diverse set of tasks from drawings of basic doodles to more complex structures such as flowcharts. Previous works address recognition and synthesis of free-form sketches.

Ha et al. [38] and Ribeiro et al. [75] build LSTM/VAE-based and Transformer-based models, respectively, to generate samples from the QuickDraw dataset [34]. These approaches model the entire drawing as a single sequence of points. The different categories of drawings are modeled holistically without taking their internal structure into account.

Costagliola et al. [23] present a parsing-based approach using a grammar of shapes and symbols where shapes and symbols are independently recognized and the results are combined using a non-deterministic grammar parser. Bresler et al. [13, 14] investigated flowchart and diagram recognition using a multi-stage approach including multiple independent segmentation and recognition steps. [101] have applied graph attention networks to 1,300 diagrams from [13, 14, 23] for text/non-text classification using a hand-engineered stroke feature vector. Yang et al. [98] use graph convolutional networks for semantic segmentation at the stroke level to extensions of the QuickDraw data [54, 95]. For an in-depth treatment of free-form sketch models, we refer the reader to the recent survey by Xu et al. [97].

3 Background

In the following, we formally define the digital ink data as time-series representations, present datasets we utilize in this chapter, and provide dataset statistics.

3.1 Data Representation

Digital handwriting or sketching can be represented via sequences of pen positions or images as appear on the device screen. In this chapter, our focus lie on modeling of the digital ink in its raw format, i.e., temporally ordered points such that every point consists of (x, y) 2D pen-coordinates on the device screen and corresponding pen-up events p. While the pen-coordinates are integer values bounded by screen resolution of the device, *pen-up* takes value 1 when the pen is lifted off the screen and 0, otherwise (Fig. 2).

An ink sample is formally defined as a sequence $\mathbf{x} = \{u_t\}_{t=1}^{T}$ of length T where u_t represents a single point as $u_t = (x_t, y_t, p_t)$. Note that the distribution of sample lengths T is primarily determined by the device's sampling frequency as well as the data pre-processing.

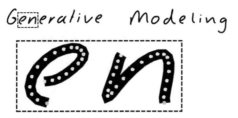

Fig. 2 Discretization of digital handwriting. A handwriting sample (top) is represented by a sequence of temporarily ordered strokes. Yellow and green nodes illustrate sampled points. The green nodes correspond to *pen-up* events

Fig. 3 Strokes are illustrated in different colors for various ink samples, namely flowchart (left), cat and elephant drawings (right) and handwritten text (bottom). A stroke may correspond to both semantically meaningful or arbitrary building blocks. A semantic entity (e.g., shapes or letters) may consist of a single or multiple strokes

Depending on the underlying application, additional labels can be of great importance. In handwriting recognition and synthesis systems, for example, character labels are required. For every point in an ink sample, we can set a collection of semantic labels analogous to segmentation in images. Without loss of generality, each point u can be assigned with the corresponding entity label c_t or an indicator for the end of the entity e_t. While c_t specifies which character or shape a stroke u_t belongs to, e_t is binary-valued and set to 1 if u_t corresponds to the last point of a semantic category c (i.e., a character, shape, or a stroke).

We additionally define a more coarse-grained but a semantically more informative representation. To this end we treat the entire ink sample $\mathbf{x}$ as an ordered or unordered collection of strokes $\mathbf{x} = \{s_k\}_{k=1}^K$. Strokes split an ink sequence into segments by the points with pen-up events (Fig. 3). In other words, anything we draw until we lift the pen up is defined as a stroke. It is straightforward to use a stroke-based ink representation as the *pen* labels already available in the data. More formally a stroke $\mathbf{s}_k = \{(x_t, y_t)\}_{t=1}^{\bar{T}}$ where $\bar{T}$ denotes the length of the ink segment and $\bar{T} \leq T$.

Fig. 4 (Top) Our dataset
offers different level of
annotation, including
sentence-wide annotation
(**a**), as well as fine-grained
segmentation at word (**b**) and
character (**c**) level. (Bottom)
Samples from our dataset,
with color-coded character
segmentation. Different
styles are available,
including challenging styles
to segment (e.g., joined-up
cursive, right)

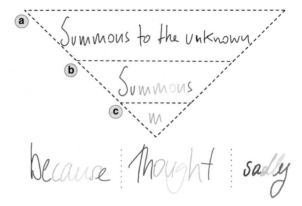

3.2 Datasets

In this section, we provide a summary of the digital ink datasets we use throughout
the chapter. Our models are trained on IAM-OnDB, Deepwriting, DiDi, and
QuickDraw datasets.

3.2.1 IAM-OnDB and Deepwriting Handwriting Datasets

IAM On-Line Handwriting Database (IAM-OnDB) is the established handwriting
dataset for learning tasks [57]. It was captured with a low-resolution and low-accuracy
digital whiteboard and only contains annotations at the sequence level. In our first
work (Sect. 4), we require more fine-grained annotations to disentangle handwriting
content and style. Hence, we contribute a novel dataset of handwritten text with
character level annotations.

The proposed dataset accumulates the IAM-OnDB with newly collected samples
and provides character level annotations for the IAM-OnDB samples. The unified
dataset contains data from 294 unique authors, for a total of 85181 word instances
(writer median 292 words) and 406956 handwritten characters (writer median 1349
characters), with further statistics reported in Table 1.

We developed a web tool to collect samples from 94 authors (see Fig. 5). Inline
with IAM-OnDB we asked each subject to write extracts of the Lancaster-Oslo-
Bergen (LOB) text corpus [46] using an iPad Pro. Besides stylus information, we
recorded age, gender, handedness, and native language of each author. The data is
again segmented at the character level and misspelled or unreadable samples have
been removed.

Samples from 200 authors in the dataset stem from the IAM-OnDB dataset and
were acquired using a smart whiteboard. The data provide stylus information (i.e.,
x-y coordinates, pen events, and timestamps) as well as transcription of the written
text, on a per-line basis (Fig. 4a). We purged 21 authors from the original data

Table 1 Data statistics. In bold, the final *unified* dataset

Avg. age (SD)	IAM-OnDB	Deepwriting	Unified
	24.84 (± 6.2)	23.55 (± 5.7)	24.85 (± 6.19)
Females %	34.00	32.63	33.55
Right-handed %	91.50	96.84	93.22
# sentences	11242	63182	17560
# unique words	11059	6418	12718
# word instances	59141	26040	85181
# characters	262981	143975	406956

Fig. 5 Deepwriting data collection interface. Users are presented with text to write (**a**) in the scrollable collection canvas (**b**). A progress bar (**c**) informs the user on the status. A writer can save, reject, or correct samples using the toolbox buttons (**d**)

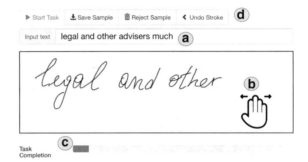

due to low-quality samples or missing annotations. Furthermore, to improve the granularity of annotations we process the remaining samples, segmenting them down to the character level, obtaining ASCII labels for each character (Fig. 4B, C). For segmentation, we used a commercial tool [65] and manually cleaned-up the results.

3.2.2 DiDi Flowchart Dataset

DiDi is a dataset of flowchart drawings by asking participants to draw the shown diagram image [33] (Fig. 6). The reference images are created with GraphViz tool, based on randomly generated dot files. The dataset contains 22,287 diagrams with textual labels and 36,368 diagrams without textual labels. The data was collected from a total of 364 participants where the number of individual drawings any participant created was between 1 and 1291.

Diagrams are created by using a set of basic shapes including box, diamond, octagon, oval, parallelogram, and arrow. The dataset reflects the variations in user drawings as well as the compositional nature of the strokes. The only annotation available for the dataset is the reference diagrams. It is not straightforward to extract the correspondences between the shapes and the strokes. The collected drawings use between 1 and 161 strokes (median 14) and contain between 2 and 17980 points (median 1559).

Fig. 6 DiDi data collection interface. The users are requested to replicate the diagram and the text provided in the reference image

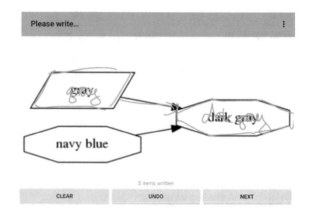

In our work, presented in Sect. 5, we use samples with shape only and ignored the textual labels. We re-sample all the data points by using the available timestamps such that the sampling frequency becomes 20. Samples with less than 4 strokes and points are discarded during training.

3.2.3 QuickDraw Sketch Dataset

QuickDraw dataset is a collection of more than 50 million sketches across 345 categories, collected via the online game *Quick, Draw!*.[1] The game challenges the participants to draw a verbally given object or abstract term within a time limit.

We use samples from the *cat* and *elephant* categories only in our work in Sect. 5. There are 106902 samples for the *cat* category. Samples contain between 4 and 92 (median 10) strokes and the number of points ranges between 18 and 1418 (median 236). In the *elephant* category, we use 66735 samples with having between 4 and 82 strokes (median 7). The samples contain minimum 8 and maximum 1177 (median 357) points. The data is resampled by using Ramer–Douglas–Peucker algorithm.

4 Editable Digital Ink via Deep Generative Modeling

We explore novel ways to combine the benefits of digital ink with the versatility and efficiency of typing, allowing for a seamless transition between handwritten and digital text. Our focus lies on a generative handwriting model to achieve editable digital ink representation via disentanglement of style and content.

We seek a model that is capable of capturing and reproducing local variability of handwriting and can mimic different user styles with high-fidelity. Importantly, the model is expected to provide full control over the content of the synthetic sequences,

---

[1] https://quickdraw.withgoogle.com/.

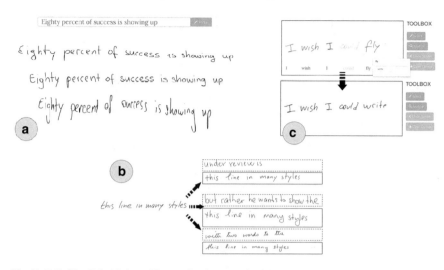

Fig. 7 Editable digital ink enables applications synthesizing handwriting from typed text while giving users control over the visual appearance (**a**), transferring style across handwriting samples (**b**, solid line box synthesized sample, dotted line box reference style), and editing handwritten samples at the word level (**c**)

enabling processing and editing of digital ink at the word level, enabling compelling applications such as beautification, synthesis, spell-checking, and correction (Fig. 7).

To make digital ink fully editable, one has to overcome a number of technical problems such as character recognition and synthesis of realistic handwriting. None is more important than the disentanglement of *style* and *content*. Each author has a unique style of handwriting [82, 103], but at the same time, they also display a lot of intra-variability, such as mixing connected and disconnected styles, variance in usage of glyphs, character spacing and slanting (see Fig. 8). Hence, it is hard to define or predict the appearance of a character, as often its appearance is strongly influenced by its content. A comprehensive approach to handwriting synthesis must be able to maintain *global* style while preserving *local* variability and context (e.g., many users mix cursive and disconnected styles dynamically).

Embracing this challenge we follow a data-driven approach capable of disentangling handwritten text into their content and style components, necessary to enable editing and synthesis of novel handwritten samples in a user-specified style. The key idea underlying our approach is to treat style and content as two separate latent random variables (Fig. 9a). While the *content* component is defined as the set of alphanumeric characters and punctuation marks, the *style* term is an abstraction of the factors defining appearance. It is learned by the model and projected into a continued-valued latent space. One can make use of content and style variables to *edit* either style, content or both, or one can generate entirely new samples (Fig. 9b).

In this section, we present a conditional variational recurrent neural network architecture to disentangle the handwritten text into content and style. First, we

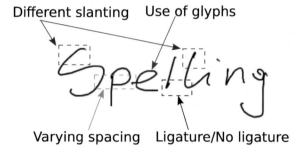

Different slanting   **Use of glyphs**

Varying spacing   **Ligature/No ligature**

Fig. 8 Example of intra-author variation that leads to entanglement of style and content, making conditional synthesis of realistic digital ink very challenging

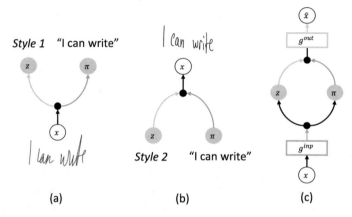

(a)   (b)   (c)

Fig. 9 High-level representation of our approach. **x**, **z** and π are random variables corresponding to handwritten text, *style* and *content*, respectively. **a** A given handwritten sample can be decomposed into *style* and *content* components. **b** Similarly, a sample can be synthesized using *style* and *content* components. **c** Our model learns inferring and using latent variables by reconstructing handwriting samples. g^{inp} and g^{out} are feed-forward networks projecting the input into an intermediate representation and predicting outputs, respectively

provide a background on the backbone architectures. Then, we introduce technical details of our proposed model along with the training and sampling algorithms. Finally, we share application scenarios of our approach and provide preliminary user evaluations.

4.1 Method Overview

We use the point-wise data representation $u_t = (x_t, y_t, p_t)$ presented in Sect. 3.1 and introduce the labels for character c_t, end of character e_t and beginning of a new word w_t. The c_t takes one of the categorical labels determined by the alphabet. The e_t and

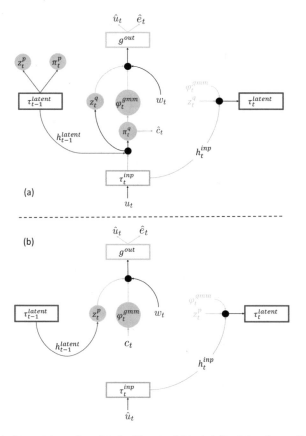

Fig. 10 Schematic overview of our handwriting model in training (**a**) and sampling phases (**b**), operating at the point level. Subscripts denote time step t. Superscripts correspond to layer names such as *input*, *latent* and *output* layers or the distributions of the random variables such as $z_t^q \sim q(z_t|u_t)$ and $z_t^p \sim p(z_t|u_t)$. (τ and h) An RNN cell and its output. (g) A multi-layer feed-forward neural network. (Arrows) Information flow color-coded with respect to source. (Colored circles) Latent random variables. Outgoing arrows represent a sample of the random variable. (Green branch) Gaussian latent space capturing style related information along with latent RNN (τ_t^{latent}) cell at individual time steps t. (Blue branch) Categorical and GMM random variables capturing content information. (Small black nodes) An auxiliary node for concatenation of incoming nodes

w_t are binary and set to 1 only if the criterion is met. The beginning of a new word label w_t correspond to the first point of a new word.

We propose a novel autoregressive neural network (NN) architecture that contains continuous and categorical latent random variables. Here, the continuous latent variable which captures the appearance properties is modeled by an isotropic Normal distribution (Fig. 10, green). Whereas the content information is captured via a Gaussian Mixture Model (GMM), where each character in the dataset is represented by an isotropic Gaussian (shown in Fig. 10, blue). We train the model by reconstructing a given handwritten sample **x** (Fig. 9c). Handwriting is inherently a temporal domain and require exploiting long-range dependencies. Hence, we leverage recurrent neural network (RNN) cells and operate in the point level u_t. Moreover, we make use of and predict c_t, e_t, w_t in auxiliary tasks such as controlling the word spacing, character segmentation, and recognition (Fig. 10).

The proposed architecture which we call conditional variational recurrent neural network (C-VRNN) builds on prior work on variational autoencoders (VAE) [48] and its recurrent variant, variational recurrent neural networks (VRNN) [22]. While VAEs only work with non-temporal data, VRNN can reconstruct and synthesize time series, albeit without conditioning, providing no control over the generated content. In contrast, our model synthesizes realistic handwriting with natural variation and conditioned on a user-specified content.

4.2   Background

Multi-layer recurrent neural networks (RNNs) [35] and variational RNN (VRNN) [22] are most related to our work. We briefly recap these and highlight differences. In our notation superscripts correspond to layer information such as *input*, *latent*, or *output* while the subscript t denote the time step. Moreover, we drop parametrization for the sake of brevity, and therefore readers should assume that all probability distributions are modeled by using neural networks.

4.2.1   Recurrent Neural Networks

RNNs model variable length input sequences $\mathbf{x} = (u_1, u_2, \cdots, u_T)$ by predicting the next time step u_{t+1} given all the inputs up to the current u_t. The probability of a sequence $\mathbf{x}$ is given by

$$
\begin{aligned}
p(\mathbf{x}) &= \prod_{t=1}^{T} p(u_{t+1}|u_t), \\
p(u_{t+1}|u_t) &= g^{out}(h_t) \\
h_t &= \tau(u_t, h_{t-1}),
\end{aligned}
\tag{1}
$$

where τ is a *deterministic* transition function of an RNN cell, updating the internal cell state h. Note that u_{t+1} implicitly depends on all inputs until step $t + 1$ through the cell state h.

The function g^{out} maps the hidden state to a probability distribution. In vanilla RNNs (e.g., LSTM, GRU), g^{out} is the only source of variability. To express the natural randomness in the data, the output function g^{out} typically parametrizes a statistical distribution (e.g., Bernoulli, Normal, GMM). The output is then calculated by sampling from this distribution. Both functions τ and g^{out} are approximated by optimizing neural network parameters via maximizing the log-likelihood:

$$\mathcal{L}_{rnn}(\mathbf{x}) = \log p(\mathbf{x}) = \sum_{t=1}^{T} \log p(u_{t+1}|u_t) \tag{2}$$

Multi-layered LSTMs with a GMM output distribution have been used for handwriting modeling [35]. While capable of conditional synthesis, they can not disentangle style from content due to the lack of latent random variables.

4.2.2 Variational Recurrent Neural Networks

VRNNs [22] modify the deterministic τ transition function by introducing a latent random variable $\mathbf{z} = (z_1, z_2, \cdots, z_T)$ increasing the expressive power of the model and to better capture variability in the data by modeling

$$p(\mathbf{x}, \mathbf{z}) = p(\mathbf{x}|\mathbf{z})p(\mathbf{z}),$$

$$p(\mathbf{x}, \mathbf{z}) = \prod_{t=1}^{T} p(u_t|z_t)p(z_t),$$

$$p(u_t|z_t) = g^{out}(z_t, h_{t-1}), \tag{3}$$

$$p(z_t) = g^{p,z}(h_{t-1}),$$

$$h_t = \tau(u_t, z_t, h_{t-1}),$$

where $g^{p,z}$ is a multi-layer feed-forward network parameterizing the prior distribution $p(z_t)$ and the latent variable $\mathbf{z}$ enforces the model to project the data variability on the prior distribution $p(\mathbf{z})$. Note that u_t still depends on the previous steps, albeit implicitly through the internal state h_{t-1}.

At each time step the latent random variable $\mathbf{z}$ is modeled as isotropic Normal distribution $z_t \sim \mathcal{N}(\mu_t, \sigma_t I)$. The transition function τ takes samples z_t as input, introducing a new source of variability.

Since we do not have access to the true distributions at training time, the posterior $p(\mathbf{z}|\mathbf{x})$ is intractable and hence makes the marginal likelihood, i.e., the objective, $p(\mathbf{x})$ also intractable. Instead, an approximate posterior distribution $q(\mathbf{z}|\mathbf{x})$ is employed, imitating the true posterior $p(\mathbf{z}|\mathbf{x})$ [48], where $q(\mathbf{z}|\mathbf{x})$ is an isotropic Normal distribution and parameterized by a neural network $g^{q,z}$ as follows:

$$q(z_t|u_t) = g^{q,z}(u_t, h_{t-1}) \tag{4}$$

The model parameters are optimized by jointly maximizing the variational lower bound:

$$\log p(\mathbf{x}) \geq \mathbb{E}_{q(z_t|u_t)} \sum_{t=1}^{T} \log p(u_t|z_t) - KL(q(z_t|u_t)||p(z_t)), \tag{5}$$

where $KL(q||p)$ is the Kullback–Leibler divergence (non-similarity) between distributions q and p. The first term in loss (5) ensures that the sample u_t is reconstructed given the latent sample $z_t \sim q(z_t|u_t)$ while the KL term minimizes the discrepancy between our approximate posterior and prior distributions. Note the difference in the inputs of the prior $g^{p,z}$ and the posterior $g^{q,z}$ functions in Eqs. 3 and 4, respectively. Hence, the KL-term never becomes 0 due to the different amount of input information to $g^{p,z}$ and $g^{q,z}$ It ensures that the prior learns to be predictive of the next step so that we can use the prior $z_t \sim p(z_t)$ for synthesis at test time. Moreover, the $q(\mathbf{z}|\mathbf{x})$ network enables inferring latent properties of a given sample, providing interesting applications. For example, a handwriting sample can be projected into the latent space z and reconstructed with different slant.

4.3   Conditional Variational Recurrent Neural Network

While multi-layer RNNs and VRNNs have appealing properties, neither is directly capable of full conditional handwriting synthesis. For example, one can synthesize a given text in a given style by using RNNs but samples will lack natural variability. Or one can generate high quality novel samples with VRNNs. However, VRNNs lack control over *what* is written. Neither model have inference networks to decouple style and content, which lies at the core of our work.

We overcome this issue by introducing a new set of latent random variables, $\mathbf{z}$ and $\boldsymbol{\pi}$, capturing style and content of handwriting samples. More precisely our new model describes the data as being generated by two latent variables $\mathbf{z}$ and $\boldsymbol{\pi}$ (Fig. 9) such that

$$p(\mathbf{x}, \mathbf{z}, \boldsymbol{\pi}) = p(\mathbf{x}|\mathbf{z}, \boldsymbol{\pi})p(\mathbf{z})p(\boldsymbol{\pi}),$$

$$p(\mathbf{x}, \mathbf{z}, \boldsymbol{\pi}) = \prod_{t=1}^{T} p(u_t|z_t)p(z_t)p(\pi_t) \tag{6}$$

$$
\begin{aligned}
p(u_t|z_t, \pi_t) &= g^{out}(z_t, \pi_t), \\
p(z_t) &= g^{p,z}(h_{t-1}^{latent}), \\
p(\pi_t) &= g^{p,\pi}(h_{t-1}^{latent}), \\
h_t^{latent} &= \tau^{latent}(u_t, z_t, \pi_t, h_{t-1}^{latent}), \\
q(z_t|u_t) &= g^{q,z}(u_t, h_{t-1}^{latent}),
\end{aligned}
\tag{7}
$$

where $p(\pi_t)$ is a K-dimensional multinomial distribution specifying the characters that are synthesized.

Similar to VRNNs, we introduce an approximate inference distribution $q(\boldsymbol{\pi}|\mathbf{x})$ for the categorical latent variable:

$$q(\pi_t | u_t) = g^{q,\pi}(u_t, h_{t-1}^{latent}) \tag{8}$$

Since we aim to decouple style and content in handwriting, we assume that the approximate distribution has a factorized form $q(z_t, \pi_t | u_t) = q(z_t | u_t)q(\pi_t | u_t)$. Both $q(\pi | \mathbf{x})$ and $q(\mathbf{z} | \mathbf{x})$ are used to infer content and style components of a given sample $\mathbf{x}$ as described earlier.

We optimize the following variational lower bound:

$$\log p(\mathbf{x}) \geq \mathcal{L}_{lb}(\cdot) = \mathbb{E}_{q(z_t, \pi_t | u_t)} \sum_{t=1}^{T} \log p(u_t | z_t, \pi_t)$$
$$-KL(q(z_t | u_t) \| p(z_t)) - KL(q(\pi_t | u_t) \| p(\pi_t)), \tag{9}$$

where the first term ensures that the input point is reconstructed by using its latent samples. We model the output by using bivariate Gaussian and Bernoulli distributions for $2D$-pixel coordinates and binary *pen-up* events, respectively.

Note that our output function g^{out} does not employ the internal cell state h. By using only the latent variables z and π for synthesis, we aim to enforce the model to capture the patterns only in the latent variables z and π.

4.4 High Quality Digital Ink Synthesis

The C-VRNN architecture as discussed so far enables the crucial component of separating continuous components from categorical aspects (i.e., characters) which potentially would be sufficient to conditionally synthesize individual characters. However, to fully address the entire handwriting task several extension to control important aspects such as word spacing and to improve quality of the predictions are necessary.

4.4.1 Character Classification Loss

Although we assume that the latent random variables $\mathbf{z}$ and π capture style and content information, respectively, and make a conditional independence assumption, in practice full disentanglement is an ambiguous task. Since we essentially ask the model to learn by itself what style and what content are we found further guidance at training time to be necessary.

To prevent divergence during training we make use of character labels at training time and add an additional cross-entropy classification loss $\mathcal{L}_{classification}$ on the content component $q(\pi_t | u_t)$.

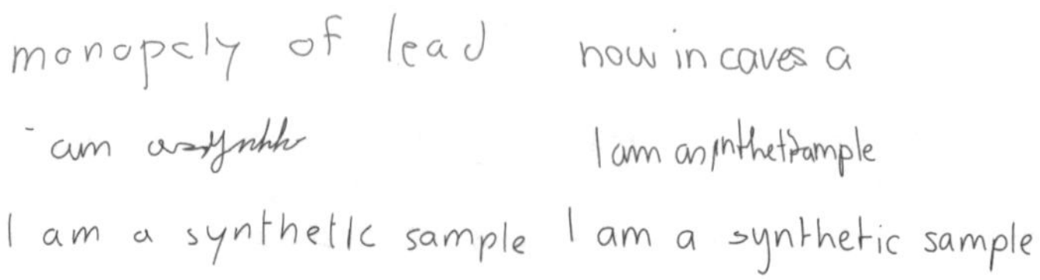

monopoly of lead   now in caves a

¯ am a~synthe   I am a synthetr ample

I am a synthetic sample I am a synthetic sample

Fig. 11 (top, green) Input samples used to infer style. (middle, red) Synthetic samples of a model with π only. They are generated using one-hot-encoded character labels, causing problems with *pen-up* events and with character placement. (bottom, blue) Synthetic samples of our model *with* GMM latent space

4.4.2 GMM Latent Space

Conditioning generative models is typically done via one-hot encoded labels. While we could directly use samples from $q(\pi_t|u_t)$, we prefer using a continuous representation. We hypothesize and experimentally validate (see Fig. 11) that the synthesis model can shape the latent space with respect to the loss caused by the content aspect.

For this purpose, we use a Gaussian mixture model where each character in K is represented by an isotropic Gaussian

$$p(\varphi_t) = \sum_{k=1}^{K} \pi_{t,k} \mathcal{N}(\varphi_t|\mu_k, \sigma_k), \tag{10}$$

where $\mathcal{N}(\varphi_t|\mu_k, \sigma_k)$ is the probability of sampling from the corresponding mixture component k. π corresponds to the content variable in Eq. (8) which is here interpreted as weight of the mixture components. This means that we use $q(\pi_t|u_t)$ to select a particular Gaussian component for a given point sample u_t. We then sample φ_t from the k-th Gaussian component and apply the "re-parametrization trick" [37, 48] so that the gradients can flow through the random variables, enabling the learning of GMM parameters via standard backpropagation.

$$\varphi_t = \mu_k + \sigma_k \epsilon, \tag{11}$$

where $\epsilon \sim \mathcal{N}(0, 1)$. Our continuous content representation results in similar letters being located closer in the latent space while dissimilar letters or infrequent symbols being pushed away. This effect is visualized in Fig. 12.

Importantly, the GMM parameters are sampled from a time-invariant distribution. That is they remain the same for all data samples and across time steps of a given input $\mathbf{x}$, whereas z_t is dynamic and employs new parameters per time step. For each Gaussian component in φ, we initialize μ_k, $1 \leq k \leq K$, randomly by using a uniform distribution $\mathcal{U}(-1, 1)$ and σ_k with a fixed value of 1. The GMM components are trained alongside the other network parameters.

In order to increase model convergence speed and to improve results, we use ground-truth character labels during training. More precisely, the GMM components

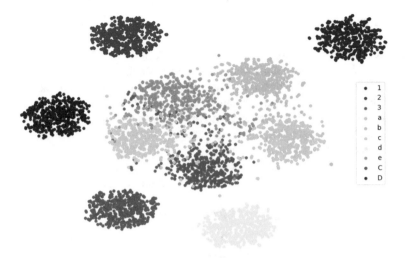

Fig. 12 Illustration of our GMM latent space φ^{gmm}. We select a small subset of our alphabet and draw 500 samples from corresponding GMM components. We use the tSNEalgorithm [61] to visualize 32-dimensional samples in 2D space. Note that the tSNEalgorithm finds an arbitrary placement and hence the positioning does not reflect the true latent space. Nevertheless, letters form separate clusters

are selected by using the ground-truth character labels c instead of predictions of the inference network $q(\pi_t|u_t)$. Hence, $q(\pi_t|u_t)$ is trained only by using the classification loss $\mathcal{L}_{classification}$ and not affected by the gradients of GMM with respect to π_t.

4.4.3 Word Spacing and Character Limits

At sampling time the model needs to automatically infer word spacing and which character to synthesize (these are a priori unknown). In order to control when to leave a space between words or when to start synthesizing the next character, we introduce two additional signals during training, namely e and w signaling the *end* of a character and *beginning* of a word, respectively. These labels are attained from ground-truth character level segmentation.

The w signal is fed as input to the output function g^{out}, and the output distribution of our handwriting synthesis takes the following form:

$$p(u_t|z_t, \pi_t) = g^{out}(z_t, \varphi_t, w_t), \tag{12}$$

forcing the model to learn when to leave empty space at training and sampling time.

The e signal, on the other hand, is provided to the model at training so that it can predict when to stop synthesizing a given character. It is included in the loss function in the form of Bernoulli log-likelihood $\mathcal{L}_e$. Along with the reconstruction of the input point u_t, the e_t label is predicted.

4.4.4 Input RNN Cell

Our model consists of two LSTM cells in the latent and at the input layers. Note that the latent cell is originally contributing via the transition function τ^{latent} in Eq. (6). Using an additional cell at the input layer increases model capacity (similar to multi-layered RNNs) and adds a new transition function τ^{inp}. Thus, the synthesis model can capture and modulate temporal patterns at the input levels. Intuitively, this is motivated by the strong temporal consistency in handwriting where the previous letter influences the appearance of the current (cf. Fig. 8).

We now use a temporal representation h_t^{inp} of the input points u_t. With the cumulative modifications, our C-VRNN architecture becomes

$$p(u_t|z_t, \pi_t) = g^{out}(z_t, \varphi_t, w_t), \tag{13}$$

$$z_t^p \sim p(z_t) = g^{p,z}(h_{t-1}^{latent}), \tag{14}$$

$$\pi_t^p \sim p(\pi_t) = g^{p,\pi}(h_{t-1}^{latent}), \tag{15}$$

$$h_t^{inp} = \tau^{inp}(u_t, h_{t-1}^{inp}), \tag{16}$$

$$z_t^q \sim q(z_t|u_t) = g^{q,z}(h_t^{inp}, h_{t-1}^{latent}), \tag{17}$$

$$\pi_t^q \sim q(\pi_t|u_t) = g^{q,\pi}(h_t^{inp}, h_{t-1}^{latent}), \tag{18}$$

$$h_t^{latent} = \tau^{latent}(h_t^{inp}, z_t, \varphi_t, h_{t-1}^{latent}). \tag{19}$$

Finally, we train our handwriting model by optimizing the following loss:

$$\mathcal{L}(\cdot) = \mathcal{L}_{lb} + \mathcal{L}_{classification} + \mathcal{L}_e. \tag{20}$$

In our style transfer applications, we first pass a reference sample to the model and get the internal state of the latent LSTM cell h^{latent} carrying style information. We then initialize the sampling phase (see Fig. 10) by calculating the style and content via corresponding prior distributions as in Eqs. 14 and 15.

4.5 Application Scenarios

By disentangling content from style, our approach makes digital ink truly editable. This allows the generation of novel writing in user-defined styles and, similarly to typed text, of seamless editing of handwritten text. Further, it enables a wide range of exciting application scenarios, of which we discuss proof-of-concept implementations.

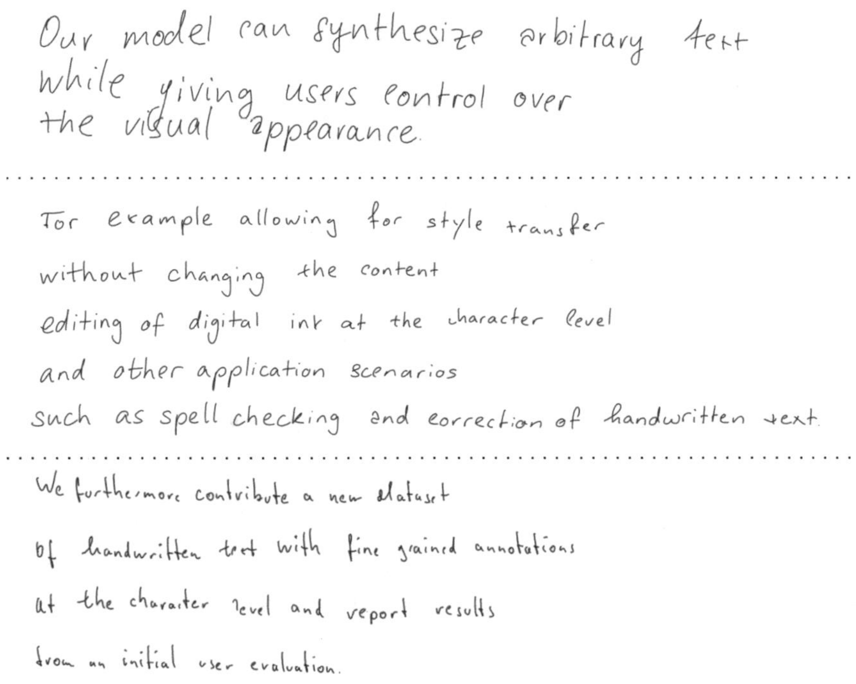

Our model can synthesize arbitrary text
while giving users control over
the visual appearance.

. . . .

For example allowing for style transfer
without changing the content
editing of digital ink at the character level
and other application scenarios
such as spell checking and correction of handwritten text

. . . .

We furthermore contribute a new dataset
of handwritten text with fine grained annotations
at the character level and report results
from an initial user evaluation.

Fig. 13 Handwritten text synthesized from the paper abstract. Each sentence is "written" in the style of a different author. For full abstract, see Appendix

4.5.1 Conditional Handwriting Generation

To illustrate the capability to synthesize *novel* text in a user-specific style we have implemented an interface that allows user to type text, browse a database of handwritten samples from different authors, and generate novel handwriting. The novel sequence takes the content from the typed text and matches the style to a single input sample. This could be directly embedded in existing note-taking applications to generate personalized handwritten notes from typed text or email clients could turn typed text into handwritten, personalized letters. For demonstration we have synthesized extracts of this paper's abstract in three different styles (see Fig. 13).

4.5.2 Content Preserving Style Transfer

Our model can furthermore transfer *existing* handwritten samples to *novel* styles, thus preserving their content while changing their appearance. We implemented an interactive tablet application that allows users to recast their own handwriting into a selected style (see Fig. 14 for results). After scribbling on the canvas and selecting an author's handwriting sample, users see their strokes morphed to that style in

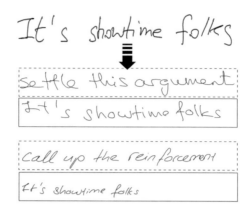

Fig. 14 Style transfer. The input sequence (top) is transferred to a selected reference style (black ink, dotted outlines). The results (blue ink, solid outline) preserve the input content, and its appearance matches the reference style

real time. Such solution could be beneficial for a variety of domains. For example, artist and comic authors could include specific handwritten lettering in their work, or preserving style during localization to a foreign language.

Beautification

When using the users own input style as target style, our model re-generates smoother versions of the original strokes, while maintaining natural variability and diversity. Thus obtaining an averaging effect that suppresses local noise and preserves global style features. The resulting strokes are then beautified (see Fig. 17), in line with previous work that solely relied on token averaging for beautification (e.g., [104]) or denoising (e.g., [15]).

4.5.3   Word-Level Editing

At the core of our technique lies the ability to edit digital ink at the same level of fidelity as typed text, allowing users to change, delete, or replace individual words. Figure 15 illustrates a simple prototype allowing users to edit handwritten content, while preserving the original style when re-synthesizing it. Our model recognizes individual words and characters and renders them as (editable) overlays. The user may select individual words, change the content, and regenerate the digital ink reflecting the edits while maintaining a coherent visual appearance. We see many applications, for example, note-taking apps, which require frequent edits but currently do not allow for this without loosing visual appearance.

Handwriting Spell-checking and Correction

A further application of the ability to edit digital ink at the word level is the possibility to spell-check and correct handwritten text. As a proof of concept, we implemented

Fig. 15 Our model allows editing of handwritten text at the word level. **a** Handwriting is recognized, with each individual word fully editable. **b** Edited words are synthesized and embedded in the original text, preserving the style

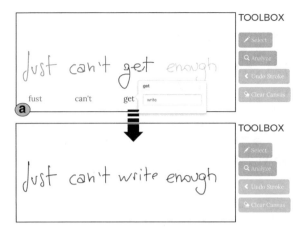

Fig. 16 Our spell-checking interface. **a** Spelling and grammar mistakes are detected and highlighted directly on the handwriting. Alternative spelling is offered (red box). **b** Corrected words are synthesized and embedded in the original text (blue ink), preserving the writer style

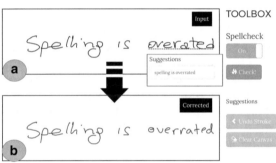

a functional handwriting spell-checker that can analyze digital ink, detect spelling mistakes, and correct the written samples by synthesizing the corrected sentence in the original style (see Fig. 16). For the implementation we rely on existing spell-checking APIs, feeding recognized characters into it and re-rendering the retrieved corrections.

4.6 Preliminary User Evaluation

So far we have introduced our neural network architecture and have evaluated its capability to synthesize digital ink. We now shift our focus on initially evaluating users' perception and the usability of our method. To this end, we conducted a preliminary user study gathering quantitative and qualitative data on two separate tasks. Throughout the experiment, 10 subjects ($M = 27.9$; $SD = 3.34$; 3 female) from our institution evaluated our model using an iPad Pro and Apple Pencil.

Handwriting Beautification

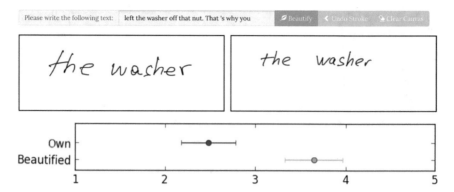

Fig. 17 Task 1. Top: Experiment Interface. Participants input on the left; beautified version on the right. Bottom: Confidence interval plot on a 5-point Likert scale

The first part of our experiment evaluates text beautification. Users were asked to compare their original handwriting with its beautified counterpart. Specifically, we asked our subjects to repeatedly write extracts from the LOB corpus [46], for a total of 12 trials each. In each trial, the participant copied down the sample, and we beautified the strokes with the results being shown side-by-side (see Fig. 17, top). Users were then asked to rate the aesthetics of their own script (Q: *I find my own handwriting aesthetically pleasing*) and the beautified version (Q: *I find the beautified handwriting aesthetically pleasing*), using a 5-point Likert scale. Importantly, these were treated as independent questions (i.e., users were allowed to like both).

Handwriting Spell-Checking

In the second task, we evaluate the spell-checking utility (see Fig. 16). We randomly sampled from the LOB corpus and perturbed individual words such that they contained spelling mistakes. Participants then used our tool to correct the written text (while maintaining its style), and subsequently were asked to fill in a standard system usability scale (SUS) questionnaire and take part in an exit interview.

Results

Our results, summarized in Fig. 17 (bottom), indicate that users' reception of our technique is overall positive. The beautified strokes were on average rated higher ($M = 3.65$, 95% CI [3.33–3.97]) with non-overlapping confidence intervals. The SUS results further support this trend, with our system scoring positively ($SUS = 85$). Following the analysis technique suggested in [53], our system can be classified as Rank A, indicating that users are likely to recommend it to others.

The above results are also echoed by participants' comments during the exit interviews (e.g., *I have never seen anything like this*, and *Finally others can read my notes.*). Furthermore, some suggested additional applications that would naturally fit our model capabilities (e.g., *This would be very useful to correct bad or illegible handwriting, I can see this used a lot in education, especially when teaching how*

Fig. 18 Potential starting positions are illustrated as heatmaps for the next stroke for handwritten text (left), animal drawings (middle), and a flowchart sample (right)

to write to kids and *This would be perfect for note taking, as one could go back in their notes and remove mistakes, abbreviations and so on*). Interestingly, the ability to preserve style while editing content were mentioned frequently as the most valued feature of our approach (e.g., *Having a spell-checker for my own handwriting feels like writing personalized text messages!*).

5 Compositional Stroke Embeddings

We have shown that generative modeling of the handwritten text promises to combine the flexibility and aesthetics of handwriting and the ability to process, search and edit digital text, offering an improved user experience. Handwriting is the basis of note taking, yet it is usually much more involved as we often rely on sketching as well (Fig. 1). Handwriting is relatively a more structured task as we follow an order while writing. In a free-form sketch, strokes are composed into more complex structures by following underlying semantics. The order of strokes in a drawing can be arbitrary and yet very similar sketches can be achieved. The sequences **x** representing the drawing sample will be different though due to the ordering of the strokes. This observation indicates the compositional nature of drawings, introducing a new challenge to the data representations and models we have been using for relatively more structured handwriting data.

The existing work, including our handwriting model, considers the entire drawing as a single sequence of points [1, 17, 38, 75]. Instead, in our paper [2], we explore a novel *compositional* generative model, called CoSE, for complex stroke-based data such as drawings, diagrams, and sketches. To this end, we treat a drawing sample **x** as an *unordered* collection of strokes $\mathbf{x}=\{\mathbf{s}_k\}_{k=1}^{K}$. Our key insight is to factor *local* appearance of a stroke from the *global* structure of the drawing. Since the stroke ordering does not impact the semantic meaning of the diagram, this modeling decision has profound implications. In our approach, the model does not need to understand the difference between the $(K-1)!$ potential orderings of the previous strokes to predict the k-th stroke, leading to a much more efficient utilization of modeling capacity.

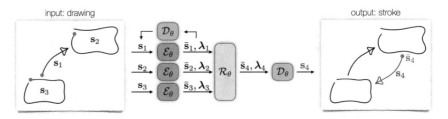

Fig. 19 Architecture overview—(left) the input drawing as a collection of strokes $\{s_k\}$; (middle) our embedding architecture, consisting of a shared encoder $\mathcal{E}_\theta$, a shared decoder $\mathcal{D}_\theta$, and a relational model $\mathcal{R}_\theta$; (right) the input drawing with the next stroke s_4 and its starting position $\bar{s}_4$ predicted by $\mathcal{R}_\theta$ and decoded by $\mathcal{D}_\theta$. Note that the relational model $\mathcal{R}_\theta$ is permutation-invariant

In our generative modeling task, we follow a predictive setup where the model is expected to complete a given sample. We consider a collaborative scenario between the model and the user such that the model follows the user drawing, understands the scene, and provides strokes when asked for. Such a task requires to know where and what to draw next, heavily depending on the context. In handwriting, localization of the next stroke is rather easy and often determined by the previous stroke while in sketches the next stroke depends on the semantic category and the order of the strokes is determined by the user. For a diagram sample, on the other hand, the next stroke is not tied to global semantics and the start position is an important degree of freedom (Fig. 18).

We demonstrate the predictive capabilities via a proof-of-concept interactive demo[2] in which the model suggests diagram completions based on initial user input. We also show that our model outperforms existing models quantitatively and qualitatively and we analyze the learned latent space to provide insights into how predictions are formed.

5.1 Method Overview

We use the stroke-based representation $\mathbf{x}=\{s_k\}_{k=1}^{K}$ presented in Sect. 3.1. The *pen-up* labels p_t are no longer required as the ink samples are split by the *pen-up* positions. We follow a fully unsupervised approach and do not use any additional labels.

We decompose the sample $\mathbf{x}$ into strokes and ignore the ordering, requiring the model to capture the semantics of a sketch and learn the relationships between its strokes. Our model first projects variable-length strokes into a fixed-dimensional latent space, and then models their relationships in this latent space to predict future strokes. This approach is illustrated in Fig. 19. More formally, given an initial set of strokes (e.g. $\{s_1, s_2, s_3\}$), we wish to predict the next stroke (e.g. s_4). We decompose the joint distribution of the sequence of strokes $\mathbf{x}$ as a product of conditional

---

[2] https://eth-ait.github.io/cose.

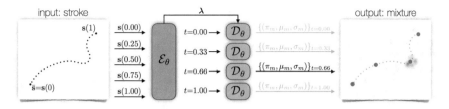

Fig. 20 Stroke embedding—The input stroke **s** is passed to the encoder, which produces a latent code λ. The decoder parameterizes a Gaussian mixture model for arbitrary positions $t \in [0, 1]$ from which we sample points on the stroke. We only visualize the mixture model associated with $t = .66$ (non-grayed out arrow)

distributions over the set of existing strokes:

$$p(\mathbf{x}; \theta) = \prod_{k=1}^{K} p(\mathbf{s}_k, \bar{\mathbf{s}}_k | \mathbf{s}_{<k}, \bar{\mathbf{s}}_{<k}; \theta), \tag{21}$$

with $\bar{\mathbf{s}}_k$ referring to the starting position of the k-th stroke, and $<k$ denotes $\{1 \ldots k-1\}$. Note that we assume a fixed but not chronological ordering of K. An encoder $\mathcal{E}_\theta$ first encodes each stroke **s** to its corresponding latent code λ. A decoder $\mathcal{D}_\theta$ reconstructs the corresponding **s**, given a code λ and the starting position $\bar{\mathbf{s}}$. A transformer-based relational model $\mathcal{R}_\theta$ processes the latent codes $\{\lambda_{<k}\}$ and their corresponding starting positions $\{\bar{\mathbf{s}}_{<k}\}$ to generate the next stroke starting position $\bar{\mathbf{s}}_k$ and embedding λ_k, from which $\mathcal{D}_\theta$ reconstructs the output stroke $\mathbf{s}_k$. Overall, our architecture factors into a *stroke embedding* model ($\mathcal{E}_\theta$ and $\mathcal{D}_\theta$) and a *relational model* ($\mathcal{R}_\theta$).

Stroke Embedding

We force the embedding model to capture *local* information such as the shape, size, or curvature by preventing it from accessing *any* global information such as the canvas position or existence of other strokes and their inter-dependencies. The autoencoder generates an abstraction of the variable-length strokes **s** by encoding them into fixed-length embeddings $(\lambda, \bar{\mathbf{s}}) = \mathcal{E}_\theta(\mathbf{s})$ and decoding them into strokes $\mathbf{s} = \mathcal{D}_\theta(\lambda, \bar{\mathbf{s}})$.

Relational Model

Our relational model learns how to *compose* individual strokes to create a sketch by considering the relationship between latent codes. Given an input drawing encoded as $\mathbf{x} = \{(\lambda_{<k}, \bar{\mathbf{s}}_{<k})\}$, we predict: i) a starting position for the next stroke $\bar{\mathbf{s}}_k$, and ii) its corresponding embedding λ_k. Introducing the embeddings into Eq. 21, we obtain our *compositional stroke embedding* model that decouples *local* drawing information from *global* semantics:

$$p(\mathbf{x}; \theta) = \prod_{k=1}^{K} p(\lambda_k, \bar{\mathbf{s}}_k | \lambda_{<k}, \bar{\mathbf{s}}_{<k}; \theta) \tag{22}$$

Fig. 21 Sampling frequency in decoding. For arrow (top) and circle (bottom) shapes, we decode the corresponding stroke embedding λ in different resolutions by controlling the number of output points

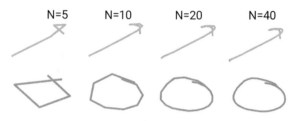

N=5   N=10   N=20   N=40

We train by maximizing the log-likelihood of the network parameters θ on the training set.

5.2 Stroke Embeddings

We represent variable-length strokes $\mathbf{s}$ with fixed-length embeddings $\lambda \in \mathbb{R}^D$. The goal is to learn a representation space of the strokes such that it is informative both for *reconstruction* of the original strokes, and for *prediction* of future strokes. We now detail our autoencoder architecture: the encoder $\mathcal{E}_\theta$ is based on transformers [88], while the decoder $\mathcal{D}_\theta$ extends ideas from neural modeling of differential geometry [36]. The parameters of both networks are trained via:

$$\arg\max_\theta \;\; \mathbb{E}_{t\sim[0,1]} \sum_{m=1}^{M} \pi_{t,m} \, \mathcal{N}(\mathbf{s}_k(t) \mid \mu_{t,m}, \sigma_{t,m}),$$

$$\{\mu_{t,m}, \sigma_{t,m}, \pi_{t,m}\} = \mathcal{D}_\theta(t \mid \mathcal{E}_\theta(\mathbf{s}))$$

(23)

where we use mixture densities [11, 35] with M Gaussians with mixture coefficients π, mean μ and variance σ; $t \in [0, 1]$ is the curve parameter. Note that we use log-likelihood rather than Chamfer Distance as in [36]. While we do interpret strokes as 2D curves, we observe that modeling of prediction uncertainity is commonly done in the ink modeling literature [1, 35, 38] and has been shown to result in better regression performance compared to minimizing an L2 metric [52].

CoSE Encoder—$\mathcal{E}_\theta(\mathbf{s})$

We encode a stroke by viewing it as a sequence of 2D points, and generate the corresponding latent code with a transformer $\mathcal{T}_\theta^t$, where the superscript t denotes use of positional encoding in the temporal dimension [88]. The encoder outputs $(\bar{\mathbf{s}}, \lambda) = \mathcal{E}_\theta(\mathbf{s})$, where $\bar{\mathbf{s}}$ is the starting position of a stroke and $\lambda = \mathcal{T}_\theta^t(\mathbf{s} - \bar{\mathbf{s}})$. The use of positional encoding induces a point ordering and emphasizes the geometry, where most sequence models focus strongly on capturing the drawing dynamics. Furthermore, avoiding the modeling of explicit temporal dependencies between time steps allows for inherent parallelism and is hence computationally advantageous over RNNs.

CoSE Decoder—$\mathcal{D}_\theta(t|\bar{s}, \lambda)$

We consider a stroke as a curve in the differential geometry sense: a 1D manifold embedded in 2D space. As such, there exists a differentiable map $s : \mathbb{R} \to \mathbb{R}^2$ between $t \subset [0, 1]$ and the 2D planar curve $s(t)=(x_t, y_t)$. Groucix ct al. [36] proposed to represent 2D (curves) and 3D (surfaces) geometry via MLPs that approximate $s(t)$. Recently, it has been shown that representing curves via dense networks induces an implicit smoothness regularizer [32, 93] akin to the one that CNNs induce on images [87]. Since we do not want to reconstruct a single curve [32], we employ the latent code provided by $\mathcal{E}_\theta$ to condition our decoder jointly with the curve parameter t: $\mathcal{D}_\theta(t|\lambda, \bar{s}) = \bar{s} + \text{MLP}_\theta([t, \lambda])$ [36] which parameterizes the Gaussian mixture from Eq. 23. Our decoder allows us to determine the number of points in the decoded stroke. We control the output resolution by defining the sampling frequency for $t \in [0, 1]$ (Fig. 21).

Inference

At inference time, a stroke is reconstructed by using t values sampled at (consecutive) regular intervals as determined by an arbitrary sampling rate; see Fig. 20. Note how compared to RNNs, we do not need to predict an "end of stroke" token, as the decoder output for $t=1$ corresponds to the end of a stroke. Therefore, the length of the reconstructed sequence depends on how densely we sample the parameter t.

5.3 CoSE Relational Model—$\mathcal{R}_\theta$

We propose a generative model that autoregressively estimates a joint distribution over stroke embeddings and positions given a latent representation of the current drawing in the form $\mathbf{x}=\{(\lambda_{<k}, \bar{s}_{<k})\}$. We hypothesize that, in contrast to handwriting, local context and spatial layout are important factors that are not influenced by the drawing order of the user. We exploit the self-attention mechanism of the transformer [88] to learn the *relational dependencies* between strokes in the latent space. In contrast to the stroke embedding model (Sect. 5.2), we *do not* use positional encoding to prevent any temporal information to flow through the relational model.

Prediction Factorization

In drawings, the starting position is an important degree of freedom. Hence, we split the prediction of the next stroke into two tasks: (i) the prediction of the stroke's starting position $\bar{s}_k$, and (ii) the prediction of the stroke's embedding λ_k. Given the (latent codes of) initial strokes, and their starting positions $\{(\lambda_{<k}, \bar{s}_{<k})\}$, this results in the factorization of the joint distribution over the strokes $\mathbf{s}_k$ and positions $\bar{s}_k$ as a product of conditional distributions:

$$p(\lambda_k, \bar{s}_k|\lambda_{<k}, \bar{s}_{<k}; \theta) = \underbrace{p(\bar{s}_k|\lambda_{<k}, \bar{s}_{<k}; \theta)}_{\text{starting position prediction}} \underbrace{p(\lambda_k|\bar{s}_k, \lambda_{<k}, \bar{s}_{<k}; \theta)}_{\text{latent code prediction}} \quad (24)$$

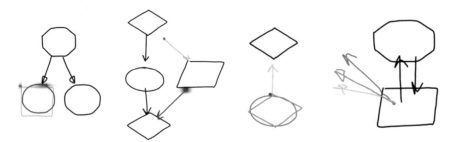

Fig. 22 Relational model—A few snapshots from our live demo. (Left) Given a drawing, our model proposes *several* starting position for auto-completion (we draw the most likely strokes associated with the two most likely starting positions (red, gray)). (Right) Given a stating position, our model can predict *several* stroke alternatives; here we show the top 3 most likely predictions (orange, light blue, dark blue)

By conditioning on the starting position, the attention mechanism in $\mathcal{R}_\theta$ focuses on a *local* context, allowing our model to perform more effectively. (see also Sect. 5.5.3). We use two separate transformers with the same network configuration yet slightly different inputs and outputs: (i) the position prediction model takes the set $\{(\mathbf{s}_{<k}, \bar{\mathbf{s}}_{<k})\}$ as input and produces $\bar{\mathbf{s}}_k$; (ii) the embedding prediction model takes the next starting position $\bar{\mathbf{s}}_k$ as additional input to predict λ_k. Factorizing the prediction in this way has two advantages: (i) all strokes start at the origin, hence we can employ the translational-invariant embeddings from Sect. 5.2; (ii) it enables interactive applications, where the user specifies a starting position and the model predicts an auto-completion; see video in the supplementary and Fig. 22.

Starting Position Prediction

The prediction of the next starting positions is inherently multi-modal, since there may be multiple equally good predictions in terms of drawing continuation; see Fig. 22 (left). We employ multi-modal predictions in the form of a 2-dimensional Gaussian Mixture. In the fully generative scenario, we sample a position $\bar{\mathbf{s}}_k$ from the predicted GMM, rather than expecting a user input or ground-truth data as at training time.

Latent Code Prediction

Given a starting position, multiple strokes can be used to complete a given drawing; see Fig. 22 (right). We again use a Gaussian Mixture to capture this multi-modality. At inference time, we sample from $p(\lambda_k | \bar{\mathbf{s}}_k, \lambda_{<k}, \bar{\mathbf{s}}_{<k}; \theta)$ to generate λ_k. Thanks to order-invariant relational model, CoSE can predict over long prediction horizons (see Fig. 23).

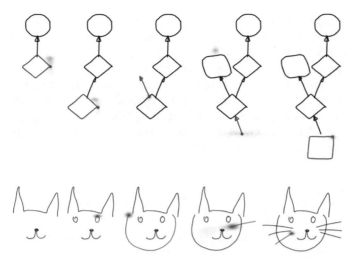

Fig. 23 Autoregressive completion. Performed by CoSE trained on `DiDi` and `QuickDraw` datasets

5.4 Training

Given a random pair of target $(\lambda_k, \bar{s}_k)$ and a subset of inputs $\{(\lambda_{\neq k}, \bar{s}_{\neq k})\}$, we make a prediction for the position and the embedding of the target stroke. This subset is obtained by selecting $H \in [1, K]$ strokes from the drawing. We either pick H strokes i) in order or ii) at random. This allows the model to be good in completing existing partial drawings but also be robust to arbitrary subsets of strokes. During training, the model has access to the ground-truth positions $\bar{s}$ (like teacher forcing [94]). Note that while we train all three sub-modules (encoder, relational model, decoder) in parallel, we found that the performance is slightly better if gradients from the relational model (Eq. 22) are not backpropagated through the stroke embedding model. We apply augmentations in the form of random rotation and re-scaling of the entire drawing (see supplementary for details).

5.5 Experiments

We evaluate our model on the recently released `DiDi` dataset [33]. In contrast to existing drawing [34] or handwriting datasets [62], this task requires learning of the *compositional structure* of flowchart diagrams, consisting of several shapes. In this paper, we focus on the predictive setting in which an existing (partial) drawing is extended by adding more shapes or by connecting already drawn ones. State-of-the-art techniques in ink modeling treat the entire drawing as a *single* sequence. Our experiments demonstrate that this approach does not scale to complex structures such as flowchart diagrams (cf. Fig. 25). We compare our method to the state-of-the-art [38] via the Chamfer Distance [74] between the ground-truth strokes and the model outputs (i.e. reconstructed or predicted strokes).

The task is inherently stochastic as the next stroke highly depends on where it is drawn. To account for the high variability in the predictions across different generative models, the ground-truth starting positions passed the models in our quantitative analysis (note that the qualitative results rely only on the predicted starting positions). Moreover, similar to most predictive tasks, there is no single, correct prediction in the stroke prediction task (see Fig. 22). To account for this multi-modality of fully generative models, we employ a *stochastic* variant of the Chamfer distance (CD):

$$\min_{\lambda_k \sim p(\lambda_k|\bar{s}_k, \lambda_{<k}, \bar{s}_{<k}; \theta)} \left\{ \text{CD}\left(\mathcal{D}_\theta(t|\hat{\lambda}_k), \, s_k\right) \right\}. \tag{25}$$

We evaluate our models by sampling one λ_k from each mixture component of the relational model's prediction which are decoded into 10 strokes (see Fig. 27). This results in a broader exploration of the predicted strokes than a strict Gaussian mixture sampling. Note that while our training objective is NLL (as is common in ink modeling), the Chamfer Distance allows for a fairer comparison since it allows to compare models trained on differently processed data (i.e., positions vs offsets).

5.5.1 Stroke Prediction

We first evaluate the performance in the *stroke prediction* setting. Given a set of strokes and a target position, the task is to predict the next stroke. For each drawing, we start with a single stroke and incrementally add more strokes from the original drawing (in the order they were drawn) to the set of given strokes and predict the subsequent one. In this setting, we evaluate our method in an ablation study, where we replace components of our model with standard RNN-based models: a sequence-to-sequence (seq2seq) architecture [86] for stroke embeddings, and an autoregressive RNN for the relational model. Furthermore, following the setting in [38], we compare to the decoder-only setup from Sketch-RNN (itself conceptually similar to Graves et al. [35]). For the seq2seq-based embedding model we use bi-directional LSTMs [43] as the encoder, and a uni-directional LSTM as decoder. Informally, we determined that a deterministic encoder with a non-autoregressive decoder outperformed other seq2seq architectures; see Sect. 5.5.2. The RNN-based relational model is an autoregressive sequence model [35].

Analysis

The results are summarized in Table 2. While the stroke-wise reconstruction performance across all models differs only marginally, the predictive performance of our proposed model is substantially better. This indicates that a standard seq2seq model is able to learn an embedding space that is suitable for accurate reconstruction; this embedding space, however, *does not* lend itself to predictive modeling.

Table 2 Stroke prediction—We evaluate reconstruction (i.e. $CD(\mathcal{D}_\theta(\mathcal{E}_\theta(s)), s)$ and prediction (i.e. $CD(\mathcal{R}_\theta(\lambda_{<k}), s_k)$ for a number of different models. Note that performing well on reconstruction does not necessarily correlate with good prediction performance

$\mathcal{E}_\theta/\mathcal{D}_\theta$	$\mathcal{R}_\theta$	Recon. CD$\downarrow$	Pred. CD$\downarrow$
seq2seq	RNN	0.0144	0.0794
seq2seq	CoSE-$\mathcal{R}_\theta$	0.0138	0.0540
CoSE-$\mathcal{E}_\theta/\mathcal{D}_\theta$	RNN	0.0139	0.0713
CoSE-$\mathcal{E}_\theta/\mathcal{D}_\theta$	CoSE-$\mathcal{R}_\theta$ (Ord.)	0.0143	0.0696
CoSE-$\mathcal{E}_\theta/\mathcal{D}_\theta$	CoSE-$\mathcal{R}_\theta$	**0.0136**	**0.0442**
Sketch-RNN Decoder [38]	N/A	0.0679

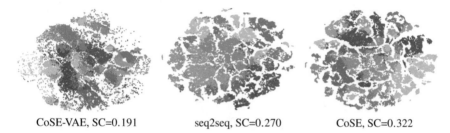

CoSE-VAE, SC=0.191   seq2seq, SC=0.270   CoSE, SC=0.322

Fig. 24 tSNE Embedding—Visualization of the latent spaces for different models (for quantitative analysis see Table 3). We employ k-means in latent space ($k = 10$), and color by cluster ID. While a VAE regularized objective leads to an overall compact latent space, clusters are not well separated, ours produces the most compact clusters (from left to right) which we show to be correlated with prediction quality

The combination of our embedding model (CoSE-$\mathcal{E}_\theta/\mathcal{D}_\theta$) with our relational model (CoSE-$\mathcal{R}_\theta$) outperforms all other models in terms of predicting consecutive strokes, giving an indication that the learned embedding space is better suited for the predictive downstream tasks. The results also indicate that the contributions of both are necessary to attain the best performance. This can be seen by the increase in prediction performance of the seq2seq when augmented with our relational model (CoSE-$\mathcal{R}_\theta$). However, a significant gap remains to the full model (cf. row 2 and 5).

We also evaluate our full model with additional positional encoding in the relational CoSE-$\mathcal{R}_\theta$ (Ord.). The results support our hypothesis that an order-invariant model is beneficial for the task of modeling compositional structures. It is also observed in sequential modeling of the stroke embeddings by using an RNN (row 3). Similarly, our model outperforms Sketch-RNN which treats drawings as sequence. We show a comparison of flowchart completions by Sketch-RNN and CoSE in Fig. 25. Our model is more robust to make longer predictions.

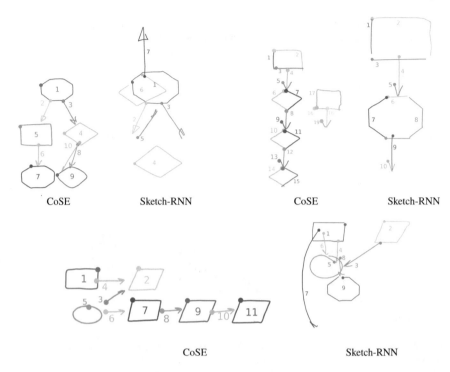

Fig. 25 Comparison with Sketch-RNN—For each pair of samples the first two strokes (denoted by 1 and 2 in blue color) are given as context, the remaining strokes (in color) are model outputs, numbers indicate prediction step. While Sketch-RNN produces meaningful completions for the first few predictions, its performance quickly decreases with increasing complexity. In contrast, CoSE is capable of predicting plausible continuations even over long prediction horizons

5.5.2 Stroke Embedding

Our analysis in Sect. 5.5.1 revealed that good reconstruction accuracy is not necessarily indicative of an embedding space that is useful for fully autoregressive predictions. We now investigate the structure of our embedding space in qualitative and quantitative measures by analyzing the performance of clustering algorithms on the embedded data. Since there is only a limited number of shapes that occur in diagrams, the expectation is that a well-shaped latent space should form clusters consisting of similar shapes, while maintaining sufficient variation.

Silhouette Coefficient (SC)

This coefficient is a quantitative measure that assesses the quality of a clustering by jointly measuring tightness of exemplars within clusters versus separation between clusters [78]. It does not require ground-truth cluster labels (e.g. whether a stroke is a box, arrow, arrow tip), and takes values between $[-1, 1]$ where a higher value is an indication of tighter and well separated clusters. The exact number of clusters

Table 3 Embedding space analysis—(Top) Variants of our model with different embedding dimensionalities and a variant of our model with VAE. (Bottom) Results for a sequence-to-sequence stroke autoencoder (seq2seq) and its variational (VAE) and/or autoregressive (AR) variants. All stroke embedding models use our Transformer relational model $\mathcal{R}_\theta$. D indicates the dimensionality of the embedding space. CD and SC denote Chamfer Distance and Silhouette Coefficient, respectively

$\mathcal{E}_\theta / \mathcal{D}_\theta$	$\mathcal{R}_\theta$	D	Recon. CD $\downarrow$	Pred. CD $\downarrow$	SC $\uparrow$
CoSE-$\mathcal{E}_\theta/\mathcal{D}_\theta$ (Table 2)	TR	8	0.0136	**0.0442**	**0.361**
CoSE-$\mathcal{E}_\theta/\mathcal{D}_\theta$	TR	16	0.0091	0.0481	0.335
CoSE-$\mathcal{E}_\theta/\mathcal{D}_\theta$	TR	32	0.0081	0.0511	0.314
CoSE-$\mathcal{E}_\theta/\mathcal{D}_\theta$-VAE	TR	8	0.0198	0.0953	0.197
seq2seq (Table 2)	TR	8	0.0138	0.0540	0.276
seq2seq	TR	16	0.0076	0.0783	0.253
seq2seq	TR	32	**0.0047**	0.0848	0.261
seq2seq-VAE	TR	8	0.0161	0.0817	0.180
seq2seq-AR	TR	8	0.0432	0.0855	0.249
seq2seq-AR-VAE	TR	8	0.2763	0.1259	0.151

is not known and we therefore compute the SC for the clustering result of k-means and spectral clustering [81] with varying numbers of clusters ({5, 10, 15, 20, 25}) with both Euclidean and cosine distance on the embeddings of all strokes in the test data. This leads to a total of 20 different clustering results. In Table 3, we report the average SC across these 20 clustering experiments for a number of different model configurations along with the Chamfer distance (CD) for stroke reconstruction and prediction. Note, the Pearson correlation between the SC and the prediction accuracy is 0.92 indicating a strong correlation between the two.

Influence of the Embedding Dimensionality (D)

We performed experiments with different values of D—the dimensionality of the latent codes. Table 3 shows that this parameter directly affects all components of the task: While a high-dimensional embedding space improves reconstructions accuracy, it is harder to predict valid embeddings in such a high-dimensional space and in consequence both the prediction performance and SC deteriorate. We observe a similar pattern with sequence-to-sequence architectures which benefit most from the increased embedding capacity by achieving the lowest reconstruction error (Recon. CD for seq2seq, $D = 32$). However, it also leads to a significantly higher prediction error. Higher-dimensional embeddings result in less compact representation space, making the prediction task more challenging.

Architectural Variants

In order to obtain a smoother latent space, we also introduce a KL-divergence regularizer [49] and follow the same annealing strategy as Ha et al. [38]. It is maybe surprising to see that a VAE regularizer (line CoSE-VAE) *hurts* reconstruction accuracy and interpretability of the embedding space. Note that the prediction task does

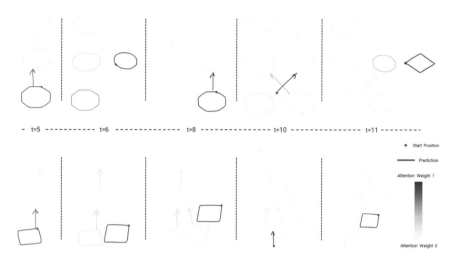

Fig. 26 Attention visualization over time—(top) with and (bottom) without conditioning on the start position to make a prediction for the next stroke's (in red) embedding. Attention weights correspond to the average of all attention layers across the network

not require interpolation or latent space walks since latent codes represent entire strokes that can be combined in a discrete fashion. The results further indicate that our architecture yields a better behaved embedding space, while retaining a good reconstruction accuracy. This is indicated by (i) the increase in reconstruction quality with larger D yet prediction accuracy and SC deteriorate; (ii) CoSE obtains much better prediction accuracy and SC at similar reconstruction accuracy; (iii) smoothing the embedding space using a VAE for regularization hurts reconstruction accuracy, prediction accuracy and SC; iv) autoregressive approach hurts reconstruction and prediction accuracy and SC—this is because autoregressive models tend to overfit to the ground-truth data (i.e., teacher forcing) and fail when forced to complete drawings based on their own predictions.

Visualizations

To further analyse the latent space properties, we provide a tSNE visualization [61] of the embedding space with color coding for cluster IDs as determined by k-means with $k = 10$ in Fig. 24. The plots indicate that the VAE objective encourages a latent space with overlapping clusters, whereas for CoSE, the clusters are better separated and more compact. An interesting observation is that the smooth and regularized VAE latent space does not translate into improved performance on either reconstruction or inference, which is inline with prior findings on the connection of latent space behavior and downstream behavior [59]. Clearly, the embedding spaces learned using a CoSE model have different properties and are more suitable for predictive tasks that are conducted in the embedding space. This qualitative finding is inline with the quantitative results of the SC and correlating performance in the stroke prediction task.

Fig. 27 Pred. CD performance of our model $\mathcal{R}_\theta$ by using different number of components in the GMM for embedding predictions

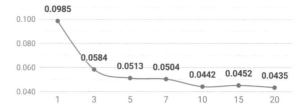

5.5.3 Ablations

Conditioning on the Start Position

The factorization in Eq. 24 allows our model to attend to a relatively local context. To show the importance of conditioning on the initial stroke positions, we train a model without this conditioning. Figure 26 shows that conditioning on the start position helps to attend to the local neighborhood, which becomes increasingly important as the number of strokes gets larger. Moreover, the Chamfer Distance on the predictions nearly double from 0.0442 to 0.0790 in the absence of the starting positions.

Number of GMM components. Using a multi-modal distribution to model the stroke embedding predictions significantly improves our model's performance (cf. Fig. 27). It is an important hyper-parameter as it is the only source of stochasticity in our relational model $\mathcal{R}_\theta$. We observe that using 10 or more components is sufficient. Our results presented in the paper are achieved with 10 components.

Backpropagating $\mathcal{R}_\theta$ gradients. Since we aim to decouple the local stroke information from the global drawing structure, we train the embedding model CoSE-$\mathcal{E}_\theta/\mathcal{D}_\theta$ via the reconstruction loss only, and do not backpropagate the relational model's gradients. We hypothesize that doing so would force the encoder to use some capacity to capture global semantics. When training our best model with all gradients flowing to the encoder CoSE-$\mathcal{E}_\theta$, increases the reconstruction error (Recon. CD) from 0.0136 to 0.0162 and the prediction error (Pred. CD) from 0.0442 to 0.0470.

5.5.4 Qualitative Results

The quantitative results from Table 2 indicate that our model performs better in the predictive modeling of complex diagrams compared to the baselines. Figure 25 provides further indication that this is indeed the case. We show predictions of SketchRNN [38] which performs well on structures with very few strokes but struggles to predict more complex drawings. In contrast ours continues to produce meaningful predictions even for complex diagrams. This is further illustrated in Fig. 28 showing a number of qualitative results from a model trained on the DiDi (left), IAM-OnDB (center) and the QuickDraw (right) datasets, respectively. Note that all predictions are in the autoregressive setting, where only the first stroke (in light

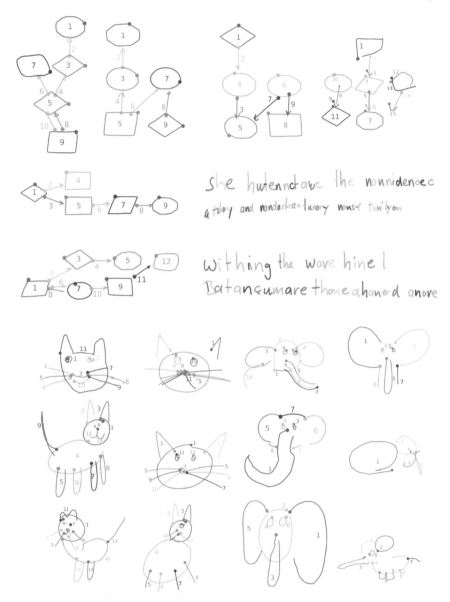

Fig. 28 Qualitative examples from CoSE—Drawings were sampled from the model given the **first stroke**. Numbers denote the drawing order of the strokes

blue) is given as input. All other strokes are model predictions (numbers indicate steps).

6 Discussion and Outlook

The advancing deep generative modeling techniques have given rise to a new class of interactive and collaborative applications in various domains by enabling manipulation of the user data or content synthesis for the users. Inspired by those novel interaction techniques and motivated by the increasing utility of digital inking, we address the problem of designing generative models for digital ink data. To this end, we introduce the *generative ink* layer for the digital ink framework, which aims to augment the inking platforms with a more fine-grained control. We present models that are able to generate realistic ink data, allowing us to create applications in interactive and collaborative scenarios.

In our handwriting work, our focus lies on the personalization of the digital ink data while preserving the versatility and efficiency of digital text. We have built a variety of proof-of-concept applications, including conditional synthesis and editing of digital ink at the word level.[3] Initial user feedback, while preliminary, indicates that users are largely positive about the capability to edit digital ink—in one's own handwriting or in the style of another author. The key idea underlying our approach is to treat style and content as two separate latent random variables with distributions learned during training.

A major challenge in learning disentangled representations and producing realistic samples of digital handwriting is that the model needs to perform auxiliary tasks, such as controlling the spacing in between words, character segmentation and recognition. It implies that such a fine-grained control requires a powerful architecture and extensive data labeling effort as we performed in our Deepwriting dataset. Considering the high amount of training data required by the deep neural networks and the cost of labeling operation, scaling of such fine-grained labeling to application domains beyond handwriting is tedious. QuickDraw transforms this expensive labeling process into a game for the users, harvesting over 50 million sketching samples, albeit to more coarse-grained and noisy labels. More work is needed to develop efficient data collection strategies as well as data-efficient models in parallel.

A potential approach for improving the data efficiency is incorporating domain priors into model design. In our second work, CoSE, we introduce compositionality as an inductive bias and show that we mitigate the complexity induced by the compositional nature of the strokes, particularly in free-form drawings. This is achieved by treating the digital ink data as a collection of strokes rather than a sequence of points as in the previous works. We follow a hierarchical design to model the local stroke appearance and global drawing semantics. We demonstrate experimentally that our model outperforms baselines and previous approaches on complex draw-

---

[3] https://www.youtube.com/watch?v=NVF-1csvVvc.

ings. Although being fully unsupervised is an advantage in terms of computational requirements, this also limits our options for applications. Our proposed model can be used in a collaborative scenario where our model observes the user and provides predictions when asked by the user.[4]

The works we have discussed in this chapter as well as the literature focus on addressing modeling tasks in controlled settings such as synthesis of handwritten text or drawings of basic shapes only. While they work well in an isolated scenario, a comprehensive note-taking experience involves various the data types including sketches, flowcharts, math equations, drawings, and handwritten text. Future works should seek more holistic approaches by embracing the challenges in modeling tasks collectively. Furthermore, to provide the model with a better understanding of the use intentions, the available material such as text or media could serve as a context in a note-taking application. Ink data, user actions, and the media can be formulated as a multi-modal problem [83] in the generative modeling framework.

Another challenge we should bear in mind is the hardware limitations as mobile devices are the number one application platform for digital ink. This introduces a significant discrepancy in the computational power between the training and inference time, enforcing us to design computationally more efficient algorithms. While compression techniques for neural architectures [20] can alleviate this problem, designing more effective architectures is a more fundamental remedy to this problem. Take the decoder component CoSE-$\mathcal{D}_\theta$ of our stroke autoencoder architecture (Sect. 5.2) as an example. It does not only improve the performance of the entire model but also allows us to control computational overhead in the decoding task. More concretely, our stroke parameterization over the scalar value t determines the sampling rate of the rendered strokes. For example, on a device with lower screen resolution, we can render the strokes with fewer points by sampling a sparser set of t values (Fig. 21), inducing smaller amount of computational load. Furthermore, we model the temporal information implicitly through the t parameter instead of following an autoregressive approach as in RNN-based architectures, enabling decoding of the points in parallel and hence achieving lower latency.

The digital ink technology has not yet matched our expectations shaped by the traditional pen and paper, and it is an open question if it will. *generative ink* layer itself may not be the approach to close this gap, however, it has potential to enhance digital inking experience by providing novel interaction schemes. We have presented in this chapter that generative modeling of digital ink bears significant potential for both human–computer interaction and machine learning research. While the synthesis and manipulation of digital ink present novel interaction scenarios for the users, it also introduces new challenges in the application and theory of modeling.

---

[4] https://www.youtube.com/watch?v=GENck9zmpMY.

References

1. Aksan E, Pece F, Hilliges O (2018) DeepWriting: making digital Ink editable via deep generative modeling, association for computing machinery, New York, NY, USA, pp 1–14. https://doi.org/10.1145/3173574.3173779
2. Aksan E, Deselaers T, Tagliasacchi A, Hilliges O (2020) Cose: compositional stroke embeddings. arXiv:200609930
3. Annett M (2017) (digitally) inking in the 21st century. IEEE Comput Graph Appl 37(1):92–99. https://doi.org/10.1109/MCG.2017.1
4. Annett M, Anderson F, Bischof WF, Gupta A (2014) The pen is mightier: Understanding stylus behaviour while inking on tablets. In: Proceedings of graphics interface 2014, Canadian information processing society, CAN, GI '14, pp 193–200
5. Arvo J, Novins K (2000) Fluid sketches: continuous recognition and morphing of simple hand-drawn shapes. In: Proceedings of the 13th annual ACM symposium on User interface software and technology. ACM, pp 73–80
6. Arvo J, Novins K (2005) Appearance-preserving manipulation of hand-drawn graphs. In: Proceedings of the 3rd international conference on Computer graphics and interactive techniques in Australasia and South East Asia. ACM, pp 61–68
7. Berninger VW (2012) Strengthening the mind's eye: the case for continued handwriting instruction in the 21st century. Principal 91:28–31
8. Bhattacharya U, Plamondon R, Chowdhury SD, Goyal P, Parui SK (2017) A sigma-lognormal model-based approach to generating large synthetic online handwriting sample databases. Int J Doc Anal Recogn (IJDAR) 1–17
9. Bhunia AK, Ghose S, Kumar A, Chowdhury PN, Sain A, Song YZ (2021a) Metahtr: towards writer-adaptive handwritten text recognition. arXiv:210401876
10. Bhunia AK, Khan S, Cholakkal H, Anwer RM, Khan FS, Shah M (2021b) Handwriting transformers. arXiv:210403964
11. Bishop CM (1995) Neural networks for pattern recognition. Oxford University Press Inc, USA
12. Brandl P, Richter C, Haller M (2010) Nicebook: supporting natural note taking. In: Proceedings of the SIGCHI conference on human factors in computing systems. ACM, New York, NY, USA, CHI '10, pp 599–608. https://doi.org/10.1145/1753326.1753417
13. Bresler M, Phan TV, Průša D, Nakagawa M, Hlaváč V (2014) Recognition system for on-line sketched diagrams. In: ICFHR
14. Bresler M, Průša D, Hlaváč V (2016) Online recognition of sketched arrow-connected diagrams. IJDAR
15. Buades A, Coll B, Morel JM (2005) A non-local algorithm for image denoising. In: 2005 IEEE computer society conference on computer vision and pattern recognition, CVPR'05, vol 2, pp 60–65. https://doi.org/10.1109/CVPR.2005.38
16. Burgert HJ (2002) The calligraphic line: thoughts on the art of writing. H-J Burgert, translated by Brody Neuenschwander
17. Carbune V, Gonnet P, Deselaers T, Rowley HA, Daryin A, Calvo M, Wang LL, Keysers D, Feuz S, Gervais P (2020) Fast multi-language LSTM-based online handwriting recognition. IJDAR
18. Chang WD, Shin J (2012) A statistical handwriting model for style-preserving and variable character synthesis. Int J Doc Anal Recogn 15(1):1–19. https://doi.org/10.1007/s10032-011-0147-7
19. Chen HI, Lin TJ, Jian XF, Shen IC, Chen BY (2015) Data-driven handwriting synthesis in a conjoined manner. Comput Graph Forum 34(7):235–244. https://doi.org/10.1111/cgf.12762
20. Cheng Y, Wang D, Zhou P, Zhang T (2017) A survey of model compression and acceleration for deep neural networks. arXiv:171009282
21. Cherubini M, Venolia G, DeLine R, Ko AJ (2007) Let's go to the whiteboard: how and why software developers use drawings. In: Proceedings of the SIGCHI conference on human

factors in computing systems. ACM, New York, NY, USA, CHI '07, pp 557–566. https://doi.org/10.1145/1240624.1240714

22. Chung J, Kastner K, Dinh L, Goel K, Courville AC, Bengio Y (2015) A recurrent latent variable model for sequential data. arXiv:1506.02216

23. Costagliola G, Deufemia V, Risi M (2006) A multi-layer parsing strategy for on-line recognition of hand-drawn diagrams. In: Visual languages and human-centric computing

24. Davis B, Tensmeyer C, Price B, Wigington C, Morse B, Jain R (2020) Text and style conditioned gan for generation of offline handwriting lines. arXiv:200900678

25. Davis RC, Landay JA, Chen V, Huang J, Lee RB, Li FC, Lin J, Morrey CB III, Schleimer B, Price MN, Schilit BN (1999) Notepals: Lightweight note sharing by the group, for the group. In: Proceedings of the SIGCHI conference on human factors in computing systems. ACM, New York, NY, USA, CHI '99, pp 338–345. https://doi.org/10.1145/302979.303107

26. Drucker J (1995) The alphabetic labyrinth: the letters in history and imagination. Thames and Hudson

27. Elarian Y, Abdel-Aal R, Ahmad I, Parvez MT, Zidouri A (2014) Handwriting synthesis: classifications and techniques. Int J Doc Anal Recogn 17(4):455–469. https://doi.org/10.1007/s10032-014-0231-x

28. Elsen C, Häggman A, Honda T, Yang MC (2012) Representation in early stage design: an analysis of the influence of sketching and prototyping in design projects. Int Des Eng Tech Conf Comput Inf Eng Conf Am Soc Mech Eng 45066:737–747

29. Espana-Boquera S, Castro-Bleda MJ, Gorbe-Moya J, Zamora-Martinez F (2011) Improving offline handwritten text recognition with hybrid hmm/ann models. Trans Pattern Recogn Mach Intell 33(4):767–779

30. Evernote Corporation (2017) How evernotes image recognition works. http://blog.evernote.com/tech/2013/07/18/how-evernotes-image-recognition-works/. Accessed 10 Aug 2017

31. Fogel S, Averbuch-Elor H, Cohen S, Mazor S, Litman R (2020) Scrabblegan: semi-supervised varying length handwritten text generation. In: Proceedings of the IEEE/CVF conference on computer vision and pattern recognition, pp 4324–4333

32. Gadelha M, Wang R, Maji S (2020) Deep manifold prior

33. Gervais P, Deselaers T, Aksan E, Hilliges O (2020) The DIDI dataset: digital ink diagram data

34. Google Creative Lab (2017) Quick, draw! The data. https://quickdraw.withgoogle.com/data. Accessed 01 May 2020

35. Graves A (2013) Generating sequences with recurrent neural networks. arXiv:1308.0850

36. Groueix T, Fisher M, Kim V, Russell B, Aubry M (2018) Atlasnet: a papier-mâché approach to learning 3D surface generation. In: CVPR

37. Gurumurthy S, Sarvadevabhatla RK, Radhakrishnan VB (2017) Deligan: generative adversarial networks for diverse and limited data. arXiv:170602071

38. Ha D, Eck D (2017) A neural representation of sketch drawings

39. Haines TS, Mac Aodha O, Brostow GJ (2016) My text in your handwriting. In: Transactions on graphics

40. Haller M, Leitner J, Seifried T, Wallace JR, Scott SD, Richter C, Brandl P, Gokcezade A, Hunter S (2010) The nice discussion room: Integrating paper and digital media to support co-located group meetings. In: Proceedings of the SIGCHI conference on human factors in computing systems. ACM, New York, NY, USA, CHI '10, pp 609–618. https://doi.org/10.1145/1753326.1753418

41. Hinckley K, Pahud M, Benko H, Irani P, Guimbretière F, Gavriliu M, Chen XA, Matulic F, Buxton W, Wilson A (2014) Sensing techniques for tablet+stylus interaction. In: Proceedings of the 27th annual ACM symposium on user interface software and technology. ACM, New York, NY, USA, UIST '14, pp 605–614. https://doi.org/10.1145/2642918.2647379

42. Hinton G, Nair V (2005) Inferring motor programs from images of handwritten digits. In: Proceedings of the 18th international conference on neural information processing systems. MIT Press, Cambridge, MA, USA, NIPS'05, pp 515–522. http://dl.acm.org/citation.cfm?id=2976248.2976313

43. Hochreiter S, Schmidhuber J (1997) Long short-term memory. Neural Comput 9(8):1735–1780
44. Huang CZA, Vaswani A, Uszkoreit J, Shazeer N, Simon I, Hawthorne C, Dai AM, Hoffman MD, Dinculescu M, Eck D (2018) Music transformer. arXiv:180904281
45. Hussain F, Zalik B (1999) Towards a feature-based interactive system for intelligent font design. In: Proceedings of the 1999 IEEE international conference on information visualization, pp 378–383. https://doi.org/10.1109/IV.1999.781585
46. Johansson S, Eric A, Roger G, Geoffrey L (1986) The tagged LOB corpus: user's manual. Norwegian computing centre for the humanities, Bergen, Norway
47. Kienzle W, Hinckley K (2013) Writing handwritten messages on a small touchscreen. In: Proceedings of the 15th international conference on human-computer interaction with mobile devices and services. ACM, New York, NY, USA, MobileHCI '13, pp 179–182. https://doi.org/10.1145/2493190.2493200
48. Kingma DP, Welling M (2013a) Auto-encoding variational bayes. In: Proceedings of the 2nd international conference on learning representations (ICLR), 2014
49. Kingma DP, Welling M (2013b) Auto-encoding variational bayes
50. Knuth DE (1986) The metafont book. Addison-Wesley Longman Publishing Co Inc, Boston, MA, USA
51. Kotani A, Tellex S, Tompkin J (2020) Generating handwriting via decoupled style descriptors. In: European conference on computer vision. Springer, pp 764–780
52. Kumar A, Marks TK, Mou W, Feng C, Liu X (2019) UGLLI face alignment: estimating uncertainty with gaussian log-likelihood loss. In: ICCV workshops, pp 0–0
53. Lewis JR, Sauro J (2009) The factor structure of the system usability scale. In: Kurosu M (ed) Proceedings of the human centered design: first international conference, HCD 2009. Springer, Berlin, Heidelberg, pp 94–103. https://doi.org/10.1007/978-3-642-02806-9_12
54. Li K, Pang K, Song YZ, Xiang T, Hospedales T, Zhang H (2019) Toward deep universal sketch perceptual grouper. Trans image processing
55. Li Y, Li W (2018) A survey of sketch-based image retrieval. Mach Vis Appl 29(7):1083–1100
56. Liu G, Reda FA, Shih KJ, Wang TC, Tao A, Catanzaro B (2018) Image inpainting for irregular holes using partial convolutions. In: Proceedings of the European conference on computer vision (ECCV), pp 85–100
57. Liwicki M, Bunke H (2005) Iam-ondb. an on-line English sentence database acquired from handwritten text on a whiteboard. In: In Proceedings of the 8th international conference on document analysis and recognition, pp 956–961
58. Liwicki M, Graves A, Bunke H, Schmidhuber J (2007) A novel approach to on-line handwriting recognition based on bidirectional long short-term memory networks. In: Proceedings of the 9th international conference on document analysis and recognition, ICDAR 2007
59. Locatello F, Bauer S, Lucic M, Rätsch G, Gelly S, Schölkopf B, Bachem O (2018) Challenging common assumptions in the unsupervised learning of disentangled representations
60. Lu J, Yu F, Finkelstein A, DiVerdi S (2012) Helpinghand: example-based stroke stylization. ACM Trans Graph 31(4):46:1–46:10. https://doi.org/10.1145/2185520.2185542
61. Maaten LVD, Hinton G (2008) Visualizing data using t-sne. JMLR 9(Nov):2579–2605
62. Marti UV, Bunke H (2002) The IAM-database: an English sentence database for offline handwriting recognition. IJDAR 5(1):39–46
63. Mueller PA, Oppenheimer DM (2014) The pen is mightier than the keyboard: Advantages of longhand over laptop note taking. Psychol Sci. https://doi.org/10.1177/0956797614524581, http://pss.sagepub.com/content/early/2014/04/22/0956797614524581.abstract
64. Mynatt ED, Igarashi T, Edwards WK, LaMarca A (1999) Flatland: new dimensions in office whiteboards. In: Proceedings of the SIGCHI conference on human factors in computing systems. ACM, New York, NY, USA, CHI '99, pp 346–353. https://doi.org/10.1145/302979.303108
65. MyScript (2016) MyScript: the power of handwriting. http://myscript.com/. Accessed 04 Oct 2016
66. Noordzij G (2005) The stroke: theory of writing. Hyphen, translated from the Dutch, London

67. Oord A, Dieleman S, Zen H, Simonyan K, Vinyals O, Graves A, Kalchbrenner N, Senior A, Kavukcuoglu K (2016) Wavenet: a generative model for raw audio. arXiv:160903499
68. Park T, Liu MY, Wang TC, Zhu JY (2019) Semantic image synthesis with spatially-adaptive normalization. In: Proceedings of the IEEE/CVF conference on computer vision and pattern recognition, pp 2337–2346
69. Perteneder F, Bresler M, Grossauer EM, Leong J, Haller M (2015) cluster: smart clustering of free-hand sketches on large interactive surfaces. In: Proceedings of the 28th annual ACM symposium on user interface software and technology. ACM, New York, NY, USA, UIST '15, pp 37–46. https://doi.org/10.1145/2807442.2807455
70. Pfeuffer K, Hinckley K, Pahud M, Buxton B (2017) Thumb + pen interaction on tablets. In: Proceedings of the 2017 CHI conference on human factors in computing systems. ACM, New York, NY, USA, CHI '17, pp 3254–3266. https://doi.org/10.1145/3025453.3025567
71. Plamondon R, Srihari SN (2000) On-line and off-line handwriting recognition: a comprehensive survey. IEEE Trans Pattern Anal Mach Intell 22(1):63–84. https://doi.org/10.1109/34.824821
72. Plamondon R, O'reilly C, Galbally J, Almaksour A, Anquetil É (2014) Recent developments in the study of rapid human movements with the kinematic theory: applications to handwriting and signature synthesis. Pattern Recogn Lett 35:225–235
73. Pulver MAE (1972) Symbolik der handschrift, new. Kindler, Munich
74. Qi CR, Su H, Mo K, Guibas LJ (2017) Pointnet: Deep learning on point sets for 3d classification and segmentation. In: CVPR, pp 652–660
75. Ribeiro L, Bui T, Collomosse J, Ponti M (2020) Sketchformer: transformer-based representation for sketched structure
76. Riche Y, Henry Riche N, Hinckley K, Panabaker S, Fuelling S, Williams S (2017) As we may ink?: Learning from everyday analog pen use to improve digital ink experiences. In: Proceedings of the 2017 CHI conference on human factors in computing systems. ACM, New York, NY, USA, CHI '17, pp 3241–3253. https://doi.org/10.1145/3025453.3025716
77. Robinson A (2007) The story of writing. Thames & Hudson, London, UK
78. Rousseeuw PJ (1987) Silhouettes: a graphical aid to the interpretation and validation of cluster analysis. J Comput Appl Math 20:53–65
79. Sellen AJ, Harper RH (2003) The myth of the paperless office. MIT Press, Cambridge, MA, USA
80. Shamir A, Rappoport A (1998) Feature-based design of fonts using constraints. In: International conference on raster imaging and digital typography. Springer, pp 93–108
81. Shi J, Malik J (2000) Normalized cuts and image segmentation. PAMI
82. Srihari S, Cha S, Arora H, Lee S (2002) Individuality of handwriting. J Forensic Sci 47(4):1–17. https://doi.org/10.1520/JFS15447J
83. Subramonyam H, Seifert C, Shah P, Adar E (2020) texsketch: active diagramming through pen-and-ink annotations. In: Proceedings of the 2020 CHI conference on human factors in computing systems, pp 1–13
84. Sutherland CJ, Luxton-Reilly A, Plimmer B (2016) Freeform digital ink annotations in electronic documents: a systematic mapping study. Comput Graph 55(C):1–20. https://doi.org/10.1016/j.cag.2015.10.014
85. Sutherland IE (1963) Sketchpad: A man-machine graphical communication system. In: Proceedings of the 21–23 May 1963, spring joint computer conference. ACM, New York, NY, USA, AFIPS '63 (Spring), pp 329–346. https://doi.org/10.1145/1461551.1461591
86. Sutskever I, Vinyals O, Le QV (2014) Sequence to sequence learning with neural networks. In: NeurIPS, pp 3104–3112
87. Ulyanov D, Vedaldi A, Lempitsky V (2018) Deep image prior. In: CVPR, pp 9446–9454
88. Vaswani A, Shazeer N, Parmar N, Uszkoreit J, Jones L, Gomez AN, Kaiser L, Polosukhin I (2017) Attention is all you need. In: NeurIPS
89. Wang J, Wu C, Xu YQ, Yeung Shum H, Ji L (2002) Learning-based cursive handwriting synthesis. In: Proceedings of the Eighth international workshop on frontiers of handwriting recognition, pp 157–162

90. Wang J, Wu C, Xu HY, Ying-Qing nd Shum, (2005) Combining shape and physical models for online cursive handwriting synthesis. Int J Doc Anal Recogn (IJDAR) 7(4):219–227. https://doi.org/10.1007/s10032-004-0131-6

91. Weibel N, Fouse A, Emmenegger C, Friedman W, Hutchins E, Hollan J (2012) Digital pen and paper practices in observational research. In: Proceedings of the SIGCHI conference on human factors in computing systems. ACM, New York, NY, USA, CHI '12, pp 1331–1340. https://doi.org/10.1145/2207676.2208590

92. Williams BH, Toussaint M, Storkey AJ (2007) Modelling motion primitives and their timing in biologically executed movements. In: Proceedings of the 20th international conference on neural information processing systems, Curran associates Inc, USA, NIPS'07, pp 1609–1616. http://dl.acm.org/citation.cfm?id=2981562.2981764

93. Williams F, Trager M, Panozzo D, Silva C, Zorin D, Bruna J (2019) Gradient dynamics of shallow univariate relu networks. In: NeurIPS, pp 8376–8385

94. Williams RJ, Zipser D (1989) A learning algorithm for continually running fully recurrent neural networks. Neural Comput

95. Wu X, Qi Y, Liu J, Yang J (2018) SketchSegNet: a RNN model for labeling sketch strokes. In: MLSP

96. Xia H, Hinckley K, Pahud M, Tu X, Buxton B (2017) Writlarge: Ink unleashed by unified scope, action, and zoom. In: Proceedings of the 2017 CHI conference on human factors in computing systems. ACM, New York, NY, USA, CHI '17, pp 3227–3240. https://doi.org/10.1145/3025453.3025664

97. Xu P, Hospedales TM, Yin Q, Song YZ, Xiang T, Wang L (2020) Deep learning for free-hand sketch: a survey.

98. Yang L, Zhuang J, Fu H, Zhou K, Zheng Y (2020) SketchGCN: semantic sketch segmentation with graph convolutional networks

99. Yoon D, Chen N, Guimbretière F (2013) Texttearing: opening white space for digital ink annotation. In: Proceedings of the 26th annual ACM symposium on user interface software and technology. ACM, New York, NY, USA, UIST '13, pp 107–112. https://doi.org/10.1145/2501988.2502036

100. Yoon D, Chen N, Guimbretière F, Sellen A (2014) Richreview: Blending ink, speech, and gesture to support collaborative document review. In: Proceedings of the 27th annual ACM symposium on user interface software and technology. ACM, New York, NY, USA, UIST '14, pp 481–490. https://doi.org/10.1145/2642918.2647390

101. Yun XL, Zhang YM, Ye JY, Liu CL (2019) Online handwritten diagram recognition with graph attention networks. In: ICIG

102. Zanibbi R, Novins K, Arvo J, Zanibbi K (2001) Aiding manipulation of handwritten mathematical expressions through style-preserving morphs. Graph Interf 2001:127–134

103. Zhang B, Srihari SN, Lee S (2003) Individuality of handwritten characters. In: Proceedings of the 7th international conference on document analysis and recognition, pp 1086–1090

104. Zitnick CL (2013) Handwriting beautification using token means. ACM Trans Graph 32(4):53:1–53:8. https://doi.org/10.1145/2461912.2461985

Bridging Natural Language and Graphical User Interfaces

Yang Li, Xin Zhou, and Gang Li

Abstract "Language as symbolic action" (https://en.wikipedia.org/wiki/Kenneth_ Burke) has a natural connection with direct-manipulation interaction (e.g., via GUI or physical appliances) that is common for modern computers such as smartphones. In this chapter, we present our efforts for bridging the gap between natural language and graphical user interfaces, which can potentially enable a broad category of interaction scenarios. Specifically, we develop datasets and deep learning models that can ground natural language instructions or command into executable actions on GUIs, and on the other hand generate natural language descriptions of user interfaces such that a user knows how to control them in language. These projects resemble research efforts intersecting Natural Language Processing (NLP) and HCI, and produce datasets and opensource code that lay a foundation for future research in the area.

1 Introduction

While natural language dominates how we human communicate with each other in everyday life, Graphical User Interfaces (GUI), with direct manipulation, is the commonplace for us to converse with a computer system. There are inherent connections between these two communication mediums. In natural language, the semantics is realized via a sequence of word tokens, and in GUIs, a task is accomplished by manipulating a set of graphical objects where each fulfills a building block action. The attempt of combining Natural Language Processing (NLP) and Human–Computer Interaction (HCI) research can be dated back to the early work on conversational agents, which was an excellent example showing the synergy between the HCI and

Y. Li (✉) · X. Zhou · G. Li
Google Research, Mountain View, CA, USA
e-mail: liyang@google.com

X. Zhou
e-mail: zhouxin@google.com

G. Li
e-mail: leebird@google.com

AI fields. With the advance in modern AI methods, such a vision becomes more obtainable than ever.

In this chapter, we particularly focus on two directions of work, which have been pursued in our research group, for bridging the gap between natural language and graphical user interfaces—we will review two recent papers on natural language grounding [13] and generation [15] in the context of mobile user interfaces. There are a rich collection of interaction scenarios where mobile interaction can benefit from natural language grounding techniques. For example, mobile devices offer a myriad of functionalities that can assist in our everyday activities. However, many of these functionalities are not easily discoverable or accessible to users, forcing users to look up how to perform a specific task, e.g., how to turn on the traffic mode in maps or change notification settings in YouTube. While searching the web for detailed instructions for these questions is an option, it is still up to the user to follow these instructions step by step and navigate UI details through a small touchscreen, which can be tedious and time-consuming, and results in reduced accessibility. As such, it is important to develop a computational agent to turn these language instructions into actions and automatically execute them on the user's behalf.

On the other hand, we want to equip mobile interfaces, which are highly graphical and unconventional compared to traditional desktop applications, with language descriptions so that they can be communicated with users verbally. We refer to the language description of a UI element as a *widget caption*. For example, accessibility services such as screen readers rely on widget captions to make UI elements accessible to visually impaired users via text-to-speech technologies. In general, widget captions are a foundation for conversational agents on GUIs where UI elements are building blocks. The lack of widget captions has stood out as a primary issue for mobile accessibility [25, 26]. More than half of image-based elements have missing captions [26]. Beyond image-based ones, our analysis of a UI corpus here showed that a wide range of elements have missing captions.

For the rest of the chapter, we will dive into two projects, one for each of these research directions. For each project, we start with problem formulation and dataset creation. We then detail on the design and training of deep models, and lastly report and discuss our findings from experiments.

2   Natural Language Grounding in User Interfaces

An important area of language grounding involves tasks like completion of multi-step actions in a graphical user interface conditioned on language instructions [3, 4, 8, 18]. These domains matter for accessibility, where language interfaces could help visually impaired individuals perform tasks with interfaces that are predicated on sight. This also matters for *situational impairment* [27] when one cannot access a device easily while encumbered by other factors, such as cooking.

We focus on a domain of task automation in which natural language instructions must be interpreted as a sequence of actions on a mobile touchscreen UI. Existing web search is quite capable of retrieving multi-step natural language instructions for user queries, such as "How to turn on flight mode on Android." Crucially, the missing piece for fulfilling the task automatically is to map the returned instruction to a sequence of actions that can be automatically executed on the device with little user intervention. This task automation scenario does not require a user to maneuver through UI details, which is useful for average users and is especially valuable for visually or situationally impaired users. The ability to execute an instruction can also be useful for other scenarios such as automatically examining the quality of an instruction.

Our approach (Fig. 1) decomposes the problem into an *action phrase extraction* step and a *grounding* step. The former extracts operation, object, and argument descriptions from multi-step instructions; for this, we use Transformers [28] and test three span representations. The latter matches extracted operation and object descriptions with a UI object on a screen; for this, we use a Transformer that contextually represents UI objects and grounds object descriptions to them.

We construct three new datasets.[1] To assess full task performance on *naturally occurring* instructions, we create a dataset of 187 multi-step English instructions for operating Pixel Phones and produce their corresponding action-screen sequences using annotators. For action phrase extraction training and evaluation, we obtain English How-To instructions from the web and annotate action description spans. A Transformer with spans represented by sum pooling [14] obtains 85.56% accuracy for predicting span sequences that completely match the ground truth. To train the grounding model, we synthetically generate 295k single-step commands to UI actions, covering 178K different UI objects across 25K mobile UI screens.

Our phrase extractor and grounding model together obtain 89.21% partial and 70.59% complete accuracy for matching ground-truth action sequences on this challenging task. We also evaluate alternative methods and representations of objects and spans and present qualitative analyses to provide insights into the problem and models.

2.1 Problem Formulation

Given an instruction of a multi-step task, $I = t_{1:n} = (t_1, t_2, ..., t_n)$, where t_i is the ith token in instruction I, we want to generate a sequence of automatically executable actions, $a_{1:m}$, over a sequence of user interface screens S, with initial screen s_1 and screen transition function $s_j = \tau(a_{j-1}, s_{j-1})$:

$$p(a_{1:m}|s_1, \tau, t_{1:n}) = \prod_{j=1}^{m} p(a_j|a_{<j}, s_1, \tau, t_{1:n})$$ (1)

---

[1] Our data pipeline is available at https://github.com/google-research/google-research/tree/master/seq2act.

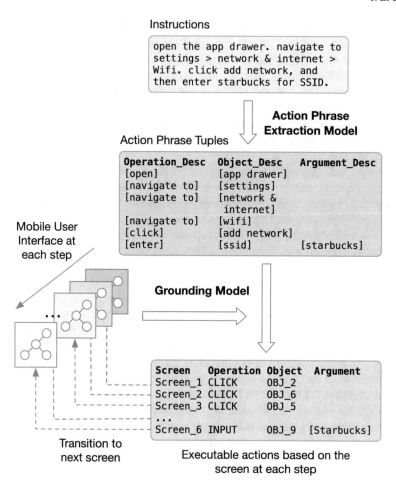

Fig. 1 Our model extracts the phrase tuple that describe each action, including its operation, object and additional arguments, and grounds these tuples as executable action sequences in the UI

An action $a_j = [r_j, o_j, u_j]$ consists of an operation r_j (e.g., Tap or Text), the UI object o_j that r_j is performed on (e.g., a button or an icon), and an additional argument u_j needed for o_j (e.g., the message entered in the chat box for Text or null for operations such as Tap). Starting from s_1, executing a sequence of actions $a_{<j}$ arrives at screen s_j that represents the screen at the jth step: $s_j = \tau(a_{j-1}, \tau(...\tau(a_1, s_1)))$:

$$p(a_{1:m}|s_1, \tau, t_{1:n}) = \prod_{j=1}^{m} p(a_j|s_j, t_{1:n}) \tag{2}$$

Each screen $s_j = [c_{j,1:|s_j|}, \lambda_j]$ contains a set of UI objects and their structural relationships. $c_{j,1:|s_j|} = \{c_{j,k} \mid 1 \leq k \leq |s_j|\}$, where $|s_j|$ is the number of objects in

s_j, from which o_j is chosen. λ_j defines the structural relationship between the objects. This is often a tree structure such as the *View* hierarchy for an Android interface[2] (similar to a DOM tree for web pages).

An instruction I describes (possibly multiple) actions. Let $\bar{a}_j$ denote the phrases in I that describes action a_j. $\bar{a}_j = [\bar{r}_j, \bar{o}_j, \bar{u}_j]$ represents a tuple of descriptions with each corresponding to a span—a subsequence of tokens—in I. Accordingly, $\bar{a}_{1:m}$ represents the description tuple sequence that we refer to as $\bar{a}$ for brevity. We also define $\bar{A}$ as all possible description tuple sequences of I, thus $\bar{a} \in \bar{A}$.

$$p(a_j|s_j, t_{1:n}) = \sum_{\bar{A}} p(a_j|\bar{a}, s_j, t_{1:n}) p(\bar{a}|s_j, t_{1:n}) \tag{3}$$

Because a_j is independent on the rest of the instruction given its current screen s_j and description $\bar{a}_j$, and $\bar{a}$ is only related to the instruction $t_{1:n}$, we can simplify (3) as (4).

$$p(a_j|s_j, t_{1:n}) = \sum_{\bar{A}} p(a_j|\bar{a}_j, s_j) p(\bar{a}|t_{1:n}) \tag{4}$$

We define $\hat{a}$ as the most likely description of actions for $t_{1:n}$.

$$\hat{a} = \arg\max_{\bar{a}} p(\bar{a}|t_{1:n})$$
$$= \arg\max_{\bar{a}_{1:m}} \prod_{j=1}^{m} p(\bar{a}_j|\bar{a}_{<j}, t_{1:n}) \tag{5}$$

This defines the action phrase extraction model, which is then used by the grounding model:

$$p(a_j|s_j, t_{1:n}) \approx p(a_j|\hat{a}_j, s_j) p(\hat{a}_j|\hat{a}_{<j}, t_{1:n}) \tag{6}$$

$$p(a_{1:m}|t_{1:n}, S) \approx \prod_{j=1}^{m} p(a_j|\hat{a}_j, s_j) p(\hat{a}_j|\hat{a}_{<j}, t_{1:n}) \tag{7}$$

$p(\hat{a}_j|\hat{a}_{<j}, t_{1:n})$ identifies the description tuples for each action. $p(a_j|\hat{a}_j, s_j)$ grounds each description to an executable action given in the screen.

---

[2] https://developer.android.com/reference/android/view/View.html.

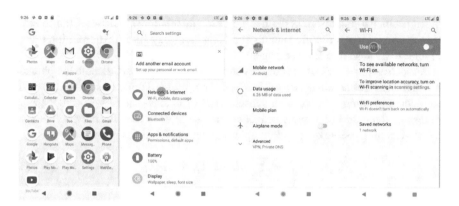

Fig. 2 PIXELHELP example: *Open your device's Settings app. Tap Network and Internet. Click Wi-Fi. Turn on Wi-Fi.* The example uses the App Drawer and Settings on the Google Pixel phone. The instruction is paired with actions, each of which is shown as a red dot on a specific screen

2.2 Data

The ideal dataset would have natural instructions that have been executed by people using the UI. Such data can be collected by having annotators perform tasks according to instructions on a mobile platform, but this is difficult to scale. It requires significant investment to instrument: different versions of apps have different presentation and behaviors, and apps must be installed and configured for each task. Due to this, we create a small dataset of this form, PIXELHELP, for full task evaluation. For model training at scale, we create two other datasets: ANDROIDHOWTO for action phrase extraction and RICOSCA for grounding. Our datasets are targeted for English. We hope that starting with a high-resource language will pave the way to creating similar capabilities for other languages.

2.2.1 PIXELHELP Dataset

Pixel Phone Help pages[3] provide instructions for performing common tasks on Google Pixel phones such as *switch Wi-Fi settings* (Fig. 2) or *check emails*. Help pages can contain multiple tasks, with each task consisting of a sequence of steps. We pulled instructions from the help pages and kept ones that can be automatically executed. Instructions that requires additional user input such as *Tap the app you want to uninstall* are discarded. Also, instructions that involve actions on a physical button such as *Press the Power button for a few seconds* are excluded because these events cannot be executed on mobile platform emulators.

---

[3] https://support.google.com/pixelphone.

We instrumented a logging mechanism on a Pixel Phone emulator and had human annotators perform each task on the emulator by following the full instruction. The logger records every user action, including the type of touch events that are triggered, each object being manipulated, and screen information such as view hierarchies. Each item thus includes the instruction input, $t_{1:n}$; the screen for each step of task, $s_{1:m}$; and the target action performed on each screen, $a_{1:m}$.

In total, PIXELHELP includes 187 multi-step instructions of 4 task categories: 88 general tasks, such as configuring accounts, 38 Gmail tasks, 31 Chrome tasks, and 30 Photos-related tasks. The number of steps ranges from two to eight, with a median of four. Because it has both natural instructions and grounded actions, we reserve PIXELHELP for evaluating full task performance.

2.2.2 ANDROIDHOWTO Dataset

No datasets exist that support learning the action phrase extraction model, $p(\hat{a}_j | \hat{a}_{<j}, t_{1:n})$, for mobile UIs. To address this, we extracted English instructions for operating Android devices by processing web pages to identify candidate instructions for how-to questions such as *how to change the input method for Android*. A web crawling service scrapes instruction-like content from various websites. We then filter the web contents using both heuristics and manual screening by annotators.

Annotators identified phrases in each instruction that describe executable actions. They were given a tutorial on the task and were instructed to skip instructions that are difficult to understand or label. For each component in an action description, they select the span of words that describes the component using a web annotation interface. The interface records the start and end positions of each marked span. Each instruction was labeled by three annotators: three annotators agreed on 31% of full instructions and at least two agreed on 84%. For the consistency at the tuple level, the agreement across all the annotators is 83.6% for operation phrases, 72.07% for object phrases, and 83.43% for input phrases. The discrepancies are usually small, e.g., a description marked as *your Gmail address* or *Gmail address*.

The final dataset includes 32,436 data points from 9,893 unique How-To instructions and split into training (8K), validation (1K), and test (900). All test examples have perfect agreement across all three annotators for the *entire* sequence. In total, there are 190K operation spans, 172K object spans, and 321 input spans labeled. The lengths of the instructions range from 19 to 85 tokens, with median of 59. They describe a sequence of actions from one to 19 steps, with a median of 5.

2.2.3 RICOSCA Dataset

Training the grounding model, $p(a_j | \hat{a}_j, s_j)$ involves pairing action tuples a_j along screens s_j with action description $\hat{a}_j$. It is very difficult to collect such data at scale. To get past the bottleneck, we exploit two properties of the task to generate a *synthetic* command-action dataset, RICOSCA. First, we have precise structured and visual knowledge of the UI layout, so we can spatially relate UI elements to each other and the overall screen. Second, a grammar grounded in the UI can cover many of the commands and kinds of reference needed for the problem. This does not capture all manners of interacting conversationally with a UI, but it proves effective for training the grounding model.

Rico is a public UI corpus with 72K Android UI screens mined from 9.7K Android apps [6]. Each screen in Rico comes with a screenshot image and a view hierarchy of a collection of UI objects. Each individual object, $c_{j,k}$, has a set of properties, including its name (often an English phrase such as *Send*), type (e.g., Button, Image, or Checkbox), and bounding box position on the screen. We manually removed screens whose view hierarchies do not match their screenshots by asking annotators to visually verify whether the bounding boxes of view hierarchy leaves match each UI object on the corresponding screenshot image. This filtering results in 25K unique screens.

For each screen, we randomly select UI elements as target objects and synthesize commands for operating them. We generate multiple commands to capture different expressions describing the operation $\hat{r}_j$ and the target object $\hat{o}_j$. For example, the Tap operation can be referred to as *tap*, *click*, or *press*. The template for referring to a target object has slots Name, Type, and Location, which are instantiated using the following strategies:

- *Name-Type*: the target's name and/or type (*the OK button* or *OK*).
- *Absolute-Location*: the target's screen location (*the menu at the top right corner*).
- *Relative-Location*: the target's relative location to other objects (*the icon to the right of Send*).

Because all commands are synthesized, the span that describes each part of an action, $\hat{a}_j$ with respect to $t_{1:n}$, is known. Meanwhile, a_j and s_j, the actual action and the associated screen, are present because the constituents of the action are synthesized. In total, RICOSCA contains 295,476 single-step synthetic commands for operating 177,962 different target objects across 25,677 Android screens.

2.3   Model Architectures

Equation 7 has two parts. $p(\hat{a}_j | \hat{a}_{<j}, t_{1:n})$ finds the best phrase tuple that describes the action at the jth step given the instruction token sequence. $p(a_j | \hat{a}_j, s_j)$ computes the probability of an executable action a_j given the best description of the action, $\hat{a}_j$, and the screen s_j for the jth step.

2.3.1   Phrase Tuple Extraction Model

A common choice for modeling the conditional probability $p(\bar{a}_j | \bar{a}_{<j}, t_{1:n})$ (see Eq. 5) is encoder–decoders such as LSTMs [10] and Transformers [28]. The output of our

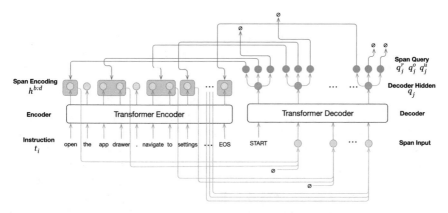

Fig. 3 The Phrase Tuple Extraction model encodes the instruction's token sequence and then outputs a tuple sequence by querying into all possible spans of the encoded sequence. Each tuple contains the span positions of three phrases in the instruction that describe the action's operation, object, and optional arguments, respectively, at each step. $\varnothing$ indicates the phrase is missing in the instruction and is represented by a special span encoding

model corresponds to positions in the input sequence, so our architecture is closely related to Pointer Networks [30].

Figure 3 depicts our model. An encoder g computes a latent representation $h_{1:n} \in R^{n \times |h|}$ of the tokens from their embeddings: $h_{1:n} = g(e(t_{1:n}))$. A decoder f then generates the hidden state $q_j = f(q_{<j}, \bar{a}_{<j}, h_{1:n})$ which is used to compute a query vector that locates each phrase of a tuple $(\bar{r}_j, \bar{o}_j, \bar{u}_j)$ at each step. $\bar{a}_j = [\bar{r}_j, \bar{o}_j, \bar{u}_j]$ and they are assumed conditionally independent given previously extracted phrase tuples and the instruction, so $p(\bar{a}_j | \bar{a}_{<j}, t_{1:n}) = \prod_{\bar{y} \in \{\bar{r}, \bar{o}, \bar{u}\}} p(\bar{y}_j | \bar{a}_{<j}, t_{1:n})$.

Note that $\bar{y}_j \in \{\bar{r}_j, \bar{o}_j, \bar{u}_j\}$ denotes a specific span for $y \in \{r, o, u\}$ in the action tuple at step j. We therefore rewrite $\bar{y}_j$ as $y_j^{b:d}$ to explicitly indicate that it corresponds to the span for r, o, or u, starting at the bth position and ending at the dth position in the instruction, $1 \leq b < d \leq n$. We now parameterize the conditional probability as

$$p(y_j^{b:d} | \bar{a}_{<j}, t_{1:n}) = \text{softmax}(\alpha(q_j^y, h^{b:d}))$$
$$y \in \{r, o, u\} \tag{8}$$

As shown in Fig. 3, q_j^y indicates task-specific query vectors for $y \in \{r, o, u\}$. They are computed as $q_j^y = \phi(q_j, \theta_y)W_y$, a multi-layer perceptron followed by a linear transformation. θ_y and W_y are trainable parameters. We use separate parameters for each of r, o, and u. $W_y \in R^{|\phi_y| \times |h|}$ where $|\phi_y|$ is the output dimension of the multi-layer perceptron. The alignment function $\alpha(\cdot)$ scores how a query vector q_j^y matches a span whose vector representation $h^{b:d}$ is computed from encodings $h_{b:d}$.

Span Representation. There are a quadratic number of possible spans given a token sequence [11], so it is important to design a fixed-length representation $h^{b:d}$ of a variable-length token span that can be *quickly* computed. Beginning–Inside–

Outside (BIO) [24]—commonly used to indicate spans in tasks such as named entity recognition—marks whether each token is beginning, inside, or outside a span. However, BIO is not ideal for our task because subsequences for describing different actions can overlap, e.g., in *click X and Y*, *click* participates in both actions *click X* and *click Y*. In our experiments, we consider several recent, more flexible span representations [11, 12, 14] and show their impact in Sect. 2.4.2.

With fixed-length span representations, we can use common alignment techniques in neural networks [2, 19]. We use the dot product between the query vector and the span representation: $\alpha(q_j^y, h^{b:d}) = q_j^y \cdot h^{b:d}$. At each step of decoding, we feed the previously decoded phrase tuples, $\bar{a}_{<j}$ into the decoder. We can use the concatenation of the vector representations of the three elements in a phrase tuple or sum their vector representations as the input for each decoding step. The entire phrase tuple extraction model is trained by minimizing the softmax cross-entropy loss between the predicted and ground-truth spans of a sequence of phrase tuples.

2.3.2 Grounding Model

Having computed the sequence of tuples that best describe each action, we connect them to executable actions based on the screen at each step with our grounding model (Fig. 4). In step-by-step instructions, each part of an action is often clearly stated. Thus, we assume the probabilities of the operation r_j, object o_j, and argument u_j are independent given their description and the screen.

$$
\begin{aligned}
p(a_j|\hat{a}_j, s_j) &= p([r_j, o_j, u_j]|[\hat{r}_j, \hat{o}_j, \hat{u}_j], s_j) \\
&= p(r_j|\hat{r}_j, s_j)p(o_j|\hat{o}_j, s_j)p(u_j|\hat{u}_j, s_j) \\
&= p(r_j|\hat{r}_j)p(o_j|\hat{o}_j, s_j)
\end{aligned}
\tag{9}
$$

We simplify with two assumptions: (1) an operation is often fully described by its instruction without relying on the screen information and (2) in mobile interaction

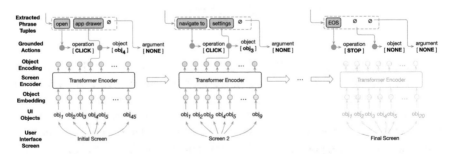

Fig. 4 The grounding model grounds each phrase tuple extracted by the phrase extraction model as an operation type, a screen-specific object ID, and an argument if present, based on a contextual representation of UI objects for the given screen. A grounded action tuple can be automatically executed

tasks, an argument is only present for the Text operation, so $u_j = \hat{u}_j$. We parameterize $p(r_j|\hat{r}_j)$ as a feedforward neural network:

$$p(r_j|\hat{r}_j) = \text{softmax}(\phi(\hat{r}'_j, \theta_r)W_r) \tag{10}$$

$\phi(\cdot)$ is a multi-layer perceptron with trainable parameters θ_r. $W^r \in R^{|\phi_r| \times |r|}$ is also trainable, where $|\phi_r|$ is the output dimension of the $\phi(\cdot, \theta_r)$ and $|r|$ is the vocabulary size of the operations. $\phi(\cdot)$ takes the sum of the embedding vectors of each token in the operation description $\hat{r}_j$ as the input: $\hat{r}'_j = \sum_{k=b}^{d} e(t_k)$ where b and d are the start and end positions of $\hat{r}_j$ in the instruction.

Determining o_j is to select a UI object from a variable-number of objects on the screen, $c_{j,k} \in s_j$ where $1 \leq k \leq |s_j|$, based on the given object description, $\hat{o}_j$. We parameterize the conditional probability as a deep neural network with a softmax output layer taking logits from an alignment function:

$$\begin{aligned}
p(o_j|\hat{o}_j, s_j) &= p(o_j = c_{j,k}|\hat{o}_j, c_{j,1:|s_j|}, \lambda_j) \\
&= \text{softmax}(\alpha(\hat{o}'_j, c'_{j,k}))
\end{aligned} \tag{11}$$

The alignment function $\alpha(\cdot)$ scores how the object description vector $\hat{o}'_j$ matches the latent representation of each UI object, $c'_{j,k}$. This can be as simple as the dot product of the two vectors. The latent representation $\hat{o}'_j$ is acquired with a multi-layer perceptron followed by a linear projection:

$$\hat{o}'_j = \phi(\sum_{k=b}^{d} e(t_k), \theta_o)W_o \tag{12}$$

where b and d are the start and end index of the object description $\hat{o}_j$. θ_o and W_o are trainable parameters with $W_o \in R^{|\phi_o| \times |o|}$, where $|\phi_o|$ is the output dimension of $\phi(\cdot, \theta_o)$ and $|o|$ is the dimension of the latent representation of the object description.

Contextual Representation of UI Objects. To compute latent representations of each candidate object, $c'_{j,k}$, we use both the object's properties and its context, i.e., the structural relationship with other objects on the screen. There are different ways for encoding a variable-sized collection of items that are structurally related to each other, including Graph Convolutional Networks (GCN) [20] and Transformers [28]. GCNs use an adjacency matrix predetermined by the UI structure to regulate how the latent representation of an object should be affected by its neighbors. Transformers allow each object to carry its own positional encoding, and the relationship between objects can be learned instead.

The input to the Transformer encoder is a combination of the *content embedding* and the *positional encoding* of each object. The content properties of an object include its name and type. We compute the content embedding by concatenating the name embedding, which is the average embedding of the bag of tokens in the object name, and the type embedding. The positional properties of an object include both its spatial position and structural position. The spatial positions include the top, left, right, and bottom screen coordinates of the object. We treat each of these coordinates as a discrete value and represent it via an embedding. Such a feature representation for coordinates was used in ImageTransformer to represent pixel positions in an image [22]. The spatial embedding of the object is the sum of these four coordinate embeddings. To encode structural information, we use the index positions of the object in the preorder and the postorder traversal of the view hierarchy tree, and represent these index positions as embeddings in a similar way as representing coordinates. The content embedding is then summed with positional encodings to form the embedding of each object. We then feed these object embeddings into a Transformer encoder model to compute the latent representation of each object, $c'_{j,k}$.

The grounding model is trained by minimizing the cross-entropy loss between the predicted and ground-truth object and the loss between the predicted and ground-truth operation.

2.4 Experiments

Our goal is to develop models and datasets to map multi-step instructions into automatically executable actions given the screen information. As such, we use PIXEL-HELP's paired natural instructions and action-screen sequences solely for testing. In addition, we investigate the model quality on phrase tuple extraction tasks, which is a crucial building block for the overall grounding quality.[4]

2.4.1 Datasets and Metrics

We use two metrics that measure how a predicted tuple sequence matches the ground-truth sequence.

- *Complete Match*: The score is 1 if two sequences have the same length and have the identical tuple $[\hat{r}_j, \hat{o}_j, \hat{u}_j]$ at each step, otherwise 0.
- *Partial Match*: The number of steps of the predicted sequence that match the ground-truth sequence divided by the length of the ground-truth sequence (ranging between 0 and 1).

We train and validate using ANDROIDHOWTO and RICOSCA, and evaluate on PIXELHELP. During training, single-step synthetic command-action examples are dynamically stitched to form sequence examples with a certain length distribution. To evaluate the full task, we use Complete and Partial Match on grounded action sequences $a_{1:m}$ where $a_j=[r_j, o_j, u_j]$.

---

[4] Our model code is released at https://github.com/google-research/google-research/tree/master/seq2act.

The token vocabulary size is 59K, which is compiled from both the instruction corpus and the UI name corpus. There are 15 UI types, including 14 common UI object types, and a type to catch all less common ones. The output vocabulary for operations includes CLICK, TEXT, SWIPE, and EOS.

2.4.2 Model Configurations and Results

Tuple Extraction. For the action-tuple extraction task, we use a six-layer Transformer for both the encoder and the decoder. We evaluate three different span representations. Area Attention [14] provides a parameter-free representation of each possible span (one-dimensional area), by summing up the encoding of each token in the subsequence: $h^{b:d} = \sum_{k=b}^{d} h_k$. The representation of each span can be computed in constant time invariant to the length of the span, using a summed area table. Previous work concatenated the encoding of the start and end tokens as the span representation, $h^{b:d} = [h_b; h_d]$ [12] and a generalized version of it [11]. We evaluated these three options and implemented the representation in [11] using a summed area table similar to the approach in area attention for fast computation. For hyperparameter tuning and training details, refer to the appendix.

Table 1 gives results on ANDROIDHOWTO's test set. All the span representations perform well. Encodings of each token from a Transformer already capture sufficient information about the entire sequence, so even only using the start and end encodings yields strong results. Nonetheless, area attention provides a small boost over the others. As a new dataset, there is also considerable headroom remaining, particularly for complete match.

Grounding. For the grounding task, we compare Transformer-based screen encoder for generating object representations $h^{b:d}$ with two baseline methods based on graph convolutional networks. The *Heuristic* baseline matches extracted phrases against object names directly using BLEU scores. *Filter-1 GCN* performs graph convolution without using adjacent nodes (objects), so the representation of each object is computed only based on its own properties. *Distance GCN* uses the distance between objects in the view hierarchy, i.e., the number of edges to traverse from one object to another following the tree structure. This contrasts with the traditional GCN definition based on adjacency, but is needed because UI objects are often leaves

Table 1 ANDROIDHOWTO phrase tuple extraction test results using different span representations $h^{b:d}$ in (8). $\hat{e}^{b:d} = \sum_{k=b}^{d} w(h_k)e(t_k)$, where $w(\cdot)$ is a learned weight function for each token embedding [11]. See the pseudocode for fast computation of these in Appendix

Span Rep. $h^{b:d}$	Partial	Complete
SumPooling $\sum_{k=b}^{d} h_k$	92.80	85.56
StartEnd $[h_b; h_d]$	91.94	84.56
$[h_b; h_d, \hat{e}^{b:d}, \phi(d-b)]$	91.11	84.33

Table 2 PIXELHELP grounding accuracy. The differences are statistically significant based on t-test over 5 runs ($p < 0.05$)

Screen encoder	Partial	Complete
Heuristic	62.44	42.25
Filter-1 GCN	76.44	52.41
Distance GCN	82.50	59.36
Transformer	89.21	70.59

in the tree, as such they are not adjacent to each other structurally but instead are connected through non-terminal (container) nodes. Both Filter-1 GCN and Distance GCN use the same number of parameters (see the appendix for details).

To train the grounding model, we first train the Tuple Extraction sub-model on ANDROIDHOWTO and RICOSCA. For the latter, only language-related features (commands and tuple positions in the command) are used in this stage, so screen and action features are not involved. We then freeze the Tuple Extraction sub-model and train the grounding sub-model on RICOSCA using both the command- and screen-action-related features. The screen token embeddings of the grounding sub-model share weights with the Tuple Extraction sub-model.

Table 2 gives full task performance on PIXELHELP. The Transformer screen encoder achieves the best result with 70.59% accuracy on Complete Match and 89.21% on Partial Match, which sets a strong baseline result for this new dataset while leaving considerable headroom. The GCN-based methods perform poorly, which shows the importance of contextual encodings of the information from other UI objects on the screen. Distance GCN does attempt to capture context for UI objects that are structurally close; however, we suspect that the distance information that is derived from the view hierarchy tree is noisy because UI developers can construct the structure differently for the same UI.[5] As a result, the strong bias introduced by the structure distance does not always help. Nevertheless, these models still outperformed the heuristic baseline that achieved 62.44% for partial match and 42.25% for complete match.

2.5 Analysis

To explore how the model grounds an instruction on a screen, we analyze the relationship between words in the instruction language that refer to specific locations on the screen, and actual positions on the UI screen. We first extract the embedding weights from the trained phrase extraction model for words such as *top*, *bottom*, *left*, and *right*. These words occur in object descriptions such as *the check box at the top of the*

---

[5] While it is possible to directly use screen visual data for grounding, detecting UI objects from raw pixels is nontrivial. It would be ideal to use both structural and visual data.

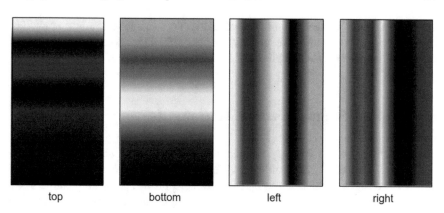

top   bottom   left   right

Fig. 5 Correlation between location-related words in instructions and object screen position embedding

screen. We also extract the embedding weights of object screen positions, which are used to create object positional encoding. We then calculate the correlation between word embedding and screen position embedding using cosine similarity. Figure 5 visualizes the correlation as a heatmap, where brighter colors indicate higher correlation. The word *top* is strongly correlated with the top of the screen, but the trend for other location words is less clear. While *left* is strongly correlated with the left side of the screen, other regions on the screen also show high correlation. This is likely because *left* and *right* are not only used for referring to absolute locations on the screen, but also for relative spatial relationships, such as *the icon to the left of the button.* For *bottom*, the strongest correlation does not occur at the very bottom of the screen because many UI objects in our dataset do not fall in that region. The region is often reserved for system actions and the on-screen keyboard, which are not covered in our dataset.

The phrase extraction model passes phrase tuples to the grounding model. When phrase extraction is incorrect, it can be difficult for the grounding model to predict a correct action. One way to mitigate such cascading errors is using the hidden state of the phrase decoding model at each step, q_j. Intuitively, q_j is computed with the access to the encoding of each token in the instruction via the Transformer encoder–decoder attention, which can potentially be a more robust span representation. However, in our early exploration, we found that grounding with q_j performs stunningly well for grounding RICOSCA validation examples, but performs poorly on PIXELHELP. The learned hidden state likely captures characteristics in the synthetic instructions and action sequences that do not manifest in PIXELHELP. As such, using the hidden state to ground remains a challenge when learning from unpaired instruction-action data.

The phrase model failed to extract correct steps for 14 tasks in PIXELHELP. In particular, it resulted in extra steps for 11 tasks and extracted incorrect steps for 3 tasks, but did not skip steps for any tasks. These errors could be caused by different language styles manifested by the three datasets. Synthesized commands in RICOSCA tend to be brief. Instructions in ANDROIDHOWTO seem to give more contextual description and involve diverse language styles, while PIXELHELP often has a more consistent language style and gives concise description for each step.

3 Natural Language Generation from UIs

In this section, we discuss *widget captioning*, a task to automatically generate captions for UI elements[6] based on their visual appearance, structural properties, and context (see Fig. 6), which can be considered the opposite task of language grounding in the previous section. This task is analogous to image captioning that generates language descriptions for images, e.g., [17, 31]. However, widget captioning raises several unique challenges. User interfaces are highly structural while traditional image captioning mostly focus on raw image pixels. Widget captioning is concerned with describing individual elements in the UI rather than the entire UI screen, while the entire screen provides useful contextual information for widget captioning. We target language generation for a broad set of UI elements, rather than only image-based ones. As we will show in our data analysis, many non-image elements also suffer the lack of captions. These challenges give rise to several interesting modeling questions such as how to combine both structural and image input and how to effectively represent each modality.

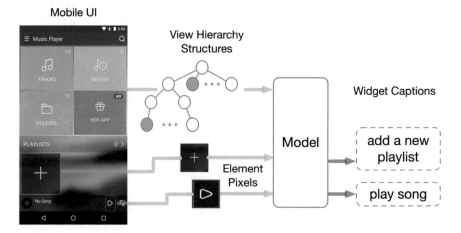

Fig. 6 Widget captioning is a task to generate language descriptions for UI elements that have missing captions, given multimodal input of UI structures and screenshot images. These captions are crucial for accessibility and language-based interaction in general. The illustration uses a screen from a Music Player app

---

[6] We use widgets and elements interchangeably.

Similar to the language grounding work, we start our investigation of widget captioning by creating the dataset. We process and analyze an existing mobile UI corpus, and then create a large dataset for widget captioning by asking crowd workers to annotate a collection of UI elements in the corpus. Based on this dataset, we train and evaluate a set of model configurations to investigate how each feature modality and the choice of learning strategies would impact caption generation quality. Our champion model that is based on a Transformer [28] to encode structural information and a ResNet [9] for image input is able to produce accurate captions for UI elements based on both automatic and human evaluation. In summary, the work makes the following contributions:

- We propose widget captioning as a task for automatically generating language descriptions for UI elements in mobile user interfaces; the task raises unique challenges for modeling and extends the popular image captioning task to the user interface domain.
- We create a dataset for widget captioning via crowdsourcing.[7] It contains 162,859 captions created by human workers for 61,285 UI elements across 21,750 unique screens from 6,470 mobile apps. Our analysis on the missing captions and the linguistic attributes of collected captions contribute new knowledge for understanding the problem.
- We investigate a set of model configurations and learning strategies for widget captioning; our benchmark models leverage multimodal input including both structural information and images of user interfaces.[8] They are able to generate accurate captions for UI elements, and yet leave enough room for improvement for future research.

3.1 Data

We first create a mobile UI corpus, and then ask crowd workers to create captions for UI elements that have missing captions, which is followed by a thorough analysis of the dataset.

3.1.1 Creating a Mobile UI Corpus

We create a mobile UI corpus based on RICO [6]. We expanded the dataset using a crawling robot to perform random clicks on mobile interfaces, which added 12K novel screens to our corpus. Each screen comes with both a screenshot JPG/PNG image and a view hierarchy[9] in JSON. The view hierarchy is a structural tree repre-

---

[7] Our dataset is released at https://github.com/google-research-datasets/widget-caption.

[8] Our model code is released at https://github.com/google-research/google-research/tree/master/widget-caption.

[9] https://developer.android.com/reference/android/view/View.

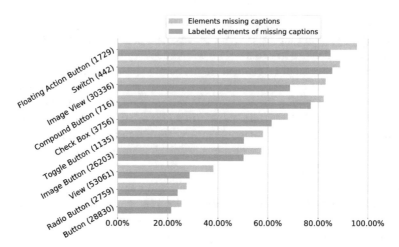

Fig. 7 The percentage of elements that have missing captions (red) for each category and elements labeled by crowd workers (green). The numbers in parentheses are total counts of the elements

sentation of the UI where each node has a set of properties such as content description, Android class information, visibility, and bounding box.

Preprocessing the UI Corpus. We first exclude UI screens with missing or inaccurate view hierarchies, which could occur when Android logging is out of sync. This filtering step was conducted by asking crowd workers to visually examine each UI and confirm that the bounding boxes of all the leaf nodes in the hierarchy match the UI elements shown on the screenshot image. We focus on leaf nodes because most interactive elements are leaf nodes. The filtering process resulted in 24,571 unique screens from 6,853 mobile apps.

We then select UI elements that are visible and clickable because they are responsible for many of the interaction tasks. Similar to previous work, we consider an element missing captions when both its contentDescription and text properties in the view hierarchy are missing, according to the Android accessibility guideline.[10] Screen readers such as the TalkBack service[1] rely on these fields to announce the widget. Overall, in our dataset, there are 74,379 UI elements with missing captions, across 10 categories of UI elements (see Fig. 7).

Understanding Missing Captions. Previous work analyzed missing captions for image-based elements [26]. We include all types of elements in our dataset and analysis. The results from analyzing image-based elements in our corpus are comparable to previous analysis, i.e., 95% of Floating Action Buttons, 83% of Image Views, and 57% of Image Buttons have missing captions. Beyond these image-based elements, we found that missing captions is a serious issue for other types of elements as well (see Fig. 7). More than 50% of the Switch, Compound Button, Check

---

[10] https://developer.android.com/guide/topics/ui/accessibility/apps.

Box, and `Toggle Button` have missing captions. 24.3% of the screens have none pre-existing captions.

Crowdsourcing Widget Captions. To best match the target scenario of predicting for elements with missing captions, we asked crowd workers to create captions for these elements, which are used as labels for training and testing. Because pre-existing captions in the corpus are not always correct, they are used as model input, to provide the context, but not as output.

We developed a web interface for crowd workers to create language descriptions for UI elements that have missing captions. The interface shows a screenshot of the mobile interface, with the UI element that needs to be captioned highlighted. Workers can input the caption using a text field, or indicate that they cannot describe the element. In the annotation guidelines, we asked the workers to caption the element for vision-impaired users to understand its functionalities and purposes. The captions need to be concise but more descriptive than generic words such as "button" or "image." We recruited over 5,454 workers from Amazon Mechanical Turk[11] over multiple batches. While the elements to be labeled by each worker are randomly selected, we instrumented the task in the way such that a worker can only label each unique element once, and each element is labeled by three different workers.

Data Analyses. Human workers can skip elements when they were not sure how to describe them. For all the elements of each type given to workers, the percentage of elements being captioned ranges from 75% to 94% (see Fig. 7). In particular, the `View` type has the lowest labeling ratio of 75%, which we suspect that elements with the `View` type, a generic widget type, tend to be quite arbitrary and are difficult for the workers to understand. We only kept the elements that received at least two captions (from different workers). On average, each element received 2.66 captions. In total, we collected 162,859 captions for 61,285 UI elements across 21,750 unique screens, from 6,470 mobile apps.

To measure inter-annotator agreement, we computed the word-level precision and recall for all the words with two or more occurrences in the collected captions (see Fig. 8), as in the COCO image captioning dataset [5]. The results were generated on about 6K most frequent words, which amount to 98.6% of all the word occurrences in the captions. Figure 8 shows that our corpus has reasonable word-level agreement among the captions of the same widget. Specifically, for the 6K most frequent words, we report the mean precision and recall of every 10 consecutive words in the vocabulary. Therefore, we have 600 data points, each representing precision/recall of 10 words. The ranks of the words in the vocabulary sorted by word frequency are used to color the data points. Lower rank indicates higher word frequencies in the corpus.

Caption Phrase Analysis. We analyzed the distribution of caption lengths created by human workers (see Fig. 9). We found most captions are brief, i.e., two to three words. But a significant number of captions have more words, which are often long-tail captions. The average length of captions from human workers is 2.72. Overall, the length distribution of captions created by human workers is similar to those pre-

---

[11] https://www.mturk.com.

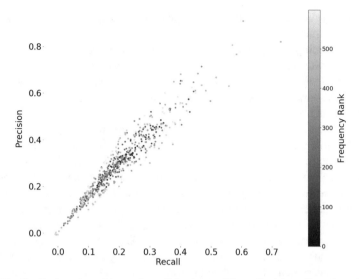

Fig. 8 The distribution of precision and recall for the top 6K words of the collected captions

Fig. 9 The length
distribution of captions
created by human workers.
The X-axis shows the
number of captions and the
Y-axis is the lengths from 1
to ≥ 10

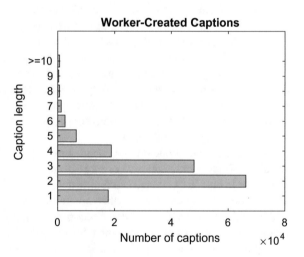

existing in the UI corpus, which are from app developers. The latter will be used as
a feature input to the model, which we will discuss later.

The captions in our dataset include a diverse set of phrases. The most frequent
caption is "go back" that amounts to 4.0% of the distribution. Other popular captions
among the top 5 are "advertisement" (2.4%), "go to previous" (0.8%), "search"
(0.7%), and "enter password" (0.6%).

A common pattern of the phrases we observe is *Predicate + Object*. Table 3 lists
the seven common predicates and their most frequent objects. As we can see, the
phrases describe highly diverse functionalities of the UI elements. It is difficult to

Table 3 In our dataset, the popular predicates are often associated with a diverse set of objects that are contextually determined

Predicate	Object
Search	Location, contact, app, music, map, image, people, recipe, flight, hotel
Enter	Password, email, username, phone, last name, first name, zip code, location, city
Select	Image, ad, color, emoji, app, language, folder, location, ringtone, theme
Toggle	Autoplay, favorite, menu, sound, advertisement, power, notification, alarm, microphone
Share (to)	Article, Facebook, Twitter, image, app, video, Instagram, recipe, location, Whatsapp
Download	App, sound, song, file, image, video, theme, game, wallpaper, effect
Close	Window, ad, screen, tab, menu, pop-up, notification, file, settings, message

classify them into a few common categories. This linguistic characteristic motivated us to choose sequence decoding for caption generation instead of classification based on a predefined phrase vocabulary. The diversity of caption phrases indicates that widget captioning is a challenging machine learning task.

Furthermore, to distinguish different objects for the same predicate, it is necessary to take into account the screen context that the element belongs to. For example, Fig. 10 shows two examples of the "search" predicate. The two UI elements have very similar images (magnifiers) although they are for searching different objects. Thus, context information is critical for models to decode the correct objects.

View Hierarchy Complexities. A unique modality in widget captioning is UI structures as represented by view hierarchy trees. To better understand the complexity of the UI structures, we analyze the size and depth of the view hierarchy of each UI. The size of a view hierarchy is the total number of nodes in the hierarchy tree, including both non-terminal nodes, i.e., layout containers and leaf nodes. The size distribution is highly skewed and with a long tail toward large view hierarchies (see the left of Fig. 11). The median size of view hierarchies is 61, with a minimum of 6 and a maximum of 1,608 nodes. Many view hierarchies have a large depth with a median depth of 11, a minimum of 3, and a maximum of 26 (see the right of Fig. 11). These show that view hierarchies are complex and contain rich structural information about a user interface.

3.2 Model Architecture

Captioning models are often designed based on an encoder–decoder architecture. We formulate widget captioning as a multimodal captioning task where the encoder takes both the structural information and the pixel appearance of the UI element, and the decoder outputs the caption based on the encodings (see Fig. 12).

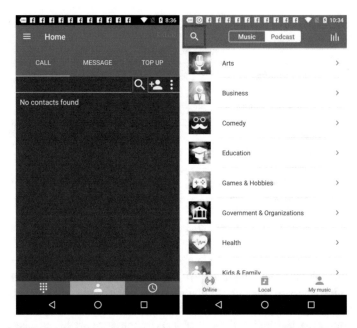

Fig. 10 Two UI elements (outlined in red) of "search" predicate. Left: search contact; Right: search music. Both screens are from the RICO dataset [6]: the left screen is from a call app and the right screen is from a music player app

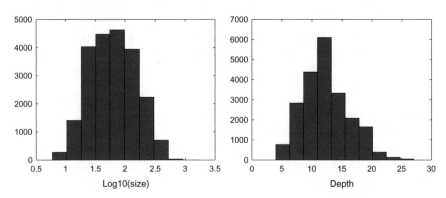

Fig. 11 The histogram of $\log_{10}$ transformed view hierarchy sizes on the left, and the histogram of tree depths on the right

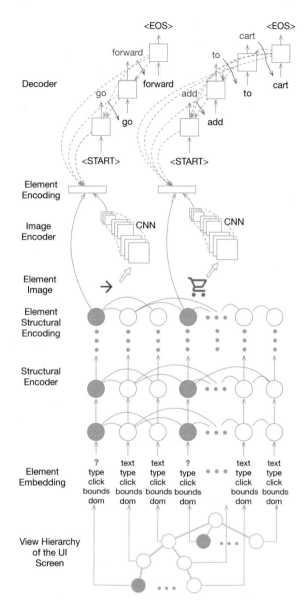

Fig. 12 Our widget captioning model takes both view hierarchy structures and element image as input, and performs parallel decoding for multiple elements on the screen missing captions. The shaded nodes represent the elements missing captions

3.2.1 Encoding the Structural Information

We hypothesize that the relationship of UI elements on the screen provides useful contextual information for representing each object and thus benefits captioning. We use a Transformer model [28] to encode the set of elements on a screen, which learns how the representation of an element should be affected by the others on the screen using multi-head neural attention. The input to a Transformer model requires both the content embedding and positional encoding. Similar to previous work [13], we derive these embeddings for each element on the screen in the following manner.

Each UI element in the view hierarchy consists of a tuple of properties. The `widget_text` property includes a collection of words possessed by the element. We acquire the embedding of the `widget_text` property of the i-th element on the screen, e_i^X, by max pooling over the embedding vector of each word in the property. When the `widget_text` property is empty, i.e., the element is missing a caption, a special embedding, $e^\emptyset$, is used. With e_i^T, the embedding of the `widget_type` property (see Fig. 7), and e_i^C, the embedding of whether the widget is clickable, $[e_i^X; e_i^T; e_i^C]$ form the content embedding of the element.

The `widget_bounds` property contains four coordinate values on the screen: `left`, `top`, `right`, and `bottom`, which are normalized to the range of [0, 100). The `widget_dom` property contains three values describing the element tree position in the view hierarchy: the sequence position in the `preorder` and the `postorder` traversal, and the `depth` in the view hierarchy tree. These are all treated as categorical values and represented as embedding vectors. The sum of these coordinate embeddings forms the positional embedding vector of the element, e_i^B.

The concatenation of all these embeddings forms the representation of a UI element: $e_i = [e_i^X; e_i^T; e_i^C; e_i^B]W^E$, where W^E is the parameters to linearly project the concatenation to the dimension expected by the Transformer model. The output of the Transformer encoder model, h_i, is the structural encoding of the i-th element on the screen.

3.2.2 Encoding Element Images

The image of an element is cropped from the UI screenshot and rescaled to a fixed dimension, which results in a $64 \times 64 \times 1$ tensor, where 64×64 are the spatial dimensions and 1 is the grayscale color channel. The image dimension strikes a good balance for representing both small and large elements, which preserves enough details for large elements after scaled down and enables a memory footprint good for model training and serving.

We use a ResNet (CNN) [9] to encode an element image. Each layer in the image encoder consists of a block of three sub-layers with a residual connection—the input of the first sub-layer is added to the input of the third sub-layer. There are no pooling used, and, instead, the last sub-layer of each block uses stride 2 that halves both the vertical and horizontal spatial dimensions after each layer. At the same, each layer doubles the channel dimension, starting from the channel dimension 4 of the first layer. Most sub-layers use a kernel size of 3×3 except the initial and ending sub-layers in the first layer that use a kernel size of 5×5. We will discuss further details of model configuration for the image encoder in the experiment section. The output of the multi-layer CNN is the encoding vector of the element image, which we refer to as g_i for the i-th element.

3.2.3 Decoding Captions

We form the latent representation of the ith element on the screen by combining its structural and image encoding: $z_i = \sigma([h_i; g_i], \theta^z) W^z$, where $\sigma(\cdot)$ is the non-linear activation function parameterized by θ^z and W^z is the trainable weights for linear projection. Based on the encoding, we use a Transformer [28] decoder model for generating a varying-length caption for the element.

$$a_{i,1:M}^l = \text{Masked\_ATTN}(x_{i,1:M}^l, W_d^Q, W_d^K, W_d^V)$$
$$x_{i,1:M}^{l+1} = \text{FFN}(a_{i,1:M}^l + z_i, \theta_d),$$

where $0 \leq l \leq L$ is the layer index and M is the number of word tokens to decode. $x_{i,1:M}^0$, the input to the decoder model, is the token embedding with the sequence positional encoding. W_d^Q, W_d^K, and W_d^V are trainable parameters for computing the queries, keys, and values. Masked_ATTN in a Transformer decoder allows multi-head attention to only attend to previous token representations. The element encoding, z_i, is added to the attention output of each decoding step, $a_{i,1:M}^l$, before feeding into the position-wise, multi-layer perception (FFN), parameterized by θ_d. The probability distribution of each token of the caption is finally computed using the softmax over the output of the last Transformer layer: $y_{i,1:M} = \text{softmax}(x_{i,1:M}^L W_d^y)$ where W_d^y is trainable parameters.

There is one instance of the decoder model for each element to be captioned. The captions for all the elements with missing captions on the same screen are decoded in parallel. The entire model, including both the encoder and decoder, is trained end to end, by minimizing $\mathcal{L}_{screen}$, the average cross-entropy loss for decoding each token of each element caption over the same screen.

$$\mathcal{L}_{screen} = \frac{1}{|\nabla|} \sum_{i \in \nabla} \frac{1}{M} \sum_{j=1}^{M} \text{Cross\_Entropy}(y'_{i,j}, y_{i,j})$$

where ∇ is the set of elements on the same screen with missing captions and $y'_{i,j}$ is the ground-truth token. Training is conducted in a teacher-forcing manner where the ground-truth caption words are fed into the decoder. During prediction time, the model decodes autoregressively.

3.3 Experiments

We first discuss the experimental setup, and then report the accuracy of our model as well as an analysis of the model behavior.

Table 4 Widget captioning dataset statistics

Split	Apps	Screens	Widgets	Captions
Training	5,170	18,394	52,178	138,342
Validation	650	1,720	4,548	12,242
Test	650	1,636	4,559	12,275
Total	6,470	21,750	61,285	162,859

3.3.1   Datasets

We split our dataset into training, validation, and test set for model development and evaluation, as shown in Table 4. The UIs of the same app may have a similar style. To avoid information leaks, the split was done app-wise so that all the screens from the same app will not be shared across different splits. Consequently, all the apps and screens in the test dataset are unseen during training, which allow us to examine how each model configuration generalizes to unseen conditions at test.

Our vocabulary includes 10,000 most frequent words (that covers more than 95% of the words in the dataset), and the rest of the words encountered in the training dataset is assigned a special unknown token <UNK>. During validation and testing, any <UNK> in the decoded phrase is removed before evaluation. Since each element has more than one caption, one of its captions is randomly sampled each time during training. For testing, all the captions of an element constitute its reference set for computing automatic metrics such as CIDEr.

The training, validation, and test datasets have a similar ratio of 40% for caption coverage, i.e., the number of elements with pre-existing captions with respect to the total number of elements on each screen, with no statistical significance ($p > 0.05$). Screens with none pre-existing captions exist in all the splits.

3.3.2   Model Configurations

We based our experiments on Transformer as it outperformed alternatives such as GCNs and LSTMs in our early exploration. We tuned our model architectures based on the training and validation datasets. We initialize the word embeddings with pre-trained 400K-vocab 300-dimensional GLOVE embeddings [23], which are then projected onto a 128-dimensional vector space. To reduce the number of parameters needed in the model, the embedding weights are shared by both the structural encoder and the decoder. Both the Transformer structural encoder and the Transformer decoder use 6 Transformer layers with a hidden size of 128 and 8-head attention. We used a 7-layer ResNet for encoding the pixels of a target element, where each layer consists of 3 sub-layers as discussed earlier, which in total involves 21 convolutional layers and the output of the final layer is flattened into a 256-sized vector. We used batch normalization for each convolutional layer. The final encoding z_i of an element is a 128-dimensional vector that is used for decoding.

3.3.3 Metrics and Results

We report our accuracy based on BLEU (unigram and bigram) [21], CIDEr [29], ROUGE-L [16] METOER [7], and SPICE [1] metrics (see Table 5). For all these metrics, a higher number means better captioning accuracy—the closer distances between the predicted and the ground-truth captions.

We investigate how model variations impact the overall accuracy of captioning (Table 5). *Template Matching* is an obvious baseline, which predicts the caption of an element based on its image similarity with elements that come with a caption. We use pixel-wise cosine similarity to compare the element images. Although this heuristic-based method is able to predict captions for certain elements, it performs poorly compared to the rest of the models that use deep architectures. *Pixel Only* model, which only uses the image encoding of an element, performs significantly better than *Template Matching*, which indicates that image encoding, g_i, is a much more efficient representation than raw pixels.

Pixel+Local, which uses both image encoding, g_i, and the structural representation computed only based on the properties of the element offers further improvement on the accuracy. Our full model, *Pixel+Local+Context*, uses both image encoding, g_i, and the screen context encoding, h_i. It achieves the best results, which indicate that screen context carries useful information about an element for generating its

Table 5 The accuracy of each model configuration on the full set and the predicate–object subset of the test dataset

Model configuration	BLEU-1	BLEU-2	ROUGE	CIDEr	METOER	SPICE
			Full test set			
Template matching	20.2	11.2	20.9	38.0	13.2	6.5
Pixel Only	35.6	24.6	35.6	71.3	24.9	11.2
Pixel+Local	42.6	29.4	42.0	87.3	29.4	15.3
Pixel+Local+Context (PLC)	**44.9**	**32.2**	**44.7**	**97.0**	**31.7**	**17.6**
PLC classification	36.2	25.7	36.9	78.9	26.0	13.6
			Predicate–object subset			
Template matching	20.8	11.2	21.3	34.5	12.6	7.5
Pixel Only	39.4	27.2	39.1	69.6	25.8	14.2
Pixel+Local	48.5	34.8	47.4	94.7	32.3	19.9
Pixel+Local+Context (PLC)	**52.0**	**38.8**	**51.3**	**110.1**	**36.4**	**23.3**
PLC classification	38.5	27.0	38.4	78.9	26.3	16.8

caption. Among all the structural features, the `widget_text` property plays an important role.

In addition to examining the impact of input modality on captioning quality, we compare strategies of caption generation: sequence decoding based on word tokens versus classification based on common caption phrases. *PLC classification* model uses the same input modality and encoding as *Pixel+Local+Context* but decodes a single predefined phrase based on a vocabulary of top 10K caption phrases—the same size as the token vocabulary for decoding. It performed poorly compared to the decoding-based approach.

To further validate the usefulness of the context and the information from view hierarchy, we evaluate the models on a subset of UI elements with one of their reference caption phrases is of the *Predicate + Object* pattern (see Table 3). This subset consists of about 40% of the UI elements from the test set. All the models achieve better accuracy because the predicate–object subset consists of more common words. *Pixel+Local+Context* remains the champion model, and more importantly acquired the most significant gain across all the metrics (see Table 5). This indicates that context information plays a crucial role for generating this type of captions whose object parts need to be contextually determined. In contrast, *PLC Classification* still performs worse than the champion decoding-based model. While the subset contains more common words, their combination can form long-tail phrases. A classification-based method such as *PLC Classification* is more vulnerable to the data sparsity of long-tail phrases.

3.3.4   Human Evaluation

To assess the quality of the generated phrases by human, we asked another group of crowd workers to manually verify the model generated captions for the entire test set, by presenting each human rater a caption and its corresponding element in a UI screenshot. For each phrase, we asked three raters to verify whether the caption phrase correctly describes the functionality and purpose of the element. We compared two of our models and the results are listed in Table 6. The overall endorsement of raters for generated captions is 78.64% for the full model and 62.42% for the *Pixel Only* model. These results indicate that our model can generate meaningful captions for UI elements. We found shorter captions tend to receive more rater endorsements than longer ones. The model with context still outperforms the one without context, which is consistent with automatic evaluation.

Table 6 The human evaluation results. N+ in the header refers to N or more raters judge that the caption correctly describes the element

Model	1+	2+	3+
Pixel Only	81.9	61.7	43.6
Pixel+Local+Context	**93.9**	**81.1**	**61.0**

3.4 Analysis

To identify opportunities for improvements, we conducted error analysis on 50 widgets sampled from the validation set whose captions generated by the model share no words with their references. We classify these errors into the following types:

- *Nearby Elements* (21): The model is confused by nearby elements on the screen, e.g., outputting "enter phone number" for "write street address" on a sign-up screen.
- *Similar Appearance* (10): The model is confused by elements with a similar appearance, e.g., predicting "delete" for an X-shaped image that is labeled as "close."
- *Too Generic* (9): The model generates captions that are too generic, e.g., "toggle on" instead of "flight search on/off."
- *Model Correct* (10): The model produces semantically correct captions but treated as errors due to the limitation of automatic evaluation, e.g., "close" for "exit."

There are two directions for future improvement. One is to improve encoders for UI images and view hierarchies to better represent UI elements. The other is to improve data sparsity, which we want to better address long-tail phrases by expanding the dataset and having more elements and screens labeled.

4 Conclusion

In this chapter, we reviewed two projects for bridging natural language and graphical user interfaces. In the first project, we discussed natural language grounding in mobile user interfaces where a multi-step natural language instruction is grounded as a sequence of executable actions on the user interfaces. Such a capability allows a computational agent to automatically execute a multi-step task on behalf of the user, which is valuable for accessibility and UI automation in general. In the second project, we discussed natural language generation for user interface elements such that these elements can be announced and communicated to mobile users. Both projects address important interaction scenarios where natural language is an essential communication medium of mobile user experiences. From these projects, we showcase research strategies at the intersection of Natural Language Processing (NLP) and Human–Computer Interaction (HCI), where we formulated novel machine learning tasks, created new datasets and deep learning models, and made these resources available to the public. These provide useful benchmarks for future research at the intersection of NLP and HCI.

Acknowledgements We would like to thank Jiacong He, Yuan Zhang, Jason Baldridge, Song Wang, Justin Cui, Christina Ou, Luheng He, Jingjie Zheng, Hong Li, Zhiwei Guan, Ashwin Kakarla, and Muqthar Mohammad who contributed to these projects.

References

1. Anderson, P., Fernando, B., Johnson, M., and Gould, S. SPICE: semantic propositional image caption evaluation. *CoRR abs/1607.08822* (2016)
2. Bahdanau, D., Cho, K., and Bengio, Y. Neural machine translation by jointly learning to align and translate. *CoRR abs/1409.0473* (2014)
3. Branavan, S., Zettlemoyer, L., and Barzilay, R. Reading between the lines: Learning to map high-level instructions to commands. In *Proceedings of the 48th Annual Meeting of the Association for Computational Linguistics*, Association for Computational Linguistics (Uppsala, Sweden, July 2010), 1268–1277
4. Branavan, S. R. K., Chen, H., Zettlemoyer, L. S., and Barzilay, R. Reinforcement learning for mapping instructions to actions. In *Proceedings of the Joint Conference of the 47th Annual Meeting of the ACL and the 4th International Joint Conference on Natural Language Processing of the AFNLP: Volume 1 - Volume 1*, ACL '09, Association for Computational Linguistics (Stroudsburg, PA, USA, 2009), 82–90
5. Chen, X., Fang, H., Lin, T.-Y., Vedantam, R., Gupta, S., Dollar, P., and Lawrence Zitnick, C. Microsoft COCO captions: Data collection and evaluation server
6. Deka, B., Huang, Z., Franzen, C., Hibschman, J., Afergan, D., Li, Y., Nichols, J., and Kumar, R. Rico: A mobile app dataset for building data-driven design applications. In *Proceedings of the 30th Annual ACM Symposium on User Interface Software and Technology*, UIST '17, ACM (New York, NY, USA, 2017), 845–854
7. Denkowski, M., and Lavie, A. Meteor universal: Language specific translation evaluation for any target language. In *Proceedings of the Ninth Workshop on Statistical Machine Translation*, Association for Computational Linguistics (Stroudsburg, PA, USA, 2014), 376–380
8. Gur, I., Rueckert, U., Faust, A., and Hakkani-Tur, D. Learning to navigate the web. In *International Conference on Learning Representations* (2019)
9. He, K., Zhang, X., Ren, S., and Sun, J. Deep residual learning for image recognition (2015). cite arxiv:1512.03385Comment: Tech report
10. Hochreiter S, Schmidhuber J (1997) Long short-term memory. Neural Comput. 9(8):1735–1780 Nov
11. Lee, K., He, L., Lewis, M., and Zettlemoyer, L. End-to-end neural coreference resolution. In *Proceedings of the 2017 Conference on Empirical Methods in Natural Language Processing*, Association for Computational Linguistics (Copenhagen, Denmark, Sept. 2017), 188–197
12. Lee, K., Kwiatkowski, T., Parikh, A. P., and Das, D. Learning recurrent span representations for extractive question answering. *CoRR abs/1611.01436* (2016)
13. Li, Y., He, J., Zhou, X., Zhang, Y., and Baldridge, J. Mapping natural language instructions to mobile ui action sequences. In *ACL 2020: Association for Computational Linguistics* (2020)
14. Li, Y., Kaiser, L., Bengio, S., and Si, S. Area attention. In *Proceedings of the 36th International Conference on Machine Learning*, K. Chaudhuri and R. Salakhutdinov, Eds., vol. 97 of *Proceedings of Machine Learning Research*, PMLR (Long Beach, California, USA, 09–15 Jun 2019), 3846–3855
15. Li, Y., Li, G., He, L., Zheng, J., Li, H., and Guan, Z. Widget captioning: Generating natural language description for mobile user interface elements. In *Proceedings of the 2020 Conference on Empirical Methods in Natural Language Processing (EMNLP)*, Association for Computational Linguistics (Online, Nov. 2020), 5495–5510
16. Lin, C.-Y., and Och, F. J. Orange: A method for evaluating automatic evaluation metrics for machine translation. In *Proceedings of the 20th International Conference on Computational Linguistics*, COLING '04, Association for Computational Linguistics (Stroudsburg, PA, USA, 2004)
17. Lin, T., Maire, M., Belongie, S. J., Bourdev, L. D., Girshick, R. B., Hays, J., Perona, P., Ramanan, D., Dollár, P., and Zitnick, C. L. Microsoft COCO: common objects in context. *CoRR abs/1405.0312* (2014)

18. Liu, E. Z., Guu, K., Pasupat, P., Shi, T., and Liang, P. Reinforcement learning on web interfaces using workflow-guided exploration. In *International Conference on Learning Representations (ICLR)* (2018)

19. Luong, T., Pham, H., and Manning, C. D. Effective approaches to attention-based neural machine translation. In *Proceedings of the 2015 Conference on Empirical Methods in Natural Language Processing*, Association for Computational Linguistics (Lisbon, Portugal, Sept. 2015), 1412–1421

20. Niepert, M., Ahmed, M., and Kutzkov, K. Learning convolutional neural networks for graphs. In *Proceedings of The 33rd International Conference on Machine Learning*, M. F. Balcan and K. Q. Weinberger, Eds., vol. 48 of *Proceedings of Machine Learning Research*, PMLR (New York, New York, USA, 20–22 Jun 2016), 2014–2023

21. Papineni, K., Roukos, S., Ward, T., and Zhu, W.-J. BLEU: a method for automatic evaluation of machine translation. In *Proceedings of the 40th Annual Meeting on Association for Computational Linguistics*, ACL '02, Association for Computational Linguistics (USA, July 2002), 311–318

22. Parmar, N., Vaswani, A., Uszkoreit, J., Kaiser, L., Shazeer, N., Ku, A., and Tran, D. Image transformer. In *Proceedings of the 35th International Conference on Machine Learning*, J. Dy and A. Krause, Eds., vol. 80 of *Proceedings of Machine Learning Research*, PMLR (Stockholmsmässan, Stockholm Sweden, 10–15 Jul 2018), 4055–4064

23. Pennington, J., Socher, R., and Manning, C. D. Glove: Global vectors for word representation. In *Empirical Methods in Natural Language Processing (EMNLP)* (2014), 1532–1543

24. Ramshaw, L., and Marcus, M. Text chunking using transformation-based learning. In *Third Workshop on Very Large Corpora* (1995)

25. Ross, A. S., Zhang, X., Fogarty, J., and Wobbrock, J. O. Epidemiology as a framework for large-scale mobile application accessibility assessment. In *Proceedings of the 19th International ACM SIGACCESS Conference on Computers and Accessibility*, ASSETS '17, ACM (New York, NY, USA, 2017), 2–11

26. Ross, A. S., Zhang, X., Fogarty, J., and Wobbrock, J. O. Examining image-based button labeling for accessibility in android apps through large-scale analysis. In *Proceedings of the 20th International ACM SIGACCESS Conference on Computers and Accessibility*, ASSETS '18, ACM (New York, NY, USA, 2018), 119–130

27. Sarsenbayeva, Z. Situational impairments during mobile interaction. In *Proceedings of the ACM on Interactive, Mobile, Wearable and Ubiquitous Technologies* (2018), 498–503

28. Vaswani, A., Shazeer, N., Parmar, N., Uszkoreit, J., Jones, L., Gomez, A. N., Kaiser, L., and Polosukhin, I. Attention is all you need. *CoRR abs/1706.03762* (2017)

29. Vedantam, R., Zitnick, C., and Parikh, D. Cider: Consensus-based image description evaluation (06 2015). 4566–4575

30. Vinyals, O., Fortunato, M., and Jaitly, N. Pointer networks. In *Advances in Neural Information Processing Systems 28*, C. Cortes, N. D. Lawrence, D. D. Lee, M. Sugiyama, and R. Garnett, Eds. Curran Associates, Inc., 2015, 2692–2700

31. Xu, K., Ba, J., Kiros, R., Cho, K., Courville, A. C., Salakhutdinov, R., Zemel, R. S., and Bengio, Y. Show, attend and tell: Neural image caption generation with visual attention. *CoRR abs/1502.03044* (2015)

Demonstration + Natural Language: Multimodal Interfaces for GUI-Based Interactive Task Learning Agents

Toby Jia-Jun Li, Tom M. Mitchell, and Brad A. Myers

Abstract We summarize our past five years of work on designing, building, and studying SUGILITE, an interactive task learning agent that can learn new tasks and relevant associated concepts interactively from the user's natural language instructions and demonstrations leveraging the graphical user interfaces (GUIs) of third-party mobile apps. Through its multi-modal and mixed-initiative approaches for Human-AI interaction, SUGILITE made important contributions in improving the usability, applicability, generalizability, flexibility, robustness, and shareability of interactive task learning agents. SUGILITE also represents a new human-AI interaction paradigm for interactive task learning, where it uses existing app GUIs as a *medium* for users to communicate their intents with an AI agent instead of the interfaces for users to interact with the underlying computing services. In this chapter, we describe the SUGILITE system, explain the design and implementation of its key features, and show a prototype in the form of a conversational assistant on Android.

1 Introduction

Interactive task learning (ITL) is an emerging research topic that focuses on enabling task automation agents to learn new tasks and their corresponding relevant concepts through natural interaction with human users [69]. This topic is also related to the concept of *end-user development* (EUD) for task automation [65, 115]. Work in this domain includes both physical agents (e.g., robots) that learn tasks that might involve sensing and manipulating objects in the real world [7; 28], as well as software agents

T. J.-J. Li (✉) · T. M. Mitchell · B. A. Myers
Carnegie Mellon University, Pittsburgh, PA, USA
e-mail: tobyli@cs.cmu.edu

T. M. Mitchell
e-mail: tom.mitchell@cs.cmu.edu

B. A. Myers
e-mail: bam@cs.cmu.edu

that learn how to perform tasks through software interfaces [3, 10, 68, 75]. This paper focuses on the latter category.

A particularly useful application of ITL is on conversational virtual assistants (e.g., Apple Siri, Google Assistant) running on mobile phones. With the widespread popularity of mobile apps, users are utilizing them to complete a wide variety of tasks [27, 150]. These apps interact with users through graphical user interfaces (GUIs), where users usually provide inputs by direct manipulation, and read outputs from the GUI display. Most GUIs are designed with usability in mind, providing non-expert users low learning barriers to commonly-used computing tasks. App GUIs also often follow certain design patterns that are familiar to users, which helps them easily navigate around GUI structures to locate the desired functionalities [2, 38, 130].

However, GUI-based mobile apps have several limitations. First, performing tasks on GUIs can be tedious. For example, the current version of the Starbucks app on Android requires 14 taps to order a cup of venti Iced Cappuccino with skim milk, and even more if the user does not have the account information stored. For such tasks, users would often like to have them automated [6, 105, 127]. Second, direct manipulation of GUIs is often not feasible or convenient in some contexts. Third, many tasks require coordination among many apps. But nowadays, data often remain siloed in individual apps [29]. Lastly, while some app GUIs provide certain mechanisms of personalization (e.g., remembering and pre-filling the user's home location), they are mostly hard-coded. Users have few means of creating customized rules and specifying personalized task parameters to reflect their preferences beyond what the app developers have explicitly designed for.

Recently, intelligent agents have become popular solutions to the the limitations of GUIs. They can be activated by speech commands to perform tasks on the user's behalf [102]. This interaction style allows the user to focus on the high-level specification of the task while the agent performs the low-level actions, as opposed to the usual direct manipulation GUI in which the user must select the correct objects, execute the correct operations, and control the environment [25, 135]. Compared with traditional GUIs, intelligent agents can reduce user burden when dealing with repetitive tasks, and alleviate redundancy in cross-app tasks. The speech modality in intelligent agents can support hand-free contexts when the user is physically away from the device, cognitively occupied by other tasks (e.g., driving), or on devices with little or no screen space (e.g., wearables) [101]. The improved expressiveness in natural language also affords more flexible personalization in tasks.

Nevertheless, current prevailing intelligent agents have limited capabilities. They invoke underlying functionalities by directly calling back-end services. Therefore, agents need to be specifically programmed for each supported application and service. By default, they can only invoke built-in apps (e.g., phone, message, calendar, music) and some integrated external apps and web services (e.g., web search, weather, Wikipedia), lacking the capability of controlling arbitrary third-party apps and services. To address this problem, providers of intelligent agents, such as Apple, Google, and Amazon, have released developer kits for their agents, so that the developers of third-party apps can integrate their apps into the agents to allow the agents to invoke these apps from user commands. However, such integration requires significant cost and engineering effort from app developers, therefore, only some of the most popular tasks in popular apps have been integrated into prevailing intelligent agents so far. The "long-tail" of tasks and apps have not been supported yet, and will likely not get supported due to the cost and effort involved.

Prior literature [143] showed that the usage of "long-tail" apps made up significant portion in user app usage. Smartphone users also have highly diverse usage patterns within apps [150] and wish to have more customizability over how agents perform their tasks [36]. Therefore, relying on third-party developers' effort to extend the capabilities of intelligent agents is not sufficient for supporting diverse user needs. It is not feasible for end users to develop for new tasks in prevailing agents on their own either, due to *(i)* their lack of technical expertise required, and *(ii)* the limited availability of openly accessible application programming interfaces (APIs) for many back-end services. Therefore, adding the support for interactive task learning from end users in intelligent agents is particularly useful.

1.1 Interactive Task Learning for Smartphone Intelligent Agents

To address this problem, We designed, implemented, and studied a new end-user programmable interactive task learning agent called SUGILITE[1] [80] Based on prior works in EUD and ITL for task automation, We identify the below key research challenges that SUGILITE seeks to address:

- **Usability:** SUGILITE should be usable for users without significant programming expertise. Some prior EUD systems (e.g., [100, 127]) require users to program in a visual programming language or a textual scripting language, which imposes a significant learning barrier and prevents users with limited programming expertise from using these systems.
- **Applicability:** SUGILITE should handle a wide range of common and long-tail tasks across different domains. Many existing EUD systems can only work with applications implemented with specific frameworks or libraries (e.g., [17, 32]), or services that provide open API access to their functionalities (e.g., [53]). This limits the applicability of those systems to a small subset of tasks.
- **Generalizability:** SUGILITE should learn generalized procedures and concepts that handle new task contexts and different task parameters without requiring users to reprogram from scratch. For example, macro recorders like [129] can record a sequence of input events (e.g., clicking on the coordinate (x, y)) and replay the same actions at a later time. But these macros are not generalizable, and will only perform the exact same action sequences but not tasks with variations

---

[1] SUGILITE is named after a purple gemstone, and stands for: **S**martphone **U**sers **G**enerating **I**ntelligent **L**ikeable **I**nterfaces **T**hrough **E**xamples.

or different parameters. Learning generalized procedures and concepts requires deeper understanding for the semantics of the medium of instruction, which in SUGILITE's case are the GUIs of existing mobile apps.

- **Flexibility:** SUGILITE should provide adequate expressiveness to allow users to express flexible automated rules, conditions, and other control structures that reflect their desired task intentions. The simple single trigger-action rule approach like [53, 56], while providing great usability due to its simplicity, is not sufficiently expressive for many tasks that users want to automate [140].

- **Robustness:** SUGILITE should be resilient to minor changes in target applications, and be able to recover from errors caused by previously unseen or unexpected situations with the user's help. Macro recorders such as [129] are usually brittle. Approaches with complicated programming synthesis or machine learning techniques (e.g., [98, 108]) usually lack transparency into the inference process, making it difficult for end users to recover from errors. Another aspect of robustness is to handle errors in natural language interactions [8, 101].

- **Shareability:** SUGILITE should support the sharing of learned task procedures and concepts among users. This requires SUGILITE to *(i)* have the robustness of being resilient to minor differences between different devices, and *(ii)* preserve the original end-user developer's privacy in the sharing process. As discussed in [75, 78], end users are often hesitant about sharing end-user-developed scripts due to the fear of accidentally including personal private information in shared program artifacts.

To address the challenges, SUGILITE takes a *multi-modal* interactive task learning approach, where it learns new tasks and concepts from end users interactively in two complementary modalities: *(i)* demonstrations by direct manipulation of third-party app GUIs, and *(ii)* spoken natural language instructions. This approach combines two popular EUD techniques—*programming by demonstration* (PBD) and *natural language programming*. In PBD, users teach the system a new behavior by directly demonstrating how to perform it. In natural language programming, users teach the system by verbally describing and explaining the desired behaviors using a natural language like English. Combining these two modalities allows users to take advantage of the easiest, most natural, and/or most effective modality based on the context for different parts of the programming task.

Through its multi-modal approach combining PBD and natural language programming, SUGILITE mitigates the shortcomings in each individual technique. Demonstrations are often too literal, making it hard to infer the user's higher level intentions. In other words, it often only records *what* the user did, but not *why* the user did it. Therefore, it is difficult to produce generalizable programs from demonstrations alone. On the other hand, natural language instructions can be very flexible and expressive for users to communicate their intentions and desired system behaviors. However, they are inherently ambiguous. In our approach, SUGILITE *grounds* natural language instructions to demonstration app GUIs, allowing *mutual disambiguation* [119], where demonstrations are used to disambiguate natural language inputs and vice versa.

1.2 Contributions

Our work contributes a new mixed-initiative multi-modal approach for intelligent agents to learn new task procedures and relevant concepts and a system that implements this approach. Specifically, this chapter describes the following contributions:

1. The SUGILITE system, a mobile PBD system that enables end users with no significant programming expertise to create automation scripts for arbitrary tasks across any or multiple third-party mobile apps through a multi-modal interface combining demonstrations and natural language instructions [80] (Sect. 4).
2. A multi-modal mixed-initiative PBD disambiguation interface that addresses the data description problem by allowing users to verbally explain their intentions for demonstrated GUI actions through multi-turn conversations with the help of an interaction proxy overlay that guides users to focus on providing effective information [84] (Sect. 5.2).
3. A technique for grounding natural language task instructions to app GUI entities by constructing semantic relational knowledge graphs from hierarchical GUI structures, along with a formative study showing the feasibility of this technique with end users [84] (Sect. 5.2).
4. A PBD script generalization mechanism that leverages the natural language instructions, the recorded user demonstration, and the GUI hierarchical structures of third-party mobile apps to infer task parameters and their possible values from a single demonstration [80] (Sect. 5.3).
5. A top-down conversational programming framework for task automation that can learn both task procedures and the relevant concepts by allowing users to naturally start with describing the task and its conditionals at a high-level and then recursively clarify ambiguities, explain unknown concepts, and define new procedures through a mix of conversations and references to third-party app GUIs [88] (Sect. 5.4).
6. A multi-modal error handling and repairing approach for task-oriented conversational agents that helps users discover, identify the causes of, and recover from conversational breakdowns caused by natural language understanding errors using existing mobile app GUIs for grounding [82] (Sect. 5.5).
7. A new self-supervised technique for generating semantic embeddings of GUI screens and components that encode their textual content, visual design and layout patterns, and app metadata without requiring manual data annotation [87] (Sect. 5.6).

2 The Human-AI Collaboration Perspective

We argue that a key problem in the ITL process is to facilitate effective Human-AI collaboration. In the traditional view, programming is viewed as the process of transforming a user's existing mental plan into a programming language that the computer can execute. However, in end-user ITL, this is not an accurate model. The user often starts with only a vague idea of what to do and needs an intelligent system's help to clarify their intents. We view ITL as a joint activity where the user and the agent share the same goal in a human-AI collaboration framework. In such mixed-initiative interactions, the user's goals and inputs come with uncertainty [4, 51]. The agent needs to show guesses of user goals, assist the user to provide more effective inputs, and engage in multi-turn dialogs with the user to resolve any uncertainties and ambiguities.

Significant progress has been made on this topic in recent years in both AI and HCI. Specifically on the AI side, advances in natural language processing (NLP) enable the agents to process users' instructions of task procedures, conditionals, concepts definitions, and classifiers in natural language [2, 6, 10], to ground the instructions (e.g., [12]), and to have dialog with users based on GUI-extracted task models (e.g., [11]). Reinforcement learning techniques allow the agent to more effectively explore action sequences on GUIs to complete tasks [13]. Large GUI datasets such as RICO [4] allow the analysis of GUI patterns at scale, and the construction of generalized models for extracting semantic information from GUIs.

The HCI community also has presented new study findings, design implications, and interaction designs in this domain. A key direction has been the design of multi-modal interfaces that leverage both natural language instructions and GUI demonstrations [1, 7]. Prior work also explored how users naturally express their task intents [10, 15, 17] and designed new interfaces to guide the users to provide more effective inputs (e.g., [8]).

On one hand, AI-centric task flow exploration and program synthesis techniques often lack transparency for users to understand the internal process, and they provide the users with little control over the task fulfillment process to reflect their personal preferences. On the other hand, machine intelligence is desired because the users' instructions are often incomplete, vague, ambiguous, or even incorrect. Therefore, the system needs to provide adequate assistance to guide the users to provide effective inputs to express their intents, while retaining the users' agency, trust, and control of the process. While relevant design principles have been discussed in early foundational works in mixed-initiative interaction [5] and demonstrational interfaces [16], incorporating these ideas into the design and implementation of actual systems remains an important challenge.

A crucial factor in human-AI collaboration is the *medium*. SUGILITE presents a new human-AI interaction paradigm for interactive task learning, where it uses the GUIs of the existing third-party mobile apps as the medium for users to communicate their intents with an AI agent instead of the interfaces for users to interact with the underlying computing services. Among common mediums for agent task learning, app GUIs sit at a nice middle ground between (1) programming language, which can be easily processed by a computing system but imposes significant learning barriers to non-expert users; and (2) unconstrained visual demonstrations in the physical work and natural language instructions, which are natural and easy-to-use for users but infeasible for computing systems to fully understand without significant human-annotated training data and task domain restrictions given the current state-of-art in natural language understanding, computer vision, and commonsense reasoning. In comparison, existing app GUIs cover a wide range of useful task domains for automation, encode the properties and relations of task-relevant entities, and encapsulate the flows and constraints of underlying tasks in formats that can be feasibly extracted and understood by an intelligent agent.

By sitting *between* the user and the GUIs of third-party apps, SUGILITE allows the user to teach the agent new task procedures and concepts by demonstrating them on existing third-party app GUIs *and* verbally explaining them in natural language. When executing a task, SUGILITE directly manipulates app GUIs on the user's behalf. This approach tackles the two major barriers in prevailing intelligent agents by *(i)* leveraging the available third-party app GUIs as a channel to access a large number of back-end services without requiring openly available APIs, and *(ii)* taking advantage of users' familiarity with app GUIs, so users can program the intelligent agent without having significant technical expertise by using app GUIs as the medium.

3　Related Work

3.1　Programming by Demonstration

SUGILITE uses the programming by demonstration (PBD) technique to enable end users to define concepts by referring to the content of GUIs from third-party mobile apps, and to teach new procedures through demonstrations with those apps. PBD is a promising technique for enabling end users to automate their activities without necessarily requiring programming knowledge—It allows users to program in the same environment in which they perform the actions. This makes PBD particularly appealing to many end users, who have little knowledge of conventional programming languages, but are familiar with how to perform the tasks they wish to automate using existing app GUIs [37, 94, 114].

A key challenge for PBD is generalization [37, 71, 94]. When an user demonstrates an instance of performing a task in a specific situation, the PBD system needs to learn the task a higher level of abstraction so that it can perform similar tasks (with different parameters, configurations etc.) in new contexts. SUGILITE improved the generalization capability compared with prior similar PBD agents such as CoScripter [75], HILC [57], Sikuli [147], and VASTA [132] through its support for parameterization (Sect. 5.3), data description disambiguation (Sect. 5.2), and concept generalization (Sect. 5.4).

SUGILITE supports domain-independent PBD by task automation by using GUIs of third-party apps. Similar approaches have also been used in prior systems. For example, Assistive Macros [129] uses mobile app GUIs, CoScripter [75], d.mix [50], Vegemite [97], Ringer [13], and PLOW [3] use web interfaces, and HILC [57] and Sikuli [147] use desktop GUIs. Macro recording tools like [129] can record a sequence of input events and replay them later. These tools are too literal—they can only replay exactly the same procedure that was demonstrated, without the ability to generalize the demonstration to perform similar tasks. They are also brittle to any UI changes in the app. Sikuli [147], VASTA [132], and HILC [57] used the visual features of GUI entities to identify the target entities for actions—while this approach has some advantages over SUGILITE's approach, such as being able to work with graphic entities without textual labels or other appropriate identifiers, the visual approach does not use the semantics of GUI entities, which also limits its generalizability.

In human–robot interaction, PBD is often used in interactive task learning where a robot learns new tasks and procedures from the user's demonstration with physical objects [7, 20, 45, 64]. The demonstrations are sometimes also accompanied by natural language instructions [112, 133] similar to SUGILITE. While many recent works have been done in enhancing computing systems' capabilities for parsing human activities (e.g., [126]), modeling human intents (e.g., [44]), representing knowledge (e.g., [149]), from visual information from the physical world, it remains a major AI challenge to recognize, interpret, represent, learn from, and reason with visual demonstrations. In comparison, SUGILITE avoids this grand challenge by using existing app GUIs as the alternative medium for task instruction, which retains the user familiarity, naturalness, and domain generality of visual demonstration but is much easier to comprehend for a computing system.

3.2 Natural Language Programming

SUGILITE uses natural language as one of the two primary modalities for end users to program task automation scripts. The idea of using natural language inputs for programming has been explored for decades [11, 18, 95, 109]. In NLP and AI communities, this approach is also known as learning by instruction [10, 33, 68, 96].

The foremost challenge in supporting natural language programming is to deal with the inherent ambiguities and vagueness in natural language [141]. To address this challenge, a prior approach was to require users to use similar expression styles that resembled conventional programming languages (e.g., [11, 77, 125]), so that the system could directly translate user instructions into code. Despite that the user instructions used in this approach seemed like natural language, it did not allow much flexibility in expressions. This approach is not adequate for end-user development, because it has a high learning barrier for users without programming expertise—users have to adapt to the system by learning new syntax, keywords, and structures.

Another approach for handling ambiguities and vagueness in natural language inputs is to seek user clarification through conversations. For example, Iris [43] asked follow-up questions and presents possible options through conversations when initial user inputs are incomplete or unclear. This approach lowered the learning barrier for end users, as it did not require them to clearly define everything up front. It also allowed users to form complex commands by combining multiple natural language instructions in conversational turns under the guidance of the system. This multi-turn interactive approach is also known as *interactive semantic parsing* in the NLP community [145, 146]. SUGILITE adopts the use of multi-turn conversations as a key strategy in handling ambiguities and vagueness in user inputs. However, a key difference between SUGILITE and other conversational instructable agents is that SUGILITE is domain-independent. All conversational instructable agents need to resolve the user's inputs into existing concepts, procedures, and system functionalities supported by the agent, and to have natural language understanding mechanisms and training data in each task domain. Because of this constraint, existing agents often limit their supported tasks to one or a few pre-defined domains, such as data science [43], email processing [10, 136], invoking Web APIs [137], or database queries [49, 61, 76].

SUGILITE supports learning concepts and procedures from existing third-party mobile apps regardless of the task domain. Users can explain new concepts, define task conditionals, and clarify ambiguous demonstrated actions in SUGILITE by referencing relevant information shown in app GUIs. The novel semantic relational graph representation of GUIs (details in Sect. 5.2) allows SUGILITE to understand user references to GUI content without having prior knowledge on the specific task domain. This approach enables SUGILITE to support a wide range of tasks from diverse domains, as long as the corresponding mobile apps are available. This approach also has a low learning barrier because end users are already familiar with the functionalities of mobile apps and how to use them. In comparison, with prior instructable agents, users are often unclear about what concepts, procedures, and functionalities already exist to be used as "building blocks" for developing new ones.

3.3 Multi-modal Interfaces

Multi-modal interfaces process two or more user input modes in a coordinated manner to provide users with greater expressive power, naturalness, flexibility, and portability [120]. SUGILITE combines speech and touch to enable a "speak and point" interaction style, which has been studied since early multi-modal systems like Put-that-there [23]. Prior systems such as CommandSpace [1], Speechify [60], Quick-Set [121], SMARTBoard [113], and PixelTone [70] investigated multi-modal interfaces that can map coordinated natural language instructions and GUI gestures to system commands and actions. In programming, similar interaction styles have also been used for controlling robots (e.g., [55, 104]). But the use of these systems are limited to specific first-party apps and task domains, in contrast to SUGILITE which aims to be general-purpose.

When SUGILITE addresses the data description problem (details in Sect. 5.2), demonstration is the primary modality; verbal instructions are used for disambiguating demonstrated actions. A key pattern used in SUGILITE is *mutual disambiguation* [119]. When the user demonstrates an action on the GUI with a simultaneous verbal instruction, our system can reliably detect what the user did and on which UI object the user performed the action. The demonstration alone, however, does not explain why the user performed the action, and any inferences on the user's intent would be fundamentally unreliable. Similarly, from verbal instructions alone, the system may learn about the user's intent, but grounding it onto a specific action may be difficult due to the inherent ambiguity in natural language. SUGILITE utilizes these complementary inputs to infer robust and generalizable scripts that can accurately represent user intentions in PBD. A similar multi-modal approach has been used for handling ambiguities in recognition-based interfaces [103], such as correcting speech recognition errors [138] and assisting the recognition of pen-based handwriting [67]. The recent DoThisHere [144] system uses a similar multi-modal interface for cross-app data query and transfer between multiple mobile apps.

In the parameterization and concept teaching components of SUGILITE, the natural language instructions come first. During the parametrization, the user first verbally describes the task, and then demonstrates the task from which SUGILITE infers parameters in the initial verbal instruction, and the corresponding possible values. In concept teaching, the user starts with describing an automation rule at a high-level in natural language, and then recursively defines any ambiguous or vague concepts by referring to app GUIs. SUGILITE's approach builds upon prior work like PLOW [3], which uses user verbal instructions to hint possible parameters, to further explore how GUI and GUI-based demonstrations can help enhance natural language inputs.

3.4 Understanding App Interfaces

A unique challenge for SUGILITE is to support multi-modal PBD on arbitrary third-party mobile app GUIs. Some of such GUIs can be complicated, with hundreds of entities, each with many different properties, semantic meanings, and relations with other entities. Moreover, third-party mobile apps only expose the low-level hierarchical representations of their GUIs at the presentation layer, without revealing information about internal program logic.

There has been some prior work on inferring semantics and task knowledge from GUIs. Prefab [40–42] introduces pixel-based methods to model interactive widgets and interface hierarchies in GUIs, and allowed runtime modifications of widget behaviors. Waken [12] also uses a computer vision approach to recognize GUI components and activities from screen captured videos. StateLens [48] and KITE [89] look at the sequence of GUI screens of completing a task, from which they can infer the task flow model with multiple different branches and states. The interaction mining approach used in ERICO [39] and RICO [38] captures the static (UI layout, visual features) and dynamic (user flows) parts of an app's design from a large corpus of user interaction traces with mobile apps. A similar approach was also used to learn the design semantics of mobile apps [99]. These approaches use a smaller number of discrete types of flows, GUI elements, and entities to represent GUI screens and their components, while our Screen2Vec uses continuous embedding in a vector space for screen representation.

Some prior techniques specifically focus on the visual aspect of GUIs. The RICO dataset [38] shows that it is feasible to train a GUI layout embedding with a large screen corpus, and retrieve screens with similar layouts using such embeddings. Chen et al.'s work [31] and Li et al.'s work [91] show that trained machine learning models can generate semantically meaningful natural language descriptions for GUI components based on their visual appearances and hierarchies. Compared with them, the Screen2Vec method (Sect. 5.6) used in SUGILITE provides a more holistic representation of GUI screens by encoding textual content, GUI component class types, and app-specific metadata in addition to the visual layout.

Another category of work in this area focuses on predicting GUI actions for completing a task objective. Pasupat et al.'s work [122] maps the user's natural language commands to target elements on web GUIs. Li et al.'s work [90] goes a step further by generating sequences of actions based on natural language commands. These works use the supervised approach that require a large amount of manually-annotated training data, which limits its utilization. In comparison, the Screen2Vec method used in SUGILITE uses a self-supervised approach that does not require any manual data annotation of user intents and tasks. Screen2Vec also does not need any annotation on the GUI screens themselves, unlike [148] which requires additional developer annotations for the metadata of GUI components.

SUGILITE faces a unique challenge—in SUGILITE, the user talks about the underlying task of an app in natural language while making references to the app's GUI. The system needs to have sufficient understanding about the content of the app GUI to be able to handle these verbal instructions to learn the task. Therefore, the goal of SUGILITE in understanding app interfaces is to abstract the semantics of GUIs from their platform-specific implementations, while being sufficiently aligned with the semantics of users' natural language instructions, so that it can leverage the GUI representation to help understanding the user's instruction of the underlying task.

4 System Overview

We present the prototype of a new task automation agent named SUGILITE.[2] This prototype integrates and implements the results from several of our prior research works [80–82, 84, 86–89]. The implementation of our system is also open-sourced on GitHub.[3] This section explains how SUGILITE learns new tasks and concepts from the multi-modal interactive instructions from the users.

The user starts with speaking a command. The command can describe either an action (e.g., "check the weather") or an automation rule with a condition (e.g., "If it is hot, order a cup of Iced Cappuccino"). Suppose that the agent has no prior knowledge in any of the involved task domains, then it will recursively resolve the unknown concepts and procedures used in the command. Although it does not know

---

[2] A demo video is available at https://www.youtube.com/watch?v=tdHEk-GeaqE.

[3] https://github.com/tobyli/Sugilite_development.

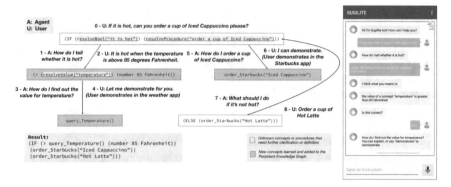

Fig. 1 An example dialog structure while SUGILITE learns a new task that contains a conditional and new concepts. The numbers indicate the sequence of the utterances. The screenshot on the right shows the conversational interface during these steps

these concepts, it can recognize the structure of the command (e.g., conditional), and parse each part of the command into the corresponding typed `resolve` functions, as shown in Fig. 1. SUGILITE uses a grammar-based executable semantic parsing architecture [92]; therefore, its conversation flow operates on the recursive execution of the `resolve` functions. Since the `resolve` functions are typed, the agent can generate prompts based on their types (e.g., "How do I tell whether..." for `resolveBool` and "How do I find out the value for..." for `resolveValue`).

When the SUGILITE agent reaches the `resolve` function for a value query or a procedure, it asks the users if they can demonstrate them. The users can then demonstrate how they would normally look up the value, or perform the procedure manually with existing mobile apps on the phone by direct manipulation (Fig. 3a). For any ambiguous demonstrated action, the user verbally explains the intent behind the action through multi-turn conversations with the help from an interaction proxy overlay that guides the user to focus on providing more effective input (see Fig. 3, more details in Sect. 5.2). When the user demonstrates a value query (e.g., finding out the value of the temperature), SUGILITE highlights the GUI elements showing values with the compatible types (see Fig. 2) to assist the user in finding the appropriate GUI element during the demonstration.

All user-instructed value concepts, Boolean concepts, and procedures automatically get generalized by SUGILITE. The procedures are parameterized so that they can be reused with different parameter values in the future. For example, for Utterance 8 in Fig. 1, the user does not need to demonstrate again since the system can invoke the newly-learned `order_Starbucks` function with a different parameter value (details in Sect. 5.3). The learned concepts and value queries are also generalized so that the system recognizes the different definitions of concepts like "hot" and value queries like "temperature" in different contexts (details in Sect. 5.4).

Fig. 2 The user teaches the value concept "commute time" by demonstrating querying the value in Google Maps. SUGILITE highlights all the duration values on the Google Maps GUI

5 Key Features

5.1 Using Demonstrations in Natural Language Instructions

SUGILITE allows users to use demonstrations to teach the agent any unknown procedures and concepts in their natural language instructions. As discussed earlier, a major challenge in ITL is that understanding natural language instructions and carrying out the tasks accordingly require having knowledge in the specific task domains. Our use of programming by demonstration (PBD) is an effective way to address this "out-of-domain" problem in both the task fulfillment and the natural language understanding processes [85]. In SUGILITE, procedural actions are represented as sequences of GUI operations, and declarative concepts can be represented as references to GUI content. This approach supports ITL for a wide range of tasks—virtually anything that can be performed with one or more existing third-party mobile apps.

Our prior study [88] also found that the availability of app GUI references can result in end users providing clearer natural language commands. In one study where we asked participants to instruct an intelligent agent to complete everyday computing tasks in natural language, the participants who saw screenshots of relevant apps used *fewer* unclear, vague, or ambiguous concepts in their verbal instructions than those who did not see the screenshots. By using demonstrations in natural language instructions, our multi-modal approach also makes understanding the user's natural language instructions easier by naturally constraining the user's expressions.

5.2   Spoken Intent Clarification for Demonstrated Actions

A major limitation of demonstrations is that they are too literal, and are, therefore, brittle to any changes in the task context. They encapsulate *what* the user did, but not *why* the user did it. When the context changes, the agent often may not know what to do, due to this lack of understanding of the user intents behind their demonstrated actions. This is known as the *data description problem* in the PBD community, and it is regarded as a key problem in PBD research [37, 94]. For example, just looking at the action shown in Fig. 3a, one cannot tell if the user meant "the restaurant with the most reviews", "the promoted restaurant", "the restaurant with 1,000 bonus points", "the cheapest Steakhouse", or any other criteria, so the system cannot generate a description for this action that accurately reflects the user's intent. A prior approach is to ask for multiple examples from the users [106], but this is often not feasible due to the user's inability to come up with useful and complete examples, and the amount of examples required for complex tasks [74, 116].

SUGILITE's approach is to ask users to verbally explain their intent for the demonstrated actions using speech. Our formative study [84] with 45 participants found that end users were able to provide useful and generalizable explanations for the intents of demonstrated actions. They also commonly used in their utterances semantic references to GUI content (e.g., "the close by restaurant" for an entry showing the text "596 ft") and implicit spatial references (e.g., "the score for Lakers" for a text object that contains a numeric value and is right-aligned to another text object "Lakers").

Based on these findings, we designed and implemented a multi-modal mixed-initiative intent clarification mechanism for demonstrated actions. As shown in Fig. 3, the user describes their intention in natural language, and iteratively refines the descriptions to remove ambiguity with the help of an interactive overlay (Fig. 3d). The overlay highlights the result from executing the current data description query, and helps the user focus on explaining the key differences between the target object (highlighted in red) and the false positives (highlighted in yellow) of the query.

a. User demonstrates the action directly on unmodified GUIs of third party apps

b. SUGILITE asks the user to describe intentions for actions

c. Multi-turn conversations help users refine ambiguous descriptions

d. User can view the result for the current query and the originally clicked UI object

e. SUGILITE generates formal executable data descrption queries to be used in automation scripts

Fig. 3 The screenshots of SUGILITE's demonstration mechanism and its multi-modal mixed-initiative intent clarification process for the demonstrated actions

To ground the user's natural language explanations about GUI elements, SUGILITE represents each GUI screen as a *UI snapshot graph*. This graph captures the GUI elements' text labels, meta-information (including screen position, type, and package name), and the spatial (e.g., `nextTo`), hierarchical (e.g., `hasChild`), and semantic relations (e.g., `containsPrice`) among them (Fig. 4). A semantic parser translates the user's explanation into a graph query on the UI snapshot graph, executes it on the graph, and verifies if the result matches the correct entity that the user originally demonstrated. The goal of this process is to generate a query that uniquely matches the target UI element and also reflects the user's underlying intent.

5.2.1 UI Snapshot Graph

Formally, we define a UI snapshot graph as a collection of *subject-predicate-object triples* denoted as (s, p, o), where the subject s and the object o are two entities, and the predicate p is a directed edge representing a relation between the subject and the object. In APPINITE's graph, an entity can either represent a view in the GUI, or a typed (e.g., string, integer, Boolean) constant value. This denotation is highly flexible—it can support a wide range of nested, aggregated, or composite queries. Furthermore, a similar representation is used in general-purpose knowledge bases such as DBpedia [9], Freebase [22], Wikidata [142], and WikiBrain [83], which can enable us to plug APPINITE's UI snapshot graph into these knowledge bases to support better semantic understanding of app GUIs in the future.

The first step in constructing a UI snapshot graph from the hierarchical tree extracted from the Android Accessibility Service is to flatten all views in the tree into a collection of view entities, allowing more flexible queries on the relations between entities on the graph. The hierarchical relations are still preserved in the graph, but converted into `hasChild` and `hasParent` relationships between the corresponding view entities. Properties (e.g., coordinates, text labels, class names) are also converted into relations, where the values of the properties are represented as entities. Two or more constants with the same value (e.g., two views with the same class name) are consolidated as a single constant entity connected to multiple view entities, allowing easy querying for views with shared properties values.

In GUI designs, horizontal or vertical alignments between objects often suggest a semantic relationship [5]. Generally, smaller geometric distance between two objects also correlates with higher semantic relatedness between them [46]. Therefore, it is important to support spatial relations in data descriptions. APPINITE adds spatial relationships between view entities to UI snapshot graphs based on the absolute coordinates of their bounding boxes, including `above`, `below`, `rightTo`, `leftTo`, `nextTo`, and `near` relations. These relations capture not only explicit spatial references in natural language (e.g., the button next to something), but also implicit ones (see Fig. 4 for an example). In APPINITE, thresholds in the heuristics for determining these spatial relations are relative to the dimension of the screen, which supports generalization across phones with different resolutions and screen sizes.

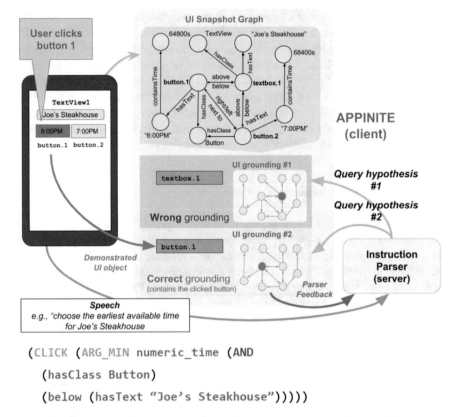

```
(CLICK (ARG_MIN numeric_time (AND
   (hasClass Button)
   (below (hasText "Joe's Steakhouse"))))))
```

Fig. 4 SUGILITE's instruction parsing and grounding process for intent clarifications illustrated on an example UI snapshot graph constructed from a simplified GUI snippet

APPINITE also recognizes some semantic information from the raw strings found in the GUI to support grounding the user's high-level linguistic inputs (e.g., "*item with the <u>lowest</u> price*"). To achieve this, APPINITE applies a pipeline of data extractors on each string entity in the graph to extract structured data (e.g., phone number, email address) and numerical measurements (e.g., price, distance, time, duration), and saves them as new entities in the graph. These new entities are connected to the original string entities by `contains` relations (e.g., `containsPrice`). Values in each category of measurements are normalized to the same units so they can be directly compared, allowing flexible computation, filtering, and aggregation.

5.2.2 Parsing

Our semantic parser uses a Floating Parser architecture [123] and is implemented with the SEMPRE framework [16]. We represent UI snapshot graph queries in a simple but flexible LISP-like query language (S-expressions) that can represent joins, conjunctions, superlatives and their compositions, constructed by the following 7 grammar rules:

$$E \rightarrow e; E \rightarrow S; S \rightarrow (\text{join } r\ E); S \rightarrow (\text{and } S\ S)$$
$$T \rightarrow (\text{ARG\_MAX } r\ S); T \rightarrow (\text{ARG\_MIN } r\ S); Q \rightarrow S \mid T$$

where Q is the root non-terminal of the query expression, e is a terminal that represents a UI object entity, r is a terminal that represents a relation, and the rest of the non-terminals are used for intermediate derivations. SUGILITE's language forms a subset of a more general formalism known as Lambda Dependency-based Compositional Semantics [93], which is a notationally simpler alternative to lambda calculus which is particularly well-suited for expressing queries over knowledge graphs. More technical details and the user evaluation are discussed in [84].

5.3 Task Parameterization Through GUI Grounding

Another way SUGILITE leverages GUI groundings in the natural language instructions is to infer task parameters and their possible values. This allows the agent to learn generalized procedures (e.g., to order *any kind of beverage* from Starbucks) from a demonstration of a specific instance of the task (e.g., ordering an iced cappuccino).

SUGILITE achieves this by comparing the user utterance (e.g., "order a cup of iced cappuccino") against the *data descriptions* of the target UI elements (e.g., click on the menu item that has the text "Iced Cappuccino") and the arguments (e.g., put "Iced Cappuccino" into a search box) of the demonstrated actions for matches. This process grounds different parts in the utterances to specific actions in the demonstrated procedure. It then analyzes the hierarchical structure of GUI at the time of demonstration, and looks for alternative GUI elements that are in parallel to the original target GUI element structurally. In this way, it extracts the other possible values for the identified parameter, such as the names of all the other drinks displayed in the same menu as "Iced Cappuccino"

The extracted sets of possible parameter values are also used for disambiguating the procedures to invoke, such as invoking the `order_Starbucks` procedure for the command "order a cup of *latte*", but invoking the `order_PapaJohns` procedure for the command "order a *cheese pizza*."

5.4 Generalizing the Learned Concepts

In addition to the procedures, SUGILITE also automatically generalizes the learned *concepts* in order to reuse parts of existing concepts as much as possible to avoid requiring users to perform redundant demonstrations [88].

For Boolean concepts, SUGILITE assumes that the type of the Boolean operation and the types of the arguments stay the same, but the arguments themselves may differ. For example, for the concept "hot" in Fig. 1, it should still mean that a temperature (of something) is greater than another temperature. But the two in comparison can be different constants, or from different value queries. For example, suppose after the interactions in Fig. 1, the user instructs a new rule "*if the oven is hot, start the cook timer.*" PUMICE can recognize that "hot" is a concept that has been instructed before in a different context, so it asks "*I already know how to tell whether it is hot when determining whether to order a cup of Iced Cappuccino. Is it the same here when determining whether to start the cook timer?*" After responding "No", the user can instruct how to find out the temperature of the oven, and the new threshold value for the condition "hot" either by instructing a new value concept, or using a constant value.

The generalization mechanism for value concepts works similarly. PUMICE supports value concepts that share the same name to have different query implementations for different task contexts. For example, following the "if the oven is hot, start the cook timer" example, suppose the user defines "hot" for this new context as "*The temperature is above 400 degrees.*" PUMICE realizes that there is already a value concept named "temperature", so it will ask "*I already know how to find out the value for temperature using the Weather app. Should I use that for determining whether the oven is hot?*", to which the user can say "No" and then demonstrate querying the temperature of the oven using the corresponding app (assuming the user has a smart oven with an in-app display of its temperature).

This mechanism allows learned concepts like "hot" to be reused at three different levels: *(i)* exactly the same (e.g., the temperature of the weather is greater than 85°F); *(ii)* with a different threshold (e.g., the temperature of the weather is greater than x); and *(iii)* with a different value query (e.g., the temperature of *something else* is greater than x).

5.5 Breakdown Repairs in Task-Oriented Dialogs

Another important challenge in facilitating effective human-AI collaboration with ITL agents is to support the discovery and repair of conversational breakdowns. Despite the advances in the agent's natural language understanding capabilities, it is still far from being able to understand the wide range of flexible user utterances and engage in complex dialog flows [47]. Existing agents employ rigid communication patterns, requiring that users adapt their communication patterns to the needs of the system instead of the other way around [14, 59]. As a result,conversational breakdowns, defined as failures of the system to correctly understand the intended meaning of the user's communication, often occur. Conversational breakdowns decrease users' satisfaction, trust, and willingness to continue using a conversational system [15, 58, 101].

Beneteau et al.'s deployment study [14] of Alexa showed that a major barrier for the users to repair conversational breakdowns is that their understandings of the causes of the breakdowns are frequently inaccurate, as a result, the repair strategies they naturally use are often ineffective. Other studies [8, 21, 34, 59, 117, 124]

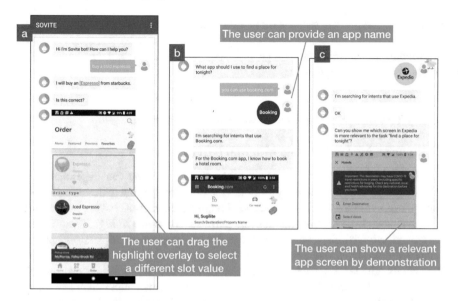

Fig. 5 The interface of SOVITE: **a** SOVITE shows a app GUI screenshot to communicates its state of understanding. The yellow highlight overlay specifies the task slot value. The user can drag the overlay to fix slot value errors. **b** To fix intent detection errors, the user can refer to an app that represents their desired task. SOVITE will match the utterance to an app on the phone (with its icon shown), and look for intents that use or are relevant to this app. **c** If the intent is still ambiguous after referring to an app, the user can show a specific app screen relevant to the desired task

reported similar findings of the types of breakdowns encountered by users and the common repair strategies. In a taxonomy of conversational breakdown repair strategies by Ashktorab et al. [8], repair strategies can be categorized into dimensions of: (1) whether there is evidence of breakdown (i.e., whether the system makes users aware of the breakdown); (2) whether the system attempts to repair (e.g., provide options of potential intents), and (3) whether assistance is provided for user self-repair (e.g., highlight the keywords that contribute to the intent classifier's decision). Among them, the most preferred option by the users was to have the system attempt to help with the repair process by providing options of potential intents. However, as discussed, this approach requires domain-specific "deep knowledge" about the task and error handling flows manually programmed by the developers [5, 107], and therefore, is not practical for user-instructed tasks. The second most preferred strategy in [8] was for the system to provide more transparency into the cause of the breakdown, such as highlighting the keywords that contribute to the results.

Informed by these results, we developed SOVITE,[4] a new interface for SUGILITE that helps users discover, identify the causes of, and recover from conversational breakdowns using a app-grounded multi-modal approach (Fig. 5). Compared with

---

[4] SOVITE is named after a type of rock. It is also an acronym for **S**ystem for **O**ptimizing **V**oice **I**nterfaces to **T**ackle **E**rrors.

the domain-specific approaches that require "deep knowledge", our approach does not require any additional efforts from the developers. It only requires "shallow knowledge" in a domain-general generic language model to map user intents to the corresponding app screens.

5.5.1   The Design of the Breakdown Handling Interface

Communicating System State with App GUI Screenshots

The first step for SOVITE in supporting the users in repairing conversational break-downs is to provide transparency into the state of understanding in the system, allow-ing the users to discover breakdowns and identify their causes. SOVITE leverages the GUI screenshots of mobile apps for this purpose. As shown in Fig. 5a, for the user command, SOVITE displays one or more (when there are multiple slots spanning many screens) screenshots from an app that corresponds to the detected user intent. For intents with slots, it shows screens that contain the GUI widgets corresponding to where the slots would be filled if the task was performed manually using the app GUI. SOVITE also adds a highlight overlay, shown in yellow in Fig. 5a, on top of the app's GUI, which indicates the current slot value. If the slot represents selecting an item from a menu in the GUI, then the corresponding menu item will be high-lighted on the screenshot. For an intent without a slot, SOVITE displays the last GUI screen from the procedure of performing the task manually, which usually shows the result of the task. After displaying the screenshot(s), SOVITE asks the user to confirm the understanding of the user's intent. by asking, "I will…[the task], is this correct?", to which the user can verbally respond.

Design Rationale SOVITE's references to app GUIs help with *grounding* in human-agent interactions. In communication theory, the concept of grounding describes conversation as a form of collaborative action to come up with common ground or mutual knowledge [35]. For conversations with computing systems, when the user provides an utterance, the system should provide evidence of understanding so that the user can evaluate the progress toward their goal [26]. As described in the *gulf of evaluation* and *gulf of execution* framework [54, 118] and shown in prior studies of conversational agents [8, 14], execution and evaluation are interdependent—in order to choose an effective strategy for repairing a conversational breakdown, the user needs to first know the current state of understanding in the system and be able to understand the cause of the breakdown. We believe this approach should help users to more effectively identify the understanding errors because it provides better *closeness of mapping* [46] to how the user would naturally approach this task.

Intent Detection Repair with App GUI References

When an intent detection result is incorrect, as evidenced by the wrong app or the wrong functionality of app shown in a confirmation screenshot, or when the agent fails to detect an intent from the user's initial utterance at all (i.e., the system responds

"I don't understand the command."), the user can fix the error by indicating the correct apps and app screens for their desired task.

References to Apps After the user says that the detected intent is incorrect after seeing the app GUI screenshots, or when the system fails to detect an intent, SOVITE asks the user "What app should I use to perform... [the task]?", for which the user can say the name of an app for the intended task (shown in Fig. 5b). SOVITE looks up the collection of all supported task intents for not only the intents that *use* this underlying app, but also intents that are semantically *related* to the supplied app.

References to App Screens In certain situations, the user's intent can still be ambiguous after the user indicates the name of an app; there can be multiple intents associated with the app (for example, if the user specifies "Expedia" which can be used for booking flights, cruises, or rental cars), or there can be no supported task intent in the user-provided app and no intent that meets the threshold of being sufficiently "related" to the user-provided app. In these situations, SOVITE will ask the user a follow-up question "Can you show me which screen in... [the app]] is most relevant to... [the task]?" (shown in Fig. 5c). SOVITE then launches the app and asks the user to navigate to the target screen in the app. SOVITE then finds intents that are the most semantically related to this app screen among the ambiguous ones, or asks the user to teach it a new one by demonstration.

Ease of Transition to Out-of-Domain Task Instructions An important advantage of SOVITE's intent disambiguation approach is that it supports the easy transition to the user *instruction* of a new task when the user's intended task is out of scope. An effective approach to support handling out of scope errors is programming-by-demonstration (PBD) [85]. SOVITE's approach can directly connect to the user instruction mode in SUGILITE. Since at this point, SOVITE already knows the most relevant app and app screen for the user's intended task and how to navigate to this screen in the app, it can simply ask the user "Can you teach me how to... [the task] using... [the app] in this screen", switch back to this screen, and have the user to continue demonstrating the intended task to teach the agent how to fulfill the previously out of scope task intent. The user may also start over and demonstrate from scratch if they do not want to start the instruction from this screen.

Design Rationale The main design rationale of supporting intent detection repairs with app GUI references is to make SOVITE's mechanism of fixing intent detection errors *consistent* with how users discover the errors from SOVITE's display of intent detection results. When users discover the intent detection errors by seeing the wrong apps or the wrong screens displayed in the confirmation screenshots, the most intuitive way for them to fix these errors is to indicate the correct apps and screens that should be used for the intended tasks. Their references to the apps and the screens also allow SOVITE to extract richer semantic context (e.g., the app store descriptions and the text labels found on app GUI screens) than having the user simply rephrase their utterances, helping with finding semantically related task intents.

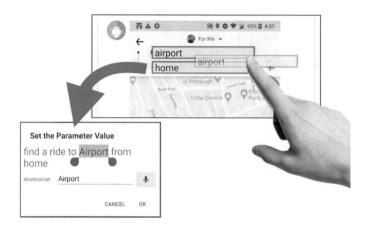

Fig. 6 SOVITE provides multiple ways to fix text-input slot value errors: *LEFT*: the user can click the corresponding highlight overlay and change its value by adjusting the selection in the original utterance, speaking a new value, or just typing in a new value. *RIGHT*: the user can drag the overlays on the screenshot to move a value to a new slot, or swap the values between two slots

Slot Value Extraction Repair with Direct Manipulation

If the user finds that the intent is correct (i.e., the displayed app and app screen correctly match the user's intended task), but there are errors in the extracted task slot values (i.e., the highlighted textboxes, the values in the highlighted textboxes, or the highlighted menu items on the confirmation screenshots are wrong), the user can fix these errors using direct manipulation on the screenshots.

All the highlight overlays for task slots can be dragged-and-dropped. For slots represented by GUI menu selections, the user can simply drag the highlight overlay to select a different item, as shown in Fig. 5a. The same interaction technique also works for fixing mismatches in the text-input type slot values. For example, if the agent swaps the order between starting location and destination in a "requesting Uber ride" intent, the user can drag these overlays with location names to move them to the right fields in the app GUI screenshot (Fig. 6). When a field is dragged to another field that already has a value, SOVITE performs a *swap* rather than a *replace* so as not to lose any user-supplied data.

Alternatively, when the value for a text-input type slot is incorrect, the user can repair it using the popup dialog shown in Fig. 6. After the user clicks on the highlight overlay for a text-input slot, a dialog will pop up, showing the slot's current value in the user's original utterance. The user can adjust the text selection by dragging the highlight boundaries in the identified entities. The same dialog alternatively allows the user to just enter a new slot value by speech or typing.

Design Rationale We believe these direct manipulation interactions in SOVITE are intuitive to the users. The positions and the contents of the highlight overlays represent where and what slot values would be entered if the task was performed using the GUI of the corresponding app. Therefore, if what SOVITE identified does not match what the users would do for the intended task, the users can directly fix these *inconsistencies* through simple physical actions such as drag-and-drop and text selection gestures, and see immediate feedback on the screenshots, which are major advantages of direct manipulation [134].

5.6 The Semantic Representation of GUIs

With the rise of data-driven computational methods for modeling user interactions with graphical user interfaces (GUIs), the GUI screens have become not only interfaces for human users to interact with the underlying computing services, but also valuable data sources that encode the underlying task flow, the supported user interactions, and the design patterns of the corresponding apps, which have proven useful for AI-powered applications. For example, programming-by-demonstration (PBD) intelligent agents such as [80, 88, 132] use task-relevant entities and hierarchical structures extracted from GUIs to parameterize, disambiguate, and handle errors in user-demonstrated task automation scripts. ERICA [39] mines a large repository of mobile app GUIs to enable user interface (UI) designers to search for example design patterns to inform their own design. Kite [89] extracts task flows from mobile app GUIs to bootstrap conversational agents.

We present a new self-supervised technique Screen2Vec for generating semantic representations of GUI screens and components using their textual content, visual design and layout patterns, and app context metadata. Screen2Vec's approach is inspired by the popular word embedding method Word2Vec [111], where the embedding vector representations of GUI screens and components are generated through the process of training a prediction model. But unlike Word2Vec, Screen2Vec uses a two-layer pipeline informed by the structures of GUIs and GUI interaction traces and incorporates screen- and app-specific metadata.

The embedding vector representations produced by Screen2Vec can be used in a variety of useful downstream tasks such as nearest neighbor retrieval, composability-based retrieval, and representing mobile tasks. The self-supervised nature of Screen2Vec allows its model to be trained without any manual data labeling efforts—it can be trained with a large collection of GUI screens and the user interaction traces on these screens such as the RICO [38] dataset.

Screen2Vec addresses an important gap in prior work about computational HCI research. The lack of comprehensive semantic representations of GUI screens and components has been identified as a major limitation in prior work in GUI-based interactive task learning (e.g., [88, 132]), intelligent suggestive interfaces (e.g., [30]), assistive tools (e.g., [19]), and GUI design aids (e.g., [72, 139]). Screen2Vec embeddings can encode the semantics, contexts, layouts, and patterns of GUIs, providing representations of these types of information in a form that can be easily and effectively incorporated into popular modern machine learning models.

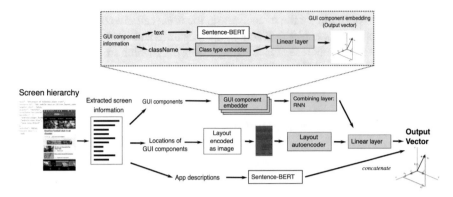

Fig. 7 The two-level architecture of Screen2Vec for generating GUI component and screen embeddings. The weights for the steps in teal color are optimized during the training process

5.6.1 Screen2Vec's Approach

Figure 7 illustrates the architecture of Screen2Vec. Overall, the pipeline of Screen2Vec consists of two levels: the GUI component level (shown in the gray shade) and the GUI screen level. We will describe the approach at a high-level here, you may refer to [87] for the implementation details.

The GUI component level model encodes the textual content and the class type of a GUI component into a 768-dimensional embedding vector to represent the GUI component (e.g., a button, a textbox, a list entry etc.) This GUI component embedding vector is computed with two inputs: (1) a 768-dimensional embedding vector of the text label of the GUI component, encoded using a pre-trained Sentence-BERT [128] model; and (2) a 6-dimensional class embedding vector that represents the class type of the GUI component. The two embedding vectors are combined using a linear layer, resulting in the 768-dimensional GUI component embedding vector that represents the GUI component. The class embeddings in the class type embedder and the weights in the linear layer are optimized through training a Continuous Bag-of-Words (CBOW) prediction task: for each GUI component on each screen, the task predicts the current GUI component using its context (i.e., all the other GUI components on the same screen). The training process optimizes the weights in the class embeddings and the weights in the linear layer for combining the text embedding and the class embedding.

The GUI screen level model encodes the textual content, visual design and layout patterns, and app context of a GUI screen into an 1536-dimensional embedding vector. This GUI screen embedding vector is computed using three inputs: (1) the collection of the GUI component embedding vectors for all the GUI components on the screen (as described in the last paragraph), combined into a 768-dimension vector using a recurrent neural network model (RNN); (2) a 64-dimensional layout embedding vector that encodes the screen's visual layout; and (3) a 768-dimensional embedding vector of the textual App Store description for the underlying app, encoded with a pre-trained Sentence-BERT [128] model. These GUI and layout vectors are combined using a linear layer, resulting in a 768-dimensional vector. After training, the description embedding vector is concatenated on, resulting in the 1536-dimensional GUI screen embedding vector (if included in the training, the description dominates the entire embedding, overshadowing information specific to that screen within the app). The weights in the RNN layer for combining GUI component embeddings and the weights in the linear layer for producing the final output vector are similarly trained on a CBOW prediction task on a large number of interaction traces (each represented as a sequence of screens). For each trace, a sliding window moves over the sequence of screens. The model tries to use the representation of the context (the surrounding screens) to predict the screen in the middle.

In the training process, we trained `Screen2Vec`[5] on the open-sourced RICO[6] dataset [38]. The RICO dataset contains interaction traces on 66,261 unique GUI screens from 9,384 free Android apps collected using a hybrid crowdsourcing plus automated discovery approach. The models are trained on a cross entropy loss function with an Adam optimizer [63]. In training the GUI screen embedding model, we use *negative sampling* [110, 111] so that we do not have to recalculate and update every screen's embedding on every training iteration, which is computationally expensive and prone to over-fitting. In each iteration, the prediction is compared to the correct screen and a sample of negative data that consists of: a random sampling of size 128 of other screens, the other screens in the batch, and the screens in the same trace as the correct screen, used in the prediction task. We specifically include the screens in the same trace to promote screen-specific learning in this process: This way, we can disincentive screen embeddings that are based solely on the app[7], and emphasize on having the model learn to differentiate the different screens within the same app. You can refer to [87] for details on the training process.

Prediction Task Results

In the screen prediction task, the `Screen2Vec` model performs better than three baseline models (`TextOnly`, `LayoutOnly`, and `VisualOnly`; see [87] for details on the baseline models) in top-1 prediction accuracy, top-k prediction accuracy, and the *normalized* rooted mean square error (RMSE) of the predicted screen embedding vector. See [87] for details on the results and the relevant discussions.

---

[5] Available at: https://github.com/tobyli/screen2vec.

[6] Available at: http://interactionmining.org/rico.

[7] Since the next screen is always within the same app, and therefore, shares an app description embedding, the prediction task favors having information about the specific app (i.e., app store description embedding) dominate the embedding

5.6.2 Sample Downstream Tasks

Nearest Neighbors

The nearest neighbor task is useful for data-driven design, where the designers want to find examples for inspiration and for understanding the possible design solutions [38]. The task focuses on the similarity between GUI screen embeddings: for a given screen, what are the top-N most similar screens in the dataset? The similar technique can also be used for unsupervised clustering in the dataset to infer different types of GUI screens. In our context, this task also helps demonstrate the different characteristics between Screen2Vec and the three baseline models.

We conducted a study with 79 Mechanical Turk workers, where we compared the human-rated similarity of the nearest neighbors results generated by Screen2Vec with the baseline models on 5,608 pairs of screen instances. The Mechanical Turk workers rated the nearest neighbor screens generated by the Screen2Vec model to be, on average, more similar ($p < 0.0001$) to their source screens than the nearest neighbor screens generated by the baseline models (details on study design and results in [87]).

Subjectively, when looking at the nearest neighbor results, we can see the different aspects of the GUI screens that each different model captures. Screen2Vec can create more comprehensive representations that encode the textual content, visual design and layout patterns, and app contexts of the screen compared with the two baselines, which only capture one or two aspects. For example, Fig. 8 shows the example nearest neighbor results for the "request ride" screen in the Lyft app. Screen2Vec model retrives the "get direction" screen in the Uber Driver app, "select navigation type" screen in the Waze app, and "request ride" screen in the Free Now (My Taxi) app. Visual and component layout wise, the result screens all feature a menu/information card at the bottom 1/3 to 1/4 of the screen, with a MapView taking the majority of the screen space. Content and app domain wise, all these screens are from transportation-related apps that allow the user to configure a trip. In comparison, the TextOnly model retrieves the "request ride" screen from the zTrip app, the "main menu" screen from the Hailo app (both zTrip and Hailo are taxi hailing apps), and the home screen of the Paytm app (a mobile payment app in India). The commonality of these screens is that they all include text strings that are semantically similar to "payment" (e.g., add payment type, wallet, pay, add money), and texts that are semantically similar to "destination" and "trips" (e.g., drop off location, trips, bus, flights). But the model neither considers the visual layout and design patterns of the screens, nor the app context. Therefore, the result contains the "main menu" (a quite different type of screen) in the Hailo app and the "home screen" in the Paytm app (a quite different type of screen in a different type of app). The LayoutOnly model, on the other hand, retrieves the "exercise logging" screens from the Map My Walk app and the Map My Ride app, and the tutorial screen from the Clever Dialer app. We can see that the content and app-context similarity of the result of the LayoutOnly model is quite lower than those of the Screen2Vec and TextOnly models. However, the result screens all share similar layout features as the source screen, such as the

Fig. 8 The example nearest neighbor results for the Lyft "request ride" screen generated by the Screen2Vec, TextOnly, and LayoutOnly models

menu/information card at the bottom of the screen and the screen-wide button at the bottom of the menu (Fig. 8).

Embedding Composability

A useful property of embeddings is that they are composable—meaning that we can add, subtract, and average embeddings to form a meaningful new one. This property is commonly used in word embeddings. For example, in Word2Vec, analogies such as "man is to woman as brother is to sister" is reflected in that the vector $(man - woman)$ is similar to the vector $(brother - sister)$. Besides representing analogies, this embedding composability can also be utilized for generative purposes—for example, $(brother - man + woman)$ results in an embedding vector that represents "sister".

This property is also useful in screen embeddings. For example, we can run a nearest neighbor query on the composite embedding of (Marriott app 's "hotel booking" screen + (Cheapoair app's "search result" screen − Cheapoair app's "hotel booking" screen)). The top result is the "search result" screen in the Marriott app.

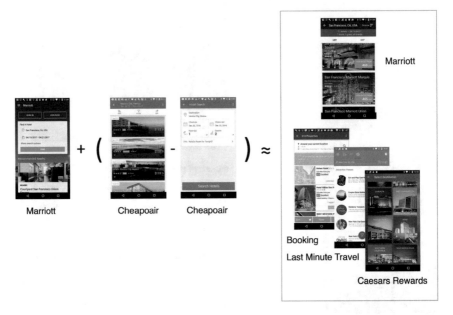

Fig. 9 An example showing the composability of Screen2Vec embeddings: running the nearest neighbor query on the composite embedding of (Marriott app 's hotel booking page + Cheapoair app's hotel booking page − Cheapoair app's search result page) can match the Marriott app's search result page, and the similar pages of a few other travel apps

When we filter the result to focus on screens from apps other than Marriott, we get screens that show list results of items from other travel-related apps such as Booking, Last Minute Travel, and Caesars Rewards.

The composability can make Screen2Vec particularly useful for GUI design purposes—the designer can leverage the composability to find inspiring examples of GUI designs and layouts.

Screen Embedding Sequences for Representing Mobile Tasks

GUI screens are not only useful data sources individually on their own, but also as building blocks to represent a user's task. A task in an app, or across multiple apps, can be represented as a sequence of GUI screens that makes up the user interaction trace of performing this task through app GUIs. We conduct a preliminary evaluation on the effectiveness of embedding mobile tasks as sequences of Screen2Vec screen embedding vectors (details in [87]).

While the task embedding method we explored is quite primitive, it illustrates that the Screen2Vec technique can be used to effectively encode mobile tasks into the vector space where semantically similar tasks are close to each other. For the next steps, we plan to further explore this direction. For example, the current method of averaging all the screen embedding vectors does not consider the order of the screens in the sequence. In the future, we may collect a dataset of human annotations of task similarity, and use techniques that can encode the sequences of items, such as recurrent neural networks (RNN) and long short-term memory (LSTM) networks, to create the task embeddings from sequences of screen embeddings. We may also incorporate the Screen2Vec embeddings of the GUI components that were interacted with (e.g., the button that was clicked on) to initiate the screen change into the pipeline for embedding tasks.

5.6.3   Potential Applications of Screen2Vec

This section describes several potential applications where the new Screen2Vec technique can be useful based on the downstream tasks described in Sect. 5.6.2.

Screen2Vec can enable new GUI design aids that take advantage of the nearest neighbor similarity and composability of Screen2Vec embeddings. Prior work such as [38, 52, 66] has shown that data-driven tools that enable designers to curate design examples are quite useful for interface designers. Unlike [38], which uses a content-agnostic approach that focuses on the visual and layout similarities, Screen2Vec considers the textual content and app metadata in addition to the visual and layout patterns, often leading to different nearest neighbor results as discussed in section. This new type of similarity results will also be useful when focusing on interface design beyond just visual and layout issues, as the results enable designers to query, for example, designs that display similar content or screens that are used in apps in a similar domain. The composability in Screen2Vec embeddings enables querying for design examples at a finer granularity. For example, suppose a designer wishes to find examples for inspiring the design of a new checkout page for app A. They may query for the nearest neighbors of the synthesized embedding App A's order page $+$ (App B's checkout page $-$ App B's order page). Compared with simply querying for the nearest neighbors of App B's checkout page, this synthesized query can encode the interaction context (i.e., the desired page should be the checkout page for App A's order page) in addition to the "checkout" semantics.

The Screen2Vec embeddings can also be useful in generative GUI models. Recent models such as the neural design network (NDN) [73] and LayoutGAN [79] can generate realistic GUI layouts based on user-specified constraints (e.g., alignments, relative positions between GUI components). Screen2Vec can be used in these generative approaches to incorporate the semantics of GUIs and the contexts of how each GUI screen and component gets used in user interactions. For example, the GUI component prediction model can estimate the likelihood of each GUI component given the context of the other components in a generated screen, providing a heuristic of how likely the GUI components can fit well with each other. Similarly, the GUI screen prediction model may be used as a heuristic to synthesize GUI screens that can better fit with the other screens in the planned user interaction flows. Since Screen2Vec has been shown effective in representing mobile tasks in Sect. 5.6.2, where similar tasks will yield similar embeddings, one may also use the task embeddings of performing the same task on an existing app to inform the generation of new screen designs. The embedding vector form of `Screen2Vec` representations made them particularly suitable for use in the recent neural network based generative models.

`Screen2Vec`'s capability of embedding tasks can also enhance interactive task learning systems. Specifically, `Screen2Vec` may be used to enable more powerful procedure generalizations of the learned tasks. We have shown that the `Screen2Vec` model can effectively predict screens in an interaction trace. Results in Sect. 5.6.2 also indicated that `Screen2Vec` can embed mobile tasks so that the interaction traces of completing the same task in different apps will be similar to each other in the embedding vector space. Therefore, it is quite promising that `Screen2Vec` may be used to generalize a task learned from the user by demonstration in one app to another app in the same domain (e.g., generalizing the procedure of ordering coffee in the Starbucks app to the Dunkin' Donut app). In the future, we plan to further explore this direction by incorporating `Screen2Vec` into open-sourced mobile interactive task learning agents such as SUGILITE.

6   User Evaluations

We conducted several lab user studies to evaluate the usability, efficiency, and effectiveness of SUGILITE. The results of these study showed that end users without significant programming expertise were able to successfully teach the agent the procedures of performing common tasks (e.g., ordering pizza, requesting Uber, checking sports score, ordering coffee) [80], conditional rules for triggering the tasks [88], and concepts relevant to the tasks (e.g., the weather is *hot*, the traffic is *heavy*) [88] using SUGILITE. The users were also able to clarify their intents when ambiguities arise [84] and successfully discover, identify the sources of, and repair conversational breakdowns caused by natural language understanding errors [82]. Most of our participants found SUGILITE easy and natural to use [80, 84, 88]. Efficiency wise, teaching a task usually took the user 3–6 times longer than how long it took to perform the task manually in our studies [80], which indicates that teaching a task using SUGILITE can save time for many repetitive tasks.

7   Limitations

7.1   Platform

SUGILITE and its follow-up work have been developed and tested only on Android phones. SUGILITE retrieves the hierarchical tree structure of the current GUI screen and manipulates the app GUI through Android's Accessibility API. However, the approach used in SUGILITE should apply to any GUI-based apps with hierarchical-based structures (e.g., the hierarchical DOM structures in web apps). In certain platforms like iOS, while the app GUIs still use hierarchical tree structures, the access to extracting information from and sending inputs to third-party apps has been restricted by the operating system due to security and privacy concerns. In such platforms, implementing a SUGILITE-like system likely requires collaboration with the OS provider (e.g., Apple) or limiting the domain to first-party apps. We also expect working with desktop apps to be more challenging than with mobile apps due to the increased difficulty in inferring their GUI semantics, as the desktop apps often have more complex layouts and more heterogeneous design patterns.

7.2 Runtime Efficiency

An important characteristic of SUGILITE is that it interacts with the underlying third-party app in the same way as a human user do, meaning that it reads information by navigating to the corresponding app screen through the app GUI menu and performs a task by manipulating the app GUI controls. While this approach provides excellent applicability for SUGILITE, allowing the invocation of millions of existing third-party apps without any modification to these apps, it also means that performing a task in SUGILITE is much slower than in an agent that directly invokes the under-the-hood API. It usually takes SUGILITE a few seconds to execute a task automation script. This includes the time needed for SUGILITE to process each screen, plus the extra time for the underlying app to load and to render its GUI.

Another implication of how SUGILITE interacts with the underlying apps is that it needs to run in the foreground of the phone. If an automation script is triggered when the user is actively using the phone at the same time, the user's current task will be interrupted. Similarly, if an external event (e.g., an incoming phone call) interrupts in the middle of executing an automation script, the script execution may fail. One possible way to address the problem is to execute SUGILITE scripts in a virtual machine running in the background, similar to X-Droid [62]. We will leave this for future work.

7.3 Expressiveness

SUGILITE has made several contributions in improving the user expressiveness in programming by demonstration and interactive task learning systems. However, there are still several limitations in SUGILITE's expressiveness, which we plan to address in future work.

The first type of limitations originates from SUGILITE's domain-specific language (DSL) used to specify its automation scripts. For example, it has no support for nested arithmetic operations in the DSL (e.g., one can say "if the price of a Uber ride is greater than 10 dollars" and "if the price of a Uber ride is greater than the price of a

Lyft ride", but not "if the price of a Uber ride is at least 10 dollars more expensive than the price of a Lyft ride.") mostly due to the extra complication in semantic parsing. Correctly parsing the user's natural language description of arithmetic operations into our DSL would likely require a more complicated parsing architecture with a much larger training corpus. It also does not support loops in automation (e.g., "order one of each item in the "Espresso Drinks" category in the Starbucks app"). This is due to SUGILITE's limited capability to capture the internal "states" within the apps and to return to a specific previous state. For example, in the "ordering one of each item" task, the agent needs to return to the GUI state showing the list of items after completing the ordering of the first item in order to order the second item. This cannot be easily done with the current SUGILITE agent. Even if SUGILITE was able to find the "same" (visually similar or have the same activity name) screen, SUGILITE cannot know if the internal state of the underlying app has changed (e.g., adding the first item to the cart affects what other items are available for purchase).

Another limitation in expressiveness is due to the input modalities that SUGILITE tracks in the user demonstrations—it only records a set of common input types (clicks, long-clicks, text entries, etc.) on app GUIs. Gestures (e.g., swipes, flicks), sensory inputs (e.g., tilting or shaking the phone detected by the accelerometer and the gyroscope, auditory inputs from the microphone), and visual inputs (from the phone camera) are not recorded.

7.4 Brittleness

While many measures have been taken to help SUGILITE handle minor changes in app GUIs, SUGILITE scripts can still be brittle after the a change in the underlying app GUI due to either an app update or an external event. As discussed in Sect. 5.2, SUGILITE uses a graph query to locate the correct GUI element to operate on when executing an automation script. Instead of using the absolute (x, y) coordinates for identifying a GUI element like some prior systems do, SUGILITE picks one or more features such as the text label, the ordinal position in a list (e.g., first item in the search result), or the relative position to another GUI element (e.g., the "book" button next to the cheapest flight) that corresponds to the user's intent. Therefore, if a GUI change does not affect the result of the graph query, the automation should still work. In the future, it is possible to further enhance SUGILITE's capability of understanding screen semantics, so that it can automatically detect and handle some of these unexpected screens that do not affect the task without user intervention.

8 Future Work

8.1 Generalization in Programming by Demonstration

Generalization is a central challenge in programming by demonstration [37, 94]. SUGILITE has made several important improvements to the generalization capabilities of the current state-of-art programming by demonstration systems through (1) its multi-modal approach for parameterizing task procedures by combining entities from the user's spoken instructions with information extracted from the hierarchical app GUI structures; and (2) its app-based abstraction model for generalizing learned concepts such as "hot" and "busy" across different apps.

However, there are still opportunities for supporting more powerful generalization. The embedding technique described in Sect. 5.6 opens up the opportunity of cross-app generalization, i.e., when the user has taught performing a task in an app, can the agent generalize the learned procedure to perform a similar task in a different app? Sect. 5.6.2 shows that a task procedure can be represented as a sequence of actions that each consists of (1) the embedding of the screen where the action is performed; and (2) the embedding of the GUI component on which the action is performed, while Sect. 5.6.2 illustrates that it is feasible to find the "equivalence" of a screen in a new app (e.g., locating the search screen in the Cheapoair app based on the search screen in the Marriott app) through arithmetic operations on the screen embeddings. In future work, We plan to explore the design of new mechanisms and their corresponding interfaces that leverage these characteristics of screen embeddings to allow the agent to generalize the learned tasks across different apps with the help from the user.

This approach is inspired by our observation on how human users use unfamiliar apps. In most cases, a user would be able to use an unfamiliar app to perform a task if they have used a similar app before because (1) they have the domain-agnostic knowledge of how mobile apps *generally* work; and (2) they have the app-agnostic knowledge about the task domain. In this planned approach, the domain-agnostic knowledge of app design patterns and layouts is encoded in the app screen embedding model, while the task-domain-specific knowledge can be acquired by the agent through the user's instruction of a similar task in a different app.

Another opportunity for facilitating generalization is to enhance the reasoning of user intents by connecting to large pre-trained commonsense models like COMET [24] and Atomic [131]. While the current SUGILITE agent can be taught new concepts (e.g., hot, busy, and late), procedures (e.g., setting alarms and requesting Uber rides), and if-else rules, the agent does not understand the rationale and reasoning process among these entities (e.g., the user requests a Uber ride when it is late *because* the Uber ride is faster and the user does not want to be late for an event). Understanding such rationale would allow the agent to better generalize user instructions to different contexts and to suggest alternative approaches.

8.2   Field Study of SUGILITE

Another future direction is to study the user adoption of SUGILITE through a longitudinal field study. While the usability and the effectiveness of SUGILITE have been validated through task-based lab studies, deploying it to actual users can still be useful for *(i)* further validating the feasibility and robustness of the system in various contexts, *(ii)* measuring the usefulness of SUGILITE in real-life scenarios, and *(iii)* studying the characteristics of how users use SUGILITE. The key goal of the deployment is to study SUGILITE within its intended context of use.

9   Conclusion

We described SUGILITE, a task automation agent that can learn new tasks and relevant concepts interactively from users through their GUI-grounded natural language instructions and demonstrations. This system provides capabilities such as intent clarification, task parameterization, concept generalization, breakdown repairs, and embedding the semantics of GUI screens. SUGILITE shows the promise of using app GUIs for grounding natural language instructions, and the effectiveness of resolving unknown concepts, ambiguities, and vagueness in natural language instructions using a mixed-initiative multi-modal approach.

Acknowledgements This research was supported in part by Verizon through the Yahoo! InMind project, a J.P. Morgan Faculty Research Award, NSF grant IIS-1814472, AFOSR grant FA95501710218, and Google Cloud Research Credits. Any opinions, findings or recommendations expressed here are those of the authors and do not necessarily reflect views of the sponsors. We thank Amos Azaria, Yuanchun Li, Fanglin Chen, Igor Labutov, Xiaohan Nancy Li, Xiaoyi Zhang, Wenze Shi, Wanling Ding, Marissa Radensky, Justin Jia, Kirielle Singarajah, Jingya Chen, Brandon Canfield, Haijun Xia, and Lindsay Popowski for their contributions to this project.

References

1. Adar E, Dontcheva M, Laput G (2014) CommandSpace: modeling the relationships between tasks, descriptions and features. In: Proceedings of the 27th annual ACM symposium on user interface software and technology, UIST '14, pp 167–176. ACM, New York, NY, USA. https://doi.org/10.1145/2642918.2647395. http://doi.acm.org/10.1145/2642918.2647395
2. Alharbi K, Yeh T (2015) Collect, decompile, extract, stats, and diff: mining design pattern changes in android apps. In: Proceedings of the 17th international conference on human-computer interaction with mobile devices and services, MobileHCI '15, pp 515–524. ACM, New York, NY, USA. https://doi.org/10.1145/2785830.2785892. http://doi.acm.org/10.1145/2785830.2785892
3. Allen J, Chambers N, Ferguson G, Galescu L, Jung H, Swift M, Taysom W (2007) PLOW: a collaborative task learning agent. In: Proceedings of the 22Nd national conference on artificial intelligence - volume 2, AAAI'07, pp 1514–1519. AAAI Press, Vancouver, British Columbia, Canada

4. Allen JF, Guinn CI, Horvtz E (1999) Mixed-initiative interaction. IEEE Intell Syst Appl 14(5):14–23
5. Amazon: Alexa Design Guide (2020). https://developer.amazon.com/en-US/docs/alexa/alexa-design/get-started.html
6. Antila V, Polet J, Lämsä A, Liikka J (2012) RoutineMaker: towards end-user automation of daily routines using smartphones. In: 2012 IEEE international conference on pervasive computing and communications workshops (PERCOM workshops), pp 399–402. https://doi.org/10.1109/PerComW.2012.6197519
7. Argall BD, Chernova S, Veloso M, Browning B (2009) A survey of robot learning from demonstration. Robot Auton Syst 57(5):469–483. https://doi.org/10.1016/j.robot.2008.10.024
8. Ashktorab Z, Jain M, Liao QV, Weisz JD (2019) Resilient chatbots: repair strategy preferences for conversational breakdowns. In: Proceedings of the 2019 CHI conference on human factors in computing systems, p 254. ACM
9. Auer S, Bizer C, Kobilarov G, Lehmann J, Cyganiak R, Ives Z (2007) Dbpedia: a nucleus for a web of open data. The semantic web, pp 722–735. http://www.springerlink.com/index/rm32474088w54378.pdf
10. Azaria A, Krishnamurthy J, Mitchell TM (2016) Instructable intelligent personal agent. In: Proceedings of the 30th AAAI conference on artificial intelligence (AAAI), vol 4
11. Ballard BW, Biermann AW (1979) Programming in natural language "NLC" as a prototype. In: Proceedings of the 1979 annual conference, ACM '79, pp 228–237. ACM, New York, NY, USA. https://doi.org/10.1145/800177.810072. http://doi.acm.org/10.1145/800177.810072
12. Banovic N, Grossman T, Matejka J, Fitzmaurice G (2012) Waken: reverse engineering usage information and interface structure from software videos. In: Proceedings of the 25th annual ACM symposium on user interface software and technology, UIST '12, pp 83–92. ACM, New York, NY, USA. https://doi.org/10.1145/2380116.2380129. http://doi.acm.org/10.1145/2380116.2380129
13. Barman S, Chasins S, Bodik R, Gulwani S (2016) Ringer: web automation by demonstration. In: Proceedings of the 2016 ACM SIGPLAN international conference on object-oriented programming, systems, languages, and applications, OOPSLA 2016, pp 748–764. ACM, New York, NY, USA. https://doi.org/10.1145/2983990.2984020. http://doi.acm.org/10.1145/2983990.2984020
14. Beneteau E, Richards OK, Zhang M, Kientz JA, Yip J, Hiniker A (2019) Communication breakdowns between families and alexa. In: Proceedings of the 2019 CHI conference on human factors in computing systems, CHI '19, pp 243:1–243:13. ACM, New York, NY, USA. https://doi.org/10.1145/3290605.3300473. http://doi.acm.org/10.1145/3290605.3300473
15. Bentley F, Luvogt C, Silverman M, Wirasinghe R, White B, Lottridge D (2018) Understanding the long-term use of smart speaker assistants. Proc ACM Interact Mob Wearable Ubiquitous Technol 2(3). https://doi.org/10.1145/3264901
16. Berant J, Chou A, Frostig R, Liang P (2013) Semantic parsing on freebase from question-answer pairs. In: Proceedings of the 2013 conference on empirical methods in natural language processing, pp 1533–1544
17. Bergman L, Castelli V, Lau T, Oblinger D (2005) DocWizards: a system for authoring follow-me documentation wizards. In: Proceedings of the 18th annual ACM symposium on user interface software and technology, UIST '05, pp 191–200. ACM, New York, NY, USA. https://doi.org/10.1145/1095034.1095067. http://doi.acm.org/10.1145/1095034.1095067
18. Biermann AW (1983) Natural Language Programming. In: Biermann AW, Guiho G (eds) Computer program synthesis methodologies, NATO advanced study institutes series. Springer, Netherlands, pp 335–368
19. Bigham JP, Lau T, Nichols J (2009) Trailblazer: enabling blind users to blaze trails through the web. In: Proceedings of the 14th international conference on intelligent user interfaces, IUI '09, pp 177–186. ACM, New York, NY, USA. https://doi.org/10.1145/1502650.1502677
20. Billard A, Calinon S, Dillmann R, Schaal S (2008) Robot programming by demonstration. In: Springer handbook of robotics, pp 1371–1394. Springer. http://link.springer.com/10.1007/978-3-540-30301-5_60

21. Bohus D, Rudnicky AI (2005) Sorry, I didn't catch that!-An investigation of non-understanding errors and recovery strategies. In: 6th SIGdial workshop on discourse and dialogue

22. Bollacker K, Evans C, Paritosh P, Sturge T, Taylor J (2008) Freebase: a collaboratively created graph database for structuring human knowledge. In: Proceedings of the 2008 ACM SIGMOD international conference on Management of data, pp 1247–1250. ACM. http://dl.acm.org/citation.cfm?id=1376746

23. Bolt RA (1980) "Put-that-there": voice and gesture at the graphics interface. In: Proceedings of the 7th annual conference on computer graphics and interactive techniques, SIGGRAPH '80, pp 262–270. ACM, New York, NY, USA

24. Bosselut A, Rashkin H, Sap M, Malaviya C, Celikyilmaz A, Choi Y (2019) COMET: commonsense transformers for automatic knowledge graph construction. In: Proceedings of the 57th annual meeting of the association for computational linguistics, pp 4762–4779. ACL, Florence, Italy. https://doi.org/10.18653/v1/P19-1470. https://www.aclweb.org/anthology/P19-1470

25. Brennan SE (1991) Conversation with and through computers. User Model User-Adap Int 1(1):67–86. https://doi.org/10.1007/BF00158952

26. Brennan SE (1998) The grounding problem in conversations with and through computers. Social and cognitive approaches to interpersonal communication, pp 201–225

27. Böhmer M, Hecht B, Schöning J, Krüger A, Bauer G (2011) Falling asleep with angry birds, facebook and kindle: a large scale study on mobile application usage. In: Proceedings of the 13th international conference on human computer interaction with mobile devices and services, MobileHCI '11, pp 47–56. ACM, New York, NY, USA. https://doi.org/10.1145/2037373.2037383. http://doi.acm.org/10.1145/2037373.2037383

28. Chai JY, Gao Q, She L, Yang S, Saba-Sadiya S, Xu G (2018) Language to action: towards interactive task learning with physical agents. In: IJCAI, pp 2–9

29. Chandramouli V, Chakraborty A, Navda V, Guha S, Padmanabhan V, Ramjee R (2015) Insider: towards breaking down mobile app silos. In: TRIOS workshop held in conjunction with the SIGOPS SOSP 2015

30. Chen F, Xia K, Dhabalia K, Hong JI (2019) Messageontap: a suggestive interface to facilitate messaging-related tasks. In: Proceedings of the 2019 CHI conference on human factors in computing systems, CHI '19. ACM, New York, NY, USA. https://doi.org/10.1145/3290605.3300805

31. Chen J, Chen C, Xing Z, Xu X, Zhu L, Li G, Wang J (2020) Unblind your apps: predicting natural-language labels for mobile gui components by deep learning. In: Proceedings of the 42nd international conference on software engineering, ICSE '20

32. Chen JH, Weld DS (2008) Recovering from errors during programming by demonstration. In: Proceedings of the 13th international conference on intelligent user interfaces, IUI '08, pp 159–168. ACM, New York, NY, USA. https://doi.org/10.1145/1378773.1378794. http://doi.acm.org/10.1145/1378773.1378794

33. Chkroun M, Azaria A (2019) Lia: a virtual assistant that can be taught new commands by speech. Int J Hum–Comput Interact 1–12

34. Cho J, Rader E (2020) The role of conversational grounding in supporting symbiosis between people and digital assistants. Proc ACM Hum-Comput Interact 4(CSCW1)

35. Clark HH, Brennan SE (1991) Grounding in communication. In: Perspectives on socially shared cognition, pp 127–149. APA, Washington, DC, US. https://doi.org/10.1037/10096-006

36. Cowan BR, Pantidi N, Coyle D, Morrissey K, Clarke P, Al-Shehri S, Earley D, Bandeira N (2017) "what can i help you with?": Infrequent users' experiences of intelligent personal assistants. In: Proceedings of the 19th international conference on human-computer interaction with mobile devices and services, MobileHCI '17, pp 43:1–43:12. ACM, New York, NY, USA. https://doi.org/10.1145/3098279.3098539. http://doi.acm.org/10.1145/3098279.3098539

37. Cypher A, Halbert DC (1993) Watch what I do: programming by demonstration. MIT Press

38. Deka B, Huang Z, Franzen C, Hibschman J, Afergan D, Li Y, Nichols J, Kumar R (2017) Rico: a mobile app dataset for building data-driven design applications. In: Proceedings of the 30th annual ACM symposium on user interface software and technology, UIST '17, pp 845–854. ACM, New York, NY, USA. https://doi.org/10.1145/3126594.3126651. http://doi.acm.org/10.1145/3126594.3126651

39. Deka B, Huang Z, Kumar R (2016) ERICA: interaction mining mobile apps. In: Proceedings of the 29th annual symposium on user interface software and technology, UIST '16, pp 767–776. ACM, New York, NY, USA. https://doi.org/10.1145/2984511.2984581. http://doi.acm.org/10.1145/2984511.2984581

40. Dixon M, Fogarty J (2010) Prefab: implementing advanced behaviors using pixel-based reverse engineering of interface structure. In: Proceedings of the SIGCHI conference on human factors in computing systems, CHI '10, pp 1525–1534. ACM, New York, NY, USA. https://doi.org/10.1145/1753326.1753554. http://doi.acm.org/10.1145/1753326.1753554

41. Dixon M, Leventhal D, Fogarty J (2011) Content and hierarchy in pixel-based methods for reverse engineering interface structure. In: Proceedings of the SIGCHI conference on human factors in computing systems, CHI '11, pp 969–978. ACM, New York, NY, USA. https://doi.org/10.1145/1978942.1979086. http://doi.acm.org/10.1145/1978942.1979086

42. Dixon M, Nied A, Fogarty J (2014) Prefab layers and prefab annotations: extensible pixel-based interpretation of graphical interfaces. In: Proceedings of the 27th annual ACM symposium on user interface software and technology, UIST '14, pp 221–230. ACM, New York, NY, USA. https://doi.org/10.1145/2642918.2647412. http://doi.acm.org/10.1145/2642918.2647412

43. Fast E, Chen B, Mendelsohn J, Bassen J, Bernstein MS (2018) Iris: a conversational agent for complex tasks. In: Proceedings of the 2018 CHI conference on human factors in computing systems, CHI '18, pp 473:1–473:12. ACM, New York, NY, USA. https://doi.org/10.1145/3173574.3174047. http://doi.acm.org/10.1145/3173574.3174047

44. Gao X, Gong R, Zhao Y, Wang S, Shu T, Zhu SC (2020) Joint mind modeling for explanation generation in complex human-robot collaborative tasks. In: 2020 29th IEEE international conference on robot and human interactive communication (RO-MAN), pp 1119–1126. IEEE

45. Gluck KA, Laird JE (2019) Interactive task learning: humans, robots, and agents acquiring new tasks through natural interactions, vol 26. MIT Press

46. Green TR (1989) Cognitive dimensions of notations. People and Computers V pp 443–460. https://books.google.com/books?hl=en&lr=&id=BTxOtt4X920C&oi=fnd&pg=PA443&dq=Cognitive+dimensions+of+notations&ots=OEqg1By_Rj&sig=dpg1zZFRHpBVC_r0--XLyLr6718

47. Grudin J, Jacques R (2019) Chatbots, humbots, and the quest for artificial general intelligence. In: Proceedings of the 2019 CHI conference on human factors in computing systems, pp 1–11

48. Guo A, Kong J, Rivera M, Xu FF, Bigham JP (2019) StateLens: a reverse engineering solution for making existing dynamic touchscreens accessible. In: Proceedings of the 32nd annual ACM symposium on user interface software and technology (UIST 2019), p 15

49. Gur I, Yavuz S, Su Y, Yan X (2018) DialSQL: dialogue based structured query generation. In: Proceedings of the 56th annual meeting of the association for computational linguistics (volume 1: long papers), pp 1339–1349. ACL, Melbourne, Australia. https://doi.org/10.18653/v1/P18-1124. https://www.aclweb.org/anthology/P18-1124

50. Hartmann B, Wu L, Collins K, Klemmer SR (2007) Programming by a sample: rapidly creating web applications with d.mix. In: Proceedings of the 20th annual ACM symposium on user interface software and technology, UIST '07, pp 241–250. ACM, New York, NY, USA. https://doi.org/10.1145/1294211.1294254. http://doi.acm.org/10.1145/1294211.1294254

51. Horvitz E (1999) Principles of mixed-initiative user interfaces. In: Proceedings of the SIGCHI conference on human factors in computing systems, CHI '99, pp 159–166. ACM, New York, NY, USA. https://doi.org/10.1145/302979.303030

52. Huang F, Canny JF, Nichols J (2019) Swire: sketch-based user interface retrieval. In: Proceedings of the 2019 CHI conference on human factors in computing systems, CHI '19, pp 1–10. ACM, New York, NY, USA. https://doi.org/10.1145/3290605.3300334

53. Huang THK, Azaria A, Bigham JP (2016) InstructableCrowd: creating IF-THEN rules via conversations with the crowd, pp 1555–1562. ACM Press. https://doi.org/10.1145/2851581. 2892502. http://dl.acm.org/citation.cfm?doid=2851581.2892502
54. Hutchins EL, Hollan JD, Norman DA (1986) Direct manipulation interfaces
55. Iba S, Paredis CJJ, Khosla PK (2005) Interactive multimodal robot programming. Int J Robot Res 24(1):83–104. https://doi.org/10.1177/0278364904049250
56. IFTTT (2016) IFTTT: connects the apps you love. https://ifttt.com/
57. Intharah T, Turmukhambetov D, Brostow GJ (2019) Hilc: domain-independent pbd system via computer vision and follow-up questions. ACM Trans Interact Intell Syst 9(2-3):16:1–16:27. https://doi.org/10.1145/3234508. http://doi.acm.org/10.1145/3234508
58. Jain M, Kumar P, Kota R, Patel SN (2018) Evaluating and informing the design of chatbots. In: Proceedings of the 2018 designing interactive systems conference, pp 895–906. ACM
59. Jiang J, Jeng W, He D (2013) How do users respond to voice input errors?: lexical and phonetic query reformulation in voice search. In: Proceedings of the 36th international ACM SIGIR conference on research and development in information retrieval, pp 143–152. ACM
60. Kasturi T, Jin H, Pappu A, Lee S, Harrison B, Murthy R, Stent A (2015) The cohort and speechify libraries for rapid construction of speech enabled applications for android. In: Proceedings of the 16th annual meeting of the special interest group on discourse and dialogue, pp 441–443
61. Kate RJ, Wong YW, Mooney RJ (2005) Learning to transform natural to formal languages. In: Proceedings of the 20th national conference on artificial intelligence - volume 3, AAAI'05, pp 1062–1068. AAAI Press, Pittsburgh, Pennsylvania. http://dl.acm.org/citation. cfm?id=1619499.1619504
62. Kim D, Park S, Ko J, Ko SY, Lee SJ (2019) X-droid: a quick and easy android prototyping framework with a single-app illusion. In: Proceedings of the 32nd annual ACM symposium on user interface software and technology, UIST '19, pp 95–108. ACM, New York, NY, USA. https://doi.org/10.1145/3332165.3347890
63. Kingma DP, Ba J (2015) Adam: a method for stochastic optimization. In: Bengio Y, LeCun Y (eds) 3rd international conference on learning representations, ICLR 2015, San Diego, CA, USA, May 7–9, 2015, Conference Track Proceedings. http://arxiv.org/abs/1412.6980
64. Kirk J, Mininger A, Laird J (2016) Learning task goals interactively with visual demonstrations. Biol Inspired Cogn Archit 18:1–8
65. Ko AJ, Abraham R, Beckwith L, Blackwell A, Burnett M, Erwig M, Scaffidi C, Lawrance J, Lieberman H, Myers B, Rosson MB, Rothermel G, Shaw M, Wiedenbeck S (2011) The state of the art in end-user software engineering. ACM Comput Surv 43(3), 21:1–21:44. https:// doi.org/10.1145/1922649.1922658. http://doi.acm.org/10.1145/1922649.1922658
66. Kumar R, Satyanarayan A, Torres C, Lim M, Ahmad S, Klemmer SR, Talton JO (2013) Webzeitgeist: design mining the web. In: Proceedings of the SIGCHI conference on human factors in computing systems, CHI '13, pp 3083–3092. ACM, New York, NY, USA. https:// doi.org/10.1145/2470654.2466420
67. Kurihara K, Goto M, Ogata J, Igarashi T (2006) Speech pen: predictive handwriting based on ambient multimodal recognition. In: Proceedings of the SIGCHI conference on human factors in computing systems, pp 851–860. ACM
68. Labutov I, Srivastava S, Mitchell T (2018) Lia: a natural language programmable personal assistant. In: Proceedings of the 2018 conference on empirical methods in natural language processing: system demonstrations, pp 145–150
69. Laird JE, Gluck K, Anderson J, Forbus KD, Jenkins OC, Lebiere C, Salvucci D, Scheutz M, Thomaz A, Trafton G, Wray RE, Mohan S, Kirk JR (2017) Interactive task learning. IEEE Intell Syst 32(4):6–21. https://doi.org/10.1109/MIS.2017.3121552
70. Laput GP, Dontcheva M, Wilensky G, Chang W, Agarwala A, Linder J, Adar E (2013) Pixel-Tone: a multimodal interface for image editing. In: Proceedings of the SIGCHI conference on human factors in computing systems, CHI '13, pp 2185–2194. ACM, New York, NY, USA. https://doi.org/10.1145/2470654.2481301. http://doi.acm.org/10.1145/2470654.2481301

71. Lau T (2009) Why programming-by-demonstration systems fail: lessons learned for usable AI. AI Mag 30(4):65–67. http://www.aaai.org/ojs/index.php/aimagazine/article/view/2262
72. Lee C, Kim S, Han D, Yang H, Park YW, Kwon BC, Ko S (2020) Guicomp: a gui design assistant with real-time, multi-faceted feedback. In: Proceedings of the 2020 CHI conference on human factors in computing systems, CHI '20, pp 1–13. ACM, New York, NY, USA. https://doi.org/10.1145/3313831.3376327
73. Lee HY, Yang W, Jiang L, Le M, Essa I, Gong H, Yang MH (2020) Neural design network: graphic layout generation with constraints. In: European conference on computer vision (ECCV)
74. Lee TY, Dugan C, Bederson BB (2017) Towards understanding human mistakes of programming by example: an online user study. In: Proceedings of the 22nd international conference on intelligent user interfaces, IUI '17, pp 257–261. ACM, New York, NY, USA. https://doi.org/10.1145/3025171.3025203. http://doi.acm.org/10.1145/3025171.3025203
75. Leshed G, Haber EM, Matthews T, Lau T (2008) CoScripter: automating & sharing how-to knowledge in the enterprise. In: Proceedings of the SIGCHI conference on human factors in computing systems, CHI '08, pp 1719–1728. ACM, New York, NY, USA. https://doi.org/10.1145/1357054.1357323. http://doi.acm.org/10.1145/1357054.1357323
76. Li F, Jagadish HV (2014) Constructing an interactive natural language interface for relational databases. Proc VLDB Endow 8(1):73–84. https://doi.org/10.14778/2735461.2735468
77. Li H, Wang YP, Yin J, Tan G (2019) Smartshell: automated shell scripts synthesis from natural language. Int J Softw Eng Knowl Eng 29(02):197–220
78. Li I, Nichols J, Lau T, Drews C, Cypher A (2010) Here's What I Did: sharing and reusing web activity with ActionShot. In: Proceedings of the SIGCHI conference on human factors in computing systems, CHI '10, pp 723–732. ACM, New York, NY, USA. https://doi.org/10.1145/1753326.1753432. http://doi.acm.org/10.1145/1753326.1753432
79. Li J, Yang J, Hertzmann A, Zhang J, Xu T (2019) Layoutgan: synthesizing graphic layouts with vector-wireframe adversarial networks. IEEE Trans Pattern Anal Mach Intell
80. Li TJJ, Azaria A, Myers BA (2017) SUGILITE: creating multimodal smartphone automation by demonstration. In: Proceedings of the 2017 CHI conference on human factors in computing systems, CHI '17, pp 6038–6049. ACM, New York, NY, USA. https://doi.org/10.1145/3025453.3025483. http://doi.acm.org/10.1145/3025453.3025483
81. Li TJJ, Chen J, Canfield B, Myers BA (2020) Privacy-preserving script sharing in gui-based programming-by-demonstration systems. Proc ACM Hum-Comput Interact 4(CSCW1). https://doi.org/10.1145/3392869
82. Li TJJ, Chen J, Xia H, Mitchell TM, Myers BA (2020) Multi-modal repairs of conversational breakdowns in task-oriented dialogs. In: Proceedings of the 33rd annual ACM symposium on user interface software and technology, UIST 2020. ACM. https://doi.org/10.1145/3379337.3415820
83. Li TJJ, Hecht B (2014) WikiBrain: making computer programs smarter with knowledge from wikipedia
84. Li TJJ, Labutov I, Li XN, Zhang X, Shi W, Mitchell TM, Myers BA (2018) APPINITE: a multi-modal interface for specifying data descriptions in programming by demonstration using verbal instructions. In: Proceedings of the 2018 IEEE symposium on visual languages and human-centric computing (VL/HCC 2018)
85. Li TJJ, Labutov I, Myers BA, Azaria A, Rudnicky AI, Mitchell TM (2018) Teaching agents when they fail: end user development in goal-oriented conversational agents. In: Studies in conversational UX design. Springer
86. Li TJJ, Li Y, Chen F, Myers BA (2017) Programming IoT devices by demonstration using mobile apps. In: Barbosa S, Markopoulos P, Paterno F, Stumpf S, Valtolina S (eds) End-user development. Springer, Cham, pp 3–17
87. Li TJJ, Popowski L, Mitchell TM, Myers BA (2021) Screen2vec: semantic embedding of gui screens and gui components. In: Proceedings of the 2021 CHI conference on human factors in computing systems, CHI '21. ACM

88. Li TJJ, Radensky M, Jia J, Singarajah K, Mitchell TM, Myers BA (2019) PUMICE: a multi-modal agent that learns concepts and conditionals from natural language and demonstrations. In: Proceedings of the 32nd annual ACM symposium on user interface software and technology (UIST 2019), UIST 2019. ACM. https://doi.org/10.1145/3332165.3347899

89. Li TJJ, Riva O (2018) KITE: building conversational bots from mobile apps. In: Proceedings of the 16th ACM international conference on mobile systems, applications, and services (MobiSys 2018). ACM

90. Li Y, He J, Zhou X, Zhang Y, Baldridge J (2020) Mapping natural language instructions to mobile UI action sequences. In: Proceedings of the 58th annual meeting of the association for computational linguistics, pp 8198–8210. ACL, Online. https://doi.org/10.18653/v1/2020.acl-main.729. https://www.aclweb.org/anthology/2020.acl-main.729

91. Li Y, Li G, He L, Zheng J, Li H, Guan Z (2020) Widget captioning: generating natural language description for mobile user interface elements. In: Proceedings of the 2020 conference on empirical methods in natural language processing (EMNLP), pp 5495–5510. ACL, Online. https://doi.org/10.18653/v1/2020.emnlp-main.443. https://www.aclweb.org/anthology/2020.emnlp-main.443

92. Liang P (2016) Learning executable semantic parsers for natural language understanding. Commun ACM 59(9):68–76

93. Liang P, Jordan MI, Klein D (2013) Learning dependency-based compositional semantics. Comput Linguist 39(2):389–446

94. Lieberman H (2001) Your wish is my command: programming by example. Morgan Kaufmann

95. Lieberman H, Liu H (2006) Feasibility studies for programming in natural language. In: End user development, pp 459–473. Springer

96. Lieberman H, Maulsby D (1996) Instructible agents: software that just keeps getting better. IBM Syst J 35(3.4):539–556. https://doi.org/10.1147/sj.353.0539

97. Lin J, Wong J, Nichols J, Cypher A, Lau TA (2009) End-user programming of mashups with vegemite. In: Proceedings of the 14th international conference on intelligent user interfaces, IUI '09, pp 97–106. ACM, New York, NY, USA. https://doi.org/10.1145/1502650.1502667. http://doi.acm.org/10.1145/1502650.1502667

98. Liu EZ, Guu K, Pasupat P, Shi T, Liang P (2018) Reinforcement learning on web interfaces using workflow-guided exploration. CoRR. http://arxiv.org/abs/1802.08802

99. Liu TF, Craft M, Situ J, Yumer E, Mech R, Kumar R (2018) Learning design semantics for mobile apps. In: Proceedings of the 31st annual ACM symposium on user interface software and technology, UIST '18, pp 569–579. ACM, New York, NY, USA. https://doi.org/10.1145/3242587.3242650

100. LlamaLab: Automate: everyday automation for Android (2016). http://llamalab.com/automate/

101. Luger E, Sellen A (2016) "like having a really bad pa": the gulf between user expectation and experience of conversational agents. In: Proceedings of the 2016 CHI conference on human factors in computing systems, CHI '16, pp 5286–5297. ACM, New York, NY, USA. https://doi.org/10.1145/2858036.2858288. http://doi.acm.org/10.1145/2858036.2858288

102. Maes P (1994) Agents that reduce work and information overload. Commun ACM 37(7):30–40. https://doi.org/10.1145/176789.176792. http://doi.acm.org/10.1145/176789.176792

103. Mankoff J, Abowd GD, Hudson SE (2000) Oops: a toolkit supporting mediation techniques for resolving ambiguity in recognition-based interfaces. Comput Graph 24(6):819–834

104. Marin R, Sanz PJ, Nebot P, Wirz R (2005) A multimodal interface to control a robot arm via the web: a case study on remote programming. IEEE Trans Ind Electron 52(6):1506–1520. https://doi.org/10.1109/TIE.2005.858733

105. Maués RDA, Barbosa SDJ (2013) Keep doing what i just did: automating smartphones by demonstration. In: Proceedings of the 15th international conference on human-computer interaction with mobile devices and services, MobileHCI '13, pp 295–303. ACM, New York, NY, USA. https://doi.org/10.1145/2493190.2493216. http://doi.acm.org/10.1145/2493190.2493216

106. McDaniel RG, Myers BA (1999) Getting more out of programming-by-demonstration. In: Proceedings of the SIGCHI conference on human factors in computing systems, CHI '99, pp 442–449. ACM, New York, NY, USA. https://doi.org/10.1145/302979.303127. http://doi.acm.org/10.1145/302979.303127

107. McTear M, O'Neill I, Hanna P, Liu X (2005) Handling errors and determining confirmation strategies–an object-based approach. Speech Commun 45(3):249–269. https://doi.org/10.1016/j.specom.2004.11.006. http://www.sciencedirect.com/science/article/pii/S0167639304001426. Special Issue on Error Handling in Spoken Dialogue Systems

108. Menon A, Tamuz O, Gulwani S, Lampson B, Kalai A (2013) A machine learning framework for programming by example, pp 187–195. http://machinelearning.wustl.edu/mlpapers/papers/ICML2013_menon13

109. Mihalcea R, Liu H, Lieberman H (2006) NLP (Natural Language Processing) for NLP (Natural Language Programming). In: Gelbukh A (ed) Computational linguistics and intelligent text processing. Lecture notes in computer science. Springer, Berlin, Heidelberg, pp 319–330

110. Mikolov T, Chen K, Corrado G, Dean J (2013) Efficient estimation of word representations in vector space. arXiv:1301.3781 [cs]. http://arxiv.org/abs/1301.3781. ArXiv: 1301.3781

111. Mikolov T, Sutskever I, Chen K, Corrado GS, Dean J (2013) Distributed representations of words and phrases and their compositionality. In: Advances in neural information processing systems, pp 3111–3119. http://papers.nips.cc/paper/5021-distributed-representations-of-words-and-phrases-and-their-compositionality

112. Mohan S, Laird JE (2014) Learning goal-oriented hierarchical tasks from situated interactive instruction. In: Proceedings of the twenty-eighth AAAI conference on artificial intelligence, AAAI'14, pp 387–394. AAAI Press

113. Myers B, Malkin R, Bett M, Waibel A, Bostwick B, Miller RC, Yang J, Denecke M, Seemann E, Zhu J et al (2002) Flexi-modal and multi-machine user interfaces. In: Proceedings of the fourth IEEE international conference on multimodal interfaces, pp 343–348. IEEE

114. Myers BA (1986) Visual programming, programming by example, and program visualization: a taxonomy. In: Proceedings of the SIGCHI conference on human factors in computing systems, CHI '86, pp 59–66. ACM, New York, NY, USA. https://doi.org/10.1145/22627.22349. http://doi.acm.org/10.1145/22627.22349

115. Myers BA, Ko AJ, Scaffidi C, Oney S, Yoon Y, Chang K, Kery MB, Li TJJ (2017) Making end user development more natural. In: New perspectives in end-user development, pp 1–22. Springer, Cham. https://doi.org/10.1007/978-3-319-60291-2_1. https://link.springer.com/chapter/10.1007/978-3-319-60291-2_1

116. Myers BA, McDaniel R (2001) Sometimes you need a little intelligence, sometimes you need a lot. Your wish is my command: programming by example. Morgan Kaufmann Publishers, San Francisco, CA, pp 45–60. http://citeseerx.ist.psu.edu/viewdoc/download?doi=10.1.1.2.8085&rep=rep1&type=pdf

117. Myers C, Furqan A, Nebolsky J, Caro K, Zhu J (2018) Patterns for how users overcome obstacles in voice user interfaces. In: Proceedings of the 2018 CHI conference on human factors in computing systems, pp 1–7

118. Norman D (2013) The design of everyday things: revised and expanded edition. Basic Books

119. Oviatt S (1999) Mutual disambiguation of recognition errors in a multimodel architecture. In: Proceedings of the SIGCHI conference on human factors in computing systems, pp 576–583. ACM

120. Oviatt S (1999) Ten myths of multimodal interaction. Commun ACM 42(11):74–81 https://doi.org/10.1145/319382.319398. http://doi.acm.org/10.1145/319382.319398

121. Oviatt S, Cohen P (2000) Perceptual user interfaces: multimodal interfaces that process what comes naturally. Commun ACM 43(3):45–53

122. Pasupat P, Jiang TS, Liu E, Guu K, Liang P (2018) Mapping natural language commands to web elements. In: Proceedings of the 2018 conference on empirical methods in natural language processing, pp 4970–4976. ACL, Brussels, Belgium. https://doi.org/10.18653/v1/D18-1540. https://www.aclweb.org/anthology/D18-1540

123. Pasupat P, Liang P (2015) Compositional semantic parsing on semi-structured tables. In: Proceedings of the 53rd annual meeting of the association for computational linguistics and the 7th international joint conference on natural language processing. http://arxiv.org/abs/1508.00305. ArXiv: 1508.00305

124. Porcheron M, Fischer JE, Reeves S, Sharples S (2018) Voice interfaces in everyday life. In: Proceedings of the 2018 CHI conference on human factors in computing systems, CHI '18. ACM, New York, NY, USA. https://doi.org/10.1145/3173574.3174214

125. Price D, Rilofff E, Zachary J, Harvey B (2000) NaturalJava: a natural language interface for programming in java. In: Proceedings of the 5th international conference on intelligent user interfaces, IUI '00, pp 207–211. ACM, New York, NY, USA. https://doi.org/10.1145/325737.325845. http://doi.acm.org/10.1145/325737.325845

126. Qi S, Jia B, Huang S, Wei P, Zhu SC (2020) A generalized earley parser for human activity parsing and prediction. IEEE Trans Pattern Anal Mach Intell

127. Ravindranath L, Thiagarajan A, Balakrishnan H, Madden S (2012) Code in the air: simplifying sensing and coordination tasks on smartphones. In: Proceedings of the twelfth workshop on mobile computing systems & applications, HotMobile '12, pp 4:1–4:6. ACM, New York, NY, USA. https://doi.org/10.1145/2162081.2162087. http://doi.acm.org/10.1145/2162081.2162087

128. Reimers N, Gurevych I (2019) Sentence-bert: sentence embeddings using siamese bert-networks. In: Proceedings of the 2019 conference on empirical methods in natural language processing. ACL. http://arxiv.org/abs/1908.10084

129. Rodrigues A (2015) Breaking barriers with assistive macros. In: Proceedings of the 17th international ACM SIGACCESS conference on computers & accessibility, ASSETS '15, pp 351–352. ACM, New York, NY, USA. https://doi.org/10.1145/2700648.2811322. http://doi.acm.org/10.1145/2700648.2811322

130. Sahami Shirazi A, Henze N, Schmidt A, Goldberg R, Schmidt B, Schmauder H (2013) Insights into layout patterns of mobile user interfaces by an automatic analysis of android apps. In: Proceedings of the 5th ACM SIGCHI symposium on engineering interactive computing systems, EICS '13, pp 275–284. ACM, New York, NY, USA. https://doi.org/10.1145/2494603.2480308. http://doi.acm.org/10.1145/2494603.2480308

131. Sap M, Le Bras R, Allaway E, Bhagavatula C, Lourie N, Rashkin H, Roof B, Smith NA, Choi Y (2019) Atomic: an atlas of machine commonsense for if-then reasoning. Proc AAAI Conf Artif Intell 33:3027–3035

132. Sereshkeh AR, Leung G, Perumal K, Phillips C, Zhang M, Fazly A, Mohomed I (2020) Vasta: a vision and language-assisted smartphone task automation system. In: Proceedings of the 25th international conference on intelligent user interfaces, pp 22–32

133. She L, Chai J (2017) Interactive learning of grounded verb semantics towards human-robot communication. In: Proceedings of the 55th annual meeting of the association for computational linguistics (volume 1: long papers), pp 1634–1644. ACL, Vancouver, Canada. https://doi.org/10.18653/v1/P17-1150. https://www.aclweb.org/anthology/P17-1150

134. Shneiderman B (1983) Direct manipulation: a step beyond programming languages. Computer 16(8):57–69. https://doi.org/10.1109/MC.1983.1654471

135. Shneiderman B, Plaisant C, Cohen M, Jacobs S, Elmqvist N, Diakopoulos N (2016) Designing the user interface: strategies for effective human-computer interaction, 6, edition. Pearson, Boston

136. Srivastava S, Labutov I, Mitchell T (2017) Joint concept learning and semantic parsing from natural language explanations. In: Proceedings of the 2017 conference on empirical methods in natural language processing, pp 1527–1536

137. Su Y, Hassan Awadallah A, Wang M, White RW (2018) Natural language interfaces with fine-grained user interaction: a case study on web apis. In: The 41st international ACM SIGIR conference on research and development in information retrieval, SIGIR '18, pp 855–864. ACM, New York, NY, USA. https://doi.org/10.1145/3209978.3210013

138. Suhm B, Myers B, Waibel A (2001) Multimodal error correction for speech user interfaces. ACM Trans Comput-Hum Interact 8(1):60–98. https://doi.org/10.1145/371127.371166. http://doi.acm.org/10.1145/371127.371166

139. Swearngin A, Dontcheva M, Li W, Brandt J, Dixon M, Ko AJ (2018) Rewire: interface design assistance from examples. In: Proceedings of the 2018 CHI conference on human factors in computing systems, CHI '18, pp 1–12. ACM, New York, NY, USA. https://doi.org/10.1145/3173574.3174078

140. Ur B, McManus E, Pak Yong Ho M, Littman ML (2014) Practical trigger-action programming in the smart home. In: Proceedings of the SIGCHI conference on human factors in computing systems, CHI '14, pp 803–812. ACM, New York, NY, USA. https://doi.org/10.1145/2556288.2557420. http://doi.acm.org/10.1145/2556288.2557420

141. Vadas D, Curran JR (2005) Programming with unrestricted natural language. In: Proceedings of the Australasian language technology workshop 2005, pp 191–199

142. Vrandečić D, Krötzsch M (2014) Wikidata: a free collaborative knowledgebase. Commun ACM 57(10):78–85. http://dl.acm.org/citation.cfm?id=2629489

143. Xu Q, Erman J, Gerber A, Mao Z, Pang J, Venkataraman S (2011) Identifying diverse usage behaviors of smartphone apps. In: Proceedings of the 2011 ACM SIGCOMM conference on internet measurement conference, IMC '11, pp 329–344. ACM, New York, NY, USA. https://doi.org/10.1145/2068816.2068847. http://doi.acm.org/10.1145/2068816.2068847

144. Yang JJ, Lam MS, Landay JA (2020) Dothishere: multimodal interaction to improve cross-application tasks on mobile devices. In: Proceedings of the 33rd annual ACM symposium on user interface software and technology, UIST '20, pp 35–44. ACM, New York, NY, USA. https://doi.org/10.1145/3379337.3415841

145. Yao Z, Su Y, Sun H, Yih WT (2019) Model-based interactive semantic parsing: a unified framework and a text-to-SQL case study. In: Proceedings of the 2019 conference on empirical methods in natural language processing and the 9th international joint conference on natural language processing (EMNLP-IJCNLP), pp 5447–5458. ACL, Hong Kong, China. https://doi.org/10.18653/v1/D19-1547. https://www.aclweb.org/anthology/D19-1547

146. Yao Z, Tang Y, Yih WT, Sun H, Su Y (2020) An imitation game for learning semantic parsers from user interaction. In: Proceedings of the 2020 conference on empirical methods in natural language processing (EMNLP), pp 6883–6902. ACL, Online. https://doi.org/10.18653/v1/2020.emnlp-main.559. https://www.aclweb.org/anthology/2020.emnlp-main.559

147. Yeh T, Chang TH, Miller RC (2009) Sikuli: using GUI screenshots for search and automation. In: Proceedings of the 22nd annual ACM symposium on user interface software and technology, UIST '09, pp 183–192. ACM, New York, NY, USA. https://doi.org/10.1145/1622176.1622213. http://doi.acm.org/10.1145/1622176.1622213

148. Zhang X, Ross AS, Fogarty J (2018) Robust annotation of mobile application interfaces in methods for accessibility repair and enhancement. In: Proceedings of the 31st annual ACM symposium on user interface software and technology, UIST '18

149. Zhang Z, Zhu Y, Zhu SC (2020) Graph-based hierarchical knowledge representation for robot task transfer from virtual to physical world. In: 2020 IEEE/RSJ international conference on intelligent robots and systems (IROS)

150. Zhao S, Ramos J, Tao J, Jiang Z, Li S, Wu Z, Pan G, Dey AK (2016) Discovering different kinds of smartphone users through their application usage behaviors. In: Proceedings of the 2016 ACM international joint conference on pervasive and ubiquitous computing, UbiComp '16, pp 498–509. ACM, New York, NY, USA. https://doi.org/10.1145/2971648.2971696. http://doi.acm.org/10.1145/2971648.2971696

Human-Centered AI for Medical Imaging

Yuan Liang, Lei He, and Xiang 'Anthony' Chen

Abstract Medical imaging is the primary data source most physicians refer to when making a diagnosis. However, examination of medical imaging data, due to its density and uncertainty, can be time-consuming and error-prone. The recent advent of data-driven artificial intelligence (AI) provides a promising solution, yet the adoption of AI in medicine is often hindered by the 'black box' nature. This chapter reviews how AI can distil new insights from medical imaging data and how a human-centered approach can transform AI's role as one that engages patients with self-assessment and personalized models and as one that enables physicians to comprehend and control how AI performs a diagnosis, thus able to collaborate with AI in making a diagnosis.

1   Introduction

Medical diagnosis and treatment is contingent upon our ability to see and understand the human body. Medical imaging is a class of imaging technology that achieves such purposes by non-invasively creating a visual representation of the interior of the human body—everything from a skeletal map to the histology of cells.

Imaging is the primary data source in medicine, followed by clinical notes and lab reports [43]. Physicians rely on medical imaging data to facilitate the differential diagnosis process [26]. For example, consider meningioma—the primary major brain tumor among adults. Physicians might start by using radiographs to formulate the initial hypotheses; then tissue samples are collected where histological data is examined to further confirm the detection of the tumor and the subsequent grading to

Y. Liang · L. He · X. 'Anthony' Chen (✉)
UCLA, Los Angeles, USA
e-mail: xac@ucla.edu

Y. Liang
e-mail: liangyuandg@ucla.edu

L. He
e-mail: lhe@ee.ucla.edu

Y. Li and O. Hilliges (eds.), *Artificial Intelligence for Human Computer Interaction: A Modern Approach*, Human–Computer Interaction Series,
https://doi.org/10.1007/978-3-030-82681-9_16

539

determine severity; further immunohistochemical tests can be conducted that stain the tissue to better assist the examination. On the patient's side, the decreasing cost and increasing availability of obtaining imaging data (exemplified by the popular smartphone cameras) provide abundant opportunities to inform patients of their own conditions, allowing patients to perform self-assessment complementary to seeking professional medical help.

Despite its ubiquitous use and promises, medical imaging remains an uncertain process where the visual representation of the body is merely an approximation with a limited fidelity and often appears ambiguous. For example, a radiologist examining a radiograph relies on different shades of X-ray 'shadows' to detect certain abnormal patterns for identifying a condition. Further, some medical imaging data comes with a large amount of information, e.g., digitalized tissue slices, and is time-consuming for physicians to perform a thorough examination. One patient's case comprising over 10 slides could take a pathologist several hours to go through it.

The challenges of uncertainty and overwhelming information call for an automatic process that can provide assistance to physicians in processing medical imaging data. As medical diagnosis is "inherently an information-management task" [86], there is an opportunity to augment physicians' work by leveraging the recent development in data-driven artificial intelligence (AI). In fact, the idea of incorporating a computer-based solution for diagnosis is not new—systems like MYCIN [85] were developed and deployed among the earliest expert systems. However, historically there has been a resistance to adopt AI-enabled diagnosis in clinical decision support systems [12], not merely because of a lack of performant AI models, but primarily due to AI's 'black box' nature and a lack of user-centered integration into physicians' workflow [10, 24, 25, 65, 100]. Similarly, for patients' self-assessment, one main challenge of adopting an intelligent sensing solution is to bridge the gulf of expertise, i.e., to develop a workflow that guides non-medical experts to easily and accurately obtain medical imaging data and to comprehend AI's findings.

Similar to how a user-centered approach revolutionized the development of early computer systems among individuals, we believe the rise of AI in medicine should be built upon both its computational performance and its ability to center itself on physicians. As a point of departure, this chapter focuses on medical imaging data in two specialties—radiology and pathology[1]: we first review recent advances in AI's ability to mine new insights that were previously not possible in how we processed medical imaging data; we then summarize the existing limitations and challenges, which lead to two threads of work on human-centered AI: *(i)* how a patient-centered approach can enable self-assessment and closely involve patients in clinical diagnosis and treatment; *(ii)* how a physician-centered approach can enable physicians to comprehend AI's findings, to use AI as tools, and to collaborate with AI.

---

[1] We consider pathology as a type of medical imaging specialty, as the recent development in digital pathology has fostered a growing body of work on processing digitalized whole slide images, although traditionally images obtained from removed tissues for studying pathology are not considered medical imaging.

2 Leveraging Data-Driven AI to Distill New Insights from Medical Imaging

2.1 Advances in AI-Enabled Radiology

Radiology alleviates phenomena such as electromagnetic radiation and radioactivity to generate scans of internal body tissues without invasion [13], whereas the most commonly used modalities include X-ray, computed tomography (CT), magnetic resonance imaging (MRI), positron emission tomography (PET), and ultrasound. Radiology AI has the potential to immensely benefit radiologists because of the large volume of scans produced annually [88] and the continuously increasing use of radiology imaging among adults [87]. Inspired by the success of deep learning in computer vision, AI algorithms have been developed for radiology in analogous, but with the consideration of the unique properties of radiology data, i.e., three dimensional, anatomically structured, and with medical knowledge embedded. According to the intended task, existing radiology AI applications by and large fall into two categories: diagnostic and non-diagnostic.

Diagnostic applications aid radiologists by offering second opinions and flagging concerning scans/areas, formulating tasks like classification, segmentation, or detection. With the recent availability of large amounts of training data [60], many AI applications have achieved physician-level accuracy, which includes classifying the existence of tuberculosis from chest X-ray [50], segmenting hemorrhage on head CT [49], and localizing breast lesion in mammograms [48]. The outputs of the above algorithms are the predicted probabilities of a target scan, voxel, or bounding box to contain a positive finding of a medical condition. However, such deterministic output does not capture confidential information, or the level of uncertainty, about the diagnosis that can arise from those diagnostic tasks that are inherently challenging. As an example, it is reported that radiologists strive to detect all nodules that might have relevance to cancer diagnosis in lung CT when the nodule size falls below 8–10 mm [80], due to the lack of an absolute reference standard of the nodule size for actionability. To estimate the uncertainty in deep learning models, one popular solution is approximative Bayesian inferences with dropout neural networks as proposed by Gal et al. [35]. Following this path, radiology AI studies have explored scan-level [73], voxel-level [69], and instance-level [109] uncertainty estimation, which produce consistent accuracy improvement for models. More importantly, information about model uncertainty can also be vital for risk management when radiologists adopt AI-enabled tools in their diagnosis pipeline [2], since out-of-distribution observations could be rated with high uncertainty, posing as alerts to physicians when reviewing the AI's results.

Non-diagnostic AI applications generate auxiliary information from radiology scans to assist radiologists' decision-making, which can include a variety of technical tasks, e.g., anatomical localization, image reconstruction, and image registration. The anatomical localization of organs, regions, and landmarks is the most common task, since it benefits many clinical applications including therapy planning, surgical navigation, and pathological change quantification. For example, Alansary et al. pinpoints right and left cerebellum and cavum septum pellucidum from head ultrasound [1], and several works focus on producing masks of brain MRI for up to 133 functional regions [14, 40]. While U-Net-like architectures are the most well-known for the anatomical localization [21, 32, 67], recent studies have shown that better accuracy and robustness can be achieved by incorporating anatomical invariances, e.g., organ's shapes and adjacency conditions, into modeling as priors [56, 57]. Image reconstruction, which aims to form high-quality scans from low does and/or fast acquisitions, is another practical task made possible with recent AI advances. Typical works include Shan et al. introducing a CNN to reduce the noise of low-dose CT, which achieve comparable fidelity with commercial methods in largely reduced time [83]; Song et al. provide low-dose three-dimensional bone structures from two-dimensional panoramic dental X-ray, using prior knowledge learned with a generative adversarial network (GAN) [90]. Image registration aims to spatially align a radiology scan into a specific coordinate system. It acts as an essential prepossessing step for many clinical studies, e.g., population analysis of anatomies from large-scale data and longitudinal analysis of temporal structural changes across a patient's multiple scans. Traditional optimization-based methods are mostly time-consuming, costing up to a few hours to register one three-dimensional scan [6]. However, recent predictive CNN models have shown the ability to reduce that time to a few seconds by estimating the deformation map from a target scan, while achieving comparable aligning accuracy with traditional methods [8, 64].

2.2 Advances in AI-Enabled Digital Pathology

According to Holzinger et al., digital pathology is "not just the transformation of the classical microscopic analysis of histological slides by pathologists to a digital visualization, it is an innovation that will dramatically change medical workflows in the coming years" [39]. The increase of data collection in digital pathology [59, 78, 97, 101] has triggered a recent surge of data-driven techniques in a broad range of applications, such as carcinoma detection [3, 9, 11], histological feature detection [22, 98], and tumor grading [5, 29]. While some of this work reported expert-level performance of AI models, human involvement remains indispensable, primarily in the provision of training labels. However, labeling histological data is a nontrivial task, since it usually suffers from a high variance in tissue appearance [47], subjectivity in medical guidelines [15], and, most importantly, a rare availability of trained specialists [81]. Those barriers result in a low throughput in the medical image processing pipeline. Schaekermann et al. try to break this dilemma by training more available general clinicians—their comprehension of difficult cases could be improved by being exposed to specialist adjudication feedback [81]. However, the validation study shows that labeling performance does not increase significantly, since training humans without comprehensive, informative teaching would incur confusion.

In lieu of training humans, another way to reduce labeling cognitive workload is by using human labels more efficiently. Specifically, multiple projects [70, 89, 116] have employed the concept of active learning [82], where machines could learn from previous input iteratively and recommend the most uncertain cases to users for annotation. For example, Sommer et al. propose Ilastik for cell segmentation model training, which allows users to annotate by drawing strokes over cells [89]. However, the microscopic nature of such labels demands much user effort to achieve gigapixel whole slide-level performance. Nalisnik et al. implement HistomicsML to perform nucleus identification with a random forest classifier, which dynamically recommends the most uncertain patches for annotation in each training iteration [70]. Going beyond selecting the most uncertain samples, Zhu et al. add a diverse constraint to reduce recommended samples' over-concentration in a localized area [116]. However, due to the high variation of histological features, merely relying on limited human annotations without exposing the model to a comprehensive training set, would cause bias. This would result in a dispersion of sensitive false positives across the whole slide image, and humans would lose trust in machines while being overwhelmed with false-positive information.

To address this 'low information input' issue without significantly increasing human burden, recent work [16, 41, 108] applied multiple instance learning (MIL) [7, 115] approaches to digital pathology, where MIL learners could even learn from whole slide-level labels, thus dispensing with the need for users to label at the pixel level. For example, Xu et al. employ MIL [108] to train a patch-level classifier to identify colon cancer based on slide-level annotations. Ilse et al. use an attention-based deep MIL approach to learn a CNN with image-level annotations. The learned CNN can highlight breast or colon cancer areas, with reported performance on par with other MIL approaches without sacrificing interpretability [41]. Campanella et al. combine MIL with Recurrent Neural Network (RNN) techniques and train with a slide-level diagnosis for prostate cancer, basal cell carcinoma, and breast cancer metastases [16]. However, it usually requires a large amount of slide-level annotations for training (for example, [16] used >44,000 slides from >15,000 patients for training); otherwise, there is often a performance drop compared to using strongly supervised labels on the same set of slides.

2.3 Advances in Other AI-Enabled Medical Imaging Modalities

Given the ubiquitous use of visual information for diagnosis and treatment, there exist many other medical imaging modalities in clinics. In this section, we cover three of the modalities that have been widely discussed in the AI research community: colonoscopy, dermatology, and eye imaging.

Colonoscopy images have been mainly studied for the automated detection of polyps, a clinical task that not only is laborious but also suffers from a high mis-detection rate for endoscopists [52]. This is because AI-enabled systems are the potential to function as a second observer to improve endoscopist's performance by indicating the presence of polyps in real time during colonoscopies. With CNN models trained on large-scale colonoscopy datasets with manual annotations, studies have shown that AI can achieve a per-image sensitivity of 92%, a perpolyp sensitivity of 100%, and polyp tracking accuracy of 89% [95, 99]. However, the above studies have treated images independently with CNNs, without considering that colonoscopy data is mostly in the format of videos in clinics. As such, several recent works target to further reduce false-positive detections from AI by exploring the temporal dependency between images in a colonoscopy video: intuitively, a polyp should show among consecutive frames with correlated positions and appearances [76, 111]. Moreover, considering the high variations of polyps, recent work also proposes to adopt the knowledge learnt from a heterogeneous polyp dataset collected from multiple sites to benefit the detection of polyp in site-specific colonoscopy videos by pseudo labeling [112].

Dermatology. Since inspection can assist dermatologists to diagnose many types of skin lesions, there is continuous interest in developing automated diagnostic algorithms for skin issues with photos as input. For example, Vardell et al. introduce a clinical decision support tool for diagnosing multiple skin-related issues (e.g., drug reactions) by indexing archived studies using skin photos and metadata (e.g., body location and surface type) [96], and Wolf et al. explore classifying photos of benign and malignant lesions by using detected lesion border information [105]. With the recent availability of large-scale clinical photo datasets with expert annotations for supervised training, a few studies have reported CNNs that outperform the average dermatologist in the task of diagnosing skin malignancy for a single lesion [31, 38]. Despite the success, one of the challenges is the gap between the retrospective data used for model training/validation and the real-world data: some study suggests that artifacts that are less seen during training, e.g., skin markings, can significantly reduce the CNN's accuracy by increasing its false-positive rate [104].

Eye imaging. Fundus photography is the most used modality for eyes, which can help physicians detect many eye health conditions, e.g., glaucoma, neoplasms of the retina, macular degeneration, and diabetes retinopathy. Two anatomies that are of particular interest for diagnosis are the blood vessels and the optic disk. As such, many AI studies have focused on the task of automated extracting of the two structures, which can potentially assist physician's diagnostic process. For example, existing researches have achieved high accuracy for the detailed segmentation of vessel networks [33, 34, 63] and optic disks [63, 117] with CNNs. Regarding the automated detection of diseases, Gulshan et al. [37] examined the performance of a CNN for classifying the existence of referable diabetic retinopathy from a fundus photo, which shows that comparable accuracy with a panel of at least seven ophthalmologists can be achieved.

2.4 Limitations and Challenges

Parallel to the development of data-driven AI, several limitations and challenges have arisen.

Explainability. Despite its ever-growing accuracy in identifying patterns of specific conditions, medical imaging AI models, in the foreseeable future, will always make mistakes from time to time due to the uncertain and inexact nature of the data and the limitation in the learning methods (e.g., overfitting to the training data loses generalizability). However, being imperfect is not the deal-breaker. Humans are not perfect, either—even the most experienced physicians err from time to time. The 'break-down' seems to be a lack of ability to explain AI's findings as human physicians do with each other. Unlike humans, AI's mistakes are obscured by its 'black box' nature—physicians using AI-enabled diagnostic tools will not be able to tell when AI makes mistakes, why it makes mistakes, or how to fix such mistakes. Likewise, patients using an AI-enabled self-assessment app will hesitate to trust AI's findings, especially when in doubt upon seeing the results. Caruana et al. reported a hospital choosing a rule-based system over a neural model, which is considered too risky because it could not be understood; rules, on the other hand, allow physicians to see an error and prevent it by modifying the rules [19]. This is an example of trading off performance with explainability, a reflection of how high-stake decision-making in medicine imposes requirements on an AI model beyond that it simply works. In order to enable human-centered AI for medical imaging, we need to enable physicians to comprehend AI's findings so that they can trust and act on such findings, which we discuss in Sect. 4.1; explainability should also be addressed in designing AI-enabled self-assessment workflow for patients, which we discuss in Sect. 3.1.

Teachability. Most AI models are developed in a data-driven manner (i.e., trained with annotated datasets)—a process loosely connected with physicians. For example, it is typical to only have just a few labels associated with a radiograph (e.g., keywords extracted from radiologists' reports); as a result, a learning method can only tell a model what condition an image is associated with but not why or how such a conclusion is reached. To address this limit, we can ask physicians to convey their knowledge by providing more annotations than simple labels (e.g., pixel-level annotations that outline the contours of tumor cells); however, such approaches risk adding too much efforts, thus unscalable for constructing large datasets required by training most data-driven AI models. In order to enable human-centered AI for medical imaging, we should strive to make AI more teachable by *(i)* enabling physicians to cost-effectively express their domain knowledge, which is then translated to structured data learnable by a model or alternative models that can be 'incorporated' with the existing model; *(ii)* allowing physicians to alter an AI's behavior (e.g., controlling which range of threshold values to use and which subset of features is more/less relevant given a patient' case). Both approaches are nascent research areas, which we will discuss in Sect. 4.3.

Integrability. Researchers have long realized the limitation of using AI as a 'Greek Oracle'. Miller and Masarie pointed out that a 'mixed initiative system' is mandatory whereby "physician-user and the consultant program should interact symbiotically" [66]. Despite the plethora of AI models, there remain limited discussions on how physicians would use such models amid their day-to-day work: Would their work be reduced to clicking a button? Would they be using new type of clinical decision support systems? Would they interact with AI models before, during, or after their normal workflow? Ideally, given that physicians often have limited time, an AI model should embed itself as a natural part of what a physician already does rather than an extra task. Further, rather than open-endedly interacting with AI, there should be well-defined goals. For example, we will discuss in Sect. 4.3, rather than asking a pathologist to open-endedly label unknown patterns on a whole slide image, there should be clear feedback that shows the (expected) outcome of such labeling and whether they should proceed or stop. Rather than using AI as yet another computer-based tool (Sect. 4.2), perhaps we should seek to define a more collaborative relationship between AI and physicians, similar to how different medical professionals work together (Sect. 4.3).

3 Patient-Centered AI for Medical Imaging

3.1 Enabling Patients to Perform Self-Assessment

With the advent of diagnostic AI for medical imaging, AI-enabled tools provide a promising solution to detect health issues for everyday users as a supplement to clinical visits. Moreover, photography, an imaging modality that can be conveniently and cost-effectively captured by patients, has become the most popular medium for self-assessment. As such, existing research has explored using the widely available and increasingly ubiquitous platform of smartphone cameras for the purpose of health sensing [62]. To investigate the design of patient-centered diagnostic tools, we describe the example of OralCam [54], an interactive tool for enabling the self-examination of oral health. OralCam targeted at detecting five common oral conditions (diseases or early disease signals) that are visually diagnosable using images of one's oral cavity: periodontal disease, caries, soft deposit, dental calculus, and dental discoloration. Early detection of potential oral diseases is important, since it enables interventions that alter its natural course and prevents the onset of adverse outcomes with a minimized cost [27]. A routine dental visit is the most effective way for oral disease detection [23]. However, due to the lack of dental care resources and awareness of oral health, many oral health issues are often left unexamined and untreated, affecting about 3.5 billion people worldwide according to an estimation in [46]. From interviews with three dentists, three key requirements were identified for such a tool to be clinically valid and user-friendly.

Requirement #1: Leveraging additional modalities: In clinical diagnosis, dentists often rely on more than the visuals of a patient's oral cavity. Other factors, e.g., oral cleaning routines, smoking habits, and patients' descriptions of symptoms, also contribute to diagnosis and should be taken into consideration in tandem with smartphone-captured images.

Requirement #2: Providing contextualized results: It is insufficient to simply show whether a condition exists or not. To help users comprehensively understand the self-examination results, it is useful to show the localization of oral diseases as well as related background knowledge on demand, e.g., a layman description with exemplar images of symptoms. Dentists also pointed out that such contextual information (location, background, etc.) can also help gain trust from users, since it sheds light on the mechanism of the underlying detection model.

Requirement #3: Accurate detection: Automatic assessment should be accurate so that users can be informed of possible oral conditions without being misled by false detection. Given that automatic detection algorithms have imperfect accuracy, the level of confidence needs to be clearly conveyed to the user to ensure a comprehensive understanding of their oral conditions.

Guided by the requirements, a prototype of OralCam was designed and implemented as shown in Fig. 1. It has been evaluated with *(i)* 3,182 oral photos with expert annotations for the accuracy of AI model; *(ii)* 18 users over a one-week period for the usability; *(iii)* 2 board-certified dentists for the clinical validity of the design. We describe the implementation of OralCam from the three aspects of **input, modeling**, and **output**, and summarize the corresponding lessons learnt from the evaluation.

Input: OralCam allows users to provide multiple photos on various locations of the oral cavity (Fig. 1b), hygiene habits and medical history from a questionnaire (Fig. 1a), and descriptions of symptoms (e.g., pain and bleeding) by directly drawing on the captured photos (Fig. 1c) (**Requirement #1**). The design of the information collecting mechanism has taken usability into consideration: the questionnaire is designed to consist of only multiple-choice questions; and the photo taking is guided with marks to help users align the camera. All the information collected is incorporated into the model which serves as model priors to enhance AI's performance. According to the evaluation, the information collection design was validated by dentists and found usable by the majority of the users.

Modeling: OralCam formulates the diagnosis as a mix of object localization and image classification by considering the clinical nature of the conditions: object localization is formulated for periodontal disease, caries, and dental calculus since their findings are sparse in locations, while classification is formulated for soft deposit and dental discoloration since the findings usually spread over the whole oral cavity. In order to provide contextualized results for the classification tasks, OralCam further localizes related regions by reasoning the model attention with activation map (**Requirement #2**). To fuse all information of photo, questionnaire, and drawing for the prediction, OralCam proposes to encode questionnaire and draw into one-hot feature maps, and concatenate them channel-wise with deep features from photos. The whole model is end-to-end trainable, and only a small amount of additional parameters are introduced due to the feature fusion mechanism. The evaluation showed high agreements between the AI's predicted localization of and experts' opinion, while the activation maps can miss some regions of findings. Moreover, the information fusion

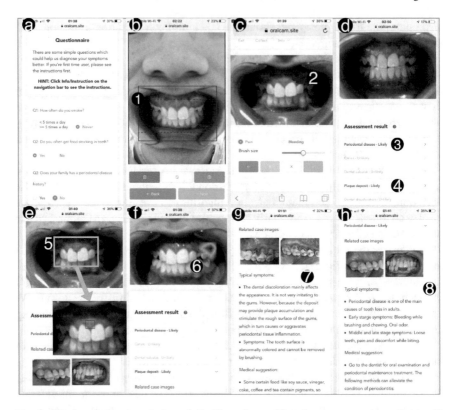

Fig. 1 The key interaction design of OralCam for enabling layman users to perform self-examination of oral health

from different modalities boosted the prediction accuracy for four of the conditions, and by up to 4.80% measured in the area under the curve values.

Output: To convey the confidence of the model on a finding (**Requirement #3**), OralCam sets two operating points for the model to enable trade-offs between miss rate and false positive for the imperfect model: a high-sensitivity point with higher probability thresholds to highlight AI's confident findings, and a high-specificity point with lower probability thresholds for reducing misses. According to such threshold settings, OralCam correspondingly visualizes the likelihood of having each type of disease by grouping them into the following levels: (*i*) unlikely, (*ii*) likely, and (*iii*) very likely (Fig. 1d). To provide contextualized results (**Requirement #2**), Oral-Cam highlights the related regions with either bounding boxes (Fig. 1e) or heatmaps (Fig. 1f) on the input image once a user clicks on a detected condition. Moreover, OralCam expands the disease label with hierarchy information, e.g., typical appearances of such disease, common symptoms, and backgrounds of the disease (Fig. 1g, h). All this information serves to contextualize the user's understanding of an oral condition beyond a simple textual label. With the mentioned designs, the evaluation showed that all the 18 users had no trouble understanding the AI's results (i.e., confidence level and condition visualization). Meanwhile, it was found that most of the users believe the results, with 12 out of 18 of them believing they were having some oral conditions that they were not aware of or could not confirm before the study.

OralCam makes several attempts to improve the explainability of AI-enabled self-assessment tools: By visualizing where the AI model is 'looking at', OralCam allows users to glance into the process of result generation. By showing hierarchical information about a type of detection, OralCam further contextualizes the user's understanding. By presenting predictions probabilistically, OralCam conveys richer information of model confidence. While the study showed the effectiveness of those measures, there were cases that users can still remain skeptical about AI when the results conflict with users' beliefs. For future studies, we advocate that besides showing the regions of conditions, it would help users to understand by giving reasons why the regions are flagged out, e.g., what patterns trigger the prediction, and how the patterns are related to medical knowledge. Challenging as the task is, recent progress of explainable AI [113] aimed to unbox models by interpreting that the learnt deep features might provide a promising solution. Moreover, regarding gaining user's trust, external evidence, e.g., the confirmation of physicians, Food and Drug Administration approvals, and more comprehensive clinical trials, should be investigated.

3.2 Involving Patients in Clinical Diagnosis and Treatment

Patient-centered care is defined as providing care that is respectful of, and responsive to, individual patient preferences, needs, and values, and ensuring that patient values guide all clinical decisions [18]. The concept has been recognized as a key dimension of quality within health care, whereas the patient-physician communication is a vital part of it. According to [68, 79, 91, 94], patients who understand their physicians and procedures are more likely to follow medication schedules, feel satisfied about treatments, and have better medical outcomes. Due to the educational barriers between the patients and the clinicians, conventional verbal instructions may not be effective for involving patients in the clinical process of diagnosis and treatment. As such, a few researchers have investigated visualization and HCI techniques to improve patients' understanding. The most common approach is by accompanying the education with the static 3D visualization of anatomy templates, where example systems include those for abdominal [58], cardiac system [71, 103], and more [102]. The above systems have observed improved understanding from patients about clinical procedures and decisions with the aid of visualization. With the recent advent of computer graphics and AI, construction and interactive manipulation of patient-specific 3D models have become possible, and have shown to be helpful for physician's decision-making [30, 75]. For example, Capuano et al. [17, 61] apply the cardiovascular reconstruction from MRI combined with computational fluid dynamics to assist surgical planning by simulating post-operative pulmonary flow patterns; Yang et al. [110] show that the preoperative simulation with reconstructed heads from

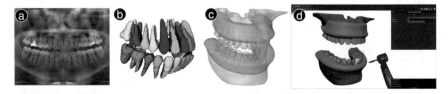

Fig. 2 OralViewer takes a patient's 2D X-ray (**a**) as input, and reconstructs the 3D teeth structure (**b**) with a novel deep learning model. The system then generates the complete oral cavity model (**c**) by registering the pre-defined models of jaw bone and gum to the dental arch curve. Finally, a dentist can demonstrate the forthcoming surgeries to a patient by animating the steps with our virtual dental instruments (**d**)

CT can make condyle surgeries more accurate and more convenient; Endo et al. [28] demonstrate a simulation system with detailed tissue and vein segmentations to navigate operations. Despite those efforts, only limited work has studied the application of AI for the purpose of involving patients in clinical diagnosis and treatment.

Here, we take the example of OralViewer [55] to discuss how the combination of HCI and AI can help improve patient-physician communication. OralViewer is a web-based tool to enable dentists to virtually demonstrate dental surgeries on 3D oral cavity models. The need for dental surgery demonstration arises not only from patient-centered care but also from relieving the anxiety of oral surgeries: up to every fourth adult reports dental fear [72], and an effective solution is to unveil the surgical steps with patient education to decrease patients' fear of the unknown [4, 44]. To inform the design of OralViewer, three dentists were interviewed and two key requirements for the visualization were elicited from a clinical point of view.

Requirement #1: Providing patient-specific 3D model from 2D imaging: Dental surgical steps, e.g., how a fractured tooth is extracted or repaired, often depend on an individual's teeth condition. Thus, a patient-specific teeth model should be provided to make demonstrations contextualized to the patient's conditions. Moreover, 3D screening of oral cavity (e.g., Cone-beam CT) is not standard practice for the clinical diagnosis of many common surgeries, e.g., apicoectomy and root canal treatment, for its high radiation and cost. As such, it is preferred to generate a patient's 3D teeth model from his/her 2D X-ray image to enable the widely available application of the tool.

Requirement #2: Modeling complete oral cavity: Both the target oral structure of a surgery and its nearby anatomies need to be incorporated into a surgical demonstration. For example, when a dentist removes a root tip in apicoectomy, procedures on other structures should be simulated as well. Thus, to help patients understand what to expect in a surgery, a complete oral cavity including teeth, gum, and jawbones should be modeled.

Informed by the aforementioned requirements, a prototype of OralViewer was designed and implemented as shown in Fig. 2. Overall, OralViewer consists of two cascaded parts: *(i)* a 3D reconstruction pipeline for generating a patient's oral cavity from a single 2D panoramic X-ray with the aid of AI (Fig. 2a→c), and *(ii)* a demon-

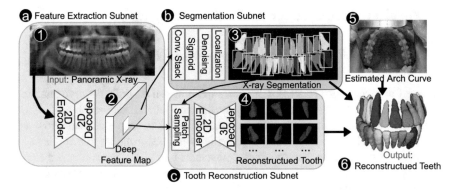

Fig. 3 OralViewer reconstructs 3D patient-specific tooth structures (6) from a single panoramic X-ray (1)

stration interface for dentist's animating steps on the 3D model with virtual dental instruments (Fig. 2d). To meet the requirements of complete and patient-specific oral cavity modeling, OralViewer combines the recent technique of 3D reconstruction with deformable template modeling. In the first step, a novel deep CNN as shown in Fig. 3 (**Requirement #1**) is proposed to estimate the patient's 3D teeth structures from a single 2D panoramic X-ray (Fig. 3 1). The task is more challenging than anatomy modeling in surgical planning scenarios, where detailed 3D medical imaging (e.g., CT and MRI) are available for extracting 3D virtual models. To tackle it, the model decomposes it into two easier sub-tasks of teeth localization (Fig. 3b) and patch-wise single tooth reconstruction (Fig. 3c); meanwhile, feature maps (Fig. 3a) are shared to increase the generalization of the model. A semi-automatic pipeline is applied to extract the dental arch curve (Fig. 3 5) from occlusal surface photos of the patient, since such information is lost during the rotational screening process of a panoramic X-ray. In the second step, 3D templates of gum and jawbones are defined from existing 3D head CTs, and non-rigidly registered to the estimated teeth to tailor for specific patients' oral anatomy, since the 3D structures of gum and jaw cannot be well-reflected from X-ray. Finally, the deformed gum and jawbone model can be assembled with the 3D reconstructed teeth for the complete oral cavity model (**Requirement #2**). The technical evaluation with data of 10 patients showed that the CNN-based 3D teeth reconstruction achieved an average intersection over a union of 0.771 ± 0.062. The expert study with 3 board-certificated dentists further confirmed that reconstructed oral cavity models could appropriately reflect patient-specific conditions, and was clinically valid for patient education.

4   Physician-Centered AI for Medical Imaging

4.1   Enabling Physicians to Comprehend AI's Findings

Since AI ultimately is a processor of data, explaining an AI boils down to enabling physicians to comprehend how data is transformed when processed by AI. If we understand how physicians currently interact with data in an AI-less workflow, we can design an AI-enabled system that presents data transformation in a similar way to promote a better understanding by the physicians. In [107], we conducted a preliminary interview study that collected six medical professionals' reflections of how they interact with data for diagnosis and treatment purposes. Our data reveals when and how doctors prioritize various types of data as a central part of their diagnosis process. Based on these findings, we outline directions of explainability in the medical domain when designing XAI systems, as shown in Fig. 4.

To instantiate this design space, we focus on one of the most common modalities—chest X-ray (CXR) images. We took a user-centered approach to design a system that encapsulates a CXR AI to explainably present its findings, allowing referring physicians to see and understand such findings [106]. As shown in Fig. 5, we started with a survey, which informed a user-centered design to formulate CheXplain—a

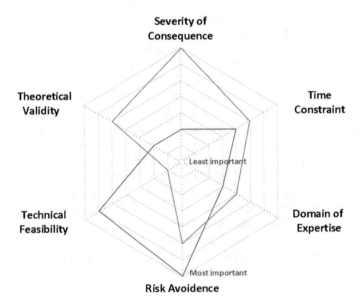

Fig. 4 A diagram that compares the prioritization matrices held by two different medical professionals (blue versus orange line) when making diagnosis decisions. While one doctor uses severity as the primary parameter to weigh various data during diagnosis/treatment, the other cares most about the calculation of risks and responsibilities

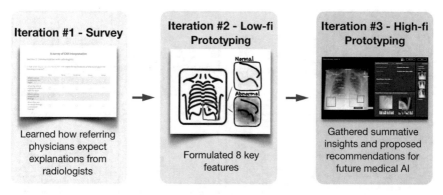

Fig. 5 To enable physicians to comprehend AI's findings, we conducted three user-centered activities to formulate the design of CheXplain [106]—a system that enables physicians to explore and understand AI-enabled chest X-ray analysis

system for physicians to interactively explore and understand CXR analysis generated by a state-of-the-art AI [42].

Iteration #1: Survey We conducted a paired survey on both referring physicians (N = 39) and radiologists (N = 38) to learn about how radiologists currently explain their analysis to referring physicians and how referring physicians expect explanations from both human and (hyperthetical) AI radiologists. The findings reveal whether, when, and what kinds of explanations are needed between referring physicians and radiologists. By juxtaposing referring physicians' responses to these questions with respect to human versus AI radiologists, we elicit system requirements that encompass the current practices and a future of AI-enabled diagnosis.

Iteration #2: Low-fi prototype co-designed with three physicians manifested the survey-generated system requirements into eight specific features (Fig. 6a–f): augmenting input CXR images with specific inquiries, mediating system complexity by the level of urgency, presenting explanation hierarchically, calibrating regional findings with contrastive examples, communicating results probabilistically, contextualizing impressions with additional information, and comparing with images in the past or from other patients.

Iteration #3: High-fi prototype integrates the eight features into CheXplain (Fig. 7)—a functional system front-end that allows physician users to explore *real* results generated by an AI [42] while all the other explanatory information either comes from real clinical reports or is manually generated by a radiologist collaborator. An evaluation with six medical professionals provides summative insights on each feature. Participants provided more detailed and accurate explanations of the underlying AI after interacting with CheXplain. We summarize the design and implementation recommendations for the future development of explainable medical AI.

One meaningful finding in this process is the distinction between explanation and justification. Our research started with a focus on explanations of AI, which enables

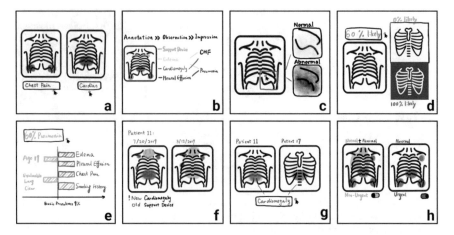

Fig. 6 Low-fidelity prototypes of eight key system designs of CheXplain formulated by co-design sessions with physicians from UCLA Health

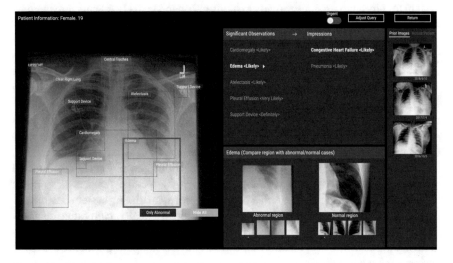

Fig. 7 The High-fidelity prototype of CheXplain, which was evaluated in work sessions involving eight physicians across the US

physicians to understand AI with an *intrinsic* process of producing certain output given certain input data, e.g., processing pixels of a CXR image to arrive at certain observations. Later, as we co-designed CheXplain with physicians, a different set of ideas emerged, which tried to draw on the *extrinsic* sources of information to justify AI's results. Such justifications include the prevalence of a disease, contrastive examples from other CXR images, and a patient's history. Thus, we consider explanations and justifications as two categories of methods that help physicians understand AI.

Two design recommendations arise:

Use more explanation for medical data analysis (e.g., radiologists), and more justification for medical data consumers (e.g., referring physicians). We find that radiologists tend to expect more explanations for details such as low-level annotations of CXR images, while referring physicians are generally less concerned about the intrinsic details but care more about the extrinsic validity of AI's results. Retrospectively, we can see that five of CheXplain's features are a justification (#3-7).

Enable explanation and justification at different levels of abstraction, similar to how CheXplain employs the examination-observation-impression hierarchy to scaffold both explanation and justification. Holistically, as a physician follows a bottom-up or top-down path to understand an AI's diagnosis of a patient, at any step along the way, they should be able to seek both explanation and justification. To achieve this, the XAI community needs to consider explanation regulated by a user-specified level of abstraction; research on Content-Based Image Retrieval (CBIR) should enable search criteria at multiple levels of abstraction, e.g., from a region of specific visual features to a global image that presents a specific impression.

4.2 Enabling Physicians to Use AI as Tools

With the extensive study of medical imaging AI as we have introduced in Sect. 2, many AI-enabled tools have been proposed to assist physicians in various clinical tasks. The tools can be roughly classified into *(i)* diagnostic tools, which provide diagnostic decisions with predictive modeling, and *(ii)* non-diagnostic tools, which supply information of potential use to physician's decision-making. Diagnostic tools are potential to assist physicians in ways, including reducing human error by acting as a second reader, decreasing human fatigue by handling simple routine tasks, and eliciting new knowledge for physicians by extracting previously unrecognized associations between image patterns and diagnosis [74]. Meanwhile, different non-diagnostic tools are under investigation, e.g., computer-aided design systems with implant auto-generation [53], clinical decision support systems with patient-specific assessment reasoning from scans and records [92], and surgery planning with automated anatomy segmentation [21]. In this section, we will use OralViewer [55], the patient education tool for dentists as we have mentioned in Sect. 3.2, and SmartReporting [84], a medical report generation system, to contextualize our introduction. We then discuss the challenges for the deployment of existing AI-enabled tools in clinics.

4.2.1 OralViewer

The demonstration interface of OralViewer was developed in collaboration with three dentists, after the satisfactory AI modeling of the oral cavity had been achieved. To make the tool effective for patient education and convenient for dentists to use in the clinical setting, the following requirement was raised by the dentists.

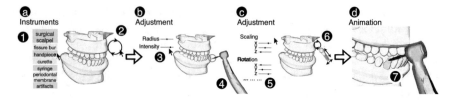

Fig. 8 Overall workflow for demonstrating dental surgeries with OralViewer

Requirement: The dentists consider it important to show for each surgery step: (*i*) how the step is performed—illustrating the applied instruments, and (*ii*) what happens in the step—animating the dental structure changes upon the application of instruments. Moreover, the demonstration should be carried out by dentists using simple interaction techniques, which is more important than having to achieve realistic effects with high fidelity.

Guided by the requirement, a prototype of OralViewer's interface was developed, with the overall workflow as shown in Fig. 8. OralViewer provides a web-based interface for dentists to demonstrate surgery steps with a set of virtual dental instruments. The dental instruments allow dentists to express what and where an action is applied to the oral cavity, and demonstrate the effect on the model in real time. A dentist starts by importing a reconstructed 3D oral cavity model (Fig. 8a), which can be viewed freely with rotation and scaling. To apply a virtual dental instrument, the dentist selects the instrument from a list (Fig. 8l). Upon the selection, the corresponding instrument model (Fig. 8(4, 6)) is visualized, and can be controlled with a mouse to move and operate on the oral cavity model. Moreover, dentists can use simple sliders to customize the animation effect of the instruments to better suit their particular needs and preferences Fig. 8(3, 5). The selected instrument can be directly applied to a dental structure for demonstrating effects with clicking, pressing, and dragging (Fig. 8d). Since a typical dental surgery consists of sequential steps using multiple dental instruments, the aforementioned steps of instrument selection, adjusting, and animating can be repeated to demonstrate.

OralViewer was validated for the demonstration of two common but complex dental surgeries, crown lengthening and apicoectomy, each of which involves multiple steps. The user study involving 12 patients compared the effectiveness of patient education using OralViewer and the common practice of verbal descriptions, and the result indicated that OralViewer led to a significantly better understanding of a forthcoming surgery ($p < 0.05$). The expert study with three dentists, who had the user experience of OralViewer showed a high preference for the tool, pointed out that such tool can be very necessary with the patients' recently growing need for improved dentist visit experience and their willingness to involve in treatment planning. Regarding the usability, experts pointed out that the virtual instrument control with a mouse was unfamiliar to dentists: it is different from the way dentists use real dental instruments in a surgery, which can lead to a steep learning curve. As such, an implementation on a touch screen, e.g., iPad, with the control using a stylus can be more intuitive to dentists.

4.2.2 SmartReporting

For every medical study (e.g., X-ray, CT, and MRI) performed, a physician is required to generate a report describing all the pertinent findings (i.e., both positive findings and pertinent negative ones). Since reports need to be comprehensive and accurate, the act of generating reports usually takes a large amount of physicians' time for each study performed. At the same time, with the large number of medical imaging studies conducted annually [87, 88], it is imperative that physicians make diagnoses based on studies efficiently and accurately. Thus, there is a need for tools that can reduce the time cost of physicians generating a report. The state-of-the-art systems enable the physician to input findings by voice while reading a study, which is converted to textual sentences automatically in real time with voice recognition algorithms [77, 77, 93]. However, such systems can lead to fatigue, since the physician needs to consistently speak into a microphone on a typical workday. Moreover, they are vulnerable to speech interpretation accuracy—the variety of speaker accents and uncommon medical terminologies predispose them to errors, which from time to time requires physicians to revise or re-enter the findings.

Different from those systems, SmartReporting alleviates medical knowledge and AI-enabled automated awareness of anatomy/finding to save a physician's effort in creating reports. First, a template is pre-defined for each finding type at each anatomy, which can include entries and options for detailing different aspects of a finding. An example of such a template is shown in Fig. 9. The physician can fill in the template by one or more types of human-machine interactions, such as mouse clicks, screen taps, typing, and speaking into a microphone. By encoding medical knowledge, such templates reduce the amount of physician's inputs from the full narration of findings to the selecting or key value entering. Next, to enable the fast retrieving of templates and their automated filling, SmartReporting defines two working modes: semi-auto mode and auto mode.

Semi-auto mode: captures mouse clicks from the physician on the location of interest, and prompts the physician to select a template from a list to fill in for describing the finding (Fig. 10a). The list is filtered to consist only of the templates that are related to the anatomies around the cursor location of activation. To achieve anatomy awareness, a CNN-based anatomical segmentation algorithm is applied, which incorporates structural invariances to enhance model robustness to possible pathologies [56]. Figure 11b demonstrates the segmentation of 65 anatomies for an input head CT as an example.

Auto mode: It makes use of the computer-aided diagnosis of a medical scan. As shown in Fig. 10b, upon the activation, the physician is prompted with a list of templates that are related to the findings around the selected location. Moreover, the templates selected are also pre-filled with information from the automated diagnosis for extra time saving. For example, the dimension of a hemorrhage can be calculated

Fig. 9 An example of the interactive template of SmartReporting, which is used to guide the physician to fill in descriptions of a finding

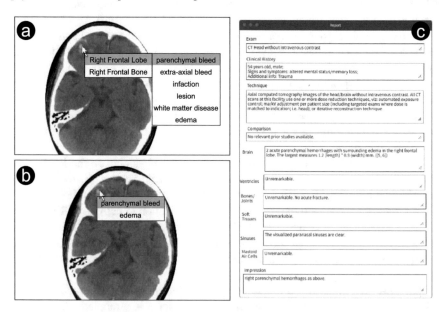

Fig. 10 SmartReporting's interactive study display interface with its response to the physician's selections in the **a** semi-auto mode and **b** auto mode. **c** An example of the SmartReporting's report screen with an auto-generated readable report

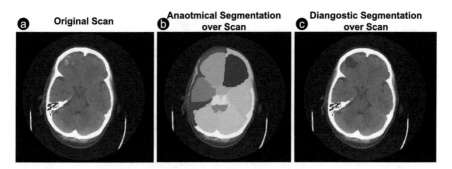

Fig. 11 Given a head CT scan (**a**), SmartReporting's AI enables the segmentation of 65 anatomies (**b**) for both semi-auto and auto modes, and the segmentation of multiple types of positive finding, e.g., hemorrhage and edema (**c**), for the auto mode

with the AI's predicted region and the voxel spacing information that is stored in the metadata of a scan. The physician can edit or confirm the template with the pre-filled text. To achieve the automated diagnosis, SmartReporting applies multiple CNN models that are known in the art [20], with each for detecting the existence of one type of finding and generating a mask for it. As an example, Fig. 11c illustrates the detection and segmentation of hemorrhage and edema from an input head CT.

Once the physician finishes describing all the findings, SmartReporting converts the filled templates into a medical report, as the example shows in Fig. 11c. Such conversion is done using a pre-defined mapping protocol that maps template entry-option pairs to readable sentences.

SmartReporting has the potential to provide multiple advantages over the state-of-the-art voice-based reporting systems: *(i)* it can reduce the time to complete diagnosis by using pre-defined templates to describe findings, using image-based AI to accelerate the template retrieval/filling, and automatically converting filled templates into reports; *(ii)* it can reduce interpretation mistakes, since the physician instead describing findings by mainly making selections based on the options provided via templates; *(iii)* it is more adaptable for multiple language interchange, since it mostly uses built-in entries and options for describing findings, which are stored with encodings that are independent of languages; *(iv)* it also has the potential to ease the mining of medical records, which is a meaningful task for disease prediction and improving the clinical decision-making [45], since all the findings generated are standard in wordings and structured in formats.

Despite the achievements of the above-mentioned computer tools, they all have a relatively simple working mode of first presenting the AI's result as is, and then the physician diagnoses by accepting/declining the result or basing the practice on the result. As such, the performance of the tools can be largely affected by the mispredictions from AI. Some study has suggested that a physician can possibly be more likely to miss a diagnosis with the presence of a false-negative AI detection than without the AI system [51]. However, errors are almost inevitable for current AI algorithms due to multiple reasons, e.g., the ambiguity exists in medical imaging, medical images can be heterogeneous with differences in equipment/scan protocols, and dataset annotations can be sparse and noisy [114]. As such, how to better integrate AI into physician's clinical workflows to reach their full potential for clinical assistance is a key.

4.3 Enabling Physicians to Collaborate with AI

As mentioned above, one major challenge of AI-enabled diagnosis is finding a way to integrate AI with how physicians currently perform diagnoses: how can a human physician collaborate with AI? Among various medical imaging techniques, histological data in digital pathology [39], in particular, presents some of the most difficult challenges for achieving AI-automated diagnosis, thus serving as an ideal arena to explore the interactional relationship between physicians and AI.

Focusing on digital pathology as a point of departure, we propose a series of physician-AI collaboration techniques, based on which we prototype Impetus—a tool where an AI aids a pathologist in histological slide tumor detection using multiple degrees of initiatives [36]. Trained on a limited-sized dataset, our AI model cannot fully automate the examination process; instead, Impetus harnesses AI to *(i)* guide pathologists' attention to regions of major outliers, thus helping them prioritize the manual examination process (Fig. 12a); *(ii)* use agile labeling to train and adapt itself on-the-fly by learning from pathologists (Fig. 12b); *(iii)* take initiatives appropriately for the level of performance confidence, from automation to pre-filling diagnosis, and to defaulting back to manual examination (Fig. 12c).

We used the Impetus prototype as a medium to engage eight pathologists and observe how they perform diagnosis with AI involved in the process and elicit pathologists' qualitative reactions and feedback on the aforementioned collaborative techniques. We summarize lessons learned as follows:

Lesson #1: To explain AI's guidance, suggestions and recommendations, the system should go beyond a one-size-fits-all concept and provide instance-specific details that allow a medical user to see evidence that leads to a recommendation. **Recommendation #1**: an overview + instance-based explanation of AI's suggestions. Currently, Impetus only provides an explanation of the suggested regions at the overview level: a textual description of the outlier detection method as part of the tutorial and visualization (i.e., attention map) that shows the degree of 'outlying' across the WSI. As an addition, we can further incorporate instance-based explanation, i.e., with information specific to a particular patient and a particular region on the patient's slide. The idea is to allow pathologists to question why a specific region is recommended by clicking on the corresponding part of the slide, which prompts the system to show a comparison between the recommended region and a number of samples from non-recommended parts of the slide for the physician to contrast features in these regions extracted by AI. One important consideration is that such an additional explanation should be made available on demand rather than shown

Fig. 12 Key interactive features of Impetus: **a** as a pathologist loads a whole slide image, AI highlights areas of interest identified by outlier detection, shown as two yellow recommended boxes. **b** Agile labeling: pathologists can drag and click to provide a label that can be used to train the AI's model. **c** Diagnosis dialogue, pre-filled with AI's diagnosis, allows the pathologist to either confirm or disregard and proceed with manual diagnosis

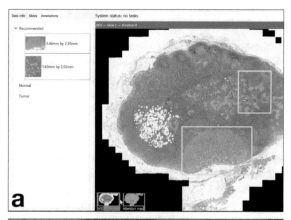

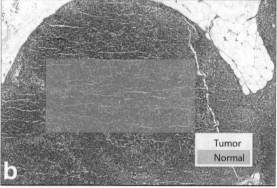

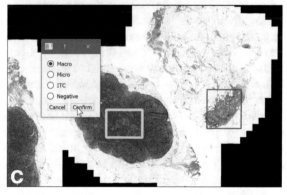

by default, which could defeat the recommendation boxes' purpose to accelerate the pathologists' examination process.

Lesson #2: Medical diagnosis is seldom a one-shot task, thus AI's recommendations need to continuously direct a medical user to filter and prioritize a large task space, taking into account new information extracted from a user's up-to-date input. **Recommendation #2**: make AI-generated suggestions always available (and constantly evolving) throughout the process of a (manual) examination. For example, in Impetus, a straightforward design idea is to show recommendation boxes one after another. We believe this is especially helpful when the pathologist might be drawn to a local, zoomed-in region and neglects looking at the rest of the WSI. The always-available recommendation boxes can serve as global anchors that inform pathologists of what might need to be examined elsewhere beyond the current view. This is an example of a multi-shot diagnosis behavior where each shot is an attempt to find tumor cells in a selected region.

Lesson #3: Medical tasks are often time-critical, thus the benefits of AI's guidance, suggestions and recommendations need to be weighed by the amount of extra efforts incurred and the actionability of the provided information. **Recommendation #3**: weigh the amount of extra efforts by co-designing a system with target medical users, as different physicians have a different notion of time urgency. Emergency room doctors often deal with urgent cases by making decisions in a matter of seconds, and internists often perform examinations in 15–20 min per patient, and oncologists or implant specialists might decide on a case via multiple meetings that span days. There is a sense of timeliness in all these scenarios, but the amount of time that can be budgeted differs from case to case. To address such differences, we further recommend modeling each interactive task in a medical AI system (i.e., how long it might take for the user to perform each task) and providing a mechanism that allows physicians to 'filter out' interactive components that might take too much time (e.g., the attention map in Impetus). Importantly, different levels of urgency should be modifiable (perhaps as a one-time setup) by physicians in different specialties.

Lesson #4: To guide the examination process with prioritization, AI should help a medical user narrow in small regions of a large task space, as well as helping them filter out information within specific regions. **Recommendation #4**: use visualization to filter out information, i.e., leverage AI's results to reduce information load for the physicians. An example would be a spotlight effect that darkens parts of a WSI where AI detects little or no tumor cells. Based on our observation that pathologists used AI's results to confirm their examination on the original H&E WSI, such an overt visualization can help them filter out subsets of the WSI patches. Meanwhile, pathologists can also reveal a darkened region if they want to examine further AI's findings (e.g., when they disagree with AI, believing a darkened spot has signs of tumor).

Lesson #5: It is possible for medical users to provide labels during their workflow with acceptable extra effort. However, the system should provide explicit feedback on how the model improves as a result, as a way to motivate and guide medical users' future inputs. **Recommendation #5**: when adapting the model on-the-fly, show a visualization that indicates the model's performance changes as the physician labels more data. There could be various designs of such information, from showing low-level technical details (e.g., the model's specificity versus sensitivity), high-level visualization (e.g., charts that plot accuracy over WSIs read), and even actionable items (e.g., 'nudging' the user to label certain classes of data to balance the training set). There are two main factors to consider when evaluating a given design: *(i)* as we observed in our study, whether the design could inform the physician of the model's performance improvement or degradation as they label more data, which can be measured quantitatively as the amount of performance gain divided by the amount of labeling work done; *(ii)* as we noted in Lesson #2, whether consuming the extra information incurs too much effort and slows down the agile labeling process and whether there is actionability given the extra information about model performance changes.

Lesson #6: Tasks treated equally by an AI might carry different weights to a medical user. Thus for medically high-staked tasks, AI should provide information to validate its confidence level. **Recommendation #6**: provide additional justification for a negative diagnosis of a high-staked disease. For example, when Impetus concludes a case as negative, the system can still display the top five regions wherein AI finds the most likely signs of tumor (albeit below a threshold of positivity). In this way, even if the result turned out to be a false negative, the physicians would be guided to examine regions where the actual tumor cells are likely to appear. Beyond such intrinsic details, it is also possible to retrieve extrinsic information, e.g., prevalence of the disease given the patient's population, or similar histological images for comparison. As suggested in [106], such extrinsic justification can complement the explanation of a model's intrinsic process, thus allowing physicians to understand AI's decision more comprehensively.

5 Outlook and Summary

Democratization of medical imaging techniques and advanced data-driven computer vision catalyze data acquisition and processing, enabling physician-centered diagnosis (e.g., radiograph reading and cancer detection from digital pathology) and patient-centered examination (e.g., self-assessment of oral conditions). Since medical diagnosis is essentially an information-management task [86], we should expect to see an increasing development of datasets, models, and systems that attempt to dispose of physicians of the onerous labor of examining imaging data. However, the main challenges are beyond what goes into a model; the medical and AI community have long realized that replacing physicians remains an unrealistic goal in the foreseeable future, given the inherent limitations of the data, the inevitability of prediction errors, and the high stakes in medical decision-making. This chapter describes a series of works with a cross-cutting theme of human-centered AI for medical imaging. For patient-facing self-assessment, this means guiding a user to capture imaging data using their personal devices, using AI to generate personalized models, and informing patients not only of AI's findings but also how to interpret such

Fig. 13 Our ultimate vision is a closed loop between physicians/patients and AI where AI presents its findings comprehensible to humans, while allowing humans to control its behavior, thus achieving human-AI collaborative diagnosis

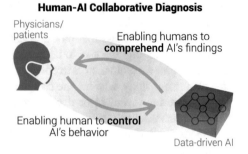

Human-AI Collaborative Diagnosis

Physicians/patients

Enabling humans to **comprehend** AI's findings

Enabling human to **control** AI's behavior

Data-driven AI

findings. For physician-facing diagnosis, human-centered AI also means enabling them to comprehend AI's findings so that physicians can decide whether to trust and how to act on such findings; in addition, AI can empower tools that augment a physician's work (e.g., making the report generation process faster and more accurate); and finally, there are various mechanisms for physicians to collaborate with AI, e.g., AI recommending regions to prioritize examinations and AI making predictions at a level appropriate for its confidence. In the future, we should expect to see more emergent work that employs a human-centered approach to enable physician-AI collaboration. As illustrated in Fig. 13, our ultimate vision is a closed loop between physicians/patients and AI where AI presents its findings comprehensibly to humans, while allowing humans to control its behavior, thus achieving a human-AI collaborative diagnosis.

References

1. Alansary A, Oktay O, Li Y, Le Folgoc L, Hou B, Vaillant G, Kamnitsas K, Vlontzos A, Glocker B, Kainz B et al (2019) Evaluating reinforcement learning agents for anatomical landmark detection. Med Image Anal 53:156–164
2. Amodei D, Olah C, Steinhardt J, Christiano P, Schulman J, Mané D (2016) Concrete problems in AI safety. arXiv preprint arXiv:1606.06565
3. Araújo T, Aresta G, Castro E, Rouco J, Aguiar P, Eloy C, Polónia A, Campilho A (2017) Classification of breast cancer histology images using convolutional neural networks. PloS ONE 12(6):e0177544
4. Armfield JM, Heaton L (2013) Management of fear and anxiety in the dental clinic: a review. Aust Dent J 58(4):390–407
5. Arvaniti E, Fricker KS, Moret M, Rupp N, Hermanns T, Fankhauser C, Wey N, Wild PJ, Rueschoff JH, Claassen M (2018) Automated Gleason grading of prostate cancer tissue microarrays via deep learning. Sci Rep 8(1):1–11
6. Avants BB, Epstein CL, Grossman M, Gee JC (2008) Symmetric diffeomorphic image registration with cross-correlation: evaluating automated labeling of elderly and neurodegenerative brain. Med Image Anal 12(1):26–41
7. Babenko B (2008) Multiple instance learning: algorithms and applications. View Article PubMed/NCBI Google Scholar, pp 1–19

8. Balakrishnan G, Zhao A, Sabuncu MR, Guttag J, Dalca AV (2019) Voxelmorph: a learning framework for deformable medical image registration. IEEE Trans Med Imaging 38(8):1788–1800

9. Bardou D, Zhang K, Ahmad SM (2018) Classification of breast cancer based on histology images using convolutional neural networks. IEEE Access 6:24680–24693

10. Bates DW, Kuperman GJ, Wang S, Gandhi T, Kittler A, Volk L, Spurr C, Khorasani R, Tanasijevic M, Middleton B (2003) Ten commandments for effective clinical decision support: making the practice of evidence-based medicine a reality. J Am Med Inform Assoc: JAMIA 10(6):523–530. https://doi.org/10.1197/jamia.M1370, https://www.ncbi.nlm.nih.gov/pmc/articles/PMC264429/

11. Bejnordi BE, Veta M, Van Diest PJ, Van Ginneken B, Karssemeijer N, Litjens G, Van Der Laak JA, Hermsen M, Manson QF, Balkenhol M et al (2017) Diagnostic assessment of deep learning algorithms for detection of lymph node metastases in women with breast cancer. JAMA 318(22):2199–2210

12. Berner ES (2007) Clinical decision support systems, vol 233. Springer, Berlin

13. Beutel J, Kundel HL, Van Metter RL (2000) Handbook of medical imaging, vol 1. SPIE Press, Bellingham

14. de Brebisson A, Montana G (2015) Deep neural networks for anatomical brain segmentation. In: Proceedings of the IEEE conference on computer vision and pattern recognition workshops, pp 20–28

15. Cai CJ, Winter S, Steiner D, Wilcox L, Terry M (2019) " Hello AI": uncovering the onboarding needs of medical practitioners for human-AI collaborative decision-making. Proc ACM Hum-Comput Interact 3(CSCW), 1–24

16. Campanella G, Hanna MG, Geneslaw L, Miraflor A, Silva VWK, Busam KJ, Brogi E, Reuter VE, Klimstra DS, Fuchs TJ (2019) Clinical-grade computational pathology using weakly supervised deep learning on whole slide images. Nat Med 25(8):1301–1309

17. Capuano F, Loke YH, Cronin I, Olivieri LJ, Balaras E (2019) Computational study of pulmonary flow patterns after repair of transposition of great arteries. J Biomech Eng 141(5)

18. Carroll JG (2002) Crossing the quality chasm: a new health system for the 21st century. Qual Manag Healthc 10(4):60–61

19. Caruana R, Lou Y, Gehrke J, Koch P, Sturm M, Elhadad N (2015) Intelligible models for healthcare: predicting pneumonia risk and hospital 30-day readmission. In: Proceedings of the ACM SIGKDD international conference on knowledge discovery and data mining. https://doi.org/10.1145/2783258.2788613

20. Chang PD, Kuoy E, Grinband J, Weinberg BD, Thompson M, Homo R, Chen J, Abcede H, Shafie M, Sugrue L et al (2018) Hybrid 3D/2D convolutional neural network for hemorrhage evaluation on head CT. Am J Neuroradiol 39(9):1609–1616

21. Çiçek Ö, Abdulkadir A, Lienkamp SS, Brox T, Ronneberger O (2016) 3D U-net: learning dense volumetric segmentation from sparse annotation. In: International conference on medical image computing and computer-assisted intervention. Springer, pp 424–432

22. Cireşan DC, Giusti A, Gambardella LM, Schmidhuber J (2013) Mitosis detection in breast cancer histology images with deep neural networks. In: International conference on medical image computing and computer-assisted intervention. Springer, pp 411–418

23. Cohen LA (2013) Expanding the physician's role in addressing the oral health of adults. Am J Public Health 103(3):408–412

24. Cooper GF, Abraham V, Aliferis CF, Aronis JM, Buchanan BG, Caruana R, Fine MJ, Janosky JE, Livingston G, Mitchell T, Monti S, Spirtes P (2005) Predicting dire outcomes of patients with community acquired pneumonia. J Biomed Inform 38(5):347–366. https://doi.org/10.1016/j.jbi.2005.02.005

25. Cooper GF, Aliferis CF, Ambrosino R, Aronis J, Buchanan BG, Caruana R, Fine MJ, Glymour C, Gordon G, Hanusa BH, Janosky JE, Meek C, Mitchell T, Richardson T, Spirtes P (1997) An evaluation of machine-learning methods for predicting pneumonia mortality. Artif Intell Med 9(2):107–138. https://doi.org/10.1016/s0933-3657(96)00367-3

26. Croskerry P, Cosby K, Graber ML, Singh H (2017) Diagnosis: interpreting the shadows. CRC Press, Boca Raton
27. Deep P (2000) Screening for common oral diseases. J-Can Dent Assoc 66(6):298–299
28. Endo K, Sata N, Ishiguro Y, Miki A, Sasanuma H, Sakuma Y, Shimizu A, Hyodo M, Lefor A, Yasuda Y (2014) A patient-specific surgical simulator using preoperative imaging data: an interactive simulator using a three-dimensional tactile mouse. J Comput Surg 1(1):1–8
29. Ertosun MG, Rubin DL (2015) Automated grading of gliomas using deep learning in digital pathology images: a modular approach with ensemble of convolutional neural networks. In: AMIA annual symposium proceedings, vol 2015. American Medical Informatics Association, p 1899
30. Eschweiler J, Stromps JP, Fischer M, Schick F, Rath B, Pallua N, Radermacher K (2016) A biomechanical model of the wrist joint for patient-specific model guided surgical therapy: part 2. Proc Inst Mech Eng Part H: J Eng Med 230(4):326–334
31. Esteva A, Kuprel B, Novoa RA, Ko J, Swetter SM, Blau HM, Thrun S (2017) Dermatologist-level classification of skin cancer with deep neural networks. Nature 542(7639), 115–118
32. Falk T, Mai D, Bensch R, Çiçek Ö, Abdulkadir A, Marrakchi Y, Böhm A, Deubner J, Jäckel Z, Seiwald K et al (2019) U-net: deep learning for cell counting, detection, and morphometry. Nat Methods 16(1):67–70
33. Fu H, Xu Y, Lin S, Wong DWK, Liu J (2016) Deepvessel: retinal vessel segmentation via deep learning and conditional random field. In: International conference on medical image computing and computer-assisted intervention. Springer, pp 132–139
34. Fu H, Xu Y, Wong DWK, Liu J (2016) Retinal vessel segmentation via deep learning network and fully-connected conditional random fields. In: 2016 IEEE 13th international symposium on biomedical imaging (ISBI). IEEE, pp 698–701
35. Gal Y, Ghahramani Z (2016) Dropout as a Bayesian approximation: representing model uncertainty in deep learning. In: International conference on machine learning, pp 1050–1059
36. Gu H, Huang J, Hung L, Chen XA (2020) Lessons learned from designing an AI-enabled diagnosis tool for pathologists. arXiv:2006.12695 null
37. Gulshan V, Peng L, Coram M, Stumpe MC, Wu D, Narayanaswamy A, Venugopalan S, Widner K, Madams T, Cuadros J et al (2016) Development and validation of a deep learning algorithm for detection of diabetic retinopathy in retinal fundus photographs. JAMA 316(22):2402–2410
38. Haenssle HA, Fink C, Schneiderbauer R, Toberer F, Buhl T, Blum A, Kalloo A, Hassen ABH, Thomas L, Enk A et al (2018) Man against machine: diagnostic performance of a deep learning convolutional neural network for dermoscopic melanoma recognition in comparison to 58 dermatologists. Ann Oncol 29(8):1836–1842
39. Holzinger A, Malle B, Kieseberg P, Roth PM, Müller H, Reihs R, Zatloukal K (2017) Towards the augmented pathologist: challenges of explainable-AI in digital pathology. arXiv preprint arXiv:1712.06657
40. Huo Y, Xu Z, Xiong Y, Aboud K, Parvathaneni P, Bao S, Bermudez C, Resnick SM, Cutting LE, Landman BA (2019) 3D whole brain segmentation using spatially localized atlas network tiles. NeuroImage 194:105–119
41. Ilse M, Tomczak JM, Welling M (2018) Attention-based deep multiple instance learning. arXiv preprint arXiv:1802.04712
42. Irvin J, Rajpurkar P, Ko M, Yu Y, Ciurea-Ilcus S, Chute C, Marklund H, Haghgoo B, Ball R, Shpanskaya K, Others (2019) Chexpert: a large chest radiograph dataset with uncertainty labels and expert comparison. In: Thirty-Third AAAI conference on artificial intelligence. http://aaai.org
43. Jiang F, Jiang Y, Zhi H, Dong Y, Li H, Ma S, Wang Y, Dong Q, Shen H, Wang Y (2017) Artificial intelligence in healthcare: past, present and future. Stroke Vasc Neurol 2(4):230–243
44. Johnson S, Chapman K, Huebner G (1984) Stress reduction prior to oral surgery. Anesth Prog 31(4):165
45. Jothi N, Husain W et al (2015) Data mining in healthcare-a review. Procedia Comput Sci 72:306–313

46. Kassebaum N, Smith A, Bernabé E, Fleming T, Reynolds A, Vos T, Murray C, Marcenes W, Collaborators GOH (2017) Global, regional, and national prevalence, incidence, and disability-adjusted life years for oral conditions for 195 countries, 1990–2015: a systematic analysis for the global burden of diseases, injuries, and risk factors. J Dent Res 96(4):380–387

47. Köbel M, Kalloger SE, Baker PM, Ewanowich CA, Arseneau J, Zhercbitskiy V, Abdulkarim S, Leung S, Duggan MA, Fontaine D et al (2010) Diagnosis of ovarian carcinoma cell type is highly reproducible: a transcanadian study. Am J Surg Pathol 34(7):984–993

48. Kooi T, Litjens G, Van Ginneken B, Gubern-Mérida A, Sánchez CI, Mann R, den Heeten A, Karssemeijer N (2017) Large scale deep learning for computer aided detection of mammographic lesions. Med Image Anal 35:303–312

49. Kuo W, Häne C, Mukherjee P, Malik J, Yuh EL (2019) Expert-level detection of acute intracranial hemorrhage on head computed tomography using deep learning. Proc Natl Acad Sci 116(45):22737–22745

50. Lakhani P, Sundaram B (2017) Deep learning at chest radiography: automated classification of pulmonary tuberculosis by using convolutional neural networks. Radiology 284(2):574–582

51. Lehman CD, Wellman RD, Buist DS, Kerlikowske K, Tosteson AN, Miglioretti DL (2015) Diagnostic accuracy of digital screening mammography with and without computer-aided detection. JAMA Intern Med 175(11):1828–1837

52. Leufkens A, Van Oijen M, Vleggaar F, Siersema P (2012) Factors influencing the miss rate of polyps in a back-to-back colonoscopy study. Endoscopy 44(05):470–475

53. Li J, Pepe A, Gsaxner C, Egger J (2021) An online platform for automatic skull defect restoration and cranial implant design. arXiv preprint arXiv:2006.00980

54. Liang Y, Fan HW, Fang Z, Miao L, Li W, Zhang X, Sun W, Wang K, He L, Chen X (2020) Oralcam: enabling self-examination and awareness of oral health using a smartphone camera. In: Proceedings of the 2020 CHI conference on human factors in computing systems, pp 1–13

55. Liang Y, Qiu L, Lu T, Fang Z, Tu D, Yang J, Zhao T, Shao Y, Wang K, Chen XA, He L(2020): Oralviewer: 3D demonstration of dental surgeries for patient education with oral cavity reconstruction from a 2D panoramic X-ray

56. Liang Y, Song W, Dym J, Wang K, He L (2019) Comparenet: anatomical segmentation network with deep non-local label fusion. In: International conference on medical image computing and computer-assisted intervention. Springer, pp 292–300

57. Liang Y, Song W, Yang J, Qiu L, Wang K, He L (2020) Atlas-aware convnet for accurate yet robust anatomical segmentation. In: Asian conference on machine learning. PMLR, pp 113–128

58. Lin C, Gao J, Zheng H, Zhao J, Yang H, Zheng Y, Cao Y, Chen Y, Wu G, Lin G et al (2019) When to introduce three-dimensional visualization technology into surgical residency: a randomized controlled trial. J Med Syst 43(3):71

59. Litjens G, Bandi P, Ehteshami Bejnordi B, Geessink O, Balkenhol M, Bult P, Halilovic A, Hermsen M, van de Loo R, Vogels R et al (2018) 1399 H&E-stained sentinel lymph node sections of breast cancer patients: the CAMELYON dataset. GigaScience 7(6), giy065

60. Litjens G, Kooi T, Bejnordi BE, Setio AAA, Ciompi F, Ghafoorian M, Van Der Laak JA, Van Ginneken B, Sánchez CI (2017) A survey on deep learning in medical image analysis. Med Image Anal 42:60–88

61. Loke YH, Capuano F, Mandell J, Cross RR, Cronin I, Mass P, Balaras E, Olivieri LJ (2019) Abnormal pulmonary artery bending correlates with increased right ventricular afterload following the arterial switch operation. World J Pediatr Congenit Hear Surg 10(5):572–581

62. Majumder S, Deen MJ (2019) Smartphone sensors for health monitoring and diagnosis. Sensors 19(9):2164

63. Maninis KK, Pont-Tuset J, Arbeláez P, Van Gool L (2016) Deep retinal image understanding. In: International conference on medical image computing and computer-assisted intervention. Springer, pp 140–148

64. Miao S, Wang ZJ, Liao R (2016) A CNN regression approach for real-time 2D/3D registration. IEEE Trans Med Imaging 35(5):1352–1363

65. Miller RA, Masarie FE (1990) The demise of the 'Greek Oracle' model for medical diagnostic systems. ISSN: 00261270 Publication Title: Methods of Information in Medicine

66. Miller RA, Masarie FE (1990) The demise of the 'Greek Oracle' model for medical diagnostic systems

67. Milletari F, Navab N, Ahmadi SA (2016) V-net: fully convolutional neural networks for volumetric medical image segmentation. In: 2016 fourth international conference on 3D vision (3DV). IEEE, pp 565–571

68. Mills I, Frost J, Cooper C, Moles DR, Kay E (2014) Patient-centred care in general dental practice-a systematic review of the literature. BMC Oral Health 14(1):64

69. Nair T, Precup D, Arnold DL, Arbel T (2020) Exploring uncertainty measures in deep networks for multiple sclerosis lesion detection and segmentation. Med Image Anal 59:101557

70. Nalisnik M, Amgad M, Lee S, Halani SH, Vega JEV, Brat DJ, Gutman DA, Cooper LA (2017) Interactive phenotyping of large-scale histology imaging data with HistomicsML. Sci Rep 7(1):14588

71. Olivieri LJ, Zurakowski D, Ramakrishnan K, Su L, Alfares FA, Irwin MR, Heichel J, Krieger A, Nath DS (2018) Novel, 3D display of heart models in the postoperative care setting improves CICU caregiver confidence. World J Pediatr Congenit Hear Surg 9(2):206–213

72. Oosterink FM, De Jongh A, Hoogstraten J (2009) Prevalence of dental fear and phobia relative to other fear and phobia subtypes. Eur J Oral Sci 117(2):135–143

73. Pedoia V, Norman B, Mehany SN, Bucknor MD, Link TM, Majumdar S (2019) 3D convolutional neural networks for detection and severity staging of meniscus and PFJ cartilage morphological degenerative changes in osteoarthritis and anterior cruciate ligament subjects. J Magn Reson Imaging 49(2):400–410

74. Poplin R, Varadarajan AV, Blumer K, Liu Y, McConnell MV, Corrado GS, Peng L, Webster DR (2018) Prediction of cardiovascular risk factors from retinal fundus photographs via deep learning. Nat Biomed Eng 2(3):158

75. Prinz A, Bolz M, Findl O (2005) Advantage of three dimensional animated teaching over traditional surgical videos for teaching ophthalmic surgery: a randomised study. Br J Ophthalmol 89(11):1495–1499

76. Qadir HA, Balasingham I, Solhusvik J, Bergsland J, Aabakken L, Shin Y (2019) Improving automatic polyp detection using CNN by exploiting temporal dependency in colonoscopy video. IEEE J Biomed Health Inform 24(1):180–193

77. Rosenthal DF, Bos JM, Sokolowski RA, Mayo JB, Quigley KA, Powell RA, Teel MM (1997) A voice-enabled, structured medical reporting system. J Am Med Inform Assoc 4(6):436–441

78. Roux L, Racoceanu D, Loménie N, Kulikova M, Irshad H, Klossa J, Capron F, Genestie C, Le Naour G, Gurcan MN (2013) Mitosis detection in breast cancer histological images an ICPR 2012 contest. J Pathol Inform 4

79. Rozier RG, Horowitz AM, Podschun G (2011) Dentist-patient communication techniques used in the united states: the results of a national survey. J Am Dent Assoc 142(5):518–530

80. Rubin GD (2015) Lung nodule and cancer detection in CT screening. J Thorac Imaging 30(2):130

81. Schaekermann M, Cai CJ, Huang AE, Sayres R (2020) Expert discussions improve comprehension of difficult cases in medical image assessment. In: Proceedings of the 2020 CHI conference on human factors in computing systems, pp 1–13

82. Settles B (2009) Active learning literature survey. University of Wisconsin-Madison Department of Computer Sciences, Technical Report

83. Shan H, Padole A, Homayounieh F, Kruger U, Khera RD, Nitiwarangkul C, Kalra MK, Wang G (2019) Competitive performance of a modularized deep neural network compared to commercial algorithms for low-dose CT image reconstruction. Nat Mach Intell 1(6):269–276

84. Shiping X, Jean-Paul D, Yuan L (2020) System for generating medical reports for imaging studies. US Patent App. 17/006,590

85. Shortliffe EH (1974) A rule-based computer program for advising physicians regarding antimicrobial therapy selection. In: Proceedings of the 1974 annual ACM conference-volume 2, p 739

86. Shortliffe EH (1993) The adolescence of AI in medicine: will the field come of age in the '90s? Artif Intell Med. https://doi.org/10.1016/0933-3657(93)90011-Q
87. Smith-Bindman R, Kwan ML, Marlow EC, Theis MK, Bolch W, Cheng SY, Bowles EJ, Duncan JR, Greenlee RT, Kushi LH et al (2019) Trends in use of medical imaging in us health care systems and in Ontario, Canada, 2000–2016. JAMA 322(9):843–856
88. Smith-Bindman R, Miglioretti DL, Larson EB (2008) Rising use of diagnostic medical imaging in a large integrated health system. Health Aff 27(6):1491–1502
89. Sommer C, Straehle C, Koethe U, Hamprecht FA (2011) Ilastik: interactive learning and segmentation toolkit. In: 2011 IEEE international symposium on biomedical imaging: from nano to macro. IEEE, pp 230–233
90. Song W, Liang Y, Wang K, He L (2021) Oral-3D: reconstructing the 3D bone structure of oral cavity from 2D panoramic X-ray. In: Proceedings of the AAAI conference on artificial intelligence
91. Stewart MA (1995) Effective physician-patient communication and health outcomes: a review. CMAJ: Can Med Assoc J 152(9):1423
92. Sutton RT, Pincock D, Baumgart DC, Sadowski DC, Fedorak RN, Kroeker KI (2020) An overview of clinical decision support systems: benefits, risks, and strategies for success. NPJ Digit Med 3(1):1–10
93. Teel MM, Sokolowski R, Rosenthal D, Belge M (1998) Voice-enabled structured medical reporting. In: Proceedings of the SIGCHI conference on human factors in computing systems, pp 595–602
94. Travaline JM, Ruchinskas R, D'Alonzo GE Jr (2005) Patient-physician communication: why and how. J Am Osteopat Assoc 105(1):13
95. Urban G, Tripathi P, Alkayali T, Mittal M, Jalali F, Karnes W, Baldi P (2018) Deep learning localizes and identifies polyps in real time with 96% accuracy in screening colonoscopy. Gastroenterology 155(4):1069–1078
96. Vardell E, Bou-Crick C (2012) VisualDX: a visual diagnostic decision support tool. Med Ref Serv Q 31(4):414–424
97. Veta M, Heng YJ, Stathonikos N, Bejnordi BE, Beca F, Wollmann T, Rohr K, Shah MA, Wang D, Rousson M et al (2019) Predicting breast tumor proliferation from whole-slide images: the TUPAC16 challenge. Med Image Anal 54:111–121
98. Veta M, Van Diest PJ, Willems SM, Wang H, Madabhushi A, Cruz-Roa A, Gonzalez F, Larsen AB, Vestergaard JS, Dahl AB et al (2015) Assessment of algorithms for mitosis detection in breast cancer histopathology images. Med Image Anal 20(1):237–248
99. Wang P, Xiao X, Brown JRG, Berzin TM, Tu M, Xiong F, Hu X, Liu P, Song Y, Zhang D et al (2018) Development and validation of a deep-learning algorithm for the detection of polyps during colonoscopy. Nat Biomed Eng 2(10):741–748
100. Wears RL, Berg M (2005) Computer technology and clinical work: still waiting for Godot. JAMA 293(10):1261–1263. https://doi.org/10.1001/jama.293.10.1261
101. Weinstein JN, Collisson EA, Mills GB, Shaw KRM, Ozenberger BA, Ellrott K, Shmulevich I, Sander C, Stuart JM, Network CGAR et al (2013) The cancer genome atlas pan-cancer analysis project. Nat Genet 45(10):1113
102. Welker SA (2014) Urogynecology patient education: visualizing surgical management of pelvic organ prolapse. PhD thesis, Johns Hopkins University
103. Whitman RM, Dufeau D (2017) Visualization of cardiac anatomy: new approaches for medical education. FASEB J 31(1_supplement), 736–8
104. Winkler JK, Fink C, Toberer F, Enk A, Deinlein T, Hofmann-Wellenhof R, Thomas L, Lallas A, Blum A, Stolz W et al (2019) Association between surgical skin markings in dermoscopic images and diagnostic performance of a deep learning convolutional neural network for melanoma recognition. JAMA Dermatol 155(10):1135–1141
105. Wolf JA, Moreau JF, Akilov O, Patton T, English JC, Ho J, Ferris LK (2013) Diagnostic inaccuracy of smartphone applications for melanoma detection. JAMA Dermatol 149(4):422–426

106. Xie Y, Chen M, Kao D, Gao G, Chen XA (2020) CheXplain: enabling physicians to explore and understand data-driven, AI-enabled medical imaging analysis. In: Proceedings of the 2020 CHI conference on human factors in computing systems, CHI '20. Association for Computing Machinery, New York, pp 1–13. https://doi.org/10.1145/3313831.3376807

107. Xie Y, Gao G, Chen XA (2019) Outlining the design space of explainable intelligent systems for medical diagnosis

108. Xu Y, Zhu JY, Chang E, Tu Z (2012) Multiple clustered instance learning for histopathology cancer image classification, segmentation and clustering. In: 2012 IEEE conference on computer vision and pattern recognition. IEEE, pp 964–971

109. Yang J, Liang Y, Zhang Y, Song W, Wang K, He L (2020) Exploring instance-level uncertainty for medical detection

110. Yang X, Hu J, Zhu S, Liang X, Li J, Luo E (2011) Computer-assisted surgical planning and simulation for condylar reconstruction in patients with osteochondroma. Br J Oral Maxillofac Surg 49(3):203–208

111. Yu L, Chen H, Dou Q, Qin J, Heng PA (2016) Integrating online and offline three-dimensional deep learning for automated polyp detection in colonoscopy videos. IEEE J Biomed Health Inform 21(1):65–75

112. Zhan ZQ, Fu H, Yang YY, Chen J, Liu J, Jiang YG (2020) Colonoscopy polyp detection: domain adaptation from medical report images to real-time videos

113. Zhang QS, Zhu SC (2018) Visual interpretability for deep learning: a survey. Front Inf Technol Electron Eng 19(1):27–39

114. Zhou SK, Greenspan H, Davatzikos C, Duncan JS, van Ginneken B, Madabhushi A, Prince JL, Rueckert D, Summers RM (2020) A review of deep learning in medical imaging: image traits, technology trends, case studies with progress highlights, and future promises. arXiv preprint arXiv:2008.09104

115. Zhou ZH (2004) Multi-instance learning: a survey. Department of Computer Science & Technology, Nanjing University, Technical Report

116. Zhu Y, Zhang S, Liu W, Metaxas DN (2014) Scalable histopathological image analysis via active learning. In: International conference on medical image computing and computer-assisted intervention. Springer , pp 369–376

117. Zilly J, Buhmann JM, Mahapatra D (2017) Glaucoma detection using entropy sampling and ensemble learning for automatic optic cup and disc segmentation. Comput Med Imaging Graph 55:28–41

3D Spatial Sound Individualization with Perceptual Feedback

Kazuhiko Yamamoto and Takeo Igarashi

Abstract Designing an interactive system tailored appropriately for each user's physical and cognitive characteristics is important for providing optimal user experience. In this chapter, we discuss how we could address such problems leveraging modern interactive machine learning techniques. As a case study, we introduce a method to individualize 3D spatial sound rendering with perceptual feedback. 3D spatial sound rendering traditionally required time-consuming measurement of individual user using an expensive device. By taking data-driven approach, one can replace such expensive measurement with simple calibration. We first describe how to train a generic deep learning model with an existing measured data set. We then describe how to adapt the model to a specific user with simple calibration process consisting of pairwise comparisons. Through this case study, the readers will get insight on how to adapt an interactive system for a specific user's characteristics, taking advantage of the high expressiveness of modern machine learning techniques.

1 Introduction

1.1 User Modeling and System Adaptation

User modeling is important in the design of interactive systems. Each user has their own physical and cognitive characteristics or preference biases. We can significantly improve user experience by adapting a system to individual users by taking such char-

K. Yamamoto (✉)
Hamamatsu-si, Shizuoka-ken, Japan
e-mail: yamo_o@acm.org

T. Igarashi
Bunkyo, Tokyo, Japan

acteristics into account. To provide tailored experience, we need to model individual user appropriately and then adapt the system to the model. However, it is difficult to represent the human physical and cognitive property by simple hand-crafted parameters. For example, the user's preference of appearance of images, sensation during listening a music, and controllability of a game user interface, are difficult to be represented by simple parameters. How could we parameterize such complicated characteristics of individual users?

Data-driven approach—machine learning—is an effective solution for this. Machine learning takes a lot of example data during training and approximates its probability distribution as a function. The parameters in the approximated function implicitly parameterize the target distribution, so they are useful for implicitly expressing the targets that can not be expressed explicitly, such as the user's characteristics. The ability of machine learning, in particular deep neural network (DNN), has been advanced dramatically in this decade, and becoming capable of approximating functions for various complex phenomena. This chapter discusses how we train a machine learning system to model the user characteristics and adapt them to a specific user.

We focus on the methods for adapting machine learning systems, in particular generative models of images, videos, languages, and sounds, to a specific user's characteristics (e.g., preference, aesthetics, and his or her mood of the day). An inherent difficulty here is that adaptation to individuals is fundamentally contradicts with generalization. Generally, the most important aspect of machine learning is *"generalization"*. This is quite different from *"optimization"* and *"adaptation"*. Generalization refers to maximize the model's ability to adapt properly to new, previously unseen data, drawn from the same distribution as the one used to create the model. In other words, a generalized model with data from many people can not produce optimal results for any particular target person, while the generalization maximizes the expressiveness of the model. Therefore, we have conflicting demands on machine learning system: we want to take advantage of the machine learning which frees us from hand-crafted feature design, while we also want it to produce an optimal result for a specific target through adaptation.

This chapter describes a method to address this challenging problem taking 3D spatial sound individualization as an example. We believe the basic idea presented here is applicable to other user modeling problems in broader fields. In the reminder of this section, we first describe our target application, 3D spatial sound individualization. We then describe the outline of the individualization method combining deep learning and perceptual feedback. Finally, we give an outline of this chapter.

1.2   3D Spatial Sound Individualization

3D spatial sound with a two-channels (stereo) headphone is a technique to enrich audio applications such as 3D games, virtual reality (VR), and immersive audio listening. In these applications, when the user changes the position or angle of the

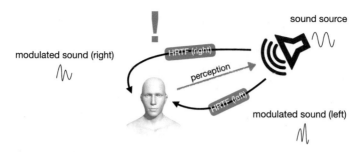

Fig. 1 We can recognize the localization of the sound source by spectral transforms of both ear's sounds. These two-channel transforms of the spectrums can be represented as finite impulse response filters and are called human-related transfer functions (HRTFs)

head, the perceived direction of the sound naturally changes accordingly. This allows the user to feel as if the sound source is fixed in a space regardless of the user's motion. How is it possible to change the direction of sound perception even though the positional relationship between the headphone and the ears remains unchanged?

The human auditory system perceives the directions of incoming sounds using both ears. According to the direction from which a sound arrives to the head, an arrival time difference to the left and right ears can be determined. In addition, the sound is intricately diffracted by the shape of the person's head and ears. This diffraction effect depends on the frequency and incoming direction of the sound. Therefore, the spectrums of the sounds that arrive at each ear are modulated (Fig. 1). The human auditory system recognizes the location of the sound by these sound modulations. These two-channel modulations of the spectrums can be represented as finite impulse response filters and are called human-related transfer functions (HRTFs). 3D spatial sound manipulates the perceived direction of incoming sound by convoluting this HRTFs with the original stereo source according to the relative positions between the user and virtual source.

HRTFs are highly specific to individuals because they depend considerably on the shape of indivisual user's ears and head. We call the proper HRTFs for individual users as an individualized HRTFs. We know that inappropriate HRTFs can lead to improper localization of the sound source accompanied by an unexpected equalization of the timbre. Such improper localization especially includes front-back and up-down confusions [1–3]. Because of this, we must essentially measure the individualized HRTF for each user.

The traditional method for acquiring individualized HRTFs is acoustic measurement in an anechoic chamber. Loud speaker arrays are spherically arranged around the subject's head and two small microphones are inserted into both ears. The subject sits with his or her head placed at the center of these spherical speaker arrays and is instructed to remain still during the long measurement periods. Specific test signals (such as sine sweep signals) are played one by one from the different loud speakers and the signals at the microphones are recorded. By comparing these recordings with those obtained from a microphone placed at the center of the speaker arrays (without the subject), the individual HRTFs can be computed. Many variants exist for conducting these measurements.

However, because such measurements usually require expensive equipment as well as tedious procedures, using these measurements with each end user is impractical and thus prevents their widespread use. Thus, using individualized HRTFs for each end user has been impractical, and most 3d spatial sound applications are forced to use the averaged (not optimized for any people) HRTFs, resulting in sub-optimal user experience. This may explain why 3D spatial sound rendering has not been as popular as visual rendering.

This chapter introduces a method to obtain individualized HRTFs without acoustic measurement by leveraging machine learning and perceptual feedback. To achieve this, we first design a deep neural network-based HRTF generative model trained by the publicity available HRTF database. However, of course, the database does not contain the optimal HRTFs for the target user, and it could be difficult to produce the target HRTFs directly. To address this, we train a model in such a way to extract the unique features of each individual's HRTFs, and it produces new tailored HRTFs for the target user by blending them at the calibration phase. This can be conducted by optimizing the embedded user-adaptable parameters with a human-in-the-loop manner.

1.3 Adapting Generative Model to a Specific User with Perceptual Feedback

This subsection gives an outline of adapting generative model to a specific user with perceptual feedback. The details are explained in Sects. 2 and 3. The generative model $y = G(z)$ produces an output y with the latent variable z as input. For example, in this chapter, this output y becomes HRTF. If we change the latent variable z, the output y will also change accordingly. In other words, if we can find the latent variable that produces the optimal output for the target user by exploration, we can expect to be able to adapt the generative model. However, there are two problems with this method.

The first problem is that a well generalized pre-trained model, as described in Sect. 1.1, has a difficulty producing a truly optimal output for any particular target user. To address this problem, we first transform the generative model as $y = G(z, \beta)$, where β represents a vector that has the dimension of the number of subjects in the training dataset. During training, β becomes a one-hot vector that indicates the subject to which the inputted data belongs. Thus, if the current input x is the p-th subject's, the corresponding element of β became 1; otherwise, 0. In this way, the model can explicitly handle who the currently input data belongs to. By using β, this model separates the characteristic factors that are common among the different subjects from the factors that are unique to each individual subject. Then, we train the model so that the factors that are common among subjects are generalized, and the part that handles factors that are not common among subjects but are unique to each individual subject is optimized and not generalized. By doing this, the model is able to generate a tailored output for all the subjects in the training data. At calibration phase, in order to make it possible to generate the optimal output for a certain target user who is not included in the training dataset, β is not a one-hot vector but a vector of continuous values. Then, the model can generate the optimal output for the target user by blending the feature factors unique to each subject that was separated during training. In this way, if the variance of the subject data included in the training data is sufficiently large, it would be possible to generate the optimal output for the target user. This specific method is discussed in detail in Sect. 2.

The second problem for exploring the latent space to obtain the optimal output for a specific user is that it is difficult for the user to directly correct the errors of the output from the model. Since the target user does not know the specific form of output that suits them, they can not answer specifically what is wrong with the output from the model. For example, in this chapter, it is impractical to answer with concrete values which parts of the spectrum of the generated HRTFs are suitable for oneself and which parts are not. Therefore, it is necessary to use other indirect methods to properly evaluate the errors in the model output. A solution to this is perceptual feedback, in which the target user is asked to evaluate the output by answering a simple perceptual question, rather than specifically pointing out the errors in the model output. However, it is often very difficult for users to express their perceptual score of the model output in absolute values (absolute assessment) [4, 5]. For this reason, it is desirable to use relative comparative evaluation (relative assessment) instead of absolute scoring [5–7]. In relative assessment, an evaluator is provided multiple options and chooses the one that seems better among them. The number of options may be two in the simplest form but can be more than two. In latent space exploration, we repeatedly conduct this evaluation, and the model output is evaluated based on the relationship of the evaluations among the queries. We explore the latent space so that the evaluation is maximized. The method presented in this chapter also introduces such relative assessment to explore the latent space of the model. This will be explained in detail in Sect. 3.2.

There are several methods to explore the latent space of the model from such the perceptual feedback (e.g., generic algorithm [18], preferential Bayesian optimization koyama, and evolution strategy [8]). A common requirement for all of these is the ability to complete the exploration with as few queries as possible. This is especially important when we treat what are called expensive-to-evaluate problems, where the user's evaluation cost is high. For example, the cost for a person to listen/watch and evaluate a sound/image is much higher than the cost for a computer to compute one iteration of the optimization. In such a problem, it is not practical to make the user evaluate many times because the cost of one query is too high. Therefore, minimizing the number of queries is very important. In Sect. 3.3, we introduce a hybrid combination of evolution strategy and gradient descent method as a way to achieve this. This method combines evolution strategy, which is a sampling-based optimization method, with gradient information to improve the convergence in a smaller number of queries. However, since the user's perceptual evaluation is done by sampling discrete points in the latent space, we can not directly observe the function that represents the user's evaluation score, and thus can not obtain the gradient. In the method introduced in this chapter, the gradient is estimated by inferring the landscape of the function, assuming that the latent model evaluation values follow random variables with a certain posterior distribution (e.g., Gaussian process).

Chapter Organization This chapter is organized as follows. Section 2 describes how we could embed user-adaptable nonlinear space parameters into a generative pre-trainable neural network model and extract the characteristic features of individual user's data. We discuss these techniques without limiting it specifically to HRTF individualization problem. Then, Sect. 3 illustrates how the internal parameters could be optimized for a specific user through perceptual feedback of the user: pairwise comparison queries. We also introduce some techniques to accelerate the adaptation by reducing the number of queries. Section 4 presents an actual example of 3D spatial sound adaptation as an application of the methods introduced in this chapter. We also demonstrate a user study that shows how the localization qualities are improved through our framework as an example (Sect. 4). Finally, we discuss the possibilities and some future directions of the introduced methods (Sect. 5), and then summarize this chapter (Sect. 6).

2 Embedding Individualization Parameters into a Generative Model

2.1 Variational AutoEncoder

We first review a general neural network-based generative model. We use conditional variational AutoEncoder [10, 11] here, but one can choice other types of generative model (e.g., generative adversarial network [9]). Conditional variational AutoEncoder is a generative model of a deep neural network. It consists of a decoder $p_\theta(x, c|z)$ and the variational posterior encoder $q_\phi(z|x, c)$, where x, c, and z are input, description label (condition), and latent variable, respectively. For example, if we want to generate digit image 0–9, the input x is the original image and the condition c is the corresponding digit number id 0–9. In the model, the encoder computes latent variable z from the input x and the condition c so that z follows some prior distribution (e.g., Gaussian distribution). Finally, the decoder reconstructs an output x' from a sampled latent variable z and condition c (Fig. 2).

Both the model (θ) and variational (ϕ) parameters will be jointly optimized with stochastic gradient variational Bayes (SGVB) algorithm according to a lower bound on the log-likelihood. The variation lower bound can be formulated as

$$
\begin{aligned}
log\ p_\theta(c|x) = &-KL(q_\phi(z|x, c)||p_\theta(z|x, c)) \\
&+ \mathbb{E}_{q_\phi(z|x,c)}\left[-log\ q_\phi(z|x, c) + log\ p_\theta(c, z|x)\right]
\end{aligned}
$$

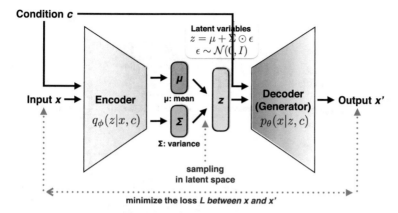

Fig. 2 Conditional variational AutoEncoder. This model consists of the encoder and decoder and reconstructs the output from input so that the latent variable follows some prior distribution

$$\geq -KL(q_\phi(z|x,c)||p_\theta(z|x)) + \mathbb{E}_{q_\phi(z|x,c)}\left[log\ p_\theta(c|x,z)\right], \quad (1)$$

where $KL()$ denotes Kullback–Leibler divergence. Suppose that the latent variables follow Gaussian distribution $z = g_\phi(x, \epsilon)$, $\epsilon \sim \mathcal{N}(0, I)$, where $g_\phi(\cdot, \cdot)$ is a deterministic differentiable function, the empirical lower bound that can be written as

$$\mathcal{L}(x, c; \theta, \phi) = -KL(q_\phi(z|x,c)||p_\theta(z|x)) + \frac{1}{L}\sum_{l=1}^{L} log\ p_\theta(c|x, z^{(l)}), \quad (2)$$

where L is the number of samples. In addition, the first term on the right hand side of Eq. (2) can be analytically computed as

$$- KL(q_\phi(z|x,c)||p_\theta(z|x)) = \frac{1}{2}\sum_{j=1}^{J}\left(1 + log(\Sigma_j) - \mu_j^2 - \Sigma_j\right), \quad (3)$$

where μ and Σ denote the variational mean and variance, and J is the dimensionality of z. This loss function is totally differentiable at each parameter in the neural network. So, we can train this model by stochastic gradient descent methods like Adam [20].

Fig. 3 An adaptive layer that decomposes the function approximation into individual feature and non-individual feature. A one-hot vector *s* works like switching function depending on the inputted subject's data. ⊗ denotes tensor product

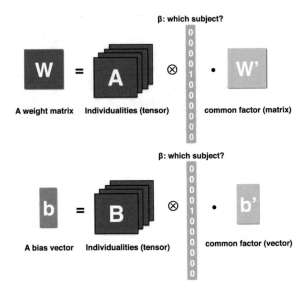

2.2 Decomposing the Individualities

In this subsection, we introduce an adaptive layer that separates the individual and non-individual factors from a training dataset during training. This is a new type of layer: a layer in neural network means a combination of a linear function and nonlinear function. Generally, a neural network consists of several numbers of layers. We can use arbitrary type of functions for a layer as long as they are differentiable. The model we are aiming for in this chapter not only reconstructs the input x, but also aims to extract the personality of the subjects in the database.

As described above, a common layer in a neural network can be written as a combination of linear and nonlinear functions:

$$y = F(x) = f(Linear(x)) = f(W \cdot x + b), \tag{4}$$

where $x \in \mathbb{R}^N$ and $y \in \mathbb{R}^M$ are the input and output of this layer, respectively. $Linear()$ denotes a linear layer function of the neural network. $W \in \mathbb{R}^{N \times M}$ is a matrix, $b \in \mathbb{R}^M$ is a bias vector, and $f()$ is an arbitrary nonlinear function (e.g., sigmoid). We introduce *blending vector* β to represent individuality in the model. β has same dimensions with the number of subjects K in the training dataset. It is a one-hot vector during training and each dimension corresponds to a subject in the training data. We train the model by setting β according to the training data. We now consider to isolate the latent individualities into a tensor from the weight matrix in an unsupervised manner. The assumption here is that subjects in the training data sufficiently cover the wide variety of individual factors and the target user's characteristics are approximated by a combination of the separated individualities.

The adaptive layer is based on tensor factorization that employs stochastic gradient descent optimization [12]. We decompose this W and b as follows by introducing a new parameter β (Fig. 3):

$$y = f(Adapt(x, \beta)) = f(A \otimes_3 \beta \cdot W' \cdot x + B \otimes_3 \beta \cdot b'), \tag{5}$$

where $\beta = [\beta_1, \ldots, \beta_K]^T$, $\beta_k \in \{0, 1\}$ is a binary subject label (a one-hot vector that represents the subject to which the inputted data belongs). Thus, if the current input x is the p-th subject's, the corresponding element of β became 1; otherwise, 0. $A \in \mathbb{R}^{N \times M \times K}$, and $B \in \mathbb{R}^{M \times M \times K}$ are tensors. $W' \in \mathbb{R}^{N \times M}$ is a matrix, and $b' \in \mathbb{R}^M$ is a vector. $\otimes_d$ is the dot product between the d-mode expansion of a tensor and vector.

We replace the linear layers in the variational AutoEncoder with this adaptive layer, and iteratively input the training data of a randomly selected subject during training. The adaptive layer gradually inserts the individualities of the input feature into the tensor A and B as if the β becomes a switcher with respect to the selected subject. In addition, non-individualities that are shared with all subjects are included in the matrix W' and the vector b' during stochastic optimization.

2.3 Blending the Individualizing Parameters

After training, we aim to calibrate the generator (the decoder of the neural network) to obtain an individualized data for a target user. To this end, we assume that the output optimized for an individual user can be expressed as a blending of the trained individualities of features in the dataset in a nonlinear space.

Thus, we now reinterpret the binary subject label β in Eq. (5) with a continuous personalization weight vector. Each β_i takes $[0,1]$ continuous value and is constrained as $\sum_i^K \beta_i = 1$. Then, in Eq. (5), we can say the optimized individualization transformation matrices to the user can be expressed as $A \otimes_3 \beta$ and $B \otimes_3 \beta$, which are blends of the individualities of the subjects included in the trained data set. Similarly, the latent variables z, which are necessary for generating a new HRTF, are also transformed using β as

$$\bar{z}_{mean} = Z_{mean}(c) \cdot \beta, \quad \bar{z}_{var} = Z_{mean}(c) \cdot \beta, \tag{6}$$

$$\bar{z} \sim \mathbb{N}\left(\bar{z}_{mean}, \frac{1}{2}\bar{z}_{var}\right), \tag{7}$$

where $Z_{mean} \in \mathbb{R}^{L \times K}$, $Z_{var} \in \mathbb{R}^{L \times K}$ are matrices in which each column is the pre-computed latent vector $(z_{mean}^1(c), \ldots, z_{mean}^K(c))$ and $(z_{var}^1(c), \ldots, z_{var}^K(c))$ that correspond to the subject. Furthermore, $z_{mean}^k(c)$ and $z_{var}^k(c)$ are switched by the con-

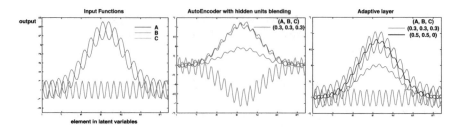

Fig. 4 A comparison between hidden units interpolation approach (bottom-left) and our adaptive layers (bottom-right). We trained two networks with three nonlinear functions A, B, and C (Top). Red, blue, green lines at bottom two graphs represent the reconstructed functions respectively. Purple lines denote a blending of three functions equally, and black line denotes a blending of A and B. Hidden units interpolation approach diminishes the details of each function while our method preserves them

dition c. L denotes the dimensions of the latent variables. We use the blended $\bar{z}$ for the latent variables in the individual feature vector of the user.

The system optimizes the blending vector β for an individual user by fixing the other parameters A and B, as well as the matrices W' and bias vectors b'. This approach has the advantage of dramatically reducing the DoFs of the design variables for optimization purposes because it can eliminate the need for multiple optimization runs when considering all dimensions of the condition. This means optimizing only a blending vector β covers the individualities of the user through all conditions.

2.4 Blending Example

This adaptive layer allows us to interpolate, emphasize, diminish, and blend each individuality in the trained dataset by adjusting the blending vector $\beta \in \mathbb{R}^K$ at runtime as an additional input. Several approaches exist that morph data into different categorized data continuously by interpolating several sampled hidden units extracted with AutoEncoder (e.g., using procedural modeling of a 3D mesh [13] and controlling and stylizing the human character motion [14]). However, this corresponds to the approach in which exploring only in the generalized space as described in Sect. 1.1. Then, these approaches are limited in terms of their ability to distinguish many nonlinear functions, which is crucial to solving our target problem.

Figure 4 shows a comparison of three simple functions morphing between hidden units interpolation approach and our approach after performing the same number of iterations (although this number is unfavorable with our approach). We use a dual-stacked AutoEncoder for our experiment. (Note that for hidden units interpolation, we replace each adaptive layer with a common fully connected layer.)

The hidden units interpolation approach diminishes each characteristic feature of the functions. This is crucial when the target function to reconstruct is complex and has sharp peaks and dips. However, our adaptive layer successfully enables us to reconstruct the details of characteristic features and blend them.

3 Adaptation with Perceptual Feedback

3.1 Optimizing the Blending Vector

The optimization procedure for the blending vector β is interactive with the user. The user gives relative scores for two blending vector β_i and β_j through pairwise comparison as described in Sect. 1.3. The user is presented with two test outputs of the model, and rates the relative score (evaluates which is better and how much better). With this input, our optimization problem is reformulated into a minimization problem $\mathrm{argmin}_\beta \ Q(\beta)$ where the absolute cost values $Q(\beta)$ are computed from the relative scores as described in a Sect. 3.2. By running this procedure iteratively, the system optimizes the β for the target user.

To optimize this black-box system, we use a hybrid optimization scheme [15] as an evolutional strategy (we use CMA-ES [8]) and a gradient descent approach (we use the BGFS-quasi-Newton method). The optimization procedure is shown in Algorithm 1. We introduce local Gaussian process regression (GPR) [16] to accelerate the optimization. This method estimates the local landscape of the cost function from discrete sampling to obtain the gradients.

ALGORITHM 1: Hybrid CMA-ES assisted by Local GPR

1: **Until convergence**
2:     Generate β samplings using Eq.(14)
       and make P test pairs $\mathbb{P}$.
3:     Gathering the user feedbacks for each pair.
4:     Computes absolute cost q for each β samplings.
5:     Estimating the cost function of each sampling using GPR
6:     Sort the samplings by the order of the cost
       to form the new parent population in CMA-ES
7:     The weighted mean $y_w^{(g)}$ is computed
       from the new parent population.
8:     Quasi-Newton updates of $y_w^{(g)}$
       using the gradients estimated by GPR.
9:     Update the covariance matrix $C^{(g)}$ and global step size
       in CMA-ES using Chen et al. [15],
       respectively.
10: **end**

Figure 5 shows a comparison between with and without using gradient information estimated by GPR. We minimize the EggHolder function for this evaluation using four conditions (N = 8, 32). CMA-ES requires N times of function evaluation (pairwise comparisons) at each iteration. In our target problem, the number of samplings should be small because the sampling size is proportional to the user's effort. However, when the number of samplings N seeded by CMA-ES is few, the optimization without GPR tends to be trapped by a bad local minima. As shown in

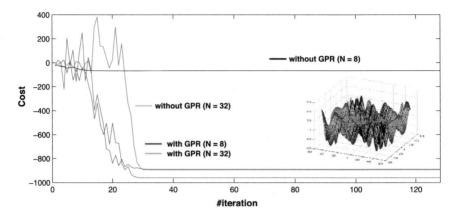

Fig. 5 Comparison of convergence curves between CMA-ES with/without GPR. We use EggHolder function for this evaluation. When the number of samplings seeded by CMA-ES is fewer, the optimization without GPR fails to bad local minima while our technique converges to better solution with much fewer iterations

Fig. 5, our technique addresses this problem and converges to a better solution with considerably fewer iterations than in previous methods.

At a single iteration during optimization, we first sample N sets of β samplings $\beta_1, \ldots, \beta_N$ using common CMA-ES procedure. Let $\mathbb{P}$ be a set of pairs of indices $(1, 2), \ldots, (N - 1, N)$. For each $(i, j) \in \mathbb{P}$, the system generates two test outputs $S(\beta_i), S(\beta_j)$, presents the pair to the user side by side to the user, and requests the user to rate each to generate a relative score ($N - 1$ queries of pairwise comparisons). After collecting the user feedback for all pairs, the system stores $N - 1$ pairs of different βs and their relative scores. After computing the absolute value of the cost q for each β samplings using these relative scores, we estimate the local landscape of the continuous cost function $Q(\beta)$ from the discrete q. We represent $\mathbb{Q} = (q_1, \ldots, q_N)$ as a set of indices of sampling points. Using this estimated cost function, the system computes the gradients and updates the covariance matrix in CMA-ES with quasi-Newton. We detail this procedure in the next subsection.

3.2 Estimating the Local Landscape of the Perceptual Function

The system requests that the user provides feedback regarding the two test outputs of the model that correspond to each β pair. The system then has a set of β pairs $\mathbb{P}$ and corresponding the relative scores. Given these relative scores, we compute the absolute value of the sampling cost q for each sampling β. Our formulation is derived from Koyama et al. [7], which estimates the consistent goodness field of high dimensional parameters through unreliable crowd sourced rating tasks. Their approach solves a minimization problem with two constraints:

$$\arg \min_{q} \left(E_{relative}(q) + \omega E_{continuous}(q) \right), \tag{8}$$

where $\omega > 0$ balances the two constraints (we set 5.0). $E_{relative}(q)$ is the relative score-based constraint and is represented as

$$E_{relative}(q) = \sum_{(i,j) \in \mathbb{P}} ||q_i - q_j + d_{i,j}||^2, \tag{9}$$

where $d_{i,j}$ denotes the offset determined by the rating between i-th and j-th samples. Here, we set $d_{i,j} = (3 - RelativeScore)/2$, where $RelativeScore \in \{1, 2, 3, 4, 5\}$. We evaluate the rating as linear scale, but this depends on the target problem. Note that the sign of $d_{i,j}$ is opposite to Koyama et al. [7] because we assume a minimization problem here. In addition, we enforce the continuity of the cost function by $E_{continuous}(q)$:

$$E_{continuous}(q) = \sum_{i \in \mathbb{Q}} \left\| q_i - \sum_{i \neq j} \left(1 - \frac{|\beta_i - \beta_j|}{\sum_{i \neq k} |\beta_i - \beta_k|} \right) q_j \right\|^2. \tag{10}$$

In this equation, we constrain the absolute costs of two sampling β to become closer when the distance of the two β diminishes. This minimization problem Eq. (8) can be solved as a linear least square problem.

Finally, we estimate the local landscape of the cost function $Q(\beta)$ using multidimensional GPR. We include discrete q samplings obtained by Eq. (8) into Gaussian process regression (GPR). GPR is a non-parametric, Bayesian approach to regression. This approximate function can be used to estimate the gradients, which are required by the quasi-Newton method as described below (Sect. 3.3). Note that although GPR is expensive with high dimensions, it is not a serious problem in our case because the dimension of a design parameter would not increase to such a high dimension.

3.3 Optimization

We illustrate a hybrid optimization scheme [15] of an evolutional strategy to minimize $Q(\beta)$ with respect to β. Note that we used CMA-ES [8] and a gradient descent approach (quasi-Newton method.) This hybrid approach first updates the design parameter using gradient information to search for the local optima in the area sampled by evolutional strategy, and to escape from bad local optima by evolutional strategy vice versa.

CMA-ES generates λ offsprings (sampling) and selects μ best offsprings among them at an iteration. Each offsprings are generated according to the strategy of using two characteristic variation operators, weighted recombination, and additive Gaussian mutation.

$$q^{(g)} = QuasiNewtonUpdate(y^{(g)}),   \tag{11}$$

$$y^{(g+1)} = q^{(g)} + \rho^{(g)} B^{(g)} D^{(g)} z^{(g)},   \tag{12}$$

$$B^{(g)} D^{(g)} z^{(g)} \sim N(0, C^{(g)}),   \tag{13}$$

where $y^{(g)}$, g and $\rho^{(g)}$ are the design parameters, iteration step and a global step size respectively. $z^{(g)} \sim N(0, I)$ are independent realizations of a normally distributed random vector with zero mean and covariance matrix equal to the identity matrix I. The columns of the orthogonal matrix $B^{(g)}$ are the normalized eigenvectors of The covariance matrix $C^{(g)}$, and $D^{(g)}$ is a diagonal matrix with the square roots of the corresponding eigenvalues. $C^{(g)}$ can be computed as

$$C^{(g+1)} = (1 - \alpha)C^{(g)} + \alpha \frac{1}{\tau} p^{(g)}(p^{(g)})^T$$

$$+ \alpha \left(1 - \frac{1}{\tau}\right) \sum_{i=1}^{\mu} \frac{\omega_i}{\rho^{(g)2}} (y_i^{(g+1)} - q^{(g)})(y_i^{(g+1)} - q^{(g)})^T,   \tag{14}$$

where α and τ are learning rates, and ω_i denotes the weight determined by the rank in the offsprings i. $p^{(g)}$ is also the learning rate, but not a hyper parameter. It is computed using $q^{(g)}$ at each iteration (please see [15] for details). $QuasiNewtonUpdate()$ represents the gradient descent part. We use quasi-Newton method, but one can use any other gradient-based methods such as Adam [20] alternately.

For our initial guess, we first randomly generate the offsprings $y^{(g)}$ within a user-defined range by means of Gaussian distribution, and then enforce a constraint $\sum y^{(g)} = 1$ by dividing all the offsprings by $\sum y^{(g)}$. This constraint can be considered as a portion of the user feedback function. In addition, in most case, optimal β for a specific user has a sparsity because when too much personal factors are blended together, individuality would disappear. Thus, the optimizer randomly drops the elements under the average to zero in β offsprings of CMA-ES (we dropped them with 30% probability). In most case, this constraint reduces training error.

4   Example: 3D Spatial Sound Individualization

This section describes a practical example of generative model adaptation for a specific user with perceptual feedback. We treat the personalization problem of HRTF used in 3D spatial sound as described in Sect. 1.2.

4.1 Generative Model for 3D Spatial Sound

We first design a generative model of HRTF. We use an extension of conditional variational AutoEncoder that includes adaptive layers described in Sect. 2. In our model, the input x and condition vector c in Eq. (1) become HRTF (power spectrum and phases of left and right ear's impulse response) and a sampled incoming direction of sound, respectively. In addition, each adaptive layer takes a subject label as blending vector β that is used for decomposing the individualities of the input HRTFs. The model outputs the reconstructed HRTFs x' for both ears, and we train this model to have x' be similar to x using Adam optimizer [20]. The model treats HRTF in a spectral domain. The original HRTFs in a time domain can be recovered from both the power spectrum and phase information outputted from the system. This section provides only an overview of our model. For more details of the network architecture, please see [21].

4.1.1 Input Format

To construct the HRTF input data structure of x, we include not only the impulse response of the HRTF at the exact sampled direction c, but also its several surrounding neighboring impulse responses (Fig. 6). In total, we sample 25 directions with 5×5 rectangular grid shapes, in which the center becomes the HRTF at the direction c. The stride of the grid is $\pm 0.08\pi$ rotations for both yaw and pitch on a unit sphere direction from the head. In addition, we obtain the power spectrums and LR time domain impulse responses at each direction using bilinear interpolation in frequency domain on the unit sphere [22, 23]. To reconstruct an interpolated time signals, we use both interpolated power spectrums and phases. We call this 5×5 grid that stores HRTF information as the *Patch*. This patch representation is expected to encode the correlations with surrounding directions. Finally, this input data structure becomes a 3D voxel patch with $5 \times 5 \times 128$ dimensions (128 power spectrums or 128 sample time signals) and each voxel has four color channels (power spectrums and time signals of LR channels) as shown in Fig. 6. This becomes the input x of our neural network.

4.1.2 Output Format

Our neural network reconstructs the HRTF x' to minimize the difference between the input and output HRTF with an AutoEncoder manner. However, solving a regression problem of a signal that shows a large fluctuation (e.g., time domain audio signal and power spectrum) using a generative neural network is difficult. This is because a neural network smoothes the output throughout the training data. Therefore, the trained result tends to be an "averaged signal," which causes a fatal error. To address this, we use a quantized format similar to WaveNet [24].

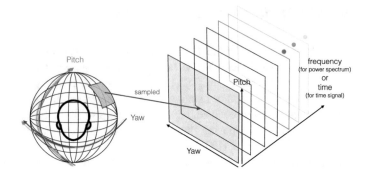

Fig. 6 The input data structure of our neural network (We call HRTF patch). This HRTF patch has voxel-like data structure, which encodes spatial correlations of HRTFs. Each voxel has four properties (LR channels of power spectrums and time signals) like color channels of image

WaveNet predicts time domain audio signals using an image-like quantized format (width: time, height: amplitude), which successfully solves a regression problem of large fluctuated signals. Similarly, we quantize the power spectrums and time signals of HRTFs into 256 steps using μ-law compression. As a result, the output format becomes an image-like representation. Unlike in WaveNet, we do not use one-hot vectors for the final layer nor the softmax function. The softmax function generalizes all the output of the neural network into [0, 1] probabilities. This is equivalent to solving an unconstrained optimization problem which requires extensive training data. However, the size of our setting's training data is considerably less than that of WaveNet, which can lead to optimization failure.

Alternatively, we construct an array of normal distributions on each quantized vector, in which mean values are equal to each quantized value. In addition, we set all the variances to 5 and minimize the mean squared error of these multiple normal distributions. This addresses the aforementioned problem because it is equivalent to constraining the value range of the solution. To generate a final HRTF, we first compute each quantized value by maximum likelihood estimation from the output and then obtain the result by decoding the quantized values using inverse μ-law compression.

4.1.3   3D Convolutional Layer for HRTF Patch

We introduce 3d convolutions at the beginning of the model so that they expect to encode the correlations between the HRTF at the sample direction and its surrounding neighboring directions within an HRTF patch.

A typical 3D convolutional layer [25] in a neural network shares the filter coefficients of the kernel over the weight tensor. Instead of using this type of layer, we employ a convolutional layer that shares the kernel coefficients only in spatial domains (the yaw and pitch axis) but uses different filters along the frequency axis

Fig. 7 3D convolutional
layer for HRTF patch which
packs multiple proximity
HRTFs around the target
direction c

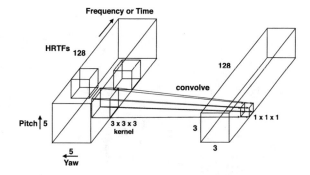

(Fig. 7). This is because the spectral correlation of an HRTF with its surroundings
generally has a different structure between the lower and higher frequencies as a
result of the frequency dependent diffraction by the subject's head and ears.

We use two convolutional layers for each channel (for four total channels). We set
the kernel size of each convolution as $3\times3\times3$ (yaw $\times$ pitch $\times$ frequency axis), and
add zero padding to the frequency axis only. For all directions, we set the stride as 1.
Thus, the first convolutional layer transforms each channel of a patch from $5\times5\times128$
to $3\times3\times128$, and the second layer further transforms them to $1\times1\times128$. Note that
we did not add bias parameters to this convolutional layer in our experiment.

4.1.4   Dataset

For training dataset, we used the publicly available CIPIC data set [17] which contains
HRTFs of both ears measured in an anechoic chamber for 45 subjects at 25 azimuths
and 50 elevations. In total, it includes 1250 sample directions of HRTF per subject
and ear. Each set of data for a direction, subject, and ear is recorded as an impulse
response of 200 wave samples with a 44.1 kHz sampling rate audio file. Impulse
signals are played by a loud speaker array spherically arranged around the head. They
are recorded using two small microphones inserted into the ears of each subject.

4.2   User Interface

We designed a GUI application for calibration (Fig. 8). This application first presents
a pair of test signals and its intended direction. The user then plays the test sound by
pressing an A/B selection button. Each of these two test signals is generated from
different HRTFs (personalization weights), respectively, and has the same intended
direction. We randomly select an audio source from 10 predefined test sounds (e.g.,
speech, helicopter, short music phrase) and then filter the audio using the generated
HRTFs. The intended direction continuously moves spherically around a head and

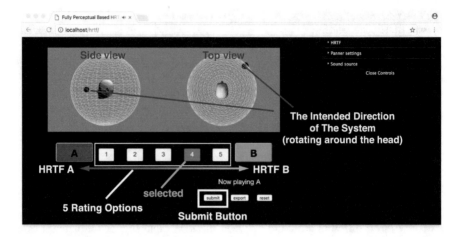

Fig. 8 The user interface pane for gathering the user feedbacks. It runs on web browser. When the user push A (red) or B (blue) button, one of the test signal pair is played. The 3D graphics show the intended direction of the system from the side and top views. The user rates the pair by 5 pt scale with radio buttons and submits it. Finally, the user exports his/her individualized HRTF data by pressing the export button

is shown as a moving sphere from side and top views. The user listens to the test signals and provides feedback by selecting one of the 5-scale options that represent the sound that is perceptually closer to the intended direction. "1" means that the test signal A is definitely better, and "5" means B is definitely better. "3" means neutral. By iterating this simple pairwise comparisons (approximately $150 \sim 200$ times), the system automatically individualizes the HRTFs by optimizing the blending vector for the target user. The user can stop the calibration at an arbitrary timing (usually when the user is satisfied or can not distinguish two test signals).

4.3 User Study

We employed 20 participants (male:female = 13:7, age: $22 \sim 62$) and optimized HRTFs for them using our system. The experiment consisted of three steps. In the first step, we investigated the best-fitted CIPIC HRTF for each participant. Here, we conducted a progressive comparison [19] to estimate the best-fitted HRTF. Therefore, a participant compared 44 pairs of HRTFs because 45 CIPIC HRTFs exist. We showed each participant 44 pairs of test sounds convolved by two CIPIC HRTFs using the same GUI in our system (Fig. 8); the participant indicated the best among them. This task consumed $15 \sim 20$ min. The best CIPIC HRTFs were used in the third step as baselines to evaluate our optimized HRTF.

One might question the robustness of the selection of the best CIPIC HRTF. We, therefore, run an informal pilot study to answer the concern. We requested a

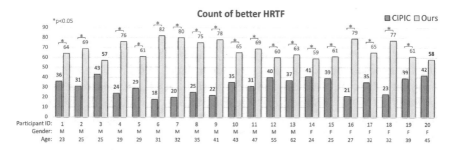

Fig. 9 The result of user study. The third column shows how many numbers of options are selected as better HRTF for each participant between best-fitted CIPIC HRTF and optimized HRTF by our system

participant to find the best HRTF six times. Unfortunately, this was not perfectly repeatable, but we observed the participant selected same HRTF three times in the six explorations. We can consider this small variation in the result is not a critical problem in our experiment because it means that the selected HRTFs are equally good.

We next requested that the participants calibrate their HRTFs using our system. We asked each participant to answer at least 100 pairwise comparisons. We did not decide the maximum times of comparisons and when a participant indicated that he or she was satisfied, we stopped the calibration. We measured calibration time and the number of mouse clicks (number of pairwise comparisons) for each participant. The participants used the UI described in the previous section. The calibration took $20 \sim 35$ min for each participant. The number of pairwise comparisons was $109 \sim 202$ times. This calibration time was much shorter than the actual measurement for obtaining fitted HRTFs.

After each calibration, we conducted a blind listening test to compare the HRTFs obtained using our method and the best-fitted CIPIC HRTFs. In this step, we showed each participant 100 pairs of test sounds. One of the test sounds in each pair was convolved by an optimized HRTF and the other was convolved by the best CIPIC HRTF for the participant. The test sound to convolve was randomly selected from 10 prepared sounds (e.g., short music, helicopter, and speech) and played 100 times. We requested that each participant use the same GUI as during the calibration to select one test sound from each pair that showed better spatialization. We requested that each participant select only either 1 or 5 from among the option buttons. The order (A or B) in which test sounds were played using optimized HRTF and best CIPIC HRTF for each presented pair was random. We did not inform the participants whether the selection was the optimized HRTF or the best CIPIC HRTF.

Figure 9 shows the number of times each HRTF was selected as a better HRTF by each participant. These results show that the optimized HRTFs were significantly better for almost all participants (*p-value < 0.05 by Chi-squared test for 18/20 subjects) than were the best CIPIC HRTFs, indicating that our system successfully optimizes HRTFs for individual users.

5   Discussions

This chapter has discussed techniques for adapting the output of neural network-based generative models to specific users not included in the training data, by separating out individuality through tensor decomposition with an unsupervised manner and using perceptual feedback (pairwise comparisons) to optimize their mixture. To minimizing the number of queries, we estimated the landscape of the perceptual function of the target user's preference from the relative assessments, and used it for gradient estimation which improves the convergence of the optimization. This section discusses the possibilities and some future directions of these methods.

5.1   Tensor Decomposition for Adaptation

To separating individualities from the input dataset, we conducted tensor decomposition at each neural network layer with an unsupervised manner. The decomposed individualities are blended in the blend vector ratio to adapt to the target user. This adaptive layer can be used not only for generative models, but also general neural network models such as image classification and speech recognition. It works by simply replacing each layer of neural network with an adaptive layer. Although we explained the adaptive layer as an extension of fully connected layer, convolutional layer can also be extended to similar form. In such case, the adaptive layer can be represented as tensor products of the filter kernels (tensors for number of channels and individualities), blending vector, and matrices for number of channels which represents the common factors among the input data. Of course, the target to be switched by the blending vector does not have to be an individual, and we can select arbitrary domains (e.g., age, gender, and physique) from which we want to extract features. The adaptive layer would be expected to extract the domain-specific features that can be switched by the blending vector.

In our example, the blending vector during training is always a one-hot vector since we are switching between individual users. However, it is possible to extend the blending vector to a vector that flags multiple elements, rather than a one-hot vector, as a future direction. This extension corresponds to considering the combination of multiple factors or individuals. For example, it would be possible to consider decomposing an individual into multiple components (e.g., gender, age, and personality), extract the features obtained by combining them, and then blend them together to adapt it for a specific user. This would be an effective method when the elements that consist of an individual have been able to be analyzed in advance. However, this would be expected to require a large amount of training data as the number of combination patterns increases. To address this is an issue for the future.

5.2   Gradient Estimation from Relative Assessments

As described in Sect. 3.2, we used Gaussian process regression (GPR) [16] for estimating the landscape of the perceptual function of the user's preference. The estimated landscape is used for computing the gradient that improves the efficiency of black-box optimization Although there are many regression algorithms (e.g., support vector machine, neural network, lasso, and polynomial regression), GPR has an advantage that works well for relatively smaller numbers of data, and non-convex function. Such the gradient estimation from relative assessments is broadly useful for generic algorithm [18], Bayesian optimization [7], and other black-box optimization problems. Especially, in problems with high evaluation costs, where the evaluation of the objective function is provided by a human, it would be valuable since it reduces the number of queries as much as possible. However, the method introduced in this chapter is just a starting point in the field that estimates the gradient from perceptual relative assessments. We expect that in the future, more efficient algorithms will be able to solve the adaptation problem with perceptual feedback more effortlessly.

5.3   Possible Applications in HCI

This chapter introduced 3D spatial sound individualization as example of machine learning-based adaptation with perceptual feedback. The basic idea of the presented method could be broadly applicable to other domains in HCI. For example, recent typical user interfaces using machine learning-based recognition algorithms such as gaze tracking [26–28], hand/body gesture tracking [49, 50], and speech/face recognition [29–31] require online calibrations of the pre-trained models by each user themselves before actual use. In such a calibration, the user traces the instructions or examples presented by the system, and the system uses the feedback to fine tune the model for adapting to the user. However, since most of these fine tuning are conducted in a generalized space as described in Sect. 1.1, they could not be able to fit each user adequately. In addition, most approaches for such calibrations rely on the hand-crafted fitting models based on each domain knowledge. The presented techniques in this chapter, especially tensor decomposition for adaptation, could help to adapting such calibrations more aggressively to each user, and free us from tedious hand-crafted feature designs. It could result to obtain better results.

Typical text entry methods for computer systems also require online personalization for each user. Several studies [47, 48] presented the methods for tuning the pre-trained language generative models finely through the collection of the input data by the user at online. However, such fine tuning has a risk of leading the model in the wrong direction depending on the unseen input of the user. Even in such a situation, our approach would be able to adapt to the user in a stable manner because our method optimizes only the weights of the individualities while leaving the parameters of the model itself unchanged. For another example, recent machine learning-based speech synthesis and voice conversion techniques [32–35] basically can only output the person's voices which are included in the training dataset, leaving little room for the user to edit the output voice to their preference. Our approach could address such the problem by blending the decomposed characteristics in the training dataset for generating a new style voice. This is similar to the concept of *disentangling* [36–38] in machine learning field, which has been increasingly studied in the last few years. The idea presented here can be considered as a more aggressive exploration of such techniques.

In addition, the methods introduced in this chapter would also be useful in other domains, especially at the situations that the user want to explore more preferable result when they can judge whether the output of a machine learning-based model is good or bad perceptually, but can not specifically determine what is good and what is bad. For creative applications, many machine learning models that generate pictures and musics to support artists have been proposed [39–43]. However, in reality, most artists use them as if they were playing a lottery over and over again until they happen to produce output that they like, and it has been difficult for them to actively explore for more favorable output on their own. This is partly due to the fact that the artists themselves might not understand what they want specifically from the system and are vaguely looking for better results through their senses. To address this problem, several methods have been proposed using perceptual relative assessments that aim to efficiently explore the learned latent space to find the output that the user wants [44–46]. However, again, since these methods still explore in generalized spaces, it is difficult to obtain extreme results (which is what artists often want). This results in the problem that it often outputs only dull results for artists. In such situations, the methods presented in this chapter could be expected to give artists more benefit from machine learning models by manipulating a more distinctive set of the individualities in the training dataset and provide a more machine-human collaborative creative environment.

6 Conclusion

This chapter introduced a method to adapt the output of the generative model to a specific user using perceptual feedback. We mentioned adaptation to a specific individual is incompatible with machine learning, which essentially aims at generalization. However, by using tensor decomposition to separate the generalization part from the adaptation part, we showed the problem can be transformed into optimizing a minimum set of adaptation parameters while utilizing the versatility of machine learning. In addition, to efficiently collect perceptual feedback, we showed how to use not only sampling-based search, but also inference of the perceptual function landscape of a specific user. After describing the algorithm from the mathematical viewpoint, this chapter demonstrated the effectiveness of the method by adapting 3d spatial sound to a specific user as a practical example. As this shows, perceptual feedback is often far less labor intensive for the user than most physical measurements. Finally, we discussed the possibilities and some future of the introduced methods, especially in HCI. We showed many HCI problems requiring online calibration/personalization could be addressed by the introduced approach. We believe that personal adaptation of machine learning models using perceptual feedback will bring users experiences that have been available only to a limited number of people in many fields in the future.

References

1. Wenzel EM, Arruda DJ, Kistler DJ (1993) Localization using non-individualized head-related transfer functions. J Acoust Soc Amer 94
2. Moller H, Sorensen MF, Jensen CB, Hammershoi D (1996) Binaural technique: do we need individual recordings? J Audio Eng Soc 44:451–469
3. Middlebrooks JC (1999) Virtual localization improved by scaling non-individualized external-ear transfer functions in frequency. J Acoust Soc Amer 106
4. Brochu E, Brochu T, de Freitas N (2010) A Bayesian interactive optimization approach to procedural animation design. In: Proceedings of the SCA, pp 103–112
5. Kristi T, Gupta Maya R (2011) How to analyze paired comparison data. Technical Report UWEETR-2011-0004
6. Patrick L, Alan C, Tom T, Seetzen H (2005) Evaluation of tone mapping operators using a high dynamic range display. ACM Trans Graph
7. Koyama Y, Sakamoto D, Igarashi T (2014) Crowd-powered parameter analysis for visual design exploration. In: Proceedings of ACM UIST, pp 56–74
8. Hansen N, Muller SD, Koumoutsakos P (2003) Reducing the time complexity of the derandomized evolution strategy with covariance matrix adaptation (CMA-ES). Evolut Comput 11:1–18
9. Goodfellow I, Pouget-Abadie J, Mirza M, Xu B, Warde-Farley D, Ozair S, Courville A, Bengio Y (2014) Generative adversarial nets. In: Advances in neural information processing systems
10. Kingma, Diederik P (2014) Semi-supervised learning with deep generative models. In: Advances in Neural Information Processing Systems
11. Kihyuk S, Lee H, Yan X (2015) Learning structured output representation using deep conditional generative models. In: Advances in neural information processing systems
12. Koren Y, Bell R, Volinsky C (2009) Matrix factorization techniques for recommender systems. IEEE Comput 42(8)
13. Yehuda K, Rovert B, Chris V (2015) Procedural modeling using autoencoder networks. In: Proceeding of ACM UIST
14. Daniel H, Jun S, Taku K (2016) A deep learning framework for character motion synthesis and editing. ACM Trans Graph (SIGGRAPH)
15. Xuefeng C, Xiabi L, Yunde J (2009) Combining evolution strategy and gradient descent method for discriminative learning of bayesian classifiers. Proc Gen Evolut Comput 8:507–514
16. Matheron G (1963) Principles of geostatistics. Econ Geol 1246–1266
17. Algazi VR, Duda RO, Thompson DM, Avendano C (2001) The CIPIC HRTF database. In: IEEE Workshop on applications of signal processing to audio and electroacoustics, pp 99–102
18. John H (1992) Adaptation in natural and artificial systems. MIT Press, Cambridge
19. Takahama R, Kamishima T, Kashima H (2016) Progressive comparison for ranking estimation. In: Proceedings of IJCAI
20. Kingma D, Ba JP (2014) Adam: a method for stochastic optimization. arXiv:1412.6980
21. Kazuhiko Y, Takeo I (2017) Fully perceptual-based 3D spatial sound individualization with an adaptive variational autoEncoder. ACM Trans Graph (SIGGRAPH Asia)
22. Wenzel EM, Foster SH (1993) Fully perceptual consequences of interpolating head-related transfer functions during spatial synthesis. In: Proceedings of workshop on applications of signal processing to audio and acoustics

23. Langendijk EHA, Bronkhorst AW (2000) Fidelity of three-dimensional-sound reproduction using a virtual auditory display. J Acoust Soc Am
24. Oord AVD, Dieleman S, Zen H, Simonyan K, Vinyals O, Graves A, Kalchbrenner N, Senior A, Kavukcuoglu K, (2016) A generative model for raw audio. arXiv:1609.03499
25. Tran D, Bourdev L, Fergus R, Torresani L, Paluri M (2015) Learning spatiotemporal features with 3D convolutional networks. In: Proceedings of IEEE ICCV
26. Tobias F, Chang HJ, Demiris Y (2018) Real-time eye gaze estimation in natural environments. In: Proceedings of ECCV, RT-GENE
27. Fischer T, Liu G, Yu Y, Mora KAF, Odobez J-M (2018) R differential approach for gaze estimation with calibration. In: Proceeding of BMVC
28. Xucong Z, Yusuke S, Andreas B (2019) Evaluation of appearance-based methods and implications for gaze-based applications. In: Proceedings of CHI
29. Shi X, Shan S, Kan M, Wu S, Chen X (2020) Real-Time rotation-invariant face detection with progressive calibration networks. In: Proceedings of INTERSPEECH
30. Kumar A, Singh S, Gowda D, Garg A, Singh S, Kim C (2018) Utterance confidence measure for end-to-end speech recognition with applications to distributed speech recognition scenarios. In: Proceedings of CVPR
31. Li C, Zhu L, Xu S, Gao P, Xu B (2018) Recurrent neural network based small-footprint wake-up-word speech recognition system with a score calibration method. In: International conference on pattern recognition
32. Erica C, Cheng-I L, Yusuke Y, Fuming F, Xin W, Nanxin C, Yamagishi J (2020) Zero-shot multi-speaker text-to-speech with state-of-the-art neural speaker embeddings. In: Proceeding of ICASSP
33. Naoki K, Michinari K, Jun R (2019) SottoVoce: an ultrasound imaging-based silent speech interaction using deep neural networks. In: Proceedings of CHI
34. Shahan N (2020) Zeo-shot singing voice conversion. In: Proceedings of ISMIR
35. Zining Z, Bingsheng H, Zhang Z (2020) GAZEV, GAN-based zero shot voice conversion over non-parallel speech corpus. In: Proceedings of INTERSPEECH
36. Tero K, Samuli L, Aila T (2019) A style-based generator architecture for generative adversarial networks. In: Proceedings of CVPR
37. Wonkwang L, Donggyun K, Seunghoon H, Lee H (2020) High-fidelity synthesis with disentangled representation. In: Proceedings of ECCV
38. William P, John P, Jun-Yan Z, Alexei E, Torralba A (2020) The Hessian penalty: a weak prior for unsupervised disentanglement. In: Proceedings of ECCV
39. Ramesh A, Pavlov M, Goh G, Gray S, Voss C, Radford A, Chen M, Sutskever I (2021) Zero-shot text-to-image generation. arXiv:2102.12092
40. Songwei G, Vedanuj G, Larry Z, Parikh D (2021) Creative sketch generation. In: Proceeding of ICLR
41. Gaetan H, Francois P, Frank N (2017) Deepbach: a steerable model for bach chorales generation. In: Proceedings of international conference on machine learning
42. Dong H-W, Hsiao W-Y, Yang L-C, Yang Y-H (2020) Jukebox: a generative model for music. arXiv:2005.00341
43. Dhariwal P, Jun H, Payne C, Kim JW, Radford A, Sutskever I (2018) Musegan: multi-track sequential generative adversarial networks for symbolic music generation and accompaniment. In: Proceedings of AAAI
44. Yijun Z, Yuki K, Masataka G, Igarashi T (2020) Generative melody composition with human-in-the-loop bayesian optimization. In: Proceedings of CSMC-MuMe
45. Yuki K, Issei S, Goto M (2020) Sequential gallery for interactive visual design optimization. ACM Trans Graph (SIGGRAPH)
46. Chia-Hsing C, Yuki K, Yu-Chi L, Takeo I, Yue Y (2020) Human-in-the-loop differential subspace search in high-dimensional latent space. ACM Trans Graph (SIGGRAPH)
47. Mengwei XU, Feng QIAN, Qiaozhu MEI, Huang K, Liu X (2018) DeepType: on-device deep learning for input personalization service with minimal privacy concern. ACM interactive, mobile, wearable and ubiquitous technologies

48. Liu J, Liu C, Belkin NJ (2020) Personalization in text information retrieval: a survey. J Ass Inf Sci Technol
49. Helten T, Baak A, Bharaj G, Muller M, Seidel H-P, Theobalt C (2013) Personalization and evaluation of a real-time depth-based full body tracker. In: 3DV-Conference
50. Anastasia T, Andrea T, Remelli E, Pauly M, Fitzgibbon AW (2017) Online generative model personalization for hand tracking. ACM Trans Graph (SIGGRAPH Asia)

Printed in the United States
by Baker & Taylor Publisher Services